Distance in miles

City labels (along the diagonal): (FORT WIL)LIAM, (GL)ASGOW, GLOUCESTER, HARWICH, HOLYHEAD, HULL, INVERNESS, KENDAL, LEEDS, LEICESTER, LINCOLN, LIVERPOOL, LONDON, MANCHESTER, NEWCASTLE UPON TYNE, NORWICH, NOTTINGHAM, OXFORD, PENZANCE, PERTH, PLYMOUTH, PORTSMOUTH, SALISBURY, SHEFFIELD, SHREWSBURY, SOUTHAMPTON, SOUTHEND-ON-SEA, STOKE-ON-TRENT, STRANRAER, THURSO, WORCESTER, YORK

```
561 502 153 139 456 514 431 344 103 262 314 400 372 332 493 332 225 471 374 477 673 81 603 556 526 347 384 542 511 365 225 191 428 304
191 56 424 321 106 282 101 221 479 182 167 150 192 99 213 124 259 277 157 157 302 362 232 219 172 156 73 198 252 109 326 587 99 192
437 358 135 36 332 412 266 243 200 138 207 298 271 208 397 208 146 369 273 353 548 97 479 431 401 235 260 418 409 245 49 313 303 206
157 168 389 286 51 164 148 128 444 147 107 43 84 89 113 80 199 159 50 67 288 326 198 144 112 74 43 131 145 46 293 552 26 122
263 220 303 200 157 216 150 65 351 61 10 99 74 65 195 35 96 173 74 166 374 237 304 245 219 37 99 232 213 68 207 460 128 33
74 140 471 368 34 197 205 211 525 229 197 114 166 159 118 162 290 213 316 69 185 408 115 90 47 173 101 70 158 127 375 633 62 212
223 270 451 347 121 67 246 129 482 215 142 68 85 187 55 152 227 63 82 79 334 367 264 128 138 116 142 129 61 139 386 590 114 149
106 104 474 371 56 227 195 243 529 233 220 135 191 162 148 169 311 245 154 100 214 412 148 131 87 179 104 110 188 138 378 637 73 235
346 286 196 93 241 321 217 152 248 47 112 207 179 117 305 117 58 278 182 261 457 133 387 340 310 140 169 327 318 149 99 356 212 115
163 197 409 305 58 144 173 118 463 167 116 24 74 114 94 99 203 139 50 49 274 346 205 127 104 78 68 114 126 65 313 571 43 126
197 196 371 268 92 163 154 92 416 129 69 29 51 80 125 58 160 133 16 99 308 301 239 177 147 36 64 163 157 34 275 524 67 83
250 235 337 234 141 183 167 46 369 96 29 68 38 84 162 51 113 140 44 140 362 254 292 219 197 18 102 205 180 66 241 477 116 34
242 325 592 465 181 127 348 249 600 342 260 182 202 289 76 275 345 164 200 133 353 485 283 128 156 234 243 141 84 240 488 708 190 267
438 378 131 44 333 393 309 223 154 139 193 278 251 209 372 209 104 350 253 353 549 42 479 432 402 226 260 418 389 241 121 262 304 183
207 543 439 106 250 277 284 597 301 273 186 238 231 170 234 365 282 208 141 109 480 43 124 88 232 171 106 210 199 447 705 133 285
476 380 148 328 157 280 537 240 226 205 247 157 249 182 317 332 212 201 319 420 249 236 188 215 129 215 289 164 320 645 148 250
```

(FORT WIL)LIAM
```
102 437 518 384 348 65 243 312 404 376 313 502 313 235 475 378 458 800 102 584 537 507 340 365 523 515 346 183 175 409 311
```
(GL)ASGOW
```
334 414 287 250 168 140 209 300 273 210 399 210 142 371 281 355 703 57 481 433 403 237 262 420 411 242 84 276 305 208
```
GLOUCESTER
```
175 177 178 492 196 158 80 132 130 102 128 250 184 102 48 217 375 147 106 69 125 76 87 142 94 341 600 28 173
```
HARWICH
```
313 187 549 282 209 135 143 254 75 219 294 63 150 129 361 434 291 152 165 183 208 157 59 206 453 657 178 181
```
HOLYHEAD
```
210 449 171 156 176 197 93 266 117 248 290 170 222 388 351 318 281 247 152 104 261 298 119 228 559 152 181
```
HULL
```
380 123 57 95 44 125 178 95 118 146 80 167 395 265 326 246 224 64 153 233 196 113 253 488 159 38
```
INVERNESS
```
299 349 435 407 369 528 369 260 506 410 514 715 112 640 593 562 382 421 580 546 402 248 110 464 368
```
KENDAL
```
79 170 175 81 265 77 99 276 160 223 415 191 347 307 266 117 131 290 306 111 154 409 177 89
```
LEEDS
```
339          96 67 71 188 41 93 166 71 163 381 234 311 242 216 34 105 229 206 72 216 457 136 24
722 612       51 108 100 88 179 114 26 71 298 320 228 149 127 62 76 135 132 57 308 524 67 102
275 198 482   117 131 84 152 102 36 123 349 293 280 199 178 44 119 187 148 85 285 515 109 71
252 92 562 127 208 33 153 211 96 164 343 251 273 242 196 71 57 229 239 51 210 476 102 96
283 153 700 273 154 193 273 111 126 57 281 413 211 71 85 159 161 76 40 158 406 636 112 194
318 71 655 282 109 82 145 193 82 158 350 262 281 241 201 39 70 224 241 45 225 480 112 72
149 200 594 130 115 174 188 254 160 255 477 155 409 339 325 130 213 321 293 194 163 376 239 99
428 286 850 427 303 160 211 334 126 145 405 423 336 203 208 155 203 200 98 201 385 641 187 182
189 152 594 124 67 141 136 54 310 97 318 295 248 176 153 38 83 163 147 49 288 518 76 78
399 190 419 159 150 288 245 247 439 233 252 396 182 78 63 129 103 65 96 115 362 621 57 173
467 235 814 444 268 183 164 339 179 311 409 591 77 237 200 343 282 218 321 310 557 816 244 396
273 129 659 257 114 41 58 155 203 132 257 203 521 474 444 267 302 460 431 283 141 220 345 224
357 269 827 359 262 114 196 263 92 254 411 233 156 167 130 274 213 148 252 241 488 746 175 326
624 636 1151 668 613 479 562 552 452 563 768 651 512 405 42 210 178 19 111 193 441 700 129 253
565 427 180 308 376 514 471 403 665 422 249 680 475 637 951 184 143 23 124 161 408 670 95 231
512 524 1030 558 501 367 450 440 340 453 658 541 399 293 124 839 83 195 180 47 244 489 102 52
452 396 954 493 389 239 321 390 114 388 545 327 283 125 381 762 268 156 193 37 273 528 48 129
397 360 905 429 348 204 286 316 136 323 523 335 246 101 321 714 209 68 116 179 427 686 109 239
245 104 615 189 54 100 71 114 256 63 209 249 61 208 552 429 440 337 295 191 439 654 152 213
167 246 678 211 169 123 192 92 259 113 343 327 133 166 454 486 342 286 231 134 249 508 65 95
421 375 932 466 368 217 302 368 123 360 517 322 262 104 351 741 239 30 36 314 252 362 312 215
479 315 879 493 332 212 239 386 65 387 471 158 236 155 516 693 405 179 200 281 311 187 572 447
192 182 646 179 115 92 137 82 255 73 312 323 79 185 499 455 387 311 259 76 59 288 308 148
367 407 399 248 347 495 458 338 653 362 262 620 463 583 897 228 785 710 656 392 440 688 706 401
900 786 177 658 735 873 829 766 1023 773 604 1031 834 999 1313 354 1201 1126 1077 787 850 1103 1053 817 582
245 256 747 285 218 107 176 163 180 180 384 301 123 92 393 556 281 208 153 164 77 176 244 105 503 921
292 60 592 144 39 164 114 154 313 116 143 292 125 274 637 361 525 407 372 83 207 384 343 153 346 720 238
```

istance in kilometres

Collins 2009
COMPACT ATLAS
BRITAIN

Contents

Information

Key to map pages	ii-iii
Key to map symbols	iv-v
Route planning maps	vi-xi

Road maps   2-191

Urban area maps and city centre maps

London urban area	192-193
London city centre	194-195
Birmingham urban area	196-197
Birmingham city centre	198-199
Merseyside urban area	200-201
Liverpool city centre	202-203
Manchester urban area	204-205
Manchester city centre	206-207
Leeds urban area	208-209
Leeds city centre	210-211
Glasgow urban area	212-213
Glasgow city centre	214-215
Edinburgh urban area	216-217
Edinburgh city centre	218-219

Index   220-278

Collins

This edition specially produced for The Book People Ltd.,
Hall Wood Avenue, Haydock, St. Helens, WA11 9UL

Published by Collins
An imprint of HarperCollins Publishers
77-85 Fulham Palace Road, Hammersmith, London W6 8JB

www.collinsworld.com

Copyright © HarperCollins Publishers Ltd 2008

Collins® is a registered trademark of HarperCollins Publishers Limited

Mapping generated from Collins Bartholomew digital databases

The grid on this map is the National Grid taken from the Ordnance Survey map with the permission of the Controller of Her Majesty's Stationery Office.

The representation of a road, track or footpath is no evidence of a right of way.

Please note that roads and other facilities which are under construction at the time of going to press, and are due to open before the end of 2008, are shown in this atlas as open. Roads due to start construction before the end of June 2009 are shown as 'proposed or under construction'.

Printed in China by South China Printing Co. Ltd

ISBN 978 0 00 782254 6   Imp 001   VG12381

e-mail: roadcheck@harpercollins.co.uk

Information on fixed speed camera locations provided by PocketGPSWorld.Com Ltd.

Information on alternative refuelling site locations provided by the Energy Saving Trust Ltd.
www.energysavingtrust.org.uk

With thanks to the Wine Guild of the United Kingdom for help with researching vineyards.

Information regarding blue flag beach awards is current as of summer 2007. For latest information please visit www.blueflag.org.uk

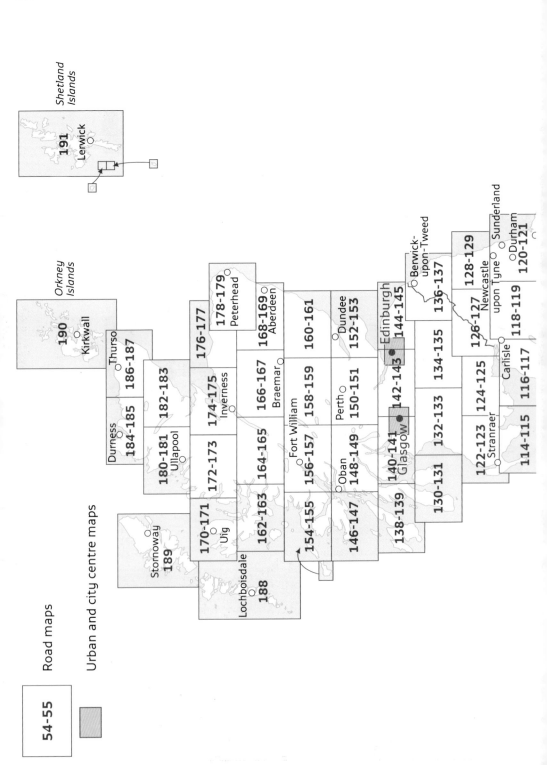

Road maps

54-55

Urban and city centre maps

Shetland Islands

191 Lerwick

Orkney Islands

190 Kirkwall

Thurso

186-187

184-185 Durness

182-183

180-181 Ullapool

176-177

178-179 Peterhead

174-175 Inverness

168-169 Aberdeen

166-167 Braemar

160-161

Dundee

152-153

Edinburgh

144-145

Berwick-upon-Tweed

136-137

128-129 Sunderland

Newcastle upon Tyne Durham

126-127 **120-121**

118-119

Carlisle

116-117

172-173

164-165

Fort William

158-159

Perth

150-151

142-143

134-135

124-125

Stranraer

114-115

170-171 Uig

162-163

156-157

Oban

148-149

140-141 Glasgow

132-133

130-131

122-123

Stornoway

189

Lochboisdale

188

154-155

146-147

138-139

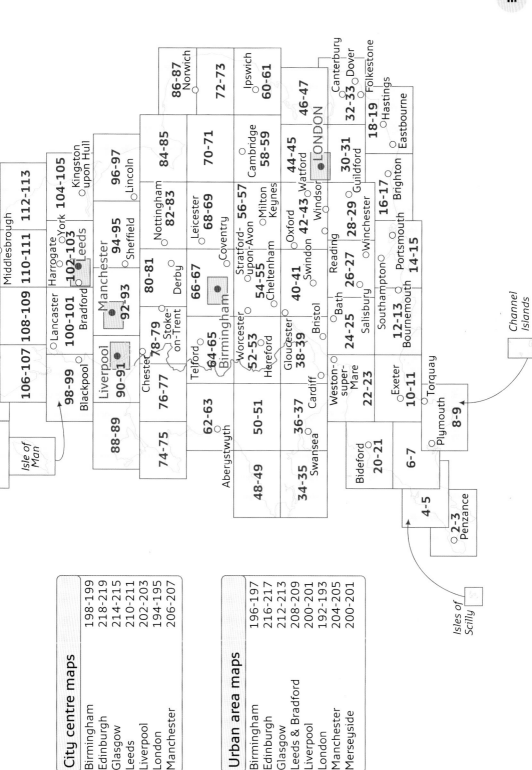

City centre maps

Birmingham	198-199
Edinburgh	218-219
Glasgow	214-215
Leeds	210-211
Liverpool	202-203
London	194-195
Manchester	206-207

Urban area maps

Birmingham	196-197
Edinburgh	216-217
Glasgow	212-213
Leeds & Bradford	208-209
Liverpool	200-201
London	192-193
Manchester	204-205
Merseyside	200-201

Key to map symbols

iv

Road maps

Scale: All 1: 266,667 / 4.2 miles to 1 inch except Western Isles, Orkney and Shetland Islands 1: 411,840 / 6.5 miles to 1 inch

Pages 2-191

M5	Motorway
M6Toll	Toll motorway
8 / 9	Motorway junction with full / limited access (in congested areas there is just a numbered symbol)
Maidstone Birch / Sarn	Motorway service area with off road / full / limited access
A556	Primary route dual / single carriageway
	24 hour service area on primary route
Peterhead	Primary route destination. Primary route destinations are places of major traffic importance linked by the primary route network. They are shown on a green background on direction signs.
A30	'A' road dual / single carriageway
B1403	'B' road dual / single carriageway
	Minor road
	Road with restricted access
	Roads with passing places
	Road proposed or under construction
33	Multi-level junction with full / limited access (with junction number)

	Roundabout
4	Road distance in miles between markers
	Road tunnel
	Steep hill (arrows point downhill)
Toll	Level crossing / Toll
St. Malo 8hrs	Car ferry route with journey times
	Railway line / station / tunnel
South Downs Way	National Trail / Long Distance Route
	Fixed safety camera sites / fixed average-speed safety camera sites
	Alternative fuel site: LPG / Bioethanol / Biodiesel / Natural Gas / Electric recharging
	Airport with / without scheduled services
H	Heliport
PaR PaR	Park and Ride site operated by bus / rail (runs at least 5 days a week)

	Built up area
Hythe	Seaside destination
	National boundary
KENT	County / Unitary Authority boundary and name
	National Park boundary
	Regional / Forest Park boundary
	Heritage Coast
	Woodland
Danger Zone	Military range
468 / 941	Spot / Summit height (in metres)
	Lake / Dam / River / Waterfall
	Canal / Dry canal / Canal tunnel
	Beach / Lighthouse
SEE PAGE 206	Area covered by urban area map

Land height reference bar

	metres	0	150	300	500	700	900
water	feet	0	490	985	1640	2295	2950

Places of interest

A selection of tourist detail is shown on the mapping. It is advisable to check with the local tourist information centre for opening times and facilities.

Any of the following symbols may appear on the map in red ★ which indicates that the site has World Heritage status.

- Tourist information centre (open all year)
- Tourist information centre (open seasonally)
- Ancient monument
- Aquarium
- Aqueduct / Viaduct
- Arboretum
- 1643 Battlefield
- Blag beach
- ...te / Caravan site
- ...rk

- County cricket ground
- Distillery
- Ecclesiastical building
- Event venue
- Farm park
- Garden
- Golf course
- Historic house
- Historic ship
- Major football club
- Major shopping centre / Outlet village
- Major sports venue
- Motor racing circuit
- Mountain bike trail
- Museum / Art gallery

- Nature reserve (NNR indicates National Nature Reserve)
- Racecourse
- Rail Freight Terminal
- Ski slope (artificial / natural)
- Spotlight nature reserve (best sites for access to nature)
- Steam railway centre / Preserved railway
- Surfing beach
- Theme park
- University
- Vineyard
- Wildlife park / Zoo
- Other interesting feature
- (NT) (NTS) National Trust / National Trust for Scotland property

Urban area maps — Scale 1: 82,019 / 1.3 inches to 1 mile — Pages 192-219

12 / 15	Motorway junctions with full / limited access
LEICESTER SERVICES	Motorway service area
M6Toll	Toll motorway
A316	Primary route with dual / single carriageway
A4054	'A' road with dual / single carriageway
B7078	'B' road with dual / single carriageway
	Minor road with dual / single carriageway
═══ ::::: •••••	Road proposed or under construction
:::::::::::	Road tunnel
○ ○ ● ○	Roundabout
T	Toll / Level crossing
→	One way street
P&R / P&R	Park and Ride site operated by bus / rail (runs at least 5 days a week)
Dublin 8 hrs	Car ferry route with destination and journey time
──── ────	Railway line / Railway tunnel
⇌ •	Railway station / Light rail station
⊖ Ⓢ	Underground stations (London / Glasgow)
✈	Airport
▓▓▓▓	Extent of London congestion charging zone
▬	Public building
362 ▲ / 🗼	Spot height (in metres) / Lighthouse
	Built up area
	National Park
	Woodland / Park
SEE PAGES 194-195	Area covered by city centre map

City centre maps — Scale 1: 12,461 / 5 inches to 1 mile — Pages 192 -219

M8	Motorway
A4 ②	Primary route dual / single carriageway and junction
A40	'A' road dual / single carriageway
B507	'B' road dual / single carriageway
	Other road dual / single carriageway
→ ②	One way street/Orbital route
•	Access restriction
	Pedestrian street
	Street market
:::::-------	Track / Footpath
	Road under construction
⇌ ⊕	Main/other National Rail stations
⊖ ⊕	London underground / Light rail station
⬤	Bus / Coach station
P&R	Park and Ride site - rail operated (runs at least 5 days a week)
⊖	Ferry
P	Car park
ℹ	Visitor Information centre
⊎	Theatre
⊟	Major hotel
⚟	Public house
Pol	Police station
Lib	Library
PO	Post Office
⌐ JAPAN	Embassy
⚟	Cinema
◼+	Cathedral / Church
☾ ✡ ■ Mormon	Mosque / Synagogue / Other place of worship
	Leisure and tourism
	Shopping
	Administration and law
	Health and welfare
	Education
	Major office
	Industry and commerce
	N

Land's End / Lizard Point / Mount's Bay / Penzance

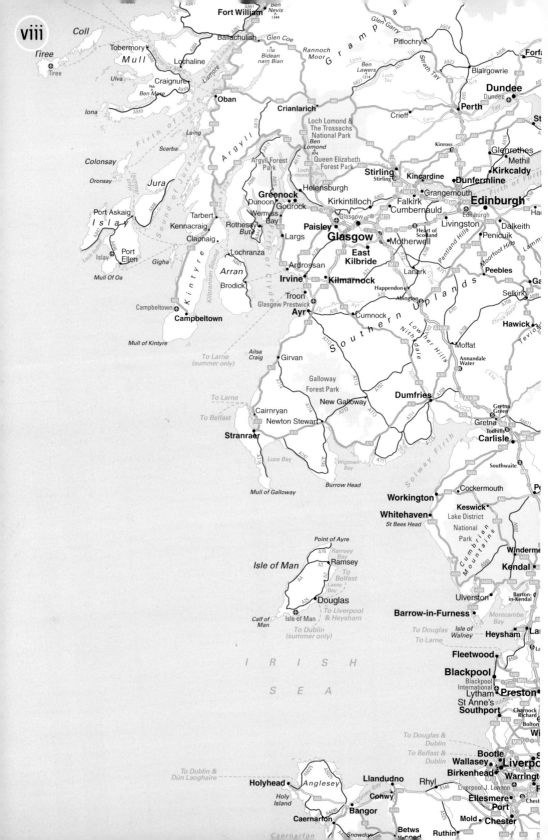

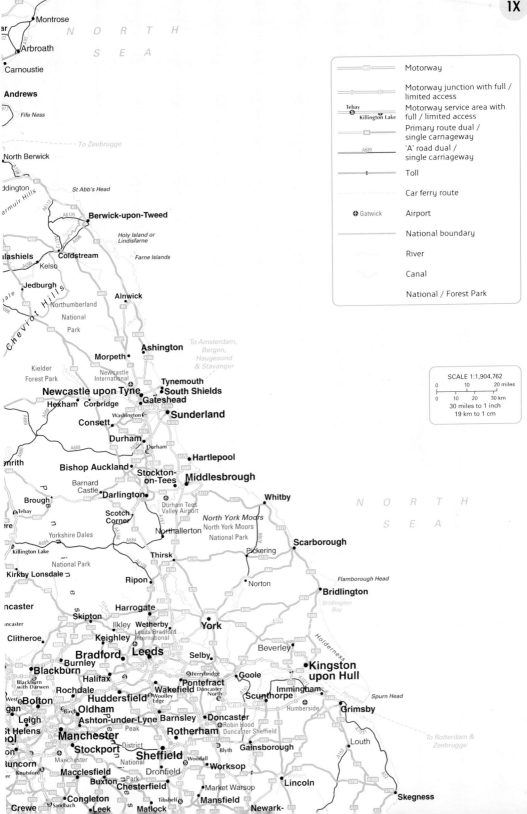

NORTH SEA

Montrose

Arbroath

Carnoustie

Andrews

Fife Ness

To Zeebrugge

North Berwick

ddington

St Abb's Head

ermuir Hills

Berwick-upon-Tweed

Holy Island or
Lindisfarne

llashiels Coldstream Kelso Farne Islands

Jedburgh

ale

Cheviot Hills

Alnwick

Northumberland
National
Park

Kielder
Forest Park

Morpeth Ashington

To Amsterdam,
Bergen,
Haugesund
& Stavanger

Newcastle International

Newcastle upon Tyne Tynemouth
Hexham Corbridge Gateshead South Shields

Consett Washington

Sunderland

Durham
Durham

Bishop Auckland Hartlepool
Stockton-
on-Tees Middlesbrough

Barnard
Castle Darlington

Brough Tebay

Whitby

NORTH SEA

Scotch
Corner

Durham Tees
Valley Airport

North York Moors
North York Moors
National Park

re

Yorkshire Dales

Northallerton

Killington Lake National Park

Kirkby Lonsdale

Thirsk

Ripon

Scarborough

Pickering

Norton

Flamborough Head

Bridlington

Bridlington
Bay

ncaster

Harrogate

Skipton Ilkley Wetherby

Keighley Leeds Bradford
International

Clitheroe

York

Beverley

Holderness

Bradford Leeds Selby

Burnley

Kingston
upon Hull

Blackburn Halifax

Ferrybridge Goole

Blackburn
with Darwen

Rochdale Wakefield Pontefract
Woolley
Edge

Immingham

Spurn Head

West Huddersfield Doncaster
North

Scunthorpe Grimsby

Bolton Oldham Humberside
gan

Ashton-under-Lyne Barnsley Doncaster

Leigh Peak

St Helens Manchester Rotherham Doncaster Sheffield

To Rotterdam &
Zeebrugge

on Stockport

Louth

Sheffield Blyth Gainsborough

uncan Manchester

Woodall

Knutsford National Worksop
Macclesfield Park Dronfield

Buxton Chesterfield Lincoln

Market Warsop

Congleton Tibshelf Mansfield
Crewe Sandbach Leek Matlock Newark- Skegness

Legend:

Motorway

Motorway junction with full /
limited access

Tebay Killington Lake

Motorway service area with
full / limited access

Primary route dual /
single carriageway

A689 'A' road dual /
single carriageway

Toll

Car ferry route

Gatwick Airport

National boundary

River

Canal

National / Forest Park

SCALE 1:1,904,762

0   10   20 miles
0   10   20   30 km
30 miles to 1 inch
19 km to 1 cm

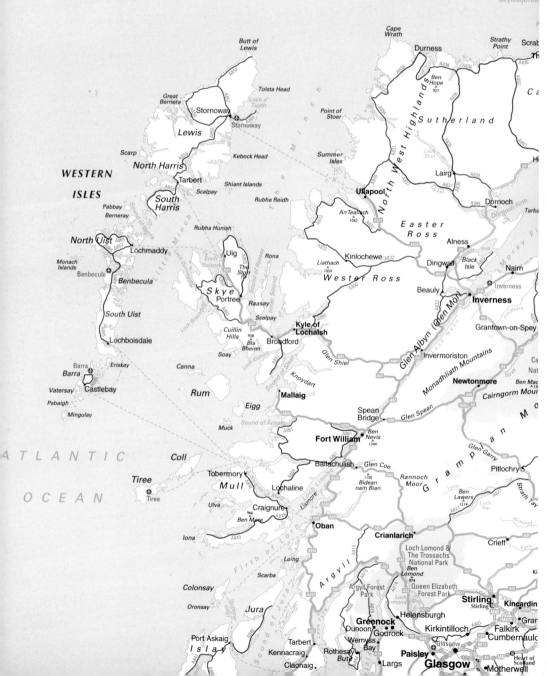

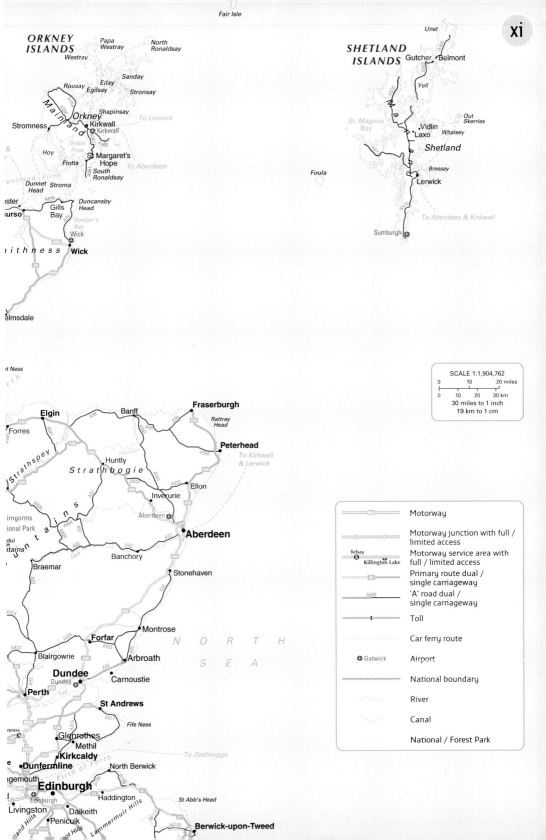

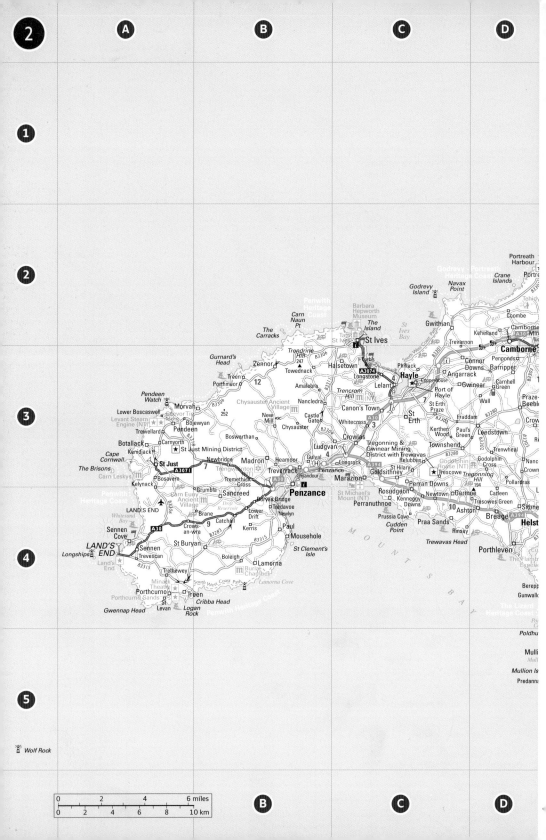

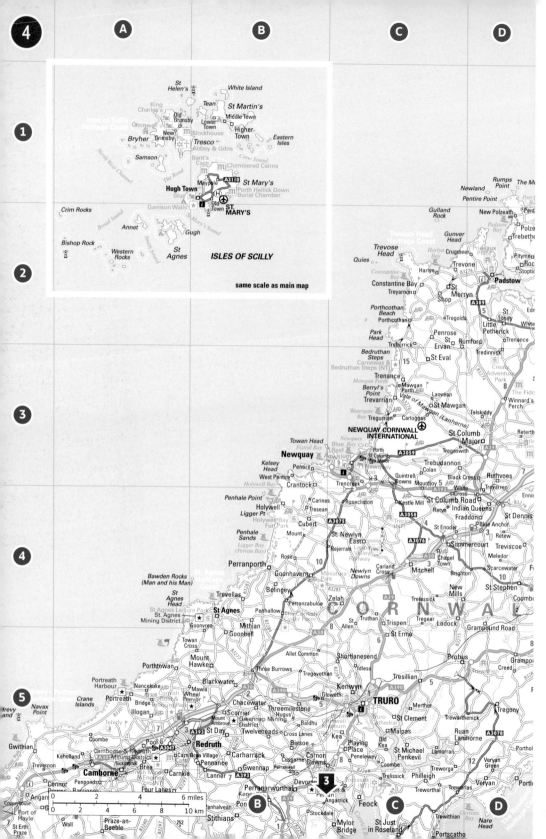

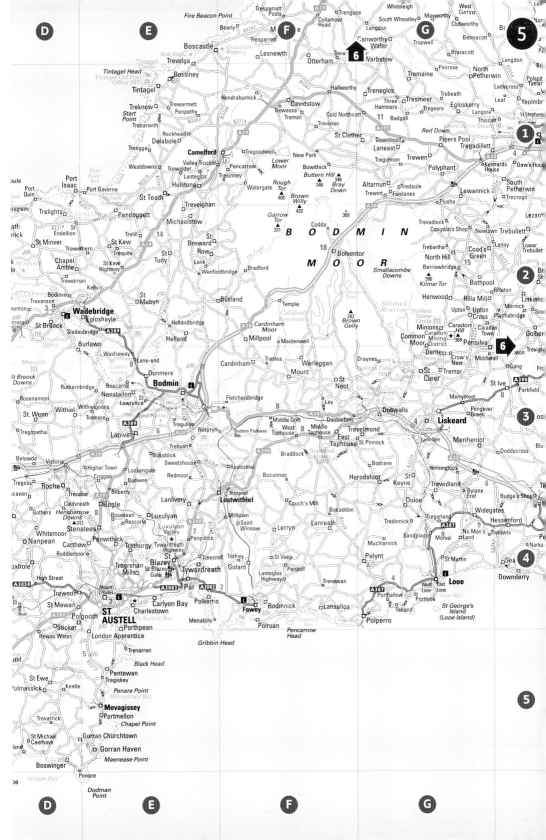

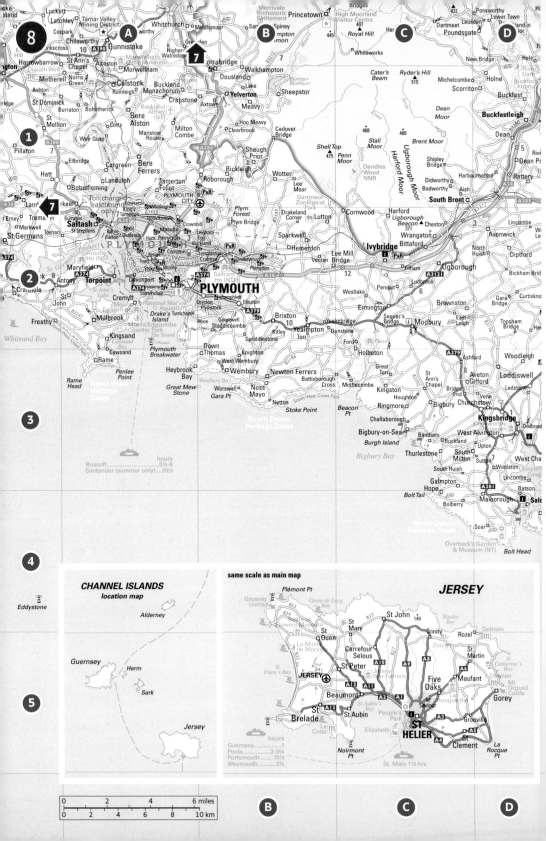

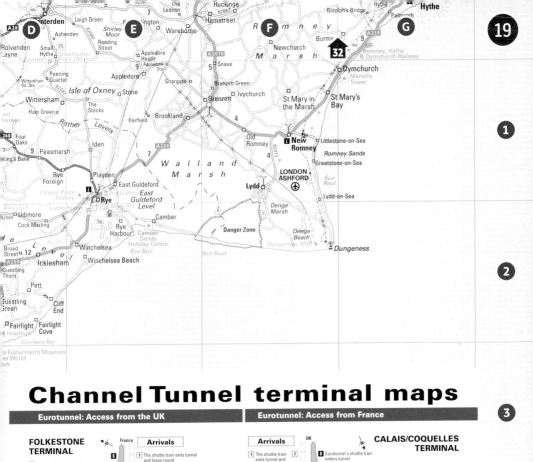

Channel Tunnel terminal maps

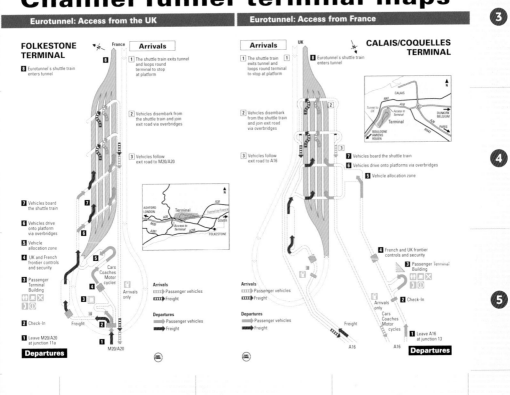

A   B   C   D

North West Point
Lundy Heritage Coast
LUNDY
Lundy Island (NT)
Lundy NNR
Rat Island
Shutter Rock

BARNS
BA
(BIDE
BA

Hartland Point
Hartland Heritage Coast
Titchberry
South West Coast Path
Windbury Point
Gallantry Bower
Clovelly
Clovelly Bay
Hartland Abbey
Sierra
Dyke
Clovelly Cross
Hartland Quay
Stoke
Hartland
Milford
Philham
Milky Way Adventure Park
Elmscott
Edistone
Tosberry
Woolfardisworthy

South Hole
Almis
Co
Knaps Longpeak
Welcombe
Ashmansworthy
Mead
Darracott
Torridge
Gooseham
Woolley
Meddon
Kis
Morwenstow
Eastcott
14
East Youlstone
Dinworthy
Bradwort
Higher Sharpnose Point
Shop
West Youlstone
Lower Sharpnose Point
Woodford
Suttcom
Taylors Cross
Upper Tamar Lake
Alfardisworthy
Soldon
Coombe
Kilkhampton
Thurdon
Lower Tamar Lake
Soldon Cross
Stibb
Youldonmoor Cross
Youldon
Holsw
Stratton
Dunsdon NNR
Maer
Poughill
Hersham Bush
Grimscott
Lana
Chilsworthy
Bude Haven
Flexbury
Stratton
Launcells Cross
Pancrasweek
Bude
Launcells
Lynstone
Stratton Museum
3
Red Post
5
Derril
Rydon
Upton
Helebridge
Marhamchurch
Bridgerule
Pyworthy
Derriton
Chasty
Widemouth Bay
Titson
Yeomadon
BUDE BAY
Box's Shop
Week Orchard
Pentire Point - Widemouth Heritage Coast
Ceppathorne
Tinney
Corfcott Green
Dizzard Point
Poundsto
eskinnick Cross
6
Penlean
North Tamerton
Tregole
W ne
Tetcott
St Genn
Trewint
19
W St
15
Trebarrow
ington Haven
Jacobstow
Cambeak
Rosecare
Crackington

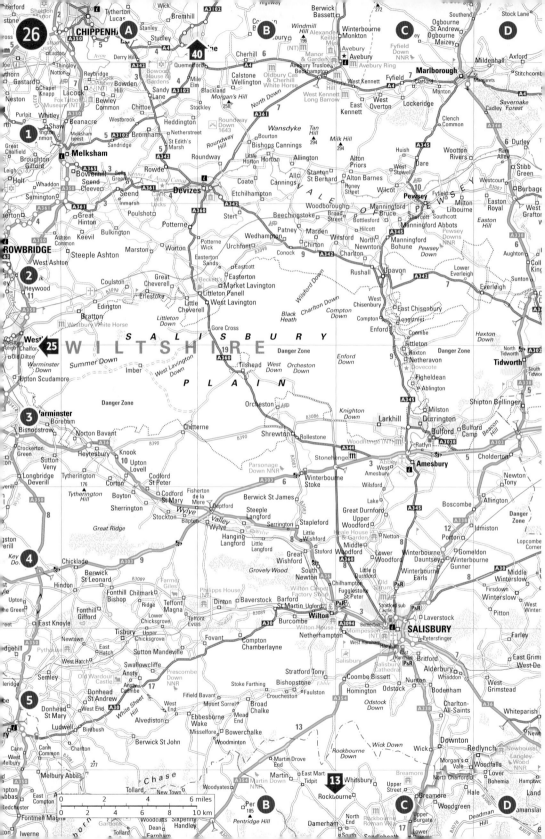

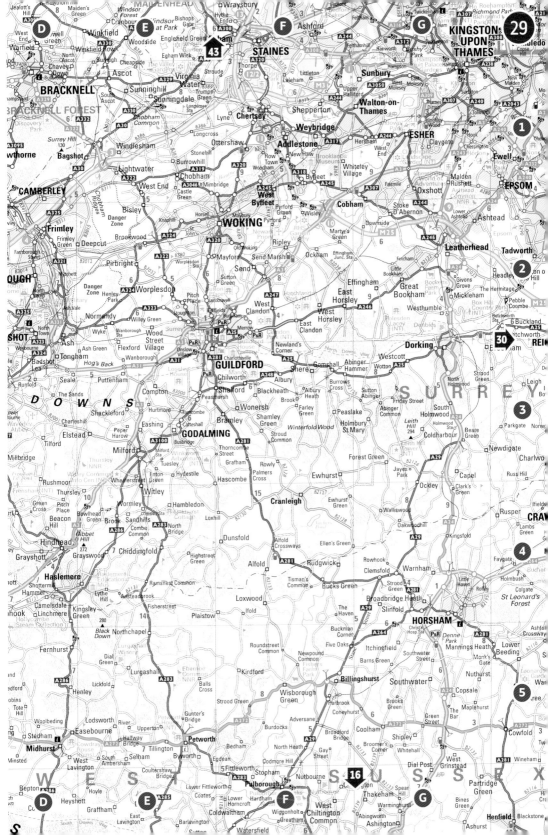

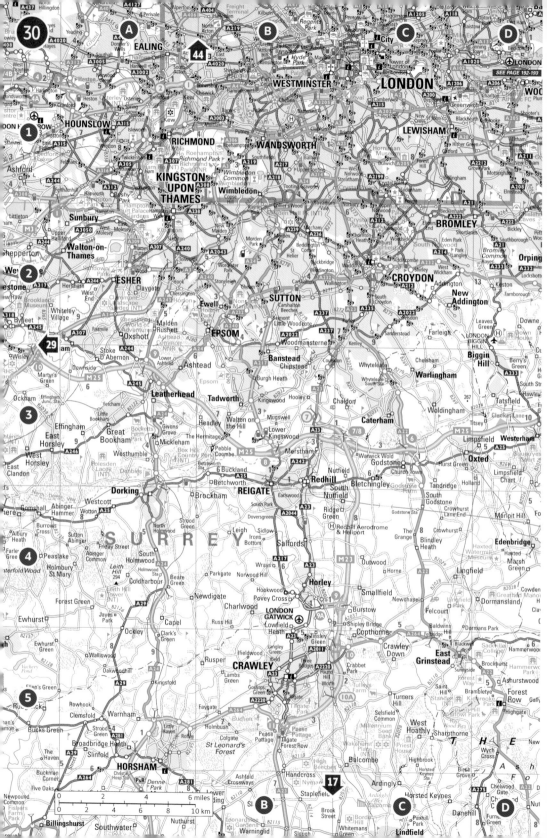

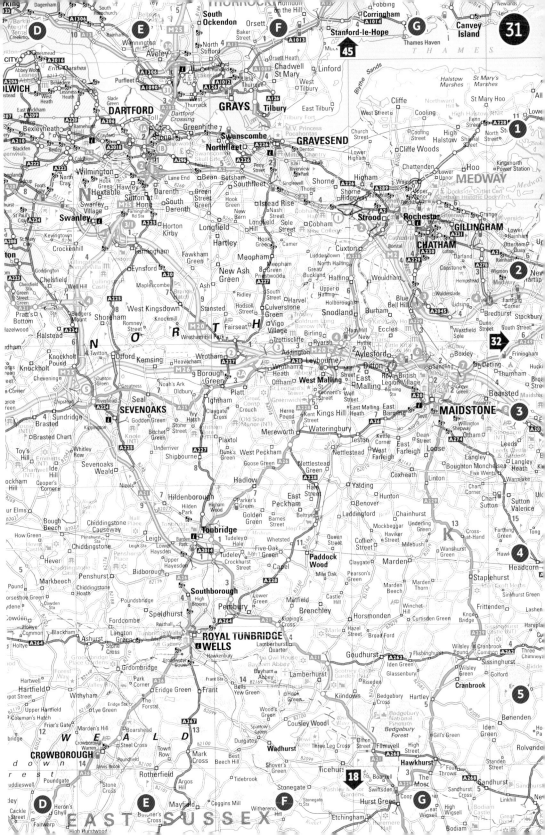

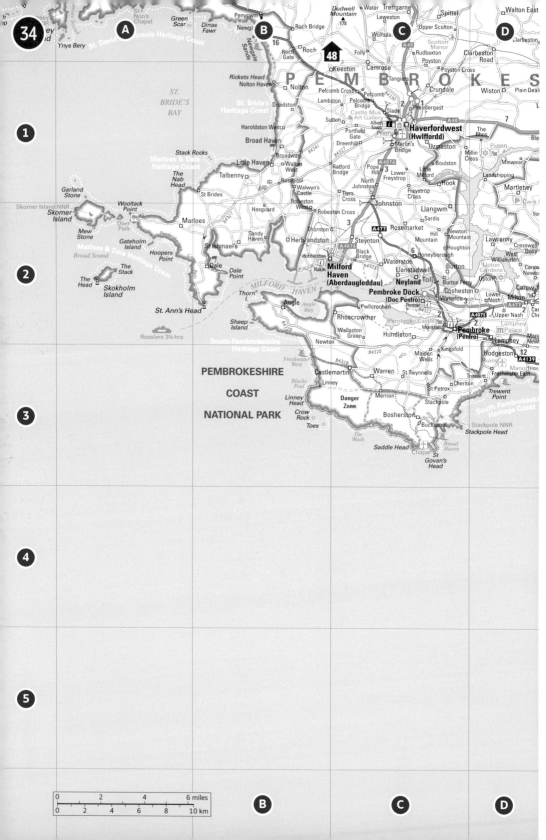

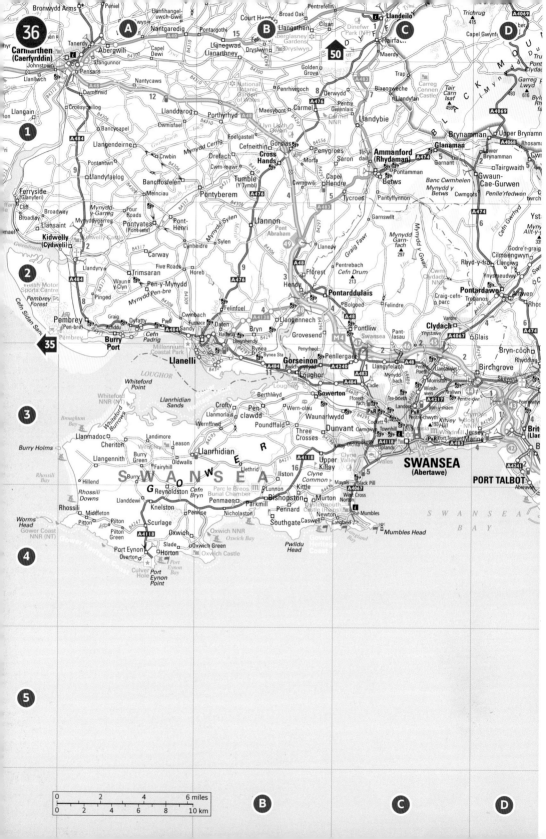

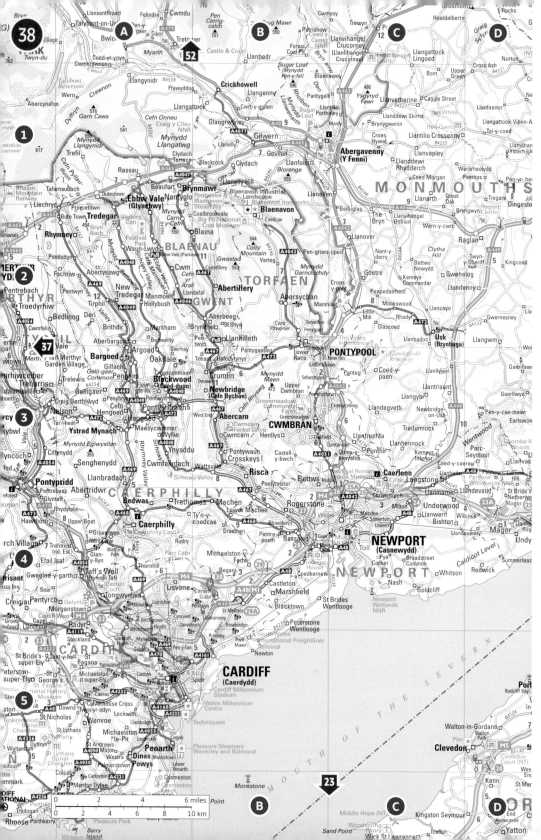

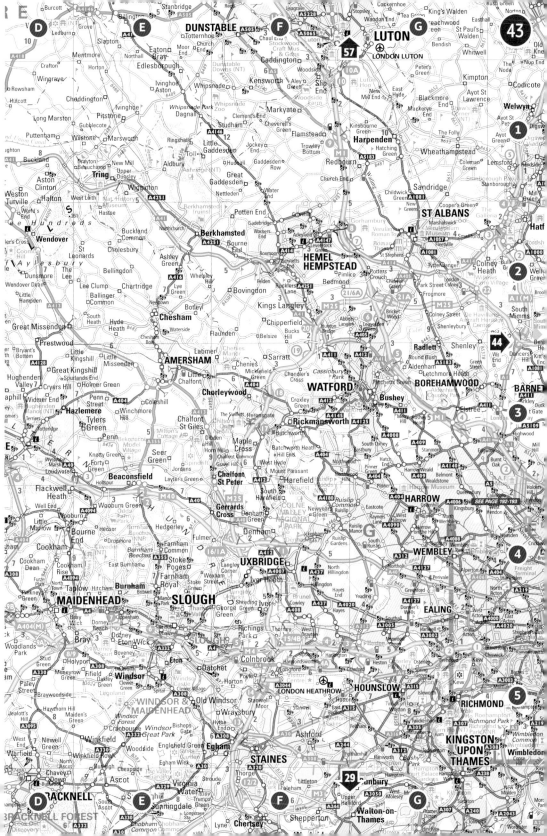

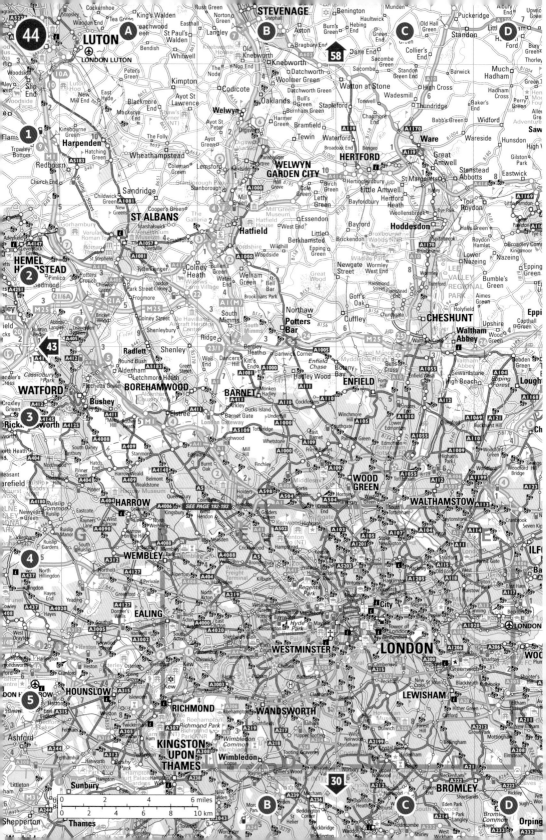

A   B   C   D

1

2

3

Rosslare 1¼-3½ hrs

Strumble Head   Carregwastad   Crincoed   Dinas Head   Dinas   Newport
St David's Peninsula   Point   Point   Dinas   Head   Bay
Heritage Coast   Fishguard   Island   Cwm-yr-Eglwys
                Pen Brush   Pen Caer   Goodwick   Bay   Bryn-   Parrog
                        Trefasser   (Wdig)   Fishguard   henllan   Dinas
PEMBROKESHIRE   Rhosycaerau   Dyffryn   (Abergwaun)   Cross
COAST   Penbwchdy   Lower   Mynydd   Myr
NATIONAL PARK   St Nicholas   Manorowen   Town   Melyn   Carr
                        Penmorfa   Scleddau   Llanychaer Bridge   Mynydd
        Ynys Deullyn   Granston   Cilrhedyn Bridge   Caregog
                Abercastle   Jordanston   A40   Pontfaen   Cwm Gwaun
4
        Penclegyr   Trefin   Llangloffan   Trecwn   Mynydd
                Mathry   Newbridge   Cilcifeth
St David's Peninsula   Porthgain   Llanrhian   Penparc   Corsydd   334   Morvil
Heritage Coast   Abereiddy   14   Castle   Llangloffan   Little   Mynydd
                Bereia   Croesgoch   Morris   NNR   Newcastle   Puncheston   Castlebythe
        Penclegyr   Carreg-   Letterston   Sealyham
        gwylan-fach   Treglemais   Treffynnon   Treddog   15   St Dogwells   Woodstock
North   Penllechwen   Tretio   Llanreithan   Welsh   Wolf's   Ambleston
Bishop   St David's Head   Carnhedryn   Newton   Hook   Castle   Wallis   Llys-y-
        Treleddyd-fawr   Ford   Rinaston   frân Res
Carreg   St David's   Rhodiad-   Caerfarchell   Hayscastle   Hayscastle   Brimaston   Walton East
rhoson   Head   y-brenin   Middle Mill   Llandeloy   Trefgarn   Cross
                Rhosson   Whitchurch   Owen   Mountain   Treffgarne   Spittal
        Point   St David's   Dudwell   Water   Leweston   Upper Scolton   Clarbeston
uth   St John   St Non's   (Tyddewi)   Brawdy   Mountain   Wolfsdale   Scolton
hop   Ramsey   Chapel   Solva   178   Manor   Clarbeston
        Island NNR   Green   Dinas   Penycwm   Roch Bridge   Rudbaxton   Road
Ramsey   Scar   Fawr   Newgale   Roch   Folly   A40   Poyston Cross
Island   Ynys Bery   16   Roch   Camrose   Crundale   Wisto   Plain Dea
        St David's Peninsula Heritage Coast   Newgale   Gate   Tangiers
                                Sands   Rickets Head   P E M B R O K E S   Pelcomb Cross   Pelcomb   Poyston   7
0   2   4   6 miles   Nolton Haven   34   Lambston   Pelcomb   Crundale
0   2   4   6   8   10 km   St   Nolton   Druidston   Bridge   Slade   Prendergast
        Heritage Coast   B   C   Sutton   Castle Mus   D

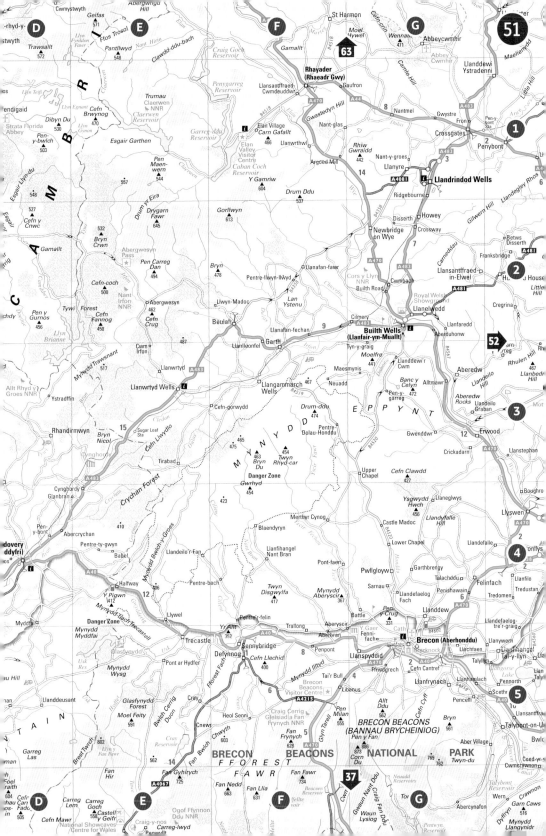

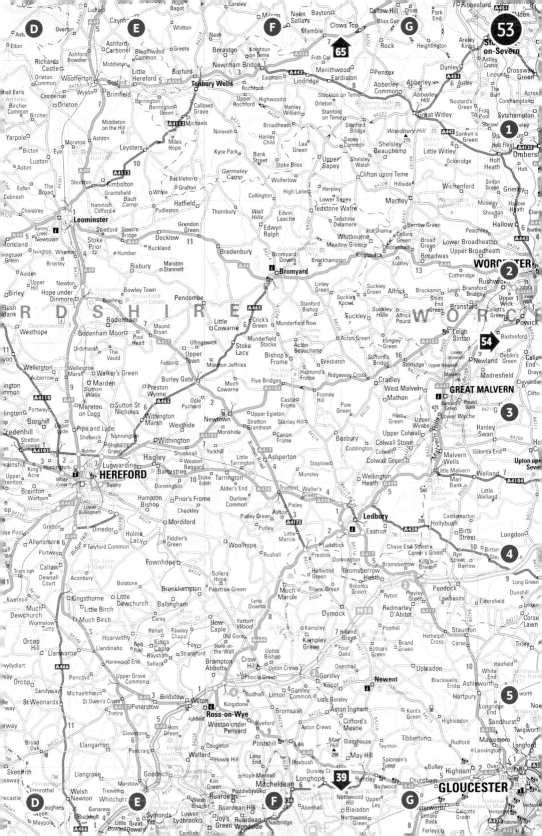

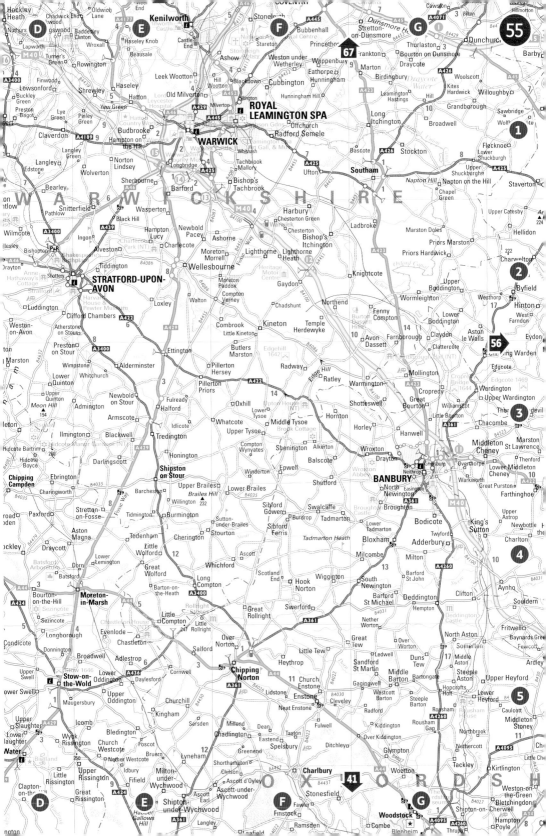

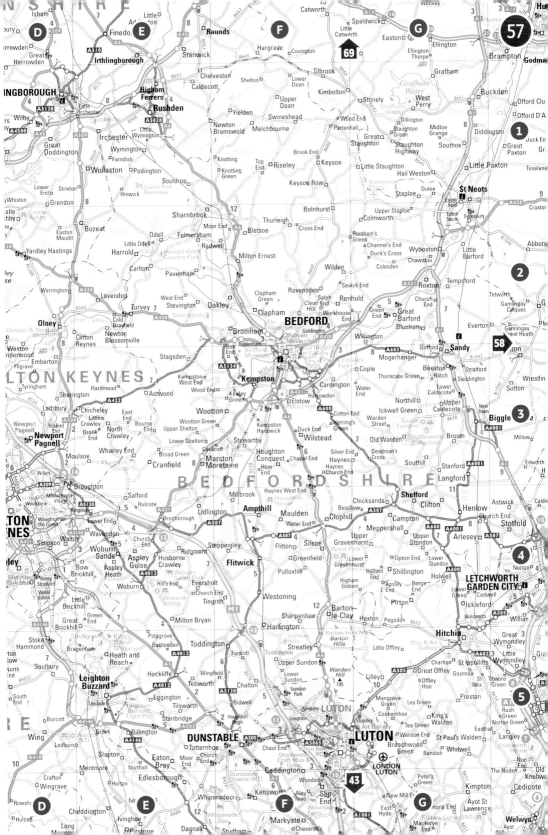

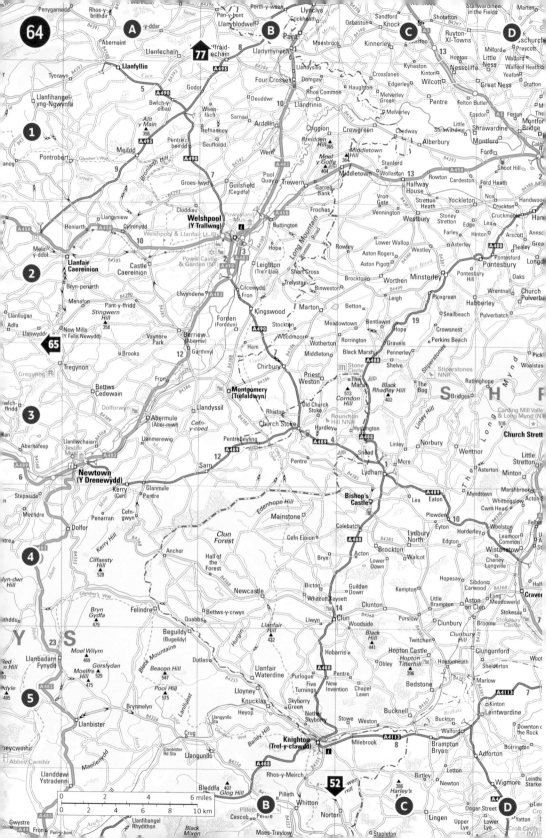

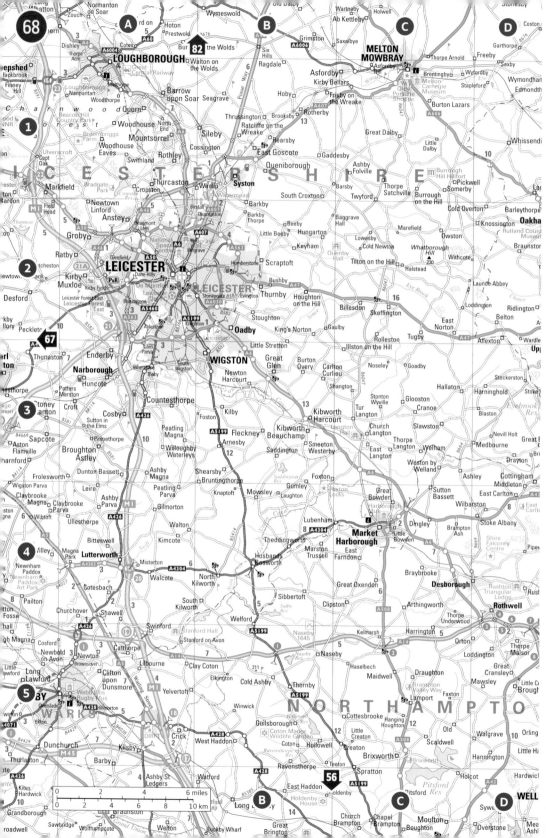

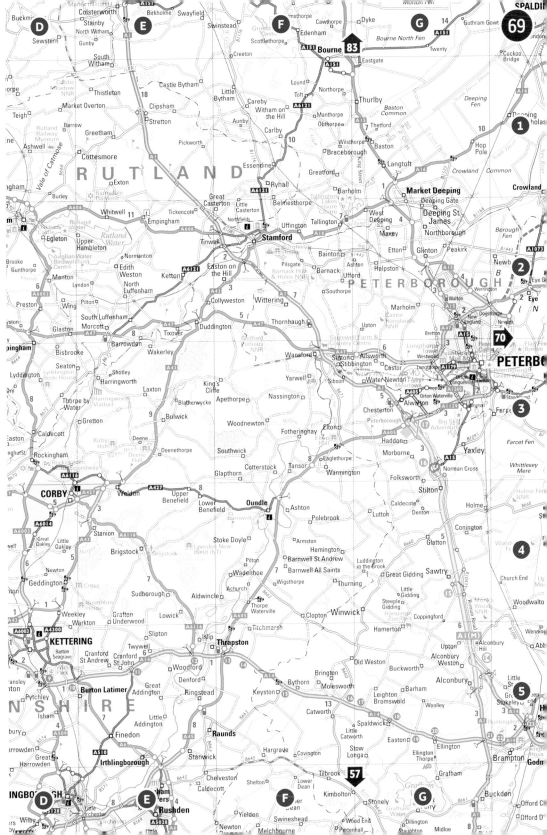

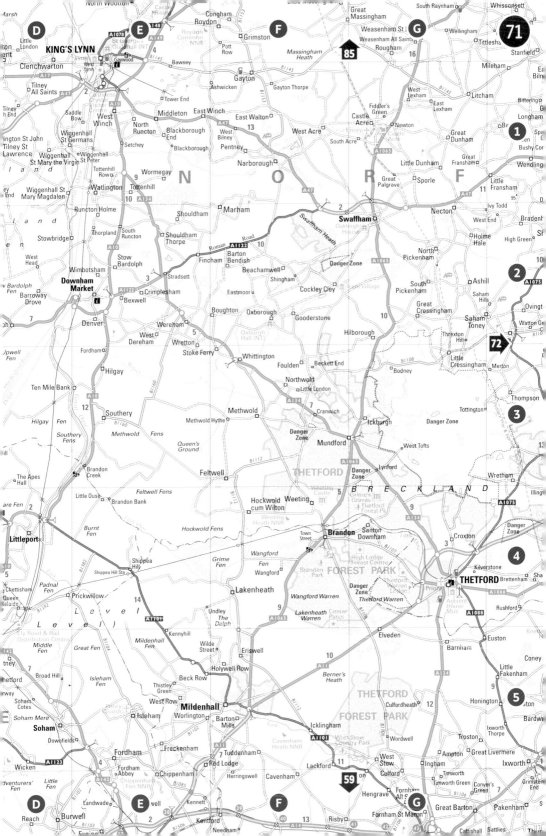

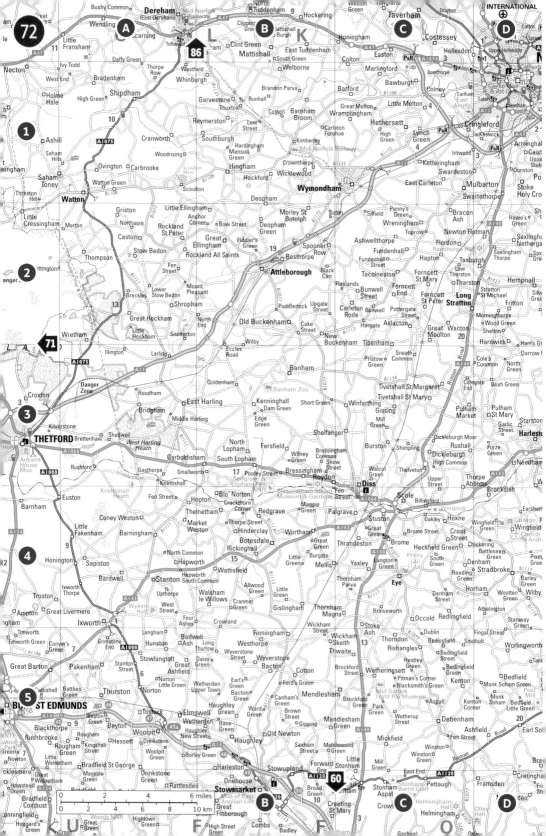

A   B   C   D

88

Rhosneigr
Pencarnisiog
A4080
Llanfaelog
Aberffraw
Langadwaladr
Trefdraeth
Hermon
10
Malltraeth
Bodorgan
A4080
Malltraeth Sands
Newborough
(Niwbwrch)
Pen-llan
Aberffraw Bay
Heritage Coast
Newborough
Warren
Llanddwyn
Island
Newborough
Warren NNR
Abermenai Point
The Bar

C A E R N A R F O N
B A Y

Dinas Dinlle
Llandwrog
A499
Pontllyfni
Trwyn Maen
Dylan
Aberdesach   10
Tai'n Lôn
Capeluchaf
Clynnog-fawr
Gyrn Goch
Bwlch
Mawr
509
Gyrn Ddu
522
Trwyn y
Gorlech
Yr Eifl
564
Llanaelhaearn
Pen-sarn
A499
Cefn-caer-Fer
St Cybi's
Well
Llangybi
Llanarmon
Chwilo
Carreg Ddu
Porth
Dinllaen
Pistyll
6
Llithfaen
Pencaenewydd
Y Ffôr
B4354
Penrhyn Fawr
Medie
Morfa Nefyn
Nefyn
Llwyndyrys
Fron
Rhos-
fawr
Afon V
Groesffordd
Edern
Garn
Boduan
B4354
Tan-y-graig
Bodfuan
A497
Abererch
Penychain Sta
Ceidio Fawr
Hendre
Llannor
Denio
1
Pwllheli
Pen-
Rhos-y-llan
Efailnewydd
Tudweiliog
Cors Geirch
NNR
Dinas
Carn Fadryn
Rhyd-y-clafdy
Carreg yr Imbill
Penllech
Garnfadryn
371
Penrhos
Porth Colmon
Pen-y-Graig   Bryn-mawr
Llaniestyn
Rhedyn
Sarn Meyllteyrn
7
Llanbedrog
Porth Ysgaden
Penrhyn
Mawr
Ty-
hen
Bryncroes
Botwnnog
B4413
Nanhoron
Y Gamlas
Trwyn Llanbedrog
Methlem
Rhydlios
Llandegwning
Mynytho
A499
Porth
Oer
Capel Carmel
Rhoshirwaun
Mynydd Rhiw
305
Plas-yn-Rhiw (NT)
Llangian
Braich Anelog
Anelog
Rhiw
Llaw-y-drel
Abersoch
St
Tudwal's
Road
Mynydd Anelog
191
Rhydolion
Llanengan
Pwlldefaid
Sarn Bach
Bwlchtocyn
St Tudwal's Islands
Braich y Pwll
Uwchmynydd
Porth
Neigwl
(Hell's Mouth)
Cilan Uchaf
Trwyn yr Wylfa
Pen y Cil
Ynys Gwylan-fawr
Aberdaron
Bay
Bardsey
Sound (Swnt Enlli)
Porth
Ceiriad
Trwyn Cilan
**Bardsey Island
(Ynys Enlli)**
St Mary's Abbey
Bardsey Island
(Ynys Enlli) NNR
Lleyn
Heritage Coast

L L E Y N   P E N I N S U L A
(PEN LLYN)

0   2   4   6 miles
0   2   4   6   8   10 km

B   C   D

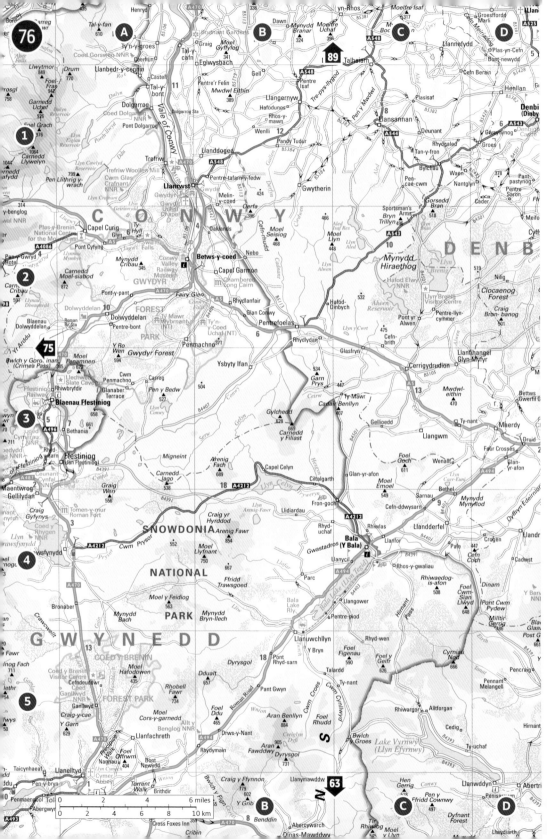

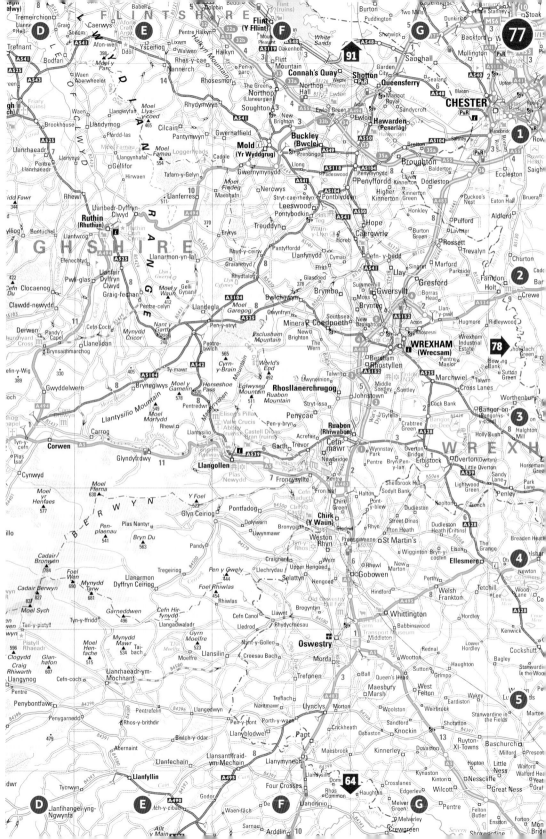

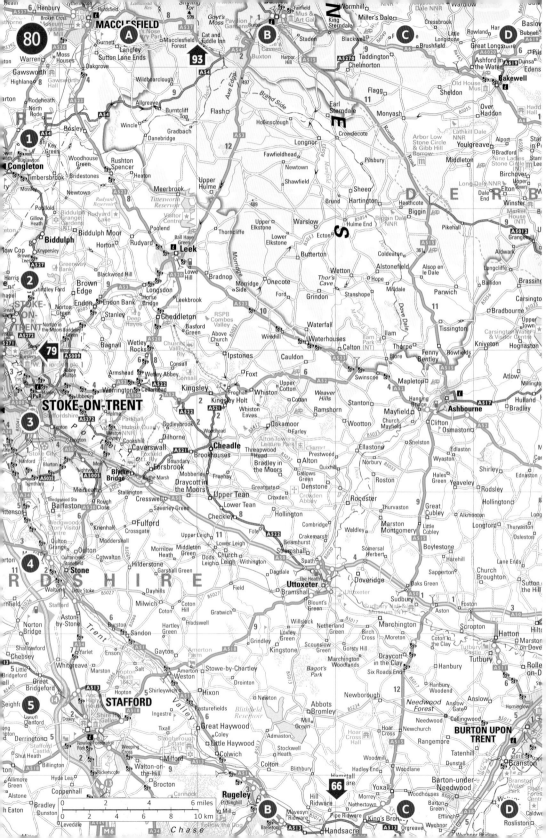

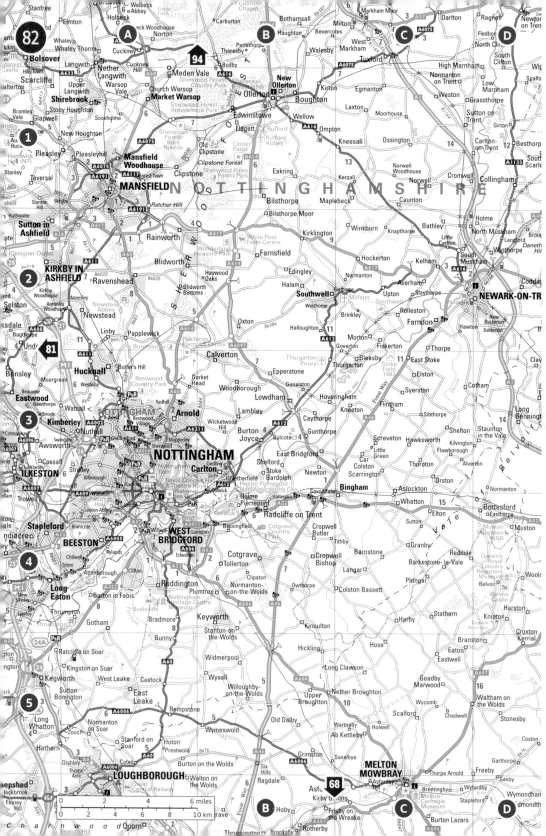

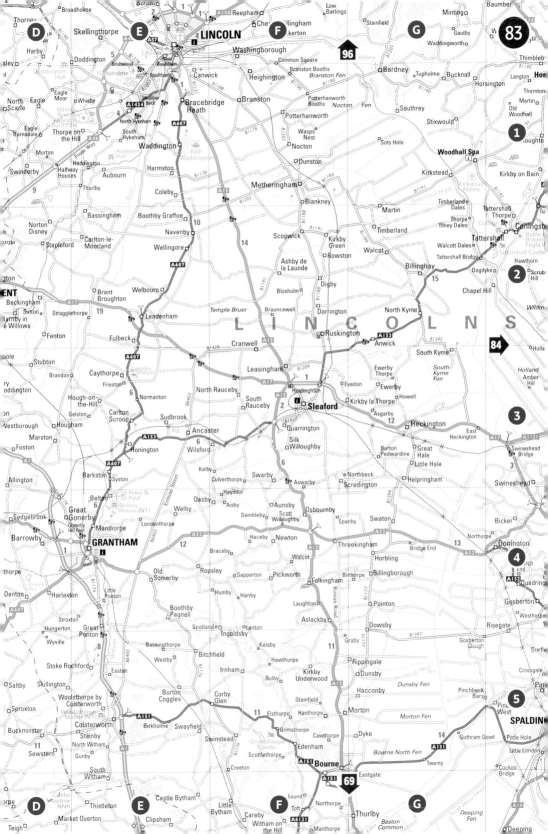

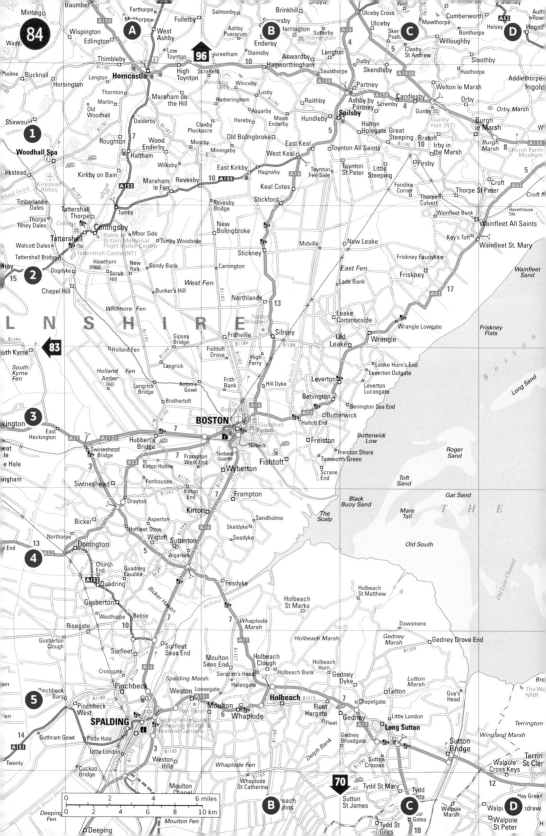

1

2

Ingoldmells
Point
Fantasy Island
Butlins Family
Entertainment Resort
Skegness Water
Leisure Park
Seathorne

Skegness

Skegness Natureland
Seal Sanctuary

Seacroft

Gibraltar
Point NNR

Gibraltar

Gibraltar Pt

W A S H

D e e p s

L y n n   D e e p s

Scolt Head
Island
NNR

Holkham
Bay

Brancaster Bay

Norton

Holme Dunes
NNR

Holme next the Sea

Brancaster
Staithe

Burnham
Deepdale

Burnham
Norton

Burnham
Over Staithe

Holkham
NNR

3

Wells-next-th

Thornham

A149

Titchwell

Brancaster

Burnham
Over Town

Burnham

Holkham

A149

17

Burnham
Market

B1355

Holkham
Hall

Peddars Way &
Norfolk Coast Path

Ringstead

Burnham Thorpe

Wighton

Sea Life Centre

Hunstanton

Summerfield

Norfolk
Lavender

Creake
Abbey

North
Creake

B1153

Stanhoe

South
Creake

Egmere

Wells &
Walsingham
Lt. Rly

Shrine of Our Lady
of Walsingham

Shirehall
Museum

4

Heacham

Eaton

Sedgeford

Docking

B1454

B1454

Barmer

North
Barsham

Slipper
Chapel

ighton
iles

Fring

Bircham
Newton

B1155

Syderstone

West
Barsham

Snettisham

13

Southgate

Shernborne

Great Bircham

Bircham
Tofts

Bagthorpe

Sculthorpe

B1355

Sn

A149

Ingoldisthorpe

Dersingham

Anmer

Houghton Hall

Tattersett

Coxford

B1454

Dunton

Shereford

Hempton

86

Fakenhan

Fakenham

Peter Black
Sand

A148

Fatterford

Toftrees

Dersingham
Bog NNR

Sandringham
House

West Newton

New Houghton

East Rudham

West Rudham

Helhoughton

A1065

Colkirk

Bulldog
Sand

St Mary
Magdalene
Chapel

Flitcham

A148

Harpley

17

West Raynham

East
Raynham

5

Whissonsett

t Sand

Trinity
Hospital

Castle Rising

Hillington

Little Massingham

Great
Massingham

South Raynham

Horningtoft

Godwick

Ongar Hill

North Wootton

Castle
Rising

A148

Congham
Roydon

Grimston

Weasenham St Peter

Weasenham All Saints

Rougham

Wellingham

Tittleshall

Stanfield

Little
London

KING'S LYNN

A1078

South
Wootton

A148

A149

St George's
Guildhall (NT)

Roydon
Common
NNR

Pott
Row

Massingham
Heath

16

Mileham

Gr

Bilne

Clenchwarton

A47

Gaywood

B1145

Bawsey

B1153

71

Beeston

Tilney
ints

A47

A10

Tower End

Gayton

Ashwicken

n Thorpe

Fiddler's
Green

Litcham

B1145

East
Lexham

Bitterin

Longham

Saddle
Bow

West
Winch

Middleton

East Winch

A47

East Walton

13

Castle
Acre

Newton

Litcham

Iney
ints

Guinness
Crystal
Visitor
Centre

2

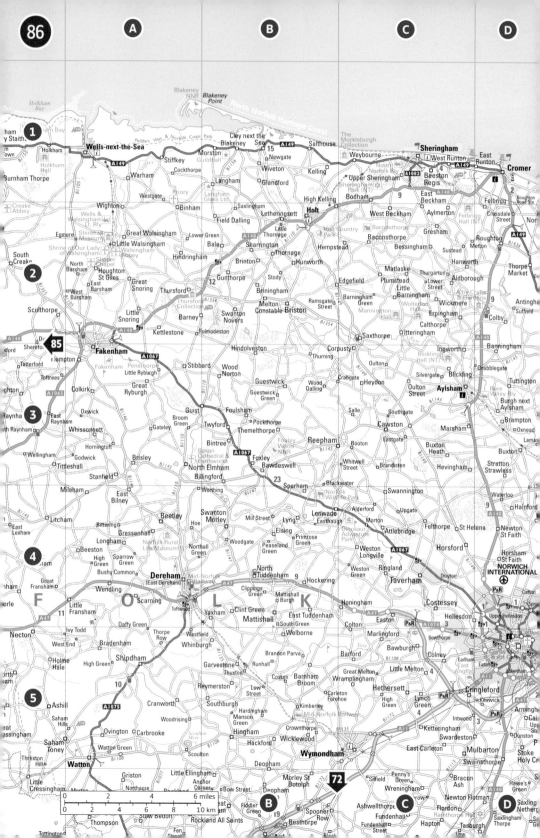

1

2

Overstrand
Sidestrand
Trimingham
repps
southrepps
Gimingham
Mundesley
Lower Street
Trunch
Paston Street
Knapton
Paston
Bacton
Bradfield
Old Hall
Street
Keswick
Edingthorpe
Walcott
Swafield
Ridlington
Happisburgh
Edingthorpe
Green
Witton Bridge
12
North
Walsham
Spa Common
Crostwight
Whimpwell
Green
Eccles-on-Sea
Tungate
Meeting
House Hill
Happisburgh
Common
Hempstead
Felmingham
Honing
Ingham Corner
Lessingham
Sea Palling
Skeyton
Corner
Bengate
Briggate
East
Ruston
Ingham
Westwick
Lyngate
Waxham
skeyton
Worstead
Dilham
Stalham
anton
Abbot
Frankfort
Smallburgh
A149
Stalham Green
Hickling
Scottow
Sloley
Sutton
Hickling Green
Little
Hautbois
Market
Street
A1151
Barton
Turf
A149
Hickling
Heath
Horsey Corner
Horsey
Sco
Ruston
Beeston St
Lawrence
Wood
Street
Hill Common
Horsey Windpump
Tunstead
Ashmanhaugh
Neatishead
Catfield
Winterton Dunes NNR
Colishall
Butcher's
Common
Irstead
Sharp
Street
Potter
Heigham
West Somerton
Threehammer
Common
Ludham
Mustard
Hyrn
East
Somerton
Winterton-on-Sea
Belaugh
Hoveton
NORFOLK
Johnson Street
Bastwick
Martham
Hemsby Holiday Centre
Wroxham
Upper
Street
Horning
A1062
16
Hemsby
Hemsby Hole
Newport
12
Repps
Thurne
Rollesby
Ormesby St
Margaret
Scratby
Crostwick
Woodbastwick
Clippesby
California
Spixworth
Ranworth
Cargate
Green
Fleggburgh
Ormesby
St Michael
Salhouse
Pilson
Green
(Burgh St Margaret)
Roman Site
Rackheath
Salhouse
Sta
Panxworth
Billockby
Filby
Caister-on-Sea
A1151
New
Rackheath
Little
Plumstead
South
Walsham
Upton
Fishley
A1064
Thrigby
Mautby
West
Caister
Thorpe
End
Pedham
North
Burlingham
Acle
Stokesby
Runham
West
End
H
Yarmouth
ORWICH
3 Great Plumstead
Witton
Damgate
7
A47
Runham
Thorpe St Andrew
Lingwood
Tunstall
Greyfriar's Cloisters
P&R
Blofield
Beighton
Sea Life Centre
Postwick
Brundall
Strumpshaw
South Burlingham
Halvergate
Water
Old Merchant's House
Row 111 House
3
Surlingham
Moulton
St Mary
Halvergate
Marshes
Breydon
Pleasure Beach
Trowse Newton
Buckenham
Freethorpe
Berney Arms Mill
Berney Arms Sta
3
Southtown
GREAT YARMOUTH
Kirby
Bedon
Bramerton
Hassingham
Wickhampton
Burgh
Castle
A146
Rockland St Mary
Freethorpe Common
Petriss Animal
Adventure
Bradwell
Gorleston-
on-Sea
St Edmund
Framingham Pigot
Claxton
Cantley
Limpenhoe
Belton
Browston
Green
Yelverton
Ashby St Mary
Carleton St Peter
Reedham
Hobland
Hall
ringland
Framingham Earl
Bergh
Apton
Hardley
Street
Norton
Marshes
Fritton
Ashby Dell
Hopton
Howe
Brooke
Thurton
Langley Street
Nogdam End
Lower
Thurlton
Somerleyton
Hall & Gdn
73
10
Seething
Sisland
14
Chedgrave
Norton
Subcourse
Thurlton
13
Thor
Blundeston
D
Kirstead
Green
E
Mundham
Loddon
Heckingham
Thor
F
Heringfleet
Somerleyton
G
The
Laurels
Hales
Hales
Hall
Haddiscoe
Ravingham
Maypole Green
Pleasurewood Hills Theme Park
Brundish

1

2

90 ▶

3

4

Great Ormes Head   Great Orme   Venue
Great Orme   Cabin   Cymru
Country Park   Lift
Toll   **Llandudno**   Little Ormes Head
Gogarth   Penrhyn-side
Great Orme   **Penrhyn Bay** (Bae Penrhyn)
Tramway   A546   4   Glanwydden
Conwy   Rhos-on-Sea
Sands

Puffin Island   St Seiriol's   Penmon Priory
(Priestholm)   Well   (ruins)
CONWY
BAY
Mariandyrys   Glan-y-afon   Caim   Penmon
Bay   Degaawy
Aberconwy House (NT)   **Llandudno**   Esgyryn
Llanddona   Junction   17   **Colwyn Bay**
Llan-faes   Dutchman   A55   18   **Mochdre**   **(Bae Colwyn)**
PLlangoed   Bank   16a   **Conwy**   19   20   10   23
Beaumaris   Dwygyfylchi   Conwy Castle   18   Llansanffraid   Llandulas
Castle   Lavan   **Penmaenmawr**   Capelulo   Glan Conwy   Bryn-y-maen   A547 **Abergele**
Beaumaris   Sands   15a   Suspension   Llanelian-   Llysfaen
(Biwmares)   **Llanfairfechan**   15   Foel Lus   Bridge (NT)   yn-Rhos   Rhyd-y-foel
Llansadwrn   A545   Moelfre   Pentrefelin   Dolwen
Llandegfan   4   Nant-y-Pandy   Moelfre   Betws
Port   Garddino   Garreg   Tal-y-fan   Henryd   Llanelian   yn-Rhos
Bangor   Penrhyn   Fawr   610   Dawn   Moelfre Uchaf
Penrhyn   Abergwyngregyn   Rowen   Mynydd   396
Castle   Crymlyn   Ty'n-y-groes   Llanelian   Trofarth   Mynydd
A4087   Minffordd   Llandygai   Coedydd   Bodnant   Branar
Pen-rhos-garnedd   Tal-y-bont   Aber   Caerhun   Gdns (NT)   Llanfair Talhaiarn
Moel   NNR   Tal-y-   Moel   A548
Wnion   cafn   Gyffylog
Waen   Glasinfryn   Llanllechid   580   Drum   Eglwysbach   341   Pentre
Rhyd   Rachub   770   Castell   Mwdwl   Isaf
Tregarth   Drosgl   Llwytmor   **Llanbedr-y-cennin**   Eithin   Tre-pys-llwyd
Pentir   Coed-y-parc   758   Foel-Fras   11   **76**   389   Pen-y-Mwdwl
Bethesda   942   Tal-y-bont
Rhiwlas   Gerlan   Garnedd Uchaf   Vale of   Gernyw   dunos
Braichmelyn   Dulyn   garrog   Dolgarrog Sta   Rhos-   Mo
S N O W D O N I A   Res   Coed Dolgarrog   y-mawr
NNR   Wenlli
Pont Dolgarrog

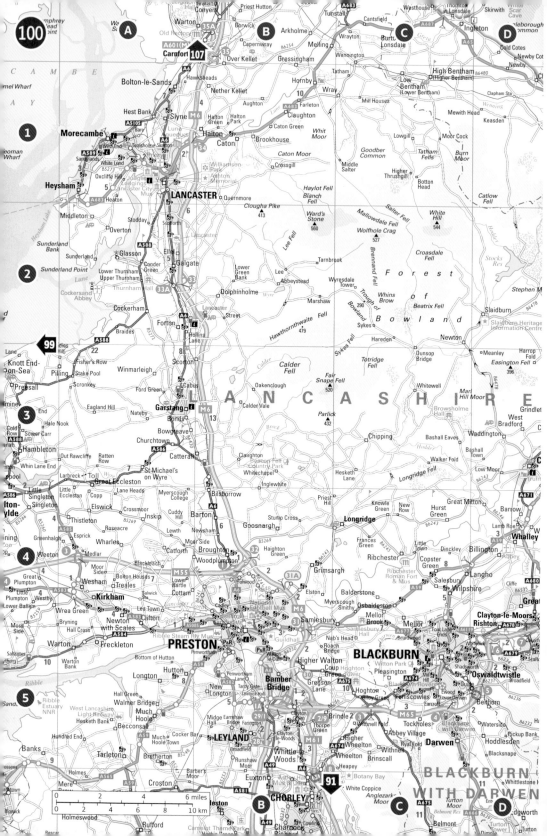

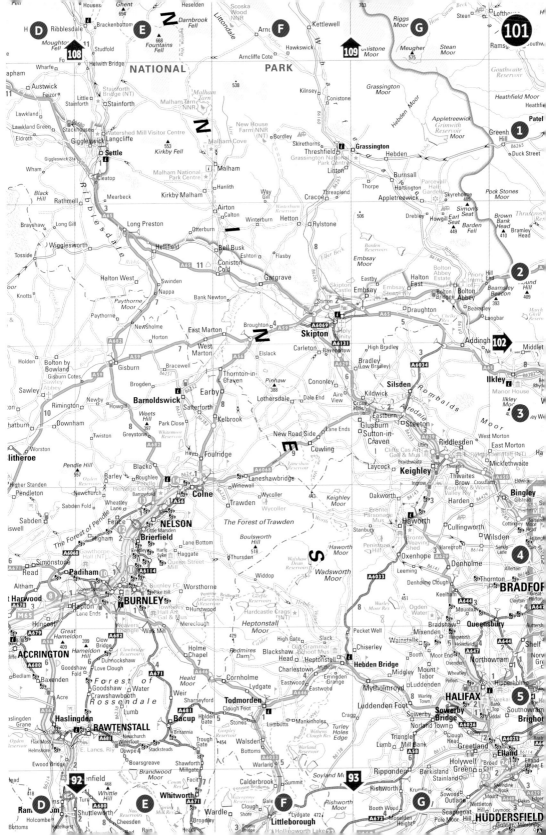

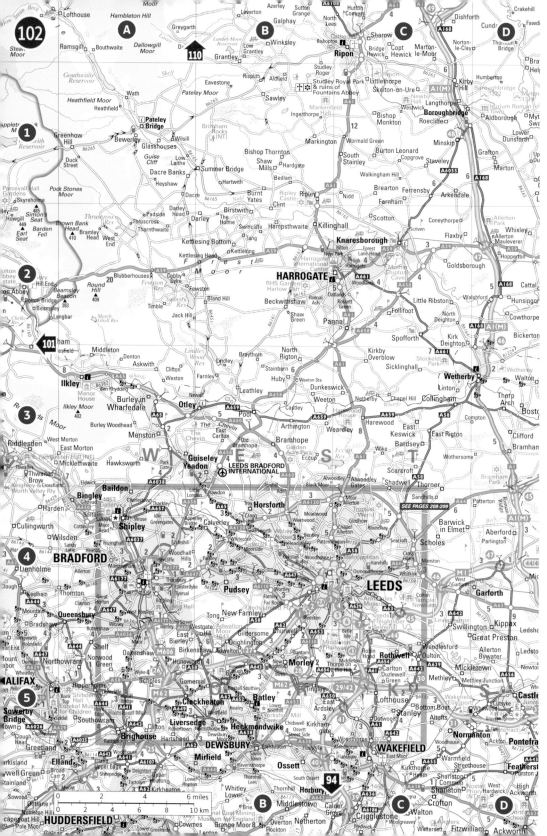

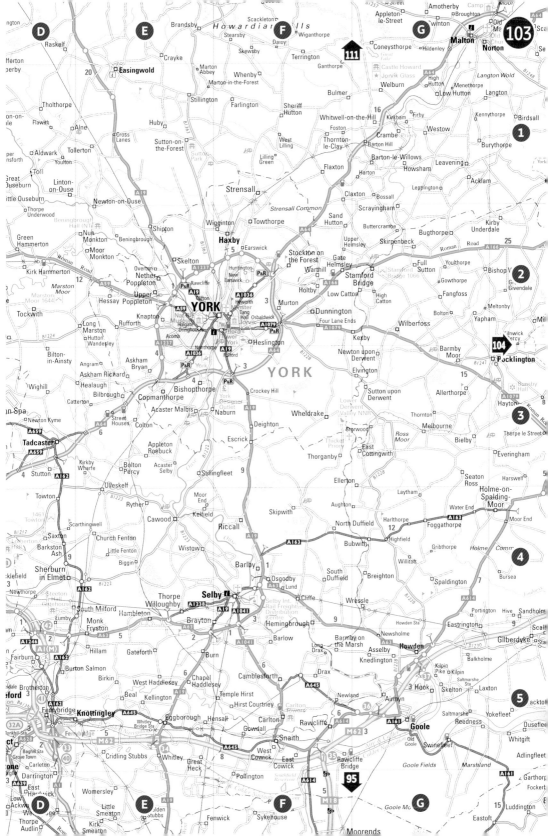

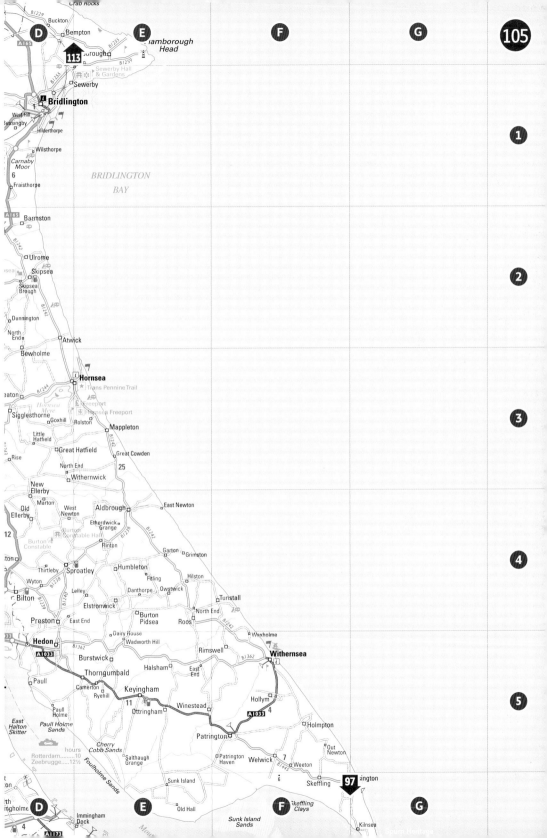

Crab Rocks
B1229
Buckton
Bempton
113
borough
E Flamborough Head
A165
D
B1255
B1229
Sewerby Hall & Gardens
B1255
Sewerby
B1259
West Hill
Bridlington
Bessingby
Hilderthorpe

1

Wilsthorpe
Carnaby Moor
6
Fraisthorpe

BRIDLINGTON
BAY

A165
Barmston
B1242

Ulrome
Skipsea
Skipsea Brough

2

Dunnington
North End
Atwick
Bewholme

B1244
Hornsea
Trans Pennine Trail
Hornsea Mere
Freeport
Hornsea Freeport
eaton
Sigglesthorne
Goxhill
Rolston
Mappleton
B1242

3

Little Hatfield
Rise
Great Hatfield
Great Cowden
North End
25
Withernwick

New Ellerby
Old Ellerby
Marton
West Newton
Aldbrough
East Newton
B1238
Etherdwick Grange
12
Burton Constable Hall
Rinton
B1242

Thirtleby
Sproatley
Humbleton
Garton
Grimston
4
Wyton
B1238
Lelley
Fitling
Hilston
Bilton
Danthorpe
Owstwick
Elstronwick
Preston
Burton Pidsea
Roos
North End
Tunstall
B1242
East End
Dairy House
Wadworth Hill
Waxholme
33
Hedon
Rimswell
B1362
Withernsea
A1033
Burstwick
Halsham
East End
B1362
Paull
Thorngumbald
Camerton
Keyingham
Winestead
Hollym

5

Ryehill
11
Ottringham
A1033
4
Paull Holme
East Halton Skitter
Paull Holme Sands
Patrington
Holmpton
Cherry Cobb Sands
Salthaugh Grange
Welwick
7
Out Newton
hours
Rotterdam......10
Zeebrugge......12½
Foulholme Sands
Patrington Haven
Weeton
B1445
6
Sunk Island
Skeffling
97
ington
mgholme
D
E
Old Hall
F
Skeffling Clays
G
4
Immingham Dock
Sunk Island Sands
Mou
Kilnsea
A1173

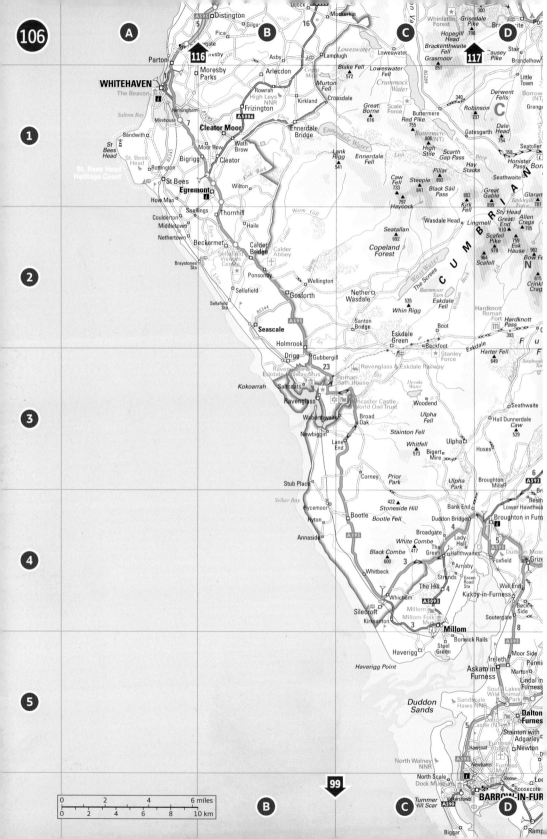

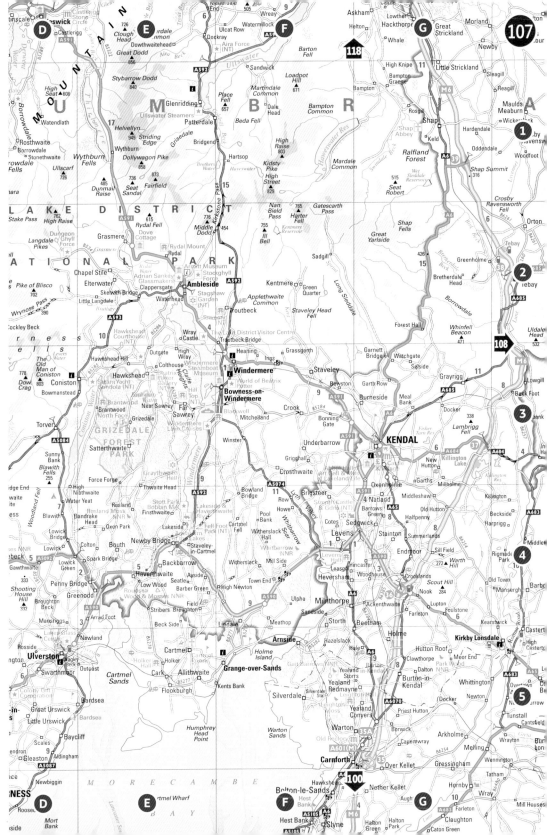

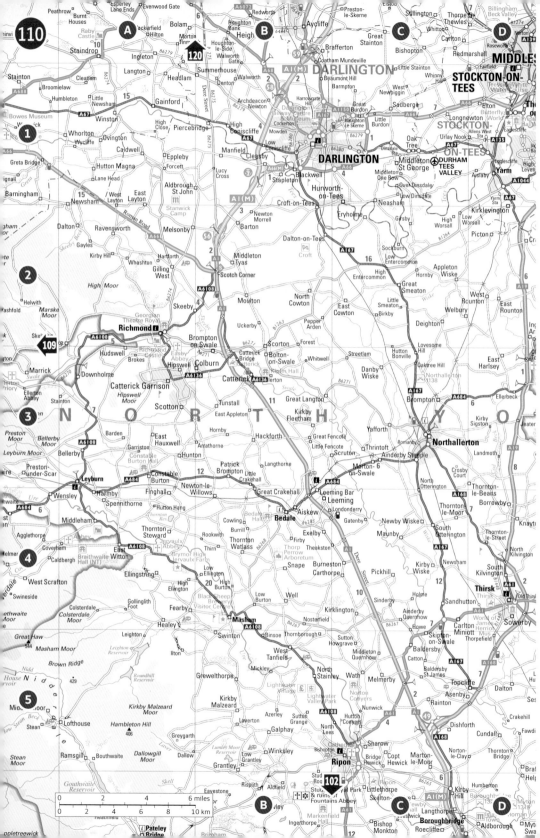

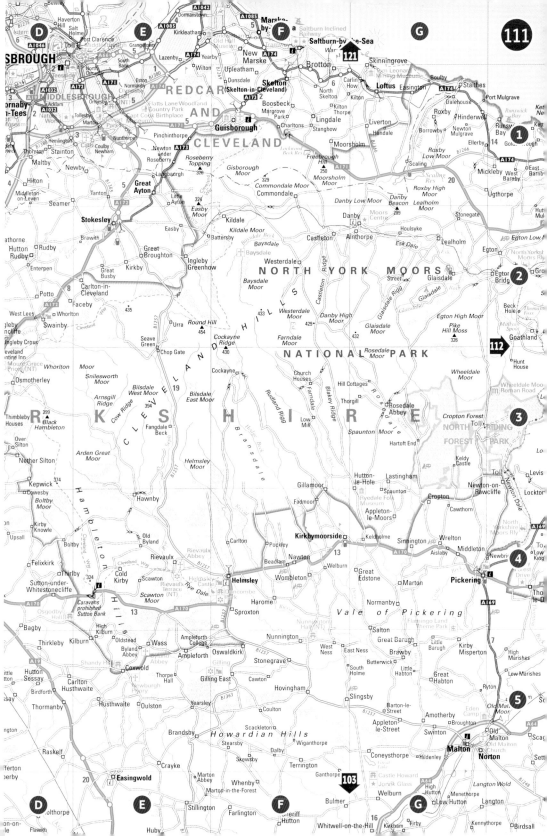

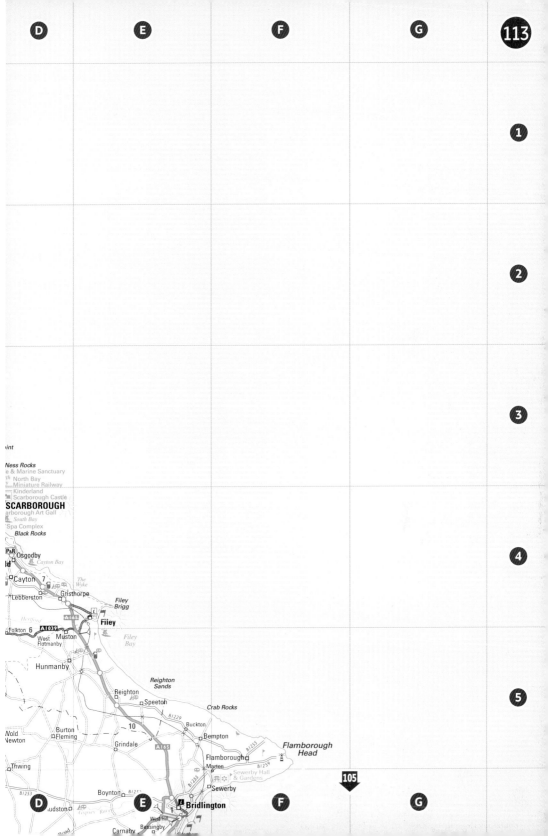

1

2

3

...int

Ness Rocks
e & Marine Sanctuary
th North Bay
Miniature Railway
Kinderland
Scarborough Castle
SCARBOROUGH
arborough Art Gall
South Bay
Spa Complex
Black Rocks

P&R Osgodby
ld
Cayton   7   *Cayton Bay*
Lebberston   Gristhorpe   *The Wyke*
             Filey
             Brigg
A165 **Filey**
Folkton 6 A1039   Muston
West   *Filey*
Flotmanby   *Bay*

Hunmanby

                  Reighton
                  Sands
       Reighton
          Speeton   *Crab Rocks*
                   B1229
Nold   10   Buckton
Newton Burton   Bempton
        Fleming Grindale A165   B1255
Thwing   Flamborough   *Flamborough*
                              Marton   *Head*
                                        Sewerby Hall
                              B1259   & Gardens
                    B1253
        Boynton B125   Sewerby

B1253
udston   *Gypsey Race*   **Bridlington**
                  West Hill
                  Bessingby
        Carnaby

4

5

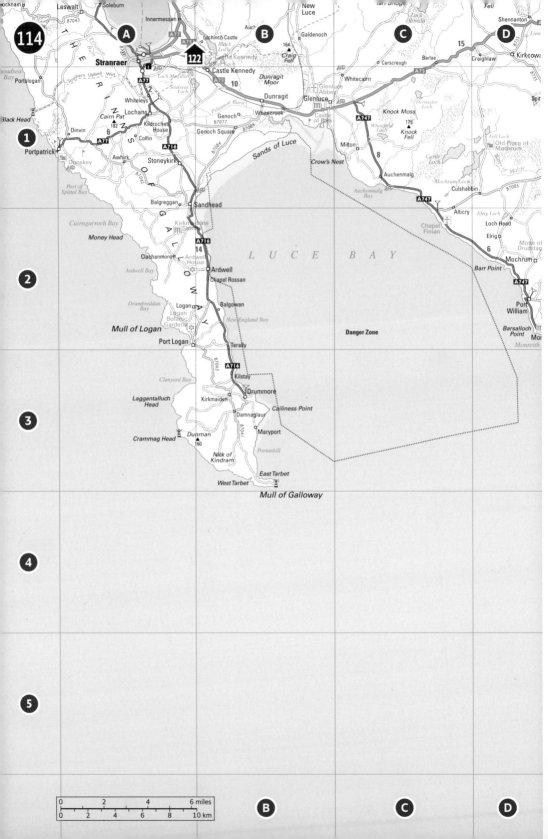

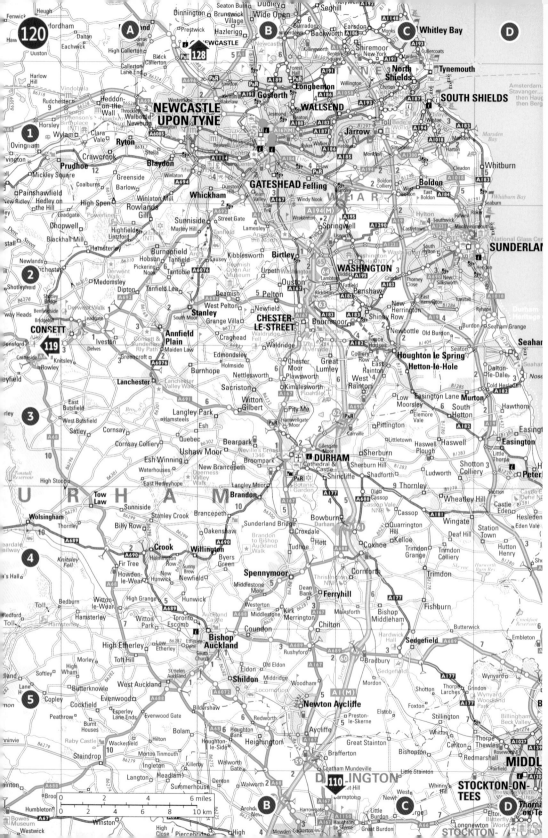

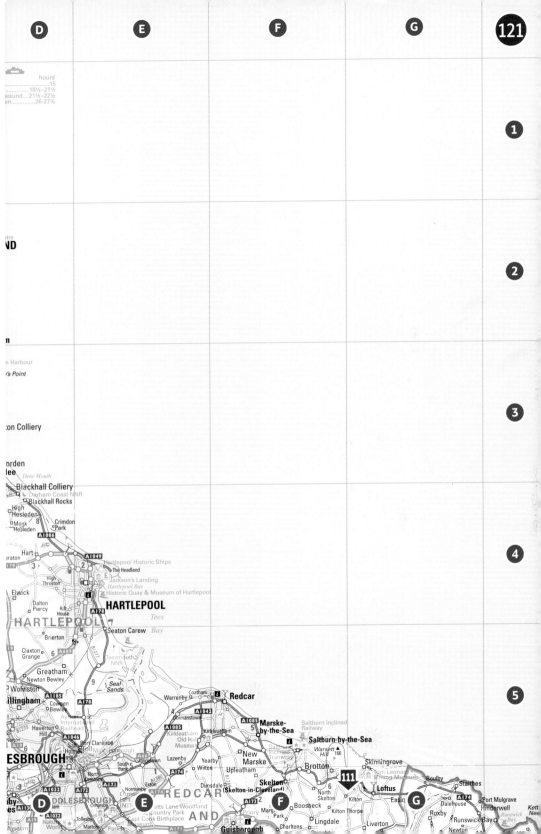

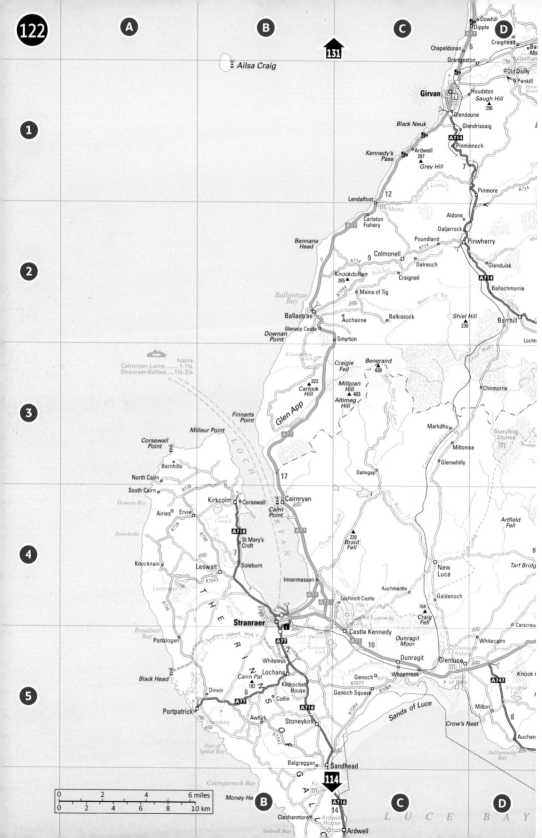

A   B   C   D

1

2

3

4

5

131

Ailsa Craig

Chapeldonan
Grangeston
Girvan
Houdston
Saugh Hill
296
Glendoune
Black Neuk
Glendrissaig
A714
Pinminnoch
Kennedy's
Pass
Ardwell
297
Grey Hill
7
Pinmore
B734
Lendalfoot   12
Motte
A77
Carleton
Fishery
Aldons
Daljarrock
Poundland
B734
Pinwherry
Bennane
Head
Colmonell
Dalreoch
Glenduisk
B734   9
Knockdolian
265
Craigneil
Water of Tig
A714
Ballochmorrie
Mains of Tig
Ballantrae
Bay
Auchairne
Balkissock
Shiel Hill
230
Barrhill
Ballantrae
Glenapp Castle
Downan
Point
Smyrton
Craigie
Fell
Beneraird
439
Carlock
Hill
323
Milljoan
Hill   403
Altimeg
Hill
Markdhu
Miltonise
Standing
Stones
Finnarts
Point
Glen App
A77
Milleur Point
Chirmorrie
Glenwhilly
Corsewall
Point
Barnhills
North Cairn
17
Dalnigap
Artfield
Fell
South Cairn
B738
Kirkcolm
Corsewall
Cairnryan
Cairn
Point
A77
Tarf Bridge
Braid
235
Fell
Airies
Ervie
B738
A718
St Mary's
Croft
7
Soleburn
New
Luce
Knocknain
Leswalt
B7043
Innermessan
Auchmantle
Galdenoch
Lochinch Castle
Craig
Fell   164
Carscreu
Portslogan
B738
Stranraer
A77
Castle Kennedy
Whitecairn
Dunragit
Moor
10
Dunragit
Glenluce
Abbey
Black Head
Whiteleys
Lochans
Genoch
B7077
Whitecrook
Glenluce
A747
Knock
Dinvin
Cairn Pat
182
Kidrochet
House
Colfin
Genoch Square
B7084
A77
6
A716
Milton
8
Portpatrick
Awhirk
Stoneykirk
Sands of Luce
Crow's Nest
Auchen
Balgreggan
Sandhead
114
A716
Cairngarroch Bay
Money He
Clachanmore
14
Ardwell
House
Ardwell
L U C E   B A Y

Cairnryan-Larne.........1-1¾
Stranraer-Belfast.....1¼-3¼   hours

0   2   4   6 miles
0   2   4   6   8   10 km

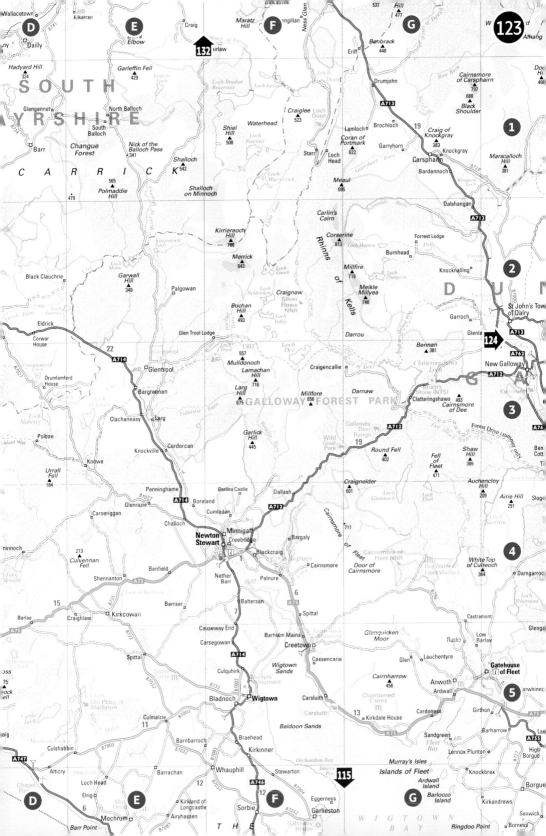

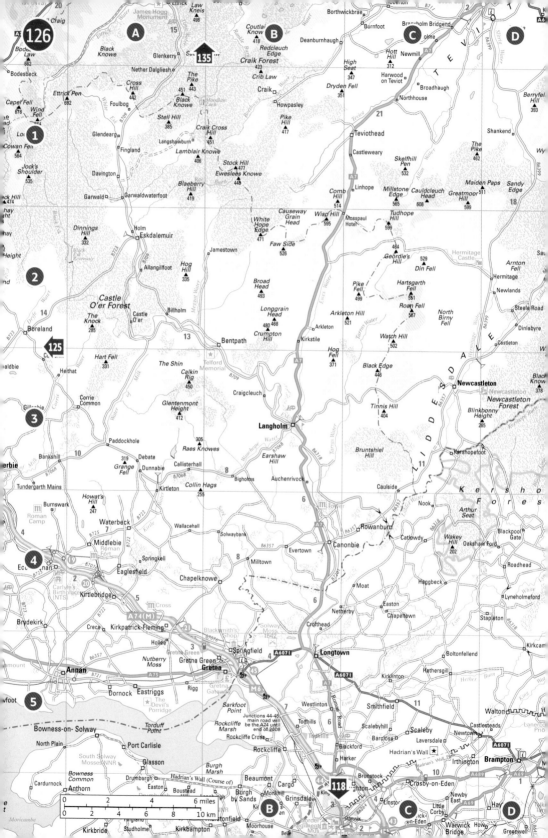

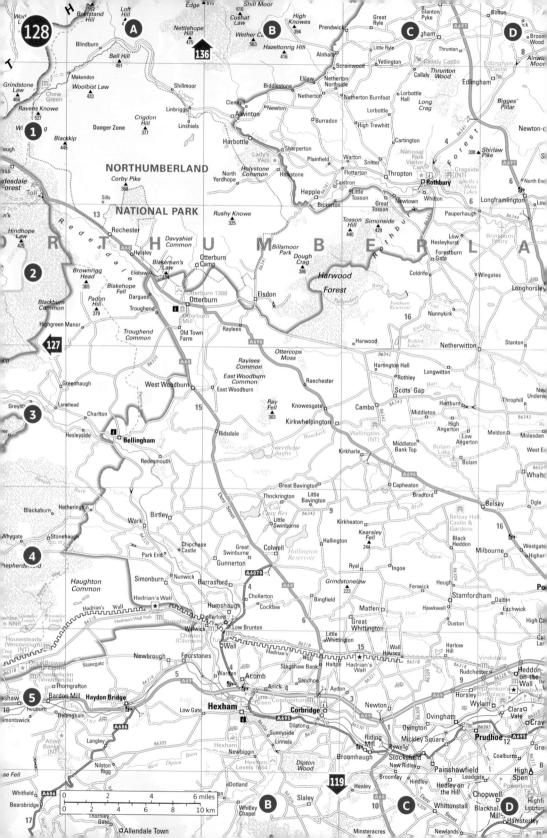

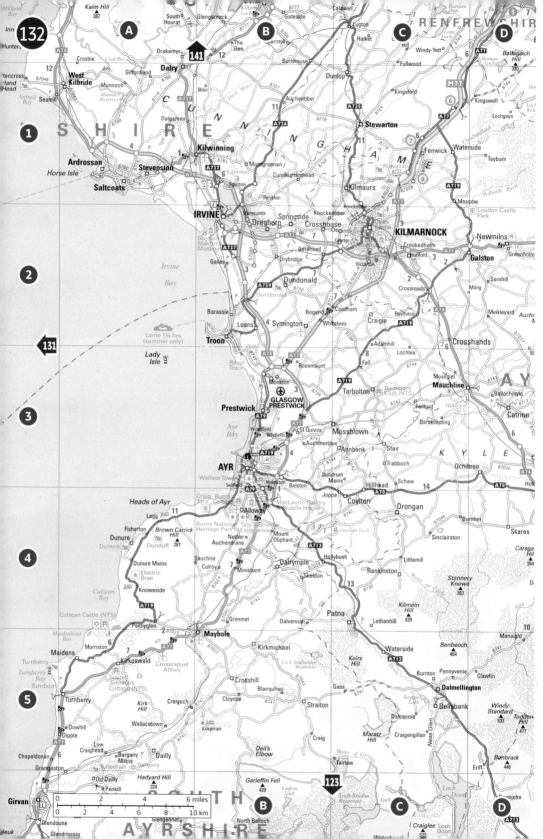

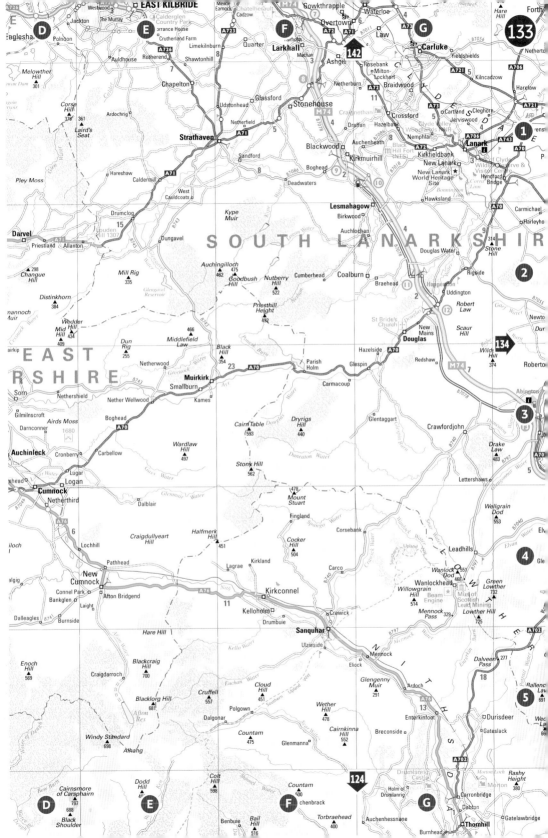

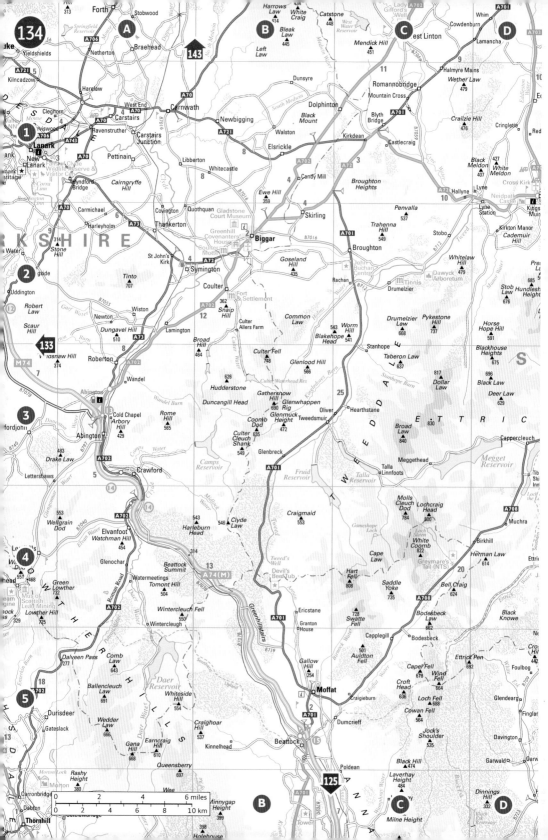

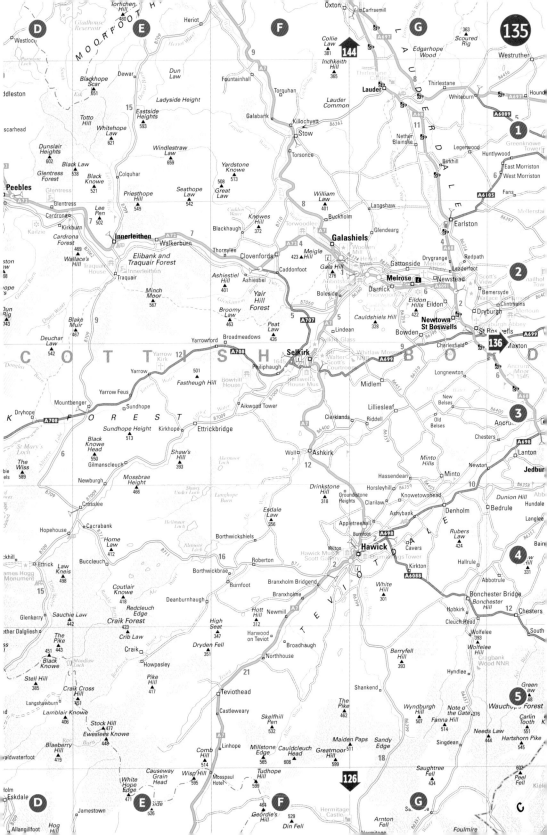

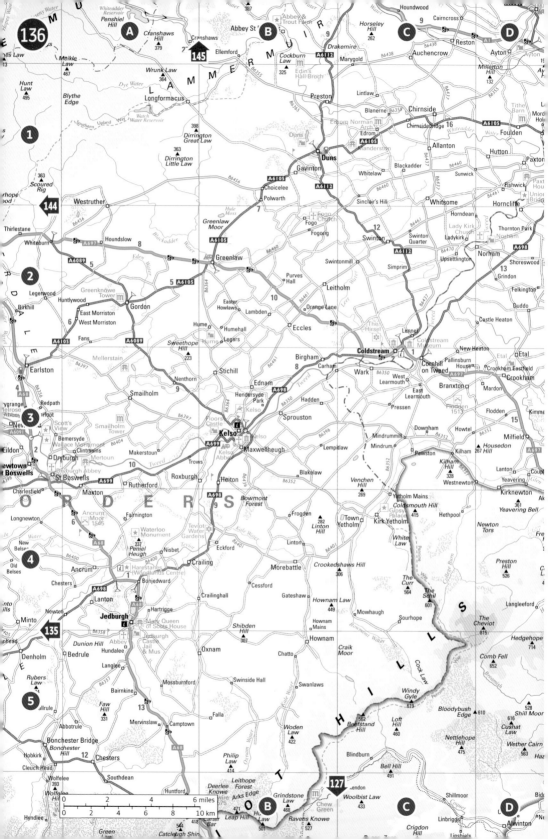

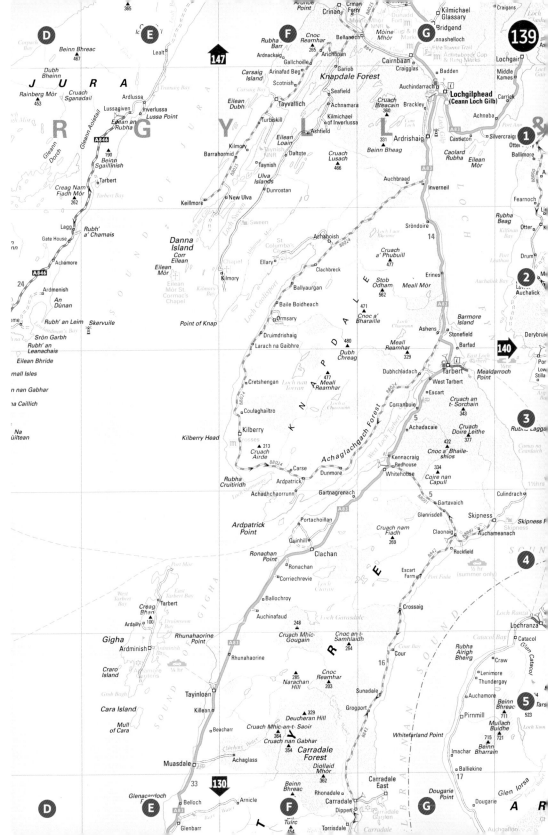

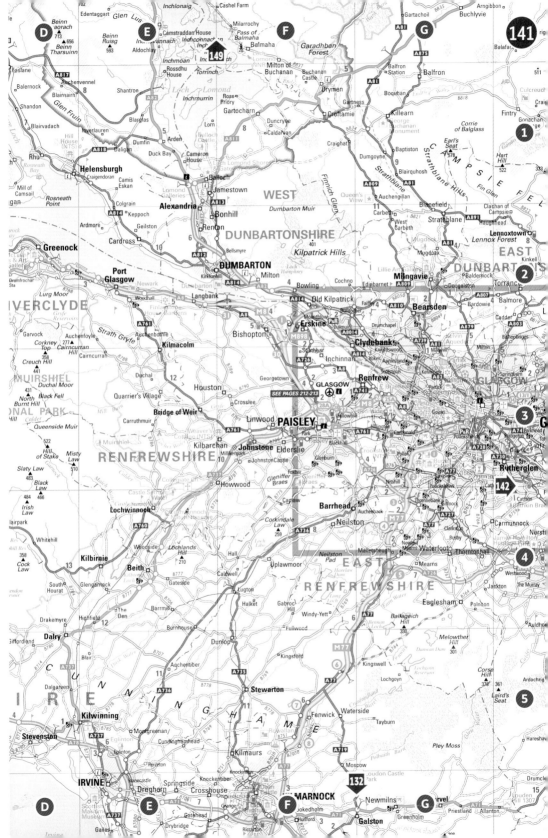

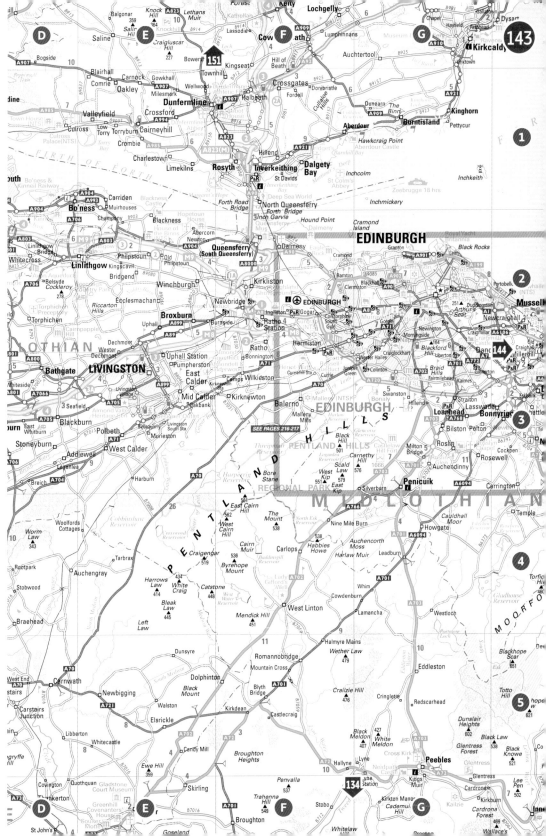

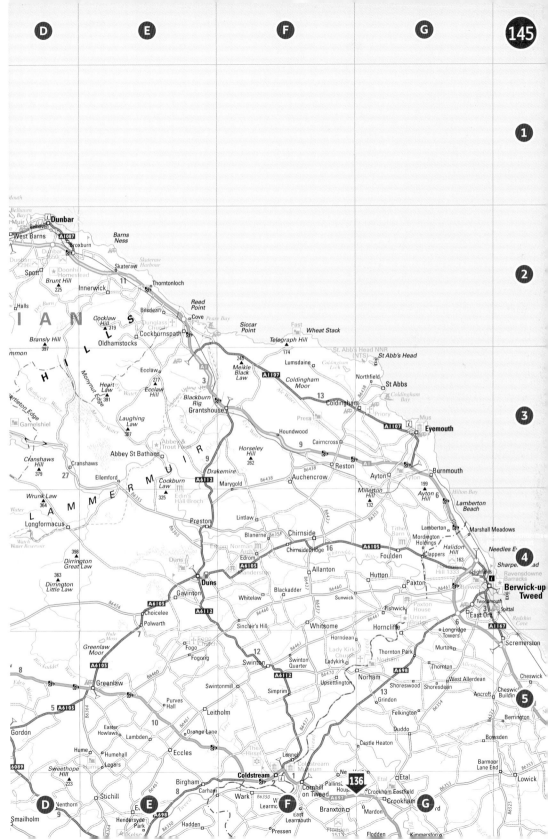

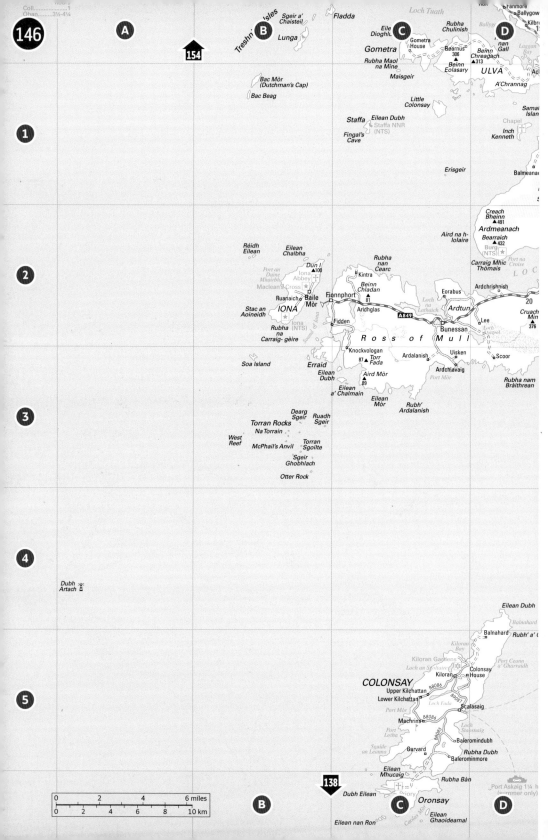

Coll.................1
Oban........3½–4¼

A   B   154   C   D

Treshnish Isles
Sgeir a'
Chaisteil   Fladda
Lunga

Eile
Dioghlu   Rubha
Chulinish   Ballygow
Kilbr

Gometra   Gometra
House   Bèarnus
306   Beinn
Chreagach
▲313   nan
Gall

Rubha Maol
na Mine   Beinn
Eolasary   **ULVA**   A'Chrannag   Loggan
Bay

Bac Mòr
(Dutchman's Cap)   Maisgeir   Little
Colonsay   Samal
Islan

Bac Beag   Chapel

Staffa   Eilean Dubh   Inch
Kenneth

Fingal's
Cave   Staffa NNR
(NTS)

1   Erisgeir   Balmean

Réidh
Eilean   Eilean
Chalbha   Rubha
nan
Cearc   Creach
Bheinn
▲491   Ardmeanach
Aird na h-
Iolaire   Bearraich
▲432

Port an
Duine
Mhairbh   Dùn I
▲100   Iona
Abbey   Kintra   Beinn
Chladan
▲81   Burg
(NTS)   Carraig Mhic
Thòmais   LOC

2   Maclean's Cross   Baile
Mòr   Fionnphort   Eorabus   Ardchrishnish
Ruanaich   Aridhglas   A849   Ardtun   20
Stac an
Aoineidh   **IONA**   Loch
na
Lathaich   Lee   Cruach
Min
376
Rubha
na
Carraig- gèire   Iona
(NTS)   Fidden   Bunessan

Ross of Mull   Knockvologan
Torr
Fada   Ardalanish   Uisken   Scoor
Soa Island   87▲   Rubha nam
Bràithrean
Erraid   Eilean
Dubh   Aird Mòr   Ardchiavaig
89▲   Port Mòr
Eilean
a' Chalmain   Eilean
Mòr   Rubh'
Ardalanish

3   Dearg
Sgeir   Ruadh
Sgeir
Torran Rocks
Na Torrain   Torran
Sgoilte
West
Reef   McPhail's Anvil
Sgeir
Ghobhlach
Otter Rock

4   Dubh
Artach

Eilean Dubh
Balnahard
Balnahard   Rubh' a' C

Kiloran
Bay
Kiloran Gardens   Port Ceann
a' Gharraidh
Loch an Sgoltaire   Colonsay
House
COLONSAY   Kiloran
B8086   Port Askaig 1¼ h
(summer 1¼ h)
Upper Kilchattan
Lower Kilchattan   B8087   Scalasaig
5   Loch Fada
Port Mòr   B8086   Loch
Staosnaig
Machrins   B8085
Port
Letha   Balerominbudh
Sgaide
an Leanna   Garvard   Rubha Dubh
Balerominmore
Eilean
Mhucaig   Rubha Bàn

Dubh Eilean   138   Priory   **Oronsay**   Eilean
Ghaoideamal

Eilean nan Ron   Caolas Mòr

A   B   C   D

0   2   4   6 miles
0   2   4   6   8   10 km

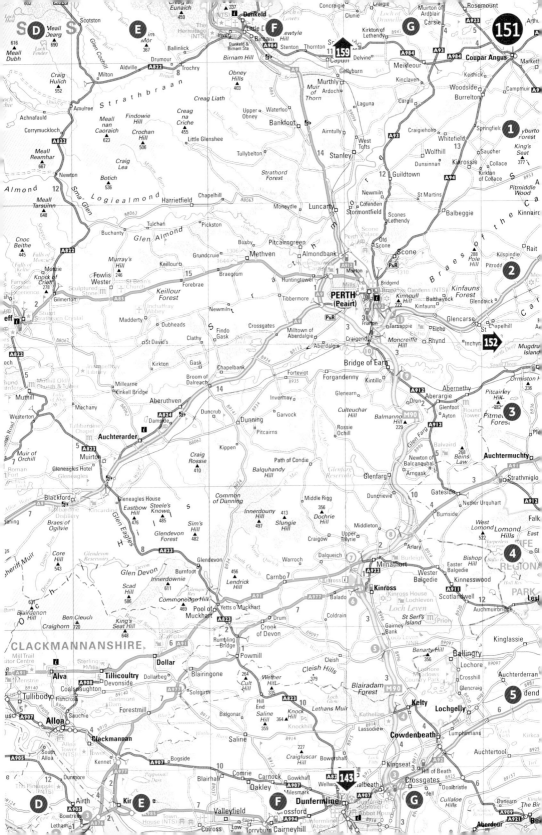

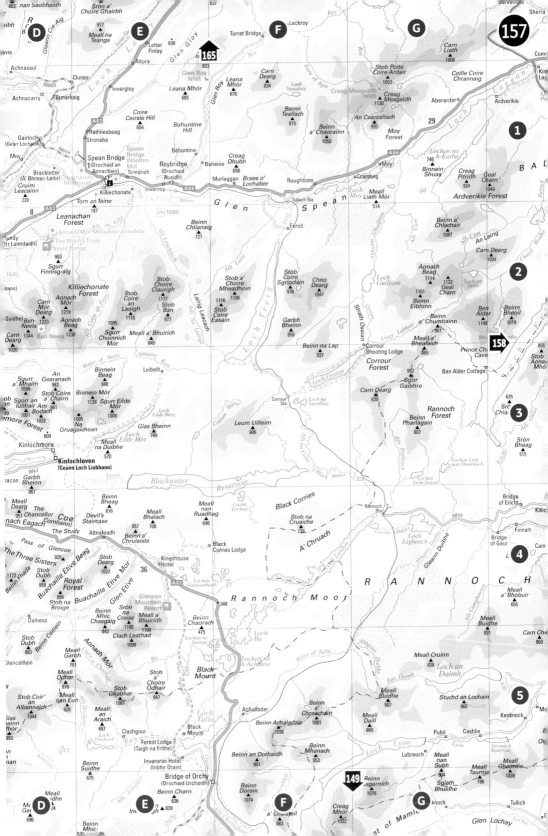

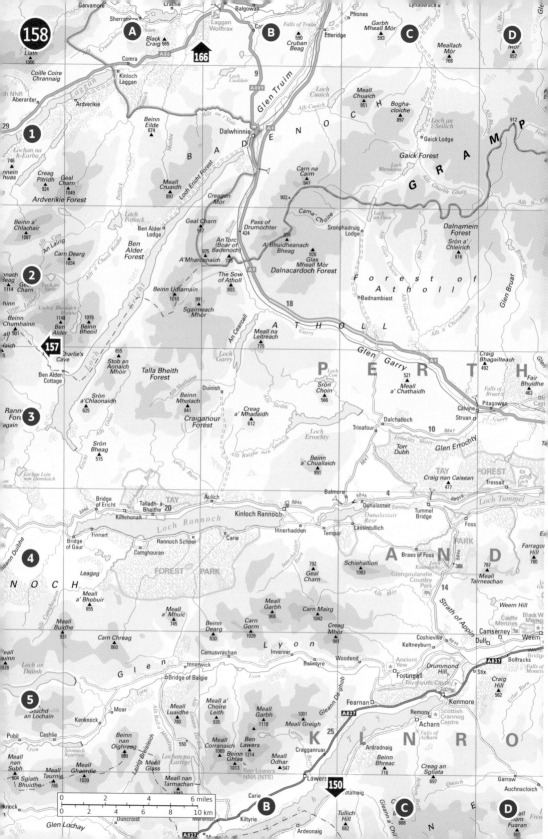

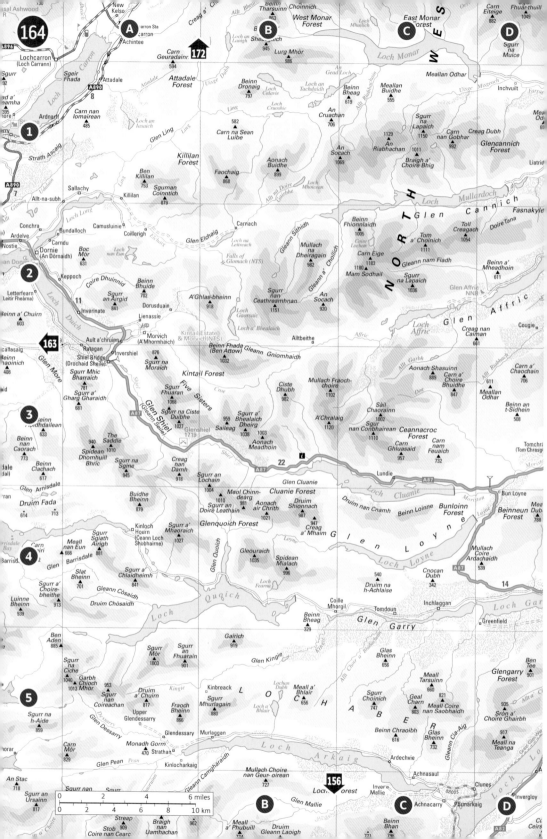

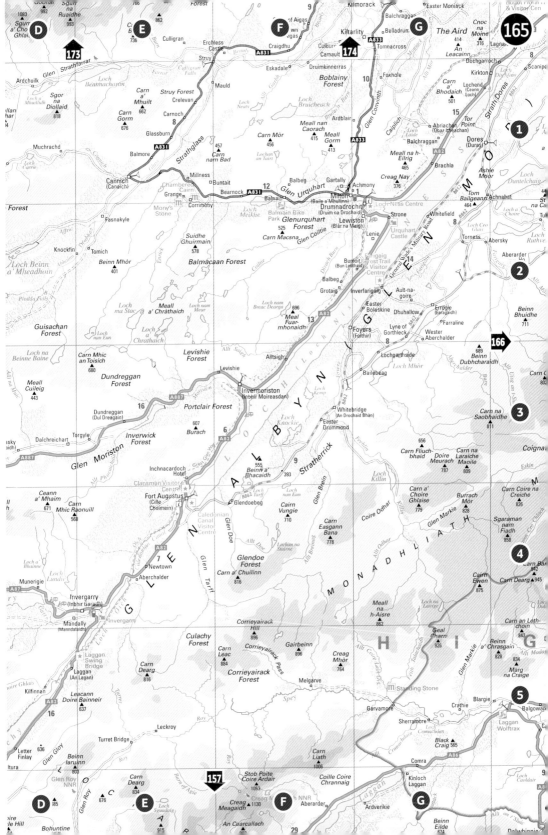

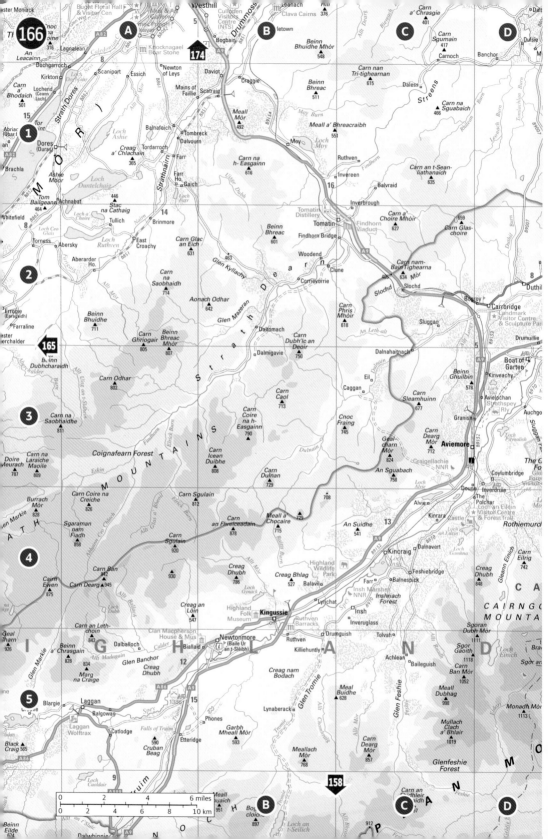

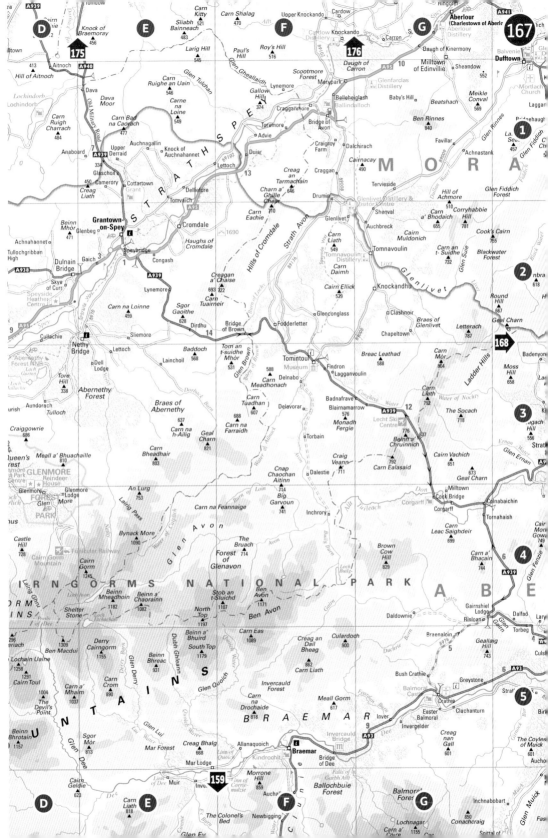

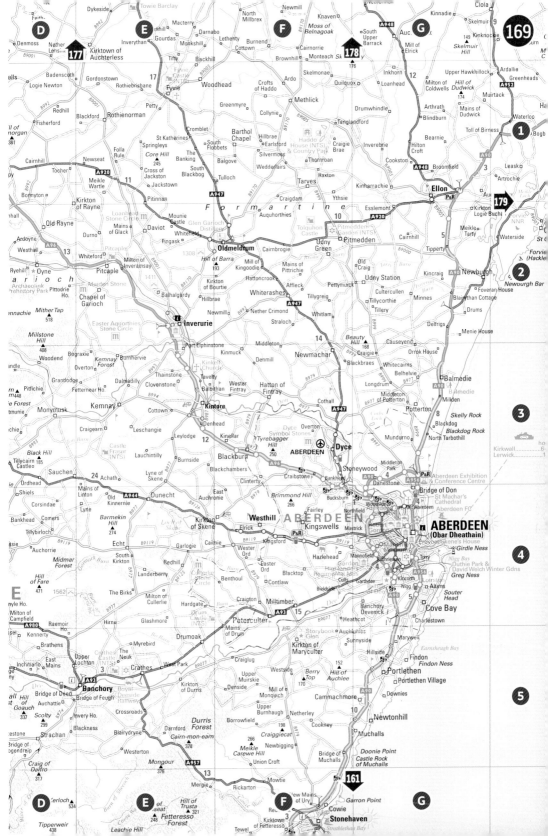

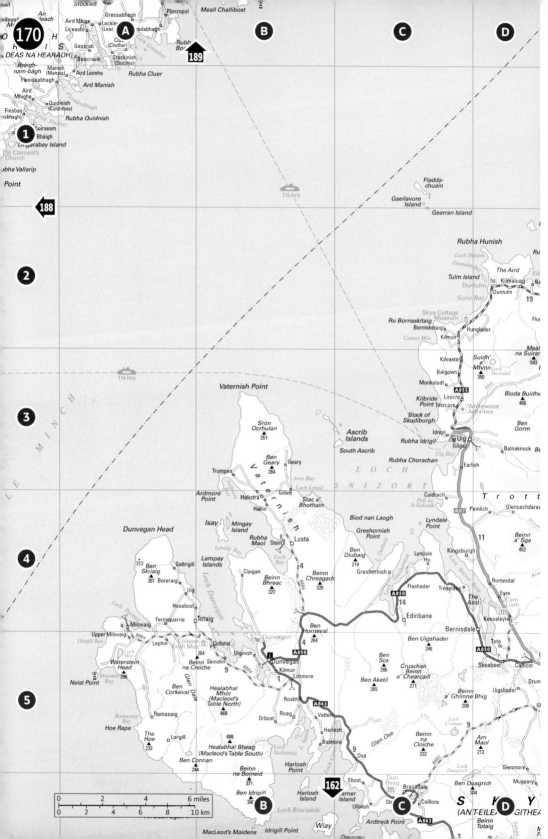

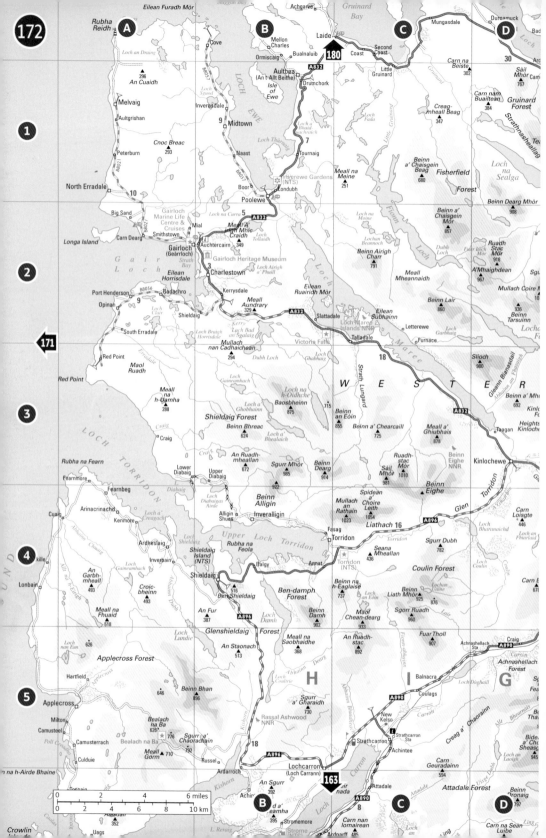

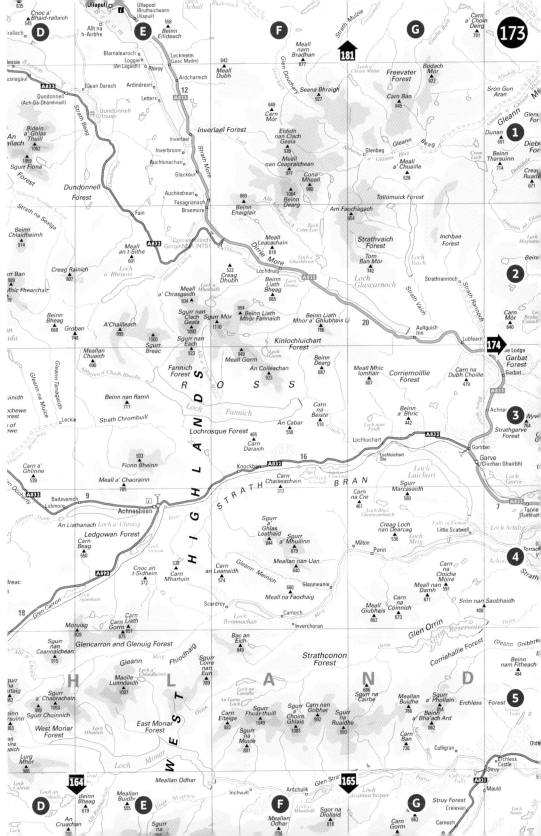

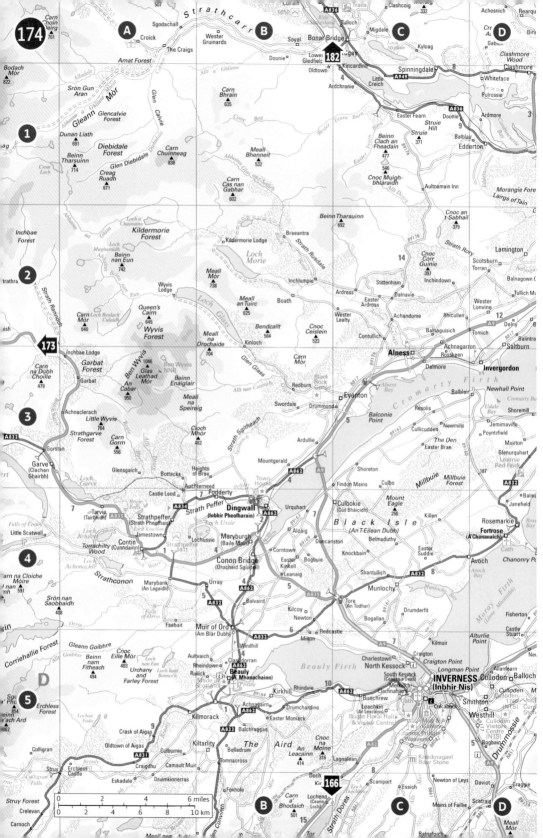

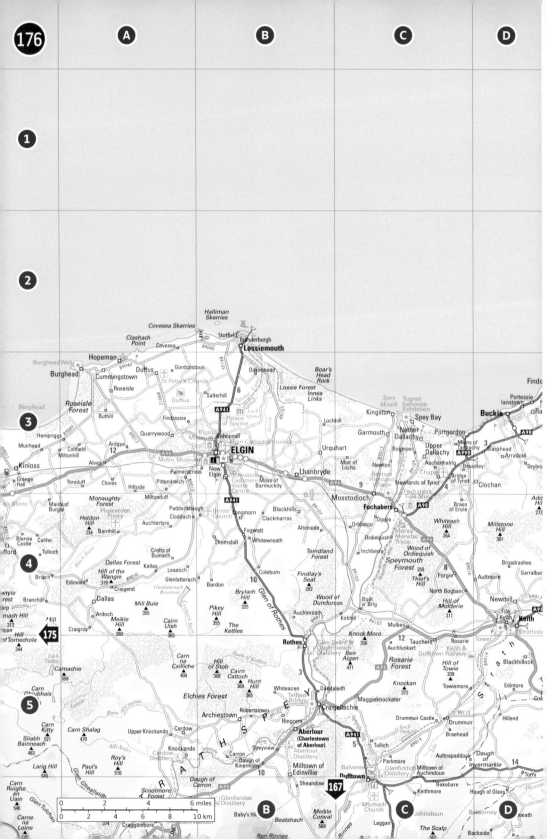

A B C D

1

2

Halliman
Skerries

Covesea Skerries

Clashach
Point   Covesea   Stotfield
Burghead Well   Hopeman   Duffus   Gordonstoun
Burghead   Cummingstown   Oakenhead
                Roseisle   St Peter's Church

Branderburgh
Lossiemouth

Boar's
Head
Rock

Findo

3

Burghead

Roseisle
Forest   Findrassie   Lossie Forest
Hempriggs   Quarrywood   Bishopmill   Innes
Muirhead   Coltfield   Ardgye   12   Elgin   Links
Kinloss   Miltonhill Alves   Cloves   Museum   Lochhill
Grange   Hillside   New Elgin   Elgin Cathedral ruins
Hall   Toreduff   Pittendreich   **ELGIN**
                                                        Motor Museum
                Mains of   Johnstons
                Burgie   Miltonduff   Cashmere Moss of
                                Monaughty   Visitor Barmuckity
fford   Blervie Califer   Forest   Paddockhaugh Centre   Blackhills
         Castle   Tulloch   Plascarden   Cloddach   Longmorn Clackmarras
s Stone Mains of   Heldon   Barnhill   Birnie   Fogwatt
         Burgie   Hill 234   Church   Whitewreath
Blervie   Auchtertyre   Altonside
Castle   Briach   Thomshill
                Dallas Forest Crofts of
4   Edinvale   Hill of the Buinach Kellas   Leanoch   Coleburn
mach Hill Branchill Wangie 319   Craigend   Bardon
313   Dallas   Mill Buie   Brylach
arp   355   Cairn   Hill
of Tomechole Ardoch Meikle   Uish   Pikey   325
344   Craigroy   Hill   280   365   Hill
                                                         355 The
175   Carn   Kettles
         Carnachie Carn na   na   Auchinroath
         359   Caillche   Stob   Kirkhill
Carn   308   Cairn   Hunt
Ghubhais   Cattoch 369   Hill
5   369   365
Carn   Whiteacen
Kitty   Carn Shalag Upper Knockando Cardow   Telford
Sliabh 470   Bridge
Bainneach   Cardow   Craigellachie
483   Distillery Knockando Speyview
Larig Hill   Roy's   Carron
545   Hill 516   Daugh of
Carn   Kinermony   Milltown of
Ruighe   Edinville
an   Scootmore   **Aberlour**
Uain   Forest   (Charlestown
546   of Aberlour)
Carne   Glenfarclas   Aberlour
na   Distillery   Distillery
Loine   Baby's Hill

A941

A96

A941

A98

175

167

0 2 4 6 miles
0 2 4 6 8 10 km

B C D

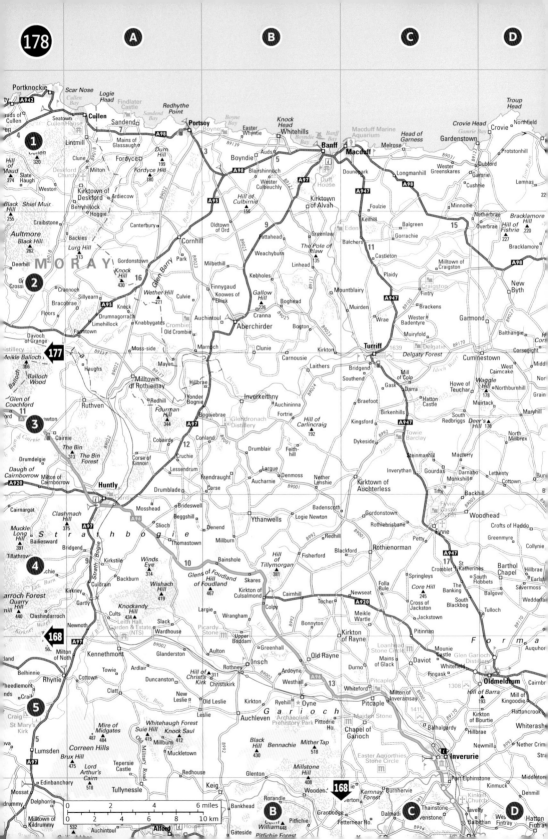

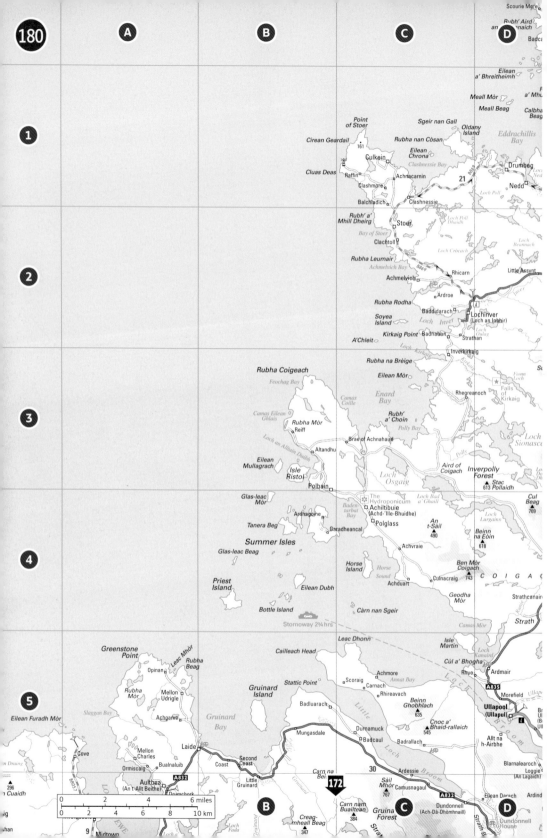

A **B** **C** **D**

1

Scourie More

Rubh' Aird
an' Fh'nnaich
Badca

Eilean
a' Bhreitheimh

Meall Mòr
Meall Beag

Rubh'
a' Mhu

Calbha
Beag

Point
of Stoer

Sgeir nan Gall

Cirean Geardail

Rubha nan Còsan

Oldany
Island

*Eddrachillis
Bay*

161

Eilean
Chrona

Culkein

Clashnessie Bay

Cluas Deas

Achnacarnin

21

Drumbeg

Raffin

*Loch
Ned*

Clashmore

Clashnessie

Nedd

Balchladich

Loch Poll

2

Rubh' a'
Mhill Dheirg

Stoer

*Loch Poll
Dhaill*

*Loch
Beannach*

Bay of Stoer

Clachtoll

B869

Loch Cròcach

Rubha Leumair

Achmelvich Bay

Rhicarn

Little Assynt

Achmelvich

Ardroe

Rubha Rodha

Baddidarach

Soyea
Island

Lochinver
(Loch an Inbhir)

*Loch
Oulag*

Kirkaig Point

Badnaban

Strathan

A'Chleit

Loch Inver

Loch Kirkaig

Inverkirkaig

3

Rubha na Brèige

Rubha Coigeach

Eilean Mòr

Feochag Bay

*Enard
Bay*

Rhegreanoch

*Fionn
Loch*

Falls
of
Kirkaig

*Camas
Coille*

*Camas Eilean
Ghlais*

Rubh'
a' Choin

*Loch
Sionasc*

Rubha Mòr
Reiff

Polly Bay

Brae of Achnahaird

Altandhu

Aird of
Coigach

Inverpolly
Forest

Eilean
Mullagrach

Isle
Ristol

Loch an Alltain Duibh

Polbain

*Loch
Osgaig*

Stac
613 Pollaidh

Cul
Beag
769

4

Glas-leac
Mòr

The
Hydroponicum

Achiltibuie
(Achd-'Ille-Bhuidhe)

An
t-Sàil
490

*Loch
Lurgainn*

Ardnagoine

*Baden-
tarbat
Bay*

Polglass

Beinn
na Eòin
618

Tanera Beg

Garadheancal

Achvraie

Ben Mòr
Coigach

Summer Isles

Glas-leac Beag

Horse
Island

*Horse
Sound*

Achduart

Culnacraig 743

C O I G A C

Priest
Island

Eilean Dubh

Geodha
Mòr

Strathcanai

Bottle Island

Stornoway 2¾ hrs

Càrn nan Sgeir

Camas Mòr

Strath

5

Greenstone
Point

Leac Dhonn

Isle
Martin

Cùl a' Bhogha

*Loch
Kanaird*

Ardmair

Opinan

Leac Mhòr

Rubha
Beag

Cailleach Head

Achmore

Rhue

A835

Morefield

Scoraig

Annat Bay

Rubha
Mòr

Mellon
Udrigle

Stattic Point

Carnach

Rhireavach

Beinn
Ghobhlach
635

Ullapool
(Ullapul)

Br

Ul

296

Eilean Furadh Mòr

Achgarve

Slaggan Bay

Gruinard
Island

Badluarach

Cnoc a'
Bhaid-rallaich
545

Allt na
h-Airbhe

UI

*Gruinard
Bay*

Laide

Little

Durnamuck

Blarnalearoch
Loggie
(An Lagaidh)

Cove

Mellon
Charles

Second
Coast

Mungasdale

Badcaul

Ormiscaig

Bualnaluib

Coast

Badrallach

30

Ardessie

Eilean Darach

Ardind

Aultbea
(An t-Allt Beithe)

A832

Little
Gruinard

Carn na
Be

172

Sàil
Mòr
767

Camusnagaul

A832

Dundonnell
(Ach-Dà-Dhòmhnaill)

9 Midtown

Carn nam
Buailtean
384

*Gruina
Forest*

Creag-
mheall Beag
347

Dundonnell
House

0   2   4   6 miles
0   2   4   6   8   10 km

B **C** **D**

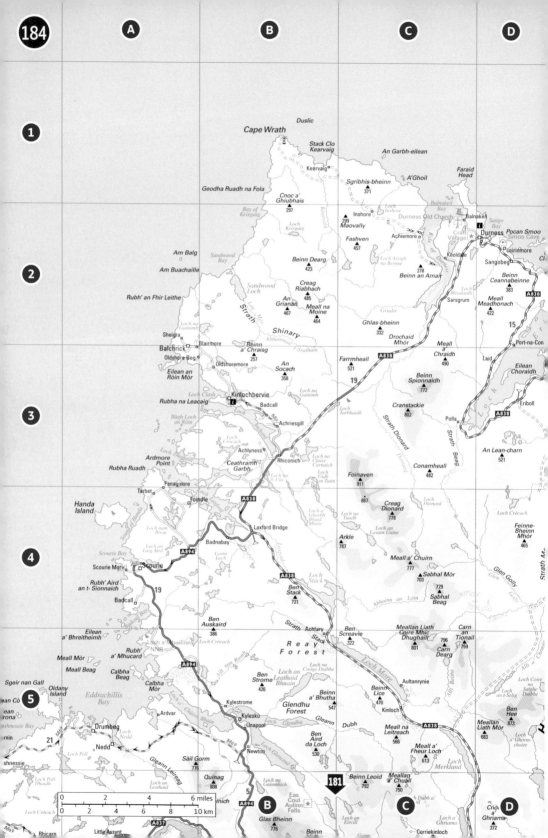

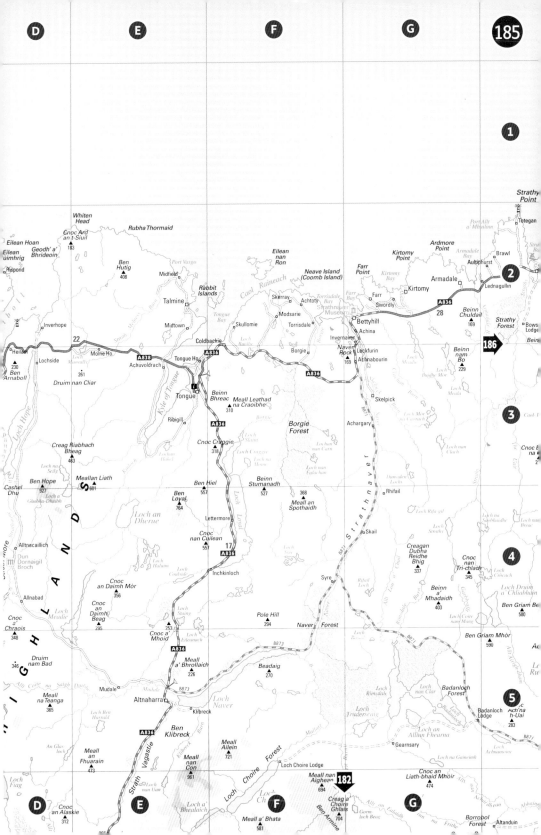

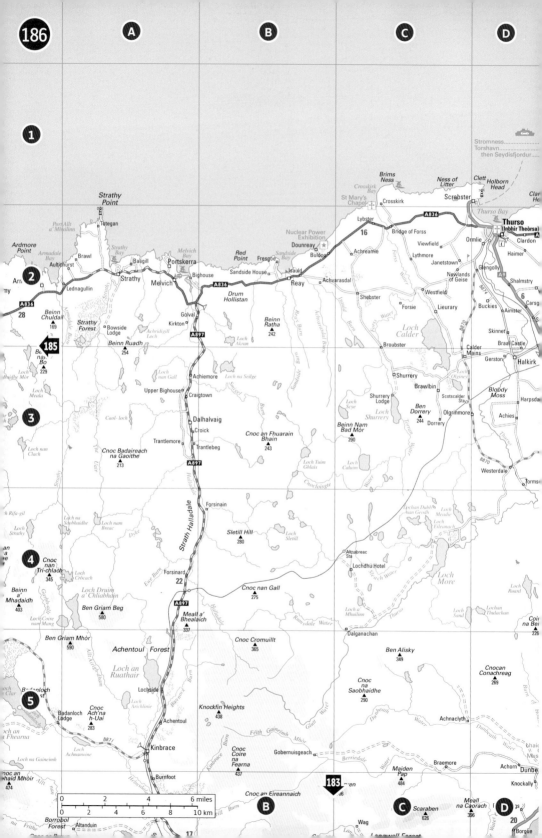

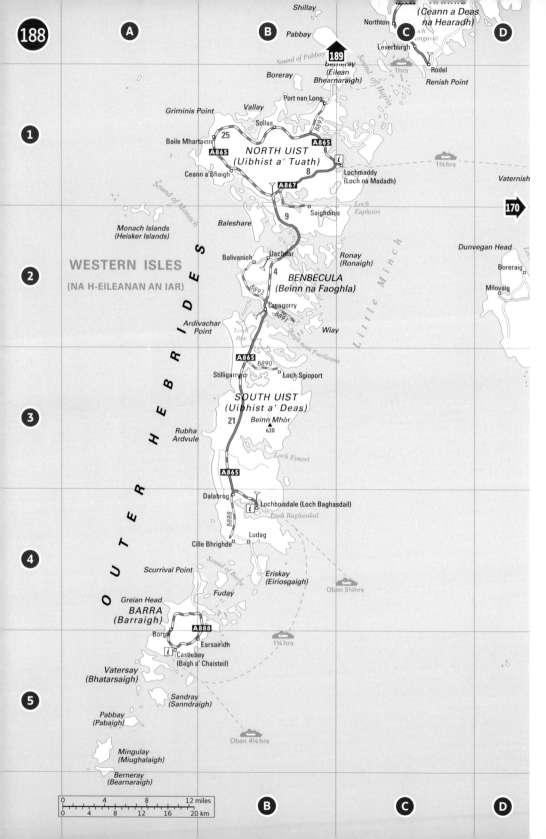

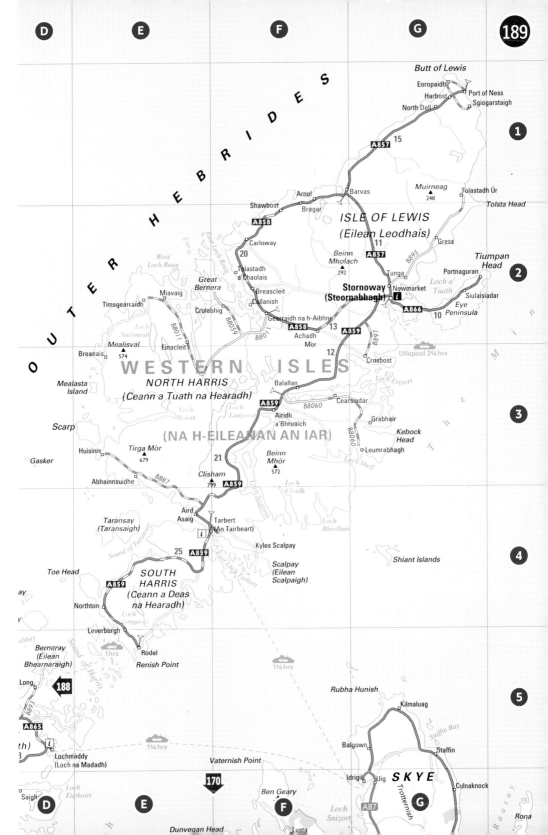

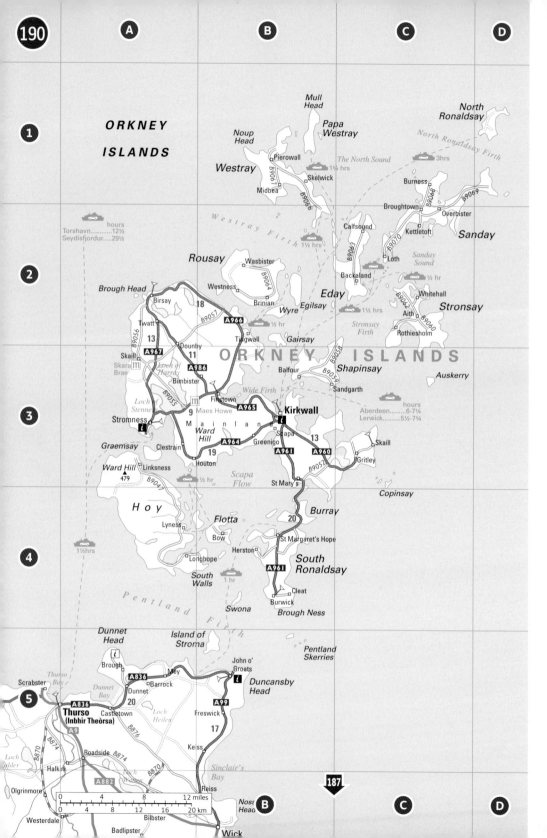

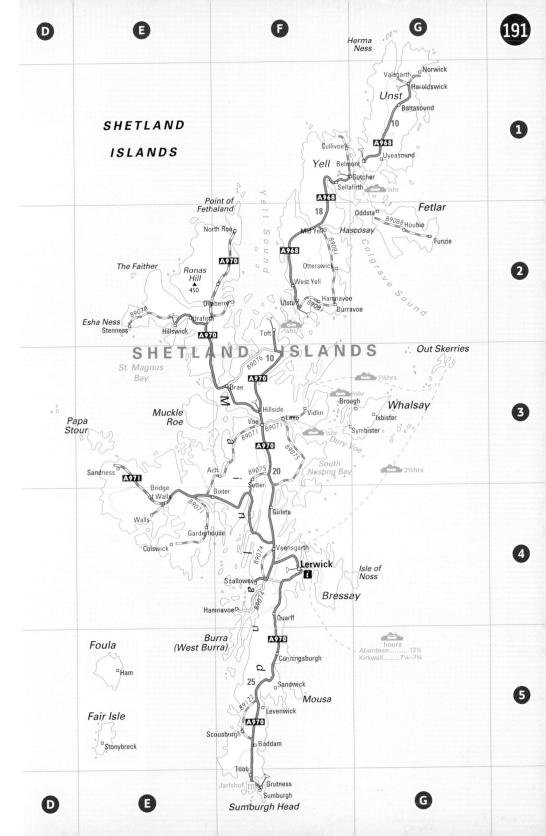

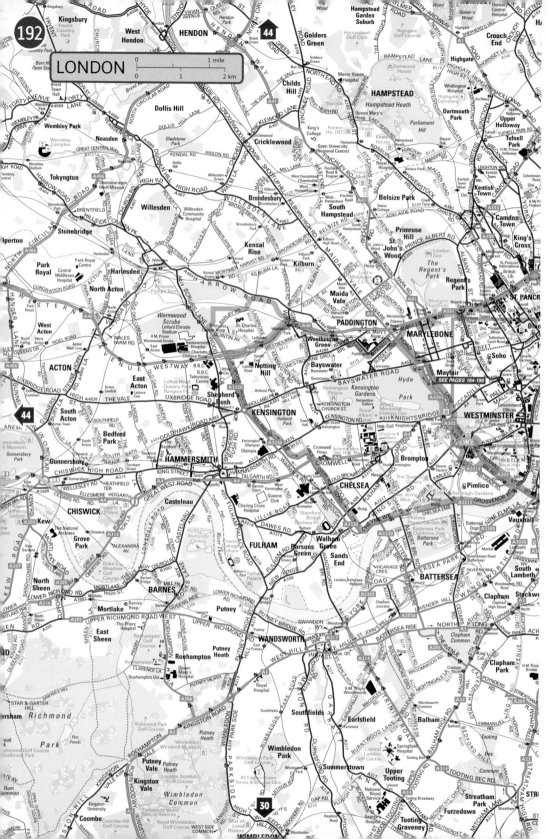

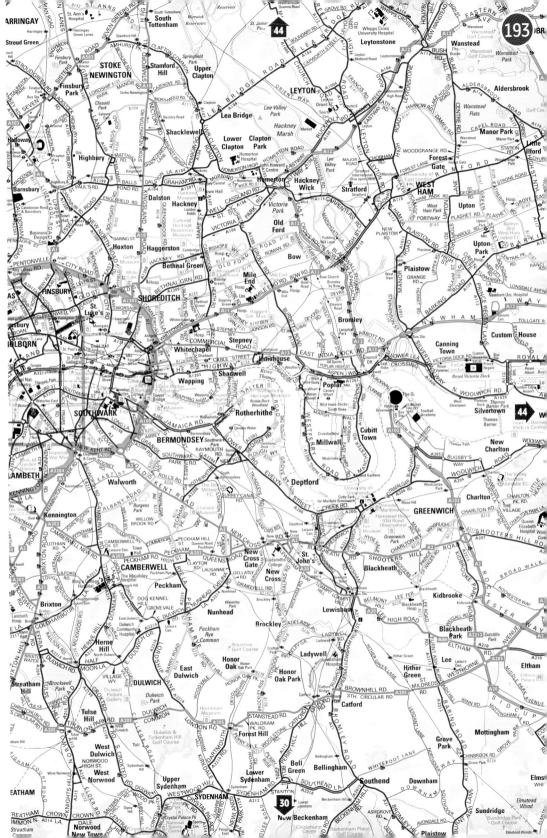

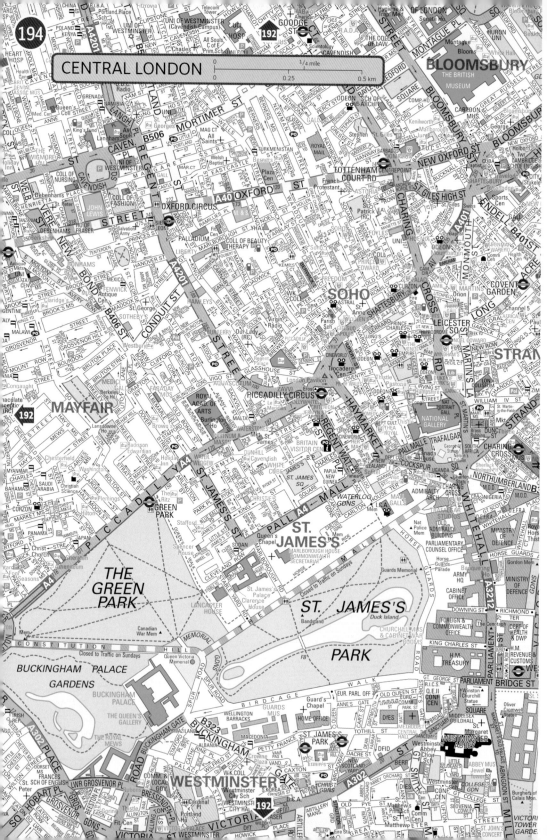

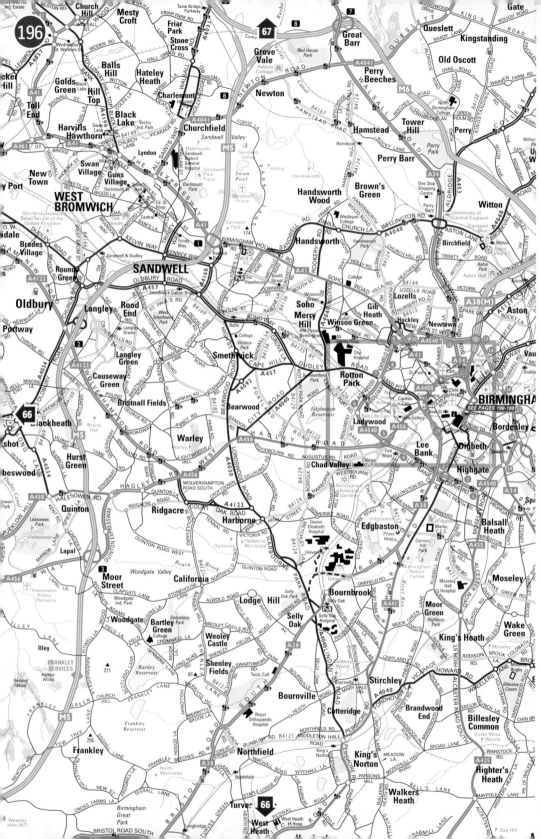

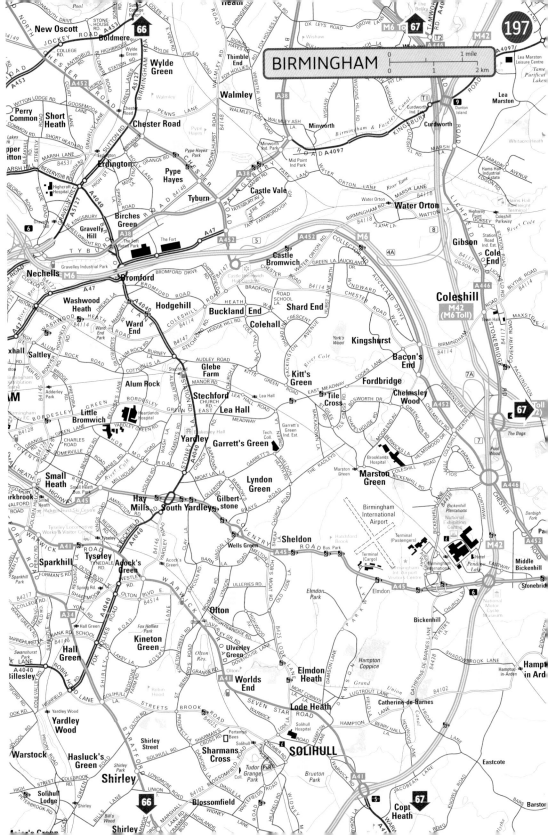

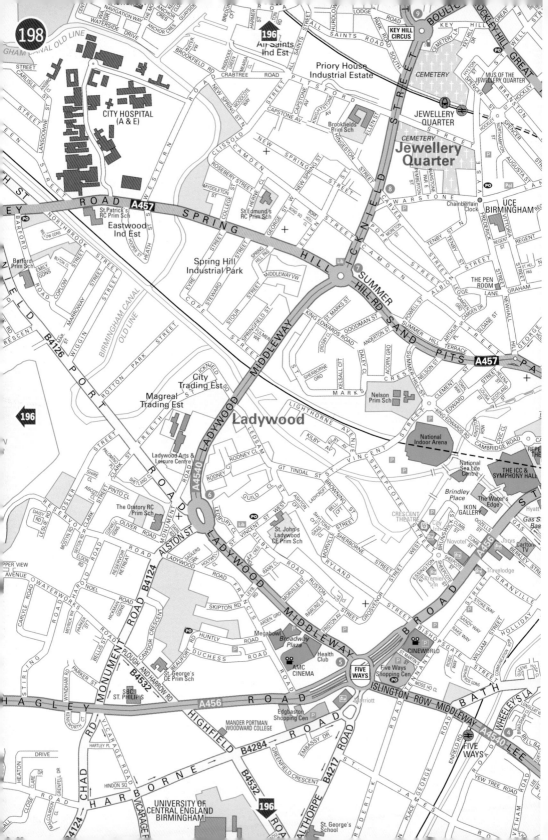

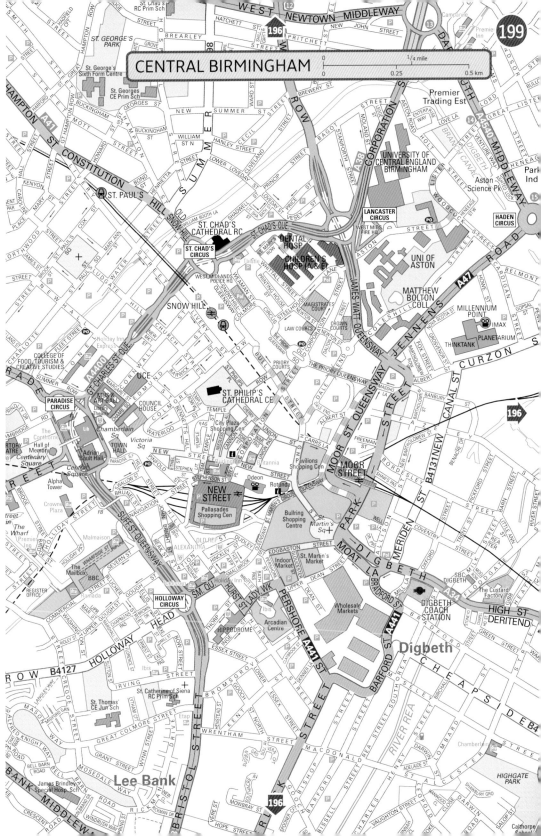

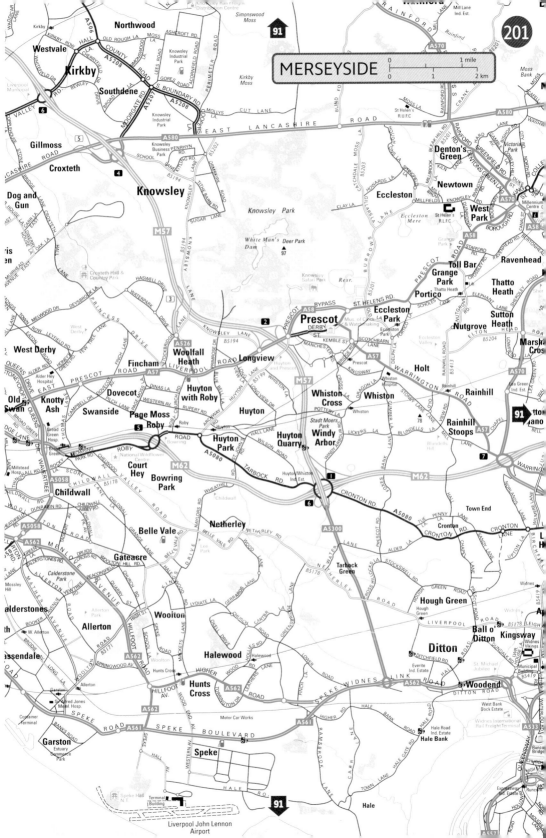

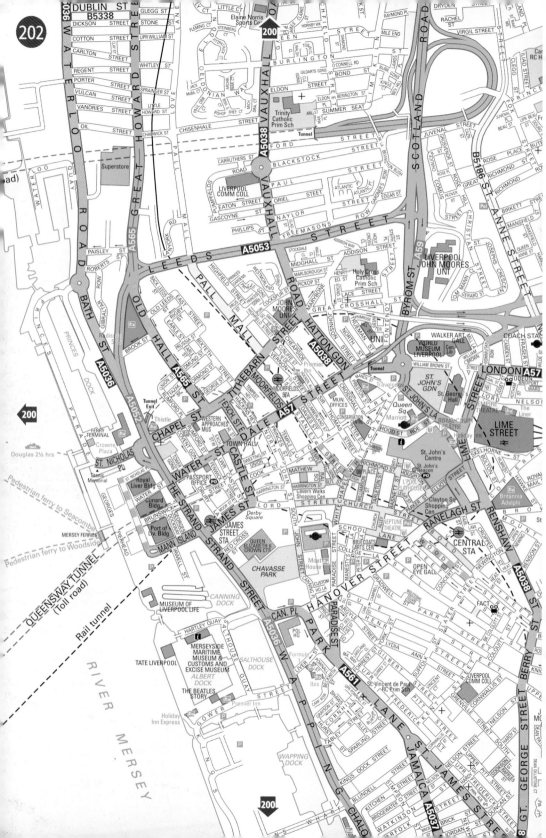

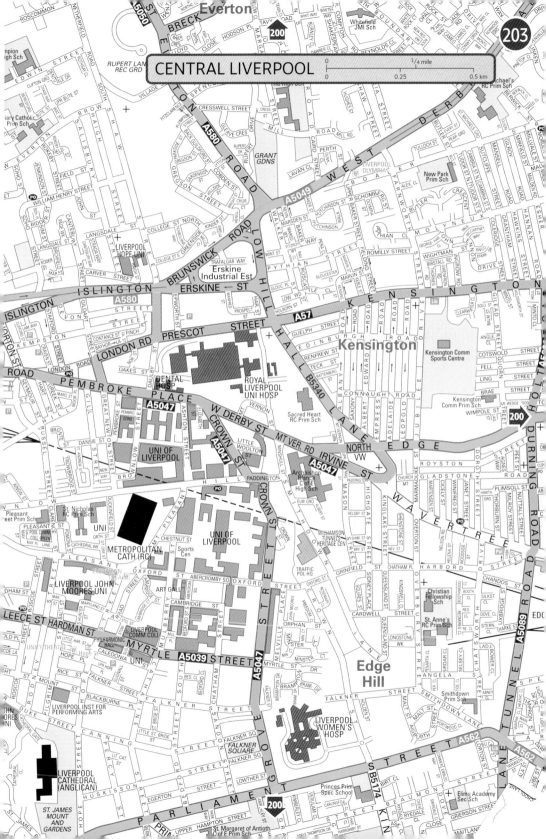

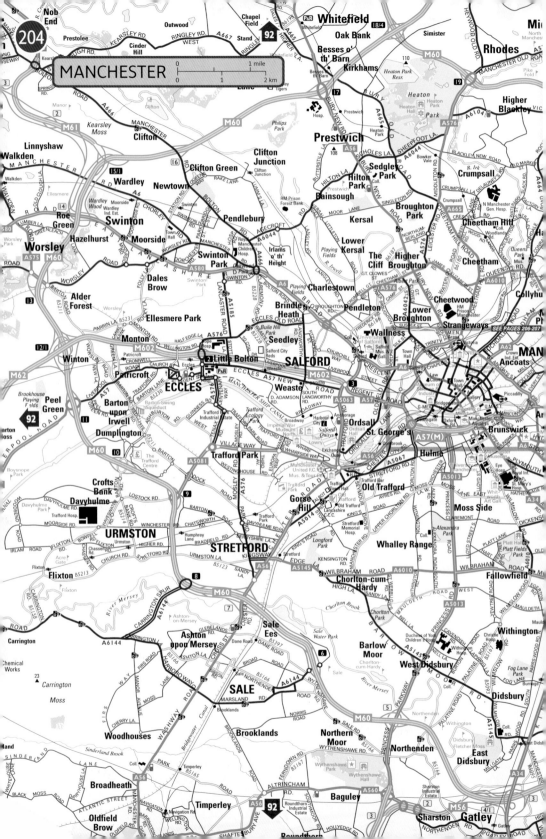

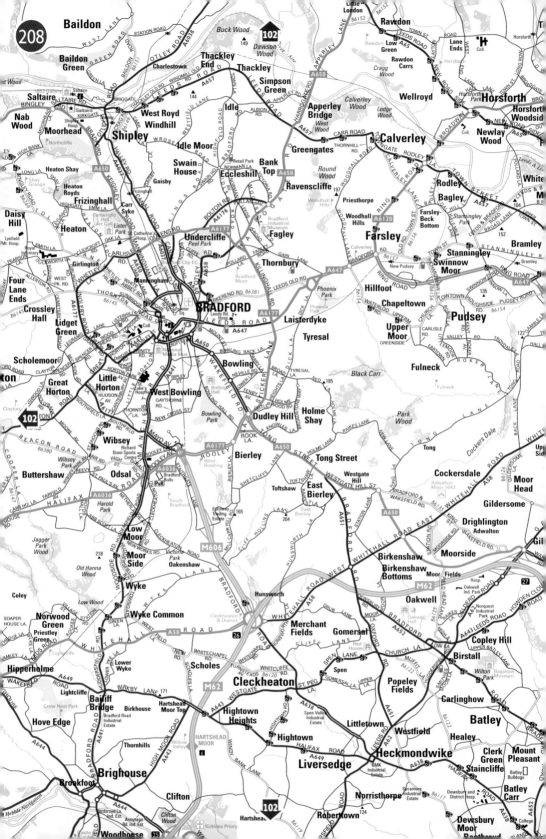

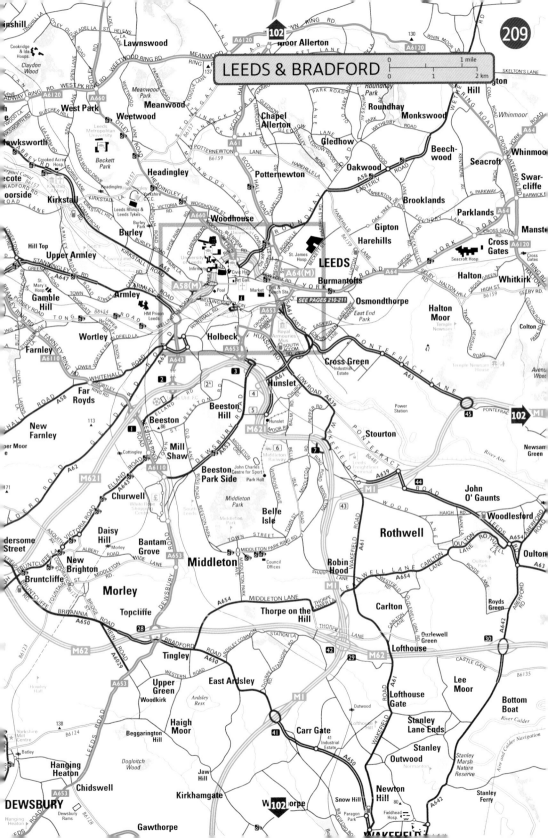

LEEDS & BRADFORD

0   1 mile

0   1   2 km

SEE PAGES 210-211

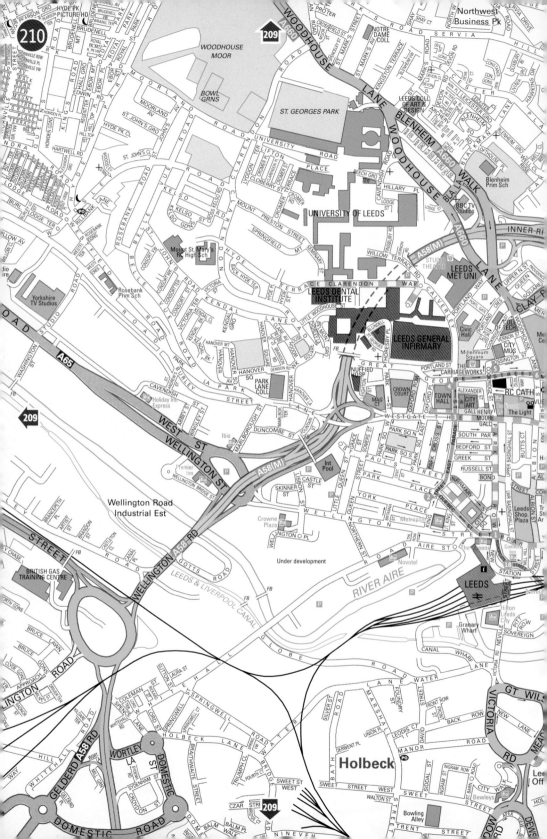

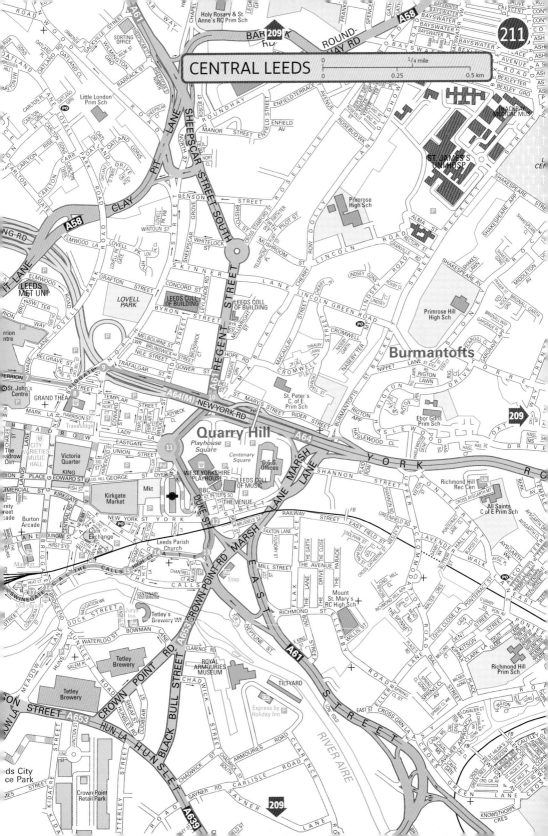

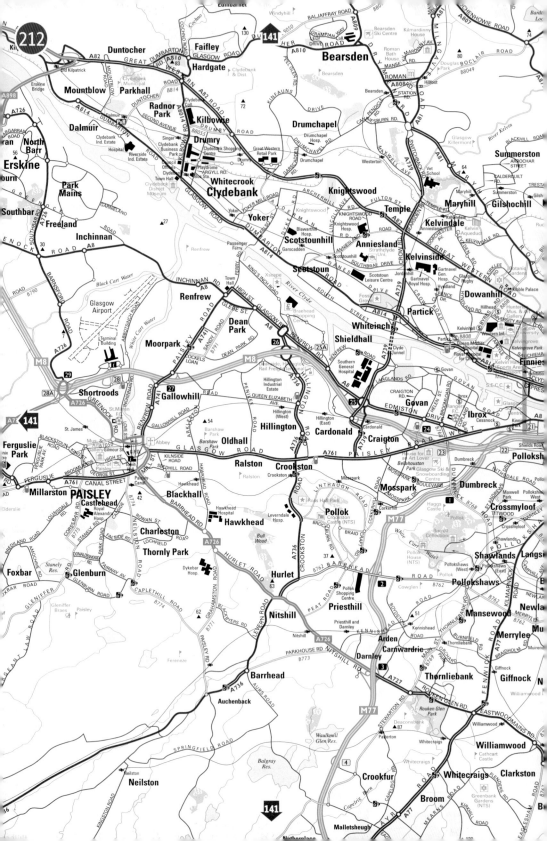

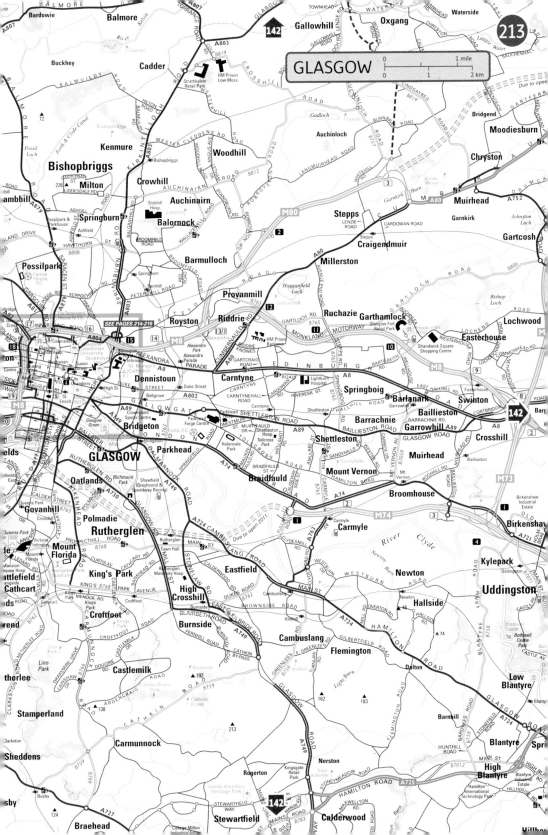

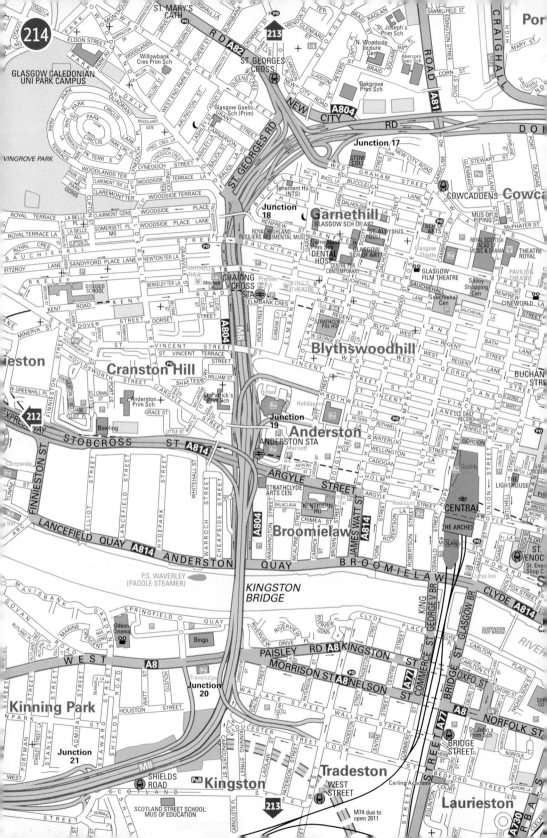

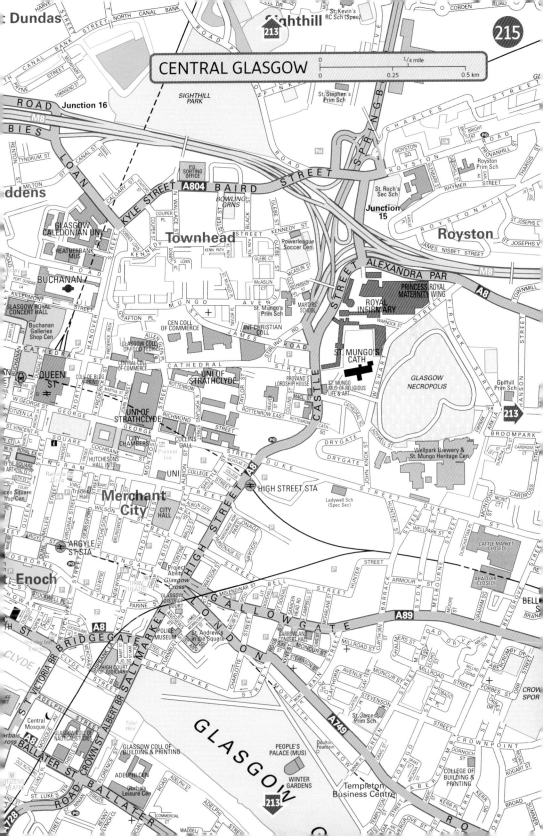

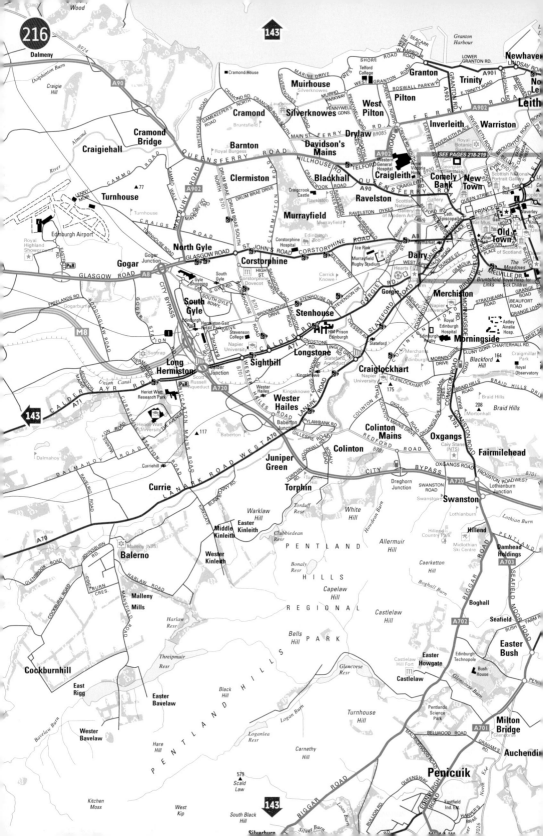

143

143

143

Dalmeny

Craigie
Hill

Dolphinton Burn

Craigiehall

Cramond
Bridge

Turnhouse

Edinburgh Airport

Royal
Highland
Showground

Gogar

North Gyle

South
Gyle

Long
Hermiston

Currie

Balerno

Malleny
Mills

Cockburnhill

East
Rigg

Easter
Bavelaw

Wester
Bavelaw

Kitchen
Moss

Wood

B974

River Almond

A90

Cramond House

Cramond

Barnton

Clermiston

Murrayfield

Corstorphine

Stenhouse

Sighthill

Longstone

Wester
Hailes

Juniper
Green

Torphin

Middle
Kinleith

Wester
Kinleith

Warklaw
Hill

Black
Hill

Harlaw
Resr

Threipmuir
Resr

West
Kip

South Black
Hill

Silverburn

Scald
Law

579

PENTLAND HILLS

Logan Burn

Carnethy
Hill

Bells
Hill

REGIONAL

Castlelaw
Hill

Clubbiedean
Resr

Bonaly
Resr

PARK

Capelaw
Hill

HILLS

PENTLAND

Colinton
Mains

Colinton

Silverknowes

Muirhouse

West
Pilton

Davidson's
Mains

Drylaw

Blackhall

Ravelston

Craigleith

Comely
Bank

Granton

Pilton

Inverleith

Trinity

Newhaven

Warriston

Leith

SEE PAGES 218-219

New
Town

Old
Town

Dalry

Merchiston

Morningside

Craiglockhart

Oxgangs

Fairmilehead

Swanston

Hillend

Damhead
Holdings

Boghall

Seafield

Easter
Bush

Howgate

Castlelaw

Milton
Bridge

Penicuik

Auchendi

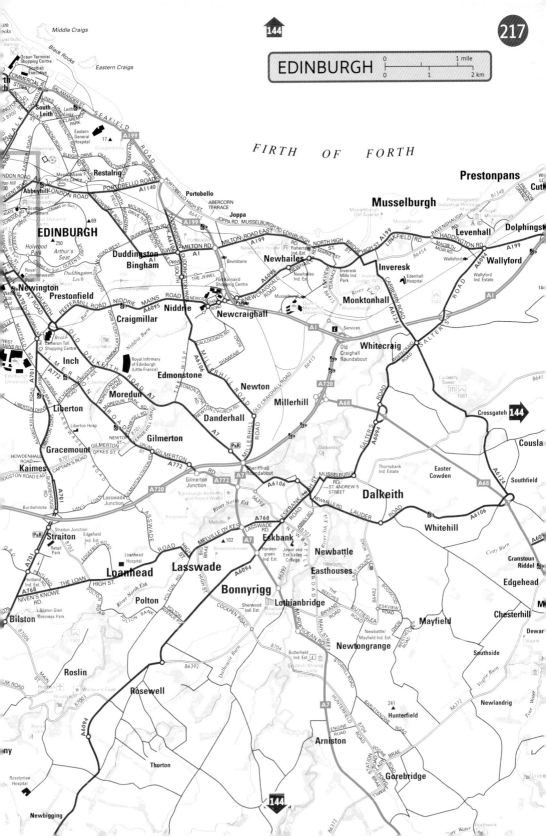

EDINBURGH

0 ____ 1 mile
0 ____ 1 ____ 2 km

FIRTH OF FORTH

Middle Craigs
Black Rocks
Eastern Craigs

Ocean Terminal Shopping Centre
Scottish Executive
COMMERCIAL

South Leith
Leith Links
CLAREMONT PARK

Eastern General Hospital
17 ▲ A199
Craigentinny

SEAFIELD ROAD
PORTOBELLO HIGH ST

Prestonpans
Cut

Restalrig
Meadowbank Sports Centre

Portobello
ABERCORN TERRACE
Joppa
JOPPA RD. MUSSELBURGH RD EDINBURGH

Musselburgh
Musselburgh Old Course
Prestongrange Industrial Heritage
Royal Musselburgh
B1348

Abbeyhill
Palace of Holyroodhouse
Scottish Parliament (Closed on Sun.)
Our Dynamic

A199 NORTH HIGH ST
MILTON ROAD EAST
Newhailes House
Fisherrow Ind. Est.
LINKFIELD RD.
Ravenshaugh
HADDINGTON RD
A199

Levenhall
Dolphings

EDINBURGH
Holyrood Park
Arthur's Seat
Royal Commonwealth

Duddingston
Bingham
A1
MILTON RD.
Brunstane

Newhailes
Newhailes Ind. Est.
A6095
NEWCRAIGHALL ROAD

Inveresk
Inveresk Mills Ind. Park
River Esk

Monktonhall
A6124 CARBERRY ROAD

Wallyford
MOIR RD.
Edenhall Hospital
Wallyford Ind. Estate
A1

Newington
Prestonfield
Duddingston Loch
A702

Craigmillar
NIDDRIE MAINS ROAD
A6095
Niddrie
Fort Kinnaird Shopping Centre
THE JEWEL
Newcraighall
P&R

Queen Margaret University

A1
i Services
Old Craighall Roundabout
Whitecraig
SALTERS ROAD

Carberry Tower
1567

Inch
Cameron Toll Shopping Centre
Royal Infirmary of Edinburgh (Little France)
Edmonstone
CAULDCOATS RD.
SHAWFAIR

Newton
OLD CRAIGHALL ROAD
A720

Millerhill
A68

Crossgatech 144

Cousla

Liberton
Liberton Hosp.
Moredun
NEWTON CHURCH RD
Danderhall
A7

A6094

Southfield
A6124

Gracemount
GILMERTON DYKES ST.
Gilmerton
DRUM
P&R

Dalkeith
ST. ANDREW'S STREET
MUSSELBURG RD.
Thornybank Ind. Estate
Easter Cowden

Kaimes
CAPTAIN'S ROAD
A772
GILMERTON RD.
Gilmerton Junction
A720
Lasswade Junction
A7
Sheriffhall Roundabout

A6106
River North Esk
Whitehill
LAUDER ROAD

Burdiehouse
Edinburgh Butterfly and Insect World ★

A6106
A68

Straiton Junction
P&R
Straiton
Retail Park
A701
Edgefield Ind. Est.
A768
MELVILLE DYKES RD.
Eskbank
BIG BRAE

Newbattle
Easthouses
Edgehead

Loanhead Hospital
▲ 102
Broomieknowe
Hardengreen Ind. Est.
Jewel and Esk Valley College
THE BEECHES

NIVEN'S KNOWE RD.
A768
Loanhead
Lasswade
A6094
Bonnyrigg
Lothianbridge
Newbattle Viaduct
Newbattle/Mayfield Ind. Est.
Mayfield
Chesterhill
Dewar

Bilston
Bilston Glen Business Park
Polton
POLTON BANK
River North Esk
Sherwood Ind. Est.
COCKPEN ROAD
Newtongrange
Southside
Vogrie

Roslin
Rosslyn Chapel
Wallace's Cave
Rosewell
B6392
Butlerfield Ind. Est. i
Scottish Mining Museum Lady Victoria
Hunterfield
241
Newlandrig

Rosslynlee Hospital
Thorton
Arniston
A7
ENGINE ROAD
Gorebridge

Newbigging

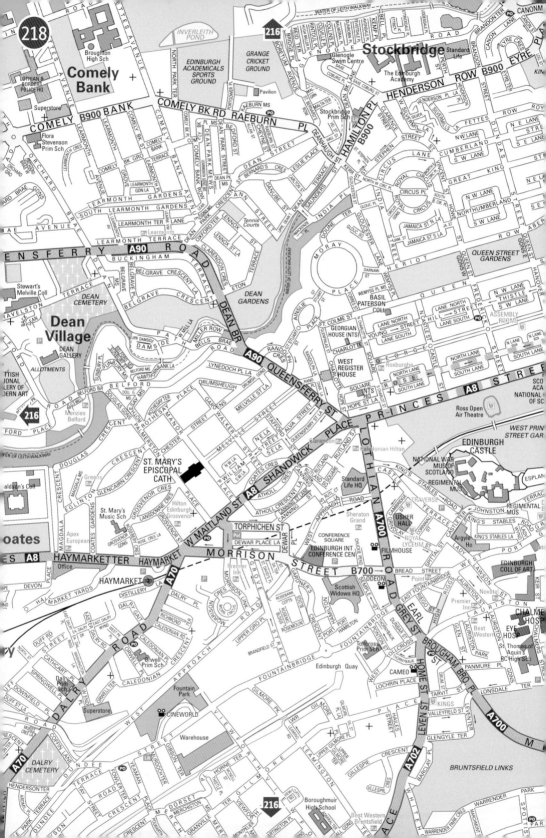

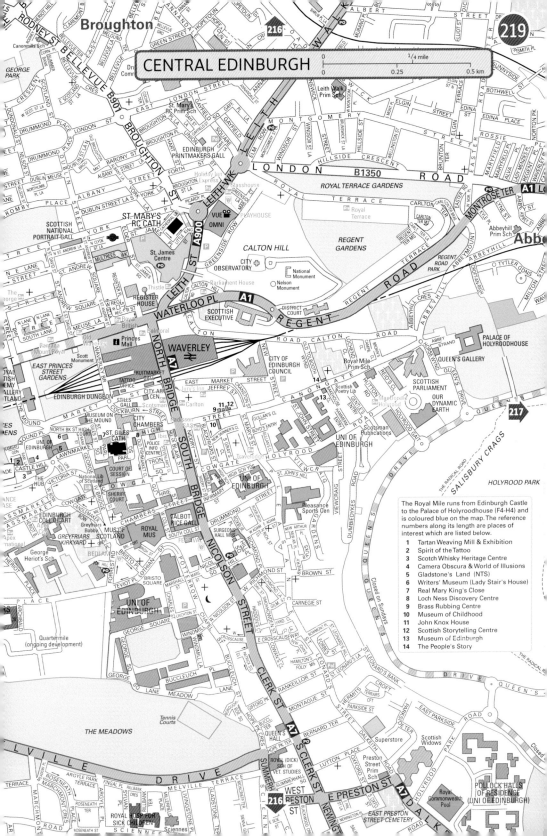

CENTRAL EDINBURGH

0   ¼ mile

0.25   0.5 km

The Royal Mile runs from Edinburgh Castle to the Palace of Holyroodhouse (F4-H4) and is coloured blue on the map. The reference numbers along its length are places of interest which are listed below.

1   Tartan Weaving Mill & Exhibition
2   Spirit of the Tattoo
3   Scotch Whisky Heritage Centre
4   Camera Obscura & World of Illusions
5   Gladstone's Land (NTS)
6   Writers' Museum (Lady Stair's House)
7   Real Mary King's Close
8   Loch Ness Discovery Centre
9   Brass Rubbing Centre
10 Museum of Childhood
11 John Knox House
12 Scottish Storytelling Centre
13 Museum of Edinburgh
14 The People's Story

In this index places are followed by a page number and a grid reference. The place can be found by searching that grid square. Where more than one place has the same name, each can be distinguished by the abbreviated county or unitary authority name shown after the place name. A list of abbreviations used for these names is shown to the right.

Aber.	Aberdeenshire	E.Riding	East Riding of Yorkshire	N.Ayr.	North Ayrshire	Shet.	Shetland
Arg. & B.	Argyll & Bute			N.E.Lincs.	North East Lincolnshire	Shrop.	Shropshire
B'burn.	Blackburn with Darwen	E.Suss.	East Sussex	N.Lan.	North Lanarkshire	Slo.	Slough
B'pool	Blackpool	Edin.	Edinburgh	N.Lincs.	North Lincolnshire	Som.	Somerset
B. & H.	Brighton & Hove	Falk.	Falkirk	N.P.T.	Neath Port Talbot	Staffs.	Staffordshire
B. & N.E.Som.	Bath & North East Somerset	Flints.	Flintshire	N.Som.	North Somerset	Stir.	Stirling
		Glas.	Glasgow	N.Yorks.	North Yorkshire	Stock.	Stockton-on-Tees
B.Gwent	Blaenau Gwent	Glos.	Gloucestershire	Norf.	Norfolk	Stoke	Stoke-on-Trent
Beds.	Bedfordshire	Gt.Lon.	Greater London	Northants.	Northamptonshire	Suff.	Suffolk
Bourne.	Bournemouth	Gt.Man.	Greater Manchester	Northumb.	Northumberland	Surr.	Surrey
Brack.F.	Bracknell Forest	Gwyn.	Gwynedd	Nott.	Nottingham	Swan.	Swansea
Bucks.	Buckinghamshire	Hants.	Hampshire	Notts.	Nottinghamshire	Swin.	Swindon
C. & W.Ches.	Chester & West Cheshire	Hart.	Hartlepool	Ork.	Orkney	T. & W.	Tyne & Wear
		Here.	Herefordshire	Oxon.	Oxfordshire	Tel. & W.	Telford & Wrekin
Caerp.	Caerphilly	Herts.	Hertfordshire	P. & K.	Perth & Kinross	Thur.	Thurrock
Cambs.	Cambridgeshire	High.	Highland	Pembs.	Pembrokeshire	V. of Glam.	Vale of Glamorgan
Carmar.	Carmarthenshire	Hull	Kingston upon Hull	Peter.	Peterborough	W'ham	Wokingham
Cere.	Ceredigion	I.o.A.	Isle of Anglesey	Plym.	Plymouth	W. & M.	Windsor & Maidenhead
Chan.I.	Channel Islands	I.o.M.	Isle of Man	Ports.	Portsmouth		
Ches.E.	Cheshire East	I.o.S.	Isles of Scilly	R. & C.	Redcar & Cleveland	W.Berks.	West Berkshire
Cornw.	Cornwall	I.o.W.	Isle of Wight	R.C.T.	Rhondda Cynon Taff	W.Dun.	West Dunbartonshire
Cumb.	Cumbria	Inclyde	Inverclyde	Read.	Reading	W.Isles	Western Isles (Na h-Eileanan an Iar)
D. & G.	Dumfries & Galloway	Lancs.	Lancashire	Renf.	Renfrewshire		
Darl.	Darlington	Leic.	Leicester	Rut.	Rutland	W.Loth.	West Lothian
Denb.	Denbighshire	Leics.	Leicestershire	S'end	Southend	W.Mid.	West Midlands
Derbys.	Derbyshire	Lincs.	Lincolnshire	S'ham.	Southampton	W.Suss.	West Sussex
Dur.	Durham	M.K.	Milton Keynes	S.Ayr.	South Ayrshire	W.Yorks.	West Yorkshire
E.Ayr.	East Ayrshire	M.Tyd.	Merthyr Tydfil	S.Glos.	South Gloucestershire	Warks.	Warwickshire
E.Dun.	East Dunbartonshire	Med.	Medway			Warr.	Warrington
		Mersey.	Merseyside	S.Lan.	South Lanarkshire	Wilts.	Wiltshire
E.Loth.	East Lothian	Middbro.	Middlesbrough	S.Yorks.	South Yorkshire	Worcs.	Worcestershire
E.Renf.	East Renfrewshire	Midloth.	Midlothian	Sc.Bord.	Scottish Borders	Wrex.	Wrexham
		Mon.	Monmouthshire				

A

Ab Kettleby 82 C5
Ab Lench 54 C2
Abbas Combe 25 E5
Abberley 53 G1
Abberley Common 53 G1
Abberton Essex 46 D1
Abberton Worcs. 54 B2
Abberwick 137 F5
Abbess Roding 45 E1
Abbey Dore 52 C4
Abbey Hulton 79 G3
Abbey St. Bathans 145 E3
Abbey Village 100 A5
Abbey Wood 45 D5
Abbeycwmhir 63 G5
Abbeydale 94 A4
Abbeystead 100 B2
Abbeytown 117 E1
Abbotrule 136 A5
Abbots Bickington 21 D4
Abbots Bromley 80 B5
Abbots Langley 43 F2
Abbots Leigh 39 E5
Abbots Morton 54 C2
Abbots Ripton 70 A5
Abbot's Salford 54 C2
Abbots Worthy 27 F4
Abbotsbury 12 B4
Abbotsfield Farm 91 G3
Abbotsham 27 E5
Abbotskerswell 9 E1
Abbotsley 58 A2
Abbotstone 27 G4
Abbotts Ann 27 E3
Abbott's Barton 27 F4
Abbottswood 27 E5
Abdon 65 E4
Abdy 94 B3
Abenhall 39 F1
Aber 50 A3
Aber Village 52 A5
Aberaeron 50 A1
Aberaman 37 G2
Aberangell 63 E2
Aber-Arad 49 G3
Abererarder 157 G1
Aberargie 151 G3
Aberarth 50 A1
Aberavon 37 D3
Aber-banc 49 G3
Aberbargoed 38 A2
Aberbeeg 38 B2
Aberbowlan 50 C4

Aberbran 51 F5
Abercanaid 37 G2
Abercarn 38 B3
Abercastle 48 B4
Abercegir 63 E2
Aberchalder 165 E4
Aberchirder 177 F4
Abercorn 143 E2
Abercraf 37 E1
Abercregan 37 E3
Abercrombie 152 D4
Abercrychan 51 D4
Abercwmboi 37 G2
Abercych 49 F3
Abercynafon 37 G1
Abercynon 37 G3
Abercywarch 63 E1
Aberdalgie 151 F2
Aberdare 37 F2
Aberdaron 74 A5
Aberdeen (Obar Dheathain) 169 G4
Aberdeen Airport 169 F3
Aberdesach 74 D2
Aberdour 143 F1
Aberdovey (Aberdyfi) 62 C3
Aberduhonw 51 G2
Aberdulais 37 D3
Aberedw 51 G3
Abereiddy 48 A4
Abererch 74 C4
Aberfan 37 G2
Aberfeldy 159 D5
Aberffraw 74 C1
Aberffrwd 62 C5
Aberford 102 D4
Aberfoyle 150 A4
Abergavenny (Y Fenni) 38 B1
Abergele 90 A5
Aber-Giâr 50 B3
Abergorlech 50 B4
Abergwesyn 51 E2
Abergwili 50 A5
Abergwydol 63 D2
Abergwynant 62 C1
Abergwynfi 37 E3
Abergwyngregyn 89 E5
Abergynolwyn 62 C2
Aberhafesp 63 G3
Aberhosan 63 E3
Aberkenfig 37 E4
Aberlady 144 B1
Aberlemno 160 D4
Aberllefenni 63 D2
Aber-Ilia 37 F1

Aberlour (Charlestown of Aberlour) 176 B5
Abermad 62 B5
Abermeurig 50 B2
Abermule (Aber-miwl) 64 A3
Abernaint 77 E5
Abernant Carmar. 49 G5
Aber-nant R.C.T. 37 G2
Abernethy 151 G3
Abernyte 152 A1
Aberporth 49 F2
Aberscross 182 C5
Abersky 165 G2
Abersoch 74 C5
Abersychan 38 B2
Aberthin 37 G5
Abertillery 38 B2
Abertridwr Caerp. 38 A4
Abertridwr Powys 63 G1
Abertysswg 38 A2
Aberuthven 151 E3
Aberyscir 51 F5
Aberystwyth 62 B4
Abhainnsuidhe 189 E3
Abingdon 41 G3
Abinger Common 29 G3
Abinger Hammer 29 F3
Abington 134 A3
Abington Pigotts 58 B3
Abingworth 16 D2
Ablington Glos. 40 D2
Ablington Wilts. 26 C3
Abney 93 E5
Above Church 80 B2
Aboyne 168 C5
Abram 92 A2
Abriachan (Obar Itheachan) 165 G1
Abridge 45 D3
Abronhill 142 B4
Abson 39 G5
Abthorpe 56 B3
Aby 97 E5
Acaster Malbis 103 E3
Acaster Selby 103 E3
Accrington 101 D5
Accurrach 148 D2
Acha 154 A4
Achacha 156 B5
Achadacaie 139 G3
Achadh Mòr 189 F2
Achadh-chaorrunn 139 F4
Achadunan 149 E3
Achagavel 155 G4
Achaglass 139 F5

Achahoish 139 F2
Achalader 159 G5
Achallader 157 F5
Achamore 139 D2
Achandunie 174 C2
Achany 182 A4
Achaphubuil 156 C2
Acharacle 155 F3
Achargary 185 G3
Acharn Arg. & B. 148 D1
Acharn P. & K. 158 C5
Acharonich 147 D1
Acharosson 140 A2
Achateny 155 E2
Achath 169 E3
Achavanich 187 D4
Achddu 36 A2
Achduart 180 C4
Achentoul 183 D1
Achfary 181 E1
Achgarve 180 A5
Achiemore High. 184 C2
Achiemore High. 186 A3
A'Chill 162 A4
Achiltibuie (Achd-'Ille-Bhuidhe) 180 C4
Achina 185 G2
Achindown 175 D4
Achinduich 182 A5
Achingills 187 D2
Achintee 172 C5
Achintee House (Achadh an t-Suidhe) 156 D2
Achintraid 163 G1
Achleanan 155 E4
Achleek 155 G4
Achlian 148 D2
Achlyness 184 B3
Achmelvich 180 C2
Achmony 165 G1
Achmore High. 163 G1
Achmore High. 180 C5
Achmore Stir. 150 A1
Achnaba 140 A1
Achnabat 165 G1
Achnabourin 185 G3
Achnacairn 148 B1
Achnacarnin 180 C1
Achnacarry 157 D1
Achnaclerach 174 A3
Achnacloich Arg. & B. 148 B1
Achnacloich High. 163 D4

Achnaclyth 183 F1
Achnacraig 155 D5
Achnacroish 156 A5
Achnadrish 154 D4
Achnafalnich 149 E2
Achnafauld 151 D1
Achnagairn 174 B5
Achnagarron 174 C2
Achnaha High. 155 F5
Achnaha High. 155 D3
Achnahanat 182 A5
Achnahannet 167 D2
Achnairn 182 A3
Achnalea 156 A3
Achnamara 139 F1
Achnanellan 155 G3
Achnasaul 157 D1
Achnasheen 173 E4
Achnashelloch 148 A5
Achnastank 167 G1
Achorn 183 G1
Achosnich High. 182 C5
Achosnich High. 154 D3
Achreamie 186 C2
Achriabhach 156 D3
Achriesgill 184 B3
Achtoty 185 F2
Achurch 69 F4
Achuvoldrach 185 E3
Achvaich 182 C5
Achvarasdal 186 B2
Achvlair 156 B4
Achvraie 180 C4
Ackenthwaite 107 G4
Ackergill 187 F3
Acklam Middbro. 111 D1
Acklam N.Yorks. 103 G1
Ackleton 65 G3
Acklington 129 E1
Ackton 102 D5
Ackworth Moor Top 94 B1
Acle 87 F4
Acock's Green 66 D4
Acol 33 F2
Acomb Northumb. 119 F1
Acomb York 103 E2
Aconbury 53 E4
Acre 101 D5
Acrefair 77 F3
Acrise Place 33 G4
Acton Ches.E. 78 D2
Acton Dorset 13 F5
Acton Gt.Lon. 44 B4
Acton Shrop. 64 C4
Acton Staffs. 79 F3
Acton Suff. 59 G3

Acton Worcs. 54 A1
Acton Wrex. 78 A2
Acton Beauchamp 53 F2
Acton Bridge 91 G5
Acton Burnell 65 E2
Acton Green 53 F2
Acton Pigott 65 E2
Acton Round 65 F3
Acton Scott 65 D4
Acton Trussell 66 B3
Acton Turville 40 A4
Adamhill 132 C2
Adbaston 79 E5
Adber 24 C5
Adderbury 55 G4
Adderley 79 D4
Adderstone 137 F3
Addiewell 143 D3
Addingham 101 G3
Addington Bucks. 56 C5
Addington Gt.Lon. 30 C2
Addington Kent 31 F3
Addiscombe 30 C2
Addlestone 29 F1
Addlethorpe 84 D1
Adel 102 B4
Adeney 65 G1
Adeyfield 43 F2
Adfa 63 G2
Adforton 64 D5
Adisham 33 G3
Adlestrop 55 E5
Adlingfleet 64 A5
Adlington Ches.E. 92 D4
Adlington Lancs. 90 C1
Admaston Staffs. 80 B5
Admaston Tel. & W. 65 F1
Admington 55 E3
Adsborough 23 F5
Adscombe 22 B4
Adstock 56 A4
Adstone 56 A2
Adversane 29 F5
Advie 167 F1
Adwalton 102 B5
Adwell 42 B3
Adwick le Street 94 C2
Adwick upon Dearne 94 B2
Adziel 179 E2
Ae Village 125 D2
Affetside 92 B1
Affleck 169 F2
Affpuddle 13 E3
Afon Wen 74 D4
Afon-wen 90 C5

Afton 14 C4
Afton Bridgend 133 E4
Agglethorpe 109 F4
Aigburth 91 E4
Aike 104 C3
Aiketgate 118 A3
Aikshaw 117 E2
Aikton 117 F1
Aikwood Tower 135 F3
Ailby 97 E5
Ailey 52 C3
Ailsworth 69 G3
Aimes Green 44 D2
Aimster 186 C2
Ainderby Quernhow 110 C4
Ainderby Steeple 110 C3
Aingers Green 60 C5
Ainsdale 91 E1
Ainsdale-on-Sea 91 E1
Ainstable 118 B3
Ainsworth 92 B1
Ainthorpe 111 G2
Aintree 91 E3
Aird Asaig 189 E4
Aird of Sleat 163 D4
Airdrie Fife 153 D4
Airdrie N.Lan. 142 B3
Aire View 101 F3
Aindh a'Bhruaich 189 F3
Aineland 124 B5
Aines 122 A4
Aingh-drishaig 163 F1
Airmyn 103 G5
Airntully 151 F1
Airor 163 F4
Airth 142 C1
Airyhassen 115 D2
Aisby Lincs. 95 F3
Aisby Lincs. 83 F4
Aisgill 108 C2
Aish Devon 8 C1
Aish Devon 9 E2
Aisholt 23 E4
Aiskew 110 B4
Aislaby N.Yorks. 112 B2
Aislaby N.Yorks. 111 G2
Aislaby Stock. 110 D1
Aisthorpe 95 G4
Aith Ork. 190 C2
Aith Shet. 191 F3
Aitnoch 167 D1
Akeld 137 D4
Akeley 56 C4
Akenham 60 C3
Albaston 7 E3
Albecq 9 E5
Alberbury 64 C1
Albert Town 34 C1
Albourne 17 E2
Albourne Green 17 E2
Albrighton Shrop. 66 A2
Albrighton Shrop. 65 D1
Alburgh 73 D3
Albury Herts. 58 C5
Albury Oxon. 42 B3
Albury Surr. 29 F3
Albury End 58 C5
Albury Heath 29 F3
Albyfield 118 B2
Aicaig 174 B4
Alcaston 65 D4
Alciston 18 A3
Alcombe 22 C3
Alconbury 69 G5
Alconbury Hill 69 G5
Alconbury Weston 69 G5
Aldborough N.Yorks. 102 D1
Aldborough Norf. 86 C2
Aldbourne 41 E5
Aldbrough 105 E4
Aldbrough St. John 110 B1
Aldbury 43 E1
Alclune 159 E3
Aldeburgh 61 F2
Aldeby 73 F2
Aldenham 44 A3
Alderbury 26 C5
Alderholt 14 A1
Alderley 39 G3
Alderley Edge 92 C5
Aldermaston 27 G1
Aldermaston Wharf 28 B1
Alderminster 55 E3

Alderney 9 G4
Alderney Airport 9 F4
Alder's End 53 F4
Aldersey Green 78 B2
Aldershot 29 D2
Alderton Glos. 54 B4
Alderton Northants. 56 C3
Alderton Suff. 61 E3
Alderton Wilts. 40 A4
Alderwasley 81 E2
Aldfield 102 B1
Aldford 78 B3
Aldham Essex 60 A5
Aldham Suff. 60 B3
Aldie Aber. 179 E5
Aldie High. 175 D1
Aldingbourne 16 B3
Aldingham 107 D5
Aldington Kent 32 C5
Aldington Worcs. 54 C3
Aldivalloch 168 A2
Aldochlay 149 F5
Aldons 122 C2
Aldous's Corner 73 E3
Aldreth 70 C5
Aldridge 66 C2
Aldringham 61 F1
Aldsworth Glos. 41 D2
Aldsworth W.Suss. 15 G2
Aldunie 168 A2
Aldville 151 E1
Aldwark Derbys. 80 D2
Aldwark N.Yorks. 103 D1
Aldwick 16 B4
Aldwincle 69 F4
Aldworth 42 A5
Alexandria 141 E2
Aley 23 E4
Aley Green 43 F1
Alfardisworthy 20 C4
Alfington 11 E3
Alfold 29 F4
Alfold Crossways 29 F4
Alford Aber. 168 C3
Alford Lincs. 97 E5
Alford Som. 24 D4
Alfreton 81 F2
Alfrick 53 G2
Alfrick Pound 53 G2
Alfriston 18 A3
Algarkirk 84 A4
Alhampton 24 D4
Alkborough 104 A5
Alkerton 55 F3
Alkham 33 E4
Alkington 78 C4
Alkmonton 80 C4
All Cannings 26 B1
All Saints South Elmham 73 E3
All Stretton 65 D3
Allaleigh 9 E2
Allanaquoich 167 F5
Allancreich 168 C5
Allanfearn 174 D5
Allangillfoot 126 A2
Allanton D. & G. 124 D2
Allanton E.Ayr. 133 E2
Allanton N.Lan. 142 C4
Allanton S.Lan. 142 B4
Allanton Sc.Bord. 145 F4
Allardice 161 G2
Allbrook 27 F5
Allendale Town 119 E2
Allenheads 119 E3
Allensford 119 G2
Allensmore 53 D4
Allenton 81 E4
Aller 24 B5
Allerby 117 D3
Allercombe 10 D3
Allerford Devon 7 E4
Allerford Som. 22 C3
Allerston 112 B4
Allerthorpe 103 G3
Allerton Mersey. 91 F4
Allerton W.Yorks. 102 A4
Allerton Bywater 102 D5
Allerton Mauleverer 102 D2
Allesley 67 E4
Allestree 81 E4
Allet Common 4 B5
Allexton 68 C2
Allgreave 79 G1
Allhallows 32 A1
Allhallows-on-Sea 32 A1

Alligin Shuas 172 B4
Allimore Green 66 A1
Allington Dorset 12 A3
Allington Lincs. 26 D4
Allington Wilts. 26 B1
Allington Wilts. 26 D1
Allington Wilts. 40 A5
Allithwaite 107 E5
Allnabad 185 D4
Alloa 151 D5
Allonby 117 D2
Allostock 92 B5
Alloway 132 B4
Allowenshay 11 G1
Allscot 65 G3
Allscott 65 F1
Allt na h-Airbhe 180 D5
Alltachonaich 155 G4
Alltbeithe 164 B2
Alltforgan 75 G2
Alltmawr 51 G3
Alltnacaillich 185 D4
Allt-na-subh 164 A1
Alltsigh 165 F3
Alltwalis 50 A4
Alltwen 36 D2
Alltyblaca 50 B3
Allwood Green 72 B4
Almeley 52 C2
Almeley Wootton 52 C2
Almer 13 F3
Almington 79 E4
Almiston Cross 21 D3
Almondbank 151 F2
Almondbury 93 F1
Almondsbury 39 F4
Alne 103 E1
Alness 174 C3
Alnham 137 D5
Alnmouth 137 G5
Alnwick 137 F5
Alperton 44 A4
Alphamstone 59 G4
Alpheton 59 G2
Alphington 10 C3
Alport 80 D1
Alpraham 78 C2
Alresford 60 B5
Alrewas 67 D1
Alrick 159 G3
Alsager 79 E2
Alsagers Bank 79 F3
Alsop en le Dale 80 C2
Alston Cumb. 118 D3
Alston Devon 11 G2
Alston Sutton 24 B2
Alstone Glos. 54 B4
Alstone Som. 24 A3
Alstone Staffs. 66 A1
Alstonefield 80 C2
Alswear 22 A5
Alt 92 D2
Altandhu 180 B3
Altanduin 182 D2
Altarnun 5 G1
Altass 182 A4
Altens 169 G4
Alterwall 187 F2
Altham 101 D4
Althorne 65 E5
Althorpe 95 F2
Alticry 123 D5
Altnafeadh 157 E4
Altnaharra 182 A1
Altofts 102 C5
Alton Derbys. 81 E1
Alton Hants. 28 B4
Alton Staffs. 80 B3
Alton Barnes 26 C1
Alton Pancras 12 D2
Alton Priors 26 C1
Altonside 176 B4
Altrincham 92 B4
Altura 164 D5
Alva 151 D5
Alvanley 91 F5
Alvaston 81 E4
Alvechurch 66 C5
Alvecote 67 E2
Alvediston 26 A5
Alveley 65 G4
Alverdiscott 21 F3
Alverstoke 15 F3
Alverstone 15 E4
Alverthorpe 102 C5
Alverton 82 C3
Alves 176 A3
Alvescot 41 G2
Alveston S.Glos. 39 F4

Alveston Warks. 55 E2
Alvie 166 C4
Alvingham 97 D3
Alvington 39 F2
Alwalton 69 G3
Alweston 12 C1
Alwington 21 E3
Alwinton 128 B1
Alwoodley 102 C3
Alwoodley Gates 102 C3
Alyth 160 C1
Amalebra 2 B3
Ambaston 81 F4
Amber Hill 84 A3
Ambergate 81 E2
Amberley Glos. 40 A2
Amberley W.Suss. 16 C2
Amble 129 E1
Amblecote 66 A4
Ambleside 107 E2
Ambleston 48 D5
Ambrismore 144 B4
Ambrosden 42 B1
Amcotts 95 F1
Amersham 43 D3
Amerton 79 G5
Amesbury 26 C3
Ameysford 13 G2
Amington 67 E2
Amisfield Town 125 E2
Amlwch 88 C3
Amlwch Port 88 C3
Ammanford (Rhydaman) 36 C1
Amotherby 111 G5
Ampfield 27 E5
Ampleforth 111 E5
Ampleforth College 111 E5
Ampney Crucis 40 C2
Ampney St. Mary 40 C2
Ampney St. Peter 40 C2
Amport 27 E3
Ampthill 57 F4
Ampton 71 G5
Amroth 35 E2
Amulree 151 D1
Anaboard 167 G2
Anaheilt 156 A3
Ancaster 83 E1
Anchor 64 A4
Anchor Corner 72 B2
Ancroft 145 G5
Ancrum 128 A4
Ancton 16 B3
Anderby 97 F5
Anderby Creek 97 F5
Andersea 24 A4
Andersfield 23 F4
Anderson 13 E3
Anderton 92 A5
Andover 27 E3
Andover Down 27 E3
Andoversford 40 C1
Andreas 98 C2
Anelog 74 A5
Anfield 91 E3
Angarrack 2 C3
Angarrick 3 E3
Angelbank 65 E5
Angerton 117 F1
Angle 34 B2
Angler's Retreat 62 D3
Anglesey (Ynys Môn) 88 B4
Angmering 16 C3
Angmering-on-Sea 16 C3
Angram N.Yorks. 103 E3
Angram N.Yorks. 109 D3
Anick 119 F1
Anie 150 A3
Ankerville 175 E2
Anlaby 104 C5
Anmer 85 F5
Anmore 15 F1
Anna Valley 27 E3
Annan 125 F4
Annaside 106 B4
Annat Arg. & B. 148 C2
Annat High. 172 B4
Annbank 132 C3
Annesley 81 F2
Annesley Woodhouse 81 F2
Annfield Plain 120 A2
Anniesland 141 G3
Annscroft 65 D2
Ansdell 99 G5
Ansford 24 D4

Ansley 67 E3
Anslow 80 D5
Anslow Gate 80 C5
Ansteadbrook 29 E4
Anstey Herts. 58 C4
Anstey Leics. 68 A2
Anstruther 153 D4
Ansty W.Suss. 17 E1
Ansty Warks. 67 E4
Ansty Wilts. 26 A5
Ansty Coombe 26 A5
Ansty Cross 13 D2
Anthill Common 15 F1
Anthorn 117 E1
Antingham 87 D2
Anton's Gowt 84 A3
Antony 7 D5
Antrobus 92 A5
Anvil Corner 21 D5
Anvil Green 32 D4
Anwick 83 G2
Anwoth 123 G5
Aoradh 138 A3
Apethorpe 69 F3
Apeton 66 A1
Apley 96 B5
Apperknowle 94 A5
Apperley 54 A5
Apperley Bridge 102 A4
Appersett 109 D3
Appin (An Apainn) 156 B5
Appin House 156 B5
Appleby 95 G1
Appleby Magna 67 F1
Appleby Parva 67 F2
Appleby-in-Westmorland 118 C5
Applecross 172 A5
Appledore Devon 21 E2
Appledore Devon 11 D1
Appledore Kent 19 E1
Appledore Heath 32 B5
Appleford 42 A3
Appleshaw 27 E3
Applethwaite 117 F4
Appleton Halton 91 G4
Appleton Oxon. 41 G2
Appleton Roebuck 103 E3
Appleton Thorn 92 A4
Appleton Wiske 110 C2
Appleton-le-Moors 111 G4
Appleton-le-Street 111 G4
Appletreehall 135 G4
Appletreewick 101 G1
Appley 23 D5
Appley Bridge 91 G2
Apse Heath 15 E4
Apsey Green 61 D1
Apsley 43 F2
Apsley End 57 G4
Apuldram 16 A3
Arbirlot 161 D5
Arborfield 28 C1
Arborfield Cross 28 C1
Arborfield Garrison 28 C1
Arbourthorne 94 A4
Arbroath 161 E5
Arbuthnott 161 F2
Archdeacon Newton 110 B1
Archiestown 176 B5
Arclid 79 E1
Ard a' Chapuill 140 B1
Ardacheearnbeg 140 B1
Ardacheranmor 140 B1
Ardachoil 147 G1
Ardachu 182 B4
Ardailly 139 E4
Ardalanish 146 C3
Ardallie 179 F4
Ardanaiseig 148 C2
Ardaneaskan 163 G1
Ardanstur 148 A3
Ardantiobairt 155 F4
Ardarroch 172 B5
Ardbeg Arg. & B. 140 B3
Ardbeg Arg. & B. 138 C5
Ardbeg Arg. & B. 140 C1
Ardblair 165 G1
Ardbrecknish 148 C2
Ardcharnich 173 E1
Ardchiavaig 146 C3
Ardchonnel 148 B1
Ardchonnell 148 B3
Ardchrishnish 146 D2

Ardchronie 174 C1
Ardchuilk 165 D1
Ardchullarie More 150 A3
Ardchyle 150 A2
Arddlin 64 B1
Ardechvie 164 C5
Ardeley 58 B5
Ardelve 163 G2
Arden 141 E2
Ardencaple House 147 G3
Ardens Grafton 54 D2
Ardentallan 148 A2
Ardentinny 140 C1
Ardeonaig 150 B1
Ardersier 175 D4
Ardery 155 G3
Ardessie 173 D1
Ardfad 147 G3
Ardfern 148 A4
Ardfin 138 C2
Ardgartan 149 E4
Ardgay 182 B5
Ardgenavan 149 D3
Ardgour (Corran) 156 C3
Ardgowan 140 D2
Ardgowse 168 D3
Ardgye 176 A3
Ardhallow 140 C2
Ardheslaig 172 A4
Ardiecow 177 E3
Ardinamar 147 G3
Ardindrean 173 E1
Ardingly 17 F1
Ardington 41 G4
Ardington Wick 41 G4
Ardintoul 163 G2
Ardkinglas House 149 D3
Ardlair 168 C2
Ardlamont 140 A3
Ardleigh 60 B5
Ardleigh Green 45 E4
Ardleigh Heath 60 B4
Ardleish 149 E3
Ardler 160 A5
Ardley 56 A5
Ardley End 45 E1
Ardlui (Àird Laoigh) 149 F3
Ardlussa 139 E1
Ardmaddy 148 C1
Ardmair 180 D5
Ardmaleish 140 B3
Ardmay 149 E4
Ardmenish 139 D2
Ardminish 139 E5
Ardmolich 155 G2
Ardmore Arg. & B. 138 C4
Ardmore Arg. & B. 147 G2
Ardmore Arg. & B. 141 E2
Ardmore High. 174 D1
Ardnackaig 147 G5
Ardnacross 155 E5
Ardnadam 140 C1
Ardnadrochit 147 G1
Ardnagoine 180 B4
Ardnagowan 148 D4
Ardnahein 149 D5
Ardnahoe 138 C2
Ardnarff 163 G1
Ardnastang 156 A3
Ardnave 138 A2
Ardno 149 D4
Ardo 169 F1
Ardoch D. & G. 133 G5
Ardoch Moray 176 A4
Ardoch P. & K. 151 F1
Ardochrig 142 A5
Ardoyne 169 D2
Ardpatrick 139 F3
Ardpeaton 140 D1
Ardradnaig 158 C5
Ardrishaig 139 G1
Ardroe 180 C2
Ardross 174 C2
Ardrossan 140 D5
Ardscalpsie 140 B4
Ardshave 182 C5
Ardshealach 155 F3
Ardshellach 147 G3
Ardsley 94 A2
Ardslignish 155 E3
Ardtalla 138 C4
Ardtalnaig 150 C1
Ardtaraig 140 B1
Ardteatle 148 D2
Ardtoe 155 F2

Ardtornish 155 G5
Ardtrostan 150 B2
Ardtur 156 B5
Arduaine 148 A3
Ardullie 174 B3
Ardura 147 F1
Ardvar 181 D1
Ardvasar 163 E4
Ardverikie 158 A1
Ardvorlich Arg. & B. 149 F3
Ardvorlich P. & K. 150 B2
Ardwall 123 G5
Ardwell D. & G. 114 B2
Ardwell Moray 168 A1
Ardwell S.Ayr. 122 C1
Ardwick 92 C3
Areley Kings 66 A5
Arford 28 D4
Argaty 150 C4
Argoed 38 A3
Argoed Mill 51 F1
Argos Hill 18 A1
Argrennan House 124 B5
Arichamish 148 B4
Arichastlich 149 E1
Arichonan 147 G5
Aridhglas 146 C2
Arienskill 155 G1
Arileod 154 A4
Arinacrinachd 172 A4
Arinagour 154 B4
Arisaig (Àrasaig) 155 F1
Arivegaig 155 F3
Arkendale 102 C1
Arkesden 58 C4
Arkholme 107 F2
Arkle Town 109 F2
Arkleby 117 E3
Arkleside 109 F4
Arkleton 126 B2
Arkley 44 B3
Arksey 94 C2
Arkwright Town 94 B5
Arlary 151 G4
Arle 54 B5
Arlecdon 116 D5
Arlesey 57 G4
Arleston 65 F1
Arley 92 A4
Arlingham 39 G1
Arlington Devon 21 G1
Arlington E.Suss. 18 A3
Arlington Glos. 40 D2
Arlington Beccott 21 G1
Armadale High. 185 G2
Armadale High. 163 E4
Armadale W.Loth. 142 D3
Armathwaite 118 B3
Arminghall 87 D5
Armitage 66 C1
Armitage Bridge 93 F1
Armley 102 B4
Armscote 55 E3
Armshead 79 G3
Armston 69 F4
Armthorpe 94 D2
Arnabost 154 B3
Arnaby 106 C4
Arncliffe 109 E5
Arncliffe Cote 109 E5
Arncroach 152 D4
Arne 13 F4
Arnesby 68 B3
Arngask 151 G3
Arngibbon 150 B5
Arngomery 150 B5
Arnhall 161 E3
Arnicle 130 C2
Arnipol 155 G1
Arnisdale (Arnasdal) 163 G3
Arnish 171 E5
Arniston Engine 144 A3
Arnol 189 F1
Arnold E.Riding 104 D3
Arnold Notts. 81 G3
Arnprior 150 B5
Arnside 107 F5
Arowry 78 A4
Arrad Foot 107 E4
Arradoul 176 D3
Arran 104 C3
Arran 131 E2
Arras 104 B3
Arrat 161 E4

Arrathorne 110 B3
Arreton 15 E4
Arrington 58 B2
Arrivain 149 E1
Arrochar 149 F4
Arrow 54 C2
Arscaig 182 A3
Arscott 64 D2
Arthington 102 B3
Arthingworth 68 C4
Arthog 62 C1
Arthrath 169 G1
Arthurstone 160 A5
Aruadh 138 A3
Arundel 16 C3
Aryhoulan 156 C3
Asby 117 D4
Ascog 140 C3
Ascot 29 E1
Ascott 55 F4
Ascott d'Oyley 41 F1
Ascott Earl 41 E1
Ascott-under-Wychwood 41 F1
Ascreavie 160 B4
Asenby 110 D5
Asfordby 68 C1
Asfordby Hill 68 C1
Asgarby Lincs. 84 B1
Asgarby Lincs. 83 G3
Ash Dorset 13 E1
Ash Kent 33 E3
Ash Kent 31 F2
Ash Som. 24 B5
Ash Surr. 29 D2
Ash Barton 21 F5
Ash Bullayne 10 A2
Ash Green Surr. 29 E3
Ash Green Warks. 67 F4
Ash Magna 78 C4
Ash Mill 22 A5
Ash Parva 78 C4
Ash Priors 23 E5
Ash Street 60 B3
Ash Thomas 10 D1
Ash Vale 29 D2
Ashampstead 42 A5
Ashbocking 60 C2
Ashbourne 80 C3
Ashbrittle 23 E5
Ashburnham Place 18 B2
Ashburton 9 D1
Ashbury Devon 7 F1
Ashbury Oxon. 41 E4
Ashby 95 F2
Ashby by Partney 84 C1
Ashby cum Fenby 96 C2
Ashby de la Launde 83 F2
Ashby de la Zouch 67 F1
Ashby Dell 73 F2
Ashby Folville 68 C1
Ashby Hill 96 C2
Ashby Magna 68 A3
Ashby Parva 68 A4
Ashby Puerorum 86 C1
Ashby St. Ledgers 56 A1
Ashby St. Mary 87 E5
Ashchurch 54 B4
Ashcombe Devon 10 C5
Ashcombe N.Som. 24 A1
Ashcott 24 B4
Ashdon 59 D3
Ashe 27 G3
Asheldham 46 C2
Ashen 59 F3
Ashendon 32 A5
Ashendon 42 C1
Ashens 139 G2
Ashfield Arg. & B. 139 F1
Ashfield Here. 53 E5
Ashfield Stir. 150 C4
Ashfield Suff. 60 D1
Ashfield Green Suff. 73 D4
Ashfield Green Suff. 59 F2
Ashfold Crossways 17 E1
Ashford Devon 8 C3
Ashford Devon 21 F2
Ashford Hants. 14 A1
Ashford Kent 32 A4
Ashford Surr. 43 F5
Ashford Bowdler 65 E5
Ashford Carbonel 65 E5
Ashford Hill 27 G2
Ashford in the Water 93 F5
Ashgill 142 B4

Ashiestiel 135 F2
Ashill Devon 11 D1
Ashill Norf. 71 G2
Ashill Som. 11 G2
Ashingdon 46 B3
Ashington Northumb. 129 E3
Ashington Som. 24 C5
Ashington W.Suss. 16 D2
Ashkirk 135 F3
Ashlett 15 D2
Ashleworth 54 A5
Ashleworth Quay 54 A5
Ashley Cambs. 59 E1
Ashley Ches.E. 92 B4
Ashley Devon 21 G4
Ashley Glos. 40 B3
Ashley Hants. 27 E4
Ashley Hants. 14 B3
Ashley Kent 33 F4
Ashley Northants. 68 C3
Ashley Staffs. 79 E4
Ashley Wilts. 25 F1
Ashley Down 39 E5
Ashley Green 40 B1
Ashley Heath Dorset 14 A2
Ashley Heath Staffs. 79 E4
Ashmanhaugh 87 E3
Ashmansworth 27 F2
Ashmansworthy 20 D4
Ashmore Dorset 13 F1
Ashmore P. & K. 159 G4
Ashmore Green 54 A1
Ashorne 55 F2
Ashover 81 E1
Ashover Hay 81 E1
Ashow 67 F5
Ashperton 53 F3
Ashprington 9 E2
Ashreigney 21 G4
Ashtead 29 E2
Ashton C. & W.Ches. 78 C1
Ashton Cornw. 2 D4
Ashton Cornw. 7 D4
Ashton Hants. 15 E1
Ashton Here. 53 E1
Ashton Inclyde 140 D2
Ashton Northants. 69 F4
Ashton Northants. 56 C3
Ashton Peter. 69 G2
Ashton Common 25 F2
Ashton Keynes 40 C3
Ashton under Hill 54 B4
Ashton upon Mersey 92 B3
Ashton-in-Makerfield 91 G3
Ashton-under-Lyne 92 D3
Ashurst Hants. 14 C1
Ashurst Kent 31 E5
Ashurst W.Suss. 17 D2
Ashurst Bridge 14 C1
Ashurstwood 30 D5
Ashwater 7 D2
Ashwell Herts. 58 A4
Ashwell Rut. 69 D1
Ashwell End 58 A3
Ashwellthorpe 72 C2
Ashwick 24 D3
Ashwicken 71 F1
Ashybank 135 G4
Askam in Furness 106 D5
Askern 94 C1
Askerswell 12 B3
Askett 42 B2
Askham Cumb. 118 B5
Askham Notts. 95 E5
Askham Bryan 103 E3
Askham Richard 103 E3
Asknish 148 B5
Askrigg 109 E3
Askwith 102 A3
Aslackby 83 F4
Aslacton 72 C2
Aslockton 82 C1
Asloun 168 C3
Aspall 60 C1
Aspatria 117 E2
Aspenden 58 B5
Asperton 84 A4
Aspley Guise 57 E4
Aspley Heath 57 E4
Aspull 92 A2
Asselby 103 G5
Asserby 97 E5

Assington 60 A4
Assington Green 59 F2
Astbury 79 F1
Astcote 56 B2
Asterby 96 C5
Asterley 64 C2
Asterton 64 D3
Asthall 41 E1
Asthall Leigh 41 F1
Astle 92 C5
Astley Gt.Man. 92 B2
Astley Shrop. 65 E1
Astley Warks. 67 F4
Astley Worcs. 53 G1
Astley Abbotts 65 G3
Astley Bridge 92 B1
Astley Cross 54 A1
Astley Green 92 B3
Astley Lodge 65 E1
Aston C. & W.Ches. 91 G5
Aston Ches.E. 78 D3
Aston Derbys. 93 F4
Aston Derbys. 80 C4
Aston Flints. 78 A1
Aston Here. 65 D5
Aston Here. 53 D1
Aston Herts. 58 A5
Aston Oxon. 41 F2
Aston S.Yorks. 94 B4
Aston Shrop. 78 C5
Aston Shrop. 66 A3
Aston Staffs. 79 E3
Aston Tel. & W. 65 F2
Aston W'ham 42 C4
Aston W.Mid. 66 C4
Aston Abbotts 58 D5
Aston Botterell 65 F4
Aston Cantlow 54 D2
Aston Clinton 43 D1
Aston Crews 53 F5
Aston Cross 54 B4
Aston End 58 A5
Aston Eyre 65 F3
Aston Fields 54 B1
Aston Flamville 67 G3
Aston Heath 91 G5
Aston Ingham 53 F5
Aston juxta Mondrum 79 D2
Aston le Walls 55 G2
Aston Magna 55 E4
Aston Munslow 65 E4
Aston on Carrant 54 B4
Aston on Clun 64 C4
Aston Pigott 64 C2
Aston Rogers 64 C2
Aston Rowant 42 C3
Aston Sandford 42 C2
Aston Somerville 54 C3
Aston Subedge 54 D3
Aston Tirrold 42 A4
Aston Upthorpe 42 A4
Aston-by-Stone 79 E4
Aston-on-Trent 81 F5
Astwick 58 A4
Astwood 83 F3
Astwood Bank 54 C1
Aswarby 83 F3
Aswardby 97 D5
Aswick Grange 70 B1
Atch Lench 54 C2
Atcham 65 E2
Athelhampton 13 D3
Athelington 72 D4
Athelney 24 A5
Athelstaneford 144 C2
Atherington Devon 21 F3
Atherington W.Suss. 16 C3
Athersley North 94 A2
Atherstone 67 F3
Atherstone on Stour 55 E2
Atherton 92 A2
Atlow 80 D3
Attadale 164 A1
Attenborough 81 G4
Atterby 95 G3
Attercliffe 94 A4
Atterley 65 F3
Atterton 67 F3
Attleborough Norf. 72 B2
Attleborough Warks. 67 F3
Attlebridge 86 C4
Attleton Green 59 F2
Atwick 105 D2
Atworth 25 F1
Auberrow 53 D3

Aubourn 83 E1
Auch 149 F1
Auchairne 122 C2
Auchallater 159 G1
Auchameanach 139 G4
Auchamore 139 G5
Auchar 54 A1
Auchavan 159 G3
Auchbraad 139 G1
Auchbreck 167 G2
Auchenback 141 G4
Auchenblae 161 F2
Auchenbothie 141 E2
Auchenbrack 124 B1
Auchenbreck 140 B1
Auchencairn 124 B5
Auchencrow 145 F3
Auchendinny 143 G3
Auchendolly 124 B4
Auchenfoyle 141 E2
Auchengray 143 D4
Auchenhalrig 176 C3
Auchenheath 142 C5
Auchenhessnane 124 C1
Auchenlochan 140 A1
Auchenmalg 122 D5
Auchenrivock 126 B3
Auchentiber 141 E5
Auchenvennel 141 D1
Auchessan 149 G2
Auchgourish 166 D3
Auchinafaud 139 F4
Auchincruive 132 A3
Auchindarrach 139 G1
Auchindarroch 156 C4
Auchindrain 148 C4
Auchindrean 173 E1
Auchininna 177 F5
Auchinleck 132 D3
Auchinloch 142 A2
Auchinner 150 B3
Auchinroath 176 B4
Auchintoul Aber. 168 C3
Auchintoul Aber. 177 E5
Auchintoul High. 182 A5
Auchiries 179 G1
Auchleven 168 D2
Auchlochan 133 D2
Auchlunachan 173 E1
Auchlunies 169 F5
Auchlunkart 176 C5
Auchlyne 150 A2
Auchmacoy 169 G1
Auchmair 168 A2
Auchmantle 122 C4
Auchmithie 161 E5
Auchmuirbridge 152 A4
Auchmull 161 D2
Auchnabony 116 A2
Auchnabreac 148 C4
Auchnacloich 150 D1
Auchnacraig 147 G1
Auchnacree 160 C3
Auchnafree 150 C1
Auchnagallin 167 E1
Auchnagatt 179 E5
Auchnaha 140 A1
Auchnangoual 148 C4
Auchnotteroch 122 A4
Aucholzie 168 A5
Auchorrie 169 D4
Auchrannie 160 A4
Auchraw 150 A2
Auchreoch 149 F2
Auchronie 160 C1
Auchterarder 151 E3
Auchtercairn 172 B2
Auchterderran 152 A4
Auchterhouse 152 B1
Auchtermuchty 152 A3
Auchterneed 174 A4
Auchtertool 152 A5
Auchtertyre Angus 160 A5
Auchtertyre (Uachdar Thìre) High. 163 G2
Auchtertyre Moray 176 A4
Auchtertyre Stir. 149 F2
Auchtubh 150 A2
Auckengill 187 F2
Auckley 94 D2
Audenshaw 92 D3
Audlem 79 D3
Audley 79 E2
Audley End Essex 58 D4
Audley End Essex 59 G4

Audley End Suff. 59 G4
Audmore 79 F5
Auds 177 F3
Aughton E.Riding 103 G4
Aughton Lancs. 91 E2
Aughton Lancs. 100 B1
Aughton S.Yorks. 94 B4
Aughton Wilts. 26 D2
Aughton Park 91 F2
Auldearn 175 D4
Aulden 53 D2
Auldgirth 124 D2
Auldhame 144 C1
Auldhouse 142 A4
Aulich 158 B4
Ault a'chruinn 164 A2
Ault Hucknall 81 F1
Aultanrynie 181 F1
Aultbea (An t-Allt Beithe) 172 B1
Aultgrishan 172 A1
Aultguish Inn 173 G2
Aultibea 183 F2
Aultiphurst 186 A2
Aultmore 176 D4
Ault-na-goire 165 G2
Aultnamain Inn 174 C1
Aultnapaddock 176 C5
Aulton 168 D2
Aultvaich 174 B5
Aultvoulin 163 F4
Aunby 69 F1
Aundorach 167 D3
Aunk 10 D2
Aunsby 83 F2
Auquhorthies 169 F2
Aust 39 G4
Austerfield 95 D3
Austrey 67 E2
Austwick 101 D1
Authorpe 97 E4
Authorpe Row 97 F5
Avebury 40 D5
Avebury Trusloe 26 B1
Aveley 45 E4
Avening 40 A3
Averham 82 C2
Avery Hill 44 D5
Aveton Gifford 8 C3
Avielochan 166 D3
Aviemore 166 C3
Avington Hants. 27 G4
Avington W.Berks. 27 E1
Avoch 174 C4
Avon 14 A3
Avon Dassett 55 G2
Avonbridge 142 D2
Avoncliff 25 F2
Avonmouth 39 E5
Avonwick 8 D2
Awbridge 27 E5
Awhirk 122 B5
Awkley 39 E4
Awliscombe 11 E2
Awre 39 G2
Awsworth 81 F3
Axbridge 24 B2
Axford Hants. 28 B3
Axford Wilts. 41 E5
Axminster 11 F3
Axmouth 11 F3
Axton 90 C4
Axtown 8 B1
Aycliffe 120 B5
Aydon 119 G1
Aylburton 39 F2
Ayle 118 D3
Aylesbeare 10 D3
Aylesbury 42 D1
Aylesby 96 C2
Aylesford 31 G3
Aylesham 33 G3
Aylestone 68 A2
Aylmerton 86 C2
Aylsham 86 C3
Aylton 53 F2
Aymestrey 52 D1
Aynho 56 A4
Ayot Green 44 B1
Ayot St. Lawrence 44 A1
Ayot St. Peter 44 B1
Ayr 132 B3
Aysgarth 109 F4
Ayshford 10 D1
Ayside 107 E4
Ayston 68 D2
Aythorpe Roding 45 E1
Ayton P. & K. 151 G3
Ayton Sc.Bord. 145 G3

Azerley **110** B5

B

Babbacombe **9** F1
Babbinswood **78** A4
Babb's Green **44** C1
Babcary **24** C5
Babel **51** E4
Babell **90** C5
Babeny **7** G3
Bablock Hythe **41** G2
Babraham **58** D2
Babworth **95** D4
Baby's Hill **167** G1
Bachau **88** C4
Back of Keppoch
   155 F1
Back Street **59** F2
Backaland **190** C2
Backbarrow **107** E4
Backburn **168** C1
Backe **35** F1
Backfolds **179** F2
Backford **91** F5
Backhill **169** E1
Backhill of Clackriach
   179 E3
Backhill of Trustach
   168 D5
Backies *High.* **182** D4
Backies *Moray* **177** E4
Backlass **187** E3
Backside **168** B1
Backwell **24** B1
Backworth **129** E4
Bacon End **45** E1
Baconend Green **45** E1
Baconsthorpe **86** C2
Bacton *Here.* **52** C4
Bacton *Norf.* **87** E2
Bacton *Suff.* **60** B1
Bacton Green **60** B1
Bacup **101** E5
Badachro **172** A2
Badanloch Lodge **182** C1
Badavanich **173** E4
Badbury **41** D4
Badbury Wick **41** D4
Badby **56** A2
Badcall *High.* **184** A4
Badcall *High.* **184** B3
Badcaul **180** C5
Baddeley Green **79** G2
Badden **139** G1
Baddesley Clinton **67** D5
Baddesley Ensor **67** E3
Baddidarach **180** C2
Badenyon **168** A3
Badgall **5** G1
Badger **65** G3
Badgerbank **92** C5
Badgers Mount **31** D2
Badgeworth **40** B1
Badgworth **24** A2
Badicaul **163** F2
Badingham **61** E1
Badintagairt **181** G3
Badlesmere **32** C3
Badley **60** B2
Badlipster **187** E4
Badluarach **180** B5
Badminton **40** A4
Badnaban **180** C2
Badnabay **184** B4
Badnafrave **167** G3
Badnagie **183** G1
Badnambiast **158** C2
Badninish **182** C5
Badrallach **180** C5
Badsey **54** C3
Badshot Lea **29** D3
Badsworth **94** B1
Badwell Ash **60** A1
Badworthy **8** C1
Badyo **159** E3
Bag Enderby **97** D5
Bagber **13** D1
Bagby **111** D4
Bagendon **40** C2
Bagginswood **65** F4
Baggrave Hall **68** B2
Baggrow **117** E2
Bagillt **90** D5
Baginton **67** F5
Baglan **36** D3
Bagley *Shrop.* **78** B5

Bagley *Som.* **24** B3
Bagmore **28** B3
Bagnall **79** G2
Bagnor **27** F1
Bagpath **40** A3
Bagshot *Surr.* **29** E1
Bagshot *Wilts.* **27** E1
Bagstone **39** F4
Bagthorpe *Norf.* **85** F4
Bagthorpe *Notts.* **81** F2
Baguley **92** C4
Bagworth **67** G2
Bagwyllydiart **52** D5
Baildon **102** A4
Baile Boidheach **139** F2
Baile Mhartainn **188** B1
Baile Mòr **146** B2
Bailebeag **165** G3
Baileguish **166** C5
Bailetonach **155** F2
Bailiesward **168** B1
Bailiff Bridge **102** A5
Baillieston **142** A3
Bainbridge **109** E3
Bainsford **142** C1
Bainshole **168** D1
Bainton *E.Riding* **104** B2
Bainton *Oxon.* **56** A5
Bainton *Peter.* **69** F2
Bairnkine **136** A5
Bakebare **168** A4
Baker Street **45** F4
Baker's End **44** C1
Bakewell **80** D1
Bala (Y Bala) **76** C4
Balachuirn **171** E5
Balado **151** F4
Balafark **150** B5
Balaldie **175** E2
Balallan **189** F3
Balavil **166** B4
Balbeg *High.* **165** F1
Balbeg *High.* **165** F1
Balbeggie **151** G2
Balbirnie **152** A4
Balbithan **169** E3
Balblair *High.* **174** D3
Balblair *High.* **182** A5
Balblair *High.* **174** D1
Balby **94** C2
Balcharn **182** A4
Balcherry **175** E1
Balchers **177** G4
Balchladich **180** C1
Balchraggan *High.*
   174 B5
Balchraggan *High.*
   165 G1
Balchrick **184** A3
Balcombe **30** C5
Balcurvie **152** B4
Baldernock **141** G2
Baldersby **79** E3
Baldersby St. James
   110 C5
Balderstone *Gt.Man.*
   92 D1
Balderstone *Lancs.*
   100 C4
Balderton *C. & W.Ches.*
   78 A1
Balderton *Notts.* **82** D2
Baldhu **4** B5
Baldinnie **152** C3
Baldock **58** A4
Baldon Row **42** A2
Baldovan **152** B1
Baldovie *Angus* **160** B4
Baldovie *Dundee* **152** C1
Baldrine **108** D3
Baldslow **18** C2
Baldwin **98** B3
Baldwinholme **117** G1
Baldwin's Gate **79** E3
Baldwins Hill **30** C5
Bale **86** B2
Balemartine **154** A2
Balendoch **160** A5
Balephuil **154** A2
Balerno **143** F3
Balernock **141** D1
Baleromindubh **146** C5
Balerominmore **146** C5
Baleshare (Bhaleshear)
   188 B2
Balevulin **147** D2
Balfield **160** D3
Balfour *Aber.* **168** C5
Balfour *Ork.* **190** B3

Balfron **141** G1
Balfron Station **141** G1
Balgonar **151** F5
Balgove **169** F1
Balgowan *D. & G.* **114** B2
Balgowan *High.* **166** A5
Balgown **170** C3
Balgreen **177** G4
Balgreggan **122** B5
Balgy **172** B4
Balhaldie **150** D4
Balhalgardy **169** E2
Balham **44** B4
Balhary **160** A5
Balhelvie **152** B2
Balhousie **152** C4
Baligill **186** A2
Baligrundle **156** A5
Balindore **148** B1
Balintore *Angus* **160** A4
Balintore *High.* **175** E2
Balintraid **174** D2
Balintyre **158** B5
Balivanich **188** B2
Balkeerie **160** B5
Balkholme **103** G5
Balkissock **122** C2
Ball **78** A5
Ball Haye Green **79** G2
Ball Hill **27** F1
Ballabeg **98** A4
Ballacannell **98** C3
Ballacarnane Beg **98** A3
Ballachulish
   (Baile a' Chaolais)
   156 C4
Balladoole **98** A5
Ballafesson **98** A4
Ballagyr **98** A3
Ballajora **98** C2
Ballakilpheric **98** A4
Ballamodha **98** A4
Ballantrae **122** B2
Ballards Gore **46** C3
Ballasalla *I.o.M.* **98** A4
Ballasalla *I.o.M.* **98** B2
Ballater **168** A5
Ballaterach **168** B5
Ballaugh **98** B2
Ballaveare **98** B4
Ballchraggan **175** D2
Ballechin **159** E4
Balleich **150** A4
Ballencrieff **144** B2
Ballidon **80** D2
Balliekine **98** C3
Balliemeanoch **148** D4
Balliemore *Arg. & B.*
   148 D5
Balliemore *Arg. & B.*
   148 A2
Ballig **98** A3
Ballimeanoch **148** C3
Ballimore *Arg. & B.*
   140 A1
Ballimore *Stir.* **150** A3
Ballinaby **138** A3
Ballindean **152** A2
Ballingdon **59** G3
Ballinger Common **43** G2
Ballingham **53** E4
Ballingry **151** G5
Ballinlick **159** E5
Ballinluig *P. & K.* **159** E4
Ballinluig *P. & K.* **159** F4
Ballintuim **159** G4
Balloch *Angus* **160** B4
Balloch *High.* **174** D5
Balloch *N.Lan.* **142** B2
Balloch *W.Dun.* **141** E1
Ballochan **168** C5
Ballochandrain **140** A1
Ballochford **168** A1
Ballochgair **123** D2
Ballochmartin **140** C4
Ballochmorrie **122** D2
Ballochmyle **132** D3
Ballochroy **139** F4
Ballogie **168** C5
Balls Cross **29** E5
Balls Green *Essex* **60** B5
Ball's Green *Glos.* **40** A3
Balls Hill **66** B3
Ballyaurgan **139** F2
Ballygown **154** D5
Ballygrant **138** B3
Ballyhaugh **154** A4
Ballymeanoch **148** A5
Ballymichael **131** E2

Balmacara (Baile Mac Ara)
   163 G2
Balmaclellan **124** A3
Balmacneil **159** E4
Balmadies **161** D5
Balmae **115** G2
Balmaha **149** G5
Balmalcolm **152** B4
Balmaqueen **170** D2
Balmeanach *Arg. & B.*
   155 F5
Balmeanach *Arg. & B.*
   146 D1
Balmedie **169** G3
Balmer Heath **78** B4
Balmerino **152** B2
Balmerlawn **14** C2
Balminnoch **123** D4
Balmore *E.Dun.* **142** A2
Balmore *High.* **175** E5
Balmore *High.* **165** E1
Balmore *High.* **170** B5
Balmore *P. & K.* **158** C4
Balmullo **152** C2
Balmungie **174** D4
Balmyle **159** F4
Balnaboth **160** B3
Balnabruaich **175** D2
Balnacra **172** C5
Balnafoich **166** A1
Balnagall **175** E1
Balnagown Castle **175** D2
Balnaguard **159** E4
Balnaguisich **174** C2
Balnahard *Arg. & B.*
   146 D5
Balnahard *Arg. & B.*
   147 D1
Balnain **165** F1
Balnakeil **184** C2
Balnaknock **170** D3
Balnamoon **160** D3
Balnapaling **175** D3
Balnespick **166** C4
Balquhidder **150** A2
Balsall **67** E5
Balsall Common **67** E5
Balsall Heath **66** C4
Balscote **55** F3
Balsham **59** D2
Baltasound **191** G1
Balterley **79** E2
Balterley Heath **79** E2
Baltersan **123** F4
Balthangie **178** D2
Balthayock **151** G2
Baltonsborough **24** C4
Baluachraig **148** A5
Balulive **138** C3
Balure *Arg. & B.* **148** C1
Balure *Arg. & B.* **148** A1
Balvaird **174** B4
Balvarran **159** F3
Balvicar **147** G3
Balvraid *High.* **163** G3
Balvraid *High.* **166** C1
Bamber Bridge **100** B5
Bamber's Green **59** D5
Bamburgh **137** F3
Bamff **160** A4
Bamford *Derbys.* **93** G4
Bamford *Gt.Man.* **92** C1
Bampton *Cumb.* **107** G1
Bampton *Devon* **22** C5
Bampton *Oxon.* **41** F2
Bampton Grange **107** G1
Banavie (Banbhaidh)
   156 D2
Banbury **55** G3
Bancffosfelen **36** A1
Banchor **175** F5
Banchory **169** E5
Banchory Devenick
   169 G4
Bancycapel **36** A1
Bancyfelin **35** G1
Bancyffordd **50** A4
Bandon **152** A4
Bandrake Head **107** E4
Banff **177** F3
Bangor **85** F3
Bangor-on-Dee
   (Bangor-is-y-coed)
   78 A3
Bangor's Green **91** E2
Banham **72** B3
Bank **14** B2
Bank End **106** C4
Bank Newton **101** F2

Bank Street **53** F1
Bank Top *Lancs.* **91** G2
Bank Top *W.Yorks.*
   102 A5
Bankend **125** E4
Bankfoot **151** F1
Bankglen **133** D4
Bankhead *Aber.* **168** D3
Bankhead *Aber.* **169** D4
Bankhead *Aberdeen*
   169 F3
Bankhead *D. & G.*
   116 A2
Bankland **24** A5
Banknock **142** B2
Banks *Cumb.* **118** A5
Banks *Lancs.* **99** G5
Bankshill **125** F2
Banningham **86** D3
Bannister Green **59** E5
Bannockburn **150** D5
Banstead **30** B3
Bantam Grove **102** B5
Bantham **8** C3
Banton **142** B2
Banwell **24** A2
Banwen Pyrddin **37** E2
Banyard's Green **73** E4
Bapchild **32** B2
Baptiston **141** G1
Bapton **26** A4
Bar End **27** F5
Bar Hill **58** B1
Barachander **148** C2
Barassie **132** B2
Baravaville **174** D2
Barber Booth **93** F4
Barber Green **107** E4
Barber's Moor **91** F1
Barbon **108** B4
Barbridge **22** A3
Barby **68** A5
Barcaldine (Am Barra
   Calltainn) **156** B5
Barcaple **124** A5
Barcheston **55** E4
Barclose **118** A1
Barcombe **17** G2
Barcombe Cross **17** G2
Barden **31** E4
Barden Park **31** E4
Bardennoch **123** G1
Bardfield Green
   59 E4
Bardney **83** G1
Bardon *Leics.* **67** G1
Bardon Mill **119** D1
Bardowie **141** G2
Bardsea **107** D5
Bardsey **102** C3
Bardsey Island (Ynys Enlli)
   74 A5
Bardwell **72** A4
Bare **100** A1
Barewood **52** C2
Barford *Norf.* **86** C5
Barford St. John **55** G4
Barford St. Martin **26** B4
Barford St. Michael **55** G4
Barfrestone **33** E3
Bargaly **123** F4
Bargany Mains **132** A5
Bargeddie **142** A3
Bargoed **38** A3
Bargrennan **123** E3
Barham *Cambs.* **69** G5
Barham *Kent* **33** E3
Barham *Suff.* **60** C2
Barharrow **124** A5
Barholm **69** F1
Barholm Mains **123** F5
Barkby **68** B2
Barkby Thorpe **68** B2
Barkers Green **78** C5
Barkestone-le-Vale **82** C4
Barkham **28** D1
Barking *Gt.Lon.* **44** D4
Barking *Suff.* **60** B2
Barking Tye **60** B2
Barkisland **101** G5
Barkston **83** E3
Barkston Ash **103** D4
Barkway **58** B4
Barlae **123** E4

Barland **52** B1
Barlaston **79** F4
Barlavington **16** B2
Barlborough **94** B5
Barlby **103** F4
Barlestone **67** G2
Barley *Herts.* **58** B4
Barley *Lancs.* **101** E3
Barley Green **72** D4
Barleycroft End **58** C5
Barleyhill **119** G2
Barleythorpe **68** D2
Barling **46** C4
Barlings **96** A5
Barlow *Derbys.* **94** A5
Barlow *N.Yorks.* **103** F5
Barlow *T. & W.* **120** D4
Barmby Moor **103** G3
Barmby on the Marsh
   103 F5
Barmer **85** G4
Barmolloch **148** A5
Barmoor Lane End
   137 E3
Barmouth (Abermaw)
   62 C1
Barmpton **110** C1
Barmston **105** D2
Barnaby Green **73** F4
Barnacabber **140** C1
Barnacarry **148** B5
Barnack **69** F2
Barnacle **67** F4
Barnamuc **156** C5
Barnard Castle **109** F1
Barnard Gate **41** G1
Barnardiston **59** F3
Barnard's Green **53** G3
Barnbarroch *D. & G.*
   123 E5
Barnbarroch *D. & G.*
   124 C5
Barnburgh **94** B2
Barnby **73** F3
Barnby Dun **94** C2
Barnby in the Willows
   83 D2
Barnby Moor **95** D4
Barndennoch **124** C2
Barne Barton **8** A2
Barnehurst **45** E5
Barnes **44** B4
Barnes Street **31** F4
Barnet **44** B3
Barnet Gate **44** B3
Barnetby le Wold **96** A1
Barney **86** A2
Barnham *Suff.* **71** G5
Barnham *W.Suss.* **16** B5
Barnham Broom **86** B5
Barnhead **161** E4
Barnhill *C. & W.Ches.*
   78 B2
Barnhill *Dundee* **152** C1
Barnhill *Moray* **176** A4
Barnhills **122** A3
Barningham *Dur.* **109** F1
Barningham *Suff.* **72** A4
Barnoldby le Beck **96** C2
Barnoldswick **101** E3
Barns Green **29** G5
Barnsley *Glos.* **40** C2
Barnsley *S.Yorks.* **94** A2
Barnsole **33** E3
Barnstaple **21** F2
Barnston *Essex* **45** F1
Barnston *Mersey.* **91** D4
Barnstone **82** C4
Barnt Green **66** C5
Barnton *C. & W.Ches.*
   92 A5
Barnton *Edin.* **143** F2
Barnwell All Saints **69** F4
Barnwell St. Andrew
   69 F4
Barnwood **40** A1
Barons' Cross **53** D2
Barr *Arg. & B.* **138** B3
Barr *High.* **155** F4
Barr *S.Ayr.* **123** D1
Barr *Som.* **23** E5
Barr Hall **59** F4
Barra (Barraigh) **188** A4
Barra (Tràigh Mhòr) Airport
   188 A4
Barrachan **115** D2
Barrackan **147** G4

Barraer 123 E4
Barrahormid 139 F1
Barran 149 D2
Barrapoll 154 A2
Barrasford 128 B4
Barravullin 148 A4
Barregarrow 98 B3
Barrets Green 78 C2
Barrhead 141 F4
Barrhill 122 D2
Barrington Cambs. 58 B3
Barrington Som. 11 G1
Barripper 2 D3
Barrisdale 163 G4
Barrmill 141 E4
Barrnacarry 148 A2
Barrock 187 E1
Barrow Glos. 54 A5
Barrow Lancs. 106 B3
Barrow Rut. 69 D1
Barrow Shrop. 65 F2
Barrow Som. 25 E4
Barrow Som. 24 C3
Barrow Suff. 59 F1
Barrow Gurney 24 C1
Barrow Hann 104 C5
Barrow Haven 104 C5
Barrow Hill 94 B5
Barrow Nook 91 F2
Barrow Street 25 F4
Barrow upon Humber
    104 C5
Barrow upon Soar 68 A1
Barrow upon Trent 81 E5
Barroway Drove 71 D2
Barrowby 83 D4
Barrowcliff 112 D4
Barrowden 69 E2
Barrowford 101 E4
Barrow-in-Furness 99 F1
Barrows Green 107 G4
Barry Angus 152 D1
Barry V. of Glam. 23 E1
Barsby 68 B1
Barsham 73 E3
Barskimming 132 C3
Barsloisnoch 148 A5
Barston 38 D1
Bartestree 53 E3
Barthol Chapel 169 F1
Bartholomew Green
    59 F5
Barthomley 79 E2
Bartley 14 C1
Bartley Green 66 C4
Bartlow 59 D3
Barton C. & W.Ches.
    78 B2
Barton Cambs. 58 C2
Barton Cumb. 118 A5
Barton Glos. 54 C5
Barton Lancs. 100 B4
Barton Lancs. 91 E2
Barton N.Yorks. 110 B2
Barton Oxon. 42 A2
Barton Torbay 9 F1
Barton Warks. 54 D2
Barton Bendish 71 F2
Barton End 40 A3
Barton Green 67 D1
Barton Hartshorn 56 B4
Barton Hill 103 G1
Barton in Fabis 81 G4
Barton in the Beans
    67 F2
Barton Mills 71 F5
Barton on Sea 14 B3
Barton St. David 24 C4
Barton Seagrave 69 F5
Barton Stacey 27 F3
Barton Turf 87 E3
Bartongate 55 G5
Barton-le-Clay 57 F4
Barton-le-Street 111 G5
Barton-le-Willows 103 G1
Barton-on-the-Heath
    55 E4
Barton-under-Needwood
    67 D1
Barton-upon-Humber
    104 C5
Barvas 189 F1
Barway 70 D5
Barwell 67 G3
Barwhinnock 124 A5
Barwick Herts. 44 C1
Barwick Som. 12 B1
Barwick in Elmet 102 C4

Barwinnock 115 D2
Baschurch 78 B5
Bascote 55 G1
Base Green 60 B1
Basford Green 79 G2
Bashall Eaves 100 C3
Bashall Town 100 D3
Bashley 14 B3
Basildon Essex 45 G4
Basildon W.Berks. 42 B5
Basingstoke 28 B2
Baslow 93 G5
Bason Bridge 24 A3
Bassaleg 38 B4
Bassenthwaite 117 F3
Basset's Cross 21 F5
Bassett 14 D1
Bassingbourn 58 B3
Bassingfield 82 B4
Bassingham 83 C2
Bassingthorpe 83 E5
Baston 69 G1
Bastonford 54 A2
Bastwick 87 F4
Batavaime 149 G1
Batch 24 A2
Batchley 54 C1
Batchworth 43 F3
Batchworth Heath 43 F3
Batcombe Dorset 12 C2
Batcombe Som. 25 D4
Bate Heath 92 A5
Bath 25 E1
Bathampton 25 E1
Bathealton 23 D5
Batheaston 25 E1
Bathford 25 E1
Bathgate 143 D2
Bathley 82 C2
Bathpool Cornw. 5 G2
Bathpool Som. 23 F5
Bathway 24 C2
Batley 102 B5
Batsford 55 D4
Batson 8 D4
Battersby 111 E2
Battersea 44 B5
Battisborough Cross 8 C3
Battisford 60 B2
Battisford Tye 60 B2
Battle E.Suss. 18 C2
Battle Powys 51 G4
Battledown 54 B5
Battlefield 65 E1
Battlesbridge 45 G3
Battlesden 57 E5
Battlesea Green 72 D4
Battleton 22 C5
Battlies Green 60 A1
Battramsley 14 C3
Batt's Corner 28 D3
Bauds of Cullen 177 D3
Baugh 154 B2
Baughton 54 A3
Baughurst 27 G1
Baulds 168 D5
Baulking 41 F3
Baumber 96 C5
Baunton 40 C2
Baveney Wood 65 F5
Baverstock 26 B4
Bawburgh 86 C5
Bawdeswell 86 B3
Bawdrip 24 A4
Bawdsey 61 E3
Bawdsey Manor 61 E4
Bawsey 71 E1
Bawtry 95 D3
Baxenden 101 D5
Baxterley 67 E3
Baxter's Green 59 F2
Bay 25 F5
Baybridge 119 F3
Baycliff 107 D5
Baydon 41 E5
Bayford Herts. 44 C2
Bayford Som. 25 E5
Bayfordbury 44 C1
Bayham Abbey 31 F5
Bayles 118 D3
Baylham 60 C2
Baynard's Green 56 A5
Baysham 53 E5
Bayston Hill 65 D2
Bayswater 44 B4
Baythorn End 59 F3
Bayton 65 F5
Bayworth 42 A2
Beach High. 155 G4

Beach S.Glos. 39 G5
Beachampton 56 C4
Beachamwell 71 F2
Beacharr 139 E5
Beachley 39 E3
Beacon Devon 11 E2
Beacon Devon 11 F2
Beacon Hill Dorset 13 F3
Beacon Hill Essex 46 B1
Beacon Hill Surr. 29 D4
Beacon's Bottom 42 C3
Beaconsfield 43 E3
Beadlam 111 F4
Beadlow 57 G4
Beadnell 137 G4
Beaford 21 F4
Beal N.Yorks. 103 E5
Beal Northumb. 137 E2
Bealach 156 B4
Bealsmill 7 D3
Beambridge 78 D2
Beamhurst 80 B4
Beaminster 12 A2
Beamish 120 B2
Beamsley 101 G2
Bean 45 E5
Beanacre 26 A1
Beanley 137 E5
Beardon 7 F2
Beardwood 100 C5
Beare 10 C2
Beare Green 29 G3
Bearley 55 D1
Bearnie 169 G1
Bearnock 165 F1
Bearnus 154 C5
Bearpark 120 B3
Bearsbridge 119 D2
Bearsden 141 G2
Bearsted 31 G3
Bearstone 79 E4
Bearwood Poole 13 G3
Bearwood W.Mid. 66 C4
Beattock 134 B5
Beauchamp Roding 45 E1
Beauchief 94 A4
Beaudesert 55 D1
Beaufort 38 A1
Beaulieu 14 C2
Beauly (A' Mhanachainn)
    174 B5
Beaumaris (Biwmares)
    89 E5
Beaumont Chan.I. 8 C5
Beaumont Cumb. 117 G1
Beaumont Essex 60 C5
Beaumont Hill 110 B1
Beaumont Leys 68 A2
Beausale 67 E5
Beauvale 81 F3
Beauworth 27 G5
Beaver Green 32 B4
Beaworthy 7 F1
Beazley End 59 F5
Bebington 91 E4
Bebside 129 E4
Beccles 73 F2
Beccles Heliport 73 F3
Becconsall 100 A5
Beck Foot 108 B3
Beck Hole 112 B3
Beck Row 71 E5
Beck Side Cumb. 106 D4
Beck Side Cumb. 107 E4
Beckbury 65 G2
Beckenham 30 C2
Beckering 96 B4
Beckermet 106 C2
Beckermonds 109 D4
Beckett End 71 F3
Beckfoot Cumb. 106 C2
Beckfoot Cumb. 117 D2
Beckford 54 B4
Beckhampton 26 B1
Beckingham Lincs. 83 D2
Beckingham Notts. 95 E4
Beckington 25 F2
Beckley E.Suss. 19 D1
Beckley Oxon. 42 A1
Beck's Green 73 E2
Beckside 108 B4
Beckton 44 D4
Beckwithshaw 102 B2
Becontree 45 D4
Bedale 110 B4
Bedburn 119 G4
Bedchester 13 E1
Beddau 37 G4
Beddgelert 75 E3

Beddingham 17 G3
Beddington 30 B2
Beddington Corner 30 B2
Bedfield 60 D1
Bedfield Little Green
    60 D1
Bedford 57 F3
Bedgebury Cross 31 G5
Bedgrove 42 D1
Bedham 29 F5
Bedhampton 15 G2
Bedingfield 60 C1
Bedingfield Green 60 C1
Bedingfield Street 60 C1
Bedingham Green 73 D2
Bedlam Lancs. 101 D5
Bedlam N.Yorks. 102 B3
Bedlar's Green 58 D3
Bedlington 129 E4
Bedlinog 37 G2
Bedminster 39 E5
Bedmond 43 F2
Bednall 66 B1
Bedol 90 D5
Bedrule 136 A5
Bedstone 64 C5
Bedwas 38 A4
Bedwell 58 A5
Bedwellty 38 A2
Bedworth 67 F4
Bedworth Woodlands
    67 F4
Beeby 68 B2
Beech Hants. 28 B4
Beech Staffs. 79 F4
Beech Hill 28 B1
Beechingstoke 26 B2
Beechwood 91 G4
Beedon 41 G5
Beeford 104 D2
Beeley 81 D1
Beelsby 96 C2
Beenham 27 G1
Beeny 6 B1
Beer 11 F4
Beer Hackett 12 C1
Beercrocombe 24 A5
Beesands 9 E3
Beesby Lincs. 97 E4
Beesby N.E.Lincs. 96 C3
Beeson 9 E3
Beeston Beds. 57 G3
Beeston C. & W.Ches.
    78 C2
Beeston Norf. 86 A4
Beeston Notts. 81 G4
Beeston W.Yorks. 102 B4
Beeston Regis 86 C1
Beeston St. Lawrence
    87 E3
Beeswing 124 C4
Beetham Cumb. 107 F5
Beetham Som. 11 F1
Beetley 86 A4
Beffcote 66 A1
Began 38 B4
Begbroke 41 G1
Begdale 70 C2
Begelly 35 E2
Beggar's Bush 52 B1
Beggearn Huish 22 D4
Beggshill 168 C5
Beguildy (Bugeildy)
    64 A5
Beighton Norf. 87 E5
Beighton S.Yorks. 94 B4
Beili-glas 38 C2
Beith 141 E4
Bekesbourne 33 D3
Belaugh 87 D4
Belbroughton 66 B5
Belchalwell 13 D2
Belchalwell Street 13 D2
Belchamp Otten 59 G3
Belchamp St. Paul 59 F3
Belchamp Walter 59 G3
Belchford 96 C5
Belfield 92 D1
Belford 137 F3
Belgrave 68 A2
Belhaven 145 D2
Belhelvie 169 G3
Belhinnie 168 B2
Bell Bar 44 B2
Bell Busk 101 F2
Bell End 66 B5
Bell Heath 66 B5
Bell Hill 28 C5
Bell o' th' Hill 78 C3

Bellabeg 168 A3
Belladrum 174 B5
Bellanoch 148 A5
Bellaty 160 A4
Belle Isle 102 C5
Belle Vue 117 G1
Belleau 87 E5
Belleheiglash 167 F1
Bellerby 110 A3
Bellever 7 G2
Bellfields 29 E2
Belliehill 161 D3
Bellingdon 43 E2
Bellingham Gt.Lon.
    44 C5
Bellingham Northumb.
    128 A3
Belloch 130 B2
Bellochantuy 130 B2
Bell's Cross 60 C2
Bells Yew Green 31 F5
Bellsbank 132 C5
Bellshill N.Lan. 142 B3
Bellshill Northumb.
    137 F3
Bellside 142 C4
Bellsmyre 141 F2
Bellsquarry 143 E3
Belluton 24 D1
Belmaduthy 174 C4
Belmesthorpe 69 F1
Belmont B'burn. 92 A1
Belmont Gt.Lon. 30 B2
Belmont Gt.Lon. 44 A3
Belmont Shet. 191 G1
Belnie 84 A4
Belowda 5 D3
Belper 81 F1
Belper Lane End 81 E3
Belsay 128 D4
Belsford 9 D2
Belsize 43 F2
Belstead 60 C3
Belston 132 B3
Belstone 7 G1
Belstone Corner 7 G1
Belsyde 143 D2
Belthorn 100 D5
Beltinge 33 D2
Beltingham 119 D1
Beltoft 95 F2
Belton Leics. 81 F5
Belton Lincs. 83 E4
Belton N.Lincs. 95 E2
Belton Norf. 87 F5
Belton Rut. 68 D2
Beltring 31 F4
Belvedere 45 D5
Belvoir 82 D4
Bembridge 15 F4
Bemersyde 135 G2
Bemerton 26 C4
Bempton 113 E5
Ben Alder Cottage 157 G3
Ben Alder Lodge 158 A2
Ben Rhydding 102 A3
Benacre 73 G3
Benbecula (Beinn na
    Faoghla) 188 B2
Benbecula (Balivanich)
    Airport 188 B2
Benbuie 124 B1
Benderloch (Meadarloch)
    148 B1
Bendish 57 G5
Benenden 32 A5
Benfield 123 E4
Benfieldside 119 G2
Bengate 87 E3
Bengeo 44 C1
Bengeworth 54 C3
Benhall 54 B5
Benhall Green 61 E1
Benhall Street 61 E1
Benholm 161 G3
Beningbrough 103 E2
Benington Herts. 58 A5
Benington Lincs. 84 B3
Benington Sea End 84 C3
Benllech 88 D4
Benmore Arg. & B.
    140 C1
Benmore Stir. 149 G2
Bennacott 6 C2
Bennan Cottage 124 A3
Bennett End 42 C3
Bennetts End 43 F2
Benniworth 96 C4
Benover 31 G4

Benson 42 B3
Benthall Northumb.
    137 G4
Benthall Shrop. 65 F2
Bentham 40 B1
Benthoul 169 F4
Bentlawnt 64 C2
Bentley E.Riding 104 C4
Bentley Essex 45 E3
Bentley Hants. 28 C3
Bentley S.Yorks. 94 C3
Bentley Suff. 60 C4
Bentley W.Mid. 66 B3
Bentley W.Yorks. 102 B4
Bentley Works. 67 E5
Bentley Heath Herts.
    44 B3
Bentley Heath W.Mid.
    67 D5
Bentley Rise 94 C2
Benton 21 G2
Benton Square 129 E4
Bentpath 126 B2
Bentworth 28 B3
Benvie 152 B1
Benville Lane 12 B2
Benwell 120 B1
Benwick 70 B3
Beoley 54 C1
Beoraidbeg 163 E5
Bepton 16 A2
Berden 58 C5
Bere Alston 8 A1
Bere Ferrers 8 A1
Bere Regis 13 E3
Berea 48 A4
Berepper 3 D4
Bergh Apton 87 E5
Berinsfield 42 A3
Berkeley 39 F3
Berkhamsted 43 E2
Berkley 25 F3
Berkswell 67 E5
Bermondsey 44 C5
Bernera 143 E3
Berneray (Eilean
    Bhearnaraigh) 188 C1
Berners Roding 45 E2
Bernice 148 D5
Bernisdale 170 D4
Berrick Prior 42 B3
Berrick Salome 42 B3
Berriedale 183 G2
Berriew (Aberriw) 64 A2
Berrington Northumb.
    137 E2
Berrington Shrop. 65 E2
Berrington Worcs. 53 E1
Berrington Green 53 E1
Berriowbridge 5 G2
Berrow Som. 23 F2
Berrow Worcs. 53 G4
Berrow Green 53 G2
Berry Cross 21 E4
Berry Down Cross 21 F1
Berry Hill Glos. 39 E1
Berry Hill Pembs. 49 D3
Berry Pomeroy 9 E1
Berryhillock 177 E3
Berrynarbor 21 F1
Berry's Green 30 C2
Bersham 78 A3
Berthlŵyd 36 B3
Berwick 18 A3
Berwick Bassett 40 D5
Berwick Hill 129 D4
Berwick St. James 26 B4
Berwick St. John 26 A5
Berwick St. Leonard 26 A4
Berwick-upon-Tweed
    145 G2
Bescar 91 E1
Bescot 66 C3
Besford Shrop. 78 C5
Besford Worcs. 54 B3
Bessacarr 94 D2
Bessels Leigh 41 G2
Besses o' th' Barn 92 C2
Bessingby 105 D1
Bessingham 86 C2
Best Beech Hill 31 F5
Besthorpe Norf. 72 B2
Besthorpe Notts. 82 D1
Bestwood Village 81 G3
Beswick E.Riding 104 C3
Beswick Gt.Man. 92 C3
Betchworth 30 B3
Bethania Cere. 50 B1
Bethania Gwyn. 76 A3

Bethel *Gwyn.* **75** E1
Bethel *Gwyn.* **76** C4
Bethel *I.o.A.* **88** B5
Bethersden **32** B5
Bethesda *Gwyn.* **75** F1
Bethesda *Pembs.* **35** D1
Bethlehem **50** C5
Bethnal Green **44** C4
Betley **79** E3
Betsham **45** F5
Betteshanger **33** F3
Bettiscombe **11** G3
Bettisfield **78** B4
Betton *Shrop.* **64** C2
Betton *Shrop.* **79** D4
Betton Strange **65** E2
Bettws *Bridgend* **37** F4
Bettws *Newport* **38** B3
Bettws Bledrws **50** B2
Bettws Cedewain **64** A3
Bettws Gwerfil Goch **76** D3
Bettws Newydd **38** C2
Bettws-y-crwyn **64** B4
Bettyhill **185** G2
Betws **36** C1
Betws Disserth **52** A2
Betws Garmon **75** E2
Betws Ifan **49** G3
Betws-y-coed **76** A2
Betws-yn-Rhos **90** A5
Beulah *Cere.* **49** F3
Beulah *Powys* **51** F2
Bevendean **17** F3
Bevercotes **95** D5
Beverley **104** C4
Beverston **40** A3
Bevington **39** F3
Bewaldeth **117** F3
Bewcastle **127** D4
Bewdley **65** G5
Bewerley **102** A1
Bewholme **105** D2
Bewley Common **26** A1
Bexhill **18** C3
Bexley **45** D5
Bexleyheath **45** D5
Bexwell **71** E2
Beyton **60** A1
Beyton Green **60** A1
Biallaid **166** B5
Bibury **40** D2
Bicester **56** A5
Bickenhall **11** F1
Bickenhill **67** D4
Bicker **84** A4
Bickershaw **92** A2
Bickerstaffe **91** F2
Bickerton *C. & W.Ches.* **78** C2
Bickerton *Devon* **9** E4
Bickerton *N.Yorks.* **103** D2
Bickerton *Northumb.* **128** B3
Bickford **66** A1
Bickham **22** C3
Bickham Bridge **8** D2
Bickham House **10** A4
Bickington *Devon* **21** F2
Bickington *Devon* **10** A5
Bickleigh *Devon* **8** B3
Bickleigh *Devon* **10** C2
Bickleton **21** F2
Bickley **30** D2
Bickley Moss **78** C3
Bickley Town **78** C3
Bicknacre **45** G2
Bicknoller **23** E4
Bicknor **32** A3
Bickton **14** A1
Bicton *Here.* **53** D1
Bicton *Shrop.* **64** D1
Bicton *Shrop.* **64** B4
Bicton Heath **65** D1
Bidborough **31** E4
Biddenden **32** A5
Biddenden Green **32** A4
Biddenham **57** F2
Biddestone **40** A5
Biddick **120** C2
Biddisham **24** A2
Biddlesden **56** B3
Biddlestone **128** B1
Biddulph **79** F2
Biddulph Moor **79** G2
Bideford **21** E3
Bidford-on-Avon **54** D2

Bidlake **7** E2
Bidston **91** D3
Bidwell **57** F5
Bielby **103** G3
Bieldside **169** F4
Bierley *I.o.W.* **15** E5
Bierley *W.Yorks.* **102** A4
Bierton **42** D1
Big Sand **172** A2
Bigbury **8** C3
Bigbury-on-Sea **8** C3
Bigby **96** A2
Bigert Mire **106** C3
Biggar *Cumb.* **99** E1
Biggar *S.Lan.* **134** B2
Biggin *Derbys.* **81** D3
Biggin *Derbys.* **80** C2
Biggin *N.Yorks.* **103** E4
Biggin Hill **30** D3
Biggin Hill Airport **30** D2
Biggleswade **57** G3
Bigholms **126** B3
Bighouse **186** A2
Bighton **28** B4
Biglands **117** F1
Bignor **16** B2
Bigrigg **116** D5
Bilberry **5** E4
Bilborough **81** G3
Bilbrook *Som.* **22** D3
Bilbrook *Staffs.* **66** A2
Bilbrough **103** E3
Bilbster **187** E3
Bilby **94** D4
Bildershaw **120** A5
Bildeston **60** A3
Billericay **45** F3
Billesdon **68** C2
Billesley **54** D2
Billholm **126** A2
Billingborough **83** G4
Billinge **91** G3
Billingford *Norf.* **72** C4
Billingford *Norf.* **86** B3
Billingham **121** D5
Billinghay **83** G2
Billingley **94** B2
Billingshurst **29** F5
Billingsley **65** G4
Billington *Beds.* **57** E5
Billington *Lancs.* **100** D4
Billington *Staffs.* **79** F5
Billockby **87** F4
Billy Row **120** A4
Bilsborrow **100** B4
Bilsby **89** G5
Bilsby Field **97** E5
Bilsdean **145** E2
Bilsham **16** B3
Bilsington **32** C5
Bilson Green **39** F1
Bilsthorpe **82** B3
Bilsthorpe Moor **82** B2
Bilston *Midloth.* **143** G3
Bilston *W.Mid.* **66** B3
Bilstone **67** G2
Bilting **32** C4
Bilton *E.Riding* **105** D4
Bilton *N.Yorks.* **102** C2
Bilton *Northumb.* **137** G5
Bilton *Warks.* **67** G5
Bilton-in-Ainsty **103** D3
Bimbister **190** B3
Binbrook **96** C3
Bincombe **12** C4
Bindal **175** F1
Bindon **21** E5
Binegar **24** D3
Bines Green **17** D2
Binfield **42** D5
Binfield Heath **42** C5
Bingfield **128** B4
Bingham **82** C4
Bingham's Melcombe **13** D2
Bingley **102** A4
Bings Heath **65** E1
Binham **86** A2
Binley *Hants.* **27** F2
Binley *W.Mid.* **67** F5
Binniehill **142** C2
Binsoe **110** B5
Binstead **15** E3
Binsted *Hants.* **28** C3
Binsted *W.Suss.* **16** B3
Binton **54** D2
Bintree **86** B3
Binweston **64** C2
Birch *Essex* **60** A5

Birch *Gt.Man.* **92** C2
Birch Cross **80** C4
Birch Green *Essex* **46** C1
Birch Green *Herts.* **44** B1
Birch Grove **17** G1
Birch Heath **78** C1
Birch Vale **93** E4
Birch Wood **11** F1
Bircham Newton **85** F4
Bircham Tofts **85** F4
Birchanger **58** D5
Bircher **53** D1
Bircher Common **53** D1
Birchfield **181** G5
Birchgrove *Cardiff* **38** A4
Birchgrove *Swan.* **36** D3
Birchington **33** G2
Birchmoor **67** E2
Birchover **80** D1
Birchwood *Lincs.* **83** E1
Birchwood *Warr.* **92** A3
Bircotes **94** D3
Bird Street **60** B2
Birdbrook **59** F3
Birdbush **25** A5
Birdfield **148** B5
Birdforth **111** D5
Birdham **16** A3
Birdingbury **55** G1
Birdlip **40** B2
Birdoswald **118** C1
Birds Green **45** E2
Birdsall **104** A1
Birdsgreen **65** G4
Birdsmoor Gate **11** G2
Birdston **142** A2
Birdwell **94** A2
Birdwood **39** G1
Birgham **136** B3
Birchen **182** C5
Birkby *Cumb.* **117** D3
Birkby *N.Yorks.* **110** C2
Birkdale *Mersey.* **91** E1
Birkdale *N.Yorks.* **109** D2
Birkenhead **91** E4
Birkenhills **177** G5
Birkenshaw **102** B5
Birkhall **168** A5
Birkhill *Angus* **152** B1
Birkhill *Sc.Bord.* **144** C5
Birkhill *Sc.Bord.* **134** B5
Birkholme **83** E5
Birkin **103** E5
Birks **102** B5
Birkwood **133** G2
Birley **53** D2
Birley Carr **94** B3
Birling *Kent* **31** F2
Birling *Northumb.* **129** E1
Birling Gap **18** A4
Birlingham **54** B3
Birmingham **66** C4
Birmingham International Airport **67** D4
Birnam **159** F5
Birsay **190** A2
Birse **190** A2
Birsemore **168** C5
Birstall **68** A2
Birstall Smithies **102** B5
Birstwith **102** B2
Birthorpe **83** G4
Birtle **92** C1
Birtley *Here.* **52** C1
Birtley *Northumb.* **128** A4
Birtley *T. & W.* **120** B2
Birts Street **53** G4
Birtsmorton **54** A4
Bisbrooke **69** D3
Biscathorpe **96** C4
Bish Mill **22** A5
Bisham **43** D4
Bishampton **54** B2
Bishop Auckland **120** B5
Bishop Burton **104** B3
Bishop Middleham **120** C4
Bishop Monkton **102** C1
Bishop Norton **95** G3
Bishop Sutton **24** C2
Bishop Thornton **102** B1
Bishop Wilton **103** G2
Bishopbridge **96** A3
Bishopbriggs **142** A2
Bishopmill **176** B3
Bishops Cannings **26** B1
Bishop's Castle **64** C4

Bishop's Caundle **12** C1
Bishop's Cleeve **54** B5
Bishop's Frome **53** F2
Bishops Gate **43** E5
Bishop's Green *Essex* **45** F1
Bishop's Green *Hants.* **27** G1
Bishop's Hull **23** F5
Bishop's Itchington **54** D2
Bishop's Lydeard **23** E5
Bishop's Norton **54** A5
Bishops Nympton **22** A5
Bishop's Offley **79** E5
Bishop's Stortford **58** C5
Bishop's Sutton **28** B4
Bishop's Tachbrook **55** F1
Bishop's Tawton **21** F2
Bishop's Waltham **15** E1
Bishop's Wood **66** A2
Bishopsbourne **33** D3
Bishopsteignton **10** C5
Bishopstoke **15** D1
Bishopston *Bristol* **39** E5
Bishopston *Swan.* **36** B4
Bishopstone *Bucks.* **42** D1
Bishopstone *Here.* **52** D3
Bishopstone *Swin.* **41** E4
Bishopstone *Wilts.* **26** B5
Bishopstrow **25** F3
Bishopsworth **24** C1
Bishopthorpe **103** E3
Bishopton *Darl.* **120** C5
Bishopton *N.Yorks.* **110** B5
Bishopton *Renf.* **141** F2
Bishopton *Warks.* **55** D2
Bishton **38** C4
Bisley *Glos.* **40** B2
Bisley *Surr.* **29** E2
Bispham **99** G4
Bispham Green **91** F1
Bissoe **4** B5
Bisterne **14** A2
Bisterne Close **14** B2
Bitchet Green **31** E3
Bitchfield **83** E5
Bittadon **21** F1
Bittaford **8** C2
Bittering **86** A4
Bitterley **65** E5
Bitterne **15** D1
Bitteswell **68** A4
Bitton **25** D1
Bix **42** C4
Bixter **191** E4
Blaby **68** A3
Black Bourton **41** E2
Black Bridge **34** C2
Black Callerton **120** A1
Black Carr **72** B2
Black Clauchrie **123** D2
Black Cornes Lodge **157** E4
Black Crofts **148** B1
Black Cross **4** D3
Black Dog **10** B2
Black Heddon **128** C4
Black Hill **55** E2
Black Marsh **64** C3
Black Moor **102** B3
Black Mount **157** E5
Black Notley **59** F5
Black Pill **36** C3
Black Street **73** G3
Black Torrington **21** E5
Blackaburn **127** F4
Blackacre **125** E1
Blackadder **145** F4
Blackawton **9** E2
Blackborough *Devon* **11** D2
Blackborough *Norf.* **71** E1
Blackborough End **71** E1
Blackboys **18** A1
Blackbraes *Aber.* **169** F3
Blackbraes *Falk.* **142** D2
Blackbrook *Derbys.* **81** E3
Blackbrook *Leics.* **67** G1
Blackbrook *Mersey.* **91** G3
Blackbrook *Staffs.* **79** E4
Blackburn *Aber.* **169** F3

Blackburn *B'burn.* **100** C5
Blackburn *W.Loth.* **143** D3
Blackbushe **28** C2
Blackcastle **175** E4
Blackchambers **169** E3
Blackcraig *D. & G.* **123** F4
Blackcraig *D. & G.* **124** D2
Blackden Heath **92** B5
Blackdog **169** G3
Blackdown *Devon* **7** F3
Blackdown *Dorset* **11** G2
Blackdown *Warks.* **55** F1
Blacker Hill **94** A2
Blackfen **45** D5
Blackfield **14** C2
Blackford *Aber.* **169** E1
Blackford *Cumb.* **126** B5
Blackford *P. & K.* **151** E2
Blackford *Som.* **25** D5
Blackford *Som.* **24** B2
Blackford Bridge **92** C1
Blackfordby **67** F1
Blackgang **15** D3
Blackhall *Edin.* **143** G2
Blackhall *Renf.* **141** F3
Blackhall Colliery **121** D4
Blackhall Mill **120** A2
Blackhall Rocks **121** D4
Blackham **31** E5
Blackhaugh **135** F2
Blackheath *Essex* **60** B5
Blackheath *Gt.Lon.* **44** C5
Blackheath *Suff.* **73** F4
Blackheath *Surr.* **29** F3
Blackheath *W.Mid.* **66** B4
Blackhill *Aber.* **179** F2
Blackhill *Aber.* **179** F3
Blackhillock **178** D5
Blackhills **176** D5
Blackland **26** B1
Blacklands **22** B4
Blackleach **100** A4
Blackley **92** C2
Blacklunans **159** G3
Blackmill **37** F4
Blackmoor *Hants.* **28** C4
Blackmoor *Som.* **11** E1
Blackmoor Gate **21** G1
Blackmore **45** F2
Blackmore End *Essex* **59** F4
Blackmore End *Herts.* **44** A1
Blackness *Aber.* **169** D5
Blackness *Falk.* **143** E2
Blackness *High.* **187** E5
Blacknest **28** C3
Blackney **12** A3
Blacko **101** E3
Blackpole **54** A2
Blackpool *B'pool* **99** G4
Blackpool *Devon* **9** E3
Blackpool Bridge **35** D1
Blackpool Gate **126** D4
Blackpool International Airport **99** G4
Blackridge **142** C3
Blackrock *Arg. & B.* **138** B3
Blackrock *Mon.* **38** B1
Blackrod **92** A1
Blackshaw **124** D3
Blackshaw Head **101** F5
Blacksmith's Green **60** C1
Blacksnape **100** D5
Blackstone **17** E2
Blackthorn **42** B1
Blackthorpe **60** A1
Blacktoft **104** A5
Blacktop **169** F4
Blacktown **38** B4
Blackwater *Cornw.* **4** B5
Blackwater *Hants.* **28** C2
Blackwater *I.o.W.* **15** E4
Blackwater *Norf.* **86** B3
Blackwater *Som.* **11** F1
Blackwaterfoot **131** G3
Blackwell *Darl.* **110** B1
Blackwell *Derbys.* **93** F5
Blackwell *Derbys.* **81** F2
Blackwell *W.Suss.* **30** C5
Blackwell *Warks.* **55** E3
Blackwell *Worcs.* **66** B5
Blackwells End **53** G5

Blackwood (Coed-duon) *Caerp.* **38** A3
Blackwood *D. & G.* **124** D2
Blackwood *S.Lan.* **142** B5
Blackwood Hill **79** G2
Blacon **78** A1
Bladbean **33** D4
Bladnoch **123** F5
Bladon **41** G1
Blaen Clydach **37** F3
Blaenannerch **49** F3
Blaenau Dolwyddelan **75** F2
Blaenau Ffestiniog **75** F1
Blaenavon **38** B2
Blaenawey **38** B1
Blaencelyn **49** G2
Blaencwm **37** F2
Blaendyryn **51** F4
Blaenffos **49** E4
Blaengarw **37** F3
Blaengeuffordd **62** C4
Blaengweche **36** C1
Blaengwrach **37** E2
Blaengwynfi **37** F3
Blaenllechau **37** G3
Blaenos **51** D4
Blaenpennal **50** C1
Blaenplwyf **62** B5
Blaenporth **49** F3
Blaenrhondda **37** F2
Blaenwaun **49** F5
Blaen-y-coed **49** G5
Blagdon *N.Som.* **24** B2
Blagdon *Torbay* **9** E1
Blagdon Hill **11** F1
Blaguegate **91** F2
Blaich **156** C2
Blaina **38** A2
Blair **141** E5
Blair Atholl **159** D3
Blair Drummond **150** C5
Blairannaich **149** F4
Blairbuie **140** C2
Blairgowrie **159** G5
Blairhall **143** E1
Blairhoyle **150** B4
Blairhullichan **149** G4
Blairingone **151** E3
Blairkip **132** D2
Blairlogie **150** D5
Blairmore *Arg. & B.* **140** C1
Blairmore *High.* **182** C4
Blairmore *High.* **184** A3
Blairnairn **141** D1
Blairnamarrow **167** G3
Blairpark **140** C4
Blairquhan **132** B5
Blairquhosh **141** G1
Blair's Ferry **140** A3
Blairshinnoch **177** F3
Blairuskinmore **149** G4
Blairvadach **141** D1
Blairydryne **169** D3
Blairythan Cottage **169** G2
Blaisdon **39** G1
Blake End **59** F5
Blakebrook **66** A5
Blakedown **66** A5
Blakelaw *Sc.Bord.* **136** B3
Blakelaw *T. & W.* **120** B1
Blakeley **66** A3
Blakelow **79** D2
Blakemere **52** C3
Blakeney *Glos.* **39** F2
Blakeney *Norf.* **86** B1
Blakenhall *Ches.E.* **79** E3
Blakenhall *W.Mid.* **66** B3
Blakeshall **66** A4
Blakesley **56** B2
Blanchland **119** F2
Bland Hill **102** B2
Blandford Camp **13** F2
Blandford Forum **13** E2
Blandford St. Mary **13** E2
Blanefield **141** G2
Blanerne **145** F4
Blankney **83** F1
Blantyre **142** A4
Blar a' Chaorainn **156** D3
Blargie **166** A5
Blarglas **141** E1
Blarmachfoldach **156** C3
Blarnalearoch **180** D5
Blashford **14** A2
Blaston **68** D3

Blatherwycke 69 E3
Blawith 107 D4
Blaxhall 61 E2
Blaxton 95 D2
Blaydon 120 A1
Bleadney 24 B3
Bleadon 24 A2
Bleak Hey Nook 93 E2
Blean 32 D2
Bleasby Lincs. 96 B4
Bleasby Notts. 82 C3
Bleasby Moor 96 B4
Bleatarn 108 C1
Bleathwood Common 53 E1
Blebocraigs 152 C3
Bleddfa 52 B1
Bledington 55 E5
Bledlow 42 C2
Bledlow Ridge 42 C3
Blencarn 118 C4
Blencogo 117 E2
Blencow 118 A4
Blendworth 15 G1
Blennerhasset 117 E2
Blervie Castle 175 G4
Bletchingdon 42 A1
Bletchingley 30 C3
Bletchley M.K. 57 D4
Bletchley Shrop. 78 D4
Bletherston 49 D5
Bletsoe 57 F2
Blewbury 42 A4
Blickling 86 C3
Blidworth 81 G2
Blidworth Bottoms 81 G2
Blindburn Aber. 169 G1
Blindburn Northumb. 136 C5
Blindcrake 117 E3
Blindley Heath 30 C4
Blisland 5 F2
Bliss Gate 65 G5
Blissford 14 A1
Blisworth 56 C2
Blithbury 80 B5
Blitterlees 117 E1
Blo' Norton 72 B4
Blockley 55 D4
Blofield 87 E5
Blofield Heath 87 E4
Blore 80 C3
Blossomfield 66 D5
Blount's Green 80 B4
Blowick 91 E1
Bloxham 55 G4
Bloxholm 83 F2
Bloxwich 13 E3
Bloxworth 13 E3
Blubberhouses 102 A2
Blue Anchor Cornw. 4 D4
Blue Anchor Som. 22 D3
Blue Bell Hill 31 G2
Bluewater 45 E5
Blundellsands 91 E3
Blundeston 73 G2
Blunham 57 G2
Blunsdon St. Andrew 40 D4
Bluntington 66 A5
Bluntisham 70 B6
Blunts 6 D4
Blurton 79 F3
Blyborough 95 G3
Blyford 73 F4
Blymhill 66 A1
Blymhill Common 65 G1
Blymhill Lawn 66 A1
Blyth Northumb. 129 F3
Blyth Notts. 94 D4
Blyth Bridge 143 F5
Blyth End 67 E3
Blythburgh 73 F4
Blythe Bridge 79 G3
Blythe Marsh 79 G3
Blyton 95 F3
Boarhills 153 D3
Boarhunt 15 F2
Boars Hill 41 G2
Boarsgreave 101 E5
Boarshead 31 E5
Boarstall 42 B1
Boarzell 18 C1
Boasley Cross 7 F1
Boat o' Brig 176 C4
Boat of Garten 166 D3
Boath 174 B2
Bobbing 32 A2
Bobbington 66 A3

Bobbingworth 45 E2
Bocaddon 5 F4
Bochastle 150 B4
Bockhampton 41 F5
Bocking 59 F5
Bocking Churchstreet 59 F5
Bockleton 53 E1
Boconnoc 5 F3
Boddam Aber. 179 G3
Boddam Shet. 191 G5
Bodden 24 D3
Boddington 54 A5
Bodedern 88 B3
Bodelwyddan 90 B5
Bodenham Here. 53 E2
Bodenham Wilts. 26 C5
Bodenham Moor 53 E2
Bodesbeck 134 C5
Bodewryd 88 C3
Bodfari 90 B5
Bodffordd 88 C5
Bodfuan 74 C4
Bodham 86 C1
Bodiam 18 C1
Bodicote 55 G4
Bodieve 5 D2
Bodinnick 5 F4
Bodior 88 A5
Bodle Street Green 18 B2
Bodmin 5 E3
Bodney 71 G3
Bodorgan 74 C1
Bodrane 5 G3
Bodsham Green 32 D4
Bodwen 5 E3
Bodymoor Heath 67 D3
Bogallan 174 C4
Bogbain 174 D5
Bogbrae 179 F4
Bogbuie 174 B4
Bogend 132 B2
Bogfern 168 C4
Bogfields 168 C4
Bogfold 178 D2
Boghead Aber. 177 F4
Boghead E.Ayr. 133 E3
Boghead S.Lan. 142 B5
Boghole Farm 175 F4
Bogmoor 176 C3
Bogniebrae 177 E5
Bognor Regis 16 B4
Bograxie 169 E3
Bogroy 166 D2
Bogside 151 E5
Bogston 168 A4
Bogton 177 F4
Bogue 124 A2
Bohemia 14 B1
Bohenie 157 E1
Bohetherick 8 A1
Bohortha 3 F3
Bohuntine 157 E1
Bojewyan 2 A3
Bokiddick 5 E3
Bolam Dur. 120 A5
Bolam Northumb. 128 C3
Bolberry 8 C4
Bold Heath 91 G4
Bolderwood 14 B2
Boldon 120 C1
Boldon Colliery 120 C1
Boldre 14 C3
Boldron 109 F1
Bole 95 E4
Bolehill 81 D2
Boleigh 2 B4
Bolenowe 3 D3
Boleside 135 F2
Bolfracks 158 D5
Bolgoed 36 C2
Bolham Devon 10 C1
Bolham Notts. 95 E4
Bolham Water 11 E1
Bolingey 4 B4
Bollington 92 D5
Bolney 17 E1
Bolnhurst 57 F2
Bolshan 161 E4
Bolsover 94 B5
Bolsterstone 93 G3
Bolstone 53 E4
Boltby 111 D4
Bolter End 42 C3
Bolton Cumb. 118 C5
Bolton E.Loth. 144 C2
Bolton E.Riding 103 G2
Bolton Gt.Man. 92 B2

Bolton Northumb. 137 F5
Bolton Abbey 101 G2
Bolton Bridge 101 G2
Bolton by Bowland 101 D3
Bolton Houses 100 A4
Bolton Low Houses 117 F2
Bolton Percy 103 E3
Bolton upon Dearne 94 B2
Bolton Wood Lane 117 F2
Boltonfellend 118 A1
Bolton-le-Sands 100 A1
Bolton-on-Swale 110 B3
Bolventor 5 F2
Bombie 116 A2
Bomere Heath 65 D1
Bonar Bridge 182 B5
Bonawe (Bun Atha) 148 C1
Bonby 96 C6
Boncath 49 F4
Bonchester Bridge 135 G4
Bonchurch 15 E5
Bondleigh 21 G5
Bonds 100 A3
Bonehill 67 D2
Bo'ness 143 D1
Bonhill 141 E2
Boningale 66 A2
Bonjedward 136 A4
Bonkle 142 C4
Bonning Gate 107 F3
Bonnington Edin. 143 F3
Bonnington Kent 32 C5
Bonnybank 152 B4
Bonnybridge 142 C1
Bonnykelly 179 D2
Bonnyrigg 144 A3
Bonnyton Aber. 169 D1
Bonnyton Angus 153 D1
Bonnyton Angus 161 E4
Bonnyton Angus 152 B1
Bonsall 81 D2
Bont 38 C1
Bont Dolgadfan 63 E2
Bont Newydd 76 A5
Bontddu 62 C1
Bont-goch (Elerch) 62 C4
Bonthorpe 97 E5
Bont-newydd Conwy 90 B5
Bontnewydd Gwyn. 75 D1
Bontuchel 77 D2
Bonvilston 37 G5
Bon-y-maen 36 C3
Boode 21 F2
Booker 42 D3
Booley 78 C5
Boor 172 B1
Boorley Green 15 E1
Boosbeck 111 F1
Boose's Green 59 G4
Boot 106 C2
Boot Street 60 D3
Booth 101 E2
Booth Bank 93 E1
Booth Green 92 D4
Booth Wood 93 E1
Boothby Graffoe 83 E2
Boothby Pagnell 83 E4
Boothstown 92 B2
Boothville 56 C1
Bootle Cumb. 106 C4
Bootle Mersey. 91 E3
Booton 86 C3
Boots Green 92 B5
Booze 109 F2
Boquhan 141 G1
Boraston 65 F5
Bordeaux 9 F4
Borden Kent 32 A2
Borden W.Suss. 28 D5
Bordley 101 F1
Bordon 28 C4
Boreham Essex 45 G2
Boreham Wilts. 25 F3
Boreham Street 18 B2
Borehamwood 44 A3
Boreland D. & G. 125 E3
Boreland D. & G. 123 E4
Boreland Stir. 150 A1
Boreley 54 A1

Boreraig 170 A4
Borgh 188 A4
Borgh 185 F3
Borgie 185 F3
Borgue D. & G. 115 G2
Borgue High. 183 G2
Borley 59 G3
Borley Green Essex 59 G3
Borley Green Suff. 60 A1
Borness 115 G2
Bornisketaig 170 C2
Borough Green 31 F3
Boroughbridge 102 C1
Borras Head 78 A2
Borrowash 81 F4
Borrowby N.Yorks. 111 G1
Borrowby N.Yorks. 110 D4
Borrowdale 117 F5
Borrowfield 169 F5
Borstal 31 G2
Borth 62 C4
Borthwick 144 A4
Borthwickbrae 135 F4
Borthwickshiels 135 F4
Borth-y-Gest 75 E4
Borve 170 D5
Borwick 107 G5
Borwick Rails 106 C5
Bosavern 2 A3
Bosbury 53 F3
Boscarne 5 E3
Boscastle 6 A1
Boscombe Bourne. 14 A3
Boscombe Wilts. 26 D4
Bosham 16 A3
Bosham Hoe 16 A3
Bosherston 34 C3
Bosley 79 G1
Bossall 103 G1
Bossiney 5 E1
Bossingham 33 D4
Bossington Hants. 27 E4
Bossington Som. 22 B3
Bostock Green 79 D1
Boston 84 B3
Boston Spa 102 D3
Boswarthan 2 B3
Boswinger 5 D5
Botallack 2 A3
Botany Bay 44 B4
Botcheston 67 G2
Botesdale 72 B4
Bothal 129 E3
Bothamsall 95 D5
Bothel 117 E3
Bothenhampton 12 A3
Bothwell 142 B4
Botley Bucks. 43 E2
Botley Hants. 15 E1
Botley Oxon. 41 G2
Botloe's Green 53 G5
Botolph Claydon 56 C5
Botolphs 17 D3
Botolph's Bridge 32 D5
Bottacks 174 A3
Bottesford Leics. 82 D4
Bottesford N.Lincs. 95 F2
Bottisham 58 D1
Bottlesford 26 C2
Bottom Boat 102 C5
Bottom of Hutton 100 A5
Bottom o'th'Moor 92 A1
Bottomcraig 152 B2
Bottoms 101 F5
Botton Head 100 C1
Botusfleming 8 A1
Botwnnog 74 B4
Bough Beech 31 D4
Boughrood 52 A4
Boughspring 39 E3
Boughton Norf. 71 F2
Boughton Northants. 56 C1
Boughton Notts. 82 B1
Boughton Aluph 32 C4
Boughton Lees 32 C4
Boughton Malherbe 32 A4
Boughton Monchelsea 31 G3
Boughton Street 32 C3
Boulby 111 G1
Bouldon 14 C4
Bouldon 65 E4
Boulge 61 D2
Boulmer 137 G5
Boulston 34 C1

Boultenstone Hotel 168 B3
Boultham 83 E1
Boundary Derbys. 67 F1
Boundary Staffs. 79 G3
Bourn 58 B2
Bourne 83 F5
Bourne End Beds. 57 E3
Bourne End Bucks. 43 D4
Bourne End Herts. 43 E2
Bournebridge 45 E3
Bournemouth 13 G3
Bournemouth Airport 14 A3
Bournheath 66 B5
Bournmoor 120 C2
Bournville 66 C4
Bourton Bucks. 56 C4
Bourton Dorset 25 E4
Bourton N.Som. 24 A1
Bourton Oxon. 41 E4
Bourton Shrop. 65 E3
Bourton Wilts. 26 B1
Bourton on Dunsmore 67 G5
Bourton-on-the-Hill 55 D4
Bourton-on-the-Water 55 D5
Bousd 154 B3
Boustead Hill 117 F1
Bouth 107 F4
Bouthwaite 110 A5
Bovain 150 A1
Boveney 43 E5
Boveridge 13 G1
Boverton 22 C1
Bovey Tracey 10 B5
Bovingdon 43 F2
Bovingdon Camp 13 E4
Bovinger 45 E2
Bovington Camp 13 G4
Bow Cumb. 117 G1
Bow Devon 10 A2
Bow Devon 9 E3
Bow Ork. 190 B4
Bow Brickhill 57 E4
Bow of Fife 152 B3
Bow Street Cere. 62 C4
Bow Street Norf. 72 B2
Bowbank 119 F5
Bowburn 120 C4
Bowcombe 15 D4
Bowd 11 E3
Bowden Devon 9 E3
Bowden Sc.Bord. 135 G2
Bowden Hill 26 A1
Bowdon 92 B4
Bower 127 F3
Bower Hinton 12 A1
Bower House Tye 60 A3
Bowerchalke 26 B5
Bowerhill 26 A1
Bowermadden 187 E2
Bowers 79 F4
Bowers Gifford 45 G4
Bowershall 151 F5
Bowertower 187 E2
Bowes 109 E1
Bowgreave 100 A3
Bowhousebog 142 C4
Bowithick 5 F1
Bowker's Green 91 F2
Bowland Bridge 107 F4
Bowley 53 E2
Bowley Town 53 E2
Bowlhead Green 29 E4
Bowling W.Dun. 141 F2
Bowling W.Yorks. 102 A4
Bowling Bank 78 A3
Bowlish 24 D3
Bowmanstead 107 E3
Bowmore 138 B3
Bowness-on-Solway 126 A5
Bowness-on-Windermere 107 F3
Bowscale 117 G3
Bowsden 145 G5
Bowside Lodge 186 A2
Bowston 107 F3
Bowthorpe 86 C5
Bowtrees 142 D1
Box Glos. 40 A2
Box Wilts. 25 F1
Box End 57 F2
Boxbush Glos. 39 G1
Boxbush Glos. 53 F5
Boxford Suff. 60 A3
Boxford W.Berks. 41 G5

Boxgrove 16 B3
Boxley 31 G3
Boxmoor 43 F2
Box's Shop 20 C5
Boxted Essex 60 A4
Boxted Suff. 59 G2
Boxted Cross 60 A4
Boxwell 40 A3
Boxworth 58 B1
Boxworth End 58 B1
Boyden Gate 33 E2
Boydston 132 C2
Boylestone 80 C4
Boyndie 177 F3
Boynton 104 D1
Boys Hill 12 C2
Boysack 161 E5
Boyton Cornw. 6 D1
Boyton Suff. 61 E3
Boyton Wilts. 26 A4
Boyton Cross 45 F2
Boyton End 59 F3
Bozeat 57 E2
Braaid 98 B4
Braal Castle 186 D2
Brabling Green 61 D1
Brabourne 32 C4
Brabourne Lees 32 C4
Brabster 187 F2
Bracadale 162 B1
Braceborough 69 F1
Bracebridge Heath 83 E1
Braceby 83 F4
Bracewell 101 E3
Brachla 165 G1
Brackenber 108 C1
Brackenbottom 108 D5
Brackenfield 81 E2
Brackens 177 G4
Bracklach 168 A2
Bracklamore 178 D2
Bracklesham 16 A4
Brackletter (A' Bhreac-Leitir) 157 D1
Brackley Arg. & B. 139 G1
Brackley High. 175 F4
Brackley Northants. 56 A4
Brackley Gate 81 E3
Brackley Hatch 56 B3
Bracknell 29 D1
Braco 150 D4
Bracobrae 177 E4
Bracon Ash 72 C2
Bracora 163 F5
Bracorina 163 F5
Bradbourne 80 D2
Bradbury 120 C5
Bradda 98 A4
Bradden 56 B3
Braddock 5 F3
Bradenham Bucks. 42 D3
Bradenham Norf. 86 A5
Bradenstoke 40 C5
Bradfield Devon 11 D2
Bradfield Essex 60 C4
Bradfield Norf. 87 D2
Bradfield W.Berks. 42 B5
Bradfield Combust 59 G2
Bradfield Green 79 D2
Bradfield Heath 60 C5
Bradfield St. Clare 60 A2
Bradfield St. George 60 A1
Bradford Cornw. 5 F2
Bradford Derbys. 80 D1
Bradford Devon 21 E5
Bradford Northumb. 137 F3
Bradford Northumb. 128 C4
Bradford W.Yorks. 102 A4
Bradford Abbas 12 B1
Bradford Leigh 25 F1
Bradford Peverell 12 C3
Bradford-on-Avon 25 F1
Bradford-on-Tone 23 E5
Bradiford 21 F2
Brading 15 F4
Bradley C. & W.Ches. 91 G5
Bradley Derbys. 80 D3
Bradley Hants. 28 B3
Bradley N.E.Lincs. 96 C2
Bradley (Low Bradley) N.Yorks. 101 G3
Bradley Staffs. 66 A1

Bradley W.Mid. 66 B3
Bradley Fold 92 B2
Bradley Green Warks. 67 E2
Bradley Green Worcs. 54 B1
Bradley in the Moors 80 B3
Bradley Mills 93 F1
Bradley Stoke 39 F4
Bradmore Notts. 81 G4
Bradmore W.Mid. 66 A3
Bradney 24 A4
Bradninch 10 D2
Bradnop 80 B2
Bradnor Green 52 B2
Bradpole 12 B4
Bradshaw Gt.Man. 92 B1
Bradshaw W.Yorks. 101 G4
Bradstone 7 D2
Bradwall Green 79 E1
Bradwell Derbys. 93 F4
Bradwell Devon 21 E1
Bradwell Essex 59 G4
Bradwell M.K. 50 B4
Bradwell Norf. 87 G5
Bradwell Grove 41 E2
Bradwell Waterside 46 C2
Bradwell-on-Sea 46 D2
Bradworthy 20 D4
Brae D. & G. 124 C3
Brae High. 181 G4
Brae Shet. 191 F3
Brae of Achnahaird 180 C3
Braeantra 174 B2
Braedownie 160 A2
Braefoot 177 G5
Braegrum 151 F2
Braehead D. & G. 123 F1
Braehead Glas. 141 G3
Braehead Moray 176 C5
Braehead S.Lan. 133 G2
Braehead S.Lan. 143 D4
Braehead of Lunan 161 E4
Braeleny 150 B3
Braemar 167 F5
Braemore High. 182 A4
Braemore High. 183 F1
Braemore High. 173 E2
Braenaloin 167 G5
Braes of Enzie 176 C4
Braes of Foss 158 C4
Braes of Ullapool (Bruthaicheann Ullapuil) 180 D5
Braeval 150 A4
Brafferton Darl. 120 B5
Brafferton N.Yorks. 110 D3
Brafield-on-the-Green 56 D2
Bragar 189 F2
Bragbury End 58 A5
Bragenham 57 E5
Bragleenbeg 148 B2
Braichmelyn 75 F1
Braides 100 A2
Braidley 109 F4
Braidwood 142 C5
Braigo 138 A3
Brailsford 81 D3
Brain's Green 39 F2
Braintree 59 F5
Braiseworth 72 C4
Braishfield 27 E5
Braithwaite Cumb. 117 F4
Braithwaite S.Yorks. 94 D1
Braithwaite W.Yorks. 101 G3
Braithwell 94 C3
Bramber 17 D2
Brambletye 30 D5
Brambridge 27 F5
Bramcote Notts. 81 G4
Bramcote Warks. 67 G4
Bramdean 28 B5
Bramerton 87 D5
Bramfield Herts. 44 B1
Bramfield Suff. 73 E4
Bramford 60 C3
Bramhall 92 C4
Bramham 102 D3
Bramhope 102 B3
Bramley Hants. 28 B2

Bramley S.Yorks. 94 B3
Bramley Surr. 29 F3
Bramley Corner 28 B2
Bramley Head 102 A2
Bramling 33 E3
Brampton Speke 10 C3
Brampton Cambs. 70 A5
Brampton Cumb. 118 B3
Brampton Cumb. 118 C5
Brampton Derbys. 94 A5
Brampton Lincs. 95 F5
Brampton Norf. 86 D3
Brampton S.Yorks. 94 B2
Brampton Suff. 73 F3
Brampton Abbotts 53 F5
Brampton Ash 68 C4
Brampton Bryan 64 C5
Brampton en le Morthen 94 B3
Brampton Street 73 F3
Bramshall 80 B4
Bramshaw 14 B1
Bramshill 28 C1
Bramshott 28 D4
Bramwell 24 B5
Bran End 59 E5
Branault 155 E3
Brancaster 85 F3
Brancaster Staithe 85 F3
Brancepeth 120 B4
Branchill 175 G4
Brand Green 53 G5
Brandelhow 117 F4
Branderburgh 176 B2
Brandesburton 104 D3
Brandeston 60 D1
Brandis Corner 21 E5
Brandiston 86 C3
Brandon Dur. 120 B4
Brandon Lincs. 83 E3
Brandon Northumb. 137 E5
Brandon Suff. 71 F4
Brandon Warks. 67 G5
Brandon Bank 71 E4
Brandon Creek 71 E3
Brandon Parva 86 B5
Brandsby 111 E5
Brandy Wharf 96 A3
Brane 2 B4
Branksome 13 E4
Branksome Park 13 G3
Bransbury 27 F3
Bransby 95 F5
Branscombe 11 E4
Bransford 53 G2
Bransgore 14 A3
Bransholme 104 D4
Branson's Cross 66 C5
Branston Leics. 82 D5
Branston Lincs. 83 E1
Branston Staffs. 80 D5
Branston Booths 83 F1
Brant Broughton 83 E2
Brantham 60 C4
Branthwaite Cumb. 117 F3
Branthwaite Cumb. 117 F4
Brantingham 104 B5
Branton Northumb. 137 E5
Branton S.Yorks. 94 D2
Brantwood 107 E3
Branxholm Bridgend 135 F4
Branxholme 135 F4
Branxton 136 C3
Brassey Green 78 C1
Brassington 80 D2
Brasted 31 D3
Brasted Chart 31 D3
Brathens 169 D5
Bratoft 84 C1
Brattleby 95 G4
Bratton Som. 22 C3
Bratton Tel. & W. 65 F1
Bratton Wilts. 26 A2
Bratton Clovelly 7 F1
Bratton Fleming 21 G2
Bratton Seymour 25 D5
Braughing 58 B5
Brauncewell 83 F2
Braunston Northants. 56 A1
Braunstone 68 A2

Braunton 21 E2
Brawby 111 G5
Brawdy 48 B5
Brawith 111 E2
Brawl 186 A2
Brawlbin 186 C3
Bray 43 E5
Bray Shop 6 D3
Bray Wick 43 D5
Braybrooke 68 C4
Braydon Side 40 C4
Brayford 21 G2
Brayshaw 101 D2
Braythorn 102 B3
Brayton 103 F4
Braywoodside 43 D5
Brazacott 6 C1
Brea 4 A5
Breach Kent 33 D4
Breach Kent 32 A2
Breachwood Green 57 G5
Breaden Heath 78 B4
Breadsall 81 B4
Breadstone 39 G2
Breage 2 D4
Bream 39 F2
Breamore 14 A1
Brean 23 F2
Breanais 189 E3
Brearton 102 C1
Breascleit 189 F2
Breaston 81 F4
Brechfa 50 B4
Brechin 161 E3
Brecklate 130 B4
Breckles 72 A2
Brecon (Aberhonddu) 51 G5
Breconside 133 G3
Bredbury 92 D3
Brede 18 D2
Bredenbury 53 F2
Bredfield 61 D2
Bredgar 32 A2
Bredhurst 31 G2
Bredon 54 B4
Bredon's Hardwick 54 B4
Bredon's Norton 54 B4
Bredwardine 52 C3
Breedon on the Hill 81 F5
Breich 143 D3
Breightmet 92 B2
Breighton 103 G4
Breinton 53 D4
Breinton Common 53 D4
Bremhill 40 B5
Bremhill Wick 40 B5
Brenachoille 148 C4
Brenchley 31 F4
Brendon Devon 22 A3
Brendon Devon 21 D4
Brendon Devon 21 D5
Brenkley 129 E4
Brent Eleigh 60 A3
Brent Knoll 24 A2
Brent Pelham 58 C4
Brentford 44 A5
Brentingby 68 C1
Brentwood 45 E3
Brenzett 19 F1
Brenzett Green 19 F1
Breoch 124 B5
Brereton 66 C1
Brereton Green 79 E1
Brereton Heath 79 F1
Breretonhill 66 C1
Bressay 191 F4
Bressingham 72 B3
Bressingham Common 72 B3
Bretby 81 D5
Bretford 67 G5
Bretforton 54 C3
Bretherdale Head 107 F2
Bretherton 100 A5
Brettenham Norf. 72 A3
Brettenham Suff. 60 A2
Bretton Derbys. 93 F5
Bretton Flints. 78 A1
Bretton Peter. 69 G2
Brewood 66 A2
Briach 175 G4
Briantspuddle 13 E3
Brick End 59 D5
Brickendon 44 C2
Bricket Wood 44 A2
Brickkiln Green 59 F4
Bricklehampton 54 B3

Bride 98 C1
Bridekirk 117 E3
Bridell 49 E3
Bridestones 79 G1
Bridestowe 7 F2
Brideswell 168 C1
Bridford 10 B4
Bridge Cornw. 4 A5
Bridge Kent 33 D3
Bridge End Cumb. 106 D4
Bridge End Devon 8 C3
Bridge End Essex 59 E4
Bridge End Lincs. 83 G4
Bridge Hewick 110 C5
Bridge o'Ess 168 C5
Bridge of Alford 168 C3
Bridge of Allan 150 C5
Bridge of Avon 167 F1
Bridge of Awe (Drochaid Abha) 148 C1
Bridge of Balgie 158 A5
Bridge of Bogendreip 169 D5
Bridge of Brewlands 159 G3
Bridge of Brown 167 F2
Bridge of Cally 159 G4
Bridge of Canny 169 D5
Bridge of Craigisla 160 A4
Bridge of Dee Aber. 167 F5
Bridge of Dee Aber. 169 D5
Bridge of Dee D. & G. 124 B4
Bridge of Don 169 G4
Bridge of Dun 161 E4
Bridge of Dye 161 E1
Bridge of Earn 151 G3
Bridge of Ericht 158 A4
Bridge of Feugh 169 D5
Bridge of Forss 186 C2
Bridge of Gairn 168 A5
Bridge of Gaur 158 A4
Bridge of Muchalls 169 F5
Bridge of Muick 168 A5
Bridge of Orchy (Drochaid Urchaidh) 149 E1
Bridge of Tynet 176 C3
Bridge of Walls 191 E4
Bridge of Weir 141 E3
Bridge Reeve 21 G4
Bridge Sollers 52 D3
Bridge Street 59 G3
Bridge Trafford 91 F5
Bridgefoot Angus 152 B1
Bridgefoot Cambs. 58 C3
Bridgefoot Cumb. 117 D4
Bridgehampton 24 C5
Bridgehaugh 168 A1
Bridgehill 119 G2
Bridgemary 15 E2
Bridgemere 79 E3
Bridgend Aber. 168 C1
Bridgend Aber. 177 G5
Bridgend Angus 160 D3
Bridgend Arg. & B. 138 B3
Bridgend Arg. & B. 148 A5
Bridgend (Pen-y-bont ar Ogwr) Bridgend 37 F5
Bridgend Cornw. 5 F4
Bridgend Cumb. 107 F1
Bridgend Fife 152 B3
Bridgend Moray 168 A1
Bridgend P. & K. 151 G3
Bridgend W.Loth. 143 E2
Bridgend of Lintrathen 160 A4
Bridgerule 20 C5
Bridges 64 C3
Bridgeton Aber. 168 C3
Bridgeton Glas. 142 A3
Bridgetown Cornw. 6 D2
Bridgetown Som. 22 C4
Bridgeyate 39 F5
Bridgham 72 A3
Bridgnorth 65 G3
Bridgtown 66 B2
Bridgwater 23 F4
Bridlington 105 D1
Bridport 12 B4
Bridstow 53 E5
Brierfield 101 E4
Brierley Glos. 39 F1

Brierley Here. 53 D2
Brierley S.Yorks. 94 B1
Brierley Hill 66 B4
Brierton 121 D5
Briery 116 A1
Briestfield 93 G1
Brig o'Turk 150 A4
Brigg 96 A2
Briggate 87 E3
Briggswath 112 B2
Brigham Cumb. 117 D3
Brigham E.Riding 104 C2
Brighouse 102 A5
Brighstone 14 D4
Brightgate 81 D2
Brighthampton 41 F2
Brightholmlee 93 G3
Brightling 18 B1
Brightlingsea 47 D1
Brighton B. & H. 17 F3
Brighton Cornw. 4 D4
Brightons 142 D2
Brightwalton 41 G5
Brightwalton Green 41 G5
Brightwell 60 D3
Brightwell Baldwin 42 B3
Brightwell Upperton 42 B3
Brightwell-cum-Sotwell 42 A3
Brignall 109 F1
Brigsley 96 C2
Brigsteer 107 F4
Brigstock 69 E4
Brill Bucks. 42 B1
Brill Cornw. 3 E4
Brilley 52 B3
Brilley Mountain 52 B2
Brimaston 48 C5
Brimfield 53 E1
Brimington 94 B5
Brimington Common 94 B5
Brimley 10 B5
Brimpsfield 40 B1
Brimpton 27 G1
Brimscombe 40 A2
Brimstage 91 E4
Brinacory 163 F5
Brindham 24 C3
Brindle 100 B5
Brindley Ford 79 F2
Brineton 66 A1
Bringhurst 68 D3
Brington 69 F5
Brinian 190 B2
Briningham 86 B2
Brinkhill 97 E5
Brinkley Cambs. 59 E2
Brinkley Notts. 82 C2
Brinklow 67 G5
Brinkworth 40 C4
Brinmore 166 A2
Brinscall 100 C5
Brinsea 24 B1
Brinsley 81 F3
Brinsop 52 D3
Brinsworth 94 B3
Brinton 86 B2
Brisco 118 A2
Brisley 86 A3
Brislington 39 F5
Brissenden Green 32 B5
Bristol 39 E5
Bristol Filton Airport 39 E4
Bristol International Airport 24 C1
Briston 86 B2
Britannia 101 E5
Britford 26 C5
Brithdir Caerp. 38 A2
Brithdir Gwyn. 63 D1
Brithem Bottom 10 D1
Briton Ferry (Llansawel) 36 D3
Britwell 43 E4
Britwell Salome 42 B3
Brixham 9 F2
Brixton Devon 8 C3
Brixton Gt.Lon. 44 C5
Brixton Deverill 25 F4
Brixworth 68 C5
Brize Norton 41 E2
Broad Alley 54 A1
Broad Blunsdon 41 D2
Broad Campden 55 D4
Broad Carr 93 E1
Broad Chalke 26 B5
Broad Ford 31 G5

Broad Green Beds. 57 E3
Broad Green Cambs. 59 E2
Broad Green Essex 59 G5
Broad Green Essex 58 C4
Broad Green Mersey. 91 F3
Broad Green Suff. 60 B2
Broad Green Worcs. 53 G2
Broad Haven 34 B1
Broad Hill 71 D5
Broad Hinton 40 D5
Broad Laying 27 F1
Broad Marston 54 D3
Broad Oak Carmar. 50 B5
Broad Oak Cumb. 106 C3
Broad Oak E.Suss. 18 D2
Broad Oak E.Suss. 18 B1
Broad Oak Here. 53 D5
Broad Road 73 D4
Broad Street E.Suss. 19 D2
Broad Street Kent 32 A3
Broad Street Kent 32 B3
Broad Street Wilts. 26 C2
Broad Street Green 46 B2
Broad Town 40 C5
Broadbottom 93 D3
Broadbridge 16 A2
Broadbridge Heath 29 G4
Broadclyst 10 C3
Broadfield Lancs. 100 D5
Broadfield Lancs. 100 B5
Broadford (An t-Ath Leathann) 163 E2
Broadford Airport 163 E2
Broadford Bridge 29 F5
Broadgate 106 C4
Broadhaugh 135 F5
Broadhaven 187 F3
Broadheath Gt.Man. 92 B4
Broadheath Worcs. 53 F1
Broadhembury 11 E2
Broadhempston 9 E1
Broadholme 95 F5
Broadland Row 18 D2
Broadlay 35 G2
Broadley Lancs. 92 C1
Broadley Moray 176 C3
Broadley Common 44 D2
Broadmayne 12 D4
Broadmeadows 135 F2
Broadmere 28 B3
Broadmoor 35 D2
Broadnymett 10 A2
Broadoak Dorset 12 A3
Broadoak Glos. 39 F1
Broadoak Kent 33 D2
Broadoak End 44 C1
Broadrashes 176 D4
Broad's Green 45 F1
Broadsea 179 E1
Broadstairs 33 F2
Broadstone Poole 13 G3
Broadstone Shrop. 65 E4
Broadstreet Common 38 C4
Broadwas 53 G2
Broadwater Herts. 57 F5
Broadwater W.Suss. 16 D3
Broadwater Down 31 E5
Broadwaters 66 A5
Broadway Carmar. 35 G2
Broadway Carmar. 35 F1
Broadway Pembs. 34 B1
Broadway Som. 11 G1
Broadway Suff. 73 E4
Broadway Worcs. 54 D4
Broadwell Glos. 55 E5
Broadwell Oxon. 41 E2
Broadwell Warks. 55 G1
Broadwell House 119 F2
Broadwey 12 C4
Broadwindsor 12 A2
Broadwoodkelly 21 G4
Broadwoodwidger 7 E2
Brobury 52 C3
Brocastle 37 F5
Brochel 171 F5
Brochloch 123 G1
Brock 154 B2
Brockamin 53 G2
Brockbridge 15 E1
Brockdish 72 D4
Brockenhurst 14 B2

Brockford Green **60** C1
Brockford Street **60** C1
Brockhall **56** B1
Brockham **29** G3
Brockhampton *Glos.* **54** C5
Brockhampton *Glos.* **54** B5
Brockhampton *Here.* **53** E4
Brockhampton *Here.* **53** F2
Brockhampton Green **12** D2
Brockholes **93** F1
Brockhurst *Hants.* **15** E2
Brockhurst *W.Suss.* **30** D5
Brocklebank **117** G2
Brocklesby **96** B1
Brockley *N.Som.* **24** B1
Brockley *Suff.* **59** G2
Brockley Green **59** F3
Brock's Green **27** F1
Brockton *Shrop.* **65** E3
Brockton *Shrop.* **65** G2
Brockton *Shrop.* **64** C2
Brockton *Shrop.* **64** C2
Brockton *Tel. & W.* **65** G1
Brockweir **39** E2
Brockwood Park **28** B5
Brockworth **40** A1
Brocton **66** B1
Brodick **131** F2
Brodsworth **94** C2
Brogaig **191** E3
Brogborough **57** E4
Brogden **101** E3
Brogyntyn **77** F4
Broken Cross *C. & W.Ches.* **92** A5
Broken Cross *Ches.E.* **92** C5
Brokenborough **40** B4
Brokes **110** A3
Bromborough **91** E4
Brome **72** C4
Brome Street **72** C4
Bromeswell **61** E2
Bromfield *Cumb.* **117** E2
Bromfield *Shrop.* **65** D5
Bromham *Beds.* **57** F2
Bromham *Wilts.* **26** A1
Bromley *Gt.Lon.* **30** D2
Bromley *S.Yorks.* **94** A3
Bromley Cross **92** B1
Bromley Green **32** B5
Brompton *Med.* **31** G2
Brompton *N.Yorks.* **110** C3
Brompton *N.Yorks.* **112** C4
Brompton *Shrop.* **65** E2
Brompton on Swale **110** B3
Brompton Ralph **23** D4
Brompton Regis **22** C4
Bromsash **53** F5
Bromsberrow **53** G4
Bromsberrow Heath **53** G4
Bromsgrove **66** B5
Bromstead Heath **66** A1
Bromyard **53** F2
Bromyard Downs **53** F2
Bronaber **76** A4
Brondesbury **44** B4
Brongest **49** G3
Bronington **78** B4
Bronllys **52** A4
Bronnant **50** C1
Bronwydd Arms **50** A5
Bronydd **52** B3
Bron-y-gaer **35** G1
Bronygarth **77** F4
Brook *Carmar.* **35** F2
Brook *Hants.* **14** B1
Brook *Hants.* **27** E5
Brook *I.o.W.* **14** C4
Brook *Kent* **32** C4
Brook *Surr.* **29** E4
Brook *Surr.* **29** F3
Brook Bottom **93** D2
Brook End *Beds.* **57** F1
Brook End *Herts.* **58** B5
Brook End *M.K.* **57** E3
Brook End *Worcs.* **54** A3
Brook Hill **14** B1
Brook Street *Essex* **45** E3
Brook Street *Kent* **32** B5
Brook Street *Suff.* **59** G3

Brook Street *W.Suss.* **17** F1
Brooke *Norf.* **73** D2
Brooke *Rut.* **58** B2
Brookend *Glos.* **39** E3
Brookend *Glos.* **39** F2
Brookfield **93** E3
Brookhampton **43** E1
Brookhouse *Ches.E.* **92** D5
Brookhouse *Denb.* **77** D1
Brookhouse *Lancs.* **100** B1
Brookhouse *S.Yorks.* **94** C4
Brookhouse Green **79** F1
Brookhouses **79** G3
Brookland **19** E1
Brooklands *D. & G.* **124** C3
Brooklands *Shrop.* **78** C3
Brookmans Park **44** B2
Brooks **64** A3
Brooks Green **29** G5
Brooksby **68** B1
Brookthorpe **40** A1
Brookwood **29** E2
Broom *Beds.* **57** G3
Broom *Fife* **152** B4
Broom *Warks.* **54** C2
Broom Green **86** A3
Broom Hill *Dorset* **13** G2
Broom Hill *Worcs.* **66** B5
Broom of Dalreach **151** F3
Broomcroft **65** E2
Broome *Norf.* **73** E2
Broome *Shrop.* **64** D4
Broome *Worcs.* **66** B5
Broome Wood **137** F5
Broomedge **92** B4
Broomer's Corner **29** G5
Broomfield *Aber.* **169** G1
Broomfield *Essex* **45** G1
Broomfield *Kent* **33** D2
Broomfield *Kent* **32** A3
Broomfield *Som.* **23** F4
Broomfleet **104** A5
Broomhall Green **78** D3
Broomhaugh **119** G1
Broomhead **179** E1
Broomhill *Bristol* **39** F5
Broomhill *Northumb.* **129** E1
Broomielaw **109** F1
Broomley **119** G1
Broompark **108** C3
Broom's Green **53** G4
Brora **183** E4
Broseley **65** F2
Brotherlee **119** F4
Brothertoft **84** A3
Brotherton **103** D5
Brotton **111** F1
Broubster **186** C2
Brough *Cumb.* **108** C1
Brough *Derbys.* **93** F4
Brough *E.Riding* **104** B5
Brough *High.* **187** E1
Brough *Notts.* **82** D2
Brough *Shet.* **191** G3
Brough Sowerby **108** C1
Broughall **78** C3
Brougham **118** B3
Broughton *Bucks.* **42** D1
Broughton *Cambs.* **70** A5
Broughton *Flints.* **78** A1
Broughton *Hants.* **27** E4
Broughton *Lancs.* **100** B4
Broughton *M.K.* **57** D3
Broughton *N.Lincs.* **95** G2
Broughton *N.Yorks.* **111** G5
Broughton *N.Yorks.* **101** F2
Broughton *Northants.* **68** D5
Broughton *Oxon.* **55** G4
Broughton *Sc.Bord.* **134** C2
Broughton *V. of Glam.* **37** F5
Broughton Astley **68** A3
Broughton Beck **107** D4
Broughton Gifford **25** F1
Broughton Green **54** B1
Broughton Hackett **54** B2

Broughton in Furness **106** D4
Broughton Mills **106** D3
Broughton Moor **117** D3
Broughton Poggs **41** E2
Broughtown **190** C2
Broughty Ferry **152** C1
Brown Candover **27** G4
Brown Edge *Lancs.* **91** E1
Brown Edge *Staffs.* **79** G2
Brown Heath **78** B1
Brown Lees **79** F2
Brown Street **80** B1
Brownber **108** C2
Browndown **15** E3
Brownheath **78** B5
Brownhill **179** D3
Brownhills *Fife* **152** D3
Brownhills *W.Mid.* **66** C2
Brownieside **137** F4
Brownlow **79** F1
Brownlow Heath **79** F1
Brown's Bank **78** D3
Brownsea Island **13** G4
Brownshill **40** A2
Brownshill Green **67** F4
Brownsover **68** A5
Brownston **8** C2
Browston Green **87** F5
Broxa **112** C3
Broxbourne **44** C2
Broxburn *E.Loth.* **145** D2
Broxburn *W.Loth.* **143** E2
Broxholme **95** G5
Broxted **59** D5
Broxton **78** B2
Broxwood **52** C2
Broyle Side **17** G2
Bruachmary **175** D3
Bruan **187** F5
Bruera **78** B1
Bruern **55** E5
Bruichladdich **138** A3
Bruisyard **61** E1
Bruisyard Street **61** E1
Brumby **95** G1
Brund **80** C1
Brundall **79** E1
Brundish *Norf.* **73** E2
Brundish *Suff.* **61** D1
Brundish Street **73** D4
Brunstock **118** A2
Brunswick Village **129** E4
Bruntingthorpe **68** B3
Bruntland **168** B2
Brunton *Fife* **152** B2
Brunton *Northumb.* **137** G4
Brunton *Wilts.* **26** D2
Brushfield **93** F5
Brushford *Devon* **21** G5
Brushford *Som.* **22** C5
Bruton **25** D4
Bryanston **13** E2
Bryant's Bottom **43** D3
Brydekirk **125** F3
Brymbo **77** F2
Brympton **7** G1
Bryn *C. & W.Ches.* **92** A5
Bryn *Caerp.* **38** A3
Bryn *Carmar.* **36** B2
Bryn *Gt.Man.* **91** G2
Bryn *N.P.T.* **37** E3
Bryn *Shrop.* **64** B4
Bryn Bwbach **75** F4
Bryn Gates **91** G2
Bryn Pen-y-lan **78** A3
Brynamman **36** D1
Brynberian **49** E4
Bryncae **37** F4
Bryncethin **37** F4
Bryncir **75** D3
Bryncoch *Bridgend* **37** F4
Bryn-côch *N.P.T.* **36** D3
Bryncroes **74** B4
Bryncrug **62** C2
Bryneglwys **77** E3
Brynford **90** C5
Bryngwran **88** B5
Bryngwyn *Mon.* **38** C2
Bryngwyn *Powys* **52** A3
Bryn-henllan **48** D3
Brynhoffnant **49** G2
Bryning **100** A4
Brynithel **38** B2
Brynmawr *B.Gwent* **38** A1
Bryn-mawr *Gwyn.* **74** B4
Brynmelyn **64** A5

Brynmenyn **37** F4
Brynna **37** F4
Brynnau Gwynion **37** F4
Brynog **50** B2
Bryn-penarth **64** A2
Brynrefail *Gwyn.* **75** E1
Brynrefail *I.o.A.* **88** C4
Brynsadler **37** G4
Brynsaithmarchog **77** D2
Brynsiencyn **75** D1
Bryn-teg *I.o.A.* **88** C4
Brynteg *Wrex.* **78** A2
Bryn-y-cochin **38** A4
Bryn-y-gwenin **38** C1
Bryn-y-maen **89** G5
Bualintur **162** C2
Bualnaluib **180** A5
Bubbenhall **67** F5
Bubwith **103** G4
Buccleuch **135** E4
Buchan **124** B4
Buchanan Castle **141** F1
Buchanhaven **179** G3
Buchanty **151** E2
Buchlyvie **150** A5
Buckabank **117** G2
Buckby Wharf **56** B1
Buckden *Cambs.* **57** G1
Buckden *N.Yorks.* **109** E5
Buckenham **87** E5
Buckerell **11** E2
Buckfast **8** D1
Buckfastleigh **8** D1
Buckhaven **152** B5
Buckholm **135** F2
Buckholt **39** E1
Buckhorn Weston **25** E5
Buckhurst Hill **44** D3
Buckie **176** D3
Buckies **186** D2
Buckingham **56** B4
Buckland *Bucks.* **43** D1
Buckland *Devon* **8** C3
Buckland *Glos.* **54** C4
Buckland *Hants.* **14** C3
Buckland *Here.* **53** E2
Buckland *Herts.* **58** B4
Buckland *Kent* **33** F4
Buckland *Oxon.* **41** F3
Buckland *Surr.* **30** B3
Buckland Brewer **21** E3
Buckland Common **43** E2
Buckland Dinham **25** E2
Buckland Filleigh **21** E5
Buckland in the Moor **10** A5
Buckland Monachorum **8** A1
Buckland Newton **12** C2
Buckland Ripers **12** C4
Buckland St. Mary **11** F1
Buckland-tout-Saints **9** D3
Bucklebury **42** A5
Bucklerheads **152** C1
Bucklers Hard **14** D3
Bucklesham **60** D3
Buckley (Bwcle) **77** F1
Buckley Green **55** D1
Bucklow Hill **92** B4
Buckman Corner **29** G5
Buckminster **83** D5
Bucknall *Lincs.* **83** G1
Bucknall *Stoke* **79** G3
Bucknell *Oxon.* **56** A5
Bucknell *Shrop.* **64** C5
Buckridge **65** G5
Buck's Cross **20** D3
Bucks Green **29** F4
Bucks Hill **43** F2
Bucks Horn Oak **28** D3
Buck's Mills **21** D3
Bucksburn **169** F4
Buckspool **34** C3
Buckton *E.Riding* **113** E5
Buckton *Here.* **64** C5
Buckton *Northumb.* **137** E3
Buckton Vale **93** D2
Buckworth **69** G5
Budby **94** D5
Buddon **152** D1
Bude **20** C5
Budge's Shop **6** D5
Budlake **10** C2
Budleigh **137** F3

Budleigh Salterton **11** D4
Budock Water **3** E3
Budworth Heath **92** A5
Buerton **79** D3
Bugbrooke **56** B2
Buglawton **79** F1
Bugle **5** E4
Bugthorpe **103** G2
Building End **58** C4
Buildwas **65** F2
Builth Road **51** G2
Builth Wells (Llanfair-ym-Muallt) **51** G2
Bulby **83** F5
Bulcote **82** B3
Buldoo **186** B2
Bulford **26** C3
Bulford Camp **26** C3
Bulkeley **78** C2
Bulkington *Warks.* **67** F4
Bulkington *Wilts.* **26** A2
Bulkworthy **21** D4
Bull Bay (Porth Llechog) **88** C3
Bull Green **32** B5
Bullbridge **81** E2
Bullbrook **29** D1
Bullen's Green **44** B2
Bulley **39** G1
Bullington **96** A5
Bullpot Farm **108** B4
Bulls Cross **44** C3
Bull's Green *Herts.* **44** B1
Bull's Green *Norf.* **73** F2
Bullwood **140** C2
Bulmer *Essex* **59** G3
Bulmer *N.Yorks.* **103** F1
Bulmer Tye **59** G4
Bulphan **45** F4
Bulstone **11** E4
Bulverhythe **18** C3
Bulwark **179** E3
Bulwell **81** G3
Bulwick **69** E3
Bumble's Green **44** D2
Bun Loyne **164** D4
Bunarkaig **157** D1
Bunbury **78** C2
Bunbury Heath **78** C2
Bunchrew **174** C5
Bundalloch **163** G2
Bunessan **146** C2
Bungay **73** E3
Bunker's Hill **84** A2
Bunlarie **122** D4
Bunloit (Bun Leothaid) **165** G2
Bunnahabhain **138** C2
Bunny **81** G5
Buntait **165** E1
Buntingford **58** B5
Bunwell **72** C2
Bunwell Street **72** C2
Burbage *Derbys.* **93** E5
Burbage *Wilts.* **26** D1
Burchett's Green **42** D4
Burcombe **26** B4
Burcot *Oxon.* **42** A3
Burcot *Worcs.* **66** B5
Burcott **57** D5
Burdale **104** A1
Burdocks **29** F5
Burdon **120** C2
Burdrop **55** F4
Bures **60** A4
Bures Green **60** A4
Burfa **52** B1
Burford *Oxon.* **41** E1
Burford *Shrop.* **53** E1
Burg **154** C5
Burgate **72** B4
Burgates **28** C5
Burge End **57** G4
Burgess Hill **17** F2
Burgh **60** D2
Burgh by Sands **117** G1
Burgh Castle **87** F5
Burgh Heath **30** B3
Burgh le Marsh **84** C1
Burgh next Aylsham **86** D3
Burgh on Bain **96** C4
Burgh St. Margaret (Fleggburgh) **87** F4
Burgh St. Peter **73** F2
Burghclere **27** F1
Burghead **176** A3
Burghfield **28** B1

Burghfield Common **28** B1
Burghfield Hill **28** B1
Burghill **53** D3
Burghwallis **94** C1
Burham **31** G2
Burland **78** D2
Burlawn **5** D3
Burleigh **29** E1
Burlescombe **11** D1
Burleston **13** D3
Burley *Hants.* **14** A2
Burley *Rut.* **69** D1
Burley *W.Yorks.* **102** B4
Burley Gate **53** E3
Burley in Wharfedale **102** A3
Burley Street **14** B2
Burley Woodhead **102** A3
Burleydam **78** D2
Burlingjobb **52** B2
Burlow **18** A2
Burlton **78** B5
Burmarsh **32** D5
Burmington **55** E4
Burn **103** E5
Burn Farm **161** E2
Burn Naze **99** G3
Burn of Cambus **150** C4
Burnage **92** C3
Burnaston **81** D4
Burnby **104** A3
Burncross **94** C4
Burndell **16** B3
Burnden **92** B2
Burnedge **92** D1
Burnend **178** D3
Burneside **107** G3
Burness **190** C2
Burneston **110** C4
Burnett **25** D2
Burnfoot *High.* **183** D2
Burnfoot *P. & K.* **151** E4
Burnfoot *Sc.Bord.* **135** G4
Burnfoot *Sc.Bord.* **135** G4
Burnham *Bucks.* **43** E4
Burnham *N.Lincs.* **96** A1
Burnham Deepdale **85** G3
Burnham Green **44** B1
Burnham Market **85** G3
Burnham Norton **85** G3
Burnham Overy Staithe **85** G3
Burnham Overy Town **85** G3
Burnham Thorpe **85** G3
Burnham-on-Crouch **46** C3
Burnham-on-Sea **24** A3
Burnhaven **179** G3
Burnhead *D. & G.* **123** G2
Burnhead *D. & G.* **124** C1
Burnhervie **169** E3
Burnhill Green **65** G2
Burnhope **120** A3
Burnhouse **141** E4
Burniston **112** D3
Burnley **101** E4
Burnmouth **145** G3
Burnopfield **120** A2
Burn's Green **58** B5
Burnsall **101** G1
Burnside *Aber.* **169** G1
Burnside *Angus* **160** D4
Burnside *E.Ayr.* **133** D4
Burnside *Fife* **151** G4
Burnside *W.Loth.* **143** E2
Burnside of Duntrune **152** C1
Burnstones **118** C2
Burnswark **125** F3
Burnt Hill **42** A5
Burnt Houses **120** A5
Burnt Oak **44** B3
Burnt Yates **102** B1
Burntcliff Top **79** G1
Burntisland **143** G1
Burnton *E.Ayr.* **132** C4
Burnton *E.Ayr.* **132** C5
Burntwood **66** C2
Burntwood Green **66** C2
Burnworthy **11** E1
Burpham *Surr.* **29** F2
Burpham *W.Suss.* **16** C3
Burra **191** F5
Burradon *Northumb.* **128** B1
Burradon *T. & W.* **129** E4

Burras **3** D3
Burraton *Cornw.* **8** A1
Burraton *Cornw.* **8** A2
Burravoe **191** F2
Burray **190** B4
Burrells **108** B1
Burrelton **152** A1
Burridge *Devon* **11** G2
Burridge *Hants.* **15** E1
Burrill **110** B4
Burringham **95** F2
Burrington *Devon* **21** G4
Burrington *Here.* **64** D5
Burrington *N.Som.* **24** B2
Burrough Green **59** G2
Burrough on the Hill **68** C1
Burrow *Som.* **22** C3
Burrow *Som.* **12** A1
Burrow Bridge **24** A4
Burrowhill **29** E1
Burrows Cross **29** F3
Bury **36** A3
Bury Green **36** A3
Bury Port **36** A2
Burscough **91** F1
Burscough Bridge **91** F1
Bursea **104** A4
Burshill **104** C3
Bursledon **15** D2
Burslem **79** F3
Burstall **60** C3
Burstock **12** A2
Burston *Norf.* **72** C3
Burston *Staffs.* **79** G4
Burstow **30** C4
Burstwick **105** E5
Burtersett **109** D4
Burthorpe **59** F1
Burthwaite **118** A3
Burtle **24** B3
Burtle Hill **24** A3
Burton *C. & W.Ches.* **91** E5
Burton *C. & W.Ches.* **78** C1
Burton *Dorset* **14** A3
Burton *Lincs.* **95** G5
Burton *Northumb.* **137** F3
Burton *Pembs.* **34** C2
Burton *Som.* **23** E3
Burton *Wilts.* **40** A5
Burton *Wilts.* **25** F4
Burton Agnes **104** D1
Burton Bradstock **12** A4
Burton Coggles **83** E5
Burton End **58** D5
Burton Ferry **34** C2
Burton Fleming **113** D5
Burton Green *Warks.* **67** E5
Burton Green *Wrex.* **78** A2
Burton Hastings **67** G4
Burton in Lonsdale **108** B5
Burton Joyce **82** B3
Burton Latimer **69** E5
Burton Lazars **68** C1
Burton Leonard **102** C1
Burton on the Wolds **91** F4
Burton Overy **68** B3
Burton Pedwardine **83** G3
Burton Pidsea **105** E4
Burton Salmon **103** D5
Burton Stather **95** F1
Burton upon Stather **95** F1
Burton upon Trent **80** D5
Burton-in-Kendal **107** G3
Burton's Green **59** G5
Burtonwood **91** G3
Burwardsley **78** C2
Burwarton **65** F4
Burwash **18** B1
Burwash Common **18** B1
Burwash Weald **18** B1
Burwell *Cambs.* **59** D1
Burwell *Lincs.* **97** D5
Burwen **88** C3
Burwick **190** B4
Bury *Cambs.* **70** A4
Bury *Gt.Man.* **92** C1
Bury *Som.* **22** C3
Bury *W.Suss.* **16** A3
Bury End **54** C4
Bury Green **58** C5

Bury St. Edmunds **59** G1
Buryas Bridge **2** B4
Burythorpe **103** G1
Busbridge **21** E3
Busby *E.Renf.* **141** G4
Busby *P. & K.* **151** E2
Buscot **41** E3
Bush **20** C5
Bush Bank **53** D2
Bush Crathie **167** G5
Bush Green **72** D3
Bushby **66** B2
Bushby **68** B2
Bushey **44** A3
Bushey Heath **44** A3
Bushley **54** A4
Bushley Green **54** A4
Bushton **40** C5
Bushy Common **86** A4
Busk **118** C3
Buslingthorpe **96** A4
Bussage **40** A2
Butcher's Common **87** E3
Butcher's Cross **18** A1
Butcher's Pasture **59** E5
Butcombe **24** C1
Bute **140** B3
Bute Town **38** A2
Buthill **176** A3
Butleigh **24** C4
Butleigh Wootton **24** C4
Butler's Cross **42** D2
Butler's Hill **81** G3
Butlers Marston **55** F3
Butlersbank **78** C5
Butley **61** E2
Butley Abbey **61** E3
Butley Low Corner **61** E3
Butley Mills **61** E2
Butley Town **79** D2
Butt Green **79** D2
Butt Lane **79** F2
Butterburn **127** E4
Buttercrambe **103** G2
Butterknowle **120** A5
Butterleigh **10** C2
Butterley **81** F2
Buttermere *Cumb.* **117** F2
Buttermere *Wilts.* **27** E1
Butters Green **79** F2
Buttershaw **102** A4
Butterstone **159** F5
Butterton *Staffs.* **80** B2
Butterton *Staffs.* **79** F3
Butterwick *Dur.* **120** C5
Butterwick *Lincs.* **84** B3
Butterwick *N.Yorks.* **112** C5
Butterwick *N.Yorks.* **111** G5
Buttington **64** B2
Buttonbridge **65** G5
Buttonoak **65** G5
Buttons' Green **60** A2
Butts **10** B4
Butt's Green *Essex* **45** G2
Butt's Green *Hants.* **27** D5
Buttsash **14** D2
Buxhall **60** B2
Buxted **17** G1
Buxton *Derbys.* **93** E5
Buxton *Norf.* **86** D3
Buxton Heath **86** C3
Buxworth **93** E4
Bwlch **52** A5
Bwlch-clawdd **49** G4
Bwlch-derwin **75** D3
Bwlchgwyn **77** F2
Bwlch-llan **50** B2
Bwlchnewydd **49** G5
Bwlchtocyn **74** C5
Bwlch-y-cibau **64** A1
Bwlch-y-ddar **77** E5
Bwlchyfadfa **50** A3
Bwlch-y-groes **49** F4
Bwlchyllyn **75** E2
Bwlchymynydd **36** B3
Bwlch-y-sarnau **63** G5
Byers Green **120** B4
Byfield **56** A2
Byfleet **29** E1
Byford **52** C3
Bygrave **58** A4
Byker **120** B1
Byland Abbey **111** E5
Bylane End **5** G4

Bylchau **76** C1
Byley **79** E1
Bynea **36** B3
Byness **127** F1
Bystock **10** D4
Bython **69** F5
Byton **52** C1
Bywell **119** G1
Byworth **29** E5

C

Cabourne **96** B2
Cabourne Parva **96** B2
Cabrach *Arg. & B.* **138** C3
Cabrach *Moray* **168** A2
Cabus **100** A3
Cackle Street *E.Suss.* **18** D2
Cackle Street *E.Suss.* **17** G1
Cacrabank **135** E4
Cadboll **175** E2
Cadbury **10** C2
Cadbury Barton **21** G4
Cadbury Heath **39** F5
Cadder **142** A2
Cadderlie **148** C1
Caddington **43** F1
Caddleton **147** G3
Caddonfoot **135** F2
Cade Street **18** B1
Cadeby *Leics.* **67** G2
Cadeby *S.Yorks.* **94** C2
Cadeleigh **10** C2
Cader **76** D1
Cadgwith **3** E5
Cadham **152** A4
Cadishead **92** B3
Cadle **36** C3
Cadley *Lancs.* **100** B4
Cadley *Wilts.* **26** D1
Cadmore End **42** C3
Cadnam **14** B1
Cadney **96** A2
Cadole **77** F1
Cadover Bridge **8** B1
Cadoxton **23** E1
Cadoxton-Juxta-Neath **37** D3
Cadwell **57** G4
Cadwst **76** D4
Cadzow **142** B4
Cae Ddafydd **75** F3
Caeathro **75** E1
Caehopkin **37** E1
Caen **183** D1
Caenby **96** A4
Caenby Corner **95** G4
Caer Llan **39** D2
Caerau *Bridgend* **37** E3
Caerau *Cardiff* **38** A5
Caerdeon **62** C1
Caerfarchell **48** A5
Caergeiliog **88** B5
Caergwrle **78** A2
Caerhun **89** F5
Caer-Lan **37** E1
Caerleon **38** C3
Caernarfon **75** D1
Caerphilly **38** A4
Caersws **63** G3
Caerwedros **49** G2
Caerwent **39** D3
Caerwys **90** C5
Caethle Farm **62** C3
Caggan **166** C3
Caggle Street **38** C1
Caim *High.* **156** E3
Caim *I.o.A.* **89** E4
Caio **50** C1
Cairnargat **168** B1
Cairnbaan **148** A5
Cairnbeathie **168** C4
Cairnbrogie **169** F2
Cairnbulg **179** F1
Cairncross *Angus* **160** D2
Cairncross *Sc.Bord.* **145** F3
Cairncurran **141** E3
Cairndoon **115** D3
Cairndow **149** D3
Cairness **179** F1
Cairney Lodge **152** B3
Cairneyhill **143** E1
Cairnhill *Aber.* **169** G2
Cairnhill *Aber.* **169** F4
Cairnie *Aber.* **169** F4
Cairnie *Aber.* **177** D5

Cairnorrie **179** D3
Cairnryan **122** B4
Cairnsmore **123** F4
Caister-on-Sea **87** G4
Caistor **96** B2
Caistor St. Edmund **86** D5
Cakebole **66** A5
Calbourne **14** D4
Calceby **97** D5
Calcoed **90** C5
Calcot **42** B5
Calcott *Kent* **33** D2
Calcott *Shrop.* **64** D1
Calcotts Green **39** G1
Calcutt **40** D3
Caldarvan **141** F1
Caldbeck **117** G3
Caldbergh **109** F4
Caldecote *Cambs.* **58** B2
Caldecote *Cambs.* **69** G4
Caldecote *Herts.* **58** A4
Caldecote *Northants.* **56** B2
Caldecote *Warks.* **67** F3
Caldecott *Northants.* **57** E1
Caldecott *Oxon.* **41** G3
Caldecott *Rut.* **69** D3
Calder Bridge **106** B2
Calder Grove **94** A1
Calder Mains **186** C3
Calder Vale **100** B3
Calderbank **142** B3
Calderbrook **92** D1
Caldercruix **142** C3
Calderglen **142** A4
Caldermill **142** A5
Caldey Island **35** E3
Caldicot **39** D4
Caldwell *Derbys.* **67** E1
Caldwell *E.Renf.* **141** F4
Caldwell *N.Yorks.* **110** A1
Caldy **90** B4
Calebreck **117** G3
Caledrhydiau **50** A2
Calford Green **59** E3
Calfsound **190** C2
Calgary **154** C4
Califer **175** G4
California *Falk.* **142** D2
California *Norf.* **87** G4
California *Suff.* **60** D3
Calke **81** E5
Callakille **171** F4
Callaly **128** C1
Callander **150** B4
Callanish **189** F2
Callaughton **65** F3
Callerton Lane End **120** A1
Calliburn **130** C3
Calligarry **163** E4
Callington **7** D4
Callingwood **80** C5
Callisterhall **126** A3
Callow **53** D4
Callow End **54** A3
Callow Hill *Wilts.* **40** C4
Callow Hill *Worcs.* **65** G5
Callow Hill *Worcs.* **54** C1
Callows Grave **53** E1
Calmore **14** C1
Calmsden **40** C2
Calne **40** B5
Calow **94** B5
Calrossie **175** D2
Calshot **15** D2
Calstock **7** E4
Calstone Wellington **26** B1
Calthorpe **86** C2
Calthwaite **118** A3
Calton *N.Yorks.* **101** F2
Calton *Staffs.* **80** C2
Calveley **78** C2
Calver **93** G5
Calver Hill **52** C3
Calverhall **78** C4
Calverleigh **10** C1
Calverley **102** B4
Calvert **56** B5
Calverton *M.K.* **56** C4
Calverton *Notts.* **82** B3
Calvine **158** C2
Calvo **117** E1
Cam **39** G3

Camasnacroise **156** A4
Camastianavaig **162** D1
Camasunary **162** D3
Camault Muir **174** B5
Camber **19** E2
Camberley **29** D1
Camberwell **44** C5
Camblesforth **103** F5
Cambo **128** C3
Cambois **129** F3
Camborne **3** D3
Cambourne **58** B2
Cambridge *Cambs.* **58** C2
Cambridge *Glos.* **39** G1
Cambridge City Airport **58** C2
Cambus **151** D5
Cambus o'May **168** B5
Cambusbarron **150** C5
Cambuskenneth **150** D5
Cambuslang **142** A3
Cambusnethan **142** C4
Camden Town **44** B4
Camel Hill **24** C3
Cameley **24** D2
Camelford **5** F1
Camelon **142** C1
Camelsdale **29** D4
Camer **31** F2
Cameron House **141** E1
Camerory **167** E1
Camer's Green **53** G4
Camerton *B. & N.E.Som.* **25** D2
Camerton *Cumb.* **116** D3
Camerton *E.Riding* **105** E5
Camghouran **158** A4
Camis Eskan **141** E1
Cammachmore **169** G5
Cammeringham **95** G4
Camore **182** C5
Camp Hill *Pembs.* **35** E1
Camp Hill *Warks.* **67** F3
Campbeltown (Ceann Loch Chille Chiarain) **130** C3
Campbeltown Airport **130** B3
Camperdown **129** E4
Campmuir **152** A1
Camps **143** F3
Camps End **59** E3
Camps Heath **73** G2
Campsall **94** C1
Campsea Ashe **61** E2
Campton **57** G4
Camptown **136** A5
Camquhart **140** A1
Camrose **48** C3
Camserney **158** D5
Camster **182** C5
Camstraddan House **149** F5
Camus Croise **163** G5
Camus-luinie **164** A2
Camusnagaul *High.* **156** C2
Camusnagaul *High.* **173** D1
Camusrory **163** G5
Camusteel **172** A5
Camusterrach **172** A5
Camusurich **150** B1
Camusvrachan **158** B5
Canada **14** B1
Canaston Bridge **35** D1
Candacraig **168** A5
Candlesby **84** C1
Candy Mill **143** E5
Cane End **42** B5
Canewdon **46** B3
Canfield End **59** D5
Canford Bottom **13** G2
Canford Cliffs **13** G4
Canford Magna **13** G3
Canham's Green **60** B1
Canisbay **187** F1
Canley **67** F5
Cann **25** F5
Cann Common **25** F5
Canna **162** A4
Cannard's Grave **24** D3
Cannich (Canaich) **165** E1
Canning Town **44** D4
Cannington **23** F4
Cannock **66** B2
Cannock Wood **66** C1
Cannop **39** F1
Canon Bridge **52** D3

Canon Frome **53** F3
Canon Pyon **53** D3
Canonbie **126** B4
Canons Ashby **56** A2
Canon's Town **2** C3
Canterbury *Aber.* **177** E4
Canterbury *Kent* **32** D3
Cantley *Norf.* **87** E5
Cantley *S.Yorks.* **94** D2
Cantlop **65** E2
Canton **38** A5
Cantray **175** D5
Cantraydoune **175** D5
Cantraywood **175** D5
Cantsfield **108** B3
Canvey Island **45** G4
Canwell Hall **66** D2
Canwick **83** E1
Canworthy Water **6** C1
Caol **156** D2
Caolas **154** B2
Caolasnacon **156** D3
Capel *Kent* **31** F4
Capel *Surr.* **29** G3
Capel Bangor **62** C1
Capel Betws Lleucu **50** D2
Capel Carmel **74** A5
Capel Celyn **76** B3
Capel Coch **88** C4
Capel Cung **76** A2
Capel Cynon **49** G3
Capel Dewi *Carmar.* **50** A5
Capel Dewi *Cere.* **62** C4
Capel Dewi *Cere.* **50** A3
Capel Garmon **76** B2
Capel Gwyn *Carmar.* **50** A5
Capel Gwyn *I.o.A.* **88** B5
Capel Gwynfe **50** D5
Capel Hendre **36** B1
Capel Isaac **50** B5
Capel Iwan **49** F4
Capel le Ferne **33** E5
Capel Llanilltern **37** G4
Capel Mawr **88** C5
Capel Parc **88** C4
Capel St. Andrew **61** E3
Capel St. Mary **60** B4
Capel St. Silin **50** B2
Capel Seion **62** C5
Capel Tygwydd **49** F3
Capelulchaf **74** D3
Capelulo **89** F5
Capel-y-ffin **52** B4
Capel-y-graig **75** E1
Capenhurst **91** E5
Capernwray **107** G5
Capheaton **128** C3
Caplaw **141** F4
Capon's Green **61** D1
Cappercleuch **134** D3
Capplegill **134** C5
Capstone **31** G2
Capton *Devon* **9** E2
Capton *Som.* **23** D4
Caputh **159** F5
Car Colston **82** C3
Caradon Town **5** G2
Carbellow **133** E3
Carbeth **141** G2
Carbis Bay **2** C3
Carbost *High.* **170** D5
Carbost *High.* **162** B1
Carbrain **142** B2
Carbrooke **86** A5
Carburton **94** D5
Carcary **161** E4
Carco **133** E3
Carcroft **94** C1
Cardenden **152** A5
Cardeston **64** C1
Cardew **117** G2
Cardiff (Caerdydd) **38** A5
Cardiff International Airport **23** D1
Cardigan (Aberteifi) **49** E3
Cardinal's Green **59** E3
Cardington *Beds.* **57** F3
Cardington *Shrop.* **65** E3
Cardinham **5** F3
Cardno **179** D3
Cardonald **141** G3
Cardoness **123** G5
Cardow **176** A5
Cardrona **135** D2
Cardross **141** E2
Cardurnock **117** E1

Careby **69** F1
Careston **160** D4
Carew **34** D2
Carew Cheriton **34** D2
Carew Newton **34** D2
Carey **53** E4
Carfin **142** B4
Carfrae **144** C3
Carfraemill **144** C4
Cargate Green **87** E4
Cargen **125** D3
Cargenbridge **125** D3
Cargill **151** E2
Cargo **117** G3
Cargreen **8** A1
Carham **136** B3
Carhampton **22** D3
Carharrack **4** B5
Carie *P. & K.* **158** B4
Carie *P. & K.* **150** B1
Carines **4** B4
Carisbrooke **15** D4
Cark **107** E5
Carkeel **8** A1
Carland Cross **4** C4
Carlatton **118** B2
Carlby **69** F1
Carlecotes **93** F2
Carleen **2** D4
Carleton *Cumb.* **118** A2
Carleton *Cumb.* **118** B5
Carleton *Lancs.* **99** G3
Carleton *N.Yorks.* **101** F3
Carleton *W.Yorks.* **103** D5
Carleton Fishery **122** C2
Carleton Forehoe **86** B3
Carleton Rode **72** C2
Carleton St. Peter **87** E5
Carlin How **111** G4
Carlisle **118** A2
Carloggas **4** C3
Carlops **143** F4
Carloway **189** F2
Carlton *Beds.* **57** E2
Carlton *Cambs.* **59** E2
Carlton *Leics.* **67** F2
Carlton *N.Yorks.* **103** F5
Carlton *N.Yorks.* **109** F4
Carlton *N.Yorks.* **109** F1
Carlton *Notts.* **82** B3
Carlton *S.Yorks.* **94** A1
Carlton *Stock.* **120** C5
Carlton *Suff.* **61** E1
Carlton *W.Yorks.* **102** C5
Carlton Colville **73** G2
Carlton Curlieu **60** B2
Carlton Green **59** E2
Carlton Husthwaite
111 D5
Carlton in Lindrick **94** C4
Carlton Miniott **110** C4
Carlton Scroop **83** E3
Carlton-in-Cleveland
111 E2
Carlton-le-Moorland
83 E2
Carlton-on-Trent **82** D1
Carluke **142** C4
Carlyon Bay **5** E4
Carmacoup **133** F3
Carmarthen (Caerfyrddin)
50 A5
Carmel *Carmar.* **36** B1
Carmel *Flints.* **90** C5
Carmel *Gwyn.* **75** D2
Carmel *I.o.A.* **88** B4
Carmichael **134** A2
Carmont **161** G2
Carmunnock **141** G4
Carmyle **142** A3
Carmyllie **161** D5
Carn **138** A4
Carn Brea Village **4** A5
Carn Dearg **172** A2
Carnaby **104** D1
Carnach *High.* **164** B2
Carnach *High.* **180** C5
Carnassarie **148** A4
Carnbee **152** B4
Carnbo **151** F4
Camdu **163** G2
Carnduncan **138** A3
Carnforth **107** F5
Carnhedryn **48** B5
Carnhell Green **2** D3
Carnichal **179** E2
Carnkie *Cornw.* **3** D3
Carnkie *Cornw.* **3** E3
Carnmore **138** B5

Carno **63** F3
Carnoch *High.* **165** E1
Carnoch *High.* **173** F4
Carnoch *High.* **175** E5
Carnock **143** E1
Carnon Downs **4** C5
Carnousie **177** F4
Carnoustie **153** D1
Carntyne **142** A3
Carnwath **143** D5
Carnyorth **2** A3
Carol Green **67** E5
Carperby **109** F4
Carr **94** C3
Carr Hill **95** D3
Carr Houses **91** E2
Carr Shield **119** E3
Carr Vale **94** B3
Carradale **130** C2
Carradale East **130** C2
Carrbridge **166** B2
Carrefour Selous **8** C5
Carreg-lefn **88** B4
Carreg-wen **49** F3
Carrhouse **95** E2
Carrick **140** A1
Carrick Castle **149** D5
Carriden **143** E1
Carrine **130** B5
Carrington *Gt.Man.*
92 B3
Carrington *Lincs.* **84** B2
Carrington *Midloth.*
144 A3
Carroch **124** A1
Carrog *Conwy* **76** A3
Carrog *Denb.* **77** E3
Carroglen **150** C2
Carrol **182** D2
Carron *Arg. & B.* **148** B5
Carron *Falk.* **142** C1
Carron *Moray* **176** B5
Carron Bridge **142** B1
Carronbridge **124** C1
Carronshore **142** C1
Carrot **160** C5
Carrow Hill **38** D3
Carrutherstown **125** F3
Carruthmuir **141** E3
Carrville **120** C3
Carry **140** A3
Carsaig **147** E2
Carscreugh **122** D4
Carse **139** F3
Carse of Ardersier **175** E4
Carsegowan **123** F5
Carseriggan **123** E4
Carsethorn **125** D5
Carsgoe **186** D5
Carshalton **30** B2
Carshalton Beeches
30 B2
Carsie **159** G5
Carsington **81** D2
Carsluith **123** F5
Carsphairn **123** G1
Carstairs **142** D5
Carstairs Junction **143** D5
Carswell Marsh **41** F3
Carter's Clay **27** E5
Carterton **41** E2
Carterway Heads **119** G2
Carthew **5** E4
Carthorpe **110** C4
Cartington **128** C1
Cartland **142** C5
Cartmel **107** E5
Cartmel Fell **107** F4
Cartworth **93** F2
Carway **36** A2
Cascob **52** B1
Cashel Farm **149** G5
Cashes Green **40** A2
Cashlie **157** G5
Cashmoor **13** F1
Caskieberran **152** A3
Cassencarie **123** F5
Cassington **41** G1
Cassop **120** C4
Castell **76** A1
Castell Gorfod **49** F5
Castell Howell **50** A3
Castellau **37** G4
Casterton **108** B5
Castle Acre **71** G1
Castle Ashby **57** D2
Castle Bolton **109** F3
Castle Bromwich **66** D4

Castle Bytham **69** E1
Castle Caereinion **64** A2
Castle Camps **59** E3
Castle Carrock **118** B2
Castle Cary **24** D4
Castle Combe **40** A5
Castle Donington **81** F5
Castle Douglas **124** B4
Castle Eaton **40** D3
Castle Eden **120** D4
Castle End **67** E5
Castle Frome **53** F3
Castle Gate **3** B3
Castle Green **29** E1
Castle Gresley **67** E1
Castle Heaton **145** G5
Castle Hill *Kent* **31** F4
Castle Hill *Suff.* **60** C3
Castle Kennedy **122** C5
Castle Leod **174** A4
Castle Levan **140** D2
Castle Madoc **51** G4
Castle Morris **48** C4
Castle O'er **126** A2
Castle Rising **85** E5
Castle Stuart **174** D5
Castlebay (Bàgh a'
Chaisteil) **188** A5
Castlebythe **48** D5
Castlecary **142** B2
Castlecraig *High.* **175** E3
Castlecraig *Sc.Bord.*
143 F5
Castlefairn **124** B2
Castleford **102** B5
Castlemartin **34** C3
Castlemilk *D. & G.*
125 F3
Castlemilk *Glas.* **142** A4
Castlemorton **53** G2
Castlerigg **117** F4
Castleside **119** G3
Castlesteads **118** B1
Castlethorpe **56** C3
Castleton *Aber.* **174** C2
Castleton *Angus* **160** B5
Castleton *Arg. & B.*
139 G1
Castleton *Derbys.* **93** F4
Castleton *Gt.Man.* **92** C1
Castleton *N.Yorks.*
111 F2
Castleton *Newport* **38** B4
Castleton *Sc.Bord.*
126 D2
Castletown *Dorset* **12** C5
Castletown *High.* **187** D2
Castletown *High.* **174** D5
Castletown *I.o.M.* **98** A5
Castletown *T. & W.*
120 C2
Castleweary **135** F5
Castlewigg **115** E2
Castley **102** B3
Caston **72** A2
Castramont **123** G4
Caswell **36** B4
Cat & Fiddle Inn **93** E5
Catacol **140** A5
Catbrain **39** E4
Catbrook **39** E2
Catchall **2** B4
Catcleugh **127** F1
Catcliffe **94** B2
Catcott **24** A4
Caterham **30** C3
Catfield **87** E3
Catford **44** C5
Catforth **100** A4
Cathays **38** A5
Cathcart **141** G3
Cathedine **52** A5
Catherine-de-Barnes
67 D4
Catherington **15** F1
Catherton **65** F5
Cathkin **142** A4
Catisfield **15** E2
Catlodge **166** A5
Catlowdy **126** C4
Catmere End **58** C4
Catmore **41** G4
Caton *Devon* **10** A5
Caton *Lancs.* **100** B1

Caton Green **100** B1
Cator Court **7** G3
Catrine **132** D3
Catsfield **18** C2
Catsfield Stream **18** C2
Catshaw **93** G2
Catshill **66** B5
Cattadale **138** B3
Cattal **102** D2
Cattawade **60** B4
Catterall **100** B3
Catterick **110** B3
Catterick Bridge **110** B3
Catterick Garrison **110** A3
Catterlen **118** A4
Catterline **161** G2
Catterton **29** E3
Catthorpe **68** A5
Cattishall **59** G1
Cattistock **12** B2
Catton *N.Yorks.* **110** C5
Catton *Norf.* **86** D4
Catton *Northumb.*
119 E2
Catton Hall **67** E1
Catwick **104** D3
Catworth **69** F5
Caudle Green **40** B1
Caulcott *Beds.* **57** F3
Caulcott *Oxon.* **56** A5
Cauldcots **161** E5
Cauldhame *Stir.* **150** B5
Cauldhame *Stir.* **150** D4
Cauldon **80** B3
Caulkerbush **124** D5
Caulside **126** C3
Caundle Marsh **12** C1
Caunton **82** C1
Causeway End *D. & G.*
123 F4
Causeway End *Essex*
45 E1
Causeway End *Lancs.*
91 F1
Causewayhead *Cumb.*
117 E1
Causewayhead *Stir.*
150 D5
Causey **120** B2
Causey Park **129** D2
Causeyend **169** G3
Cautley **108** B3
Cavendish **59** G3
Cavendish Bridge **81** F5
Cavenham **59** F1
Cavens **125** D5
Cavers **135** G4
Caversfield **56** A5
Caversham **42** C5
Caverswall **79** G3
Cawdor **175** E4
Cawkeld **104** B2
Cawkwell **96** C4
Cawood **103** E4
Cawsand **8** A3
Cawston *Norf.* **86** C3
Cawston *Warks.* **67** G5
Cawthorn **111** G4
Cawthorne **93** G2
Cawthorpe **83** F5
Cawton **111** F5
Caxton **58** B2
Caxton Gibbet **58** A1
Caynham **65** E5
Caythorpe *Lincs.* **83** E3
Caythorpe *Notts.* **82** B3
Cayton **113** D4
Ceann a' Bhàigh **188** B1
Cearsiadar **189** F3
Cedig **76** C5
Cefn Berain **76** C1
Cefn Canol **77** F4
Cefn Cantref **51** G5
Cefn Coch **77** E2
Cefn Cribwr **37** E4
Cefn Cross **37** E4
Cefn Einion **64** B4
Cefn Hengoed **38** A3
Cefn Llwyd **62** C4
Cefn Rhigos **37** F2
Cefn-brith **76** C2
Cefn-caer-Ferch **74** D3
Cefn-coch **77** E5
Cefn-coed-y-cymmer
37 G2
Cefn-ddwysarn **76** C4
Cefndeuddwr **76** A5

Cefneithin **36** B1
Cefn-gorwydd **51** F3
Cefn-gwyn **64** A4
Cefn-mawr **77** F3
Cefnpennar **37** G2
Cefn-y-bedd **78** A2
Cefn-y-pant **49** E5
Ceidio **88** C4
Ceidio Fawr **74** B4
Ceint **88** C5
Cellan **50** C3
Cellardyke **153** D4
Cellarhead **79** G3
Cemaes **88** B3
Cemmaes **65** E2
Cemmaes Road
(Glantwymyn) **63** E2
Cenarth **49** F4
Cennin **75** D3
Ceres **152** C3
Cerist **63** F4
Cerne Abbas **12** C2
Cerney Wick **40** C3
Cerrigceinwen **88** C5
Cerrigydrudion **76** C3
Cessford **136** B4
Ceunant **75** E1
Chaceley **54** A4
Chacewater **4** B5
Chackmore **56** B4
Chacombe **55** G3
Chad Valley **66** C4
Chadderton **92** D2
Chadderton Fold **92** C2
Chaddesden **81** E4
Chaddesley Corbett **66** A5
Chaddleworth **41** G5
Chadlington **55** F5
Chadshunt **55** F2
Chadstone **57** D2
Chadwell *Leics.* **82** C5
Chadwell *Shrop.* **65** G1
Chadwell St. Mary **45** F5
Chadwick End **67** E5
Chaffcombe **11** G1
Chafford Hundred **45** F5
Chagford **10** A4
Chailey **17** G2
Chainhurst **31** G4
Chalbury **13** G2
Chalbury Common **13** G2
Chaldon **30** C3
Chaldon Herring (East
Chaldon) **13** D4
Chale **15** D4
Chale Green **15** D4
Chalfont Common **43** F3
Chalfont St. Giles **43** E3
Chalfont St. Peter **43** F3
Chalford *Glos.* **40** A2
Chalford *Wilts.* **25** F3
Chalgrove **42** B3
Chalk **45** F5
Chalk End **45** F1
Challaborough **8** C3
Challacombe **21** G1
Challoch **123** E4
Challock **32** C3
Chalmington **12** B2
Chalton *Beds.* **57** F5
Chalton *Hants.* **15** G1
Chalvey **43** E5
Chalvington **18** A3
Champany **143** E2
Chancery **62** B5
Chandler's Cross **43** F3
Chandler's Ford **27** F5
Channel Islands **8** A5
Channel's End **57** G2
Chantry *Som.* **25** E3
Chantry *Suff.* **60** C3
Chapel **152** A5
Chapel Allerton *Som.*
24 B2
Chapel Allerton *W.Yorks.*
102 C4
Chapel Amble **5** D2
Chapel Brampton **56** C1
Chapel Chorlton **79** F4
Chapel Cleeve **22** D3
Chapel Cross **18** B1
Chapel End **57** F3
Chapel Green *Warks.*
67 E4
Chapel Green *Warks.*
55 G1
Chapel Haddlesey **103** E5
Chapel Hill *Aber.* **179** F4
Chapel Hill *Lincs.* **84** A2

Chapel Hill *Mon.* **39** E2
Chapel Hill *N.Yorks.*
102 C3
Chapel Knapp **25** F1
Chapel Lawn **64** C5
Chapel Leigh **23** E5
Chapel Milton **93** E4
Chapel of Garioch **169** E2
Chapel Rossan **114** B2
Chapel Row *W.Berks.*
27 G1
Chapel St. Leonards **97** F5
Chapel Stile **107** E2
Chapel Town **4** C4
Chapelbank **151** F3
Chapeldonan **131** G5
Chapelend Way **59** F4
Chapel-en-le-Frith **93** E4
Chapelgate **84** C5
Chapelhall **142** B3
Chapelhill *High.* **175** E2
Chapelhill *P. & K.* **152** A2
Chapelhill *P. & K.* **151** F1
Chapelknowe **126** B4
Chapel-le-Dale **108** C5
Chapelthorpe **94** A1
Chapelton *Aber.* **161** G1
Chapelton *Angus* **161** E5
Chapelton *Devon* **21** F3
Chapelton *S.Lan.* **142** A5
Chapeltown *B'burn.*
92 B1
Chapeltown *Cumb.*
126 C4
Chapeltown *Moray*
167 G2
Chapeltown *S.Yorks.*
94 A3
Chapmans Well **7** D1
Chapmanslade **25** F3
Chapmore End **44** C1
Chappel **59** G5
Charaton **6** C4
Chard **11** G2
Chard Junction **11** G2
Chardleigh Green **11** G1
Chardstock **11** G2
Charfield **39** G3
Charing **32** B4
Charing Cross **14** A1
Charing Heath **32** B4
Charingworth **55** D4
Charlbury **41** F1
Charlcombe **25** E1
Charlcote **55** E2
Charles **21** G2
Charles Tye **60** B2
Charlesfield **135** G3
Charleshill **29** D3
Charleston **160** B5
Charlestown *Aber.*
179 F1
Charlestown *Aberdeen*
169 G4
Charlestown *Cornw.* **5** E4
Charlestown *Derbys.*
93 E3
Charlestown *Dorset*
12 C5
Charlestown *Fife* **143** E1
Charlestown *Gt.Man.*
92 C2
Charlestown *High.*
172 B2
Charlestown *High.*
174 C5
Charlestown *W.Yorks.*
102 A4
Charlestown *W.Yorks.*
101 F5
Charlestown of Aberlour
(Aberlour) **176** B5
Charlesworth **93** E3
Charleton **152** C4
Charlinch **23** F4
Charlotteville **29** F3
Charlton *Gt.Lon.* **44** D5
Charlton *Hants.* **27** E3
Charlton *Herts.* **57** G5
Charlton *Northants.*
56 A4
Charlton *Northumb.*
128 C3
Charlton *Oxon.* **41** G4
Charlton *Som.* **25** D2
Charlton *Som.* **24** D3
Charlton *Som.* **23** F5
Charlton *Tel. & W.* **65** E1

Charlton *W.Suss.* **16** A2
Charlton *Wilts.* **26** A5
Charlton *Wilts.* **40** B4
Charlton *Wilts.* **26** C2
Charlton *Worcs.* **54** C5
Charlton Abbots **54** C5
Charlton Adam **24** C5
Charlton Down **12** C3
Charlton Horethorne **25** D5
Charlton Kings **54** B5
Charlwood **30** B4
Charminster **12** C3
Charmouth **11** G3
Charndon **56** B5
Charney Bassett **41** F3
Charnock Richard **91** G1
Charsfield **61** D2
Chart Corner **31** G4
Chart Sutton **32** A4
Charter Alley **27** C2
Charterhouse **24** B2
Charterville Allotments **41** F2
Chartham **32** D3
Chartham Hatch **32** D3
Chartridge **43** E2
Charvil **42** C5
Charwelton **56** A2
Chase End Street **53** G4
Chase Terrace **66** C2
Chasetown **66** C2
Chastleton **55** E5
Chasty **20** D5
Chatburn **101** D3
Chatcull **79** E4
Chatham **31** G2
Chatham Green **45** G1
Chathill **137** F4
Chattenden **45** G5
Chatteris **70** B4
Chattisham **60** B3
Chatto **136** B5
Chatton **137** E4
Chaul End **57** F5
Chavey Down **29** D1
Chawleigh **10** A1
Chawley **41** G2
Chawston **57** G2
Chawton **28** C4
Chazey Heath **42** B5
Cheadle *Gt.Man.* **92** C4
Cheadle *Staffs.* **80** B3
Cheadle Heath **92** C4
Cheadle Hulme **92** C4
Cheam **30** B2
Cheapside **29** E1
Chearsley **42** C1
Chebsey **79** F5
Checkendon **42** B4
Checkley *Ches.E.* **79** E3
Checkley *Here.* **53** E4
Checkley *Staffs.* **80** B4
Checkley Green **79** E3
Chedburgh **59** F2
Cheddar **24** B2
Cheddington **43** E1
Cheddleton **79** G2
Cheddon Fitzpaine **23** F5
Chedglow **40** B3
Chedgrave **73** E2
Chedington **12** A2
Chediston **73** E4
Chediston Green **73** E4
Chedzoy **24** A4
Cheesden **92** C1
Cheeseman's Green **32** C5
Cheetham Hill **92** C2
Cheglinch **21** F1
Cheldon **10** A1
Chelford **92** C5
Chellaston **81** E4
Chells **58** A5
Chelmarsh **65** G2
Chelmondiston **60** D4
Chelmorton **80** C1
Chelmsford **45** G2
Chelmsley Wood **67** D4
Chelsea **44** B5
Chelsfield **31** D2

Chelsham **30** C3
Chelston Heath **23** E5
Chelsworth **60** A3
Cheltenham **54** B5
Chelveston **57** E1
Chelvey **24** B1
Chelwood **24** D1
Chelwood Common **17** G1
Chelwood Gate **17** G1
Chelworth **40** B3
Cheney Longville **64** D4
Chenies **43** F3
Chepstow (Cas-gwent) **39** E3
Cherhill **40** C5
Cherington *Glos.* **40** B3
Cherington *Warks.* **55** E4
Cheriton *Devon* **22** A3
Cheriton *Hants.* **27** B5
Cheriton *Kent* **33** D5
Cheriton *Pembs.* **34** C3
Cheriton *Swan.* **36** B3
Cheriton Bishop **10** A3
Cheriton Cross **10** A3
Cheriton Fitzpaine **10** B2
Cherrington **79** D5
Cherry Burton **104** B3
Cherry Green **59** D5
Cherry Hinton **58** C2
Cherry Willingham **96** A5
Chertsey **29** F1
Cheselbourne **13** D3
Chesham **43** E2
Chesham Bois **43** E2
Cheshunt **44** C2
Cheslyn Hay **66** B2
Chessington **29** G1
Chestall **66** C1
Chester **78** B1
Chester Moor **120** B3
Chesterblade **25** D4
Chesterfield *Derbys.* **94** A3
Chesterfield *Staffs.* **66** D2
Chester-le-Street **120** B2
Chesters *Sc.Bord.* **136** A5
Chesters *Sc.Bord.* **136** A4
Chesterton *Cambs.* **58** C1
Chesterton *Cambs.* **69** G3
Chesterton *Oxon.* **56** A5
Chesterton *Shrop.* **65** G3
Chesterton *Staffs.* **79** F3
Chesterton *Warks.* **55** F2
Chesterton Green **55** F2
Chestfield **32** D2
Cheston **8** D2
Cheswardine **79** E5
Cheswick **137** E2
Cheswick Buildings **137** E2
Cheswick Green **66** D5
Chetnole **12** C1
Chettiscombe **10** C1
Chettisham **70** D4
Chettle **13** F1
Chetton **65** F3
Chetwode **56** B5
Chetwynd Aston **65** G1
Chetwynd Park **79** E5
Cheveley **59** E1
Chevening **31** D3
Cheverell's Green **43** F1
Chevington **59** F2
Chevington Drift **129** E2
Chevithorne **10** C1
Chew Magna **24** C1
Chew Moor **92** A2
Chew Stoke **24** C1
Chewton Keynsham **24** D1
Chewton Mendip **24** C2
Chichacott **7** G1
Chicheley **57** E3
Chichester **16** A3
Chickerell **12** C4
Chickering **72** D4
Chicklade **26** A4
Chickney **59** G4
Chicksands **57** G4
Chidden **15** F1
Chidden Holt **15** F1
Chiddingfold **29** E4
Chiddingly **18** A2
Chiddingstone **31** D4
Chiddingstone Causeway **31** E4
Chiddingstone Hoath **31** D4
Chideock **12** A3

Chidham **15** G2
Chidswell **102** B5
Chieveley **41** G5
Chignall St. James **45** F2
Chignall Smealy **45** F1
Chigwell **44** D3
Chigwell Row **45** D3
Chilbolton **27** E3
Chilcomb **27** G5
Chilcombe **12** B3
Chilcompton **25** D2
Chilcote **67** E1
Child Okeford **13** E1
Childer Thornton **91** E5
Childerditch **45** F4
Childrey **41** F4
Child's Ercall **79** D1
Childs Hill **44** B4
Childswickham **54** C4
Childwall **91** F4
Childwick Green **44** A1
Chilfrome **12** B3
Chilgrove **16** A2
Chilham **32** C3
Chilhampton **26** B4
Chilla **21** E5
Chillaton **7** E2
Chillenden **33** E3
Chillerton **15** D4
Chillesford **61** E2
Chilley **9** D2
Chillingham **137** E4
Chillington *Devon* **9** D3
Chillington *Som.* **11** G1
Chilmark **26** A4
Chilson *Oxon.* **41** F1
Chilson *Som.* **11** G2
Chilsworthy *Cornw.* **7** E3
Chilsworthy *Devon* **20** D5
Chilthorne Domer **12** B1
Chilton *Bucks.* **42** C1
Chilton *Devon* **10** B2
Chilton *Dur.* **120** B5
Chilton *Oxon.* **41** G4
Chilton *Suff.* **59** G3
Chilton Candover **27** G4
Chilton Cantelo **24** C5
Chilton Foliat **41** F5
Chilton Polden **24** A4
Chilton Street **59** F3
Chilton Trinity **23** F4
Chilvers Coton **67** F3
Chilwell **81** G4
Chilworth *Hants.* **14** D1
Chilworth *Surr.* **29** F3
Chimney **41** F2
Chimney Street **59** F3
Chineham **28** B2
Chingford **44** C3
Chinley **93** E4
Chinley Head **93** E4
Chinnor **42** C2
Chipchase Castle **128** A4
Chipley **23** E5
Chipnall **79** E4
Chippenham *Cambs.* **59** E1
Chippenham *Wilts.* **40** B5
Chipperfield **43** F2
Chipping *Herts.* **58** B4
Chipping *Lancs.* **100** C3
Chipping Campden **55** D4
Chipping Hill **46** B1
Chipping Norton **55** F5
Chipping Ongar **45** E2
Chipping Sodbury **39** G4
Chipping Warden **55** G3
Chipstable **22** D5
Chipstead *Kent* **31** D3
Chipstead *Surr.* **30** B3
Chirbury **64** B3
Chirk (Y Waun) **77** F4
Chirk Green **77** F4
Chirmorrie **122** D3
Chirnside **145** F4
Chirnsidebridge **145** F4
Chirton *T. & W.* **120** C1
Chirton *Wilts.* **26** B2
Chisbury **27** D1
Chiscan **130** B4
Chiselborough **12** A1
Chiseldon **41** D5
Chiserley **101** G5
Chislehampton **42** A3
Chislehurst **44** D5
Chislet **33** E2
Chiswell Green **44** A2
Chiswick **44** B5

Chiswick End **58** B3
Chisworth **93** D3
Chithurst **28** D5
Chittering **70** C5
Chitterne **26** A3
Chittlehamholt **21** G3
Chittlehampton **21** G3
Chittoe **26** A1
Chivelstone **9** D4
Chivenor **21** F2
Chobham **29** E1
Choicelee **145** E4
Cholderton **26** D3
Cholesbury **43** E2
Chollerford **128** B4
Chollerton **128** B4
Cholmondeston **78** D2
Cholsey **42** A4
Cholstrey **53** D2
Cholwell *B. & N.E.Som.* **24** D2
Cholwell *Devon* **7** E3
Chop Gate **111** E3
Choppington **129** E3
Chopwell **120** A2
Chorley *Ches.E.* **78** C2
Chorley *Lancs.* **91** G1
Chorley *Shrop.* **65** F4
Chorley *Staffs.* **66** C1
Chorleywood **43** F3
Chorlton **79** E2
Chorlton Lane **78** B3
Chorlton-cum-Hardy **92** C3
Chowley **78** B2
Chrishall **58** C4
Chrishall Grange **58** C3
Chrisswell **140** D2
Christchurch *Cambs.* **70** C3
Christchurch *Dorset* **14** A3
Christchurch *Glos.* **39** E1
Christchurch *Newport* **38** C4
Christian Malford **40** B5
Christleton **78** B1
Christmas Common **42** C3
Christon **24** A2
Christon Bank **137** G4
Christow **10** B4
Chrststkirk **168** D2
Chryston **142** A2
Chudleigh **10** B5
Chudleigh Knighton **10** B5
Chulmleigh **21** G4
Chunal **93** E3
Church **100** D5
Church Aston **65** G1
Church Brampton **56** C1
Church Brough **108** C1
Church Broughton **80** D4
Church Charwelton **56** A2
Church Common **61** E2
Church Crookham **28** D2
Church Eaton **66** B1
Church End *Beds.* **57** E5
Church End *Beds.* **57** E5
Church End *Beds.* **57** G2
Church End *Beds.* **57** E4
Church End *Beds.* **57** E4
Church End *Cambs.* **70** B2
Church End *Cambs.* **70** B5
Church End *Cambs.* **70** A4
Church End *E.Riding* **104** C2
Church End *Essex* **59** D3
Church End *Essex* **59** F5
Church End *Glos.* **54** A4
Church End *Hants.* **28** B2
Church End *Herts.* **44** A1
Church End *Herts.* **58** C5
Church End *Lincs.* **84** A4
Church End *Lincs.* **97** E3
Church End *Warks.* **67** E3
Church End *Wilts.* **40** C5
Church Enstone **55** F5
Church Fenton **103** E4
Church Green **11** E3
Church Gresley **67** E1
Church Hanborough **41** G1
Church Hill *C. & W.Ches.* **78** D1

Church Hill *Derbys.* **81** F1
Church Houses **111** F3
Church Knowle **13** F4
Church Laneham **95** F5
Church Langley **45** D2
Church Langton **68** C3
Church Lawford **67** G5
Church Lawton **79** F2
Church Leigh **80** B4
Church Lench **54** C2
Church Mayfield **80** C3
Church Minshull **79** D1
Church Norton **16** A4
Church Preen **65** E3
Church Pulverbatch **64** D2
Church Stoke **64** B3
Church Stowe **56** B2
Church Street *Essex* **59** F3
Church Street *Kent* **45** G5
Church Stretton **65** D3
Church Town *Leics.* **67** F1
Church Town *Surr.* **30** C3
Church Village **37** G4
Church Warsop **81** G1
Church Westcote **55** E5
Church Wilne **81** F4
Churcham **39** G1
Churchdown **40** A1
Churchend *Essex* **46** D3
Churchend *Essex* **59** E5
Churchend *S.Glos.* **39** G3
Churchfield **66** C3
Churchgate **44** C2
Churchgate Street **45** D1
Churchill *Devon* **21** F1
Churchill *Devon* **11** E2
Churchill *N.Som.* **24** B2
Churchill *Oxon.* **55** E5
Churchill *Worcs.* **54** B2
Churchill *Worcs.* **66** A5
Churchingford **11** F1
Churchover **68** A4
Churchstanton **11** E1
Churchstow **8** D3
Churchtown *Devon* **21** G1
Churchtown *I.o.M.* **98** C2
Churchtown *Lancs.* **100** A3
Churchtown *Mersey.* **91** E1
Churnsike Lodge **127** E4
Churston Ferrers **9** F2
Churt **29** D4
Churton **78** B2
Churwell **102** B5
Chute Cadley **27** E2
Chute Standen **27** E2
Chwilog **74** D4
Chyandour **2** B3
Chysauster **2** B3
Cilan Uchaf **74** B5
Cilcain **77** E1
Cilcennin **50** B1
Cilcewydd **64** B2
Cilfrew **37** D2
Cilfynydd **37** G3
Cilgerran **49** E3
Cilgwyn *Carmar.* **50** D4
Cilgwyn *Pembs.* **49** D4
Ciliau Aeron **50** B2
Cille Bhrighde **188** B4
Cilmaengwyn **36** D2
Cilmery **51** G2
Cilrhedyn **49** F4
Cilrhedyn Bridge **48** D4
Cilsan **50** B5
Ciltalgarth **76** B3
Cilwendeg **49** F4
Cilybebyll **36** D2
Cilycwm **51** D3
Cimla **37** D3
Cinderford **39** F1
Cippenham **43** E4
Cippyn **49** E3
Cirencester **40** C2
City *Gt.Lon.* **44** C4
City *V. of Glam.* **37** F5
City Airport **44** D4
City Dulas **88** C4
Clabhach **154** A4
Clachaig **140** C1
Clachan *Arg. & B.* **149** D3
Clachan *Arg. & B.* **136** A5
Clachan *Arg. & B.* **139** F4
Clachan *High.* **163** D1

Clachan Mòr **154** A4
Clachan of Campsie **142** A2
Clachan of Glendaruel **140** A1
Clachandhu **147** D1
Clachaneasy **123** E3
Clachanmore **114** A2
Clachan-Seil **147** G3
Clachanturn **167** G5
Clachbreck **139** F2
Clachnabrain **160** B3
Clachnaharry **174** C5
Clachtoll **180** C2
Clackmannan **151** E2
Clackmarras **176** B4
Clacton-on-Sea **47** E1
Cladich (An Cladach) **148** C2
Cladswell **54** C2
Claggan *High.* **155** G5
Claggan (An Claigeann) *High.* **156** D2
Claigan **170** B4
Claines **54** A2
Clandown **25** D2
Clanfield *Hants.* **15** G1
Clanfield *Oxon.* **41** E2
Clannaborough Barton **10** A2
Clanville **27** E3
Claonaig **139** G4
Claonaigh **148** C4
Claonel **182** A4
Clapgate **58** C5
Clapham *Beds.* **57** F2
Clapham *Devon* **10** B4
Clapham *Gt.Lon.* **44** B5
Clapham *N.Yorks.* **100** D1
Clapham *W.Suss.* **16** C3
Clapham Green **57** F2
Clapham Hill **32** D2
Clappers **145** G4
Clappersgate **107** E2
Clapton *Som.* **12** A2
Clapton *Som.* **24** D2
Clapton-in-Gordano **39** D5
Clapton-on-the-Hill **41** E1
Clapworthy **21** G3
Clara Vale **120** A1
Clarach **62** C4
Clarbeston **49** D5
Clarbeston Road **48** D5
Clarborough **95** E4
Clardon **186** D2
Clare **59** F3
Clarebrand **124** B4
Clarencefield **125** E4
Clanlaw **135** G4
Clark's Green **29** G4
Clarkston **141** G4
Clashban **182** B5
Clashcoig **182** B5
Clashdorran **174** B5
Clashgour **157** E5
Clashindarroch **168** B1
Clashmore *High.* **174** D1
Clashmore *High.* **180** C1
Clashnessie **180** C1
Clashnoir **167** G2
Clatford **26** C1
Clathy **151** E2
Clatt **168** C2
Clatter **83** F2
Clattercote **55** G3
Clatterford **15** D4
Clatterford End **45** E2
Clatterin Brig **161** E2
Clatteringshaws **123** G3
Clatworthy **23** D4
Claughton *Lancs.* **100** B1
Claughton *Lancs.* **100** B3
Clavelshay **23** F4
Claverdon **55** D1
Claverham **24** B1
Clavering **58** C4
Claverley **65** G3
Claverton **25** E1
Claverton Down **25** E1
Clawdd-côch **37** G5
Clawdd-newydd **77** D2
Clawfin **132** D5
Clawthorpe **107** G5
Clawton **7** D1
Claxby **96** B3
Claxby Pluckacre **84** B1
Claxby St. Andrew **97** E5

Claxton *N.Yorks.* 103 F1
Claxton *Norf.* 87 E5
Claxton Grange 121 D5
Clay Common 73 F3
Clay Coton 68 A5
Clay Cross 81 E1
Clay End 58 B5
Clay Hill 39 F5
Clay of Allan 175 E2
Claybrooke Magna 67 G4
Claybrooke Parva 67 G4
Claydene 31 D4
Claydon *Oxon.* 55 G2
Claydon *Suff.* 60 C3
Claygate *Kent* 31 G4
Claygate *Surr.* 29 G1
Claygate Cross 31 F3
Clayhanger *Devon* 22 D5
Clayhanger *W.Mid.* 66 C2
Clayhidon 11 E1
Clayhill *E.Suss.* 18 D1
Clayhill *Hants.* 14 C1
Clayhithe 58 D1
Clayock 187 D3
Claypit Hill 58 B2
Claypits 59 G2
Claypole 82 D3
Claythorpe 97 E5
Clayton *S.Yorks.* 94 B2
Clayton *Staffs.* 79 F3
Clayton *W.Suss.* 17 E2
Clayton *W.Yorks.* 102 A4
Clayton Green 100 B5
Clayton West 93 G1
Clayton-le-Moors 100 D4
Clayton-le-Woods 100 B5
Clayworth 95 E4
Cleadale 155 D1
Cleadon 120 C1
Clearbrook 8 B1
Clearwell 39 E2
Cleasby 110 B1
Cleat 190 B4
Cleatlam 110 A1
Cleatop 101 E1
Cleator 116 D5
Cleator Moor 116 D5
Cleckheaton 102 A5
Clee St. Margaret 65 E4
Cleedownton 65 E4
Cleehill 65 E5
Cleestanton 65 E5
Cleethorpes 96 D2
Cleeton St. Mary 65 F5
Cleeve *N.Som.* 24 B1
Cleeve *Oxon.* 42 B4
Cleeve Hill 54 B5
Cleeve Prior 54 C3
Cleghorn 142 C5
Clehonger 53 D4
Cleigh 148 A2
Cleish 151 F5
Cleland 142 B4
Clement's End 43 F1
Clemsfold 29 G4
Clench Common 26 C1
Clenchwarton 85 D5
Clennell 128 B1
Clent 66 B5
Cleobury Mortimer 65 F5
Cleobury North 65 F4
Clephanton 175 E4
Clerklands 135 G3
Clermiston 143 F2
Clestrain 190 A3
Cleuch Head 135 G4
Cleughbrae 125 E3
Clevancy 40 C5
Clevedon 38 D5
Cleveland Tontine Inn
  110 D3
Cleveley 55 F5
Cleveleys 99 G3
Clevelode 54 A3
Cleverton 40 B4
Clewer 24 B2
Clewer Green 43 E5
Clewer Village 43 E5
Cley next the Sea 86 B1
Cliburn 118 B5
Cliddesden 28 B3
Cliff *Carmar.* 35 G2
Cliff *High.* 155 F3
Cliff End 19 D2
Cliff Grange 78 D4
Cliffe *Lancs.* 100 D4
Cliffe *Med.* 45 G5
Cliffe *N.Yorks.* 103 F4
Cliffe Woods 45 G5

Clifford *Here.* 52 B3
Clifford *W.Yorks.* 102 D3
Clifford Chambers 55 D2
Clifford's Mesne 53 F5
Cliffs End 33 F2
Clifton *Beds.* 57 G4
Clifton *Bristol* 39 E5
Clifton *Cumb.* 118 B5
Clifton *Derbys.* 80 C3
Clifton *Devon* 21 F1
Clifton *Lancs.* 100 A4
Clifton *N.Yorks.* 102 A3
Clifton *Northumb.*
  129 E3
Clifton *Nott.* 81 G4
Clifton *Oxon.* 55 G4
Clifton *S.Yorks.* 94 C3
Clifton *Stir.* 149 F1
Clifton *W.Yorks.* 102 A5
Clifton *Worcs.* 54 A3
Clifton *York* 103 E2
Clifton Campville 67 E1
Clifton Hampden 42 A3
Clifton Maybank 12 B1
Clifton Reynes 57 E2
Clifton upon Dunsmore
  68 A5
Clifton upon Teme 53 G1
Cliftonville 33 F1
Climping 16 C3
Climpy 142 D4
Clink 25 E3
Clint 102 B2
Clint Green 86 B4
Clinterty 169 F3
Clintmains 136 A3
Clippesby 87 F4
Clippings Green 86 B4
Clipsham 69 E1
Clipston *Northants.*
  68 C4
Clipston *Notts.* 82 B4
Clipstone 81 G1
Clitheroe 100 D3
Clive 78 C3
Clixby 96 B2
Clocaenog 77 D2
Clochan 176 D3
Clochtow 179 F4
Clock Face 91 G3
Clockhill 179 F3
Cloddach 176 A4
Cloddiau 64 A2
Clodock 52 C5
Cloford 25 E3
Clopton *Here.* 60 D2
Clopton Corner 60 D2
Clopton Green *Suff.*
  59 F2
Clopton Green *Suff.*
  60 D2
Close Clark 98 A4
Closeburn 124 C1
Closworth 12 B1
Clothall 58 A4
Clotton 78 C1
Clough *Cumb.* 108 C3
Clough *Gt.Man.* 92 D2
Clough *Gt.Man.* 92 D1
Clough *W.Yorks.* 93 E1
Clough Foot 101 F1
Clough Head 101 G5
Cloughfold 101 E5
Cloughton 112 D3
Cloughton Newlands
  112 D3
Clounlaid 155 G4
Clova *Aber.* 168 B2
Clova *Angus* 160 B2
Clove Lodge 109 E1
Clovelly 6 C1
Clovelly Cross 20 D3
Clovenfords 135 F2
Clovenstone 169 E3
Cloves 176 A3
Clovullin 156 C3
Clow Bridge 101 E5
Clowne 94 B5
Clows Top 65 G5
Cloyntie 132 B5
Cluanach 138 B4
Clubworthy 6 C1
Cluddley 65 F1
Clun 64 B4
Clunas 175 E5

Clunbury 64 C4
Clunderwen 35 E1
Clune *High.* 166 B2
Clune *Moray* 177 E3
Clunes 157 E1
Clungunford 64 C5
Clunie *Aber.* 177 F4
Clunie *P. & K.* 159 G5
Clunton 64 C4
Cluny 152 A5
Clutton *B. & N.E.Som.*
  24 D2
Clutton *C. & W.Ches.*
  78 B2
Clwt-y-bont 75 F1
Clwydyfagwyr 37 G2
Clydach *Mon.* 38 B1
Clydach *Swan.* 36 C2
Clydach Terrace 38 A1
Clydach Vale 37 F3
Clydebank 141 F2
Clydey 49 F4
Clynder 140 D1
Clyne 37 E2
Clynelish 183 D4
Clynfyw 49 F4
Clynnog-fawr 74 D3
Clyro 52 B3
Clyst Honiton 10 C3
Clyst Hydon 10 D2
Clyst St. George 10 C4
Clyst St. Lawrence 10 D2
Clyst St. Mary 10 C4
Clyst William 11 D2
Cnewr 51 E5
Cnwch Coch 62 C5
Coachford 177 D5
Coad's Green 5 G2
Coal Aston 94 A5
Coalbrookdale 65 F2
Coalbrookvale 38 A2
Coalburn 133 G2
Coalburns 120 A1
Coalcleugh 119 E3
Coaley 39 G2
Coalmoor 65 F2
Coalpit Heath 39 F4
Coalpit Hill 79 F2
Coalport 65 F2
Coalsnaughton 151 E5
Coaltown of Balgonie
  152 B5
Coaltown of Wemyss
  152 B5
Coalville 67 G1
Coalway 39 E1
Coanwood 118 C2
Coast 180 B5
Coat 24 B5
Coatbridge 142 B3
Coate *Swin.* 41 D4
Coate *Wilts.* 26 B1
Coates *Cambs.* 70 B3
Coates *Glos.* 40 B2
Coates *Lincs.* 95 F4
Coates *Notts.* 95 F4
Coates *W.Suss.* 16 B2
Coatham 121 E5
Coatham Mundeville
  120 B5
Cobairdy 177 E5
Cobbaton 21 G3
Cobbler's Plain 39 D2
Cobby Syke 102 A2
Cobden 10 D3
Coberley 40 B1
Cobhall Common 53 D4
Cobham *Kent* 31 F2
Cobham *Surr.* 29 C1
Cobleland 150 A5
Cobley Hill 66 C5
Cobnash 53 D1
Coburty 179 F1
Cochno 141 F2
Cock Alley 81 F1
Cock Bank 78 A3
Cock Bevington 54 C2
Cock Bridge 167 G4
Cock Clarks 46 B1
Cock Green 45 G1
Cock Marling 19 D2
Cockayne 111 F3
Cockayne Hatley 58 A3
Cockburnspath 145 E2
Cockenzie & Port Seton
  144 B2
Cocker Bar 100 B5
Cockerham 100 A2

Cockermouth 117 E3
Cockernhoe 57 G5
Cockerton 110 B1
Cockett 36 C3
Cockfield *Dur.* 120 A5
Cockfield *Suff.* 60 A2
Cockfosters 44 B3
Cocking 16 B2
Cockington 9 E1
Cocklake 23 G5
Cocklaw 128 B4
Cockle Park 129 E2
Cockleford 40 B1
Cockley Beck 106 D2
Cockley Cley 71 F2
Cockpen 144 A3
Cockpole Green 42 C4
Cockshutt 78 B5
Cockthorpe 86 A1
Cockwood *Devon* 10 C4
Cockwood *Som.* 23 F3
Cockyard 93 E4
Codda 5 F2
Coddenham 60 C2
Coddington *C. & W.Ches.*
  78 B2
Coddington *Here.* 53 G3
Coddington *Notts.* 82 D2
Codford St. Mary 26 A4
Codford St. Peter 26 A4
Codicote 44 B1
Codmore Hill 16 C2
Codnor 81 F3
Codnor Park 81 F2
Codrington 39 G5
Codsall 66 A2
Codsall Wood 66 A2
Coed Morgan 38 C1
Coed Ystumgwern 75 D5
Coedcae 38 B1
Coedely 37 G4
Coederkernew 38 B4
Coedpoeth 77 F2
Coedway 64 C1
Coed-y-bryn 49 G3
Coed-y-caerau 38 C3
Coed-y-paen 38 C3
Coed-y-parc 75 F1
Coed-yr-ynys 52 A5
Coelbren 37 E1
Coffinswell 9 E1
Cofton 10 C4
Cofton Hackett 66 C5
Cogan 38 A5
Cogenhoe 56 D1
Cogges 41 F2
Coggeshall 59 G5
Coggeshall Hamlet 59 G5
Coggins Mill 18 A1
Coilantogle 150 A4
Coileitir 156 D5
Coilessan 149 E4
Coillag 45 D2
Coille Mhorgil 164 B4
Coille-righ 164 A2
Coillore 162 B1
Coity 37 F4
Colaboll 182 A3
Colan 4 C3
Colaton Raleigh 11 D4
Colbost 170 B5
Colburn 110 B3
Colbury 14 C1
Colby *Cumb.* 118 C5
Colby *I.o.M.* 98 A4
Colby *Norf.* 86 D2
Colchester 60 A5
Colchester Green 60 A2
Colcot 23 E1
Cold Ash 27 G1
Cold Ashby 68 B5
Cold Ashton 39 G5
Cold Aston 40 D1
Cold Blow 35 E1
Cold Brayfield 57 E2
Cold Chapel 134 A3
Cold Cotes 108 C5
Cold Hanworth 96 A4
Cold Harbour 42 B4
Cold Hatton 78 D5
Cold Hatton Heath 78 D5
Cold Hesledon 120 D3
Cold Higham 56 B2
Cold Inn 35 E2
Cold Kirby 111 E4
Cold Newton 68 C2
Cold Northcott 5 G1
Cold Norton 46 B2
Cold Overton 68 D2

Cold Row 99 G3
Coldbackie 185 F2
Coldblow 45 E5
Coldean 17 F3
Coldeast 10 B5
Coldeaton 80 C2
Colden Common 27 F5
Coldfair Green 61 F1
Coldrain 151 F4
Coldred 33 E4
Coldrey 28 C3
Coldridge 21 G5
Coldrife 128 C2
Coldstream 136 C3
Coldvreath 5 D4
Coldwaltham 16 C2
Coldwells 179 G3
Cole 25 D4
Cole End 67 D4
Cole Green 44 B1
Cole Henley 27 F2
Colebatch 64 C4
Colebrook 10 D2
Colebrooke 10 A2
Coleburn 176 B4
Coleby *Lincs.* 83 E1
Coleby *N.Lincs.* 95 F1
Coleford *Devon* 10 A2
Coleford *Glos.* 39 E1
Coleford *Som.* 25 D3
Colegate End 72 C3
Colehill 13 G2
Coleman Green 44 A1
Coleman's Hatch 30 D5
Colemere 78 B4
Colemore 28 C4
Colemore Green 65 G3
Colenden 151 G2
Coleorton 67 G1
Colerne 40 A5
Cole's Common 72 D3
Cole's Cross 9 D3
Cole's Green 61 D1
Colesbourne 40 C1
Colesden 57 G2
Coleshill *Bucks.* 43 E3
Coleshill *Oxon.* 41 E3
Coleshill *Warks.* 67 E4
Colestocks 11 D2
Coley *B. & N.E.Som.*
  24 C2
Coley *Staffs.* 80 B5
Colfin 122 B5
Colgate 30 B5
Colgrain 141 E2
Colindale 44 B4
Colinsburgh 152 C4
Colinton 143 G3
Colintraive 140 B2
Colkirk 86 A3
Coll 154 A4
Collace 152 A1
Collafirth 191 C2
Collamoor Head 6 B1
Collaton St. Mary 9 E1
Collessie 152 A3
Colleton Mills 21 G4
Collett's Green 54 A2
Collier Row 45 E3
Collier Street 31 G4
Collier's End 58 B5
Collier's Wood 44 B5
Colliery Row 120 C3
Collieston 179 F5
Collin 125 F2
Collingbourne Ducis
  26 D2
Collingbourne Kingston
  26 D2
Collingham *Notts.* 82 D1
Collingham *W.Yorks.*
  102 C3
Collington 53 F1
Collingtree 56 D2
Collins End 42 B5
Collins Green *Warr.*
  91 G3
Collins Green *Worcs.*
  53 G2
Colliston 161 E2
Colliton 11 D2
Collmuir 168 C4
Collycroft 67 F4
Collyhurst 92 C2
Collynie 169 F1

Collyweston 69 E2
Colmonell 122 C2
Colmworth 57 G2
Coln Rogers 40 C2
Coln St. Aldwyns 40 D2
Coln St. Dennis 40 C1
Colnabaichin 167 G4
Colnbrook 43 F5
Colne *Cambs.* 70 B5
Colne *Lancs.* 101 E4
Colne Engaine 59 G4
Colney 86 C5
Colney Heath 44 B2
Colney Street 44 A2
Colonsay 146 C5
Colonsay House 146 C5
Colpy 168 D2
Colquhar 144 A5
Colsterdale 110 A4
Colsterworth 83 E5
Colston Bassett 82 C4
Coltfield 176 A3
Colthouse 107 E3
Coltishall 87 D4
Coltness 142 C4
Colton *Cumb.* 107 E4
Colton *N.Yorks.* 103 E3
Colton *Norf.* 86 C5
Colton *Staffs.* 80 B5
Colton *W.Yorks.* 102 C4
Colva 52 B2
Colvend 124 C5
Colwall 53 G3
Colwall Green 53 G3
Colwall Stone 53 G3
Colwell 128 B4
Colwich 80 B5
Colwick 82 B3
Colwinston 37 F5
Colworth 16 B3
Colwyn Bay (Bae Colwyn)
  89 G5
Colyford 11 F3
Colyton 11 F3
Combe *Here.* 52 C1
Combe *Oxon.* 41 G1
Combe *Som.* 24 B5
Combe *W.Berks.* 27 E1
Combe Common 29 E4
Combe Cross 10 A5
Combe Down 25 E1
Combe Florey 23 E4
Combe Hay 25 E2
Combe Martin 21 F1
Combe Pafford 9 F1
Combe Raleigh 11 E2
Combe St. Nicholas 11 G1
Combeinteignhead 10 B5
Comberbach 92 A5
Comberford 67 D2
Comberton *Cambs.*
  58 B2
Comberton *Here.* 53 D1
Combpyne 11 F3
Combridge 80 B4
Combrook 55 F2
Combs *Derbys.* 93 E5
Combs *Suff.* 60 B2
Combs Ford 60 B2
Combwich 23 F3
Comer 149 F2
Comers 169 D4
Comhampton 54 A1
Comins Coch 62 C4
Commercial End 59 D1
Commins Coch 63 E2
Common Edge 99 G4
Common Moor 5 G2
Common Platt 40 D4
Common Side 94 A5
Commondale 111 F1
Commonside 80 C2
Compstall 93 D3
Compton *Devon* 9 E1
Compton *Hants.* 27 F5
Compton *Plym.* 8 A2
Compton *Staffs.* 66 A4
Compton *Surr.* 29 E3
Compton *W.Berks.* 42 A5
Compton *W.Suss.* 15 G1
Compton *W.Yorks.*
  102 D3
Compton *Wilts.* 26 C2
Compton Abbas 13 E1
Compton Abdale 40 C1
Compton Bassett 40 C5
Compton Beauchamp
  41 E4

Compton Bishop **24** A2
Compton Chamberlayne **26** B3
Compton Dando **24** D1
Compton Dundon **24** B4
Compton Martin **24** A2
Compton Pauncefoot **24** D5
Compton Valence **12** B3
Compton Verney **55** F2
Compton Wynyates **55** F3
Comra **165** G5
Comrie *Fife* **143** E1
Comrie *P. & K.* **150** C2
Conchra *Arg. & B.* **140** B1
Conchra *High.* **163** G2
Concraigie **159** F5
Conder Green **100** A2
Conderton **54** B4
Condicote **54** D5
Condorrat **142** B2
Condover **65** D2
Coney Weston **72** A4
Coneyhurst **29** E5
Coneythorpe **111** G5
Coneysthorpe **102** C2
Conford **28** D4
Congash **167** E2
Congdon's Shop **5** G2
Congerstone **67** F2
Congham **85** F5
Congleton **79** F1
Congresbury **24** B1
Congreve **66** B1
Conicavel **175** F4
Coningsby **84** A2
Conington *Cambs.* **69** G4
Conington *Cambs.* **58** B1
Conisbrough **94** C3
Conisby **138** A3
Conisholme **97** G3
Coniston *Cumb.* **107** E3
Coniston *E.Riding* **105** D4
Coniston Cold **101** F2
Conistone **101** F1
Conland **177** F5
Connah's Quay **77** F1
Connel (A' Choingheal) **148** C1
Connel Park **133** E4
Connor Downs **2** C3
Conock **26** B2
Conon Bridge (Drochaid Sgùideil) **174** B4
Cononish **149** F2
Cononley **101** F3
Cononsyth **161** D5
Consall **79** G3
Consett **120** A2
Constable Burton **110** A3
Constantine **3** E4
Constantine Bay **4** C2
Contin (Cunndainn) **174** A4
Contlaw **169** F4
Contullich **174** C2
Conwy **89** F5
Conyer **32** B2
Conyer's Green **59** G1
Cooden **18** C3
Coodham **132** C2
Cooil **98** B4
Cookbury **21** E5
Cookbury Wick **21** D5
Cookham **43** D4
Cookham Dean **43** D4
Cookham Rise **43** D4
Cookhill **54** C2
Cookley *Suff.* **73** E4
Cookley *Worcs.* **66** A4
Cookley Green *Oxon.* **42** B3
Cookley Green *Suff.* **73** E4
Cookney **169** F5
Cook's Green **60** A2
Cooksbridge **17** F2
Cooksey Green **54** B1
Cookshill **79** G3
Cooksmill Green **45** F2
Cookston **169** G1
Coolham **29** G5
Cooling **45** G5
Cooling Street **45** G5
Coombe *Cornw.* **5** D4
Coombe *Cornw.* **20** C4
Coombe *Cornw.* **4** A5

Coombe *Cornw.* **4** C5
Coombe *Devon* **9** D3
Coombe *Devon* **10** B4
Coombe *Devon* **11** E3
Coombe *Som.* **23** F5
Coombe *Som.* **12** A2
Coombe *Wilts.* **26** C2
Coombe Bissett **26** C5
Coombe End **22** D5
Coombe Hill **54** A5
Coombe Keynes **13** E4
Coombes **17** D3
Coombes Moor **52** C1
Cooper's Corner *E.Suss.* **18** C1
Cooper's Corner *Kent* **31** D4
Cooper's Green **44** A2
Coopersale **45** D2
Coopersale Street **45** D2
Cootham **16** C2
Cop Street **33** E3
Copdock **60** C3
Copford Green **60** A5
Copgrove **102** C1
Cople **57** G3
Copley *Dur.* **119** G5
Copley *W.Yorks.* **101** G5
Coplow Dale **93** F5
Copmanthorpe **103** E3
Compere End **79** F5
Copp **100** A4
Coppathorne **20** C5
Coppenhall **66** B1
Coppenhall Moss **79** E2
Copperhouse **2** C3
Coppicegate **65** G4
Coppingford **69** G4
Copplebridge **25** F5
Copplestone **10** A2
Coppull **91** G1
Coppull Moor **91** G1
Copsale **29** G5
Copse Hill **30** B2
Copster Green **100** C4
Copston Magna **67** G4
Copt Heath **67** D5
Copt Hewick **110** C5
Copt Oak **67** G1
Copthall Green **44** D2
Copthorne **30** C5
Copy Lake **21** G4
Copythorne **14** C1
Coralhill **179** F1
Corbets Tey **45** E4
Corbiegoe **187** F4
Corbridge **119** F1
Corby **69** D4
Corby Glen **83** F5
Cordach **168** D5
Cordorcan **123** E3
Coreley **65** F5
Corfcott Green **6** D1
Corfe **11** F1
Corfe Castle **13** F4
Corfe Mullen **13** F3
Corfton **65** D2
Corgarff **167** G4
Corhampton **28** B5
Corley **67** F4
Corley Ash **67** E4
Corley Moor **67** E4
Cornabus **138** B5
Cornard Tye **60** A3
Corndon **7** G2
Corney **106** C3
Cornforth **120** C4
Cornhill **177** E4
Cornhill on Tweed **136** C3
Cornholme **101** F5
Cornish Hall End **59** E4
Cornriggs **119** E3
Cornsay **120** A3
Cornsay Colliery **120** A3
Corntown *High.* **174** B4
Corntown *V. of Glam.* **37** F5
Cornwell **55** E5
Cornwood **8** C2
Cornworthy **9** E2
Corpach (A' Chorpaich) **156** D2
Corpusty **86** C3
Corrachree **168** B4
Corran *Arg. & B.* **149** E5
Corran *High.* **163** G4
Corran (Ardgour) *High.* **156** C3
Corranbuie **139** G3

Corranmore **147** G4
Corrany **98** C3
Corribeg **156** B2
Corrie **140** B5
Corrie Common **126** A3
Corriechrevie **139** F4
Corriecravie **131** E3
Corriedoo **124** A2
Corriekinloch **181** F2
Corrielorne **148** A3
Corrievorrie **166** B2
Corrimony **165** E1
Corringham *Lincs.* **95** F3
Corringham *Thur.* **45** G4
Corris **63** D2
Corris Uchaf **62** D2
Corrlarach **156** B2
Corrour Shooting Lodge **157** G3
Corrow **149** D4
Corry **163** E2
Corrychurrachan **156** C3
Corrylach **130** C2
Corrymuckloch **151** D1
Corsback **187** E2
Corscombe **12** B2
Corse *Aber.* **177** F5
Corse *Glos.* **53** G5
Corse Lawn **54** A4
Corse of Kinnoir **177** E5
Corsebank **133** G4
Corsegight **178** D2
Corsehill **187** E2
Corsewall **122** B4
Corsham **40** A5
Corsindae **169** E3
Corsley **25** F3
Corsley Heath **25** F3
Corsock **124** B3
Corston *B. & N.E.Som.* **25** D1
Corston *Wilts.* **40** B4
Corstorphine **143** E2
Cortachy **160** B4
Corton *Suff.* **73** G2
Corton *Wilts.* **26** A3
Corton Denham **24** D5
Corwar House **123** D3
Corwen **77** D3
Coryton *Devon* **7** E2
Coryton *Thur.* **45** G4
Cosby **68** A3
Coscote **42** A4
Coseley **66** B3
Cosford *Shrop.* **65** G2
Cosford *Warks.* **68** A5
Cosgrove **56** C3
Cosham **15** F2
Cosheston **34** D2
Coshieville **158** C5
Coskills **96** A2
Cosmeston **23** E1
Cossall **81** F3
Cossington *Leics.* **68** B1
Cossington *Som.* **24** A3
Costessey **86** C4
Costock **81** G5
Coston *Leics.* **82** D5
Coston *Norf.* **86** B5
Cote *Oxon.* **41** F2
Cote *Som.* **24** A3
Cotebrook **78** C1
Cotehill **118** C2
Cotes *Cumb.* **107** F4
Cotes *Leics.* **81** G5
Cotes *Staffs.* **79** F4
Cotesbach **68** A4
Cotford St. Luke **23** E5
Cotgrave **82** B4
Cothall **169** F3
Cotham **82** C3
Cothelstone **23** E4
Cotheridge **53** G2
Cotherstone **109** F1
Cothill **41** E2
Cotleigh **11** F2
Cotmanhay **81** F3
Coton *Cambs.* **58** C2
Coton *Northants.* **68** B5
Coton *Staffs.* **79** G4
Coton *Staffs.* **79** D2
Coton *Staffs.* **79** F5
Coton Clanford **79** F5
Coton Hill **79** D4
Coton in the Clay **80** C5
Coton in the Elms **67** E1
Cotonwood *Shrop.* **78** C4
Cotonwood *Staffs.* **79** F5
Cott **9** D1

Cottam *Lancs.* **100** A4
Cottam *Notts.* **95** F4
Cottartown **167** E1
Cottenham **58** C1
Cotterdale **108** D3
Cottered **58** B5
Cotteridge **66** C5
Cotterstock **69** F3
Cottesbrooke **68** C5
Cottesmore **69** E1
Cottingham *E.Riding* **104** C4
Cottingham *Northants.* **68** D3
Cottingley **102** A4
Cottisford **56** A4
Cotton *Staffs.* **80** B3
Cotton *Suff.* **60** B1
Cotton End **57** F3
Cottonworth **27** E4
Cottown *Aber.* **168** C2
Cottown *Aber.* **178** D3
Cottown *Aber.* **169** E3
Cotts **8** A1
Cottwood **21** G4
Cotwall **65** F1
Cotwalton **79** G4
Couch's Mill **5** F4
Coughton *Here.* **53** E5
Coughton *Warks.* **54** C1
Cougie **164** D2
Coulaghailtro **139** F3
Coulags **172** C5
Coulby Newham **111** E1
Coulderton **106** A2
Coull **168** C4
Coulport **140** D1
Coulsdon **30** B3
Coulston **26** A2
Coulter **134** B2
Coultershaw Bridge **16** B2
Coultings **23** F3
Coulton **111** F5
Coultra **152** B2
Cound **65** E2
Coundlane **65** E2
Coundon *Dur.* **120** B5
Coundon *W.Mid.* **67** F4
Countersett **109** E4
Countess Wear **10** C3
Countesthorpe **68** A3
Countisbury **22** A3
Coup Green **100** B5
Coupar Angus **160** A5
Coupland *Cumb.* **108** C1
Coupland *Northumb.* **136** D3
Cour **139** G5
Court Colman **37** E4
Court Henry **50** B5
Court House Green **67** F4
Court-at-Street **32** C5
Courteenhall **56** C2
Courtsend **46** D3
Courtway **23** F4
Cousland **144** A3
Cousley Wood **31** F5
Coustonn **140** B2
Cove *Arg. & B.* **140** D1
Cove *Devon* **10** C1
Cove *Hants.* **28** D2
Cove *High.* **180** A5
Cove *Sc.Bord.* **145** E2
Cove Bay **169** G4
Cove Bottom **73** F3
Covehithe **73** G3
Coven **66** B2
Coveney **70** C4
Covenham St. Bartholomew **96** D3
Covenham St. Mary **96** D3
Coventry **67** F5
Coventry Airport **67** F5
Coverack **3** E5
Coverham **110** A4
Covesea **176** D3
Covingham **41** D4
Covington *Cambs.* **69** F5
Covington *S.Lan.* **134** A2
Cowan Bridge **108** B5
Cowbeech **18** B2
Cowbit **70** A1
Cowbridge *Som.* **22** C3
Cowbridge *V. of Glam.* **37** F5
Cowden **31** D4
Cowden Pound **31** D4
Cowdenbeath **151** G5

Cowdenburn **143** G4
Cowers Lane **81** E3
Cowes **15** D3
Cowesby **111** D4
Cowesfield Green **27** D5
Cowey Green **60** B5
Cowfold **17** E1
Cowgill **108** C4
Cowie *Aber.* **161** G4
Cowie *Stir.* **142** C1
Cowlam Manor **104** B1
Cowley *Devon* **10** C3
Cowley *Glos.* **40** B1
Cowley *Gt.Lon.* **43** F4
Cowley *Oxon.* **42** A2
Cowling *Lancs.* **91** G1
Cowling *N.Yorks.* **101** F3
Cowling *N.Yorks.* **110** B4
Cowlinge **59** F2
Cowmes **93** F1
Cowpe **101** E5
Cowpen **129** E3
Cowpen Bewley **121** D5
Cowplain **15** F1
Cowsden **54** B2
Cowshill **119** E3
Cowthorpe **102** D2
Cox Common **73** E3
Coxbank **79** D3
Coxbench **81** E3
Coxbridge **24** C4
Coxford **85** G5
Coxheath **31** G3
Coxhoe **120** C4
Coxley **24** C3
Coxley Wick **24** C3
Coxpark **7** E3
Coxtie Green **45** E3
Coxwold **111** E5
Coychurch **37** F5
Coylet **140** C1
Coylton **132** C4
Coylumbridge **166** D3
Coynach **168** B4
Coynachie **168** B1
Coytrahen **37** E4
Crabbet Park **30** C5
Crabgate **86** B3
Crabtree *Plym.* **8** B2
Crabtree *S.Yorks.* **94** A4
Crabtree *W.Suss.* **17** E1
Crabtree Green **78** A3
Crackaig **138** D3
Crackenthorpe **118** C5
Crackington **6** B1
Crackington Haven **6** B1
Crackley **79** E2
Crackleybank **65** G1
Crackpot **109** E3
Crackthorn Corner **72** B4
Cracoe **101** F1
Craddock **11** D3
Cradley *Here.* **53** G3
Cradley *W.Mid.* **66** B4
Cradley Heath **66** B4
Crafthole **7** D5
Crafton **43** D1
Cragg **101** G5
Cragg Hill **102** B4
Craggan *Moray* **167** F1
Craggan *P. & K.* **150** D3
Cragganmore **167** F1
Cragganruar **158** B5
Craggie *High.* **166** B1
Craggie *High.* **183** D3
Craghead **120** B2
Craibstone *Aberdeen* **169** F3
Craibstone *Moray* **177** D5
Craichie **160** D5
Craig *Arg. & B.* **148** C1
Craig *Arg. & B.* **147** E1
Craig *D. & G.* **124** A4
Craig *High.* **172** A3
Craig *High.* **172** D5
Craig *S.Ayr.* **132** B5
Craig Berthlŵyd **37** G3
Craigans **148** A5
Craigbeg **157** G2
Craig-cefn-parc **36** C2
Craigcleuch **126** B3
Craigculter **179** E2
Craigdallie **152** A2
Craigdam **169** F1
Craigdarroch *D. & G.* **124** B1
Craigdarroch *E.Ayr.* **133** E5

Craigdhu *D. & G.* **115** D2
Craigdhu *High.* **174** A5
Craigearn **169** E3
Craigellachie **176** B5
Craigellie **179** F1
Craigencallie **123** G3
Craigend *Moray* **176** A4
Craigend *P. & K.* **151** G2
Craigendive **140** B1
Craigendoran **141** E1
Craigengillan **132** C5
Craigenputtock **124** B2
Craigens **138** A3
Craigglas **148** A5
Craighall **152** C3
Craighat **141** F1
Craighead *Fife* **153** E3
Craighead *High.* **175** D3
Craighlaw **123** E4
Craighouse **138** D3
Craigie *Aber.* **169** G3
Craigie *Dundee* **152** C3
Craigie *P. & K.* **159** G5
Craigie *S.Ayr.* **132** C3
Craigie Brae **169** F1
Craigieburn **125** G5
Craigieholm **152** A1
Craigielaw **144** B2
Craiglockhart **143** G2
Craiglug **169** F5
Craigmaud **179** D2
Craigmillar **143** G2
Craigmore **140** C3
Craigmyle House **168** D4
Craignafeoch **140** A2
Craignant **77** F4
Craignavie **150** A1
Craigneil **122** C2
Craigneuk **142** B4
Craignure **147** G1
Craigo **161** E3
Craigoch **132** A5
Craigow **151** F4
Craigrothie **152** B3
Craigton *Aberdeen* **169** F4
Craigton *Angus* **152** D1
Craigton *Angus* **160** B4
Craigton *High.* **174** C5
Craigton *Stir.* **142** A1
Craigtown **186** A3
Craig-y-nos **37** E1
Craik *Aber.* **168** B2
Craik *Sc.Bord.* **135** E5
Crail **153** E4
Crailing **136** A4
Crailinghall **136** A4
Crakehill **110** D5
Crakemarsh **80** B4
Crambe **103** F3
Cramlington **129** E4
Cramond **143** F2
Cranage **79** E1
Cranberry **79** F4
Cranborne **13** G1
Cranbourne **43** E4
Cranbrook *Gt.Lon.* **44** D4
Cranbrook *Kent* **31** G5
Cranbrook Common **31** G5
Crane Moor **94** A2
Cranfield **57** E2
Cranford *Devon* **20** D3
Cranford *Gt.Lon.* **44** A5
Cranford St. Andrew **69** E5
Cranford St. John **69** E5
Cranham *Glos.* **40** A1
Cranham *Gt.Lon.* **45** E4
Crank **91** G3
Cranleigh **29** F3
Cranmer Green **72** B4
Cranmore *I.o.W.* **14** C4
Cranmore *Som.* **25** D3
Cranna **177** F4
Crannoch **177** D4
Cranoe **68** C3
Cransford **61** E1
Cranshaws **145** D3
Cranstal **98** C1
Crantock **4** B3
Cranwell **83** F3
Cranwich **71** F3
Cranworth **86** A5
Craobh Haven **147** G4

Crapstone 8 B1
Crarae 148 B5
Crask Inn 182 A2
Crask of Aigas 174 A5
Craskins 168 C4
Craster 137 G5
Craswall 52 B4
Crateford 66 B2
Cratfield 73 E4
Crathes 169 E5
Crathie Aber. 167 G5
Crathie High. 165 G5
Crathorne 110 D2
Craven Arms 64 D4
Craw 139 G5
Crawcrook 120 A1
Crawford Lancs. 91 F2
Crawford S.Lan. 134 A3
Crawfordjohn 133 G3
Crawfordton 124 B1
Crawick 133 F4
Crawley Devon 11 E2
Crawley Hants. 27 F4
Crawley Oxon. 41 F1
Crawley W.Suss. 30 B5
Crawley Down 30 C5
Crawleyside 119 F3
Crawshawbooth 101 E5
Crawton 161 G2
Crawyn 98 B2
Cray N.Yorks. 109 E5
Cray P. & K. 159 G3
Cray Powys 51 E5
Crayford 45 E5
Crayke 111 E5
Crays Hill 45 G3
Cray's Pond 42 B4
Crazies Hill 42 C4
Creacombe 10 B1
Creagan 156 B5
Creagbheitheachain 156 B3
Creagorry 188 B2
Creamore Bank 78 C4
Creaton 68 C5
Creca 126 A4
Credenhill 53 D3
Crediton 10 B2
Creebridge 123 F4
Creech Heathfield 23 F5
Creech St. Michael 23 F5
Creed 4 D5
Creedy Park 10 B2
Creekmouth 45 D4
Creeting St. Mary 60 B2
Creeton 83 F5
Creetown 123 F5
Creggans 148 C4
Cregneash 98 A5
Cregrina 52 A2
Creich 152 B2
Creigiau 39 D3
Creigiau 37 G4
Crelevan 165 E1
Crelly 3 D3
Cremyll 8 A2
Crendell 13 G1
Cressage 65 E2
Cressbrook 93 F5
Cresselly 35 D2
Cressing 59 F5
Cresswell Northumb. 129 E2
Cresswell Staffs. 79 G4
Cresswell Quay 35 D2
Creswell 94 C5
Cretingham 60 D2
Cretshengan 139 F3
Crewe C. & W.Ches. 78 B2
Crewe Ches.E. 79 E2
Crewe Green 79 E2
Crewgreen 64 C1
Crewkerne 12 A2
Crew's Hole 39 F5
Crewton 81 E4
Crianlarich
(A' Chrìon-Làraich) 149 F2
Cribbs Causeway 39 E4
Cribyn 50 B2
Criccieth 75 D4
Crich 81 E2
Crich Carr 81 E2
Crich Common 81 E2
Crichie 179 E3
Crichton 144 A3
Crick Mon. 39 D3
Crick Northants. 68 A5
Crickadarn 51 G3

Cricket Hill 28 D1
Cricket St. Thomas 11 G2
Crickham 24 B3
Crickheath 77 F5
Cricklade 40 D3
Cricklewood 44 B4
Crick's Green 53 F2
Criddlestyle 14 A1
Cridling Stubbs 103 E5
Cneff 151 D2
Criftins (Dudleston Heath) 78 A4
Criggan 5 E3
Criggion 64 B1
Crigglestone 94 A1
Crimble 92 C1
Crimchard 11 G2
Crimdon Park 121 D4
Crimond 179 F2
Crimonmogate 179 F2
Crimplesham 71 E2
Crinan 147 G5
Crinan Ferry 147 G5
Cringleford 86 C5
Cringletie 143 G5
Crinow 35 E1
Cripplestyle 13 G1
Cripp's Corner 18 C1
Crix 45 G1
Crizeley 52 D4
Croalchapel 124 D1
Croasdale 117 D5
Crock Street 11 G1
Crockenhill 31 E2
Crocker End 42 C4
Crockerhill 15 E2
Crockernwell 10 A3
Crockerton 25 F3
Crockerton Green 25 F3
Crocketford (Ninemile Bar) 124 C3
Crockey Hill 103 F3
Crockham Hill 30 D3
Crockhurst Street 31 F4
Crockleford Heath 60 B5
Croes Hywel 38 C1
Croesau Bach 77 F5
Croeserw 37 E3
Croesgoch 48 B4
Croes-lan 49 G3
Croesor 75 F3
Croespenmaen 38 A3
Croesyceiliog Carmar. 36 A1
Croesyceiliog Torfaen 38 C3
Croes-y-mwyalch 38 C3
Croes-y-pant 38 C2
Croesywaun 75 E2
Croford 23 E5
Croft Here. 53 D1
Croft Leics. 68 A3
Croft Lincs. 84 D1
Croft Warr. 92 A3
Croftamie 141 F1
Crofthead 126 B4
Croftmore 159 D3
Crofton W.Yorks. 94 A1
Crofton Wilts. 27 D1
Croft-on-Tees 110 B2
Crofts 124 B3
Crofts of Benachielt 183 G1
Crofts of Buinach 176 A4
Crofts of Haddo 169 F1
Crofty 36 B3
Crogen 76 D4
Croggan 147 G2
Croglin 118 B3
Croick High. 181 G5
Croick High. 186 A3
Croig 154 D4
Croit e Caley 98 A5
Cromarty (Cromba) 175 D3
Crombie 143 E1
Crombie Mill 152 D1
Cromblet 89 E1
Cromdale 167 E2
Cromer Herts. 58 A5
Cromer Norf. 86 A5
Cromford 81 D2
Cromhall 39 F3
Cromhall Common 39 F4
Crompton Fold 93 D1
Cromwell 82 C1
Cronberry 133 G3
Crondall 28 C3

Cronk-y-Voddy 98 B3
Cronton 91 F4
Crook Cumb. 107 F3
Crook Dur. 120 A4
Crook of Devon 151 F4
Crooked Soley 41 F5
Crookedholm 132 C2
Crookham Northumb. 136 D3
Crookham W.Berks. 27 G1
Crookham Eastfield 136 D3
Crookham Village 28 C2
Crooklands 107 G4
Cropredy 55 G3
Cropston 68 A1
Cropthorne 54 B3
Cropton 111 G4
Cropwell Bishop 82 B4
Cropwell Butler 82 B4
Crosbie 140 D5
Crosbost 189 G3
Crosby Cumb. 117 D3
Crosby I.o.M. 98 B4
Crosby Mersey. 91 E3
Crosby N.Lincs. 95 F1
Crosby Court 110 C3
Crosby Garrett 108 C2
Crosby Ravensworth 108 B1
Crosby Villa 117 D3
Crosby-on-Eden 118 A2
Croscombe 24 C3
Crosemere 78 B5
Crosland Hill 93 F1
Cross 24 B2
Cross Ash 38 D1
Cross Bank 65 G5
Cross End Beds. 57 F2
Cross End Essex 59 G4
Cross Foxes Inn 63 D1
Cross Gates 102 C4
Cross Green Devon 7 D2
Cross Green Staffs. 66 B2
Cross Green Suff. 60 A2
Cross Green Suff. 59 G2
Cross Green Suff. 59 G2
Cross Hands Carmar. 36 B1
Cross Hands Pembs. 35 D1
Cross Hill 81 F3
Cross Hills 101 G3
Cross Houses 65 E2
Cross in Hand 18 A1
Cross Inn Cere. 49 G2
Cross Inn Cere. 50 B1
Cross Inn R.C.T. 37 G4
Cross Keys 40 A5
Cross Lane 15 E3
Cross Lane Head 65 G3
Cross Lanes Cornw. 4 B5
Cross Lanes Cornw. 3 D4
Cross Lanes N.Yorks. 103 E1
Cross Lanes Wrex. 78 A3
Cross of Jackston 169 E1
Cross o'th'hands 81 D3
Cross Street 72 C4
Crossaig 139 G4
Crossapol 154 A4
Crossapoll 154 A2
Cross-at-Hand 31 G4
Crossbush 16 C3
Crosscanonby 117 D3
Crossdale Street 86 D2
Crossens 91 E1
Crossflatts 102 A3
Crossford D. & G. 124 C2
Crossford Fife 143 E1
Crossford S.Lan. 142 C5
Crossgate Lincs. 84 A5
Crossgate Staffs. 79 G4
Crossgatehall 144 A3
Crossgates Fife 143 F1
Crossgates N.Yorks. 112 D4
Crossgates P. & K. 151 F2
Crossgates Powys 51 G1
Crossgill 100 B1
Crosshands 132 C2
Crosshill Fife 151 G5
Crosshill S.Ayr. 132 B5
Crosshouse 132 B2
Crosskeys 38 B3
Crosskirk 186 C1
Crosslanes 64 C1
Crosslee Renf. 141 F3

Crosslee Sc.Bord. 135 E4
Crossmichael 124 B4
Crossmoor 100 A4
Crossroads Aber. 169 E5
Crossroads E.Ayr. 132 C2
Crossway Mon. 38 D1
Crossway Powys 51 G2
Crossway Green Mon. 39 E3
Crossway Green Worcs. 54 A1
Crossways Dorset 13 D4
Crossways Glos. 39 E1
Crosswell 49 E4
Crosthwaite 107 F3
Croston 91 F1
Crostwick 87 D4
Crostwight 87 E3
Crouch 31 F3
Crouch End 44 B4
Crouch Hill 12 D1
Croucheston 25 B5
Croughton 56 A4
Crovie 178 D2
Crow 14 A2
Crow Edge 93 F2
Crow Green 45 E3
Crow Hill 53 F5
Crowan 2 D3
Crowborough 31 E5
Crowborough Warren 31 E5
Crowcombe 23 E4
Crowdecote 80 C1
Crowden 93 E3
Crowdhill 27 F5
Crowell 42 C3
Crowfield Northants. 56 B3
Crowfield Suff. 60 C2
Crowhurst E.Suss. 18 C3
Crowhurst Surr. 30 C4
Crowhurst Lane End 30 C4
Crowland Lincs. 70 A1
Crowland Suff. 72 B4
Crowlas 2 C3
Crowle N.Lincs. 95 E1
Crowle Worcs. 54 B2
Crowle Green 54 B2
Crowmarsh Gifford 42 B4
Crown Corner 73 D4
Crownhill 8 A2
Crownthorpe 86 B5
Crowntown 2 D3
Crow's Nest 5 G3
Crows-an-wra 2 A4
Crowsnest 64 C2
Crowthorne 28 D1
Crowton 91 G5
Croxall 67 E1
Croxby 96 B3
Croxdale 120 B4
Croxden 80 B4
Croxley Green 43 F3
Croxton Cambs. 58 A2
Croxton N.Lincs. 96 A1
Croxton Norf. 71 G4
Croxton Staffs. 79 E4
Croxton Green 78 C2
Croxton Kerrial 82 D5
Croxtonbank 79 E4
Croy High. 175 D5
Croy N.Lan. 142 B2
Croyde 21 E2
Croyde Bay 21 E2
Croydon Cambs. 58 A3
Croydon Gt.Lon. 30 C2
Cruach 138 B4
Cruchie 177 E5
Cruckmeole 64 D2
Cruckton 64 D1
Cruden Bay 179 F4
Crudgington 65 F1
Crudwell 40 B3
Crug 64 A5
Crugmeer 4 D2
Crugybar 50 C4
Crùlabhig 189 F2
Crumlin 38 B3
Crumpsall 92 C2
Crumpsbrook 65 F5
Crundale Kent 32 C4
Crundale Pembs. 35 C1
Crunwere Farm 35 E1
Crutherland Farm 142 A4
Cruwys Morchard 10 B1
Crux Easton 27 F2
Crwbin 36 A1

Cryers Hill 43 D3
Crymlyn 89 E5
Crymych 49 E4
Crynant 37 D2
Crystal Palace 44 C5
Cuaig 172 A4
Cubbington 55 F1
Cubert 8 A4
Cubley 93 G2
Cublington Bucks. 56 D5
Cublington Here. 52 D4
Cuckfield 17 F1
Cucklington 25 E5
Cuckney 24 C5
Cuckold's Green 73 F3
Cuckoo Bridge 84 A5
Cuckoo's Corner 28 C3
Cuckoo's Nest 78 A1
Cuddesdon 42 A2
Cuddington Bucks. 42 C1
Cuddington C. & W.Ches. 91 G5
Cuddington Heath 78 B3
Cuddy Hill 100 A4
Cudham 30 D3
Cudliptown 7 F3
Cudworth S.Yorks. 94 A2
Cudworth Som. 11 G1
Cuerdley Cross 91 G4
Cuffley 44 C2
Cuidrach 170 C4
Cuilmuich 149 D5
Cuil-uaine 148 B1
Culag 149 F5
Culbo 174 C3
Culbokie (Cùil Bhàicidh) 174 C3
Culbone 22 B3
Culburnie 174 A5
Culcabock 174 C5
Culcharan 148 B1
Culcharry 175 E4
Culcheth 92 A3
Culdrain 168 C1
Culduie 172 A5
Culford 59 G1
Culfordheath 71 G5
Culgaith 118 C5
Culgower 183 E3
Culham 42 A3
Culindrach 140 A4
Culkein 180 C1
Culkerton 40 B3
Cullachie 167 D2
Cullen 177 E3
Cullercoats 129 F4
Cullicudden 174 C3
Culligran 173 G5
Cullingworth 101 G4
Cullipool 147 G3
Cullivoe 191 F1
Culloch 150 C3
Culloden 174 D5
Cullompton 10 D2
Culmaily 182 D5
Culmalzie 123 E5
Culmington 65 D4
Culmstock 11 E1
Culnacraig 180 C2
Culnadalloch 148 B1
Culnaknock 171 E3
Culnamean 162 C2
Culpho 60 D3
Culquhirk 123 F5
Culrain 182 A5
Culross 143 D1
Culroy 132 B4
Culsh 168 A5
Culshabbin 123 E5
Culswick 191 E4
Culter Allers Farm 134 B2
Cultercullen 169 G2
Cults Aber. 168 B1
Cults Aberdeen 169 F4
Cults D. & G. 123 F5
Cultybraggan Camp 150 C3
Culverhouse Cross 38 A5
Culverstone Green 31 F2
Culverthorpe 83 F3
Culvie 177 E4
Culworth 56 A3
Cumberhead 133 F2
Cumberlow Green 58 B4
Cumbernauld 142 B2
Cumberworth 97 F5
Cuminestown 178 D3
Cumloden 123 F4
Cummersdale 117 G2

Cummertrees 125 F4
Cummingstown 176 A3
Cumnock 133 D3
Cumnor 41 G2
Cumrew 118 B2
Cumrue 125 E2
Cumstoun 124 A5
Cumwhinton 118 A2
Cumwhitton 118 B2
Cundall 110 B3
Cunninghamhead 141 E5
Cunningsburgh 191 F5
Cunnoquhie 152 B3
Cupar 152 B3
Cupar Muir 152 B3
Curbar 93 G5
Curborough 66 D1
Curbridge Hants. 15 E1
Curbridge Oxon. 41 F2
Curdridge 15 E1
Curdworth 67 D3
Curland 11 F1
Curlew Green 61 E1
Curling Tye Green 46 B2
Curload 24 A5
Curridge 41 G5
Currie 143 F3
Curry Mallet 24 A5
Curry Rivel 24 A5
Curteis' Corner 32 A5
Curtisden Green 31 G4
Curtisknowle 8 D2
Cury 3 D4
Cusgarne 4 B5
Cushnie 177 G3
Cushuish 23 E4
Cusop 52 B3
Cusworth 94 C2
Cutcloy 115 E3
Cutcombe 22 C4
Cutgate 92 C1
Cuthill 175 D1
Cutiau 62 C1
Cutlers Green 59 D4
Cutnall Green 54 A1
Cutsdean 54 C4
Cutsyke 102 D5
Cutthorpe 94 A5
Cuttyhill 179 F2
Cuxham 42 B3
Cuxton 31 G2
Cuxwold 96 B2
Cwm B.Gwent 38 A2
Cwm Denb. 90 B5
Cwm Ffrwd-oer 38 B2
Cwm Gwaun 48 D4
Cwm Head 64 D4
Cwm Irfon 51 E3
Cwm Penmachno 76 A3
Cwm Plysgog 49 E3
Cwmafan 37 D3
Cwmaman 37 G3
Cwmann 50 B3
Cwmbach Carmar. 49 F5
Cwmbach Carmar. 36 A2
Cwmbach Powys 52 A4
Cwmbach Powys 51 G2
Cwmbach R.C.T. 37 G2
Cwmbelan 38 B3
Cwmbrân 38 B3
Cwmbrwyno 62 D4
Cwmcarn 38 B3
Cwmcarvan 39 D2
Cwm-Cewydd 63 E1
Cwm-cou 49 F3
Cwmcrawnon 38 A1
Cwmdare 37 F2
Cwmdu Carmar. 50 C4
Cwmdu Powys 52 A5
Cwmduad 49 G4
Cwmerfyn 62 D4
Cwmfelin 37 G2
Cwmfelin Boeth 35 E1
Cwmfelin Mynach 49 E5
Cwmfelinfach 38 A3
Cwmffrwd 36 A1
Cwmgiedd 37 D1
Cwmgors 36 D1
Cwmgwili 36 B1
Cwmgwrach 37 E2
Cwmgwyn 36 C3
Cwmhiraeth 49 G4
Cwmifor 50 C5
Cwmisfael 36 A1
Cwm-Llinau 63 E2
Cwmllyfri 35 G1
Cwmllynfell 36 D1
Cwm-mawr 36 B1
Cwm-miles 49 E5

Cwm-Morgan 49 F4
Cwm-parc 37 F3
Cwmpengraig 49 G4
Cwmpennar 37 G2
Cwmsychbant 50 A3
Cwmsymlog 62 G4
Cwmtillery 38 B2
Cwm-twrch Isaf 37 D1
Cwm-twrch Uchaf 37 D1
Cwm-y-glo 75 E1
Cwmyoy 52 C5
Cwm-yr-Eglwys 48 D3
Cwmyrhaiadr 63 D3
Cwmystwyth 63 D5
Cwrt 62 C2
Cwrt-newydd 50 A3
Cwrt-y-cadno 50 C3
Cwrt-y-gollen 38 B1
Cyffylliog 77 D2
Cyfronydd 64 A2
Cymau 77 F2
Cymmer N.P.T. 37 E3
Cymmer R.C.T. 37 G3
Cyncoed 38 A4
Cynghordy 51 E4
Cynheidre 36 A2
Cynwyd 77 D3
Cynwyl Elfed 49 G5

D

Dabton 124 C1
Daccombe 9 F1
Dacre Cumb. 118 A5
Dacre N.Yorks. 102 A1
Dacre Banks 102 A1
Dadford 56 B4
Dadlington 67 G3
Dafen 36 B2
Daffy Green 86 A5
Dagdale 80 B4
Dagenham 45 D4
Daggons 14 A1
Daglingworth 40 B2
Dagnall 43 E1
Dail 148 C1
Dailly 132 A5
Dailnamac 148 B1
Dainton 9 E1
Dairsie (Osnaburgh) 152 C3
Dairy House 105 E5
Daisy Bank 66 C3
Daisy Green 60 B1
Dalabrog 188 B4
Dalavich 148 B3
Dalballoch 166 A5
Dalbeattie 124 C4
Dalblair 133 E4
Dalbog 161 D2
Dalbreck 182 C3
Dalbury 81 D4
Dalby I.o.M. 98 A4
Dalby Lincs. 84 C1
Dalby N.Yorks. 111 F5
Dalcairnie 132 C5
Dalchalloch 158 C3
Dalchalm 183 E4
Dalchenna 148 C4
Dalchirach 167 F1
Dalchork 182 A3
Dalchreichart 165 D3
Dalchruin 150 C3
Dalcross 175 D5
Dalderby 84 A1
Dalditch 10 D4
Daldownie 167 G4
Dale Cumb. 118 B3
Dale Gt.Man. 93 D2
Dale Pembs. 34 B2
Dale Abbey 81 F4
Dale End Derbys. 80 D1
Dale End N.Yorks. 101 F3
Dale Head 107 F1
Dale Park 16 B2
Dalehouse 111 G1
Dalelia 155 G3
Daless 166 C1
Dalestie 167 F3
Dalfad 168 A4
Dalganachan 186 C4
Dalgarven 141 D5
Dalgety Bay 143 F1
Dalgig 133 D4
Dalginross 150 C2
Dalgonar 133 F5
Dalguise 159 E5
Dalhalvaig 186 A3

Dalham 59 F1
Daligan 141 E1
Dalinlongart 140 C1
Dalivaddy 130 B3
Daljarrock 122 C2
Dalkeith 144 A3
Dallachulish 156 B5
Dallas 176 A4
Dallaschyle 175 E5
Dallash 123 F4
Dalleagles 133 D4
Dallinghoo 61 D2
Dallington E.Suss. 18 B2
Dallington Northants. 56 C1
Dallow 110 A5
Dalmadilly 169 E3
Dalmally (Dail Mhàilidh) 149 D2
Dalmarnock 159 F5
Dalmary 150 A5
Dalmellington 132 C5
Dalmeny 143 F2
Dalmichy 182 A3
Dalmigavie 166 B3
Dalmore 174 C3
Dalmuir 141 F2
Dalmunzie House Hotel 159 F2
Dalnabreck 155 G3
Dalnacarn 159 F3
Dalnaglar Castle 159 G3
Dalnaha 147 F2
Dalnahaitnach 166 C3
Dalnamain 182 C5
Dalnatrat (Dail na Tràghad) 156 B4
Dalnavert 166 C4
Dalnavie 174 C2
Dalness 157 D4
Dalnessie 182 B3
Dalnigap 122 C3
Dalqueich 151 F4
Dalreoch 122 C2
Dalriech 150 C1
Dalroy 175 D5
Dalrulzian 159 G4
Dalry 141 D5
Dalrymple 132 B4
Dalscote 56 B2
Dalserf 142 B4
Dalshangan 123 G2
Dalskairth 124 C3
Dalston 117 G1
Dalswinton 124 D2
Daltomach 166 B2
Dalton Cumb. 107 G5
Dalton D. & G. 125 F3
Dalton Lancs. 91 F2
Dalton N.Yorks. 110 D5
Dalton N.Yorks. 110 A2
Dalton Northumb. 128 D4
Dalton Northumb. 119 F2
Dalton S.Yorks. 94 B3
Dalton Magna 94 B3
Dalton Piercy 121 D4
Dalton-in-Furness 106 D5
Dalton-le-Dale 120 D3
Dalton-on-Tees 110 B2
Daltote 139 F1
Daltra 175 F5
Dalveich 150 B2
Dalvennan 132 B4
Dalvourn 166 A1
Dalwhinnie 158 B3
Dalwood 11 F2
Dam Green 72 B3
Damask Green 58 A5
Damerham 14 A1
Damgate 87 F5
Damnaglaur 114 B3
Damside 151 E3
Danaway 32 A2
Danbury 45 G2
Danby 111 G2
Danby Wiske 110 C3
Dancers Hill 44 B3
Dandaleith 176 B5
Danderhall 144 A3
Dane Bank 92 D3
Dane End 58 B5
Dane Hills 68 A2
Danebridge 79 G1
Danehill 17 G1
Danesmoor 81 F1
Danestone 169 G3

Daniel's Water 32 B4
Danskine 144 C3
Danthorpe 105 E4
Danzey Green 54 D1
Darby End 66 B4
Darby Green 28 D1
Darenth 45 C4
Daresbury 91 G4
Darfield 94 B3
Dargate 32 C2
Dargues 128 A2
Dante 5 G3
Darland 31 G2
Darlaston 66 B3
Darley 102 B2
Darley Bridge 81 D1
Darley Dale 81 D1
Darley Head 102 A2
Darley Hillside 81 D1
Darlingscott 55 E3
Darlington 110 B1
Darliston 78 C4
Darlton 95 E5
Darnabo 177 G5
Darnall 94 A4
Darnconner 133 D3
Darnford 169 E5
Darngarroch 124 A4
Darnick 135 G2
Darowen 63 E2
Darra 177 G5
Darracott 20 C4
Darras Hall 129 D4
Darrington 94 B1
Darrow Green 73 D3
Darsham 61 F1
Dartfield 179 F2
Dartford 45 E5
Dartington 9 D1
Dartmeet 7 G3
Dartmouth 9 E2
Darton 94 A1
Darvel 133 D2
Darwell Hole 18 B2
Darwen 100 C5
Datchet 43 E5
Datchworth 44 B1
Datchworth Green 44 B1
Daubhill 92 A2
Daugh of Kinermony 176 B5
Dauntsey 40 B4
Dauntsey Green 40 B4
Dauntsey Lock 40 B4
Dava 167 E1
Davaar 130 C4
Davan 168 B4
Davenham 92 A5
Davenport Green 92 C4
Daventry 56 A1
Davidstow 5 F1
Davington 134 D5
Daviot Aber. 169 E2
Daviot High. 166 B1
Davoch of Grange 177 D4
Davyhulme 92 B3
Dawley 65 F2
Dawlish 10 C5
Dawn 89 G5
Daws Heath 46 B4
Daw's House 6 B2
Dawsmere 84 C4
Day Green 79 G4
Dayhills 79 G4
Dayhouse Bank 66 B5
Daylesford 55 E5
Ddôl 90 C5
Deadman's Cross 57 G3
Deadwaters 142 B5
Deaf Hill 120 C4
Deal 33 F3
Deal Hall 46 D3
Dean Cumb. 117 D4
Dean Devon 8 D1
Dean Dorset 13 F1
Dean Hants. 15 E1
Dean Oxon. 55 F5
Dean Som. 25 D3
Dean Bank 120 B4
Dean Cross 21 F1
Dean Head 93 G3
Dean Prior 8 D1
Dean Row 92 C4
Dean Street 31 G3
Deanburnhaugh 135 E4
Deane Gt.Man. 92 A2
Deane Hants. 27 G2
Deanland 13 F1

Deanlane End 15 G1
Deans Bottom 32 A2
Deanscales 117 D4
Deansgreen 92 A4
Deanshanger 56 C4
Deanston 150 C4
Dearham 117 D3
Debach 60 D2
Debden 59 D4
Debden Cross 59 D4
Debden Green Essex 59 D4
Debden Green Essex 44 D3
Debenham 60 C1
Deblin's Green 54 A3
Dechmont 143 E2
Decker Hill 65 G1
Deddington 55 E3
Dedham 60 B4
Dedham Heath 60 B4
Dedworth 43 E5
Deecastle 168 B5
Deene 69 E3
Deenethorpe 69 E3
Deepcar 93 G3
Deepcut 29 E2
Deepdale Cumb. 108 C4
Deepdale N.Yorks. 109 D5
Deeping Gate 69 G2
Deeping St. James 69 G2
Deeping St. Nicholas 70 A1
Deepweir 39 D4
Deerhill 177 D4
Deerhurst 54 A5
Deerhurst Walton 54 A5
Deerton Street 32 B2
Defford 54 B3
Defynnog 51 F5
Deganwy 89 F5
Degnish 147 G3
Deighton N.Yorks. 110 C2
Deighton W.Yorks. 93 F1
Deighton York 103 F3
Deiniolen 75 E1
Delabole 5 E1
Delamere 78 C1
Delavorar 167 E2
Delfrigs 169 G2
Dell Lodge 167 E1
Dell Quay 16 A3
Delliefure 167 E1
Delly End 41 F1
Delnabo 167 F3
Delny 174 D2
Delph 93 D2
Delphorrie 168 B3
Delves 20 C2
Delvine 159 G5
Dembleby 83 F4
Denaby 94 B3
Denaby Main 94 B3
Denbigh (Dinbych) 76 D1
Denbury 9 E1
Denby 81 E3
Denby Dale 93 G2
Denchworth 41 F3
Dendron 106 D5
Denend 168 D1
Denford 69 E5
Dengie 46 C2
Denham Bucks. 43 F4
Denham Suff. 72 C4
Denham Suff. 59 F1
Denham Green 43 F4
Denham Street 72 C4
Denhead Aber. 169 E3
Denhead Aber. 179 F2
Denhead Fife 153 D3
Denhead of Arbirlot 161 D5
Denhead of Gray 152 B1
Denholm 135 G4
Denholme 101 G4
Denholme Clough 101 G4
Denio 74 C4
Denmead 15 F1
Denmill 169 F3
Denmoss 177 G5
Dennington 61 D1
Denny 142 C1
Dennyloanhead 142 C1
Denshaw 93 D1
Denside 169 F5
Densole 33 E4
Denston 59 F2

Denstone 80 B3
Dent 108 C4
Denton Cambs. 69 G4
Denton Darl. 110 B1
Denton E.Suss. 17 G3
Denton Gt.Man. 92 D3
Denton Kent 33 E4
Denton Kent 45 F5
Denton Lincs. 83 D4
Denton N.Yorks. 102 A3
Denton Norf. 73 D3
Denton Northants. 56 D2
Denton Oxon. 42 A2
Denton's Green 91 F3
Denver 71 E2
Denvilles 15 G2
Denwick 137 G5
Deopham 86 B5
Deopham Green 72 B2
Depden 59 F2
Depden Green 59 F2
Deptford Gt.Lon. 44 C5
Deptford Wilts. 26 B4
Derby 81 E4
Derbyhaven 98 A5
Dereham (East Dereham) 86 A4
Dererach 147 E2
Deri 20 D5
Derril 20 D5
Derringstone 33 E4
Derrington 79 F5
Derriton 20 D5
Derry 150 B2
Derry Hill 40 B5
Derrythorpe 95 F2
Dersingham 85 E4
Dervaig 154 D4
Derwen 77 D2
Derwenlas 62 D3
Derwydd 38 C1
Derybruich 140 A2
Desborough 68 D4
Desford 67 G2
Detchant 137 E3
Dethick 81 E2
Detling 31 G3
Deuddwr 64 B1
Deunant 76 C1
Deuxhill 65 F4
Devauden 39 D3
Devil's Bridge (Pontarfynach) 62 D5
Devitts Green 67 E3
Devizes 26 B1
Devonport 8 A2
Devonside 151 E5
Devoran 3 E3
Dewar 144 A5
Dewlish 13 D3
Dewsall Court 53 D4
Dewsbury 102 B5
Dewsbury Moor 102 B5
Dhiseig 147 D1
Dhoon 98 C3
Dhoor 98 C2
Dhowin 98 C1
Dhuhallow 165 F4
Dial Green 29 E5
Dial Post 17 D2
Dibden 14 C2
Dibden Hill 43 E3
Dibden Purlieu 14 D2
Dickleburgh 72 D3
Dickleburgh Moor 72 C3
Didbrook 54 C4
Didcot 42 A3
Diddington 57 G1
Diddlebury 65 E4
Didley 53 D4
Didling 16 A2
Didmarton 40 A4
Didsbury 92 C3
Didworthy 8 C1
Digby 83 F2
Digg 171 D3
Diggle 93 E2
Digmoor 91 F2
Digswell 44 B1
Dihewyd 50 A2
Dildawn 124 B5
Dilham 87 E3
Dilhorne 79 G3
Dillington 57 G1
Dilston 119 F1
Dilton Marsh 25 F3
Dilwyn 52 D2
Dilwyn Common 52 D2
Dimple 92 B1

Dinas Carmar. 50 C4
Dinas Gwyn. 75 D2
Dinas Gwyn. 74 B4
Dinas Cross 48 D4
Dinas Dinlle 74 D2
Dinas Powys 38 A5
Dinas-Mawddwy 63 E1
Dinckley 100 C4
Dinder 24 C7
Dinedor 53 E4
Dingestow 39 D1
Dingley 68 C4
Dingwall (Inbhir Pheofharain) 174 B4
Dinlabyre 126 D2
Dinnet 168 B5
Dinnington S.Yorks. 94 C4
Dinnington Som. 12 A1
Dinnington T. & W. 129 E4
Dinorwig 75 E1
Dinton Bucks. 42 C1
Dinton Wilts. 26 B4
Dinvin 122 A3
Dinwoodie Mains 125 F1
Dinworthy 20 C3
Dipford 23 F5
Dippen Arg. & B. 130 C2
Dippen N.Ayr. 131 F3
Dippenhall 28 D3
Dipple Moray 176 C4
Dipple S.Ayr. 132 A5
Diptford 8 D2
Dipton 120 A2
Dirdhu 167 E2
Dirleton 144 C1
Discoed 52 B1
Diseworth 81 F5
Dishforth 110 C5
Dishley 81 F5
Disley 93 D4
Diss 72 C3
Disserth 51 G2
Distington 116 D4
Ditcheat 24 D4
Ditchingham 73 E2
Ditchley 55 F5
Ditchling 17 F2
Ditteridge 25 F1
Dittisham 9 E2
Ditton Halton 91 F4
Ditton Kent 31 G2
Ditton Green 59 E2
Ditton Priors 65 F4
Dixton Glos. 54 B4
Dixton Mon. 39 E1
Dobcross 93 D2
Dobwalls 5 G3
Doccombe 10 A4
Dochgarroch 166 A1
Dockenfield 28 D3
Docker Cumb. 107 G3
Docker Lancs. 107 G5
Docking 85 F4
Docklow 53 E2
Dockray Cumb. 117 G4
Dockray Cumb. 117 F1
Dodbrooke 8 D3
Doddenham 53 G2
Doddinghurst 45 E3
Doddington Cambs. 70 C3
Doddington Kent 32 B3
Doddington Lincs. 95 E5
Doddington Northumb. 137 D3
Doddington Shrop. 65 F5
Doddiscombsleigh 10 B4
Doddycross 6 D4
Dodford Northants. 56 B1
Dodford Worcs. 66 B5
Dodington S.Glos. 39 G4
Dodington Som. 23 S3
Dodington Ash 39 G5
Dodleston 78 A1
Dods Leigh 80 B4
Dodscott 21 F4
Dodworth 94 A2
Doehole 81 E2
Doffcocker 92 A1
Dog Village 10 C3
Dogdyke 84 A2
Dogmersfield 28 C2
Dogsthorpe 70 A2
Dol Fawr 63 E2
Dolanog 63 G1
Dolau Powys 52 A1

Dolau *R.C.T.* **37** G4
Dolbenmaen **75** E3
Doley **79** E5
Dolfach **63** F5
Dolfor **64** A4
Dolgarreg **50** D4
Dolgarrog **76** A1
Dolgellau **62** D1
Dolgoch **62** C2
Dolgran **50** A4
Doll **183** D4
Dollar **151** E5
Dollarbeg **151** E5
Dolphin **90** C5
Dolphinholme **100** B2
Dolphinton **143** F5
Dolton **21** F4
Dolwen *Conwy* **89** G5
Dolwen *Powys* **63** F2
Dolwyddelan **76** A2
Dôl-y-bont **62** C4
Dol-y-cannau **52** A3
Dolyhir **52** B2
Dolywern **77** F4
Domgay **64** B1
Doncaster **94** C2
Donhead St. Andrew **26** A5
Donhead St. Mary **26** A5
Donibristle **143** F1
Doniford **23** D3
Donington *Lincs.* **84** A4
Donington *Shrop.* **66** A2
Donington le Heath **67** G1
Donington on Bain **96** C4
Donisthorpe **67** F1
Donna Nook **97** E3
Donnington *Glos.* **55** D5
Donnington *Here.* **53** G4
Donnington *Shrop.* **65** E2
Donnington *Tel. & W.* **65** G1
Donnington *W.Berks.* **27** F1
Donnington *W.Suss.* **16** A3
Donyatt **11** G1
Dorchester *Dorset* **12** C3
Dorchester *Oxon.* **42** A3
Dordon **67** E2
Dore **94** A4
Dores (Duras) **165** G1
Dorket Head **81** G3
Dorking **29** G3
Dorley's Corner **61** E1
Dormans Park **30** C4
Dormansland **30** D4
Dormanstown **121** E5
Dormer's Wells **44** A4
Dormington **53** E3
Dormston **54** B2
Dorn **55** E4
Dorney **43** E5
Dorney Reach **43** E5
Dornie (An Dòrnaidh) **163** G2
Dornoch **175** D1
Dornock **126** A5
Dorrery **186** C3
Dorridge **67** D5
Dorrington *Lincs.* **83** F2
Dorrington *Shrop.* **65** D2
Dorsell **168** C3
Dorsington **54** D3
Dorstone **52** C3
Dorton **42** B1
Dorusduain **164** A2
Dosthill **67** E3
Dotland **119** F2
Dottery **12** A3
Doublebois **5** F3
Dougalston **141** G2
Dougarie **131** D2
Doughton **40** A3
Douglas *I.o.M.* **98** B4
Douglas *S.Lan.* **133** G2
Douglas & Angus **152** C1
Douglas Water **133** G2
Douglastown **160** C3
Doulting **24** D3
Dounby **190** A2
Doune *Arg. & B.* **149** F5
Doune *Arg. & B.* **149** F3
Doune *High.* **166** C3
Doune *High.* **181** G4
Doune *Stir.* **150** C4
Dounepark **177** G3
Douneside **168** B4

Dounie *High.* **174** C1
Dounie *High.* **182** A5
Dounreay **186** D2
Dousland **8** B1
Dovaston **78** A5
Dove Holes **93** E5
Dovenby **117** D3
Dover **33** F4
Dovercourt **60** D4
Doverdale **54** A5
Doveridge **80** C4
Doversgreen **30** B4
Dowally **159** F5
Dowdeswell **54** C5
Dowhill **132** A5
Dowlais **37** G2
Dowland **21** F4
Dowlands **11** F3
Dowlish Ford **11** G1
Dowlish Wake **11** G1
Down Ampney **40** D3
Down End **24** A3
Down Hatherley **54** A5
Down St. Mary **10** A2
Down Thomas **8** B3
Downderry **6** D5
Downe **30** D2
Downend *I.o.W.* **15** E4
Downend *S.Glos.* **39** F5
Downend *W.Berks.* **41** G5
Downfield **152** B1
Downfields **71** E5
Downgate **7** D3
Downham *Essex* **45** G3
Downham *Lancs.* **101** D3
Downham *Northumb.* **136** C3
Downham Market **71** E2
Downhead *Cornw.* **5** G1
Downhead *Som.* **25** D3
Downhead *Som.* **24** C5
Downholland Cross **91** E2
Downholme **110** A3
Downies **169** G5
Downley **43** D3
Downs **38** A5
Downside *N.Som.* **24** B1
Downside *Som.* **24** D3
Downside *Som.* **24** D2
Downside *Surr.* **29** G2
Downton *Devon* **7** F2
Downton *Devon* **9** E2
Downton *Hants.* **14** B3
Downton *Wilts.* **26** C5
Downton on the Rock **64** D5
Dowsby **83** G5
Dowthwaitehead **117** G4
Doxey **79** G5
Doynton **39** G5
Drabblegate **86** D3
Draethen **38** B4
Draffan **142** B5
Dragley Beck **107** D5
Drakeland Corner **8** B2
Drakelow **66** A4
Drakemyre **141** D4
Drakes Broughton **54** B3
Drakes Cross **66** C5
Draughton *N.Yorks.* **101** G2
Draughton *Northants.* **68** C5
Drax **103** F5
Draycot Foliat **41** D5
Draycote **55** G1
Draycott *Derbys.* **81** F4
Draycott *Glos.* **55** D4
Draycott *Shrop.* **66** A3
Draycott *Som.* **24** B2
Draycott *Worcs.* **54** A3
Draycott in the Clay **80** C5
Draycott in the Moors **79** G4
Drayford **10** A1
Draynes **5** G3
Drayton *Leics.* **68** D3
Drayton *Lincs.* **84** A4
Drayton *Norf.* **86** C4
Drayton *Oxon.* **55** G3
Drayton *Oxon.* **41** G3
Drayton *Ports.* **15** F2
Drayton *Som.* **24** B5
Drayton *Warks.* **55** D2
Drayton *Worcs.* **66** B5
Drayton Bassett **67** D2

Drayton Beauchamp **43** E1
Drayton Parslow **56** D5
Drayton St. Leonard **42** A3
Drebley **101** G2
Dreemskerry **98** C2
Dreenhill **34** C1
Drefach *Carmar.* **49** G4
Drefach *Carmar.* **36** B1
Dre-fach *Cere.* **50** B3
Drefelin **49** G4
Dreghorn **132** B2
Drem **144** C2
Drewsteignton **10** A3
Driby **97** D5
Driffield *E.Riding* **104** C2
Driffield *Glos.* **40** C3
Drigg **106** B3
Drighlington **102** B5
Drimfern **148** C3
Drimlee **148** D3
Drimnin **155** E4
Drimpton **12** A2
Drimsynie **149** D4
Drimvore **148** A5
Drinan **162** D3
Dringhouses **103** E2
Drinkstone **60** A1
Drinkstone Green **60** A1
Drishaig **149** D3
Drissaig **148** B3
Drointon **80** B5
Droitwich Spa **54** A1
Dron **151** G3
Dronfield **94** A5
Dronfield Woodhouse **94** A5
Drongan **132** C4
Dronley **152** B1
Droop **12** D1
Dropmore **43** E4
Droxford **15** F1
Droylsden **92** D3
Druid **76** D3
Druidston **34** B1
Druimarbin **156** C2
Druimavuic **156** C5
Druimdrishaig **139** F2
Druimindarroch **155** F1
Druimkinnerras **165** F1
Drum *Arg. & B.* **140** A2
Drum *P. & K.* **151** F4
Drumachloy **140** B3
Drumbeg **180** D1
Drumblade **177** E5
Drumblair **177** F5
Drumbuie *D. & G.* **133** F4
Drumbuie *High.* **163** F1
Drumburgh **117** F1
Drumchapel **141** G2
Drumchardine **174** B5
Drumchork **172** B1
Drumclog **133** E2
Drumdelgie **177** D5
Drumeldrie **152** C4
Drumelzier **134** C2
Drumfearn **163** E3
Drumfern **156** B2
Drumgarve **130** C3
Drumgley **160** C4
Drumguish **166** B5
Drumhead **168** D5
Drumin **167** F1
Drumine **175** D4
Drumjohn **123** G1
Drumlamford House **123** D3
Drumlasie **168** D4
Drumlemble **130** B4
Drumlithie **161** F1
Drummond *High.* **174** C3
Drummond *Stir.* **150** B4
Drummore **114** B3
Drummuir **176** C5
Drummuir Castle **176** C5
Drumnadrochit (Druim na Drochaid) **165** G2
Drumnagorrach **177** E4
Drumoak **169** E5
Drumore **130** C3
Drumour **151** E1
Drumrash **124** A3
Drumrunie **181** D4
Drums **169** G2
Drumsturdy **152** C1
Drumuie **171** D5

Drumuillie **166** D2
Drumvaich **150** B4
Drumwhindle **169** G1
Drumwhirn **124** B2
Drunkendub **161** E5
Druridge **129** E2
Drury **77** F1
Drws-y-nant **76** B5
Dry Doddington **82** D3
Dry Drayton **58** B1
Dry Harbour **171** F4
Dry Sandford **41** G2
Dry Street **45** F4
Drybeck **108** B1
Drybridge *Moray* **176** D3
Drybridge *N.Ayr.* **132** B2
Drybrook **39** F1
Dryburgh **135** G2
Drygrange **135** G2
Dryhope **135** D3
Drymen **141** F1
Drymuir **179** E3
Drynoch **162** C1
Dryslwyn **50** B5
Dryton **65** E2
Duachy **148** A2
Dubford **177** G3
Dubhchladach **139** G3
Dubheads **151** E2
Dublin **60** C1
Dubton **161** D4
Duchal **141** E3
Duchally **181** F3
Duchray **149** G4
Duck Bay **141** E1
Duck End *Beds.* **57** F3
Duck End *Cambs.* **58** A1
Duck End *Essex* **59** E5
Duck Street **102** A1
Duckington **78** B2
Ducklington **41** F2
Duckmanton **94** B5
Duck's Cross **57** G2
Ducks Island **44** B3
Duddenhoe End **58** C4
Duddingston **143** G2
Duddington **69** E2
Duddleswell **23** F5
Duddleswell **17** G1
Duddo **145** G5
Duddon **78** C1
Duddon Bridge **106** C4
Dudleston **78** A4
Dudleston Heath (Criftins) **78** A4
Dudley *T. & W.* **129** E4
Dudley *W.Mid.* **66** B3
Dudley Port **66** B3
Dudlow's Green **92** A4
Dudsbury **13** G3
Duffield **81** E3
Duffryn **37** E3
Dufftown **168** A1
Duffus **174** A3
Dufton **118** C5
Duggleby **104** A1
Duiar **167** F1
Duible **183** E2
Duiletter **149** D2
Duinish **158** B3
Duirinish **163** F1
Duisdealmor **163** F3
Duisky **156** C2
Duke End **67** E4
Dukestown **38** A1
Dukinfield **92** D3
Dulas **88** C4
Dulax **148** A3
Dulcote **24** C3
Dulford **11** D2
Dull **158** D5
Dullatur **142** B2
Dullingham **59** E2
Dullingham Ley **59** E2
Dulnain Bridge **167** D2
Duloe *Beds.* **57** G1
Duloe *Cornw.* **5** G4
Dulsie **175** F5
Dulverton **22** C5
Dulwich **44** C5
Dumbarton **141** E2
Dumbleton **54** C4
Dumcrieff **134** C5
Dumeath **168** B1
Dumfin **141** E1
Dumfries **125** D3
Dumgoyne **141** G1
Dummer **27** G3
Dun **161** E4

Dunach **148** A2
Dunalastair **158** C4
Dunan *Arg. & B.* **140** C2
Dunan *High.* **163** D2
Dunans **148** C5
Dunball **24** A3
Dunbar **145** D2
Dunbeath **183** G1
Dunbeg (An Dùn Beag) **148** A1
Dunblane **150** C4
Dunbog **152** A3
Dunbridge **27** E5
Duncanston *Aber.* **168** C2
Duncanston *High.* **174** B4
Dunchideock **10** B4
Dunchurch **67** G5
Duncote **56** B2
Duncow **125** D2
Duncraggan **150** A4
Duncrievie **151** G4
Duncroist **150** A1
Duncrub **151** F3
Duncryne **141** F1
Duncton **16** B2
Dundee **152** C1
Dundee Airport **152** B2
Dundon **24** B4
Dundon Hayes **24** B4
Dundonald **132** B2
Dundonnell (Ach-Dà-Dhòmhnaill) **173** D1
Dundraw **117** F2
Dundreggan (Dul Dreagain) **165** E3
Dundrennan **116** A2
Dundridge **15** E1
Dundry **24** C1
Dunearn **143** G1
Dunecht **169** E4
Dunfermline **143** E1
Dunfield **40** D3
Dunford Bridge **93** F2
Dungate **32** B3
Dungavel **133** E2
Dungworth **93** G3
Dunham **95** F5
Dunham Town **92** B4
Dunham Woodhouses **92** B4
Dunham-on-the-Hill **91** F5
Dunhampton **54** A1
Dunholme **96** A5
Dunino **152** D3
Dunipace **142** C1
Dunira **150** C2
Dunkeld **159** F5
Dunkerton **25** E2
Dunkeswell **11** E2
Dunkeswick **102** C3
Dunkirk *C. & W.Ches.* **91** E5
Dunkirk *Kent* **32** C3
Dunk's Green **31** F3
Dunlappie **161** D3
Dunley *Hants.* **27** F2
Dunley *Worcs.* **53** G1
Dunlop **141** F5
Dunloskin **140** C2
Dunmere **5** E3
Dunmore *Arg. & B.* **139** F3
Dunmore *Falk.* **142** C1
Dunn **187** E3
Dunn Street **31** G2
Dunnabie **126** A3
Dunnet **187** E1
Dunnichen **160** D5
Dunning **151** F3
Dunnington *E.Riding* **105** D2
Dunnington *Warks.* **54** C2
Dunnington *York* **103** F2
Dunnockshaw **101** E5
Dunoon **140** C2
Dunragit **122** C5
Dunrostan **139** F1
Duns **145** E4
Duns Tew **55** G5
Dunsa **93** G5
Dunsby **83** G5
Dunscore **124** C2
Dunscroft **95** D2

Dunsden Green **42** C5
Dunsfold **29** F4
Dunsford **10** B4
Dunshalt **152** A3
Dunshill **54** A4
Dunsinnan **151** G1
Dunsland Cross **21** E5
Dunsley *N.Yorks.* **112** B1
Dunsley *Staffs.* **66** A4
Dunsmore **43** D2
Dunsop Bridge **100** C2
Dunstable **57** F5
Dunstall **80** C5
Dunstall Green **59** F1
Dunstan **137** G5
Dunstan Steads **137** G4
Dunster **22** C3
Dunston *Lincs.* **83** F1
Dunston *Norf.* **86** D5
Dunston *Staffs.* **66** B1
Dunston Heath **66** B1
Dunston Hill **120** B1
Dunstone *Devon* **10** A5
Dunstone *Devon* **8** B2
Dunsville **95** D2
Dunswell **104** C4
Dunsyre **143** F5
Dunterton **7** D3
Duntisbourne Abbots **40** B2
Duntisbourne Leer **40** B2
Duntisbourne Rouse **40** B2
Duntish **12** C2
Duntocher **141** F2
Dunton *Beds.* **58** A3
Dunton *Bucks.* **56** D5
Dunton *Norf.* **85** G4
Dunton Bassett **68** A3
Dunton Green **31** E3
Dunton Waylets **45** F3
Duntulm **170** D2
Dunure **132** A4
Dunure Mains **132** A4
Dunvant **36** B3
Dunvegan **170** B5
Dunwich **73** F4
Dura **152** C3
Durdar **118** A2
Durgan **3** E4
Durgates **31** F5
Durham **120** B3
Durham Tees Valley Airport **110** C1
Durinemast **155** F4
Durisdeer **133** G5
Durleigh **23** F4
Durley *Hants.* **15** E1
Durley *Wilts.* **26** D1
Durley Street **15** E1
Durlow Common **53** F4
Durnamuck **180** C5
Durness **184** D1
Durno **169** E2
Duror **156** C4
Durran *Arg. & B.* **148** B4
Durran *High.* **187** D2
Durrants **15** G2
Durrington *W.Suss.* **16** D3
Durrington *Wilts.* **26** C3
Dursley **39** G3
Dursley Cross **39** F1
Durston **23** F5
Durweston **13** E2
Duston **56** C1
Duthil **166** D2
Dutlas **64** B5
Duton Hill **59** E5
Dutson **6** D2
Dutton **91** G5
Duxford **58** C3
Dwygyfylchi **89** F5
Dwyran **74** D1
Dyce **169** F3
Dyfatty **36** A2
Dyffryn *Bridgend* **37** E3
Dyffryn *Pembs.* **48** C4
Dyffryn *V. of Glam.* **37** G5
Dyffryn Ardudwy **75** E5
Dyffryn Castell **63** D4
Dyffryn Ceidrych **50** D5
Dyffryn Cellwen **37** E2
Dyke *Devon* **20** D3
Dyke *Lincs.* **83** G5
Dyke *Moray* **175** F4
Dykehead *Angus* **160** B3
Dykehead *N.Lan.* **142** C4

Dykehead *Stir.* **150** A5
Dykelands **161** F3
Dykends **160** A4
Dykeside **177** G5
Dylife **63** E3
Dymchurch **19** G1
Dymock **53** G4
Dyrham **39** G5
Dysart **152** B5
Dyserth **90** B5

E

Eachwick **128** D4
Eagland Hill **100** A3
Eagle **83** D1
Eagle Barnsdale **83** D1
Eagle Moor **83** D1
Eaglescliffe **110** D1
Eaglesfield *Cumb.*
  117 D4
Eaglesfield *D. & G.*
  126 A4
Eaglesham **141** G4
Eaglethorpe **69** F3
Eagley **92** B1
Eairy **98** A4
Eakley **56** D2
Eakring **82** B1
Ealand **95** E1
Ealing **44** A4
Eamont Bridge **118** B5
Earby **101** F3
Earcroft **100** C5
Eardington **65** G3
Eardisland **52** D2
Eardisley **52** C3
Eardiston *Shrop.* **78** A5
Eardiston *Worcs.* **53** F1
Eanth **70** B5
Earl Shilton **67** G3
Earl Soham **60** D1
Earl Sterndale **80** B1
Earle **137** D4
Earlestown **91** G3
Earley **42** C5
Earlham **86** C5
Earlish **170** C3
Earls Barton **57** D1
Earls Colne **59** G5
Earl's Common **54** B2
Earl's Court **44** B5
Earl's Croome **54** A3
Earl's Green **60** B1
Earlsdon **67** F5
Earlsferry **152** C4
Earlsford **169** F1
Earlsheaton **102** B5
Earlston **135** G2
Earlswood *Mon.* **39** D3
Earlswood *Surr.* **30** B4
Earlswood *Warks.* **66** D5
Earnley **16** B4
Earnshaw Bridge **100** B5
Earsairidh **188** B5
Earsdon **129** F4
Earsdon Moor **129** D2
Earsham **73** E3
Earsham Street **72** D4
Earswick **103** F2
Eartham **16** B3
Earthcott Green **39** F4
Easby **111** E2
Easdale **147** G3
Easebourne **29** D5
Easenhall **67** G5
Eashing **29** E3
Easington *Bucks.* **42** B1
Easington *Dur.* **120** D3
Easington *E.Riding* **97** D1
Easington *Northumb.*
  137 F4
Easington *Oxon.* **42** B3
Easington *Oxon.* **55** G4
Easington *R. & C.* **111** G1
Easington Colliery
  120 D3
Easington Lane **120** C3
Easingwold **103** E1
Easole Street **33** E3
Eassie **160** B5
East Aberthaw **22** D1
East Allington **9** D3
East Anstey **22** B5
East Anton **27** E4
East Appleton **110** B3
East Ardsley **102** C5

East Ashey **15** E4
East Ashling **16** A3
East Auchronie **169** F4
East Ayton **112** C4
East Barkwith **96** B4
East Barming **31** G3
East Barnby **112** B1
East Barnet **44** B3
East Barsham **86** A2
East Beckham **86** C2
East Bedfont **43** F5
East Bergholt **60** B4
East Bierley **102** A5
East Bilney **86** A4
East Blatchington **17** G4
East Boldon **120** C1
East Boldre **14** C2
East Bolton **137** F5
East Bower **24** A4
East Brent **24** A2
East Bridge **61** F1
East Bridgford **82** B3
East Brora **183** E4
East Buckland **21** G2
East Budleigh **11** D4
East Burnham **43** E4
East Burton **13** E4
East Butsfield **120** A3
East Butterleigh **10** C3
East Butterwick **95** F2
East Cairnbeg **161** F2
East Calder **143** E3
East Carleton **86** C5
East Carlton *Northants.*
  68 D4
East Carlton *W.Yorks.*
  102 B3
East Chaldon
  (Chaldon Herring)
  13 D4
East Challow **41** F4
East Charleton **9** D3
East Chelborough **12** B2
East Chiltington **17** F2
East Chinnock **12** A1
East Chisenbury **26** C2
East Clandon **29** F2
East Claydon **56** C5
East Clyne **183** E4
East Clyth **187** E5
East Coker **12** B1
East Compton *Dorset*
  13 C1
East Compton *Som.*
  24 D3
East Coombe **10** B2
East Cornworthy **9** E2
East Cottingwith **103** G3
East Cowes **15** E3
East Cowick **103** F5
East Cowton **110** C2
East Cramlington **129** E4
East Cranmore **25** D3
East Creech **13** F4
East Croachy **166** A2
East Darlochan **130** B3
East Davoch **168** B4
East Dean *E.Suss.* **18** A4
East Dean *Hants.* **27** D5
East Dean *W.Suss.* **16** B3
East Dereham (Dereham)
  86 A4
East Down **21** F1
East Drayton **95** E5
East Dundry **24** C1
East Ella **104** C5
East End *E.Riding*
  105 D4
East End *E.Riding* **105** E3
East End *Essex* **46** D2
East End *Hants.* **27** F1
East End *Hants.* **14** C3
East End *Herts.* **58** C5
East End *Kent* **32** A5
East End *Kent* **32** B1
East End *M.K.* **57** E2
East End *N.Som.* **39** D5
East End *Oxon.* **41** F1
East End *Poole* **13** F3
East End *Som.* **24** C2
East End *Suff.* **60** C2
East End *Suff.* **60** C4
East Farleigh **31** G3
East Farndon **68** C4
East Ferry **95** F3
East Firsby **96** A4
East Fleetham **137** G4
East Fortune **144** C2
East Garston **41** F5

East Ginge **41** G4
East Goscote **68** B1
East Grafton **27** D1
East Green *Suff.* **61** F1
East Green *Suff.* **59** E2
East Grimstead **26** D5
East Grinstead **30** C5
East Guldeford **19** E1
East Haddon **57** D5
East Hagbourne **42** A4
East Halton **96** D1
East Ham **44** D4
East Hanney **41** G3
East Hanningfield **45** G2
East Hardwick **94** B1
East Harling **72** A3
East Harlsey **110** D3
East Harnham **26** C5
East Harptree **24** A2
East Hartford **129** E4
East Harting **15** G1
East Hatch **26** A5
East Hatley **58** A2
East Hauxwell **110** A3
East Haven **153** D1
East Heckington **83** G3
East Hedleyhope **120** A3
East Helmsdale **183** F3
East Hendred **41** G4
East Herrington **120** C2
East Heslerton **112** C5
East Hewish **24** B1
East Hoathly **18** A2
East Holme **13** E4
East Horndon **45** F4
East Horrington **24** C3
East Horsley **29** F2
East Horton **137** E3
East Howe **13** G3
East Huntspill **24** A3
East Hyde **44** A1
East Ilsley **41** G4
East Keal **84** B1
East Kennett **26** C1
East Keswick **102** C3
East Kilbride **142** A4
East Kimber **7** E1
East Kirkby **84** B1
East Knapton **112** B5
East Knighton **13** E4
East Knowstone **22** B5
East Knoyle **25** F4
East Kyloe **137** E3
East Lambrook **12** A1
East Langdon **33** F4
East Langton **68** C5
East Langwell **182** C4
East Lavant **16** A3
East Lavington **16** B2
East Layton **110** A1
East Leake **81** G5
East Learmouth **136** C3
East Learney **168** D4
East Leigh *Devon* **10** A2
East Leigh *Devon* **10** A1
East Leigh *Devon* **9** D2
East Leigh *Devon* **8** A3
East Lexham **71** G1
East Liburn **137** E4
East Linton **144** C2
East Liss **28** C5
East Lockinge **41** G4
East Looe **5** G4
East Lound **95** E2
East Lulworth **13** E4
East Lutton **104** B1
East Lydford **24** C4
East Lyn **22** A3
East Lyng **24** A5
East Mains **169** D5
East Malling **31** G3
East Malling Heath **31** F3
East March **152** C1
East Marden **16** A2
East Markham **95** E5
East Martin **13** G1
East Marton **101** F2
East Meon **28** B5
East Mere **10** C1
East Mersea **47** D1
East Mey **187** F1
East Midlands Airport
  81 F5
East Molesey **29** G1
East Moor **102** C5
East Morden **13** F3
East Morriston **144** D5
East Morton **102** A3
East Ness **111** F5

East Newton **105** E4
East Norton **68** C2
East Oakley **27** G2
East Ogwell **10** B5
East Orchard **13** E1
East Ord **145** D4
East Panson **7** D1
East Parley **14** A3
East Peckham **31** F4
East Pennard **24** C4
East Portlemouth **8** D4
East Prawle **9** D4
East Preston **16** C3
East Pulham **12** D2
East Putford **21** D4
East Quantoxhead **23** E3
East Rainton **120** C2
East Ravendale **96** C3
East Raynham **85** G5
East Retford (Retford)
  95 E4
East Rigton **102** C3
East Rolstone **24** A1
East Rounton **110** D2
East Row **112** B1
East Rudham **85** G5
East Runton **86** D1
East Ruston **87** E3
East Saltoun **144** B3
East Shefford **41** F5
East Sleekburn **129** E3
East Somerton **87** F4
East Stockwith **95** E3
East Stoke *Dorset* **13** E4
East Stoke *Notts.* **82** C3
East Stour **25** F5
East Stourmouth **33** E2
East Stratton **27** G3
East Street **24** C4
East Studdal **33** F4
East Suisnish **163** D1
East Taphouse **5** F3
East Thirston **129** D2
East Tilbury **45** F5
East Tisted **28** C4
East Torrington **96** B4
East Town **24** D3
East Tuddenham **86** B4
East Tytherley **27** D5
East Tytherton **40** B5
East Village **10** B2
East Wall **65** E3
East Walton **71** F1
East Wellow **27** F5
East Wemyss **152** B5
East Whitburn **143** D3
East Wickham **45** D5
East Williamston **35** D2
East Winch **71** E1
East Winterslow **26** D4
East Wittering **15** G3
East Witton **110** A4
East Woodburn **128** B3
East Woodhay **27** F1
East Woodlands **25** E3
East Worldham **28** C4
East Worlington **10** A1
East Youlstone **20** C4
Eastacott **21** G3
Eastbourne **18** B4
Eastbrook **38** A5
Eastburn *E.Riding*
  104 B2
Eastburn *W.Yorks.*
  101 G3
Eastbury *Herts.* **44** A3
Eastbury *W.Berks.* **41** F5
Eastby **101** G2
Eastchurch **32** B1
Eastcombe *Glos.* **40** A2
Eastcombe *Som.* **23** E4
Eastcote *Gt.Lon.* **44** A4
Eastcote *Northants.*
  56 B2
Eastcote *W.Mid.* **67** D5
Eastcott *Cornw.* **20** C4
Eastcott *Wilts.* **26** B2
Eastcourt **40** B3
Eastdown **9** E3
Eastend **55** F5
Easter Ardross **174** C2
Easter Balgedie **151** G4
Easter Balmoral **167** G5
Easter Boleskine **165** G3
Easter Borland **150** B4
Easter Brae **174** C3
Easter Buckieburn **142** B1
Easter Compton **39** E4
Easter Drummond **165** F3

Easter Dullater **150** B4
Easter Ellister **138** A4
Easter Fearn **174** C1
Easter Galcantray **175** E5
Easter Howlaws **145** E5
Easter Kinkell **174** B4
Easter Lednathie **160** B3
Easter Moniack **174** B5
Easter Ord **169** F4
Easter Poldar **150** B5
Easter Suddie **174** C4
Easter Tulloch **161** F2
Easter Whyntie **177** F3
Eastergate **16** B3
Easterhouse **142** A3
Easterton **26** B2
Easterton Sands **26** B2
Eastertown **24** A2
Eastfield *Bristol* **39** E5
Eastfield *N.Lan.* **142** C3
Eastfield *N.Yorks.* **112** D4
Eastfield Hall **129** E1
Eastgate *Dur.* **119** F4
Eastgate *Lincs.* **69** G1
Eastgate *Norf.* **86** C3
Easthall **58** A5
Eastham *Mersey.* **91** E4
Eastham *Worcs.* **53** F1
Easthampstead **29** D1
Easthampton **52** D1
Easthaugh **86** B4
Eastheath **28** D1
Easthope **65** E3
Easthorpe *Essex* **60** A5
Easthorpe *Leics.* **82** D4
Easthorpe *Notts.* **82** C2
Easthouses **144** A3
Eastington *Devon* **10** A2
Eastington *Glos.* **40** D1
Eastington *Glos.* **39** G2
Eastleach Martin **41** E2
Eastleach Turville **41** E2
Eastleigh *Devon* **21** E3
Eastleigh *Hants.* **14** D1
Eastling **32** B3
Eastmoor *Derbys.* **94** A5
Eastmoor *Norf.* **71** F2
Eastnor **53** G4
Eastoft **95** F1
Eastoke **15** G3
Easton *Cambs.* **69** G5
Easton *Cumb.* **126** C4
Easton *Cumb.* **117** F1
Easton *Devon* **10** A4
Easton *Dorset* **12** C5
Easton *Hants.* **27** G4
Easton *I.o.W.* **14** C4
Easton *Lincs.* **83** E5
Easton *Norf.* **86** C4
Easton *Som.* **24** C3
Easton *Suff.* **61** D2
Easton *Wilts.* **40** A5
Easton Grey **40** A4
Easton Maudit **57** D2
Easton on the Hill **69** F2
Easton Royal **26** D1
Easton-in-Gordano **39** E5
Eastrea **70** A3
Eastriggs **126** A5
Eastrington **103** G4
Eastry **33** F3
East-the-Water **21** E3
Eastville **39** F5
Eastwell **82** C5
Eastwick **44** D1
Eastwood *Notts.* **81** F3
Eastwood *S'end* **46** B4
Eastwood *S.Yorks.* **94** B3
Eastwood *W.Yorks.*
  101 F5
Eastwood End **70** C3
Eathorpe **57** E1
Eaton *C. & W.Ches.* **78** C1
Eaton *Ches.E.* **79** F1
Eaton *Leics.* **82** C5
Eaton *Norf.* **86** D5
Eaton *Norf.* **85** F5
Eaton *Notts.* **95** E5
Eaton *Oxon.* **41** G2
Eaton *Shrop.* **65** E3
Eaton *Shrop.* **64** C4
Eaton Bishop **52** D4
Eaton Bray **57** E5
Eaton Constantine **65** F2
Eaton Ford **57** G2
Eaton Hall **78** B1
Eaton Hastings **41** E3
Eaton Socon **57** G2

Eaton upon Tern **79** D5
Eaves Green **67** E4
Eavestone **102** B1
Ebberston **112** B4
Ebbesborne Wake **26** A5
Ebbw Vale (Glynebwy)
  38 A2
Ebchester **120** A2
Ebdon **24** A1
Ebford **10** C4
Ebley **40** A2
Ebnal **78** B3
Ebost **162** B1
Ebrington **56** D3
Ebsworthy Town **7** F1
Ecchinswell **27** F2
Ecclaw **145** E3
Ecclefechan **125** F3
Eccles *Gt.Man.* **92** B3
Eccles *Kent* **31** G3
Eccles *Sc.Bord.* **145** E5
Eccles Green **94** A3
Eccles Road **72** B2
Ecclesall **94** A3
Ecclesfield **94** A3
Ecclesgreig **161** F3
Eccleshall **79** F5
Eccleshill **102** A4
Ecclesmachan **143** E2
Eccles-on-Sea **87** F3
Eccleston *C. & W.Ches.*
  78 N1
Eccleston *Lancs.* **91** G1
Eccleston *Mersey.* **91** F3
Eccup **102** B3
Echt **169** E4
Eckford **136** B4
Eckington *Derbys.* **94** B5
Eckington *Worcs.* **54** A3
Ecton *Northants.* **56** D1
Ecton *Staffs.* **80** B2
Edale **93** F4
Eday **190** C2
Edburton **17** E2
Edderside **117** E2
Edderton **174** D1
Eddington **27** E1
Eddleston **143** G5
Eden Park **30** C2
Eden Vale **120** D4
Edenbridge **30** D4
Edendonich **149** D2
Edenfield **92** B1
Edenhall **118** B4
Edenham **83** F5
Edensor **93** G5
Edentaggart **149** F5
Edenthorpe **94** D2
Edern **74** B4
Edgarley **24** C4
Edgbaston **66** C4
Edgcote **56** B4
Edgcott *Bucks.* **56** B5
Edgcott *Som.* **22** B4
Edgcumbe **3** E3
Edge *Glos.* **40** A2
Edge *Shrop.* **64** C2
Edge End **39** E1
Edge Green *C. & W.Ches.*
  78 B2
Edge Green *Gt.Man.*
  91 G3
Edge Green *Norf.* **72** B3
Edgebolton **78** C5
Edgefield **86** B2
Edgehead **144** A3
Edgeley **78** C3
Edgerley **64** C1
Edgerton **93** F1
Edgeworth **40** B2
Edginswell **9** E1
Edgmond **65** G1
Edgmond Marsh **79** E5
Edgton **64** C4
Edgware **44** B3
Edgworth **92** B1
Edinample **150** B2
Edinbanchory **168** B3
Edinbane **170** C4
Edinbarnet **141** G2
Edinburgh **143** G2
Edinburgh Airport **143** F2
Edinchip **150** A2
Edingale **67** E1
Edingley **82** B2
Edingthorpe **87** E2
Edingthorpe Green **87** E2
Edington *Som.* **24** A4
Edington *Wilts.* **26** A2
Edintore **176** D5

Edinvale 176 A4
Edistone 20 C3
Edith Weston 69 E2
Edithmead 24 A3
Edlaston 80 C3
Edlesborough 43 E1
Edlingham 128 D1
Edlington 96 C5
Edmondsham 13 G1
Edmondsley 120 B3
Edmondstown 37 G3
Edmondthorpe 69 D1
Edmonton Cornw. 5 D2
Edmonton Gt.Lon. 44 C3
Edmundbyers 119 G2
Ednam 136 B3
Ednaston 80 D2
Edney Common 45 F2
Edra 149 G3
Edradynate 159 D4
Edrom 145 F4
Edstaston 78 C4
Edstone 55 D1
Edvin Loach 53 F2
Edwalton 81 G4
Edwardstone 60 A3
Edwardsville 37 G3
Edwinsford 50 C4
Edwinstowe 82 B1
Edworth 58 A3
Edwyn Ralph 53 F2
Edzell 161 E3
Efail Isaf 37 G4
Efail-fâch 37 D3
Efailnewydd 74 C4
Efailwen 49 E5
Efenechtyd 77 F2
Effingham 29 G2
Efflinch 67 D1
Efford 10 B2
Egbury 27 F2
Egdon 54 B2
Egerton Gt.Man. 92 B1
Egerton Kent 32 B4
Egerton Forstal 32 A4
Egerton Green 78 C2
Egg Buckland 8 A2
Eggborough 103 E5
Eggerness 115 E2
Eggesford Barton 21 G4
Eggington 57 E5
Egginton 81 D5
Egglescliffe 110 D1
Eggleston 119 F5
Egham 43 F5
Egham Wick 43 E5
Egilsay 190 B2
Egleton 69 D2
Eglingham 137 F5
Eglinton 141 E5
Egloshayle 5 E2
Egloskerry 5 G1
Eglwys Cross 78 B3
Eglwys Fach 62 C3
Eglwys Nunydd 37 E4
Eglwysbach 89 G5
Eglwys-Brewis 22 D1
Eglwyswrw 49 E4
Egmanton 82 C1
Egmere 86 A2
Egremont 116 D5
Egton 112 B2
Egton Bridge 112 B2
Egypt 27 F3
Eigg 155 D1
Eight Ash Green 60 A5
Eignaig 155 G5
Eil 166 C3
Eilanreach 163 G3
Eildon 135 G2
Eilean Darach 173 E1
Eilean Shona 155 F2
Einacleit 189 E2
Eisingrug 75 F4
Eisteddfa Gurig 63 D4
Elan Village 51 F1
Elberton 39 F4
Elborough 24 A2
Elburton 8 B2
Elcho 151 G2
Elcombe 40 D4
Elder Street 59 D4
Eldernell 70 B3
Eldersfield 53 G4
Elderslie 141 F3
Eldon 120 B5
Eldrick 123 D2
Eldroth 101 D1

Eldwick 102 A3
Elemore Vale 120 C3
Elford Northumb. 137 F3
Elford Staffs. 67 D1
Elford Closes 70 D5
Elgin 176 B3
Elgol 162 D3
Elham 33 D4
Elie 152 C4
Elilaw 128 B1
Elim 88 B4
Eling Hants. 14 C1
Eling W.Berks. 42 A5
Eliock 133 G5
Elishader 171 D3
Elishaw 128 A2
Elkesley 95 D5
Elkington 68 B5
Elkstone 40 B1
Elland 102 A5
Elland Upper Edge
102 A5
Ellary 139 F2
Ellastone 80 C3
Ellbridge 8 A1
Ellel 100 A2
Ellemford 145 E3
Ellenabeich 147 G3
Ellenborough 116 D3
Ellenhall 79 F5
Ellen's Green 29 F4
Ellerbeck 110 D3
Ellerby 111 G1
Ellerdine 78 D5
Ellerdine Heath 78 D5
Elleric (Eileirig) 156 C5
Ellerker 104 B5
Ellerton E.Riding 103 G3
Ellerton N.Yorks. 110 B3
Ellerton Shrop. 79 E5
Ellerton Abbey 109 F3
Ellesborough 42 D2
Ellesmere 78 A4
Ellesmere Park 92 B3
Ellesmere Port 91 F5
Ellingham Hants. 14 A2
Ellingham Norf. 73 E2
Ellingham Northumb.
137 F4
Ellingstring 110 A4
Ellington Cambs. 69 G5
Ellington Northumb.
129 E2
Ellington Thorpe 69 G5
Elliot 153 E1
Elliot's Green 25 E3
Ellisfield 28 B3
Ellistown 67 G1
Ellon 169 G1
Ellonby 118 A4
Ellough 73 F3
Ellough Moor 73 F3
Elloughton 104 B5
Ellwood 39 E2
Elm 70 C2
Elm Park 45 E4
Elmbridge 54 B1
Elmdon Essex 58 C4
Elmdon W.Mid. 67 D4
Elmdon Heath 67 D4
Elmers End 30 C2
Elmer's Green 91 F2
Elmesthorpe 67 G3
Elmhurst 66 B1
Elmley Castle 54 B3
Elmley Lovett 54 A1
Elmore 39 G1
Elmore Back 39 G1
Elmscott 20 C3
Elmsett 60 B3
Elmstead Essex 60 B5
Elmstead Gt.Lon. 60 B5
Elmstead Market 60 B5
Elmstone 33 E2
Elmstone Hardwicke
54 B5
Elmswell E.Riding 104 B2
Elmswell Suff. 60 A1
Elmton 94 C5
Elphin 181 G3
Elphinstone 144 A2
Elrick Aber. 169 F4
Elrick Moray 168 B2
Elrig 114 D2
Elrigbeag 148 D3
Elsdon 128 B2
Elsecar 94 A3
Elsenham 58 D5
Elsfield 42 A1

Elsham 96 A1
Elsing 86 B4
Elslack 101 F3
Elson Hants. 15 F2
Elson Shrop. 78 A4
Elsrickle 143 E5
Elstead 29 E3
Elsted 16 A2
Elsthorpe 83 F5
Elstob 120 C5
Elston Lancs. 100 B4
Elston Notts. 82 C3
Elstone 21 G4
Elstow 57 F3
Elstree 44 A3
Elstronwick 105 E4
Elswick 100 A4
Elsworth 58 B1
Elterwater 107 E2
Eltham 44 D5
Eltisley 58 A2
Elton C. & W.Ches. 91 F5
Elton Cambs. 69 F3
Elton Derbys. 80 D1
Elton Glos. 39 G1
Elton Here. 65 D5
Elton Notts. 82 C4
Elton Stock. 110 D1
Elton Green 91 F5
Elvanfoot 134 A4
Elvaston 81 F4
Elveden 71 G5
Elvingston 144 B2
Elvington Kent 33 E3
Elvington York 103 G3
Elwick Hart. 121 D5
Elwick Northumb. 137 F3
Elworth 79 E1
Elworthy 23 D4
Ely Cambs. 70 D5
Ely Cardiff 38 A5
Emberton 57 D3
Embleton Cumb. 117 E3
Embleton Hart. 120 D5
Embleton Northumb.
137 G4
Embo 182 D5
Embo Street 182 D5
Emborough 24 D2
Embsay 101 G2
Emerson Park 45 E4
Emery Down 14 B2
Emley 93 G1
Emmington 42 C2
Emneth 70 C2
Emneth Hungate 70 D2
Empingham 69 E2
Empshott 28 C4
Empshott Green 28 C4
Emsworth 15 G2
Enborne 27 F1
Enborne Row 27 F1
Enchmarsh 65 E3
Enderby 43 A3
Endmoor 107 G4
Endon 79 G2
Endon Bank 79 G2
Enfield 44 C3
Enfield Wash 44 C3
Enford 26 C2
Engine Common 39 F4
Englefield 42 A5
Englefield Green 43 E5
Englesea-brook 79 E2
English Bicknor 39 E1
English Frankton 78 B5
Englishcombe 25 E1
Enham Alamein 27 E3
Enmore 23 F4
Ennerdale Bridge 117 D5
Enniscaven 5 D4
Ennochdhu 159 F3
Ensay 154 C5
Ensdon 64 D1
Ensis 21 F3
Enson 79 G5
Enstone 55 F5
Enterkinfoot 133 G5
Enterpen 111 D2
Enton Green 29 E3
Enville 66 A4
Eorabus 146 C2
Eoropaidh 189 G1
Epney 39 G1
Epperstone 82 B3
Epping 45 D2
Epping Green Essex
44 D2

Epping Green Herts.
44 B2
Epping Upland 44 D2
Eppleby 110 A1
Eppleworth 104 C4
Epsom 30 B3
Epwell 55 F3
Epworth 95 E2
Epworth Turbary 95 E2
Erbistock 78 A3
Erbusaig 163 F2
Erchless Castle 174 A5
Erdington 66 D3
Eredine 148 B3
Eriboll 184 D3
Ericstane 134 B4
Eridge Green 31 E5
Eriff 132 C5
Erines 139 G2
Erisey Barton 3 E5
Eriskay (Eiriosgaigh)
188 B4
Eriswell 71 F5
Erith 45 E5
Erlestoke 26 A1
Ermington 8 C2
Ernesettle 8 A1
Erpingham 86 C2
Erringden Grange 101 F5
Errogie (Earagaidh)
165 G2
Errol 152 A2
Errollston 179 F4
Erskine 141 F2
Ervie 122 A4
Erwarton 60 D4
Erwood 51 G3
Eryholme 110 C2
Eryrys 77 F2
Escart 139 G2
Escart Farm 139 G4
Escomb 120 A5
Escrick 103 F3
Esgair 49 G5
Esgairgeiliog 63 D2
Esgyryn 89 G5
Esh 120 A3
Esh Winning 120 A3
Esher 29 G1
Eshott 129 E2
Eshton 101 F2
Eskadale 165 F1
Eskbank 144 A3
Eskdale Green 106 C2
Eskdalemuir 126 A2
Eskham 97 D3
Esknish 138 B3
Esperley Lane Ends
120 A5
Espley Hall 129 D2
Esprick 100 A4
Essendine 69 F1
Essendon 44 B2
Essich 166 A1
Essington 66 B2
Esslemont 169 G2
Eston 111 E1
Etal 136 D3
Etchilhampton 26 B1
Etchingham 18 C1
Etchinghill Kent 33 D5
Etchinghill Staffs. 66 C1
Etherdwick Grange
105 E4
Etherley Dene 120 A5
Ethie Mains 161 E5
Eton 43 E5
Eton Wick 43 E5
Etteridge 166 A5
Ettiley Heath 79 E1
Ettington 55 E3
Etton E.Riding 104 B3
Etton Peter. 69 G2
Ettrick 135 D4
Ettrickbridge 135 E3
Ettrickhill 135 D4
Etwall 81 D4
Eudon George 65 F4
Eurach 148 A4
Euston 71 G5
Euxton 91 G1
Evanstown 37 G4
Evanton 174 C3
Evedon 83 F3
Evelix 182 C5
Evenjobb 52 B1
Evenley 56 A4
Evenlode 55 E5
Evenwood 120 A5

Evenwood Gate 120 A5
Evercreech 24 D4
Everdon 56 A2
Everingham 104 A3
Everleigh 26 D2
Everley High. 187 F2
Everley N.Yorks. 112 C4
Eversholt 57 E4
Evershot 12 B2
Eversley 28 C1
Eversley Cross 28 C1
Everthorpe 104 B4
Everton Beds. 58 B3
Everton Hants. 14 B3
Everton Mersey. 91 E3
Everton Notts. 95 D3
Evertown 126 B4
Eves Corner 46 C1
Evesbatch 53 F3
Evesham 54 C3
Evington 68 B2
Ewart Newtown 137 D3
Ewden Village 93 G3
Ewell 30 B2
Ewell Minnis 33 E4
Ewelme 42 B3
Ewen 40 C3
Ewenny 37 F5
Ewerby 83 G3
Ewerby Thorpe 83 G3
Ewhurst 29 F3
Ewhurst Green E.Suss.
18 C1
Ewhurst Green Surr.
29 F4
Ewloe 78 A1
Ewloe Green 77 F1
Ewood 100 C5
Ewood Bridge 101 D5
Eworthy 7 E1
Ewshot 28 D3
Ewyas Harold 52 C5
Exbourne 21 G5
Exbury 14 D2
Exceat 18 A4
Exebridge 22 C3
Exelby 110 B4
Exeter 10 C4
Exeter International Airport
10 C3
Exford 22 B4
Exfords Green 65 D2
Exhall Warks. 54 D2
Exhall Warks. 67 F4
Exlade Street 42 B4
Exminster 10 C4
Exmouth 10 D4
Exning 59 E1
Exton Devon 10 C4
Exton Hants. 28 B5
Exton Rut. 69 E1
Exton Som. 22 C4
Exwick 10 C3
Eyam 85 G5
Eydon 56 A3
Eye Here. 53 D1
Eye Peter. 70 A2
Eye Suff. 72 C4
Eye Green 70 A2
Eyemouth 145 G3
Eyeworth 58 A3
Eyhorne Street 32 A3
Eyke 61 E2
Eynesbury 57 G2
Eynort 162 B2
Eynsford 31 E2
Eynsham 41 G2
Eype 12 A3
Eyre 170 D4
Eythorne 33 E4
Eyton Here. 53 D1
Eyton Shrop. 64 C4
Eyton on Severn 65 E2
Eyton upon the Weald
Moors 65 F1
Eywood 52 C2

F

Faccombe 27 E2
Faceby 111 D2
Fachwen 75 E1
Facit 92 C1
Faddiley 78 C2
Fadmoor 111 F4
Faebait 174 A4
Faifley 141 A4
Fail 132 C3
Failand 39 E5

Failford 132 C3
Failsworth 92 C4
Fain 173 E2
Fair Isle 191 E5
Fair Oak Devon 10 D1
Fair Oak Hants. 15 D1
Fair Oak Hants. 27 G1
Fair Oak Green 28 B1
Fairbourne 62 C1
Fairburn 103 D5
Fairfield Derbys. 93 E3
Fairfield Gt.Man. 92 D3
Fairfield Kent 19 E1
Fairfield Mersey. 91 D4
Fairfield Stock. 110 D1
Fairfield Worcs. 66 B3
Fairford 40 D2
Fairgirth 124 C5
Fairhaven 99 G5
Fairhill 142 B4
Fairholm 142 B4
Fairley 169 F4
Fairlie 140 D4
Fairlight 19 D2
Fairlight Cove 19 D2
Fairmile Devon 11 D3
Fairmile Surr. 29 G1
Fairmilehead 143 G3
Fairnington 136 A4
Fairoak 78 E4
Fairseat 31 F2
Fairstead 45 G1
Fairwarp 17 G1
Fairwater 38 A5
Fairy Cross 21 E3
Fairyhill 36 A3
Fakenham 86 A3
Fala 144 B3
Fala Dam 144 B3
Falahill 144 A4
Faldingworth 96 A4
Falfield Fife 152 C4
Falfield S.Glos. 39 F3
Falin-Wnda 49 G3
Falkenham 61 D4
Falkirk 142 C2
Falkland 152 A4
Falla 136 B5
Fallgate 81 E1
Fallin 150 D5
Falmer 17 F3
Falmouth 3 F3
Falsgrave 112 D4
Falstone 127 F3
Fanagmore 184 A4
Fanans 148 C2
Fancott 57 F5
Fangdale Beck 111 E3
Fangfoss 103 G2
Fankerton 142 B1
Fanmore 154 D5
Fanner's Green 45 G1
Fans 144 D5
Far Cotton 56 C2
Far Forest 65 G5
Far Gearstones 108 C4
Far Green 39 G2
Far Moor 91 G2
Far Oakridge 40 B2
Far Royds 102 B4
Far Sawrey 107 E3
Farcet 70 A3
Farden 65 E5
Fareham 15 E2
Farewell 66 C1
Farforth 96 D5
Faringdon 41 E3
Farington 100 B5
Farlam 118 B2
Farlary 182 C4
Farleigh N.Som. 24 C1
Farleigh Surr. 30 C2
Farleigh Hungerford
25 F2
Farleigh Wallop 28 B3
Farlesthorpe 97 E5
Farleton Cumb. 107 G4
Farleton Lancs. 100 B1
Farley Derbys. 81 D1
Farley Shrop. 64 C2
Farley Staffs. 80 B3
Farley Wilts. 26 D5
Farley Green Suff. 59 F2
Farley Green Surr. 29 F3
Farley Hill 28 C1
Farleys End 39 G1
Farlington 103 F1
Farlow 65 F4
Farm Town 67 F1

Farmborough 25 D1
Farmcote 54 C5
Farmington 40 D1
Farmoor 41 G2
Farmtown 177 E4
Farnborough Gt.Lon. 30 D2
Farnborough Hants. 29 D2
Farnborough W.Berks. 41 G4
Farnborough Warks. 55 G3
Farnborough Street 29 D2
Farncombe 29 E3
Farndish 57 E1
Farndon C. & W.Ches. 78 B2
Farndon Notts. 82 C2
Farne Islands 137 G3
Farnell 161 E1
Farnham Dorset 13 F1
Farnham Essex 58 C5
Farnham N.Yorks. 102 C1
Farnham Suff. 61 E1
Farnham Surr. 28 D3
Farnham Common 43 E4
Farnham Green 58 C5
Farnham Royal 43 E4
Farningham 31 E2
Farnley N.Yorks. 102 B3
Farnley W.Yorks. 102 B4
Farnley Tyas 93 F1
Farnsfield 82 B2
Farnworth Gt.Man. 92 B2
Farnworth Halton 91 G4
Farr High. 185 E2
Farr High. 166 A1
Farr High. 166 C4
Farr House 166 A1
Farraline 165 G2
Farringdon 10 D3
Farrington Gurney 24 D2
Farsley 102 B3
Farthing Corner 32 A2
Farthing Green 32 A4
Farthinghoe 56 A4
Farthingstone 56 B2
Fartown 93 F1
Farway 11 E3
Fasag 172 B4
Fasagnanach 173 E1
Fascadale 155 E2
Faslane 140 D1
Fasnacloich 156 C5
Fasnakyle 165 E2
Fassfern 156 C2
Fatfield 120 C2
Fattahead 177 F4
Faugh 118 B2
Fauldhouse 142 D3
Faulkbourne 45 G1
Faulkland 25 E2
Fauls 78 C4
Faulston 26 B5
Faversham 32 C2
Favillar 167 G1
Fawdington 110 D5
Fawdon 120 B1
Fawfieldhead 80 B1
Fawkham Green 31 E2
Fawler 41 F1
Fawley Bucks. 42 C4
Fawley Hants. 15 D2
Fawley W.Berks. 41 F4
Fawley Chapel 53 E5
Fawsyde 161 G2
Faxfleet 104 A5
Faxton 68 C5
Faygate 30 B5
Fazakerley 91 E3
Fazeley 67 E2
Fearby 110 A4
Fearn 175 E2
Fearnan 158 C5
Fearnbeg 172 A4
Fearnhead 92 A3
Fearnmore 172 A3
Fearnoch Arg. & B. 140 B2
Fearnoch Arg. & B. 140 A1
Featherstone Staffs. 66 B2
Featherstone W.Yorks. 102 D5
Featherstone Castle 118 C1

Feckenham 54 C1
Feering 59 G5
Feetham 109 E3
Feith-hill 177 F5
Feizor 101 D1
Felbridge 30 C5
Felbrigg 86 B2
Felcourt 30 C1
Felden 43 F2
Felhampton 64 D4
Felindre Carmar. 50 D5
Felindre Carmar. 50 B5
Felindre Carmar. 49 G4
Felindre Carmar. 50 C4
Felindre Cere. 50 B2
Felindre Powys 64 A4
Felindre Powys 52 A5
Felindre Swan. 36 C2
Felinfach Cere. 50 B2
Felinfach Powys 51 G4
Felinfoel 36 B2
Felingwmisaf 50 B5
Felingwmuchaf 50 B5
Felixkirk 111 D4
Felixstowe 61 E4
Felixstowe Ferry 61 E4
Felkington 145 G5
Felldownhead 7 D2
Felling 120 B1
Fellonmore 147 F2
Felmersham 32 B2
Felmingham 87 D3
Felpham 16 B4
Felsham 60 A2
Felsted 59 E5
Feltham 44 A5
Felthamhill 44 A5
Felthorpe 86 C4
Felton Here. 53 E3
Felton N.Som. 24 C1
Felton Northumb. 129 D1
Felton Butler 64 C1
Feltwell 71 F3
Fen Ditton 58 C1
Fen Drayton 58 B1
Fen End 67 E5
Fen Street Norf. 72 A2
Fen Street Norf. 72 B4
Fen Street Suff. 72 B4
Fen Street Suff. 60 C1
Fenay Bridge 93 F1
Fence 101 E4
Fence Houses 120 C2
Fencott 42 A1
Fendike Corner 84 C1
Fenham 137 E2
Fenhouses 84 A3
Feniscowles 100 C5
Feniton 11 E3
Fenn Street 45 G5
Fenni-fach 51 G5
Fenny Bentley 80 C2
Fenny Bridges 11 E3
Fenny Compton 55 G2
Fenny Drayton 67 F3
Fenny Stratford 57 D4
Fenrother 129 D2
Fenstanton 58 B1
Fenton Cambs. 70 B5
Fenton Lincs. 95 F5
Fenton Lincs. 83 D2
Fenton Northumb. 137 D3
Fenton Notts. 95 E4
Fenton Stoke 79 F3
Fenton Barns 144 C1
Fenwick E.Ayr. 141 F5
Fenwick Northumb. 128 C4
Fenwick Northumb. 137 E2
Fenwick S.Yorks. 94 C1
Feochaig 130 C4
Feock 3 F3
Feolin 138 D3
Feolin Ferry 138 C3
Feorlan 130 B5
Feorlin 148 B5
Ferguslie Park 141 F3
Feriniquaire 170 A4
Fern 160 C3
Ferndale 37 F3
Ferndown 13 G2
Ferness 175 F5
Fernham 41 E3
Fernhill Heath 54 A2
Fernhurst 29 D5

Fernilea 162 B1
Fernilee 93 E5
Fernybank 160 D2
Ferrensby 102 C1
Ferring 16 C3
Ferry Hill 70 B4
Ferrybridge 103 D5
Ferryden 161 F1
Ferryhill 120 B4
Ferryside (Glanyferi) 35 G1
Fersfield 72 B3
Fersit 157 F2
Ferwig 49 E3
Feshiebridge 166 C4
Fetcham 29 G2
Fetlar 191 E2
Fetterangus 179 E2
Fettercairn 161 E2
Fetternear House 169 E3
Fewcott 56 A5
Fewston 102 A2
Ffairfach 50 C5
Ffair-Rhos 50 D1
Ffaldybrenin 50 C3
Ffarmers 50 C3
Ffawyddog 38 B1
Ffestiniog (Llan Ffestiniog) 76 A3
Ffordd-las Denb. 77 E1
Fforddlas Powys 52 B4
Fforest 36 B2
Fforest-fach 36 C3
Ffostrasol 49 G3
Ffos-y-ffin 50 A1
Ffridd Uchaf 75 E2
Ffrith Denb. 90 B4
Ffrith Flints. 77 F2
Ffrwdgrech 51 G5
Ffynnon 35 G1
Ffynnongroyw 90 C4
Fichlie 168 B3
Fidden 146 C2
Fiddington Glos. 54 B4
Fiddington Som. 23 F3
Fiddleford 13 E1
Fiddler's Green Glos. 54 B5
Fiddler's Green Here. 53 E4
Fiddler's Green Norf. 71 G1
Fiddler's Green Norf. 72 B2
Fiddlers Hamlet 45 D2
Field 80 B4
Field Broughton 107 E4
Field Dalling 86 B2
Field Head 67 G2
Fife Keith 176 D4
Fifehead Magdalen 25 E5
Fifehead Neville 13 D1
Fifehead St. Quintin 13 D1
Fifield Oxon. 41 E1
Fifield W. & M. 43 E5
Fifield Bavant 26 B5
Figheldean 26 C3
Filby 87 F4
Filey 113 E4
Filgrave 57 D3
Filham 6 D2
Filkins 41 E2
Filleigh Devon 21 G3
Filleigh Devon 10 A1
Fillingham 95 G4
Fillongley 67 E4
Filmore Hill 28 B5
Filton 39 F5
Fimber 104 A1
Finavon 160 C4
Fincham 71 F2
Finchampstead 28 C1
Finchdean 15 G1
Finchingfield 59 E4
Finchley 44 B3
Findern 81 E4
Findhorn 175 G3
Findhorn Bridge 166 C2
Findhuglen 150 D3
Findo Gask 161 F2
Findochty 177 D3
Findon Aber. 169 G5
Findon W.Suss. 16 D3
Findon Mains 174 C3
Findon Valley 16 D3
Findrassie 176 A3

Findron 167 F3
Finedon 69 E5
Fingask 159 G3
Fingal Street 72 D4
Fingask 169 E2
Fingerpost 65 G5
Fingest 42 C3
Finghall 110 A4
Fingland Cumb. 117 F1
Fingland D. & G. 134 D5
Fingland D. & G. 133 F4
Finglesham 33 F3
Fingringhoe 60 B5
Finkle Street 94 A3
Finlarig 150 A1
Finmere 56 B4
Finnart Arg. & B. 149 E5
Finnart P. & K. 158 A4
Finney Hill 67 G1
Finningham 60 B1
Finningley 95 D3
Finnygaud 177 F4
Finsbury 44 C4
Finstall 66 B5
Finsthwaite 107 E4
Finstock 41 F1
Finstown 190 B3
Fintry Aber. 177 G4
Fintry Stir. 142 A1
Finwood 55 D1
Finzean 168 C5
Fionnphort 146 C2
Fir Tree 120 A4
Firbank 108 B3
Firbeck 94 C4
Firby N.Yorks. 110 B4
Firby N.Yorks. 103 G1
Firgrove 92 D1
Firs Lane 92 A2
Firsby 84 C1
Firsdown 26 D4
Fishbourne I.o.W. 15 E3
Fishbourne W.Suss. 16 A3
Fishburn 120 C4
Fishcross 151 E5
Fisherford 169 D1
Fisher's Pond 27 F5
Fisher's Row 100 A3
Fishersgate 17 E3
Fisherstreet 29 E4
Fisherton High. 174 D4
Fisherton S.Ayr. 132 A4
Fisherton de la Mere 26 A4
Fishguard (Abergwaun) 48 C1
Fishlake 95 D1
Fishleigh Barton 21 F3
Fishley 87 F4
Fishnish 155 F5
Fishpond Bottom 11 G3
Fishponds 39 F5
Fishpool 92 C2
Fishtoft 84 B3
Fishtoft Drove 84 B3
Fishtown of Usan 161 F4
Fishwick 145 G4
Fiskerton Lincs. 96 A5
Fiskerton Notts. 82 C2
Fitling 105 E4
Fitstanton 26 C3
Fittleworth 16 C2
Fitton End 70 C4
Fitz 64 D1
Fitzhead 23 E5
Fitzroy 23 E5
Fitzwilliam 94 B1
Fiunary 155 F5
Five Acres 39 E1
Five Ash Down 17 G1
Five Ashes 18 A1
Five Bridges 53 F3
Five Houses 14 D4
Five Lanes 38 D3
Five Oak Green 31 F4
Five Oaks Chan.I. 8 C5
Five Oaks W.Suss. 29 F5
Five Roads 36 A2
Five Turnings 64 B5
Five Wents 32 A3
Fivehead 24 A5
Fivelanes 5 G1
Flack's Green 45 G1
Flackwell Heath 43 D4
Fladbury 54 B3
Flagg 80 C1
Flamborough 113 F5
Flamstead 43 F1

Flamstead End 44 C2
Flansham 16 B3
Flanshaw 102 C5
Flasby 101 F2
Flash 80 B1
Flashader 170 C4
Flask Inn 112 C2
Flaunden 43 F2
Flawborough 82 C3
Flawith 103 D1
Flax Bourton 24 C1
Flax Moss 101 D5
Flaxby 102 C2
Flaxholme 81 E3
Flaxlands 72 C2
Flaxley 39 F1
Flaxpool 23 E4
Flaxton 103 F1
Fleckney 68 B3
Flecknoe 56 A1
Fledborough 95 F5
Fleet Hants. 28 D2
Fleet Hants. 15 G2
Fleet Lincs. 84 B5
Fleet Hargate 84 B5
Fleetville 44 A2
Fleetwood 99 G3
Fleggburgh (Burgh St. Margaret) 87 F4
Flemingston 37 G5
Flemington 142 A4
Flempton 59 G1
Fletchersbridge 5 F3
Fletchertown 117 F2
Fletching 17 G1
Fleuchats 168 A4
Fleur-de-lis 38 A3
Flexbury 20 C5
Flexford 29 E2
Flimby 116 D3
Flimwell 31 G5
Flint (Y Fflint) 90 D5
Flint Cross 58 C3
Flint Mountain 90 D5
Flintham 82 C3
Flinton 105 E4
Flint's Green 67 E4
Flishinghurst 31 G5
Flitcham 85 F5
Flitholme 108 C1
Flitton 57 F4
Flitwick 57 F4
Flitwick 57 F4
Flixborough 95 F1
Flixton Gt.Man. 92 B3
Flixton N.Yorks. 112 D5
Flixton Suff. 73 E3
Flockton 93 G1
Flockton Green 93 G1
Flodden 136 D3
Flodigarry 171 D2
Flood's Ferry 70 B3
Flookburgh 107 E5
Floors 177 D4
Flordon 72 C2
Flore 56 B1
Flotta 190 B4
Flotterton 128 C1
Flowton 60 B3
Flushdyke 102 B5
Flushing Aber. 179 F3
Flushing Cornw. 3 F3
Flushing Cornw. 3 E4
Fluxton 11 D3
Flyford Flavell 54 B2
Foals Green 73 D4
Fobbing 45 G4
Fochabers 176 C4
Fochriw 38 A2
Fockerby 95 F1
Fodderletter 167 F2
Fodderty 174 D3
Foddington 24 C5
Foel 63 F1
Foelgastell 36 B1
Foggathorpe 103 G3
Fogo 145 E5
Fogorig 145 E5
Fogwatt 176 B4
Foindle 184 A4
Folda 159 G3
Fole 80 B4
Foleshill 67 F4
Folke 12 C1
Folkestone 33 E5
Folkingham 83 F4
Folkington 18 A3
Folksworth 69 G4
Folkton 113 D5
Folla Rule 169 E1

Follifoot 102 C2
Folly Dorset 12 D2
Folly Pembs. 48 C5
Folly Gate 7 F1
Fonmon 23 D1
Fonthill Bishop 26 A4
Fonthill Gifford 26 A4
Fontmell Magna 13 E1
Fontmell Parva 13 E1
Fontwell 16 B3
Font-y-gary 23 D1
Foolow 93 F5
Footherley 66 D2
Foots Cray 45 D5
Forbestown 168 A3
Force Forge 107 E3
Force Green 30 D3
Forcett 110 A1
Forches Cross 10 A2
Ford Arg. & B. 148 A1
Ford Bucks. 42 C1
Ford Devon 8 C2
Ford Devon 21 E3
Ford Devon 9 D3
Ford Glos. 54 C5
Ford Mersey. 91 E3
Ford Midloth. 144 A3
Ford Northumb. 137 D3
Ford Pembs. 48 C5
Ford Plym. 8 A2
Ford Shrop. 64 D1
Ford Som. 23 D5
Ford Staffs. 80 B2
Ford W.Suss. 16 B3
Ford Wilts. 40 A5
Ford End 45 F1
Ford Green 100 A3
Ford Heath 64 C1
Ford Street 11 E1
Forda 7 F1
Fordbridge 67 D4
Fordcombe 31 F4
Fordell 143 F1
Forden (Fforddun) 64 B2
Forder Green 9 D1
Fordgate 24 A4
Fordham Cambs. 71 E5
Fordham Essex 60 A5
Fordham Norf. 71 E3
Fordham Abbey 59 E1
Fordham Heath 60 A5
Fordhouses 66 B2
Fordingbridge 14 A1
Fordon 113 D5
Fordoun 161 F2
Ford's Green 60 B1
Fordstreet 60 A5
Fordwells 41 F1
Fordwich 33 D3
Fordyce 177 E3
Forebrae 151 E2
Forebridge 79 G5
Foredale 101 E1
Foreland 138 A3
Foremark 81 E5
Forest 110 B2
Forest Coal Pit 52 B5
Forest Gate 44 D4
Forest Green 29 G3
Forest Hall Cumb. 107 G2
Forest Hall T. & W. 120 B1
Forest Head 118 B2
Forest Hill Gt.Lon. 44 C5
Forest Hill Oxon. 42 A2
Forest Lane Head 102 C2
Forest Lodge (Taigh na Frithe) Arg. & B. 157 E5
Forest Lodge P. & K. 159 E2
Forest Row 30 D5
Forest Side 15 D4
Forest Town 81 G1
Forestburn Gate 128 C2
Forest-in-Teesdale 119 E5
Forestmill 151 E5
Forestside 15 G1
Forfar 160 C3
Forgandenny 151 F3
Forge 63 D3
Forgie 176 C4
Forhill 66 C5
Formby 91 D3
Forncett End 72 C2
Forncett St. Mary 72 C2
Forncett St. Peter 72 C2

Forneth **159** F5
Fornham All Saints **59** G1
Fornham St. Martin **59** G1
Fornighty **175** F4
Forres **175** G4
Forrest **142** C3
Forrest Lodge **123** G2
Forsbrook **79** G3
Forse **187** E5
Forsie **186** C2
Forsinain **186** B4
Forsinard **186** A4
Forston **12** C3
Fort Augustus (Cille Chuimein) **165** E4
Fort George **175** D4
Fort William (An Gearasdan) **156** D2
Forter **159** G3
Forteviot **151** F3
Forth **142** D4
Forthampton **54** A4
Fortingall **158** C5
Fortis Green **44** B4
Forton *Hants.* **27** F3
Forton *Lancs.* **100** A2
Forton *Shrop.* **64** D1
Forton *Som.* **11** G2
Forton *Staffs.* **79** E5
Fortrie **177** F5
Fortrose (A'Chananaich) **174** D4
Fortuneswell **12** C5
Forty Green **43** E3
Forty Hill **44** C3
Forward Green **60** B2
Fosbury **27** E2
Foscot **55** E5
Fosdyke **84** B4
Foss **158** C4
Foss Cross **40** C2
Fossdale **109** D3
Fossebridge **40** C1
Foster Street **45** D2
Fosterhouses **94** D1
Foster's Booth **56** B2
Foston *Derbys.* **80** C4
Foston *Leics.* **68** B3
Foston *Lincs.* **83** D3
Foston *N.Yorks.* **103** F1
Foston on the Wolds **104** D2
Fotherby **96** D3
Fotheringhay **69** F3
Foul Mile **18** B2
Foula **191** E5
Foulbog **134** D5
Foulden *Norf.* **71** F3
Foulden *Sc.Bord.* **145** G4
Foulness Island **46** D3
Foulridge **101** E3
Foulsham **86** B3
Foulstone **107** G4
Foulzie **177** G3
Fountainhall **144** B5
Four Ashes *Staffs.* **66** B2
Four Ashes *Staffs.* **66** A4
Four Ashes *Suff.* **72** A4
Four Crosses *Denb.* **76** D3
Four Crosses *Powys* **64** B1
Four Crosses *Powys* **63** G2
Four Crosses *Staffs.* **66** B2
Four Elms **31** D4
Four Forks **23** F4
Four Gotes **70** C1
Four Lane Ends *B'burn.* **100** C5
Four Lane Ends *C. & W.Ches.* **78** C1
Four Lane Ends *York* **103** F2
Four Lanes **3** D3
Four Marks **28** B4
Four Mile Bridge **88** A5
Four Oaks *E.Suss.* **19** D1
Four Oaks *Glos.* **53** F5
Four Oaks *W.Mid.* **67** E4
Four Oaks *W.Mid.* **66** D3
Four Oaks Park **66** D3
Four Roads **36** A2
Four Throws **18** C1
Fourlane Ends **81** E2
Fourlanes End **79** F2
Fourpenny **182** D5
Fourstones **119** E1
Fovant **26** B5
Foveran House **169** G2
Fowey **5** F4
Fowlis **152** B1
Fowlis Wester **151** E2
Fowlmere **58** C3
Fownhope **53** E4
Fox Hatch **45** E3
Fox Lane **29** D2
Fox Street **60** B5
Fox Up **109** D5
Foxbar **141** F3
Foxcombe Hill **41** G2
Foxcote *Glos.* **40** C1
Foxcote *Som.* **25** E2
Foxdale **98** A4
Foxearth **59** G3
Foxfield **106** D4
Foxham **40** B5
Foxhole *Cornw.* **5** D4
Foxhole *High.* **165** G1
Foxholes **112** D5
Foxhunt Green **18** A2
Foxley *Here.* **52** D3
Foxley *Norf.* **86** B3
Foxley *Northants.* **56** B2
Foxley *Wilts.* **40** A4
Foxt **80** B3
Foxton *Cambs.* **58** C3
Foxton *Dur.* **120** C5
Foxton *Leics.* **68** B3
Foxwist Green **78** D1
Foy **53** E5
Foyers (Foithir) **165** F2
Frachadil **154** C4
Fraddam **2** C3
Fraddon **4** D4
Fradley **67** D1
Fradswell **79** G4
Fraisthorpe **105** D1
Framfield **17** G1
Framingham Earl **87** D5
Framingham Pigot **87** D5
Framlingham **61** D1
Frampton *Dorset* **12** C3
Frampton *Lincs.* **84** B4
Frampton Cotterell **39** F4
Frampton Mansell **40** B2
Frampton on Severn **39** G2
Frampton West End **84** A3
Framsden **60** D2
Framwellgate Moor **120** B3
France Lynch **40** B2
Frances Green **100** C4
Franche **66** A5
Frandley **92** A5
Frankby **90** D4
Frankfort **87** E3
Frankley **66** B4
Franksbridge **52** A2
Frankton **67** G5
Frant **31** E5
Fraserburgh **179** E1
Frating **60** B5
Fratton **15** F2
Freasley **67** E3
Freathy **7** D5
Freckenham **71** E5
Freckleton **100** A5
Freeby **82** D5
Freefolk **27** F3
Freehay **80** B3
Freeland **41** G1
Freethorpe **87** F5
Freethorpe Common **87** F5
Freiston **84** B3
Freiston Shore **84** B3
Fremington *Devon* **21** F2
Fremington *N.Yorks.* **109** F3
Frenchay **39** F5
Frenchbeer **7** G2
Frendraught **177** F5
Frenich **149** G4
Frensham **28** D3
Fresgoe **186** B2
Freshbrook **40** D4
Freshfield **91** D2
Freshford **25** E2
Freshwater **14** C4
Freshwater Bay **14** C4
Freshwater East **34** D3
Fressingfield **73** D4
Freston **60** C4
Freswick **187** F2
Fretherne **39** G2
Frettenham **86** D4
Freuchie **152** A4
Freystrop Cross **34** C1
Friars Carse **124** D2
Friar's Gate **31** D5
Friarton **151** G2
Friday Bridge **70** C2
Friday Street *E.Suss.* **18** B3
Friday Street *Suff.* **60** D2
Friday Street *Suff.* **61** E2
Friday Street *Surr.* **29** G3
Fridaythorpe **104** A2
Friern Barnet **44** B3
Friesthorpe **96** A4
Frieston **83** E3
Frieth **42** C3
Frilford **41** G3
Frilsham **42** A5
Frimley **29** D2
Frimley Green **29** D2
Frindsbury **31** G2
Fring **85** F4
Fringford **56** B5
Friningham **32** A3
Frinsted **32** A3
Frinton-on-Sea **47** F1
Friockheim **161** D5
Friog **62** C1
Frisby on the Wreake **68** B1
Friskney **84** C2
Friskney Eaudyke **84** C2
Friston *E.Suss.* **18** A4
Friston *Suff.* **61** F1
Fritchley **81** E2
Frith **32** B3
Frith Bank **84** B3
Frith Common **53** F1
Fritham **14** B1
Frithelstock **21** E4
Frithelstock Stone **21** E4
Frithville **84** B2
Frittenden **32** A4
Frittiscombe **9** E3
Fritton *Norf.* **72** D2
Fritton *Norf.* **87** F5
Fritwell **56** A5
Frizinghall **102** A4
Frizington **116** D5
Frocester **39** G2
Frochas **64** B2
Frodesley **65** E2
Frodesley Lane **65** E2
Frodingham **95** F1
Frodsham **91** G5
Frog End **58** C2
Frog Pool **53** G1
Frogden **136** B4
Froggatt **93** G5
Froghall **80** B3
Frogham **14** A1
Frogland Cross **39** F4
Frogmore *Devon* **9** D3
Frogmore *Hants.* **28** D2
Frogmore *Herts.* **44** A2
Frogwell **6** D4
Frolesworth **68** A3
Frome **25** E3
Frome Market **25** F2
Frome St. Quintin **12** B2
Frome Whitfield **12** C3
Fromes Hill **53** F3
Fron *Gwyn.* **74** C4
Fron *Powys* **64** B2
Fron *Powys* **51** G1
Fron *Powys* **64** A3
Fron Isaf **77** F4
Froncysyllte **77** F3
Fron-goch **76** C4
Frostenden **73** F3
Frosterley **119** G4
Froxfield **27** E1
Froxfield Green **28** C5
Fryerning **45** F2
Fugglestone St. Peter **26** C4
Fulbeck **83** E2
Fulbourn **58** D2
Fulbrook **41** E1
Fulflood **27** F5
Fulford *Som.* **23** F5
Fulford *Staffs.* **79** G4
Fulford *York* **103** F3
Fulham **44** B5
Fulking **17** E2
Full Sutton **103** G2
Fullaford **21** G2
Fuller Street **45** G1
Fuller's Moor **78** B2
Fullerton **27** E4
Fulletby **96** C5
Fullwood **141** F4
Fulmer **43** F4
Fulmodeston **86** A2
Fulnetby **96** B5
Fulready **55** E3
Fulstone **93** F2
Fulstow **96** D3
Fulwell *Oxon.* **55** F5
Fulwell *T. & W.* **120** C2
Fulwood *Lancs.* **100** B4
Fulwood *S.Yorks.* **94** A4
Fundenhall **72** C2
Fundenhall Street **72** C2
Funtington **16** A3
Funtley **15** E2
Funzie **191** G2
Furley **11** F2
Furnace *Arg. & B.* **148** C4
Furnace *Carmar.* **36** B2
Furnace *Cere.* **62** C3
Furnace *High.* **172** C2
Furnace End **67** E3
Furner's Green **17** G1
Furness Vale **93** E4
Furneux Pelham **58** C5
Furnham **11** G2
Further Quarter **32** A5
Furtho **56** C3
Furze Green **72** D3
Furze Platt **43** D4
Furzehill *Devon* **22** A3
Furzehill *Dorset* **13** G2
Furzeley Corner **15** F1
Furzey Lodge **14** C2
Furzley **14** B1
Fyfett **11** F1
Fyfield *Essex* **45** E2
Fyfield *Glos.* **41** E2
Fyfield *Hants.* **27** D3
Fyfield *Oxon.* **41** G3
Fyfield *Wilts.* **26** C1
Fyfield *Wilts.* **26** C1
Fylingthorpe **112** C2
Fyning **28** D5
Fyvie **169** E1

G

Gabalfa **38** A5
Gablon **182** C5
Gabroc Hill **141** F4
Gaddesby **68** B1
Gaddesden Row **43** F1
Gadebridge **43** F2
Gadshill **45** G5
Gaer *Newport* **38** B4
Gaer *Powys* **52** A5
Gaer-fawr **38** D3
Gaerllwyd **38** D3
Gaerwen **88** C5
Gagingwell **55** G5
Gaich *High.* **167** E2
Gaich *High.* **166** A1
Gaick Lodge **158** C1
Gailes **132** B2
Gailey **66** B1
Gainford **110** A1
Gainsborough **95** F3
Gainsford End **59** F4
Gairloch (Geàrrloch) **172** A2
Gairlochy (Geàrr Lòchaidh) **157** D1
Gairney Bank **151** G5
Gairnshiel Lodge **167** G4
Gaitsgill **117** G2
Galabank **144** B5
Galashiels **135** F2
Galdenoch **122** C4
Gale **92** D1
Galgate **100** A2
Galhampton **24** D5
Gallanach **148** A2
Gallantry Bank **78** C2
Gallatown **152** A5
Gallchoille **147** G5
Gallery **161** E3
Galley Common **67** F3
Galleyend **45** G2
Galleywood **45** G2
Gallowfauld **160** C5
Gallowhill **141** F3
Gallows Green **80** B3
Gallowstree Common **42** B4
Gallowstree Elm **66** A4
Galltair **163** G2
Gallt-y-foel **75** E1
Gallypot Street **31** D5
Galmington **23** F5
Galmisdale **155** D1
Galmpton *Devon* **8** C3
Galmpton *Torbay* **9** E2
Galmpton Warborough **9** E2
Galphay **110** B5
Galston **132** C2
Galtrigill **170** A4
Gamble's Green **45** G1
Gamblesby **118** C4
Gamelsby **117** F1
Gamesley **93** E3
Gamlingay **58** A2
Gamlingay Cinques **58** A2
Gamlingay Great Heath **58** A2
Gammaton **21** E3
Gammaton Moor **21** E3
Gammersgill **109** F4
Gamrie **177** G3
Gamston *Notts.* **95** E5
Gamston *Notts.* **82** B4
Ganarew **39** E1
Gang **6** D4
Ganllwyd **76** A5
Gannochy **161** E2
Ganstead **105** D4
Ganthorpe **111** F5
Ganton **112** C5
Ganwick Corner **44** B3
Gaodhail **147** F1
Gappah **10** B5
Gara Bridge **8** D2
Garabal **149** F3
Garadheancal **180** B4
Garbat **174** A3
Garbhallt **148** C5
Garboldisham **72** B3
Garden **150** A5
Garden City **78** A1
Garden Village **93** G3
Gardeners Green **28** D1
Gardenstown **177** G3
Garderhouse **191** E4
Gardham **104** B3
Gare Hill **25** E3
Garelochhead **149** E5
Garford **41** G3
Garforth **102** D4
Gargrave **101** F2
Gargunnock **150** C5
Gariob **139** F1
Garlic Street **72** D3
Garlies Castle **123** F4
Garlieston **115** E2
Garlinge Green **32** D3
Garlogie **169** E4
Garmelow **79** F5
Garmond **178** D2
Garmony **155** F5
Garmouth **176** C3
Garmston **65** F2
Garnant **36** C1
Garndolbenmaen **75** D3
Garneddwen **63** D2
Garnett Bridge **107** G3
Garnfadryn **74** B4
Garnswllt **36** C2
Garrachra **140** B1
Garralburn **177** D4
Garras **3** E4
Garreg **75** F3
Garreg Bank **64** B1
Garrett's Green **67** D4
Garrick **150** D3
Garrigill **118** D3
Garriston **110** A3
Garroch **123** G2
Garrochty **140** B4
Garros **171** D3
Garrow **150** D1
Garryhorn **123** G1
Garsdale **108** C4
Garsdale Head **108** C3
Garsdon **40** B4
Garshall Green **79** G4
Garsington **42** A2
Garstang **100** A3
Garston **91** F4
Garswood **91** G3
Gartachoil **150** A5
Gartally **165** F1
Gartavaich **139** G4
Gartbreck **138** A4
Gartcosh **142** A3
Garth *Bridgend* **37** E3
Garth *Cere.* **62** C4
Garth *Gwyn.* **89** D5
Garth *I.o.M.* **98** B4
Garth *Powys* **51** F3
Garth *Wrex.* **77** F3
Garth Row **107** G3
Garthbrengy **51** G4
Garthdee **169** G4
Gartheli **50** B2
Garthmyl **64** A3
Garthorpe *Leics.* **82** D5
Garthorpe *N.Lincs.* **95** F1
Garths **107** G3
Garthynty **50** D3
Gartincaber **150** B4
Gartly **168** C1
Gartmore **150** A5
Gartnagrenach **139** F4
Gartnatra **138** B3
Gartness **141** G1
Gartocharn **141** F1
Garton **105** E4
Garton-on-the-Wolds **104** B1
Gartymore **183** F3
Garvald **144** C2
Garvamore **165** G5
Garvan **156** B2
Garvard **146** C5
Garve (Clachan Ghairbh) **173** G3
Garveld **130** B5
Garvestone **86** B5
Garvie **140** B1
Garvock *Aber.* **161** F2
Garvock *Inclyde* **141** D2
Garvock *P. & K.* **151** F3
Garwald **134** D5
Garwaldwaterfoot **134** D5
Garway **53** D5
Garway Hill **52** D5
Gask *Aber.* **179** F3
Gask *Aber.* **177** G5
Gask *P. & K.* **151** E3
Gaskan **156** A2
Gass **132** C5
Gastard **25** F1
Gasthorpe **72** A3
Gaston Green **45** E1
Gatcombe **15** D4
Gate Burton **95** F4
Gate Helmsley **103** F2
Gate House **139** D2
Gateacre **91** F4
Gateford **94** C4
Gateforth **103** E5
Gatehead **132** B2
Gatehouse **159** D5
Gatehouse of Fleet **124** A5
Gatelawbridge **124** D1
Gateley **86** A3
Gatenby **110** C4
Gatesgarth **117** E5
Gateshaw **136** B4
Gateshead **120** B1
Gatesheath **78** B1
Gateside *Aber.* **168** D3
Gateside *Angus* **160** C5
Gateside *Fife* **151** G4
Gateside *N.Ayr.* **141** E4
Gateslack **133** G5
Gathurst **91** G2
Gatley **92** C4
Gattonside **135** G2
Gatwick Airport **30** B4
Gaufron **51** F1
Gaulby **68** B2
Gauldry **152** B2
Gauntons Bank **78** C3
Gaunt's Common **13** G2
Gaunt's Earthcott **39** F4
Gautby **96** B5
Gavinton **145** E4
Gawber **94** A2
Gawcott **56** B4
Gawsworth **92** C5
Gawthrop **108** B4
Gawthwaite **107** D4
Gay Bowers **45** G2
Gay Street **29** F5
Gaydon **55** F2
Gayhurst **56** D3
Gayle **109** D4
Gayles **110** A2

Gayton *Mersey.* **91** D4
Gayton *Norf.* **71** F1
Gayton *Northants.* **56** C2
Gayton *Staffs.* **79** G5
Gayton le Marsh **97** E4
Gayton le Wold **96** C4
Gayton Thorpe **71** F1
Gaywood **86** E5
Gazeley **59** F1
Geanies House **175** E2
Gearach **138** A4
Gearnsary **182** C1
Gearradh **156** B3
Gearraidh na h-Aibhne **189** F2
Geary **170** B3
Gedding **60** A2
Geddington **69** D4
Gedgrave Hall **61** F3
Gedintailor **162** D1
Gedling **82** B3
Gedney **84** C5
Gedney Broadgate **84** C5
Gedney Drove End **84** C5
Gedney Dyke **84** C5
Gedney Hill **70** B1
Gee Cross **93** D3
Geilston **141** E2
Geldeston **73** E2
Gell *Conwy* **76** B1
Gell *Gwyn.* **75** D4
Gelli **37** F3
Gelli Gynan **77** E2
Gellideg **37** D2
Gellifor **77** E1
Gelligaer **38** A3
Gellilydan **75** F4
Gellioedd **76** C3
Gelly **35** D1
Gellyburn **151** F1
Gellywen **49** F5
Gelston *D. & G.* **124** B5
Gelston *Lincs.* **83** E3
Gembling **104** D2
Gemmil **147** G4
Genoch **122** C5
Genoch Square **122** C5
Gentleshaw **66** C1
George Green **43** F4
Georgeham **21** E2
Georgetown **141** F3
Gerlan **75** F1
Germansweek **7** E1
Germoe **2** C4
Gerrans **3** F3
Gerrards Cross **43** F4
Gerston **186** D3
Gestingthorpe **59** G4
Geufordd **64** B1
Geufron **63** E4
Gibbet Hill **25** E3
Gibbshill **124** B3
Gibraltar *Lincs.* **85** D2
Gibraltar *Suff.* **60** C2
Giddeahall **40** A5
Giddy Green **13** E4
Gidea Park **45** E4
Gidleigh **7** G2
Giffnock **141** G4
Gifford **144** C3
Giffordland **141** D5
Giffordtown **152** A3
Giggleswick **101** E1
Gigha **139** E5
Gilberdyke **104** A5
Gilbert's End **54** A3
Gilchriston **144** B3
Gilcrux **117** E3
Gildersome **102** B5
Gildingwells **94** C4
Gilesgate Moor **120** B3
Gileston **22** D1
Gilfach **38** A3
Gilfach Goch **37** F4
Gilfachrheda **50** A2
Gilgarran **116** D4
Gill **118** A5
Gillamoor **111** F4
Gillen **170** B3
Gillenbie **125** F2
Gillfoot **125** D3
Gilling East **111** F5
Gilling West **110** A2
Gillingham *Dorset* **25** F5
Gillingham *Med.* **31** G2
Gillingham *Norf.* **73** F2
Gillivoan **183** G1
Gillock **187** E3

Gillow Heath **79** F2
Gills **187** F1
Gill's Green **31** G5
Gilmanscleuch **135** E3
Gilmerton *Edin.* **143** G3
Gilmerton *P. & K.* **151** D2
Gilson **67** D3
Gilstead **102** A4
Gilston **144** B4
Gilston Park **44** D1
Gilwern **38** B1
Gimingham **87** D2
Gin Pit **92** A2
Ginclough **93** D5
Ginger's Green **18** B2
Gipping **72** B1
Gipsey Bridge **84** A3
Girlsta **191** F4
Girsby **110** C2
Girtford **57** G3
Girthon **124** A5
Girton *Cambs.* **58** C1
Girton *Notts.* **82** D1
Girvan **122** C1
Gisburn **101** E3
Gisburn Cotes **101** E3
Gisleham **73** G3
Gislingham **72** B1
Gissing **72** C3
Gittisham **11** E3
Givons Grove **29** G2
Glackour **173** E1
Gladestry **52** B2
Gladsmuir **144** B2
Glaic **140** B2
Glais **36** D2
Glaisdale **111** G2
Glaister **131** E2
Glame **171** E5
Glamis **160** B5
Glan Conwy **76** B2
Glanaber Terrace **76** A3
Glanaman **36** C1
Glanbran **51** E4
Glan-Denys **50** B2
Glanderston **168** C2
Glandford **86** B1
Glan-Duar **50** B3
Glandwr **35** F1
Glan-Dwyfach **75** D3
Glangrwyney **38** B1
Glanllynfi **37** E3
Glanmule **64** A3
Glan-rhyd *N.P.T.* **37** D2
Glanrhyd *Pembs.* **49** E3
Glanton **137** E5
Glanton Pyke **137** E5
Glanvilles Wootton **12** C2
Glanwern **62** C4
Glanwydden **89** G4
Glan-y-don **90** C5
Glan-y-llyn **38** A4
Glan-y-nant **63** F4
Glan-yr-afon *Gwyn.* **76** C3
Glan-yr-afon *Gwyn.* **76** D3
Glan-yr-afon *I.o.A.* **89** E4
Glan-y-Wern **75** F4
Glapthorn **69** F3
Glapwell **81** F1
Glasahoile **149** G4
Glasbury **52** A4
Glaschoil **167** E1
Glascoed *Mon.* **38** C2
Glascoed *Wrex.* **77** F2
Glascorrie **168** B5
Glascote **67** E2
Glascwm **52** A2
Glasdrum **156** C5
Glasfryn **76** C2
Glasgow (Glaschu) **141** G3
Glasgow Airport **141** F3
Glasgow Prestwick Airport **132** B3
Glashmore **169** E4
Glasinfryn **75** E1
Glasnacardoch **163** E5
Glasnakille **162** D3
Glaspant **49** F4
Glaspwll **62** D3
Glassburn **165** E1

Glassel **169** D5
Glassenbury **31** G5
Glasserton **115** E3
Glassford **142** B5
Glasshouse **53** G5
Glasshouses **102** A1
Glassingall **150** C4
Glasslie **152** A4
Glasson *Cumb.* **126** A5
Glasson *Lancs.* **100** A2
Glassonby **118** B4
Glasterlaw **161** D4
Glaston **69** D2
Glastonbury **24** B4
Glatton **69** G4
Glazebrook **92** A3
Glazebury **92** A3
Glazeley **65** G4
Gleadless **94** A4
Gleadsmoss **79** F1
Gleaston **107** D5
Glecknabae **140** B3
Gledhow **102** C4
Gledrid **77** F4
Glemsford **59** G3
Glen *D. & G.* **124** C3
Glen *D. & G.* **123** G5
Glen Auldyn **98** C2
Glen Mona **98** C3
Glen Parva **68** A3
Glen Trool Lodge **123** F2
Glen Village **142** C2
Glen Vine **98** B4
Glenae **125** D2
Glenaladale **156** A2
Glenald **149** E5
Glenamachrie **148** B2
Glenapp Castle **122** B2
Glenarm **160** B3
Glenbarr **130** B2
Glenbatrick **138** D2
Glenbeg *High.* **173** G1
Glenbeg *High.* **167** E2
Glenbeg *High.* **155** E3
Glenbeich **150** B2
Glenbervie *Aber.* **161** F1
Glenbervie *Falk.* **142** C1
Glenboig **142** B3
Glenborrodale **155** F3
Glenbranter **148** D5
Glenbreck **134** B3
Glenbrittle **162** C2
Glenburn **141** F3
Glenbyre **147** E2
Glencaple **125** D4
Glencarse **151** G2
Glencat **168** C5
Glenceitlein **156** D5
Glenclov **131** F2
Glencoe (A' Chàrnaich) **156** D4
Glenconglass **167** F2
Glencraig **151** G5
Glencripesdale **155** F4
Glencrosh **124** B2
Glencruitten **148** A2
Glencuie **168** B3
Glendearg *D. & G.* **134** D5
Glendearg *Sc.Bord.* **135** G2
Glendessary **164** A5
Glendevon **151** E4
Glendoebeg **165** F4
Glendoick **152** A2
Glendoune **122** C1
Glendrissaig **122** C1
Glenduckie **152** A3
Glenduisk **122** D2
Glendye Lodge **161** E1
Gleneagles Hotel **151** E3
Gleneagles House **151** E4
Glenearn **151** G3
Glenegedale **138** B4
Glenelg (Gleann Eilg) **163** G3
Glenfarg **151** G3
Glenfeochan **148** A2
Glenfield **68** A2
Glenfinnan (Gleann Fhionnain) **156** B1
Glenfoot **151** G3
Glengalmadale **156** A4
Glengap **124** A5
Glengarnock **141** E4
Glengarrisdale **147** F5
Glengennet **123** D1
Glengolly **186** D2

Glengrasco **170** D5
Glengyle **149** F3
Glenhead **124** C2
Glenhead Farm **160** A3
Glenhurich **156** A3
Glenkerry **135** D4
Glenkiln **131** F2
Glenkin **140** C1
Glenkindie **168** B3
Glenlair **124** B3
Glenlatterach **176** B4
Glenlean **140** C1
Glenlee *Angus* **160** C2
Glenlee *D. & G.* **124** A2
Glenlichorn **150** C2
Glenlivet **167** F2
Glenlochar **124** B4
Glenluce **122** C5
Glenmallan **149** E5
Glenmarksie **133** F5
Glenmavis **142** B3
Glenmaye **98** A4
Glenmeanie **173** E5
Glenmore *Arg. & B.* **140** B3
Glenmore *High.* **170** D5
Glenmore *High.* **167** D5
Glenmore Lodge **167** D4
Glenmoy **160** C3
Glenmuick **181** F3
Glennoe **148** C1
Glenochar **134** A4
Glenogil **160** C3
Glenprosen Village **160** B3
Glenquiech **160** C3
Glenramskill **130** C4
Glenrazie **123** E4
Glenridding **117** G5
Glenrisdell **139** G4
Glenrossal **181** G4
Glenrothes **152** A4
Glensanda **156** A5
Glensaugh **161** E2
Glensgaich **174** A3
Glenshalg **168** C4
Glenshellish **148** D5
Glensluain **148** C5
Glentaggart **133** G3
Glentham **96** A3
Glenton **168** D2
Glentress **135** D2
Glentrool **123** E3
Glentruan **98** C1
Glentworth **95** G4
Glenuachdarach **170** D4
Glenuig **155** F2
Glenure **156** C5
Glenurquhart **174** D3
Glenwhilly **122** C3
Glespin **133** G3
Glewstone **53** E5
Glinton **69** G2
Glogue **49** F4
Glooston **68** C3
Glororum **137** F3
Glossop **93** E3
Gloster Hill **129** E1
Gloucester **40** A1
Gloucestershire Airport **54** A5
Gloweth **4** B5
Glusburn **101** G3
Glympton **55** G5
Glyn **76** D2
Glyn Ceiriog **77** F4
Glynarthen **49** G3
Glyncoch **37** G3
Glyncorrwg **37** E3
Glynde **17** G2
Glyndebourne **17** G2
Glyndyfrdwy **77** E3
Glynneath (Glyn-Nedd) **37** E2
Glynogwr **37** F4
Glyntaff **37** G4
Gnosall **79** F5
Gnosall Heath **79** F5
Goadby **82** C5
Goadby Marwood **82** C5
Goatacre **40** C5
Goatfield **148** C4
Goathill **12** C1
Goathland **112** B2
Goathurst **23** F4
Gobernuisgeach **183** D1
Gobowen **78** A4
Godalming **29** E3

Goddard's Corner **61** D1
Goddards Green **17** E1
Godden Green **31** D2
Godford Cross **11** E2
Godington **56** B5
Godley **93** G3
Godmanchester **70** A5
Godmanstone **12** C3
Godmersham **32** C3
Godney **24** B3
Godolphin Cross **2** D3
Godor **64** B1
Godre'r-graig **37** D2
Godshill *Hants.* **14** A1
Godshill *I.o.W.* **15** E4
Godstone **30** C3
Godwick **86** A3
Goetre **38** C1
Goff's Oak **44** C2
Gogar **143** F1
Goginan **62** C4
Goirtean a' Chladaich **156** C2
Goirtein **140** A1
Golan **75** E3
Golant **5** F4
Golberdon **6** D3
Golborne **92** A3
Golcar **93** F1
Gold Hill *Cambs.* **70** D3
Gold Hill *Dorset* **13** E1
Goldcliff **38** C4
Golden Cross **18** A2
Golden Green **31** F4
Golden Grove **36** B1
Golden Pot **28** D3
Golden Valley *Derbys.* **81** F2
Golden Valley *Glos.* **54** B5
Goldenhill **79** F2
Golders Green **44** B4
Goldhanger **46** C2
Goldielea **124** D3
Golding **65** E2
Goldington **57** F2
Goldsborough *N.Yorks.* **112** B1
Goldsborough *N.Yorks.* **102** C2
Goldsithney **2** C3
Goldstone **79** E5
Goldthorn Park **66** B3
Goldthorpe **94** B2
Goldworthy **21** D3
Golford **31** G5
Gollanfield **175** E4
Gollinghith Foot **110** A4
Golspie **182** D5
Golval **186** A2
Gomeldon **26** C4
Gomersal **102** B5
Gometra **154** C5
Gometra House **154** C5
Gomshall **29** F3
Gonachan Cottage **142** A1
Gonalston **82** B3
Gonerby Hill Foot **83** E4
Good Easter **45** F1
Gooderstone **71** F2
Goodleigh **21** G2
Goodmanham **104** A3
Goodmayes **45** D4
Goodnestone *Kent* **33** E3
Goodnestone *Kent* **32** C2
Goodrich **39** E1
Goodrington **9** E2
Goodshaw **101** E5
Goodshaw Fold **101** E5
Goodwick (Wdig) **48** C4
Goodworth Clatford **27** E3
Goodyers End **67** F4
Goole **103** G5
Goom's Hill **54** C2
Goonbell **4** B5
Goonhavern **4** B4
Goonvrea **4** B5
Goose Green *Essex* **60** C5
Goose Green *Essex* **60** C5
Goose Green *Gt.Man.* **91** G2
Goose Green *Kent* **31** F3
Goose Green *S.Glos.* **39** F5
Goose Pool **53** D4
Gooseham **20** C4

Goosehill Green **54** B1
Goosewell **8** B2
Goosey **41** F3
Goosnargh **100** B3
Goostrey **92** B5
Gorcott Hill **54** C1
Gorddinog **89** E5
Gordon **144** D5
Gordonbush **182** D4
Gordonstoun **176** A3
Gordonstown *Aber.* **177** F4
Gordonstown *Aber.* **169** E1
Gore Cross **26** B2
Gore End **27** F1
Gore Pit **46** B1
Gore Street **33** E2
Gorebridge **144** A3
Gorefield **70** C1
Gorey **8** D5
Gorgie **143** G2
Goring **42** B4
Goring Heath **42** B5
Goring-by-Sea **16** D3
Gorleston-on-Sea **87** G5
Gorllwyn **49** G4
Gornalwood **66** B3
Gorrachie **177** G4
Gorran Churchtown **5** D5
Gorran Haven **5** E5
Gors **62** C5
Gorsedd **90** C5
Gorseinon **36** B3
Gorseybank **81** D2
Gorsgoch **50** C2
Gorslas **36** B1
Gorsley **53** F5
Gorsley Common **53** F5
Gorstage **92** A5
Gorstan **173** G3
Gorstanvorran **156** A2
Gorsty Hill **80** C5
Gorten **147** G1
Gortenbuie **147** E1
Gorteneorn **155** F3
Gorton *Arg. & B.* **154** A4
Gorton *Gt.Man.* **92** C3
Gosbeck **60** C2
Gosberton **84** A4
Gosberton Clough **83** G5
Goseley Dale **81** E5
Gosfield **59** F5
Gosford *Here.* **53** E1
Gosford *Oxon.* **42** A1
Gosforth *Cumb.* **106** B2
Gosforth *T. & W.* **120** B1
Gosland Green **78** C2
Gosmore **57** F2
Gospel End **66** A3
Gosport **15** F3
Gossington **39** G2
Gossops Green **30** B5
Goswick **137** E2
Gotham **81** G4
Gotherington **54** B5
Gothers **5** D4
Gotton **23** F5
Goudhurst **31** G5
Goulceby **96** C5
Gourdas **177** G5
Gourdon **161** G2
Gourock **140** D2
Govan **141** G3
Goverton **82** C2
Goveton **9** D3
Govilon **38** B1
Gowanhill **179** F1
Gowdall **103** F5
Gowerton **36** B3
Gowkhall **143** E1
Gowkthrapple **142** B4
Gowthorpe **103** G2
Goxhill *E.Riding* **105** D3
Goxhill *N.Lincs.* **104** D5
Goytre **37** E4
Gozzard's Ford **41** G3
Grabhair **189** G3
Graby **83** F5
Gradbach **79** G1
Grade **3** E5
Gradeley Green **78** C2
Grafham **76** B2
Grafham *Cambs.* **57** G1
Grafham *Surr.* **29** F3
Grafton *Here.* **53** D4
Grafton *N.Yorks.* **102** D1
Grafton *Oxon.* **41** E2
Grafton *Shrop.* **64** D1

Grafton Worcs. 53 E1
Grafton Worcs. 54 B4
Grafton Flyford 54 B3
Grafton Regis 56 C3
Grafton Underwood 69 E4
Grafty Green 32 A4
Graianrhyd 77 F2
Graig Carmar. 36 A2
Graig Conwy 89 G5
Graig Denb. 77 E3
Graig-fechan 77 E2
Grain 32 A1
Grainel 138 A3
Grainhow 179 D3
Grains Bar 93 D2
Grainsby 96 C3
Grainthorpe 97 D3
Graizelound 95 E3
Grampound 4 D5
Grampound Road 4 D4
Granborough 56 C5
Granby 82 C4
Grandborough 55 G1
Grandes Rocques 9 F4
Grandtully 159 F4
Grange Cumb. 117 F5
Grange E.Ayr. 132 C2
Grange High. 165 E1
Grange Med. 31 G2
Grange Mersey. 90 D4
Grange P. & K. 152 A2
Grange Crossroads 177 D4
Grange de Lings 95 G5
Grange Hall 175 G3
Grange Hill 44 D3
Grange Moor 93 G1
Grange of Lindores 152 A3
Grange Villa 120 B2
Grangemill 80 D2
Grangemouth 142 D1
Grangemuir 152 D4
Grange-over-Sands 107 F5
Grangeston 122 D1
Grangetown Cardiff 38 A5
Grangetown R. & C. 121 E5
Granish 166 D3
Gransmoor 104 D2
Granston 48 B4
Grantchester 58 C2
Grantham 83 E4
Grantley 110 B5
Grantlodge 169 E3
Granton 143 G2
Granton House 134 B5
Grantown-on-Spey 167 E2
Grantsfield 53 E1
Grantshouse 145 F3
Grappenhall 92 A4
Grasby 96 A2
Grasmere 107 E2
Grass Green 59 F4
Grasscroft 93 D2
Grassendale 91 E4
Grassgarth 107 F3
Grassholme 119 F5
Grassington 101 G1
Grassmoor 81 F1
Grassthorpe 82 C1
Grateley 27 D3
Gratwich 80 B4
Gravel Hill 43 F3
Graveley Cambs. 58 A1
Graveley Herts. 58 A5
Gravelly Hill 66 D3
Gravels 64 C2
Graveney 32 C2
Gravesend 45 F5
Grayingham 95 G3
Grayrigg 107 F2
Grays 45 F5
Grayshott 29 D4
Grayswood 29 E4
Grazeley 28 B1
Greasbrough 94 B3
Greasby 91 D4
Great Abington 58 D3
Great Addington 69 E5
Great Alne 54 D2
Great Altcar 91 E2
Great Amwell 44 C1
Great Asby 108 B1
Great Ashfield 60 A1
Great Ayton 111 E1

Great Baddow 45 G2
Great Bardfield 59 E4
Great Barford 57 G2
Great Barr 66 C3
Great Barrington 41 E1
Great Barrow 78 B1
Great Barton 59 G1
Great Barugh 111 G5
Great Bavington 128 B3
Great Bealings 60 D3
Great Bedwyn 27 D1
Great Bentley 60 C5
Great Bernera 189 F2
Great Billing 56 D1
Great Bircham 85 F4
Great Blakenham 60 C2
Great Bolas 78 D5
Great Bookham 29 G2
Great Bourton 55 G3
Great Bowden 68 C4
Great Bradley 59 E2
Great Braxted 46 B5
Great Bricett 60 B2
Great Brickhill 57 E4
Great Bridgeford 79 F5
Great Brington 56 B1
Great Bromley 60 B5
Great Broughton Cumb. 117 D3
Great Broughton N.Yorks. 111 E2
Great Buckland 31 F2
Great Budworth 92 A5
Great Burdon 110 C1
Great Burstead 45 F3
Great Busby 111 E2
Great Cambourne 58 B2
Great Canfield 45 E1
Great Canney 46 B2
Great Carlton 97 E4
Great Casterton 69 F2
Great Chalfield 25 F1
Great Chart 32 B4
Great Chatwell 65 G1
Great Chell 79 F2
Great Chesterford 58 D3
Great Cheverell 26 A2
Great Chishill 58 C4
Great Clacton 47 E1
Great Clifton 116 D4
Great Coates 96 C2
Great Comberton 54 B3
Great Corby 118 A2
Great Cornard 59 G3
Great Cowden 105 E3
Great Coxwell 41 E3
Great Crakehall 110 B4
Great Cransley 68 D5
Great Cressingham 71 G2
Great Crosby 91 E2
Great Crosthwaite 117 F4
Great Cubley 80 C4
Great Cumbrae 140 C4
Great Doddington 57 D1
Great Doward 39 E1
Great Dunham 71 G1
Great Dunmow 59 E5
Great Durnford 26 C4
Great Easton Essex 59 E5
Great Easton Leics. 68 D3
Great Eccleston 100 A3
Great Edstone 111 G4
Great Ellingham 72 B2
Great Elm 25 E3
Great Eversden 58 B2
Great Fencote 110 B3
Great Finborough 60 B2
Great Fransham 71 G1
Great Gaddesden 43 F1
Great Gidding 69 G4
Great Givendale 104 A2
Great Glemham 61 E1
Great Glen 68 B3
Great Gonerby 83 D4
Great Gransden 58 B2
Great Green Cambs. 58 A3
Great Green Norf. 73 D3
Great Green Suff. 60 A5
Great Green Suff. 72 C4
Great Green Suff. 72 B4
Great Habton 111 G5
Great Hale 83 G3
Great Hallingbury 45 E1
Great Hampden 42 D2
Great Harrowden 69 D5
Great Harwood 100 D4

Great Haseley 42 B2
Great Hatfield 105 D3
Great Haywood 80 B5
Great Heath 67 F4
Great Heck 103 E5
Great Henny 59 G4
Great Hinton 26 A2
Great Hockham 72 A2
Great Holland 47 F1
Great Horkesley 60 A4
Great Hormead 58 C4
Great Horton 102 A4
Great Horwood 56 C4
Great Houghton Northants. 56 C2
Great Houghton S.Yorks. 94 B2
Great Hucklow 93 F5
Great Kelk 104 D2
Great Kimble 42 D2
Great Kingshill 43 D3
Great Langton 110 B3
Great Leighs 45 G1
Great Limber 96 B2
Great Linford 56 D3
Great Livermere 71 G4
Great Longstone 93 G5
Great Lumley 120 B3
Great Lyth 65 D2
Great Malvern 53 G3
Great Maplestead 59 G4
Great Marton 99 G4
Great Massingham 85 F5
Great Melton 86 C5
Great Milton 42 B2
Great Missenden 43 D2
Great Mitton 100 D4
Great Mongeham 33 F3
Great Moulton 72 C2
Great Munden 58 B5
Great Musgrave 108 C1
Great Ness 64 D1
Great Notley 59 F5
Great Nurcot 22 C4
Great Oak 38 C2
Great Oakley Essex 60 C5
Great Oakley Northants. 69 D4
Great Offley 57 G5
Great Ormside 108 C1
Great Orton 117 G1
Great Ouseburn 102 D1
Great Oxendon 68 C4
Great Oxney Green 45 F2
Great Palgrave 71 G1
Great Parndon 44 D2
Great Paxton 58 A1
Great Plumpton 99 G4
Great Plumstead 87 E5
Great Ponton 83 E4
Great Potheridge 21 F4
Great Preston 102 C5
Great Purston 56 A4
Great Raveley 70 A4
Great Rissington 41 D1
Great Rollright 55 F4
Great Ryburgh 86 A3
Great Ryle 137 E5
Great Ryton 65 D2
Great Saling 59 F5
Great Salkeld 118 B4
Great Sampford 59 E4
Great Sankey 91 G4
Great Saredon 66 B2
Great Saxham 59 F1
Great Shefford 41 F5
Great Shelford 58 C2
Great Smeaton 110 C2
Great Snoring 86 A2
Great Somerford 40 B4
Great Stainton 120 C5
Great Stambridge 46 C3
Great Staughton 57 G1
Great Steeping 84 C1
Great Stonar 33 F3
Great Strickland 118 B5
Great Stukeley 70 A5
Great Sturton 96 C5
Great Sutton C. & W.Ches. 91 E5
Great Sutton Shrop. 65 E4
Great Swinburne 128 B4
Great Tew 55 F5
Great Tey 59 G5
Great Thorness 15 D3
Great Thurlow 59 E3
Great Torr 8 C3

Great Torrington 21 E4
Great Tosson 128 C1
Great Totham Essex 46 B1
Great Totham Essex 46 B1
Great Tows 96 C3
Great Urswick 107 D5
Great Wakering 46 C4
Great Waldingfield 60 A3
Great Walsingham 86 A2
Great Waltham 45 F1
Great Warley 45 E3
Great Washbourne 54 B4
Great Weeke 10 A3
Great Welnetham 59 G2
Great Wenham 60 B4
Great Whittington 128 C4
Great Wigborough 46 C1
Great Wigsell 18 C3
Great Wilbraham 58 D2
Great Wilne 81 F4
Great Wishford 26 B4
Great Witcombe 40 B1
Great Witley 53 G1
Great Wolford 55 E4
Great Wratting 59 E3
Great Wymondley 58 A5
Great Wyrley 66 B2
Great Wytheford 65 E1
Great Yarmouth 87 G5
Great Yeldham 59 F4
Greatford 69 F1
Greatgate 80 B3
Greatham Hants. 28 C4
Greatham Hart. 121 D5
Greatham W.Suss. 16 C2
Greatness 31 E3
Greatstone-on-Sea 19 F1
Greatworth 56 A3
Green 77 D1
Green Cross 29 D4
Green End Beds. 57 G2
Green End Bucks. 57 E4
Green End Cambs. 70 A5
Green End Cambs. 70 B5
Green End Herts. 58 B5
Green End Herts. 58 B4
Green End Warks. 67 E4
Green Hammerton 103 D2
Green Hill 40 C4
Green Lane 54 C1
Green Moor 93 G3
Green Ore 24 C2
Green Quarter 107 F2
Green Street E.Suss. 18 C2
Green Street Herts. 44 A3
Green Street Herts. 58 C5
Green Street W.Suss. 29 G5
Green Street Worcs. 54 A3
Green Street Green Gt.Lon. 31 D2
Green Street Green Kent 45 E5
Green Tye 44 D1
Greenburn 160 C5
Greencroft 120 A3
Greendams 161 E1
Greendykes 137 E4
Greenend 55 F5
Greenfaulds 142 B2
Greenfield Beds. 57 F4
Greenfield (Maes-Glas) Flints. 90 C5
Greenfield Gt.Man. 93 E2
Greenfield High. 146 D5
Greenfield Lincs. 97 D5
Greenfield Oxon. 42 C3
Greenford 44 A4
Greengairs 142 B2
Greengates 102 A4
Greengill 117 E3
Greenhalgh 100 A4
Greenhall 168 D2
Greenham 27 F1
Greenhaugh 127 F3
Greenheads 179 F4
Greenheys 92 D3
Greenhill Gt.Lon. 44 A4
Greenhill High. 183 E4
Greenhill S.Yorks. 94 A4
Greenhithe 45 F5
Greenholm 132 D2
Greenholme 107 G2

Greenhow Hill 102 A1
Greenigo 190 B3
Greenland 187 E2
Greenlands 42 C4
Greenlaw Aber. 177 F4
Greenlaw Sc.Bord. 145 E5
Greenloaning 150 D4
Greenmeadow 38 B3
Greenmoor Hill 42 B4
Greenmount 92 B1
Greenmyre 169 F1
Greenock 133 D2
Greenodd 107 E4
Greens Norton 56 B3
Greenscares 150 C3
Greenside T. & W. 120 A1
Greenside W.Yorks. 93 F1
Greenstead 60 B5
Greenstead Green 59 G5
Greensted 45 E2
Greensted Green 45 E2
Greenway Pembs. 49 D4
Greenway Som. 24 A5
Greenwell 118 B2
Greenwich 44 C5
Greet 54 C5
Greete 65 E5
Greetham Lincs. 96 D5
Greetham Rut. 69 E1
Greetland 101 G5
Gregson Lane 100 B5
Greinton 24 B4
Grenaby 98 A4
Grendon Northants. 57 D1
Grendon Warks. 67 E3
Grendon Common 67 E3
Grendon Green 53 E2
Grendon Underwood 56 B5
Grenofen 7 E3
Grenoside 94 A3
Gresford 78 A2
Gresham 86 C2
Greshornish 170 C4
Gress 189 G2
Gressenhall 86 A4
Gressingham 100 B1
Greta Bridge 109 F1
Gretna 126 B5
Gretna Green 126 B5
Gretton Glos. 54 C4
Gretton Northants. 69 E3
Gretton Shrop. 65 E3
Grewelthorpe 110 B5
Greygarth 110 A5
Greylake 24 A4
Greys Green 42 C4
Greysouthen 117 D4
Greystead 127 F3
Greystoke 118 A4
Greystone Aber. 167 G5
Greystone Angus 160 D5
Greystone Lancs. 101 E3
Greystones 94 A4
Greywell 28 C2
Gribthorpe 103 G4
Gribton 124 D2
Griff 67 F4
Griffithstown 38 B3
Grigadale 154 D3
Grigghall 107 F3
Grimeford Village 92 A1
Grimethorpe 94 B3
Grimley 54 A1
Grimmet 132 B4
Grimoldby 97 D4
Grimpo 78 A3
Grimsargh 100 B4
Grimsbury 55 G3
Grimsby 96 C2
Grimscote 56 B2
Grimscott 20 C5
Grimshader 189 G5
Grimston E.Riding 105 E4
Grimston Leics. 82 B5
Grimston Norf. 85 F5
Grimstone 12 C3
Grimstone End 60 A1
Grindale 113 E5
Grindle 65 G2
Grindleford 93 G5
Grindleton 101 D3
Grindley 80 B5
Grindley Brook 78 C3
Grindlow 93 F5

Grindon Northumb. 145 G5
Grindon Staffs. 80 B2
Grindon Stock. 120 C5
Grindon T. & W. 120 C2
Gringley on the Hill 95 E3
Grinsdale 117 G1
Grinshill 78 C5
Grinton 109 F3
Grisdale 108 C3
Grishipoll 154 A4
Gristhorpe 113 D4
Griston 72 A2
Gritley 190 C3
Grittenham 40 C4
Grittleton 40 A5
Grizebeck 106 D4
Grizedale 107 E3
Groby 68 A2
Groes 76 D1
Groes-faen 37 G4
Groesffordd 74 B4
Groesffordd Marli 90 B5
Groeslon Gwyn. 75 D2
Groeslon Gwyn. 75 E1
Groes-lwyd 64 B1
Groes-wen 38 A4
Grogport 139 G5
Gromford 61 E2
Gronant 90 B4
Groombridge 31 E5
Grosmont Mon. 52 D5
Grosmont N.Yorks. 112 B2
Grotaig 165 F2
Groton 60 A3
Groundistone Heights 135 F4
Grouville 8 C5
Grove Bucks. 57 E5
Grove Dorset 12 C5
Grove Kent 33 E2
Grove Notts. 95 D5
Grove Oxon. 41 G3
Grove End 32 A2
Grove Green 31 G3
Grove Park 44 D5
Grove Town 103 D5
Grovehill 43 F2
Grovesend S.Glos. 39 F4
Grovesend Swan. 36 B2
Gruids 182 A4
Grula 162 B2
Gruline 155 E5
Grumbla 2 B4
Grundcruie 151 F2
Grundisburgh 60 D2
Grutness 191 F5
Gualachulain 156 D5
Guardbridge 152 C3
Guarlford 54 A3
Guay 159 F2
Gubbergill 106 B3
Gubblecote 43 E1
Guernsey 9 F5
Guernsey Airport 9 E5
Guestling Green 19 D2
Guestling Thorn 19 D2
Guestwick 86 B3
Guestwick Green 86 B3
Guide 100 D5
Guide Post 129 E3
Guilden Down 64 C4
Guilden Morden 58 A3
Guilden Sutton 78 B1
Guildford 29 E3
Guildtown 151 G1
Guilsborough 68 B5
Guilsfield (Cegidfa) 64 B1
Guilthwaite 94 B4
Guisborough 111 F1
Guiseley 102 A3
Guist 86 B3
Guiting Power 54 C5
Gullane 144 B1
Gulval 2 B3
Gulworthy 7 E3
Gumfreston 35 E2
Gumley 68 B3
Gunby Lincs. 83 E5
Gunby Lincs. 84 C1
Gundleton 28 B4
Gunn 21 G2
Gunnersbury 44 A5
Gunnerside 109 E3
Gunnerton 128 B4
Gunness 95 F1
Gunnislake 7 E3
Gunstone 66 A2

Gunter's Bridge **29** E5
Gunthorpe *Norf.* **86** B2
Gunthorpe *Notts.* **82** B3
Gunthorpe *Rut.* **69** D2
Gunville **15** D4
Gunwalloe **3** D4
Gupworthy **22** C4
Gurnard **15** D3
Gurnett **92** D5
Gurney Slade **24** D3
Gurnos *M.Tyd.* **37** G2
Gurnos *Powys* **37** D2
Gushmere **32** E4
Gussage All Saints **13** G1
Gussage St. Andrew **13** F1
Gussage St. Michael **13** F1
Guston **33** F4
Gutcher **191** E2
Guthram Gowt **83** G5
Guthrie **161** D4
Guyhirn **70** B2
Guynd **161** D5
Guy's Head **84** C5
Guy's Marsh **25** F4
Guyzance **129** E1
Gwaelod-y-garth **38** A4
Gwaenysgor **90** B4
Gwaithla **52** B2
Gwalchmai **88** B5
Gwastad **48** D5
Gwastadnant **75** F2
Gwaun-Cae-Gurwen **36** D1
Gwaynynog **76** D1
Gwbert **49** E3
Gweek **3** E4
Gwehelog **38** C2
Gwenddwr **51** G3
Gwendreath **3** E5
Gwennap **4** B5
Gwenter **3** E5
Gwernaffield **77** F1
Gwernesney **38** D2
Gwernogle **50** B2
Gwernymynydd **77** F1
Gwern-y-Steeple **37** G5
Gwersyllt **78** A2
Gwespyr **90** C4
Gwinear **2** C3
Gwithian **2** C2
Gwredog **88** C4
Gwrhay **38** A3
Gwyddelwern **77** D3
Gwyddgrug **50** A4
Gwynfryn **7** E2
Gwystre **51** G1
Gwythenn **76** B1
Gyfelia **78** A3
Gyrn Goch **74** D3

H

Habberley **64** C2
Habin **28** D5
Habrough **96** B1
Haccombe **10** B5
Haceby **83** F4
Hacheston **61** E2
Hackbridge **30** B2
Hackenthorpe **94** B4
Hackford **86** B5
Hackforth **110** B3
Hackleton **56** D2
Hacklinge **33** F3
Hackness **112** C3
Hackney **44** C4
Hackthorn **95** G4
Hackthorpe **118** B5
Hacton **45** E4
Hadden **136** B3
Haddenham *Bucks.* **42** C2
Haddenham *Cambs.* **70** C5
Haddington *E.Loth.* **144** C2
Haddington *Lincs.* **83** E1
Haddiscoe **73** F2
Haddon **69** G3
Hade Edge **93** F2
Hademore **67** D2
Hadfield **93** E3
Hadham Cross **44** D1
Hadham Ford **58** C5
Hadleigh *Essex* **46** B3
Hadleigh *Suff.* **60** B3

Hadleigh Heath **60** A3
Hadley *Tel. & W.* **65** F1
Hadley *Worcs.* **54** A1
Hadley End **80** C3
Hadley Wood **44** B3
Hadlow **31** F4
Hadlow Down **18** A1
Hadnall **78** C5
Hadspen **25** D4
Hadstock **59** D3
Hadston **129** E2
Hadzor **54** B1
Haffenden Quarter **32** A4
Hafod Bridge **50** C4
Hafod-Dinbych **76** B2
Hafodunos **76** B1
Hafodyrynys **38** B3
Haggate **101** E4
Haggbeck **126** C4
Haggerston *Gt.Lon.* **44** C4
Haggerston *Northumb.* **137** E2
Haggs **142** B2
Hagley *Here.* **53** E3
Hagley *Worcs.* **66** B4
Hagnaby *Lincs.* **84** B1
Hagnaby *Lincs.* **97** E5
Hague Bar **93** D4
Hagworthingham **84** B1
Haigh **92** A2
Haighton Green **100** B4
Hail Weston **57** G1
Haile **106** B2
Hailes **54** C4
Hailey *Herts.* **44** C1
Hailey *Oxon.* **42** B4
Hailey *Oxon.* **41** F1
Hailsham **18** A3
Haimer **186** D2
Hainault **45** D3
Haine **33** F2
Hainford **86** D4
Hainton **96** B4
Haisthorpe **104** D1
Hakin **34** B2
Halam **82** B2
Halbeath **143** F1
Halberton **10** D1
Halcro **187** E2
Hale *Cumb.* **107** G5
Hale *Gt.Man.* **92** B4
Hale *Halton* **91** F4
Hale *Hants.* **14** A1
Hale *Surr.* **28** B3
Hale Bank **91** F4
Hale Barns **92** B4
Hale Nook **99** G3
Hale Street **31** F4
Hales *Norf.* **73** E2
Hales *Staffs.* **79** E4
Hales Green **80** C3
Hales Place **32** D3
Halesgate **84** B5
Halesowen **66** B4
Halesworth **73** E4
Halewood **91** F4
Half Way Inn **10** D3
Halford *Devon* **10** B5
Halford *Shrop.* **64** D4
Halford *Warks.* **55** E3
Halfpenny **107** G2
Halfpenny Green **66** A3
Halfway *Carmar.* **50** C4
Halfway *Carmar.* **36** B2
Halfway *Powys* **51** E4
Halfway *S.Yorks.* **94** B4
Halfway *W.Berks.* **27** F1
Halfway Bridge **29** E5
Halfway House **64** C1
Halfway Houses *Kent* **32** B1
Halfway Houses *Lincs.* **83** D1
Halghton Mill **78** B3
Halifax **101** G5
Halistra **170** B4
Halket **141** F4
Halkirk **186** D3
Halkyn **90** D5
Hall **141** F4
Hall Cross **100** A5
Hall Dunnerdale **106** D3
Hall Green *Ches.E.* **79** F2
Hall Green *Lancs.* **100** A5
Hall Green *W.Mid.* **66** D4
Hall Grove **44** B1
Hall of the Forest **64** B4

Halland **18** A2
Hallaton **68** C3
Hallatrow **24** D2
Hallbankgate **118** B2
Hallen **39** E4
Hallfield Gate **81** E2
Hallglen **142** C2
Hallin **170** B4
Halling **31** G2
Hallington *Lincs.* **96** D4
Hallington *Northumb.* **128** B4
Halliwell **92** A1
Halloughton **82** B2
Hallow **54** A2
Hallow Heath **54** A2
Hallrule **135** G4
Halls **145** C2
Halls Green *Essex* **44** D2
Hall's Green *Herts.* **58** A5
Hallsands **9** E4
Hallthwaites **106** C4
Hallwood Green **53** F4
Hallworthy **5** F1
Hallyne **143** F5
Halmer End **79** E3
Halmond's Frome **53** F3
Halmore **39** F2
Halmyre Mains **143** F5
Halnaker **16** B3
Halsall **91** E1
Halse *Northants.* **56** A3
Halse *Som.* **23** E5
Halsetown **2** C3
Halsham **105** E5
Halsinger **21** F2
Halstead *Essex* **59** G4
Halstead *Kent* **31** D2
Halstead *Leics.* **68** C2
Halstock **12** B2
Halsway **23** E4
Haltemprice Farm **104** C4
Haltham **84** B3
Haltoft End **84** B3
Halton *Bucks.* **43** D1
Halton *Halton* **91** G4
Halton *Lancs.* **100** B1
Halton *Northumb.* **119** F1
Halton *Wrex.* **78** A4
Halton East **101** G2
Halton Gill **109** D5
Halton Green **100** B1
Halton Holegate **84** C1
Halton Lea Gate **118** C2
Halton Park **100** B1
Halton West **101** E2
Haltwhistle **118** D1
Halvergate **87** F5
Halwell **9** D2
Halwill **7** E1
Halwill Junction **7** E1
Ham *Devon* **11** F2
Ham *Glos.* **39** F3
Ham *Glos.* **54** B5
Ham *Gt.Lon.* **44** A5
Ham *High.* **187** E1
Ham *Kent* **33** F3
Ham *Plym.* **8** A2
Ham *Shet.* **191** E5
Ham *Som.* **23** F5
Ham *Som.* **11** F1
Ham *Wilts.* **27** E1
Ham Common **25** F5
Ham Green *Here.* **53** G3
Ham Green *Kent* **32** A2
Ham Green *Kent* **19** D5
Ham Green *N.Som.* **39** E5
Ham Green *Worcs.* **54** C1
Ham Hill **31** F2
Ham Street **24** C4
Hambleden **42** C4
Hambledon *Hants.* **15** F1
Hambledon *Surr.* **29** E4
Hamble-le-Rice **15** D4
Hambleton *Lancs.* **99** G3
Hambleton *N.Yorks.* **103** E4
Hambridge **24** A5
Hambrook *S.Glos.* **39** F5
Hambrook *W.Suss.* **15** G2
Hameringham **84** B1
Hamerton **69** F5
Hamilton **142** B4
Hamlet *Devon* **11** E3
Hamlet *Dorset* **12** B2
Hammer **29** D4
Hammerpot **16** C3
Hammersmith **44** B5

Hammerwich **66** C2
Hammerwood **30** D5
Hammond Street **44** C2
Hammoon **13** E1
Hamnavoe *Shet.* **191** F4
Hamnavoe *Shet.* **191** F2
Hamnish Clifford **53** E2
Hamp **23** F4
Hampden Park **18** B3
Hamperden End **59** D4
Hampnett **40** D1
Hampole **94** C2
Hampreston **13** G3
Hampstead **44** B4
Hampstead Norreys **42** A5
Hampsthwaite **102** B2
Hampton *Devon* **11** F3
Hampton *Gt.Lon.* **29** G1
Hampton *Kent* **33** D2
Hampton *Peter.* **69** G3
Hampton *Shrop.* **65** G4
Hampton *Swin.* **41** D3
Hampton *Worcs.* **54** C3
Hampton Bishop **53** E4
Hampton Fields **40** A3
Hampton Heath **78** B3
Hampton in Arden **67** E4
Hampton Loade **65** G4
Hampton Lovett **54** A1
Hampton Lucy **55** E2
Hampton on the Hill **55** E1
Hampton Poyle **42** A1
Hampton Wick **29** G1
Hamptworth **14** B1
Hamsey **17** G2
Hamstall Ridware **66** D1
Hamstead **14** C3
Hamstead Marshall **27** F1
Hamsteels **120** A3
Hamsterley *Dur.* **120** A4
Hamsterley *Dur.* **120** A2
Hamstreet **32** C5
Hamworthy **13** F3
Hanbury *Staffs.* **80** C5
Hanbury *Worcs.* **54** B1
Hanbury Woodend **80** C5
Hanby **83** F4
Hanchurch **79** F3
Handa Island **184** A4
Handale **111** G3
Handbridge **78** B1
Handcross **30** B5
Handforth **92** C4
Handley *C. & W.Ches.* **78** B2
Handley *Derbys.* **81** E1
Handley Green **45** E2
Handsacre **66** C1
Handside **44** B1
Handsworth *S.Yorks.* **94** B4
Handsworth *W.Mid.* **66** C3
Handwoodbank **64** D1
Handy Cross **43** D3
Hanford *Dorset* **13** E1
Hanford *Stoke* **79** F3
Hanging Bridge **80** C3
Hanging Houghton **68** C5
Hanging Langford **26** B4
Hangingshaw **125** F2
Hanham **39** F5
Hankelow **79** E1
Hankerton **40** B3
Hankham **18** B3
Hanley **79** F3
Hanley Castle **54** A3
Hanley Child **53** F1
Hanley Swan **54** A3
Hanley William **53** F1
Hanlith **101** F1
Hanmer **78** B4
Hannah **97** E5
Hannington *Hants.* **27** G2
Hannington *Northants.* **68** D5
Hannington *Swin.* **41** D3
Hannington Wick **41** D3
Hanslope **56** D3
Hanthorpe **83** F5
Hanwell *Gt.Lon.* **44** A4
Hanwell *Oxon.* **55** G3
Hanwood **64** D2
Hanworth *Gt.Lon.* **44** A5
Hanworth *Norf.* **86** C2
Happisburgh **87** E2

Happisburgh Common **87** E3
Hapsford **91** F5
Hapton *Lancs.* **101** D4
Hapton *Norf.* **72** C2
Harberton **9** D2
Harbertonford **9** D2
Harbledown **32** D3
Harborne **66** C4
Harborough Magna **67** G5
Harbost **189** G1
Harbottle **128** B1
Harbourneford **8** D1
Harbridge **14** A1
Harbridge Green **14** A1
Harburn **143** E3
Harbury **55** F2
Harby *Leics.* **82** C4
Harby *Notts.* **95** F5
Harcombe **11** E3
Harcombe Bottom **11** G3
Harden *W.Mid.* **66** C2
Harden *W.Yorks.* **101** G6
Hardendale **107** G1
Hardenhuish **40** B5
Hardgate *Aber.* **169** E4
Hardgate *N.Yorks.* **102** B1
Hardham **16** C2
Hardhorn **99** G3
Hardingham **86** B5
Hardingstone **56** C2
Hardington **25** E2
Hardington Mandeville **12** B1
Hardington Marsh **12** B2
Hardington Moor **12** B1
Hardley **14** D2
Hardley Street **87** E5
Hardmead **57** E3
Hardraw **109** D3
Hardstoft **81** F1
Hardway *Hants.* **15** F2
Hardway *Som.* **25** E4
Hardwick *Bucks.* **42** D1
Hardwick *Cambs.* **58** B2
Hardwick *Lincs.* **95** F5
Hardwick *Norf.* **72** D3
Hardwick *Northants.* **57** D1
Hardwick *Oxon.* **41** F2
Hardwick *Oxon.* **56** A5
Hardwick *S.Yorks.* **94** B4
Hardwick *W.Mid.* **66** C3
Hardwick Village **94** D5
Hardwicke *Glos.* **54** B5
Hardwicke *Glos.* **39** G1
Hardwicke *Here.* **52** B3
Hardy's Green **60** A5
Hare Green **60** B5
Hare Hatch **42** D5
Hare Street *Herts.* **58** B5
Hare Street *Herts.* **58** B5
Hareby **84** B1
Harecroft **101** G4
Hareden **100** C2
Harefield **43** F3
Harehill **80** C4
Harehills **102** C4
Harehope **137** E4
Harelaw **142** D5
Hareplain **32** A5
Haresceugh **118** C3
Harescombe **40** A1
Haresfield **40** A1
Hareshaw *N.Lan.* **142** C3
Hareshaw *S.Lan.* **142** A5
Harestock **27** F4
Harewood **102** C3
Harewood End **53** E5
Harford *Devon* **8** C2
Harford *Devon* **10** B3
Hargate **72** C2
Hargatewall **93** F5
Hargrave *C. & W.Ches.* **78** B2
Hargrave *Northants.* **69** F5
Hargrave *Suff.* **59** F2
Hargrave Green **59** F2
Harker **126** B5
Harkstead **60** C4
Harlaston **67** E1
Harlaxton **83** D4
Harle Syke **101** E4
Harlech **75** E4
Harlequin **82** B4
Harlescott **65** E1

Harlesden **44** B4
Harleston *Devon* **9** D3
Harleston *Norf.* **72** D3
Harleston *Suff.* **60** B1
Harlestone **56** C1
Harley *S.Yorks.* **94** A3
Harley *Shrop.* **65** E2
Harleyholm **134** C2
Harlinger **170** B5
Harlington *Beds.* **57** F4
Harlington *Gt.Lon.* **43** F5
Harlosh **170** B5
Harlow **44** D2
Harlow Hill **119** G1
Harlthorpe **103** G4
Harlton **58** B2
Harlyn **4** C2
Harman's Cross **13** F4
Harmby **110** A4
Harmer Green **44** B1
Harmer Hill **78** B5
Harmondsworth **43** F5
Harmston **83** E1
Harnage **65** E2
Harnham **26** C5
Harnhill **40** C2
Harold Hill **45** E3
Harold Park **45** E3
Harold Wood **45** E3
Haroldston West **34** B1
Haroldswick **191** G1
Harome **111** F4
Harpenden **44** A1
Harpford **11** D3
Harpham **104** C1
Harpley *Norf.* **85** F5
Harpley *Worcs.* **53** F1
Harpole **56** B1
Harprigg **108** B4
Harpsdale **186** D3
Harpsden **42** C4
Harpswell **95** G4
Harpur Hill **93** E5
Harpurhey **92** C2
Harracott **21** F3
Harrapool **163** E2
Harrietfield **151** E2
Harnetsham **32** A4
Harringay **44** C4
Harrington *Cumb.* **116** C4
Harrington *Lincs.* **97** D5
Harrington *Northants.* **68** C5
Harringworth **69** E3
Harris **162** B5
Harris Green **72** D2
Harnseahead **79** F2
Harriston **117** E2
Harrogate **102** C2
Harrold **57** E2
Harrop Fold **100** D3
Harrow *Gt.Lon.* **44** A4
Harrow *High.* **187** E1
Harrow Green **59** G2
Harrow on the Hill **44** A4
Harrow Weald **44** A3
Harrowbarrow **7** E3
Harrowden **57** F3
Harrowgate Hill **110** B1
Harry Stoke **39** F5
Harston *Cambs.* **58** C2
Harston *Leics.* **82** D4
Harswell **104** A3
Hart **121** D4
Hartburn **128** C3
Hartest **59** G2
Hartfield *E.Suss.* **31** D5
Hartfield *High.* **172** A5
Hartford *C. & W.Ches.* **92** A5
Hartford *Cambs.* **70** A5
Hartford *Som.* **22** C5
Hartford End **45** F1
Hartfordbridge **28** C2
Hartforth **110** A2
Hartgrove **13** E1
Harthill *C. & W.Ches.* **78** C2
Harthill *N.Lan.* **142** D3
Harthill *S.Yorks.* **94** B4
Hartington **80** C1
Hartington Hall **128** C3
Hartland **20** C3
Hartland Quay **20** C3
Hartlebury **66** A5
Hartlepool **121** E4
Hartley *Cumb.* **108** C2
Hartley *Kent* **31** F2
Hartley *Kent* **31** G5

Hartley *Northumb.* 129 F4
Hartley Green 79 G5
Hartley Mauditt 28 C4
Hartley Wespall 28 B2
Hartley Wintney 28 C2
Hartlip 32 A2
Hartoft End 111 G3
Harton *N.Yorks.* 103 G1
Harton *Shrop.* 65 D4
Harton *T. & W.* 120 C1
Hartpury 54 A5
Hartrigge 136 A4
Hartshead 102 A5
Hartshill 67 F3
Hartshorne 81 E5
Hartsop 107 F1
Hartwell *Bucks.* 42 C1
Hartwell *Oxon.* 41 G4
Hartwell *E.Suss.* 31 D5
Hartwell *Northants.* 56 C2
Hartwith 102 B1
Hartwood 142 C4
Harvel 31 F2
Harvington *Worcs.* 54 C3
Harvington *Worcs.* 66 A5
Harwell *Notts.* 95 D3
Harwell *Oxon.* 41 G4
Harwich 60 D4
Harwood *Dur.* 119 E4
Harwood *Gt.Man.* 92 B1
Harwood *Northumb.* 128 C2
Harwood Dale 112 C3
Harwood on Teviot 135 F5
Harworth 94 D3
Hasbury 66 B4
Hascombe 29 F3
Haselbech 68 C5
Haselbury Plucknett 12 A1
Haseley 55 E1
Haseley Knob 67 E5
Haselor 54 D2
Hasfield 54 A5
Haskayne 91 E2
Hasketon 61 D2
Hasland 81 E1
Hasland Green 81 E1
Haslemere 29 E4
Haslingden 101 D5
Haslingden Grane 101 D5
Haslingfield 58 C2
Haslington 79 E2
Hassall 79 E2
Hassall Green 79 E2
Hassell Street 32 C4
Hassendean 135 G3
Hassingham 87 E5
Hassocks 17 F2
Hassop 93 G5
Haster 187 F3
Hasthorpe 84 C1
Hastigrow 187 E2
Hastingleigh 32 C4
Hastings *E.Suss.* 18 D3
Hastings *Som.* 11 G2
Hastingwood 45 D2
Hastoe 43 E2
Haswell 120 C3
Haswell Plough 120 C3
Hatch *Beds.* 57 G2
Hatch *Hants.* 28 B2
Hatch Beauchamp 24 A5
Hatch End 44 A3
Hatch Green 11 G1
Hatching Green 44 A1
Hatchmere 91 G5
Hatcliffe 96 C2
Hatfield *Here.* 53 E2
Hatfield *Herts.* 44 B2
Hatfield *S.Yorks.* 95 D2
Hatfield Broad Oak 45 E1
Hatfield Heath 45 E1
Hatfield Peverel 45 G1
Hatfield Woodhouse 95 D2
Hatford 43 G2
Hatherden 27 E2
Hatherleigh 21 F5
Hathern 81 F5
Hatherop 41 D2
Hathersage 93 G4
Hathersage Booths 93 G4
Hathershaw 92 D2
Hatherton *Ches.E.* 79 D3

Hatherton *Staffs.* 66 B1
Hatley St. George 58 A2
Hatt 7 D4
Hattingley 28 B4
Hatton *Aber.* 179 G5
Hatton *Derbys.* 80 D5
Hatton *Gt.Lon.* 44 A5
Hatton *Lincs.* 96 B5
Hatton *Shrop.* 65 D3
Hatton *Warks.* 55 E1
Hatton *Warr.* 91 G4
Hatton Castle 177 G5
Hatton Heath 78 B1
Hatton of Fintray 169 F3
Hattoncrook 169 F2
Haugh 97 E5
Haugh Head 137 E4
Haugh of Glass 168 B1
Haugh of Urr 124 C4
Haugham 96 D4
Haughley 60 B1
Haughley Green 60 B1
Haughley New Street 60 B1
Haughs 177 E5
Haughton *Ches.E.* 78 C2
Haughton *Notts.* 95 D5
Haughton *Powys* 64 C1
Haughton *Shrop.* 65 F3
Haughton *Shrop.* 65 E1
Haughton *Shrop.* 78 A5
Haughton *Staffs.* 79 F5
Haughton Green 92 D3
Haughton Le Skerne 110 C1
Haultwick 58 B5
Haunton 67 E1
Hauxton 58 C2
Havannah 79 F1
Havant 15 G2
Haven 52 D2
Havenstreet 15 E3
Havercroft 94 A1
Haverfordwest (Hwlffordd) 34 C1
Haverhill 59 E3
Haverigg 106 C5
Havering Park 45 D3
Havering-atte-Bower 45 E3
Haversham 56 D3
Haverthwaite 107 E4
Haviker Street 31 G4
Havyat 24 C4
Hawarden (Penarlâg) 78 A1
Hawbridge 54 B3
Hawbush Green 59 F5
Hawcoat 106 D5
Hawes 109 D4
Hawe's Green 72 D2
Hawick 135 G4
Hawkchurch 11 G2
Hawkedon 59 F2
Hawkenbury *Kent* 31 E5
Hawkenbury *Kent* 32 A4
Hawkeridge 25 F2
Hawkerland 31 D4
Hawkes End 67 E4
Hawkesbury 39 G4
Hawkesbury Upton 39 G4
Hawkhill 137 G5
Hawkhurst 31 G5
Hawkinge 33 E4
Hawkley 28 C5
Hawkridge 22 B4
Hawkshead 107 E3
Hawkshead Hill 107 E3
Hawksheads 100 A1
Hawksland 142 C5
Hawkswick 109 E5
Hawksworth *Notts.* 82 C3
Hawksworth *W.Yorks.* 102 A3
Hawksworth *W.Yorks.* 102 B4
Hawkwell *Essex* 46 B3
Hawkwell *Northumb.* 128 C4
Hawley *Hants.* 29 D2
Hawley *Kent* 45 E5
Hawley's Corner 30 D3
Heage 81 E2
Healaugh *N.Yorks.* 109 F3
Healaugh *N.Yorks.* 103 E3

Hawstead Green 59 G2
Hawthorn *Dur.* 120 D3
Hawthorn *Hants.* 28 B4
Hawthorn *R.C.T.* 37 G4
Hawthorn *Wilts.* 25 F1
Hawthorn Hill *Brack.F.* 43 D5
Hawthorn Hill *Lincs.* 84 A2
Hawthorpe 83 F5
Hawton 82 C2
Haxby 105 E2
Haxey 95 E2
Hay Green 70 D1
Hay Mills 66 B4
Hay Street 58 B5
Haydock 91 G3
Haydon *Dorset* 12 C1
Haydon *Swin.* 40 D4
Haydon Bridge 119 E1
Haydon Wick 40 D4
Hayes *Gt.Lon.* 43 F4
Hayes *Gt.Lon.* 30 D2
Hayes End 43 F4
Hayfield *Arg. & B.* 148 C2
Hayfield *Derbys.* 93 E4
Hayfield *Fife* 152 A5
Hayfield *High.* 187 D2
Haygrove 23 F4
Hayhillock 160 D5
Hayle 3 D4
Hayling Island 15 G2
Haymoor Green 79 D2
Hayne 10 C1
Haynes 57 G3
Haynes Church End 57 F3
Haynes West End 57 F3
Hay-on-Wye (Y Gelli Gandryll) 52 B3
Hayscastle 48 B5
Hayscastle Cross 48 C5
Hayton *Cumb.* 118 B2
Hayton *Cumb.* 117 E2
Hayton *E.Riding* 104 A3
Hayton *Notts.* 95 E4
Hayton's Bent 65 E4
Haytor Vale 10 A5
Haytown 21 D4
Haywards Heath 17 F1
Haywood Oaks 82 B2
Hazel End 58 C5
Hazel Grove 92 B4
Hazel Street 31 F5
Hazelbank *Arg. & B.* 148 C4
Hazelbank *S.Lan.* 142 C5
Hazelbury Bryan 12 D2
Hazeleigh 46 B2
Hazeley 28 C2
Hazelhurst 92 B3
Hazelside 133 G3
Hazelslack 107 F5
Hazelslade 66 C1
Hazelton Walls 152 B2
Hazelwood *Derbys.* 81 E3
Hazelwood *Gt.Lon.* 30 D2
Hazlefield 116 A2
Hazlehead *Aberdeen* 169 F4
Hazlehead *S.Yorks.* 93 F2
Hazlemere 43 D3
Hazlerigg 129 E4
Hazleton 40 C1
Hazon 129 D1
Heacham 85 E4
Head Bridge 21 G4
Headbourne Worthy 27 F4
Headcorn 32 A4
Headingley 102 B4
Headington 42 A2
Headlam 110 A1
Headless Cross 54 C1
Headley *Hants.* 28 D4
Headley *Hants.* 27 G1
Headley *Surr.* 30 B3
Headley Down 28 D4
Headley Heath 66 C5
Headon 95 E5
Heads Nook 118 A2
Heady Hill 92 C1

Heald Green 92 C4
Heale *Devon* 21 G1
Heale *Som.* 24 A5
Healey *Lancs.* 92 C1
Healey *N.Yorks.* 110 A4
Healey *Northumb.* 119 G2
Healey *W.Yorks.* 102 B5
Healeyfield 119 G3
Healing 96 C1
Heamoor 2 B3
Heanish 154 B2
Heanor 81 F3
Heanton Punchardon 21 F2
Heapham 95 F4
Heap Bridge 92 C1
Heapey 100 C5
Hearn 28 D4
Hearthstane 134 C3
Heasley Mill 22 A4
Heast 163 E3
Heath *Cardiff* 38 A4
Heath *Derbys.* 81 F1
Heath *W.Yorks.* 94 A1
Heath & Reach 57 E5
Heath End *Derbys.* 81 E5
Heath End *Hants.* 27 G1
Heath End *Hants.* 27 F1
Heath End *Surr.* 28 D3
Heath Hayes 66 C1
Heath Hill 65 G1
Heath House 24 B3
Heath Town 66 B3
Heathbrook 78 D5
Heathcot 169 F4
Heathcote *Derbys.* 80 C1
Heathcote *Shrop.* 79 D5
Heathencote 56 C3
Heather 67 F1
Heathfield *Devon* 10 B5
Heathfield *E.Suss.* 18 A1
Heathfield *N.Yorks.* 102 A1
Heathfield *Som.* 23 E5
Heathrow Airport 43 F4
Heathton 66 A3
Heatley 92 B4
Heaton *Lancs.* 100 A1
Heaton *Staffs.* 79 G1
Heaton *T. & W.* 120 B1
Heaton *W.Yorks.* 102 A4
Heaton Moor 92 C3
Heaton's Bridge 91 F1
Heaverham 31 E3
Heaviley 92 D4
Heavitree 10 C3
Hebburn 120 C1
Hebden 101 G1
Hebden Bridge 101 F5
Hebden Green 78 D1
Hebing End 58 B5
Hebron *Carmar.* 49 E5
Hebron *Northumb.* 129 D3
Heck 125 E2
Heckfield 28 C1
Heckfield Green 72 C4
Heckfordbridge 60 A5
Heckingham 73 E2
Heckington 83 G1
Heckmondwike 102 B5
Heddington 43 E1
Heddle 40 A1
Heddon 73 E2
Hedge End 15 D1
Hedgerley 43 E4
Hedging 24 A5
Hedley on the Hill 119 G2
Hednesford 66 C1
Hedon 105 D5
Hedsor 43 E4
Heeley 94 A4
Heighington *Darl.* 120 B5
Heighington *Lincs.* 83 F1
Heightington 65 G2
Heights of Brae 174 B3
Heilam 185 D2
Heisker Islands (Monach Islands) 188 A2
Heithat 125 F2
Heiton 136 B3
Hele *Devon* 21 F1
Hele *Devon* 10 C2
Hele *Devon* 6 D1

Hele *Devon* 10 A5
Hele *Som.* 23 E5
Hele *Torbay* 9 F1
Hele Bridge 21 F5
Hele Lane 10 A1
Helebridge 20 C5
Helensburgh 141 D1
Helford 3 E4
Helhoughton 85 G5
Helions Bumpstead 59 E3
Hell Corner 27 E1
Hellaby 94 C3
Helland *Cornw.* 5 E2
Helland *Som.* 24 A5
Hellandbridge 5 E2
Hellesdon 86 D4
Hellidon 56 A2
Hellifield 101 E2
Hellingly 18 A2
Hellington 87 E5
Helmdon 56 A3
Helmingham 60 C2
Helmington Row 120 A4
Helmsdale 183 F3
Helmshore 101 D5
Helmsley 111 F4
Helperby 102 D1
Helperthorpe 112 C5
Helpringham 83 G3
Helpston 69 G2
Helsby 91 F5
Helsey 97 F5
Helston 3 D4
Helstone 5 E1
Helton 118 B5
Helwith 109 F2
Helwith Bridge 101 E1
Hem 64 B2
Hemborough Post 9 E2
Hemel Hempstead 43 F2
Hemerdon 8 B2
Hemingbrough 103 F4
Hemingby 96 C5
Hemingfield 94 A4
Hemingford Abbots 70 A5
Hemingford Grey 70 A5
Hemingstone 60 C2
Hemington *Leics.* 81 F5
Hemington *Northants.* 69 F4
Hemington *Som.* 25 E2
Hemley 61 D3
Hemlington 111 D1
Hemp Green 61 E1
Hempholme 104 C2
Hempnall 72 D2
Hempnall Green 72 D2
Hempriggs 176 A3
Hempriggs House 187 F4
Hempstead *Essex* 59 E4
Hempstead *Med.* 31 G2
Hempstead *Norf.* 87 F3
Hempstead *Norf.* 86 C2
Hempsted 40 A1
Hempton *Norf.* 86 A3
Hempton *Oxon.* 55 G4
Hemsby 87 F4
Hemswell 95 F3
Hemswell Cliff 95 G4
Hemsworth 94 B1
Hemyock 11 E1
Henbury *Bristol* 39 E5
Henbury *Ches.E.* 92 C5
Henderland 124 C3
Hendersyde Park 136 B3
Hendham 8 D2
Hendon *Gt.Lon.* 44 B4
Hendon *T. & W.* 120 C2
Hendraburnick 5 F1
Hendre *Bridgend* 37 F4
Hendre *Gwyn.* 74 C3
Hendreforgan 37 F4
Hendy 36 B2
Heneglwys 88 C5
Henfield *S.Glos.* 39 F5
Henfield *W.Suss.* 17 E2
Henford 7 D1
Hengherst 32 B5
Hengoed *Caerp.* 38 A3
Hengoed *Powys* 52 B2
Hengoed *Shrop.* 77 F4
Hengrave 59 G1
Henham 59 E5
Heniarth 64 A2
Henlade 23 F5
Henley *Dorset* 12 C2
Henley *Shrop.* 65 E5
Henley *Som.* 24 B4
Henley *Som.* 12 A2

Henley *Suff.* 60 C2
Henley *W.Suss.* 29 D5
Henley Corner 24 B4
Henley Park 29 E2
Henley-in-Arden 55 D1
Henley-on-Thames 42 C4
Henley's Down 18 C2
Henllan *Carmar.* 49 G3
Henllan *Denb.* 76 D1
Henllan Amgoed 49 E5
Henllys 38 B4
Henlow 57 G4
Hennock 10 B4
Henny Street 59 G4
Henryd 89 F5
Henry's Moat 48 D5
Hensall 103 E5
Henshaw 119 D1
Hensingham 116 C5
Henstead 73 F3
Hensting 27 F5
Henstridge 12 D1
Henstridge Ash 12 D1
Henstridge Bowden 25 D5
Henstridge Marsh 25 E5
Henton *Oxon.* 42 C2
Henton *Som.* 24 B3
Henwood 5 G2
Heol Senni 51 F5
Heolgerrig 37 G2
Heol-y-Cyw 37 F4
Hepburn 137 E4
Hepburn Bell 137 E4
Hepple 128 B1
Hepscott 129 E3
Hepthorne Lane 81 F1
Heptonstall 101 F5
Hepworth *Suff.* 72 A4
Hepworth *W.Yorks.* 93 F2
Hepworth South Common 72 A4
Herbrandston 34 B2
Hereford 53 E3
Heriot 144 A4
Herm 9 G5
Hermiston 143 F2
Hermitage *D. & G.* 124 B4
Hermitage *Dorset* 12 C2
Hermitage *Sc.Bord.* 126 D2
Hermitage *W.Berks.* 42 A5
Hermitage *W.Suss.* 15 G2
Hermitage Green 92 A3
Hermon *Carmar.* 49 G4
Hermon *I.o.A.* 74 C1
Hermon *Pembs.* 49 F4
Herne 33 D2
Herne Bay 33 D2
Herne Common 33 D2
Herne Pound 31 F3
Herner 21 F3
Hernhill 32 C2
Herodsfoot 5 G3
Herongate 43 F3
Heron's Ghyll 17 G1
Heronsgate 43 F3
Herriard 28 B3
Herringfleet 73 F2
Herring's Green 57 F3
Herringswell 59 F1
Herringthorpe 94 B3
Hersden 33 D2
Hersham *Cornw.* 20 C5
Hersham *Surr.* 29 G1
Herstmonceux 18 B2
Herston 190 B4
Hertford 44 C1
Hertford Heath 44 C1
Hertingfordbury 44 C1
Hesket Newmarket 117 G3
Hesketh Bank 100 A5
Hesketh Lane 100 C3
Heskin Green 91 G1
Hesleden 120 D4
Hesleyside 128 A3
Heslington 103 F2
Hessay 103 E2
Hessenford 6 D5
Hessett 60 A1
Hessle 104 C5
Hest Bank 100 A1
Hester's Way 54 B5
Hestley Green 60 C1
Heston 44 A5
Heswall 91 D4

Hethe 56 A5
Hethelpit Cross 53 G5
Hetherington 128 A4
Hethersett 86 C5
Hethersgill 118 A1
Hethpool 136 C4
Hett 120 B4
Hetton 101 F2
Hetton-le-Hole 120 C3
Heugh 128 A4
Heugh-head *Aber.* 168 A3
Heugh-head *Aber.* 168 C5
Heveningham 73 E4
Hever 31 D4
Heversham 107 F4
Hevingham 86 C3
Hewas Water 5 D5
Hewell Grange 54 C1
Hewell Lane 54 C1
Hewelsfield 39 E2
Hewelsfield Common 39 E2
Hewish *N.Som.* 24 B1
Hewish *Som.* 12 A2
Hewood 11 G2
Heworth 103 F2
Hewton 7 F1
Hexham 119 F1
Hextable 45 E5
Hexthorpe 94 C2
Hexton 57 G4
Hexworthy 7 G3
Hey 101 E3
Hey Houses 99 G5
Heybridge *Essex* 45 F3
Heybridge *Essex* 46 B2
Heybridge Basin 46 B2
Heybrook Bay 8 A3
Heydon *Cambs.* 58 C3
Heydon *Norf.* 86 C3
Heydour 83 F4
Heylipoll 154 A2
Heyop 64 B5
Heysham 100 A1
Heyshaw 102 A1
Heyshott 16 A2
Heyside 92 D2
Heytesbury 26 A3
Heythrop 55 F5
Heywood *Gt.Man.* 92 C1
Heywood *Wilts.* 25 F2
Hibaldstow 95 G2
Hibb's Green 59 G2
Hickleton 94 B2
Hickling *Norf.* 87 F3
Hickling *Notts.* 82 B5
Hickling Green 87 F3
Hickling Heath 87 F3
Hickstead 17 E1
Hidcote Bartrim 55 D3
Hidcote Boyce 55 D3
High Ackworth 94 B1
High Angerton 128 C3
High Balantyre 148 C3
High Bankhill 118 B3
High Beach 44 D3
High Bentham (Higher Bentham) 100 C1
High Bickington 21 F3
High Birkwith 108 C5
High Blantyre 142 A4
High Borgue 124 A5
High Bradfield 93 G3
High Bradley 101 G3
High Bransholme 104 D4
High Bray 21 G2
High Bridge 117 G2
High Brooms 31 E4
High Bullen 21 F3
High Burton 110 B4
High Buston 129 E1
High Callerton 129 D4
High Casterton 108 B5
High Catton 103 G2
High Close 110 A1
High Cogges 41 F2
High Common 72 C3
High Coniscliffe 110 B3
High Crompton 92 D2
High Cross *Hants.* 28 C5
High Cross *Herts.* 44 C1
High Cross *W.Suss.* 17 E2
High Easter 45 F1
High Ellington 110 A4
High Entercommon 110 C2

High Ercall 65 E1
High Etherley 120 A5
High Ferry 84 B3
High Flatts 93 G2
High Garrett 59 F5
High Gate 101 E3
High Grange 120 A4
High Green *Norf.* 86 C5
High Green *Norf.* 86 A4
High Green *Norf.* 86 A5
High Green *S.Yorks.* 94 A3
High Green *Suff.* 59 G1
High Green *Worcs.* 54 A3
High Halden 32 A5
High Halstow 45 G5
High Ham 24 B4
High Harrington 116 D4
High Harrogate 102 C2
High Hatton 78 D5
High Hauxley 129 E1
High Hawsker 112 C2
High Heath *Shrop.* 79 D5
High Heath *W.Mid.* 66 C2
High Hesket 118 A3
High Hesleden 121 D4
High Hoyland 93 G1
High Hunsley 104 B4
High Hurstwood 17 G1
High Hutton 103 G1
High Ireby 117 F3
High Kelling 86 B2
High Kilburn 112 A5
High Kingthorpe 112 B4
High Knipe 107 G1
High Lane *Derbys.* 81 F3
High Lane *Gt.Man.* 93 D4
High Lane *Worcs.* 53 F1
High Laver 45 E2
High Legh 92 B4
High Leven 111 D1
High Littleton 24 D2
High Lorton 117 E4
High Marishes 112 B5
High Marnham 95 F5
High Melton 94 C2
High Moor 94 B4
High Newton 107 F4
High Newton-by-the-Sea 137 G4
High Nibthwaite 107 D3
High Offley 79 E5
High Ongar 45 E2
High Onn 66 A1
High Park Corner 60 B5
High Roding 45 F1
High Shaw 109 D3
High Spen 120 A1
High Stoop 120 A4
High Street *Cornw.* 5 D4
High Street Kent 31 G5
High Street *Suff.* 61 F2
High Street *Suff.* 73 E4
High Street *Suff.* 73 F4
High Street *Suff.* 59 G3
High Street Green 60 B2
High Throston 121 D4
High Town 66 B1
High Toynton 84 A1
High Trewhitt 128 C1
High Wham 120 A5
High Wigsell 18 C1
High Woolstaston 39 E3
High Worsall 110 C2
High Wray 107 E3
High Wych 45 D1
High Wycombe 43 D3
Higham *Derbys.* 81 E3
Higham Kent 45 G5
Higham *Lancs.* 101 E4
Higham *S.Yorks.* 94 A2
Higham *Suff.* 59 F1
Higham *Suff.* 60 B4
Higham Dykes 128 D4
Higham Ferrers 57 E1
Higham Gobion 57 G4
Higham on the Hill 67 F3
Higham Wood 31 F4
Highampton 21 E5
Highams Park 44 C3
Highbridge *Hants.* 27 F3
Highbridge *Som.* 24 A3
Highbrook 30 C5
Highburton 93 F1
Highbury 25 D3
Highclere 27 F1
Highcliffe 14 B3
Higher Alham 25 D3
Higher Ansty 13 D2

Higher Ashton 10 B4
Higher Ballam 99 G4
Higher Bentham (High Bentham) 100 C1
Higher Blackley 92 C2
Higher Brixham 9 F2
Higher Chenton 11 E2
Higher Combe 22 C4
Higher Folds 92 A2
Higher Gabwell 9 F1
Higher Green 92 B3
Higher Halstock Leigh 12 B2
Higher Kingcombe 12 B3
Higher Kinnerton 78 A1
Higher Muddiford 21 F2
Higher Nyland 25 E5
Higher Prestacott 7 D1
Higher Standen 101 D3
Higher Tale 11 D2
Higher Thrushgill 100 C1
Higher Town *Cornw.* 5 E3
Higher Town *I.o.S.* 4 B1
Higher Walreddon 7 F3
Higher Walton *Lancs.* 100 B3
Higher Walton *Warr.* 91 G4
Higher Wambrook 11 F2
Higher Whatcombe 13 E2
Higher Wheelton 100 C5
Higher Whiteleigh 6 C1
Higher Whitley 92 A4
Higher Wincham 92 A5
Higher Woodhill 92 B1
Higher Woodsford 13 D4
Higher Wraxall 12 B2
Higher Wych 78 B3
Highfield *E.Riding* 103 G4
Highfield *N.Ayr.* 141 E4
Highfield *Oxon.* 56 A5
Highfield *S.Yorks.* 94 A4
Highfield *T. & W.* 120 A2
Highfields *Cambs.* 58 B2
Highfields *Northumb.* 145 G4
Highgate *E.Suss.* 30 D5
Highgate *Gt.Lon.* 44 B4
Highgreen Manor 128 A2
Highlane *Ches.E.* 79 F1
Highlane *Derbys.* 94 B4
Highlaws 117 E2
Highleadon 53 G5
Highleigh *Devon* 22 C5
Highleigh *W.Suss.* 16 A4
Highley 65 G4
Highmead 50 B3
Highmoor Cross 42 B4
Highmoor Hill 39 D4
Highnam 39 G1
Highstead 33 E2
Highsted 32 B2
Highstreet 32 C2
Highstreet Green *Essex* 59 F4
Highstreet Green *Surr.* 29 E4
Hightae 125 E3
Highter's Heath 66 C5
Hightown *Hants.* 14 A2
Hightown *Mersey.* 91 D2
Hightown Green 60 A2
Highway 40 C5
Highweek 10 B5
Highwood 53 F1
Highwood Hill 44 B3
Highworth 41 E3
Hilborough 71 G2
Hilcote 81 F2
Hilcott 26 C2
Hilden Park 31 E4
Hildenborough 31 E4
Hildenley 101 G5
Hildersham 58 D3
Hilderstone 79 G4
Hilderthorpe 105 D1
Hilfield 12 C2
Hilgay 71 E3
Hill *S.Glos.* 39 F3
Hill *Warks.* 55 E1
Hill *Worcs.* 54 B3
Hill Brow 28 C5
Hill Chorlton 79 E4
Hill Common 87 F3
Hill Cottages 105 G3
Hill Croome 54 A3
Hill Deverill 25 F3
Hill Dyke 84 B3

Hill End *Dur.* 119 G4
Hill End *Fife* 151 F5
Hill End *Glos.* 54 A4
Hill End *Gt.Lon.* 43 F3
Hill End *N.Yorks.* 101 G2
Hill Green 58 C4
Hill Head 15 E2
Hill Houses 65 F5
Hill Mountain 34 C2
Hill of Beath 143 F1
Hill of Fearn 175 E2
Hill Ridware 66 C1
Hill Row 70 C5
Hill Side 93 F1
Hill Street 14 C1
Hill Top *Hants.* 14 D2
Hill Top *S.Yorks.* 94 B3
Hill Top *S.Yorks.* 93 G4
Hill View 13 F3
Hill Wootton 55 F1
Hillam 103 E5
Hillbeck 108 C1
Hillberry 98 B4
Hillborough 31 G2
Hillbrae *Aber.* 177 F5
Hillbrae *Aber.* 169 F2
Hillbrae *Aber.* 169 F1
Hillbutts 13 F2
Hillclifflane 81 D3
Hillend *Aber.* 176 D5
Hillend *Fife* 143 F1
Hillend *Midloth.* 143 G3
Hillend *N.Lan.* 142 C3
Hillend *Swan.* 36 A3
Hillend Green 53 G5
Hillersland 39 E1
Hillesden 56 B5
Hillesley 39 G4
Hillfarrance 23 E5
Hillfoot End 57 G4
Hillhead *Devon* 9 F2
Hillhead *S.Ayr.* 132 C3
Hillhead of Auchentumb 179 E2
Hillhead of Cocklaw 179 F3
Hilliard's Cross 67 D1
Hilliclay 187 D2
Hillingdon 43 F4
Hillington *Glas.* 141 G3
Hillington *Norf.* 85 F5
Hillmorton 68 A5
Hillockhead *Aber.* 168 A4
Hillockhead *Aber.* 168 B3
Hillowton 124 B4
Hillpound 15 E1
Hill's End 57 E4
Hills Town 81 F1
Hillsborough 94 A3
Hillsford Bridge 22 A3
Hillside *Aber.* 169 G5
Hillside *Angus* 161 F3
Hillside *Moray* 176 A3
Hillside *Shet.* 191 H5
Hillside *Worcs.* 53 G1
Hillswick 191 E2
Hillway 15 F4
Hillyfields 14 C1
Hilmarton 40 C5
Hilperton 25 F2
Hilsea 15 F2
Hilston 105 E4
Hilton *Cambs.* 58 A1
Hilton *Cumb.* 118 D5
Hilton *Derbys.* 80 D4
Hilton *Dorset* 13 D2
Hilton *Dur.* 120 A5
Hilton *High.* 175 F1
Hilton *Shrop.* 65 G3
Hilton *Staffs.* 66 C2
Hilton *Stock.* 111 D1
Hilton Croft 169 G1
Hilton of Cadboll 175 E2
Hilton of Delnies 175 E4
Himbleton 54 B2
Himley 66 A3
Hincaster 107 G4
Hinchley Wood 29 G1
Hinckley 67 G3
Hinderclay 72 B4
Hinderton 91 E5
Hinderwell 111 G1
Hindford 78 A4
Hindhead 29 D4
Hindley *Gt.Man.* 92 A2
Hindley *Northumb.* 119 G2
Hindley Green 92 A2
Hindlip 54 A2

Hindolveston 86 B3
Hindon *Som.* 22 C3
Hindon *Wilts.* 25 G4
Hindringham 86 A2
Hingham 86 B5
Hinksford 66 A4
Hinstock 79 D5
Hintlesham 60 B3
Hinton *Glos.* 39 F2
Hinton *Hants.* 14 B3
Hinton *Here.* 52 C4
Hinton *Northants.* 56 A2
Hinton *S.Glos.* 39 G5
Hinton *Shrop.* 64 D2
Hinton Admiral 14 B3
Hinton Ampner 27 G5
Hinton Blewett 24 C2
Hinton Charterhouse 25 E2
Hinton Martell 13 G2
Hinton on the Green 54 C3
Hinton Parva *Dorset* 13 F2
Hinton Parva *Swin.* 41 E4
Hinton St. George 12 A1
Hinton St. Mary 13 D1
Hinton Waldrist 41 F3
Hinton-in-the-Hedges 56 A4
Hints *Shrop.* 65 F5
Hints *Staffs.* 67 D2
Hinwick 57 F1
Hinxhill 32 C4
Hinxton 58 C3
Hinxworth 58 A3
Hipperholme 102 A5
Hipsburn 137 G5
Hipswell 110 A3
Hirn 169 E4
Hirnant 77 D5
Hirst 129 E3
Hirst Courtney 103 F5
Hirwaen 77 E1
Hirwaun 37 D2
Hiscott 21 F3
Histon 58 C1
Hitcham *Bucks.* 43 E4
Hitcham *Suff.* 60 A2
Hitchin 57 G5
Hither Green 44 C5
Hittisleigh 10 A3
Hittisleigh Barton 10 A3
Hive 104 A4
Hixon 80 B5
Hoaden 33 E3
Hoaldalbert 52 C5
Hoar Cross 80 C5
Hoarwithy 53 E5
Hoath 33 E2
Hobarris 64 C5
Hobbles Green 59 F2
Hobbs Cross 45 D3
Hobbs Lots Bridge 70 B5
Hobkirk 135 G4
Hobland Hall 87 G5
Hobson 120 A2
Hoby 68 B1
Hockenill 58 C5
Hockering 86 B4
Hockerton 82 C2
Hockley 46 B3
Hockley Heath 67 D5
Hockliffe 57 E5
Hockwold cum Wilton 71 F4
Hockworthy 10 D1
Hoddesdon 44 C1
Hoddlesden 100 D5
Hodgehill 79 F1
Hodgeston 34 D3
Hodnet 79 D4
Hodnetheath 78 D5
Hodsoll Street 31 F2
Hodson 41 D4
Hodthorpe 94 C5
Hoe 86 A4
Hoe Gate 15 F1
Hoff 108 B1
Hoffleet Stow 84 A4
Hoggard's Green 59 G2
Hoggeston 56 D5
Hoggie 177 E4
Hoggrill's End 67 E3
Hoghton 100 C5
Hognaston 80 D2
Hogsthorpe 97 F5
Holbeach 84 B5
Holbeach Bank 84 B5

Holbeach Clough 84 B5
Holbeach Drove 70 B1
Holbeach Hurn 84 B5
Holbeach St. Johns 70 B1
Holbeach St. Marks 84 B4
Holbeach St. Matthew 84 C4
Holbeck 94 C5
Holbeck Woodhouse 94 C5
Holberrow Green 54 C2
Holbeton 8 C2
Holborough 31 G2
Holbrook *Derbys.* 81 E3
Holbrook *Suff.* 60 C4
Holbrooks 67 F4
Holburn 137 E3
Holbury 14 D2
Holcombe *Devon* 10 C5
Holcombe *Gt.Man.* 92 B1
Holcombe *Som.* 25 D3
Holcombe Burnell Barton 10 B3
Holcombe Rogus 11 D1
Holcot 56 C1
Holden 101 D3
Holden Gate 101 E5
Holdenby 56 B1
Holdenhurst 14 A3
Holder's Green 59 E5
Holders Hill 44 B4
Holdgate 65 E4
Holdingham 83 F3
Holditch 11 G2
Hole 11 E1
Hole Park 32 A5
Hole Street 16 D3
Holehouse 93 E3
Hole-in-the-Wall 53 F1
Holford 23 E3
Holgate 103 E2
Holker 107 E5
Holkham 85 G3
Hollacombe *Devon* 21 D5
Hollacombe *Devon* 10 B2
Hollacombe Town 21 G4
Holland 30 D5
Holland Fen 84 A3
Holland-on-Sea 47 E1
Hollee 126 A5
Hollesley 61 E3
Hollicombe 9 F1
Hollingbourne 32 A3
Hollingbury 17 F3
Hollingrove 18 B1
Hollington *Derbys.* 80 D4
Hollington *E.Suss.* 18 C2
Hollington *Staffs.* 80 B4
Hollingworth 93 E3
Hollins 94 A5
Hollins Green 92 A3
Hollins Lane 100 A2
Hollinsclough 80 B1
Hollinwood *Gt.Man.* 92 D2
Hollinwood *Shrop.* 78 C4
Hollocombe 21 G4
Hollow Meadows 93 G4
Holloway 81 F2
Hollowell 68 B5
Holly Bush 78 B3
Holly End 70 C2
Holly Green 42 C2
Hollybush *Caerp.* 38 A2
Hollybush *E.Ayr.* 132 B4
Hollybush *Worcs.* 53 G4
Hollyhurst 78 C3
Hollym 105 F5
Hollywater 28 D4
Hollywood 66 C5
Holm 126 A2
Holm of Drumlanrig 124 C1
Holmbridge 93 F2
Holmbury St. Mary 29 G3
Holmbush 30 B5
Holme *Cambs.* 69 G4
Holme *Cumb.* 107 G5
Holme *N.Lincs.* 95 G2
Holme *N.Yorks.* 110 C4
Holme *Notts.* 82 D2
Holme *W.Yorks.* 93 F2
Holme Chapel 101 E5
Holme Hale 71 G2
Holme Lacy 53 E4
Holme Marsh 52 C2
Holme next the Sea 85 F3

Holme on the Wolds **104** B3
Holme Pierrepont **82** B4
Holme St. Cuthbert **117** E2
Holme-on-Spalding-Moor **104** A4
Holmer **53** E3
Holmer Green **43** E3
Holmes **91** F1
Holmes Chapel **79** E1
Holmesfield **94** A5
Holmeswood **91** F1
Holmewood **81** F1
Holmfield **101** F1
Holmfirth **93** F2
Holmhead *D. & G.* **124** B2
Holmhead *E.Ayr.* **133** D3
Holmpton **105** F5
Holmrook **106** B2
Holmside **120** B3
Holmsleigh Green **11** F2
Holmston **132** B3
Holmwrangle **118** B3
Holne **8** D1
Holnest **12** C2
Holnicote **22** C3
Holsworthy **20** D5
Holsworthy Beacon **21** D5
Holt *Dorset* **13** G2
Holt *Norf.* **86** B2
Holt *Wilts.* **25** F1
Holt *Worcs.* **54** A1
Holt *Wrex.* **78** B2
Holt End *Hants.* **28** B4
Holt End *Worcs.* **54** C1
Holt Fleet **54** A1
Holt Heath *Dorset* **13** G2
Holt Heath *Worcs.* **54** A1
Holt Wood **13** G2
Holtby **103** F2
Holton *Oxon.* **42** B2
Holton *Som.* **25** D5
Holton *Suff.* **73** F4
Holton cum Beckering **96** B4
Holton Heath **13** F3
Holton le Clay **96** C2
Holton le Moor **96** A3
Holton St. Mary **60** B4
Holtspur **43** E4
Holtye **31** D5
Holtye Common **31** D5
Holway **23** F5
Holwell *Dorset* **12** C1
Holwell *Herts.* **57** G4
Holwell *Leics.* **82** C5
Holwell *Oxon.* **41** E2
Holwell *Som.* **25** E3
Holwick **119** F5
Holworth **13** D4
Holy Cross **66** B5
Holy Island *I.o.A.* **88** A5
Holy Island (Lindisfarne) *Northumb.* **137** F2
Holybourne **28** C3
Holyfield **44** C2
Holyhead (Caergybi) **88** A4
Holymoorside **81** E1
Holyport **43** D5
Holystone **128** B1
Holytown **142** B3
Holywell *Cambs.* **70** B5
Holywell *Cornw.* **4** B4
Holywell *Dorset* **12** B2
Holywell *E.Suss.* **18** B4
Holywell (Treffynnon) *Flints.* **97** G5
Holywell *Northumb.* **129** F4
Holywell Green **93** E1
Holywell Lake **23** E5
Holywell Row **71** F5
Holywood **124** D2
Hom Green **53** E5
Homer **65** F2
Homersfield **73** D3
Homington **26** C5
Honey Hill **32** D2
Honey Street **26** C1
Honey Tye **60** A4
Honeyborough **54** C2
Honeybourne **54** D3
Honeychurch **21** G5
Honicknowle **8** A2

Honiley **67** E5
Honing **87** E3
Honingham **86** C4
Honington *Lincs.* **83** E3
Honington *Suff.* **72** A4
Honington *Warks.* **55** E3
Honiton **11** E2
Honkley **78** A2
Honley **93** F1
Hoo *Med.* **45** G5
Hoo *Suff.* **61** D2
Hoo Green **92** B4
Hoo Meavy **8** B1
Hood Green **94** A2
Hood Hill **94** A3
Hooe *E.Suss.* **18** B3
Hooe *Plym.* **8** B2
Hooe Common **18** B2
Hook *Cambs.* **70** C3
Hook *E.Riding* **103** G5
Hook *Gt.Lon.* **29** G1
Hook *Hants.* **28** C2
Hook *Hants.* **15** E2
Hook *Pembs.* **34** C1
Hook *Wilts.* **40** C4
Hook Green *Kent* **31** F5
Hook Green *Kent* **31** F2
Hook Green *Kent* **45** E5
Hook Green *Kent* **45** E5
Hook Norton **55** F4
Hook-a-Gate **65** D2
Hooke **12** B2
Hookgate **79** E4
Hookway **10** B3
Hookwood **30** B4
Hoole **78** B1
Hooley **30** B3
Hoop **39** E2
Hooton **91** E5
Hooton Levitt **94** C3
Hooton Pagnell **94** B3
Hooton Roberts **94** B3
Hop Pole **69** G1
Hopcrofts Holt **55** G5
Hope *Derbys.* **93** F4
Hope *Devon* **8** C4
Hope *Flints.* **78** A2
Hope *Powys* **64** B2
Hope *Shrop.* **64** C2
Hope *Staffs.* **80** C2
Hope Bagot **65** E5
Hope Bowdler **65** D3
Hope End Green **59** D5
Hope Mansell **39** F1
Hope under Dinmore **53** E2
Hopehouse **135** D4
Hopeman **176** A3
Hope's Green **45** G4
Hopesay **64** C4
Hopkinstown **37** G3
Hopley's Green **52** C2
Hopperton **102** D2
Hopstone **65** G3
Hopton *Derbys.* **81** D2
Hopton *Norf.* **73** G2
Hopton *Shrop.* **78** C5
Hopton *Shrop.* **78** A5
Hopton *Staffs.* **79** G5
Hopton *Suff.* **72** A4
Hopton Cangeford **65** E4
Hopton Castle **64** C4
Hopton Wafers **65** F5
Hoptonheath **64** C5
Hopwas **67** G4
Hopwood **66** C5
Horam **18** A2
Horbling **83** G4
Horbury **93** G1
Horden **120** D3
Horderley **64** D4
Hordle **14** B3
Hordley **78** A4
Horeb *Carmar.* **36** A2
Horeb *Cere.* **49** G3
Horeb *Flints.* **77** F2
Horfield **39** E5
Horham **72** D4
Horkesley Heath **60** A5
Horkstow **95** G1
Horley *Oxon.* **55** G3
Horley *Surr.* **30** B4
Horn Hill **43** F3
Hornblotton **24** C4
Hornblotton Green **24** C4
Hornby *Lancs.* **100** B1
Hornby *N.Yorks.* **110** B3
Hornby *N.Yorks.* **110** C4

Horncastle **84** A1
Hornchurch **45** E4
Horncliffe **145** G5
Horndean *Hants.* **15** G1
Horndean *Sc.Bord.* **145** G5
Horndon **7** F2
Horndon on the Hill **45** F4
Horne **30** C4
Horne Row **45** G2
Horner **22** B3
Horniehaugh **160** C3
Horning **87** E4
Horninghold **68** D3
Horninglow **80** D5
Horningsea **58** C1
Horningsham **25** F3
Horningtoft **86** A3
Horningtops **5** G3
Horns Cross *Devon* **21** D3
Horns Cross *E.Suss.* **18** D1
Horns Green **31** D3
Hornsbury **11** G1
Hornsby **118** B3
Hornsby Gate **118** B2
Hornsea **105** E3
Hornsey **44** C4
Hornton **55** F3
Horrabridge **8** B1
Horridge **10** A5
Horringer **59** G1
Horrocks Fold **92** B1
Horse Bridge **79** G2
Horsebridge *Devon* **7** E3
Horsebridge *Hants.* **27** E4
Horsebrook **66** A1
Horsecastle **24** B1
Horsehay **65** F2
Horseheath **59** E3
Horsehouse **109** F4
Horsell **22** D2
Horseman's Green **78** B3
Horsenden **42** C2
Horseshoe Green **31** D4
Horseway **70** C4
Horsey **87** F3
Horsey Corner **87** F3
Horsford **86** C4
Horsforth **102** B4
Horsham *W.Suss.* **29** G4
Horsham *Worcs.* **53** G2
Horsham St. Faith **86** D4
Horsington *Lincs.* **83** G1
Horsington *Som.* **25** E5
Horsington Marsh **25** E5
Horsley *Derbys.* **81** E3
Horsley *Glos.* **40** A3
Horsley *Northumb.* **119** G1
Horsley *Northumb.* **128** A2
Horsley Cross **60** C5
Horsley Woodhouse **81** E3
Horsleycross Street **60** C5
Horsleygate **94** A5
Horsleyhill **135** G4
Horsmonden **31** F4
Horspath **42** A2
Horstead **87** D4
Horsted Keynes **17** F1
Horton *Bucks.* **43** E1
Horton *Dorset* **13** G2
Horton *Lancs.* **101** E2
Horton *Northants.* **56** D2
Horton *S.Glos.* **39** G4
Horton *Shrop.* **78** B5
Horton *Som.* **11** G1
Horton *Staffs.* **79** G2
Horton *Swan.* **36** A4
Horton *Tel. & W.* **65** F1
Horton *W. & M.* **43** F5
Horton *Wilts.* **26** B1
Horton Cross **11** G1
Horton Grange **129** E4
Horton Green **78** B3
Horton Heath **15** D1
Horton in Ribblesdale **108** D5
Horton Inn **13** G2
Horton Kirby **31** E2
Horton-cum-Studley **42** B1
Horwich **91** F2
Horwich End **93** E4
Horwood **21** F3
Hoscar **91** F1

Hose **82** C5
Hoses **106** D3
Hosh **151** D2
Hotham **104** A4
Hothfield **32** B4
Hoton **81** G5
Houbie **191** G2
Houdston **122** C1
Hough **79** E2
Hough Green **91** F4
Hougham **83** D3
Hough-on-the-Hill **83** E3
Houghton *Cambs.* **70** A5
Houghton *Cumb.* **118** A2
Houghton *Devon* **8** C3
Houghton *Hants.* **27** E4
Houghton *Pembs.* **34** C2
Houghton *W.Suss.* **16** C2
Houghton Bank **120** B5
Houghton Conquest **57** F3
Houghton le Spring **120** C3
Houghton on the Hill **68** B2
Houghton Regis **57** F5
Houghton St. Giles **86** A2
Houghton-le-Side **120** B5
Houlsyke **111** G2
Hound **15** D2
Hound Green **28** C2
Houndslow **144** D5
Houndsmoor **23** E5
Houndwood **145** F3
Hounsdown **14** C1
Hounslow **44** A5
Househill **175** E4
Houses Hill **93** F1
Housham Tye **45** E1
Houston **141** F3
Houstry **183** G1
Houstry of Dunn **187** E3
Houton **190** A3
Hove **17** E3
Hove Edge **102** A5
Hoveringham **82** B3
Hoveton **87** E4
Hovingham **111** F5
Howe *Cumb.* **107** F4
Howe *High.* **187** F2
Howe *N.Yorks.* **110** C4
Howe *Norf.* **73** D2
Howe Green **45** G2
Howe of Teuchar **177** G5
Howe Street *Essex* **45** F1
Howe Street *Essex* **59** G4
Howegreen **46** B2
Howell **83** G3
Howey **51** G2
Howgate *Cumb.* **116** C4
Howgate *Midloth.* **143** G4
Howgill *Lancs.* **101** E3
Howgill *N.Yorks.* **101** G2
Howick **137** G5
Howle **79** D5
Howle Hill **53** F5
Howlett End **59** D4
Howley **11** F2
Hownam **136** B5
Hownam Mains **136** B4
Howpasley **135** G5
Howsham *N.Lincs.* **96** A2
Howsham *N.Yorks.* **103** G1
Howt Green **32** A2
Howtel **136** C3
Howton **52** D5
Howwood **141** F3
Hoxne **72** C4
Hoy *High.* **187** E2
Hoy *Ork.* **190** D4
Hoylake **90** D4
Hoyland **94** A2
Hoylandswaine **93** G2
Hoyle **16** B2

Huby *N.Yorks.* **102** B3
Hucclecote **40** A1
Hucking **32** A3
Hucknall **81** G3
Huddersfield **93** F1
Huddington **54** B2
Huddlesford **66** D2
Hudnall **43** F1
Hudscott **21** G3
Hudswell **110** A3
Huggate **104** A2
Hugglescote **67** G1
Hugh Town **4** B1
Hughenden Valley **43** D3
Hughley **65** E3
Hugmore **78** A2
Hugus **4** B5
Huish *Devon* **21** F4
Huish *Wilts.* **26** C1
Huish Champflower **22** D5
Huish Episcopi **24** B5
Huisinis **189** E3
Hulcote **57** E4
Hulcott **43** D1
Hulland **80** D3
Hulland Ward **81** D3
Hullavington **40** A4
Hullbridge **46** B3
Hulme **79** G3
Hulme End **80** C2
Hulme Walfield **79** F1
Hulver Street **73** F3
Hulverstone **14** C4
Humber *Devon* **10** B5
Humber *Here.* **53** E2
Humberside Airport **96** A1
Humberston **96** D2
Humberstone **68** B2
Humberton **102** D1
Humbie **144** B3
Humbleton *Dur.* **109** F1
Humbleton *E.Riding* **105** E4
Humbleton *Northumb.* **137** D4
Humby **83** F4
Hume **145** E5
Humehall **145** E5
Hummer **12** B1
Humshaugh **128** B4
Huna **187** F1
Huncoat **101** D4
Huncote **68** A3
Hundalee **136** A5
Hundall **94** A5
Hunderthwaite **119** F5
Hundleby **84** B1
Hundleton **34** C2
Hundon **59** F3
Hundred Acres **15** E1
Hundred End **100** A5
Hundred House **52** A3
Hungate End **56** C3
Hungarton **68** B2
Hungate End **56** C3
Hungerford *Hants.* **14** A1
Hungerford *Shrop.* **65** E4
Hungerford *W.Berks.* **27** E1
Hungerford Newtown **41** F5
Hungerton **83** D5
Hunglader **170** C2
Hunmanby **113** D5
Hunningham **55** F1
Hunningham Hill **55** F1
Hunny Hill **15** D4
Hunsdon **44** D1
Hunsingore **102** D2
Hunslet **102** C4
Hunsonby **118** B4
Hunspow **187** E1
Hunstanton **85** E3
Hunstanworth **119** F3
Hunston *Suff.* **60** A1
Hunston *W.Suss.* **16** A3
Hunsworth **102** A5
Hunt End **54** C1
Hunt House **112** B3
Huntercombe End **42** B4
Hunters Forstal **33** G2
Hunter's Inn **21** G1
Hunter's Quay **140** C2
Hunterston **140** C4
Huntford **127** E1
Huntham **24** A5
Huntingdon **70** A5
Huntingfield **73** E4

Huby *N.Yorks.* **102** B3
Huntingford **25** F4
Huntington *Here.* **52** B2
Huntington *Here.* **53** D3
Huntington *Staffs.* **66** B1
Huntington *Tel. & W.* **65** F2
Huntington *York* **103** F2
Huntingtower **151** F2
Huntley **39** G1
Huntly **168** C1
Huntlywood **144** D5
Hunton *Hants.* **27** F3
Hunton *Kent* **31** G4
Hunton *N.Yorks.* **110** A3
Hunton Bridge **43** F2
Hunt's Cross **91** F4
Huntscott **22** C3
Huntsham **22** D5
Huntshaw **21** F3
Huntshaw Cross **21** F3
Huntshaw Water **21** F3
Huntspill **24** A3
Huntworth **24** A4
Hunwick **120** A4
Hunworth **86** B2
Hurcott *Som.* **24** C5
Hurcott *Som.* **11** G1
Hurdley **64** B3
Hurdsfield **92** D5
Hurley *W. & M.* **42** D4
Hurley *Warks.* **67** E3
Hurley Bottom **42** D4
Hurlford **132** C2
Hurlston Green **91** E1
Hurn **14** A3
Hursley **27** F5
Hurst *N.Yorks.* **109** F2
Hurst *W'ham* **42** C5
Hurst Green *E.Suss.* **18** C1
Hurst Green *Essex* **47** D1
Hurst Green *Lancs.* **100** C4
Hurst Green *Surr.* **30** C3
Hurst Wickham **17** E2
Hurstbourne Priors **27** F3
Hurstbourne Tarrant **27** E2
Hurstpierpoint **17** E2
Hurstwood **101** E4
Hurtmore **28** C3
Hurworth-on-Tees **110** C1
Hury **119** F5
Husabost **170** A4
Husbands Bosworth **68** B4
Husborne Crawley **57** E4
Husthwaite **111** E5
Hutcherleigh **9** D2
Huthwaite **81** F2
Huttoft **97** F5
Hutton *Cumb.* **118** A5
Hutton *Essex* **45** F3
Hutton *Lancs.* **100** A5
Hutton *N.Som.* **24** A2
Hutton *Sc.Bord.* **145** G4
Hutton Bonville **110** C2
Hutton Buscel **112** C4
Hutton Conyers **110** C5
Hutton End **118** A4
Hutton Hang **110** A4
Hutton Henry **120** D4
Hutton Magna **110** A1
Hutton Mount **45** F3
Hutton Mulgrave **112** D3
Hutton Roof *Cumb.* **107** G5
Hutton Roof *Cumb.* **117** G3
Hutton Rudby **111** D2
Hutton Sessay **111** D5
Hutton Wandesley **103** E2
Hutton-le-Hole **111** G3
Huxham **10** C3
Huxham Green **24** C4
Huxley **78** C1
Huyton **91** F3
Hycemoor **106** B2
Hyde *Glos.* **40** A2
Hyde *Gt.Man.* **92** D3
Hyde End *W'ham* **28** C1
Hyde End *W.Berks.* **27** G1
Hyde Heath **43** E2
Hyde Lea **66** B1
Hydestile **29** E3
Hyndford Bridge **142** D5
Hyndlee **135** G5

Hynish **154** A3
Hyssington **64** C3
Hythe *Hants.* **14** D2
Hythe *Kent* **33** D5
Hythe End **43** F5
Hythie **179** F2
Hyton **106** B4

I

Ianstown **176** D3
Ibberton **13** D2
Ible **80** D2
Ibsley **14** A2
Ibstock **67** G1
Ibstone **42** C3
Ibthorpe **27** E2
Ibworth **27** G2
Icelton **24** A1
Ickburgh **71** G3
Ickenham **43** F4
Ickford **42** B2
Ickham **33** E3
Ickleford **57** G4
Icklesham **19** D2
Ickleton **58** C3
Icklingham **71** F5
Ickwell Green **57** G3
Icomb **55** E5
Idbury **55** E5
Iddesleigh **21** F5
Ide **10** C3
Ide Hill **31** D3
Ideford **10** B5
Iden **19** E1
Iden Green *Kent* **31** G5
Iden Green *Kent* **32** A5
Idle **102** A4
Idless **4** C5
Idlicote **55** E3
Idmiston **26** C4
Idridgehay **81** D3
Idridgehay Green **81** D3
Idrigil **170** C3
Idstone **41** E4
Idvies **160** D5
Iffley **42** A2
Ifield **30** B5
Ifieldwood **30** B5
Ifold **29** F4
Iford *Bourne.* **14** A3
Iford *E.Suss.* **17** G3
Ifton **39** D4
Ifton Heath **78** A4
Ightfield **78** B4
Ightham **31** E3
Iken **61** F2
Ilam **80** C2
Ilchester **24** C5
Ilderton **137** E4
Ilford **44** D4
Ilfracombe **21** F1
Ilkeston **81** F3
Ilketshall St. Andrew
73 E3
Ilketshall St. Lawrence
73 E3
Ilketshall St. Margaret
73 E3
Ilkley **102** A3
Illey **66** B4
Illidge Green **79** E1
Illington **72** A3
Illingworth **101** G5
Illogan **4** A5
Illston on the Hill **68** C3
Ilmer **42** C2
Ilmington **55** E3
Ilminster **11** G1
Ilsington *Devon* **10** A5
Ilsington *Dorset* **13** D3
Ilston **36** B3
Ilton *N.Yorks.* **110** A5
Ilton *Som.* **11** G1
Imachar **139** G5
Imber **26** A3
Immeroin **150** A3
Immingham **96** B1
Immingham Dock **96** C1
Impington **58** C1
Ince **91** F5
Ince Blundell **91** E2
Ince-in-Makerfield **91** G2
Inch Kenneth **146** D1
Inchbae Lodge **174** A3
Inchbare **161** E3
Inchberry **176** C4
Inchbraoch **161** F4

Inchgrundle **160** C2
Inchindown **174** C2
Inchinnan **141** F3
Inchkinloch **185** E1
Inchlaggan **164** C4
Inchlumpie **174** B2
Inchmarlo **169** D5
Inchmarnock **140** B4
Inchnabobart **160** B1
Inchnacardoch Hotel
165 E3
Inchnadamph **181** E2
Inchock **161** E5
Inchree **156** C3
Inchrory **167** F4
Inchture **152** A2
Inchvuilt **164** D1
Inchyra **151** G2
Indian Queens **4** D4
Inerval **138** D3
Ingatestone **45** F3
Ingbirchworth **93** G2
Ingerthorpe **102** B1
Ingestre **79** G5
Ingham *Lincs.* **95** G4
Ingham *Norf.* **87** E3
Ingham *Suff.* **71** G5
Ingham Corner **87** E3
Ingleborough **70** C1
Ingleby *Derbys.* **81** E5
Ingleby *Lincs.* **95** F5
Ingleby Arncliffe **110** D2
Ingleby Barwick **110** D2
Ingleby Cross **110** D2
Ingleby Greenhow
111 E2
Ingleigh Green **21** G5
Inglesbatch **25** E1
Inglesham **41** E3
Ingleton *Dur.* **120** A5
Ingleton *N.Yorks.* **108** B3
Inglewhite **100** B4
Ingliston **143** F2
Ingoe **128** C4
Ingoldisthorpe **85** E4
Ingoldmells **85** F2
Ingoldsby **83** F4
Ingon **55** E2
Ingram **137** E5
Ingrave **45** F3
Ingrow **101** G4
Ings **107** F3
Ingst **39** E4
Ingworth **86** C3
Inhurst **27** G1
Inistrynich **148** D2
Injebreck **98** B3
Inkberrow **54** C2
Inkersall **94** B5
Inkersall Green **94** B5
Inkhorn **169** G1
Inkpen **27** E1
Inkstack **187** E1
Inmarsh **26** A1
Innellan **140** C3
Innergellie **153** D4
Innerhadden **158** B4
Innerleithen **135** E2
Innerleven **152** B4
Innermessan **122** B4
Innerwick *E.Loth.* **145** E2
Innerwick *P. & K.* **158** A5
Inninbeg **155** F5
Innsworth **54** A5
Insch **168** D2
Insh **166** C4
Inshore **184** C2
Inskip **100** A4
Instow **21** E2
Intake **94** C2
Intwood **86** C5
Inver *Aber.* **167** G5
Inver *Arg. & B.* **156** B5
Inver *High.* **175** E1
Inver *High.* **183** G1
Inver *P. & K.* **159** F5
Inver Mallie **156** D1
Inverailort **155** G1
Inveralligin **172** A3
Inverallochy **179** F1
Inveran **182** A5
Inveraray (Inbhir Aora)
148 C2
Inverardoch Mains
150 C4
Inverardran **149** F2
Inverarish **163** D1
Inveranty **160** C5

Inverarnan (Inbhir Àirnein)
149 F3
Inverasdale **172** B1
Inverbain **172** A4
Inverbeg **149** F5
Inverbervie **161** G2
Inverbroom **173** E1
Inverbrough **166** C2
Invercassley **181** G4
Invercharoan **140** B2
Invercharnan **156** D5
Inverchorachan **149** E3
Inverchoran **173** F4
Invercreran **156** C5
Inverdruie **166** D3
Inverebrie **169** G1
Invereen **166** B1
Invererne **175** G3
Inveresk **144** A2
Inverey **159** F1
Inverfarigaig **165** G2
Invergarry (Inbhir Garadh)
165 E4
Invergelder **167** G5
Invergeldie **150** C2
Inverglov **157** E1
Invergordon **174** D3
Invergowrie **152** B1
Inverguseran **163** F4
Inverharroch Farm
168 A1
Inverhenve **149** F2
Inverhope **185** D2
Inverie **163** F4
Inverinan **148** B2
Inverinate **164** A2
Inverkeilor **161** E5
Inverkeithing **143** F1
Inverkeithny **177** F5
Inverkip **142** D2
Inverkirkaig **180** C3
Inverlael **173** E1
Inverlauren **141** E1
Inverliever **148** A4
Inverliver **148** C1
Inverlochlarig **149** G3
Inverlochy **149** D2
Inverlussa **139** F4
Invermay **151** F3
Invermoriston (Inbhir
Moireasdan) **165** F3
Invernaver **185** G2
Inverneil **139** G1
Inverness (Inbhir Nis)
174 C5
Inverness Airport **175** D4
Invernettie **179** G3
Invernoaden **148** D5
Inveroran Hotel (Inbhir
Orain) **157** G5
Inverquhanity **160** C4
Inverquhomery **179** F3
Inverroy **157** E1
Inversanda **156** B4
Invershiel **164** A3
Invershore **187** E5
Inversnaid Hotel **149** F4
Invertrossachs **150** A4
Inverugie **179** G3
Inveruglas (Inbhir
Dhubhghlais) **149** F4
Inveruglass **166** C4
Inverurie **169** E2
Invervar **158** B5
Inverveigain **140** B2
Invery House **169** D5
Inverythan **177** G5
Inwardleigh **7** F1
Inworth **46** B1
Iona **146** B2
Iping **29** D5
Ipplepen **9** E1
Ipsden **42** B4
Ipstones **80** B3
Ipswich **60** C3
Irby **91** D4
Irby Hill **91** D4
Irby in the Marsh **84** C1
Irby upon Humber **96** B2
Irchester **57** E1
Ireby *Cumb.* **117** F3
Ireby *Lancs.* **108** B5
Ireland's Cross **79** E3
Ireleth **106** D3
Ireshopeburn **119** E4
Irlam **92** B3
Irnham **83** F3
Iron Acton **39** F4
Iron Cross **54** C2

Ironbridge **65** F2
Irons Bottom **30** B4
Ironside **179** D2
Ironville **81** F2
Irstead **87** E3
Irthington **118** A1
Irthlingborough **69** E5
Irton **112** D4
Irvine **132** B2
Irwell **186** B2
Isauld **186** B2
Isbister **191** G2
Isfield **17** G2
Isham **69** D5
Ishriff **147** F1
Isington **28** C3
Island of Stroma **187** F1
Islawr-dref **62** C1
Islay **138** A3
Islay Airport **138** B4
Islay House **138** B3
Isle Abbotts **24** A5
Isle Brewers **24** A5
Isle of Lewis (Eilean
Leodhais) **189** G2
Isle of Man **98** B3
Isle of Man Airport **98** A5
Isle of May **153** E5
Isle of Noss **191** G4
Isle of Sheppey **32** B1
Isle of Walney **99** E1
Isle of Whithorn **115** C3
Isle of Wight **15** D4
Isle of Wight (Sandown)
Airport **15** E4
Isleham **71** E5
Isleornsay (Eilean Iarmain)
163 E3
Isles of Scilly (Scilly Isles)
4 B1
Isleworth **44** A5
Isley Walton **81** F5
Islip *Northants.* **69** E5
Islip *Oxon.* **42** A1
Isombridge **65** F1
Istead Rise **31** F2
Itchen **14** D1
Itchen Abbas **27** G4
Itchen Stoke **27** G4
Itchingfield **29** G5
Itchington **39** F4
Itteringham **86** C2
Itton *Devon* **7** G1
Itton *Mon.* **39** D3
Itton Common **39** D3
Ivegill **118** A3
Ivelet **109** E3
Iver **43** F4
Iver Heath **43** F4
Iveston **120** A2
Ivetsey Bank **66** A1
Ivinghoe **43** E1
Ivinghoe Aston **43** E1
Ivington **53** D2
Ivington Green **53** D2
Ivy Hatch **31** G3
Ivy Todd **71** G2
Ivybridge **8** C2
Ivychurch **19** F1
Iwade **32** B2
Iwerne Courtney (Shroton)
13 E1
Iwerne Minster **13** E1
Ixworth **72** A4
Ixworth Thorpe **72** A4

J

Jack Hill **102** A2
Jackfield **65** F2
Jacksdale **81** F2
Jackstown **169** E1
Jackton **141** G4
Jacobstow **6** B1
Jacobstowe **21** F5
Jacobswell **29** E2
Jameston **35** D3
Jamestown *D. & G.*
126 B2
Jamestown *High.* **174** A4
Jamestown *W.Dun.*
141 E1
Janefield **174** D4
Janetstown *High.* **186** C2
Janetstown *High.* **187** F3
Jarrow **120** C1
Jarvis Brook **31** E5
Jasper's Green **59** F5
Jawcraig **142** C2
Jayes Park **29** G3

Jaywick **47** E1
Jealott's Hill **43** D5
Jeater Houses **110** D3
Jedburgh **136** A4
Jeffreyston **35** D2
Jemimaville **174** D3
Jericho **92** C1
Jersay **142** C3
Jersey **8** C5
Jersey Airport **8** B5
Jersey Marine **36** D3
Jerviswood **142** C5
Jesmond **120** B1
Jevington **18** A3
Jockey End **43** F1
Jodrell Bank **92** B5
John o' Groats **187** F1
John's Cross **18** C1
Johnshaven **161** F2
Johnson Street **87** E4
Johnston **34** C1
Johnston Mains **161** F2
Johnstone **141** F3
Johnstone Castle **141** F3
Johnstonebridge **125** E1
Johnstown *Carmar.*
35 G1
Johnstown *Wrex.* **78** A3
Joppa **132** C4
Jordans **43** E3
Jordanston **48** C4
Jordanstone **160** A5
Joy's Green **39** F1
Jumpers Common **14** A3
Juniper Green **143** F3
Juniper Hill **56** A4
Jura **139** D1
Jura House **138** C3
Jurby East **98** B2
Jurby West **98** B2

K

Kaber **108** C1
Kaimes **143** G3
Kames *Arg. & B.* **140** A2
Kames *Arg. & B.* **148** A3
Kames *E.Ayr.* **133** E3
Kea **4** C5
Keadby **95** F1
Keal Cotes **84** B1
Kearsley **92** B2
Kearstwick **108** B5
Kearton **109** F3
Kearvaig **184** B1
Keasden **100** D1
Kebholes **177** F4
Keckwick **91** F4
Keddington **96** D4
Keddington Corner **97** D4
Kedington **59** F3
Kedleston **81** D3
Keelby **96** B1
Keele **79** F3
Keeley Green **57** F3
Keelham **101** G4
Keenthorne **23** F4
Keeres Green **45** E1
Keeston **34** B1
Keevil **26** A2
Kegworth **81** F5
Kehelland **4** A5
Keig **168** D3
Keighley **101** G3
Keil *Arg. & B.* **130** B5
Keil *High.* **156** B4
Keilhill **177** G4
Keillmore **139** E1
Keillor **160** A5
Keillour **151** E2
Keills **138** C3
Keils **138** D3
Keinton Mandeville **24** C4
Keir House **150** C5
Keir Mill **124** C1
Keisby **83** F4
Keisley **118** C3
Keiss **187** F2
Keith **176** D4
Keithick **152** A1
Keithmore **168** A1
Keithock **161** E3
Kelbrook **101** F3
Kelby **83** F3
Keld *Cumb.* **107** G1
Keld *N.Yorks.* **109** D2
Keldholme **111** G4
Keldy Castle **111** G3

Kelfield *N.Lincs.* **95** F2
Kelfield *N.Yorks.* **103** E4
Kelham **82** C2
Kella **98** B2
Kellacott **7** E2
Kellan **155** E1
Kellas *Angus* **152** C1
Kellas *Moray* **176** A4
Kellaton **9** D4
Kellaways **40** B5
Kelleth **108** C2
Kelleythorpe **104** C2
Kelling **86** B1
Kellington **103** E5
Kelloe **120** C4
Kelloholm **133** F4
Kelly *Cornw.* **5** E2
Kelly *Devon* **7** D2
Kelly Bray **7** D3
Kelmarsh **68** C5
Kelmscott **41** E3
Kelsale **61** E1
Kelsall **78** C1
Kelsay **138** A4
Kelshall **58** B4
Kelsick **117** F1
Kelso **136** D3
Kelstedge **81** E1
Kelstern **96** C3
Kelston **25** E1
Keltneyburn **158** C5
Kelton **125** D3
Kelton Hill (Rhonehouse)
124 B5
Kelty **151** G5
Kelvedon **46** B1
Kelvedon Hatch **45** E3
Kelvinside **141** G3
Kelynack **2** A4
Kemacott **21** G1
Kemback **152** C3
Kemberton **65** G2
Kemble **40** B3
Kemerton **54** B4
Kemeys Commander
38 C2
Kemeys Inferior **38** C3
Kemnay **169** E3
Kemp Town **17** F3
Kempe's Corner **32** C4
Kempley **53** F5
Kempley Green **53** F5
Kemps Green **66** D5
Kempsey **54** A3
Kempsford **41** D3
Kempshott **27** G3
Kempston **57** F3
Kempston Hardwick
57 F3
Kempston West End
57 F3
Kempton **64** C4
Kemsing **31** E3
Kemsley **32** B2
Kenardington **32** B5
Kenchester **52** B2
Kencot **41** E2
Kendal **107** F3
Kenderchurch **52** D5
Kendleshire **39** F5
Kenfig **37** D2
Kenfig Hill **37** E4
Kenidjack **2** A4
Kenilworth **67** E5
Kenknock *P. & K.* **158** A5
Kenknock *Stir.* **149** G1
Kenley *Gt.Lon.* **30** C2
Kenley *Shrop.* **65** E2
Kenmore *Arg. & B.*
148 C4
Kenmore *High.* **172** A4
Kenmore *P. & K.* **158** C5
Kenn *Devon* **10** B4
Kenn *N.Som.* **24** B1
Kennacraig **139** G3
Kennards House **5** G1
Kenneggy Downs **2** C4
Kennerleigh **10** B2
Kennerty **169** D5
Kennet **151** E5
Kennethmont **168** C2
Kennett **59** E1
Kennford **10** C4
Kenninghall **72** B3
Kennington *Kent* **32** C4
Kennington *Oxon.* **42** A2
Kennoway **152** B4
Kenny **11** G1
Kennyhill **71** E5

Kennythorpe 103 G1
Kenovay 154 A2
Kensaleyre 170 D4
Kensington 44 B4
Kenstone 78 C5
Kensworth 43 F1
Kent International Airport 33 F2
Kent Street E.Suss. 18 C2
Kent Street Kent 31 F3
Kentallen (Ceann an t-Sàilein) 156 C4
Kentchurch 52 D5
Kentford 59 F1
Kentisbeare 11 D2
Kentisbury 24 G1
Kentisbury Ford 21 G1
Kentish Town 44 B4
Kentmere 107 F2
Kenton Devon 10 C4
Kenton Suff. 60 C1
Kenton T. & W. 120 B1
Kenton Corner 60 D1
Kentra 155 F2
Kents Bank 107 E5
Kent's Green 53 G5
Kent's Oak 27 E5
Kenwick 78 B4
Kenwyn 4 C5
Kenyon 92 A3
Keoldale 184 C2
Keppanach 156 C3
Keppoch Arg. & B. 141 E2
Keppoch High. 163 G2
Kepwick 111 D3
Keresley 67 F4
Kernborough 9 D3
Kerrera 148 A2
Kerris 2 B4
Kerry (Ceri) 64 A3
Kerrycroy 140 C3
Kerry's Gate 52 C4
Kerrysdale 172 B2
Kersall 82 C1
Kersey 60 B3
Kersey Vale 60 B3
Kershopefoot 126 C3
Kerswell 11 D2
Kerswell Green 54 A3
Kerthen Wood 2 C3
Kesgrave 60 D3
Kessingland 73 G3
Kessingland Beach 73 G3
Kestle 5 D5
Kestle Mill 4 C4
Keston 30 D2
Keswick Cumb. 117 F4
Keswick Norf. 86 D5
Keswick Norf. 87 E2
Ketley Bank 65 F1
Ketsby 97 D5
Kettering 69 D5
Ketteringham 86 C5
Kettins 152 A1
Kettle Corner 31 G3
Kettlebaston 60 A2
Kettlebridge 152 B4
Kettlebrook 67 E2
Kettleburgh 61 D1
Kettlehill 152 B4
Kettleholm 125 F3
Kettleness 112 B1
Kettleshulme 93 D5
Kettlesing 102 B2
Kettlesing Bottom 102 B2
Kettlesing Head 102 B2
Kettlestone 86 A2
Kettlethorpe 95 F5
Kettletoft 190 C2
Kettlewell 109 E5
Ketton 69 E2
Kevingtown 31 D2
Kew 44 A5
Kewstoke 24 A1
Kexbrough 94 A2
Kexby Lincs. 95 F4
Kexby York 103 G2
Key Green 79 F1
Keyham 68 B2
Keyhaven 14 C3
Keyingham 105 E5
Keymer 17 F2
Keynsham 25 D1
Key's Toft 84 C2
Keysoe 57 F1

Keysoe Row 57 F1
Keyston 69 F5
Keyworth 82 B4
Kibblesworth 120 B2
Kibworth Beauchamp 68 B3
Kibworth Harcourt 68 B3
Kidbrooke 44 D5
Kiddemore Green 66 A2
Kidderminster 66 A5
Kiddington 55 G5
Kidlington 41 G1
Kidmore End 42 B5
Kidnal 78 B3
Kidsdale 115 E3
Kidsgrove 79 F2
Kidstones 109 E4
Kidwelly (Cydweli) 36 A2
Kiel Crofts 148 A1
Kielder 127 E2
Kilbarchan 141 F3
Kilbeg 163 E4
Kilberry 139 F3
Kilbirnie 141 E4
Kilblaan 148 D3
Kilbraur 182 D3
Kilbrennan 154 D5
Kilbride Arg. & B. 148 A2
Kilbride Arg. & B. 140 B3
Kilbride High. 163 D2
Kilbride Farm 140 A3
Kilbridemore 148 C5
Kilburn Derbys. 81 E3
Kilburn Gt.Lon. 44 B4
Kilburn N.Yorks. 111 E5
Kilby 68 B3
Kilchattan Bay 140 C4
Kilchenzie 130 B3
Kilcheran 148 A1
Kilchiaran 138 A3
Kilchoan Arg. & B. 147 G3
Kilchoan High. 155 D3
Kilchoman 138 A3
Kilchrenan (Cill Chrèanain) 148 C2
Kilchrist 130 B4
Kilconquhar 152 C4
Kilcoy 174 B4
Kilcot 53 F5
Kildale 111 F2
Kildary 175 D2
Kildavie 130 C4
Kildermorie Lodge 174 B2
Kildonan 131 F3
Kildonan Lodge 183 E2
Kildonnan 155 D1
Kildrochet House 122 B5
Kildrummy 168 B3
Kildwick 101 G3
Kilfinan 140 A2
Kilfinnan 165 D5
Kilgetty 35 E2
Kilgwrrwg Common 39 D3
Kilham E.Riding 104 C1
Kilham Northumb. 136 C3
Kilkenneth 154 A2
Kilkenny 40 C1
Kilkerran Arg. & B. 130 C4
Kilkerran S.Ayr. 132 B5
Kilkhampton 20 C4
Killamarsh 94 B4
Killay 36 C3
Killbeg 155 F5
Killean Arg. & B. 139 E5
Killean Arg. & B. 148 C4
Killearn 141 G1
Killellan 130 B4
Killen 174 C4
Killerby 120 A5
Killerton 10 C2
Killichonan 158 A4
Killiechoante 157 E1
Killiechronan 155 E5
Killiecrankie 159 E3
Killiehuntly 166 B5
Killiemor 147 D1
Killilan 164 A1
Killimster 187 F3
Killin High. 183 D4
Killin Stir. 150 A1
Killinallan 138 B2
Killinghall 102 B2
Killington Cumb. 108 B4
Killington Devon 21 G1

Killingworth 129 E4
Killochyett 144 B5
Killocraw 130 B2
Killunaig 147 D2
Killundine 155 E5
Kilmacolm 141 E3
Kilmaha 148 B4
Kilmahog 150 B4
Kilmalieu 156 A4
Kilmaluag 170 D2
Kilmany 152 B2
Kilmarie 162 D3
Kilmarnock 132 C2
Kilmartin 148 A5
Kilmaurs 141 F5
Kilmelford 148 A3
Kilmeny 138 B3
Kilmersdon 25 D2
Kilmeston 27 G5
Kilmichael 130 B3
Kilmichael Glassary 148 A5
Kilmichael of Inverlussa 139 F1
Kilmington Devon 11 F3
Kilmington Wilts. 25 E4
Kilmington Common 25 E4
Kilmorack 174 A5
Kilmore (A' Chille Mhòr) Arg. & B. 148 A2
Kilmore High. 163 E4
Kilmory Arg. & B. 139 F1
Kilmory Arg. & B. 139 F2
Kilmory High. 162 B4
Kilmory High. 155 E2
Kilmory N.Ayr. 131 E3
Kilmote 183 E3
Kilmuir High. 170 B5
Kilmuir High. 174 C5
Kilmuir High. 175 D2
Kilmuir High. 170 C2
Kilmun 140 C1
Kilmux 152 B4
Kiln Green Here. 39 F1
Kiln Green W'ham 42 B5
Kiln Pit Hill 119 G2
Kilnave 138 A2
Kilncadzow 142 C5
Kilndown 31 G5
Kilnhurst 94 B3
Kilninian 154 D5
Kilninver 148 A2
Kilnsea 97 E1
Kilnsey 101 F1
Kilnwick 104 B3
Kilnwick Percy 104 A2
Kiloran 146 C5
Kilpatrick 131 E3
Kilpeck 52 D5
Kilphedir 183 E3
Kilpin 103 G5
Kilpin Pike 103 G5
Kilrenny 153 D4
Kilsby 67 F5
Kilspindie 152 A2
Kilstay 114 B3
Kilsyth 142 B2
Kiltarlity 174 B5
Kiltyrie 150 B1
Kilvaxter 170 C3
Kilve 23 E3
Kilverstone 71 G4
Kilvington 82 D3
Kilwinning 141 E5
Kimberley Norf. 86 B5
Kimberley Notts. 81 G3
Kimberworth 94 B3
Kimble Wick 42 D2
Kimblesworth 120 B2
Kimbolton Cambs. 57 F1
Kimbolton Here. 53 E1
Kimbridge 27 F5
Kimcote 68 A4
Kimmeridge 13 F5
Kimmerston 137 D3
Kimpton Hants. 37 D3
Kimpton Herts. 44 A1
Kinaldy 152 D3
Kinblethmont 161 E5
Kinbrace 183 D1
Kinbreack 164 B5
Kinbuck 150 C4
Kincaldrum 160 C5
Kincaple 152 C3

Kincardine Fife 142 D1
Kincardine High. 174 C1
Kincardine O'Neil 168 C5
Kinclaven 151 G1
Kincorth 169 G4
Kincraig Aber. 169 G2
Kincraig High. 166 C4
Kincraigie 159 E5
Kindallachan 159 E4
Kindrogan Field Centre 159 F3
Kinellar 169 F3
Kineton Glos. 54 C5
Kineton Warks. 55 F2
Kineton Green 66 D4
Kinfauns 151 G2
King Sterndale 93 E5
Kingarth 140 B4
Kingcoed 38 D2
Kingerby 96 A3
Kingham 55 E5
Kingholm Quay 125 D3
Kinghorn 143 G1
Kinglassie 152 B4
Kingoodie 152 B2
King's Acre 53 D3
King's Bank 19 D1
King's Bromley 66 D1
Kings Caple 53 E5
King's Cliffe 69 F3
King's Coughton 54 C2
King's Green 53 G4
King's Heath 66 C4
Kings Hill Kent 31 F3
King's Hill W.Mid. 66 B3
King's Hill Warks. 67 F5
Kings Langley 43 F2
King's Lynn 85 E5
King's Meaburn 118 C3
Kings Mills 9 E5
King's Moss 91 G2
King's Muir 135 D2
King's Newnham 67 G5
King's Newton 81 E5
King's Norton Leics. 68 B2
King's Norton W.Mid. 66 C5
Kings Nympton 21 G4
King's Pyon 52 D2
Kings Ripton 70 A5
King's Somborne 27 E4
King's Stag 12 D1
King's Stanley 40 A2
King's Sutton 55 G4
King's Tamerton 8 A2
King's Walden 57 G5
Kings Worthy 27 F4
Kingsand 8 A2
Kingsbarns 153 D3
Kingsbridge Devon 8 D3
Kingsbridge Som. 22 C4
Kingsburgh 170 C4
Kingsbury Gt.Lon. 44 A4
Kingsbury Warks. 67 E3
Kingsbury Episcopi 24 B5
Kingscavil 143 D2
Kingsclere 27 G2
Kingscote 40 A3
Kingscott 21 F4
Kingscross 131 F3
Kingsdale 152 B4
Kingsdon 24 C5
Kingsdown Kent 33 F4
Kingsdown Swin. 40 D1
Kingsdown Wilts. 25 F1
Kingseat 151 G5
Kingsey 42 C2
Kingsfold Pembs. 34 C3
Kingsfold W.Suss. 29 G4
Kingsford Aber. 177 G5
Kingsford Aber. 168 C3
Kingsford Aberdeen 169 F4
Kingsford E.Ayr. 141 F5
Kingsford Worcs. 66 A4
Kingsgate 33 F1
Kingshall Street 60 A1
Kingshouse 151 F2
Kingshouse 150 A2
Kingshouse Hotel 157 G4
Kingshurst 67 D4
Kingskerswell 9 E1
Kingskettle 152 B4
Kingsland Here. 52 D1
Kingsland I.o.A. 88 A4
Kingsley Ches. & W.Ches. 91 G5
Kingsley Hants. 28 C4

Kingsley Staffs. 80 B3
Kingsley Green 29 D4
Kingsley Holt 80 B3
Kingslow 65 G5
Kingsmoor 44 D2
Kingsmuir Angus 160 C5
Kingsmuir Fife 152 D4
Kingsnorth 32 C5
Kingsnorth Power Station 32 A1
Kingstanding 66 C3
Kingsteignton 10 B5
Kingsteps 175 F4
Kingsthorne 53 D4
Kingsthorpe 56 C1
Kingston Cambs. 58 B2
Kingston Cornw. 7 D3
Kingston Devon 8 D3
Kingston Devon 11 D4
Kingston Dorset 12 B5
Kingston Dorset 13 F5
Kingston E.Loth. 144 C2
Kingston Gt.Man. 92 D3
Kingston Hants. 14 A2
Kingston I.o.W. 14 C4
Kingston Kent 33 D3
Kingston M.K. 57 E4
Kingston Moray 176 C3
Kingston W.Suss. 16 C3
Kingston Bagpuize 41 G3
Kingston Blount 42 C3
Kingston by Sea 17 E3
Kingston Deverill 25 F4
Kingston Gorse 16 C3
Kingston Lisle 41 F4
Kingston Maurward 12 D3
Kingston near Lewes 17 F3
Kingston on Soar 81 G5
Kingston Russell 12 B3
Kingston St. Mary 23 F5
Kingston Seymour 24 B1
Kingston Stert 42 C2
Kingston upon Hull 104 D5
Kingston upon Thames 29 G1
Kingston Warren 41 F4
Kingstone Here. 52 B2
Kingstone Here. 53 F5
Kingstone Som. 11 G1
Kingstone Staffs. 80 B5
Kingstown Winslow 41 E4
Kingstown 117 G1
Kingswear 9 E2
Kingswell 141 G5
Kingswells 169 F4
Kingswinford 66 A4
Kingswood Bucks. 42 B1
Kingswood Glos. 39 G3
Kingswood Here. 52 B2
Kingswood Kent 32 A3
Kingswood Powys 64 B2
Kingswood S.Glos. 39 F5
Kingswood Som. 23 E3
Kingswood Surr. 30 B3
Kingswood Warks. 67 D5
Kingthorpe 96 B5
Kington Here. 52 B2
Kington Worcs. 54 B2
Kington Langley 40 B5
Kington Magna 25 E5
Kington St. Michael 40 B5
Kingussie 166 B4
Kingweston 24 C4
Kinharrachie 169 G1
Kinharvie 124 D4
Kinkell 142 A2
Kinkell Bridge 151 E3
Kinknockie 179 F3
Kinlet 65 G4
Kinloch Fife 152 A3
Kinloch High. 181 F1
Kinloch High. 155 F4
Kinloch High. 162 C5
Kinloch High. 174 D2
Kinloch P. & K. 160 A5
Kinloch P. & K. 159 G5
Kinloch Hourn (Ceann Loch Shubhairne) 164 A4
Kinloch Laggan 158 A1
Kinloch Rannoch 158 B4
Kinlochan 156 A3
Kinlochard 149 G4
Kinlocharkaig 164 A5
Kinlochbeoraid 156 A1
Kinlochbervie 184 B3

Kinlocheil 156 A2
Kinlochetive 156 D5
Kinlochewe 172 D3
Kinlochlaich 156 B5
Kinlochleven (Ceann Loch Liobhann) 157 D3
Kinlochmoidart 155 G2
Kinlochmorar 163 G5
Kinlochmore 157 D3
Kinlochspelve 147 F2
Kinloss 179 E3
Kinmel Bay (Bae Cinmel) 90 A4
Kinmuck 169 F3
Kinnaber 161 F3
Kinnadie 179 E3
Kinnaird 152 A2
Kinneff 161 G2
Kinnelhead 134 B5
Kinnell Angus 161 E4
Kinnell Stir. 150 A1
Kinnerley 78 A5
Kinnersley Here. 52 C3
Kinnersley Worcs. 54 A3
Kinnerton 52 B1
Kinnerton Green 78 A1
Kinnesswood 151 G4
Kinnettles 160 C5
Kinninvie 119 G5
Kinnordy 160 B4
Kinoulton 82 B4
Kinrara 166 C4
Kinross 151 G4
Kinrossie 151 G1
Kinsbourne Green 44 A1
Kinsham Here. 52 C1
Kinsham Worcs. 54 B4
Kinsley 94 B1
Kinson 13 G3
Kintbury 27 E1
Kintessack 175 F3
Kintillo 151 G3
Kintocher 168 C4
Kinton Here. 64 D5
Kinton Shrop. 64 C1
Kintore 169 F3
Kintour 169 F3
Kintra Arg. & B. 138 B5
Kintra Arg. & B. 146 C5
Kintradwell 183 E4
Kintraw 148 A4
Kinuachdrachd 147 G5
Kinveachy 166 D3
Kinver 66 A4
Kinwarton 54 D2
Kiplaw Croft 179 F4
Kipp 150 A3
Kippax 102 A3
Kippen P. & K. 151 F3
Kippen Stir. 150 B5
Kippenross House 150 C4
Kippford (Scaur) 124 C5
Kipping's Cross 31 F4
Kippington 31 E3
Kirby Bedon 87 D5
Kirby Bellars 68 C1
Kirby Cane 73 E2
Kirby Corner 67 E5
Kirby Cross 60 D5
Kirby Fields 68 A2
Kirby Green 73 E2
Kirby Grindalythe 104 B1
Kirby Hill N.Yorks. 110 A2
Kirby Hill N.Yorks. 102 C1
Kirby Knowle 111 E4
Kirby le Soken 60 D5
Kirby Misperton 111 G5
Kirby Muxloe 68 A2
Kirby Row 73 E2
Kirby Sigston 110 D3
Kirby Underdale 104 A2
Kirby Wiske 110 C4
Kirdford 29 F5
Kirk 187 E3
Kirk Bramwith 94 D1
Kirk Deighton 102 C2
Kirk Ella 104 C5
Kirk Hallam 81 F3
Kirk Hammerton 103 D2
Kirk Ireton 81 D2
Kirk Langley 81 D4
Kirk Merrington 120 B4
Kirk Michael 98 B2
Kirk of Shotts 142 C3
Kirk Sandall 94 D2
Kirk Smeaton 94 C1
Kirk Yetholm 136 C4
Kirkandrews 115 G2

Kirkandrews-upon-Eden **117** G1
Kirkbampton **117** G1
Kirkbean **125** D5
Kirkbride **117** F1
Kirkbuddo **160** D5
Kirkburn *E.Riding* **104** B2
Kirkburn *Sc.Bord.* **135** D2
Kirkburton **93** F1
Kirkby *Lincs.* **96** A3
Kirkby *Mersey.* **91** F3
Kirkby *N.Yorks.* **111** E2
Kirkby Fleetham **110** B3
Kirkby Green **83** F2
Kirkby in Ashfield **81** F2
Kirkby la Thorpe **83** F3
Kirkby Lonsdale **108** B5
Kirkby Malham **101** E1
Kirkby Mallory **67** G2
Kirkby Malzeard **110** B5
Kirkby on Bain **84** A1
Kirkby Overblow **102** C3
Kirkby Stephen **108** C2
Kirkby Thore **108** C1
Kirkby Underwood **83** F5
Kirkby Wharfe **103** E2
Kirkby Woodhouse **81** F2
Kirkby-in-Furness **106** D4
Kirkbymoorside **111** F4
Kirkcaldy **152** A5
Kirkcambeck **118** B1
Kirkcolm **122** B4
Kirkconnel **133** F4
Kirkconnell **125** D4
Kirkcowan **123** E4
Kirkcudbright **124** A5
Kirkdale House **123** G5
Kirkdean **143** F5
Kirkfieldbank **142** C4
Kirkgunzeon **124** C4
Kirkham *Lancs.* **100** A4
Kirkham *N.Yorks.* **103** G1
Kirkhamgate **102** C5
Kirkharle **128** C3
Kirkhaugh **118** C3
Kirkheaton *Northumb.* **128** C4
Kirkheaton *W.Yorks.* **93** F1
Kirkhill *Angus* **161** E3
Kirkhill *High.* **174** B5
Kirkhill *Moray* **176** C4
Kirkhope **135** E3
Kirkibost **163** D3
Kirkinch **160** B5
Kirkinner **123** F5
Kirkintilloch **142** A2
Kirkland *Cumb.* **118** C4
Kirkland *Cumb.* **117** D5
Kirkland *D. & G.* **124** C1
Kirkland *D. & G.* **133** F4
Kirkland *D. & G.* **125** E2
Kirkland of Longcastle **115** D2
Kirkleatham **121** E5
Kirklevington **110** D1
Kirkley **73** G2
Kirklington *N.Yorks.* **110** C3
Kirklington *Notts.* **82** B2
Kirklinton **118** A1
Kirkliston **143** F2
Kirkmaiden **114** B3
Kirkmichael *P. & K.* **159** F3
Kirkmichael *S.Ayr.* **132** B5
Kirkmuirhill **142** B5
Kirknewton *Northumb.* **136** D3
Kirknewton *W.Loth.* **143** F3
Kirkney **168** C1
Kirkoswald *Cumb.* **118** B3
Kirkoswald *S.Ayr.* **132** A5
Kirkpatrick Durham **124** B3
Kirkpatrick-Fleming **126** A4
Kirksanton **106** C4
Kirkstall **102** B4
Kirkstead **83** G1
Kirkstile *Aber.* **168** C1
Kirkstile *D. & G.* **126** B2
Kirkstyle **187** F1
Kirkthorpe **102** C5
Kirkton *Aber.* **168** D2
Kirkton *Aber.* **177** F4

Kirkton *Aber.* **168** D3
Kirkton *Angus* **160** C5
Kirkton *Arg. & B.* **147** G4
Kirkton *D. & G.* **125** D2
Kirkton *Fife* **152** B2
Kirkton *High.* **166** A1
Kirkton *High.* **182** C5
Kirkton *High.* **175** D4
Kirkton *High.* **186** A2
Kirkton *High.* **163** G2
Kirkton *P. & K.* **151** E3
Kirkton *Sc.Bord.* **135** G2
Kirkton Manor **134** D2
Kirkton of Airlie **160** B4
Kirkton of Auchterhouse **152** B1
Kirkton of Barevan **175** E5
Kirkton of Bourtie **169** F2
Kirkton of Collace **151** G1
Kirkton of Craig **161** F4
Kirkton of Culsalmond **168** D1
Kirkton of Durris **169** E5
Kirkton of Glenbuchat **168** A3
Kirkton of Glenisla **160** A3
Kirkton of Kingoldrum **160** B4
Kirkton of Lethendy **159** G5
Kirkton of Logie Buchan **169** G2
Kirkton of Maryculter **169** F5
Kirkton of Menmuir **160** D3
Kirkton of Monikie **152** D1
Kirkton of Rayne **169** D1
Kirkton of Skene **169** F4
Kirkton of Tealing **152** C1
Kirkton of Auchnahannet **167** E1
Kirktonhill *Aber.* **161** E3
Kirktonhill *W.Dun.* **141** E2
Kirktown **179** F2
Kirktown of Alvah **177** F3
Kirktown of Auchterless **177** G5
Kirktown of Deskford **177** E3
Kirktown of Fetteresso **161** G1
Kirktown of Slains **179** F5
Kirkwall **190** B3
Kirkwall Airport **190** B3
Kirkwhelpington **128** B3
Kirmington **96** B1
Kirmond le Mire **96** B3
Kirn **140** C2
Kirriemuir **160** B4
Kirstead Green **73** D2
Kirtlebridge **126** A4
Kirtleton **126** A3
Kirtling **59** E2
Kirtling Green **59** E2
Kirtlington **42** A1
Kirtomy **185** G2
Kirton *Lincs.* **84** B4
Kirton *Notts.* **82** B1
Kirton *Suff.* **61** D4
Kirton End **84** A3
Kirton Holme **84** A3
Kirton in Lindsey **95** G3
Kiscadale **131** F3
Kislingbury **56** D2
Kismeldon Bridge **21** D4
Kites Hardwick **55** G1
Kitley **8** B2
Kittisford **23** D5
Kittisford Barton **23** D5
Kittle **36** B4
Kitt's End **44** B3
Kitt's Green **67** D4
Kitwood **28** B3
Kivernoll **53** D4
Kiveton Park **94** B4
Klibreck **182** A1
Knabbygates **177** E4
Knaith **95** F4
Knaith Park **95** F4
Knap Corner **25** F5
Knaphill **29** E2
Knaplock **24** A5
Knapp *P. & K.* **152** A1
Knapp *Som.* **24** A5
Knapthorpe **82** C2
Knaptoft **68** B4

Knapton *Norf.* **87** E2
Knapton *York* **103** E2
Knapton Green **52** D2
Knapwell **58** B1
Knaresborough **102** C2
Knarsdale **118** C2
Knaven **179** D3
Knayton **110** D4
Knebworth **58** A5
Knedlington **103** G5
Kneesall **82** C1
Kneesworth **58** B3
Kneeton **82** C3
Knelston **36** A4
Knenhall **79** G4
Knettishall **72** A3
Knightacott **21** G2
Knightcote **55** G2
Knightley **79** F5
Knightley Dale **79** F5
Knighton *Devon* **8** B3
Knighton *Dorset* **12** C1
Knighton *Leic.* **68** A2
Knighton *Poole* **13** E3
Knighton (Tref-y-clawdd) *Powys* **64** B5
Knighton *Som.* **23** E3
Knighton *Staffs.* **79** E3
Knighton *Staffs.* **79** E5
Knighton *Wilts.* **41** E5
Knighton on Teme **79** E5
Knightswood **141** G3
Knightwick **53** G2
Knill **52** B1
Knipoch **148** A2
Knipton **82** D4
Knitsley **120** A3
Kniveton **80** D2
Knock *Arg. & B.* **147** E1
Knock *Cumb.* **118** C5
Knock *High.* **163** E4
Knock *Moray* **177** E4
Knock of Auchnahannet **167** E1
Knockalava **148** B5
Knockally **183** G2
Knockaloe Moar **98** A3
Knockan **181** E3
Knockandhu **167** G2
Knockando **176** A5
Knockarthur **182** C4
Knockbain **174** C4
Knockban **173** F3
Knockbreck **175** D1
Knockbrex **115** F2
Knockdamph **181** E5
Knockdee **187** D2
Knockdow **140** C2
Knockdown **40** A4
Knockenkelly **131** F3
Knockentiber **132** B2
Knockfin **165** E2
Knockgray **123** G1
Knockholt **31** D3
Knockholt Pound **31** D3
Knockin **78** A5
Knockinlaw **132** C2
Knocklearn **124** B3
Knockmill **31** E2
Knocknaha **130** B4
Knocknain **122** A4
Knocknalling **123** G2
Knockrome **139** D2
Knocksharry **98** A3
Knockville **123** E3
Knockvologan **146** C3
Knodishall **61** F1
Knodishall Common **61** F1
Knodishall Green **61** F1
Knole **24** B5
Knolls Green **92** C5
Knolton **78** A4
Knook **26** A3
Knossington **68** D2
Knott End-on-Sea **99** G3
Knotting **57** F1
Knotting Green **57** F1
Knottingley **103** E5
Knotts **101** D2
Knotty Green **43** E3
Knowbury **65** E5
Knowe **123** E3
Knowes of Elrick **177** F4
Knowesgate **128** B3
Knoweside **132** A4
Knowetownhead **135** G4
Knowhead **179** E2
Knowl Green **59** F3

Knowl Hill **42** D5
Knowl Wall **79** F4
Knowle *Bristol* **39** F5
Knowle *Devon* **10** A2
Knowle *Devon* **21** E2
Knowle *Devon* **11** D4
Knowle *Shrop.* **65** E5
Knowle *Som.* **22** C3
Knowle *W.Mid.* **67** D5
Knowle Cross **10** D3
Knowle Green **100** C4
Knowle Hall **24** A3
Knowle St. Giles **11** G1
Knowlton *Dorset* **13** G1
Knowlton *Kent* **33** E3
Knowsley **91** F3
Knowstone **22** B5
Knox Bridge **31** G4
Knucklas **64** B5
Knutsford **92** B5
Knypersley **79** F2
Krumlin **93** E1
Kuggar **3** E5
Kyle of Lochalsh (Caol Loch Aillse) **163** F2
Kyleakin (Caol Acain) **163** F2
Kylerhea (Ceol Reatha) **163** F2
Kyles Scalpay **189** F4
Kylesbeg **155** F2
Kylesknoydart **163** G5
Kylesku **181** E1
Kylesmorar **163** G5
Kylestrome **181** E1
Kyloag **182** B5
Kynaston **78** A5
Kynnersley **65** F1
Kyre Park **51** F1

L

Laceby **96** C2
Lacey Green **42** D2
Lach Dennis **92** B5
Lackford **71** F5
Lacock **26** A1
Ladbroke **55** G2
Laddingford **31** F4
Lade Bank **84** B2
Ladies Hill **100** A3
Ladock **4** C4
Lady Hall **106** C4
Ladybank **152** B3
Ladycross **6** D2
Ladyfield **148** C3
Ladykirk **145** F5
Ladysford **179** E1
Ladywood **54** C1
Laga **155** F3
Lagalochan **148** A3
Lagavulin **138** C5
Lagg *Arg. & B.* **139** D2
Lagg *N.Ayr.* **131** E3
Lagg *S.Ayr.* **132** A4
Laggan *Arg. & B.* **138** A4
Laggan *High.* **166** A5
Laggan (An Lagan) *High.* **165** D5
Laggan *Moray* **168** A1
Laggan *Stir.* **150** A3
Lagganulva **155** D5
Lagganvoulin **167** F3
Laglingarten **148** D4
Lagnalean **174** C5
Lagrae **133** F4
Laguna **151** G1
Laid **184** D3
Laide **180** B5
Laight **133** E4
Lainchoil **167** E3
Laindon **45** F4
Lair **159** G3
Lairg **182** A4
Lairg Lodge **182** A4
Lairigmor **156** D3
Laisterdyke **102** A4
Laithers **177** F5
Laithes **118** A4
Lake *Devon* **21** F2
Lake *Devon* **8** B1
Lake *I.o.W.* **15** F4
Lake *Wilts.* **26** C4
Lakenham **86** D5
Lakenheath **71** F4
Lakesend **70** D3
Lakeside *Cumb.* **107** E4
Lakeside *Thur.* **45** E5

Laleham **29** F1
Laleston **37** E5
Lamancha **143** G4
Lamarsh **59** G4
Lamas **86** D3
Lamb Corner **60** B4
Lamb Roe **100** D4
Lambden **145** E5
Lamberhurst **31** F5
Lamberhurst Quarter **31** F5
Lamberton **145** G4
Lambfell Moar **98** A3
Lambley *Northumb.* **118** C2
Lambley *Notts.* **82** B3
Lambourn **41** F5
Lambourn Woodlands **41** F5
Lambourne End **45** D3
Lambs Green **30** B5
Lambston **34** C1
Lamellion **5** G3
Lamerton **7** E3
Lamesley **120** B2
Lamington *High.* **174** D2
Lamington *S.Lan.* **134** A2
Lamlash **131** F2
Lamloch **123** G1
Lamonby **118** A4
Lamorna **2** B4
Lamorran **4** C5
Lampert **127** E4
Lampeter (Llanbedr Pont Steffan) **50** B3
Lampeter Velfrey **35** E1
Lamphey **34** D2
Lamplugh **117** D4
Lamport **68** B5
Lamyatt **25** D4
Lana *Devon* **6** D1
Lana *Devon* **20** D5
Lanark **142** C5
Lanarth **3** E4
Lancaster **100** A1
Lanchester **120** A3
Lancing **17** D3
Landbeach **58** C1
Landcross **21** D4
Landerberry **169** E4
Landewednack **3** E5
Landford **14** B1
Landhallow **183** G1
Landican **91** D4
Landimore **36** A3
Landkey **21** F2
Landmoth **110** D3
Landore **36** C3
Landrake **7** D4
Land's End Airport **2** A4
Landscove **9** D1
Landshipping **34** D1
Landulph **8** A1
Landwade **59** E1
Landywood **66** B2
Lane Bottom **101** E4
Lane End *Bucks.* **42** D3
Lane End *Cumb.* **106** C3
Lane End *Derbys.* **81** F1
Lane End *Dorset* **13** E3
Lane End *Hants.* **27** G5
Lane End *Here.* **39** F1
Lane End *Kent* **45** E5
Lane End *Wilts.* **25** F3
Lane Ends *Derbys.* **80** D4
Lane Ends *Gt.Man.* **93** D3
Lane Ends *Lancs.* **101** D4
Lane Ends *N.Yorks.* **101** F3
Lane Green **66** A2
Lane Head *Dur.* **110** A1
Lane Head *Dur.* **119** G5
Lane Head *Gt.Man.* **92** A4
Lane Head *W.Yorks.* **93** F2
Lane Heads **100** A4
Lane Side **101** D5
Laneast **5** G1
Lane-end **5** E3
Lanehead *Dur.* **119** E3
Lanehead *Northumb.* **127** F3
Lanesend **35** D2
Lanesfield **66** B3
Laneshawbridge **101** F3
Langamull **154** C4

Langar **82** C4
Langbank **141** E2
Langbar **101** G2
Langbaurgh **111** E1
Langcliffe **101** E1
Langdale End **112** C3
Langdon *Cornw.* **6** C1
Langdon *Cornw.* **6** D2
Langdon *Beds.* **57** G3
Langdon Beck **119** E4
Langdon Hills **45** F4
Langdon House **10** C5
Langdyke **152** B4
Langford *Beds.* **57** G3
Langford *Essex* **46** B2
Langford *Notts.* **82** D2
Langford *Oxon.* **41** E2
Langford Budville **23** E5
Langham *Essex* **60** B4
Langham *Norf.* **86** B1
Langham *Rut.* **68** D1
Langham *Suff.* **60** A1
Langham Moor **60** B4
Langho **100** C4
Langholm **126** B3
Langland **36** C4
Langlands **124** A5
Langlee **136** A5
Langleeford **136** D4
Langley *Ches.E.* **92** D5
Langley *Derbys.* **81** F3
Langley *Essex* **58** C4
Langley *Glos.* **54** C5
Langley *Gt.Man.* **92** C2
Langley *Hants.* **14** D2
Langley *Herts.* **58** A5
Langley *Kent* **31** G3
Langley *Northumb.* **119** E1
Langley *Oxon.* **41** F1
Langley *Slo.* **43** F5
Langley *Som.* **23** D5
Langley *W.Suss.* **28** B3
Langley *Warks.* **55** D1
Langley Burrell **40** B5
Langley Corner **43** F4
Langley Green *Derbys.* **81** D4
Langley Green *W.Suss.* **30** B5
Langley Green *Warks.* **55** E1
Langley Heath **32** A3
Langley Marsh **23** D5
Langley Mill **81** F3
Langley Moor **120** B2
Langley Park **120** B3
Langley Street **87** E5
Langney **18** B3
Langold **94** C4
Langore **5** G1
Langport **24** B5
Langrick **84** A3
Langrick Bridge **84** A3
Langridge *B. & N.E.Som.* **25** E1
Langridge *Devon* **21** F3
Langridgeford **21** F3
Langrigg **117** E2
Langrish **28** C5
Langsett **93** G2
Langshaw **135** G2
Langshawburn **135** D2
Langside *Glas.* **141** G3
Langside *P. & K.* **150** C3
Langstone *Hants.* **15** G2
Langstone *Newport* **38** C3
Langthorne **110** B3
Langthorpe **102** C1
Langthwaite **109** F3
Langtoft *E.Riding* **104** C1
Langtoft *Lincs.* **69** G1
Langton *Dur.* **110** A1
Langton *Lincs.* **97** D5
Langton *Lincs.* **84** A1
Langton *N.Yorks.* **103** G2
Langton by Wragby **96** B3
Langton Green *Kent* **31** E5
Langton Green *Suff.* **72** C4
Langton Herring **12** C4
Langton Long Blandford **13** E2
Langton Matravers **13** F5
Langtree **21** E4
Langtree Week **21** E4
Langwathby **118** B4

Langwell 181 G4
Langwell House 183 G2
Langwith 94 C5
Langworth 96 A5
Lanivet 5 E3
Lank 5 E2
Lanlivery 5 E4
Lanner 4 B5
Lanoy 5 G2
Lanreath 5 F4
Lansallos 5 F4
Lansdown 25 E1
Lanteglos 5 E1
Lanteglos Highway 5 F4
Lanton Northumb. 136 D3
Lanton Sc.Bord. 136 A4
Lanvean 4 C3
Lapford 10 A2
Laphroaig 138 B5
Lapley 66 A1
Lapworth 67 D5
Larach na Gaibhre 139 F2
Larachbeg 155 F5
Larbert 142 C1
Larbreck 100 A3
Larden Green 78 C2
Larg 123 E3
Largie 168 D1
Largiemore 140 A1
Largoward 152 C4
Largs 140 D4
Largue 177 F5
Larguybaan 130 B4
Larguybeg 131 F3
Larguymore 131 F3
Lark Hall 59 D2
Larkfield 140 D2
Larkhall 142 B4
Larkhill 26 C3
Larklands 81 F3
Larling 72 A3
Larriston 126 D2
Lartington 109 F1
Lary 168 A4
Lasborough 40 A3
Lasham 28 B3
Lashbrook 21 E5
Lashenden 32 A4
Lassington 53 G5
Lassodie 151 G5
Lasswade 144 A3
Lastingham 111 G3
Latchford 92 A4
Latchingdon 46 B2
Latchley 7 E3
Lately Common 92 A3
Lathallan Mill 152 C4
Lathbury 57 D3
Latheron 183 G1
Latheronwheel 183 G1
Lathockrar 152 C3
Lathones 152 C4
Lathrisk 152 A4
Latimer 43 F3
Latteridge 39 F4
Lattiford 25 D5
Latton 40 C3
Lauchentyre 123 G5
Lauchintilly 169 E3
Lauder 144 C5
Laugharne (Lacharn) 35 G1
Laughterton 95 F5
Laughton E.Suss. 18 A2
Laughton Leics. 68 B4
Laughton Lincs. 83 F4
Laughton Lincs. 95 F3
Laughton en le Morthen 94 C4
Launcells 20 C5
Launcells Cross 20 C5
Launceston 6 D2
Launde Abbey 68 C2
Launton 56 B5
Laurencekirk 161 F2
Laurieston D. & G. 124 A4
Laurieston Falk. 142 D2
Lavendon 57 E2
Lavenham 60 A3
Laverhay 125 F1
Lavernock 23 E1
Laversdale 118 A1
Laverstock 26 C4
Laverstoke 27 F3
Laverton Glos. 54 C4
Laverton N.Yorks. 110 B5

Laverton Som. 25 E2
Lavister 78 A2
Law 142 C4
Lawers P. & K. 150 C2
Lawers P. & K. 150 B1
Lawford Essex 60 B4
Lawford Som. 23 E4
Lawhitton 7 D2
Lawkland 101 D1
Lawkland Green 101 D1
Lawley 65 F2
Lawnhead 79 F5
Lawrence Weston 39 E5
Lawrenny 34 D2
Laws 152 C1
Lawshall 59 G2
Lawshall Green 59 G2
Lawton 52 D2
Laxey 98 C3
Laxfield 73 D4
Laxfield Bridge 184 B4
Laxo 191 F3
Laxton E.Riding 103 G5
Laxton Northants. 69 E3
Laxton Notts. 82 C1
Laycock 101 G3
Layer Breton 46 C1
Layer de la Haye 46 C1
Layer Marney 46 C1
Layham 60 B3
Laymore 11 G2
Layter's Green 43 E3
Laytham 103 G4
Layton 99 G4
Lazenby 121 E5
Lazonby 118 B4
Lea Derbys. 81 E2
Lea Here. 53 F5
Lea Lincs. 95 F4
Lea Shrop. 64 C4
Lea Shrop. 64 D2
Lea Wilts. 40 B4
Lea Bridge 81 E2
Lea Green 53 F1
Lea Marston 67 E3
Lea Town 100 A4
Lea Yeat 108 C4
Leachd 148 C5
Leachkin (An Leacainn) 174 C5
Leadburn 143 G4
Leaden Roding 45 E1
Leadenham 83 E2
Leaderfoot 135 G2
Leadgate Cumb. 118 D3
Leadgate Dur. 120 A2
Leadgate Northumb. 120 A2
Leadhills 133 G4
Leadingcross Green 32 A3
Leafield 41 F1
Leagrave 57 F5
Leake Commonside 84 B2
Leake Hurn's End 84 C3
Lealands 18 A2
Lealholm 111 G2
Lealt Arg. & B. 147 F5
Lealt High. 171 E3
Leam 93 G3
Leamington Hastings 55 G1
Leamington Spa 55 F1
Leamoor Common 64 D4
Leanach Arg. & B. 148 C5
Leanach High. 175 D5
Leanaig 174 B4
Leanoch 176 A4
Leargybreck 138 D2
Leasgill 107 F4
Leasingham 83 F3
Leask 179 F4
Leason 36 A3
Leasowe 91 D3
Leat 6 D2
Leatherhead 29 G2
Leathley 102 B3
Leaton Shrop. 65 D1
Leaton Tel. & W. 65 F1
Leaveland 32 C2
Leavenheath 60 A4
Leavening 101 G1
Leaves Green 30 D2
Leavesden Green 44 A2
Lebberston 113 D4
Lechlade-on-Thames 41 E3
Leck 108 B5

Leckford 27 E4
Leckfurin 185 G3
Leckgruinart 138 A3
Leckhampstead Bucks. 56 C4
Leckhampstead W.Berks. 41 G5
Leckhampstead Thicket 41 G5
Leckhampton 40 B1
Leckie High. 173 D3
Leckie Stir. 150 B5
Leckmelm (Leac Mailm) 173 E1
Leckroy 165 E5
Leckuary 148 A5
Leckwith 38 A5
Leconfield 104 C3
Ledaig (Leideag) 148 B1
Ledard 149 G4
Ledbeg 181 E3
Ledburn 57 D5
Ledbury 53 G4
Ledcharrie 150 A2
Ledgemoor 52 D2
Ledicot 52 D1
Ledmore Arg. & B. 155 E5
Ledmore High. 181 E3
Lednagullin 186 A2
Ledsham C. & W.Ches. 91 E5
Ledsham W.Yorks. 103 D5
Ledston 102 D5
Ledstone 8 D3
Ledwell 55 G5
Lee Arg. & B. 146 D2
Lee Devon 21 E1
Lee Hants. 14 C1
Lee Lancs. 100 B4
Lee Shrop. 78 B4
Lee Brockhurst 78 C5
Lee Chapel 45 F4
Lee Clump 43 E2
Lee Mill Bridge 8 B2
Lee Moor 8 B1
Leebotwood 65 D3
Leece 99 F1
Leeds Kent 32 A3
Leeds W.Yorks. 102 B4
Leeds Bradford International Airport 102 B3
Leedstown 2 D3
Leegomery 65 F1
Leek 79 G2
Leek Wootton 55 E1
Leekbrook 79 G2
Leeming N.Yorks. 110 B4
Leeming W.Yorks. 101 G4
Leeming Bar 110 B4
Lee-on-the-Solent 15 E2
Lees Derbys. 80 D1
Lees Gt.Man. 93 D2
Leeswood 77 F2
Leftwich 92 A5
Legars 145 E5
Legbourne 97 D4
Legerwood 144 C5
Legsby 96 B4
Leicester 68 A2
Leicester Forest East 68 A2
Leigh Dorset 12 C2
Leigh Dorset 13 G3
Leigh Gt.Man. 92 A2
Leigh Kent 31 E4
Leigh Shrop. 64 C2
Leigh Surr. 30 B3
Leigh Wilts. 40 C3
Leigh Worcs. 53 G2
Leigh Beck 46 B4
Leigh Common 25 E5
Leigh Delamere 40 A5
Leigh Green 32 B5
Leigh Park 15 G2
Leigh Sinton 53 G2
Leigh upon Mendip 25 D3
Leigh Woods 39 E5
Leigham 8 B2
Leighland Chapel 22 D4
Leigh-on-Sea 46 B4
Leighterton 40 A3
Leighton N.Yorks. 110 A5
Leighton (Tre'r Llai) Powys 64 B2
Leighton Shrop. 65 F2
Leighton Som. 25 E3

Leighton Bromswold 69 G5
Leighton Buzzard 57 E5
Leinthall Earls 52 D1
Leinthall Starkes 52 D1
Leintwardine 64 D5
Leire 68 A4
Leirinmore 184 D2
Leiston 61 F1
Leitfie 160 A5
Leith 143 G2
Leitholm 145 E5
Lelant 2 C3
Lelley 105 E4
Lemington 120 A1
Lemnas 178 D1
Lempitlaw 136 B3
Lemsford 44 B1
Lenham 32 A3
Lenham Heath 32 B4
Lenie 165 G2
Lenimore 139 G5
Lennel 145 F5
Lennox Plunton 124 A5
Lennoxtown 142 A2
Lent Rise 43 E4
Lenton Lincs. 83 F4
Lenton Nott. 81 G4
Lenton Abbey 81 G4
Lenwade 86 B4
Lenzie 142 A2
Leoch 152 B1
Leochel-Cushnie 168 C3
Leominster 53 D2
Leonard Stanley 40 A2
Leorin 138 B5
Lepe 14 D3
Lephin 170 A5
Lephinchapel 148 B5
Lephinmore 148 B5
Leppington 103 G1
Lepton 93 G1
Lerags 148 A2
Lerryn 5 F4
Lerwick 191 F4
Lesbury 137 G5
Leschangie 169 E3
Leslie Aber. 168 C2
Leslie Fife 152 A4
Lesmahagow 133 G2
Lesnewth 6 B1
Lessendrum 177 E5
Lessingham 87 F3
Lessness Heath 45 D5
Lessonhall 117 F1
Leswalt 122 B4
Letchmore Heath 44 A3
Letchworth Garden City 58 A4
Letcombe Bassett 41 F4
Letcombe Regis 41 G4
Letham Angus 160 D5
Letham Falk. 142 C1
Letham Fife 152 B3
Lethanhill 32 D2
Lethenty 178 D3
Letheringham 61 D2
Letheringsett 86 B2
Lettaford 10 A4
Letter Finlay 165 D5
Letterewe 172 C2
Letterfearn (Leitir Fheàrna) 163 G2
Lettermorar 155 G2
Lettermore Arg. & B. 155 D5
Lettermore High. 185 F4
Letters 173 E1
Lettershaws 133 G3
Letterston 48 C5
Lettoch High. 167 E3
Lettoch High. 167 F1
Letton Here. 64 C5
Letton Here. 52 C3
Letty Green 44 B1
Letwell 94 C4
Leuchars 152 C2
Leumrabhagh 189 G3
Leusdon 10 A5
Levedale 66 A1
Level's Green 58 C5
Leven E.Riding 104 D3
Leven Fife 152 B4
Levencorroch 131 F3
Levenhall 144 A2
Levens 107 F4

Levens Green 58 B5
Levenshulme 92 C3
Levenwick 191 F5
Leverburgh 189 E5
Leverington 70 C1
Leverstock Green 43 F2
Leverton 84 B3
Leverton Lucasgate 84 C3
Leverton Outgate 84 C3
Levington 60 D4
Levisham 112 B3
Levishie 165 F3
Lew 41 F1
Lewannick 5 G1
Lewcombe 12 B2
Lewdown 7 E2
Lewes 17 G2
Leweston 48 C5
Lewisham 44 C5
Lewiston (Blàr na Maigh) 165 G2
Lewistown 37 F4
Lewknor 42 C3
Leworthy 21 G2
Lewson Street 32 B2
Lewth 100 A4
Lewtrenchard 7 E2
Ley Aber. 168 C3
Ley Cornw. 5 F3
Ley Green 57 G5
Leybourne 31 F3
Leyburn 110 A3
Leyland 106 B1
Leylodge 169 E3
Leymoor 93 F1
Leys Aber. 179 F2
Leys Aber. 168 B4
Leys P. & K. 152 A1
Leys of Cossans 160 B5
Leysdown-on-Sea 32 C1
Leysmill 161 E5
Leysters 53 E1
Leyton 44 C4
Leytonstone 44 C4
Lezant 6 D3
Lezerea 3 D3
Lhanbryde 176 B3
Liatrie 165 E1
Libanus 51 F5
Libberton 143 D5
Libbery 54 B2
Liberton 143 G3
Lichfield 66 D2
Lickey 66 B5
Lickey End 66 B5
Lickfold 29 E5
Liddaton Green 7 E2
Liddesdale 155 G4
Liddington 41 E4
Lidgate Derbys. 94 A5
Lidgate Suff. 59 F2
Lidget 82 B1
Lidlington 57 E4
Lidsey 16 B3
Lidsing 31 G2
Lidstone 55 F5
Lienassie 164 A2
Lieurary 186 C2
Liff 152 B1
Lifton 7 D2
Liftondown 7 D2
Lightcliffe 102 A5
Lighthorne 55 F2
Lighthorne Heath 55 F2
Lightwater 29 E1
Lightwood 79 G3
Lightwood Green Ches.E. 78 D3
Lightwood Green Wrex. 78 A3
Lilbourne 68 A5
Lilburn Tower 137 E4
Lillesdon 24 C5
Lilleshall 65 G1
Lilley Herts. 57 G5
Lilley W.Berks. 41 G5
Lilliesleaf 135 G3
Lilling Green 103 F1
Lillingstone Dayrell 56 C4
Lillingstone Lovell 56 C3
Lillington Dorset 12 C1
Lillington Warks. 55 F1
Liliput 13 G4
Lilly 21 F2
Lilstock 23 E3
Lilyhurst 65 G1
Limbury 57 F5
Lime Side 92 D2
Limefield 92 C1

Limehillock 177 E4
Limehurst 92 D2
Limekilnburn 142 B4
Limekilns 143 E1
Limerigg 142 C2
Limerstone 14 D4
Limington 24 C5
Limpenhoe 87 E5
Limpley Stoke 25 E1
Limpsfield 30 D3
Limpsfield Chart 30 D3
Linbriggs 128 A1
Linby 81 G2
Linchmere 29 D4
Lincluden 125 D3
Lincoln 95 G5
Lincomb 54 A1
Lincombe Devon 8 D2
Lincombe Devon 8 D3
Lindal in Furness 107 D5
Lindale 107 F4
Lindean 135 F2
Lindertis 160 B4
Lindfield 17 F1
Lindford 28 D4
Lindifferon 152 B3
Lindisfarne (Holy Island) 137 F2
Lindley 102 B3
Lindores 152 A3
Lindow End 92 C5
Lindridge 53 F1
Lindsaig 140 B2
Lindsell 59 E5
Lindsey 60 A3
Lindsey Tye 60 A3
Linfitts 93 D2
Linford Hants. 14 A2
Linford Thur. 45 F5
Linford Wood 56 D3
Lingague 98 A4
Lingards Wood 93 E1
Lingdale 111 F1
Lingen 52 C1
Lingfield 30 C4
Lingley Green 91 G4
Lingwood 87 E5
Linhead 177 F4
Linhope 135 F5
Liniciro 170 C3
Linkend 54 A4
Linkenholt 27 E2
Linkhill 18 D1
Linkinhorne 6 D3
Linksness 190 A3
Linktown 152 A5
Linley Shrop. 64 C3
Linley Shrop. 65 F3
Linley Green 53 F2
Linlithgow 143 E2
Linlithgow Bridge 143 D2
Linn of Muick Cottage 160 B1
Linnels 119 F1
Linney 34 B3
Linshiels 128 A1
Linsidemore 182 A5
Linslade 57 E5
Linstead Parva 73 E4
Linstock 118 A2
Linthwaite 93 F1
Lintlaw 145 F4
Lintmill 177 E3
Linton Cambs. 59 D3
Linton Derbys. 67 E1
Linton Here. 53 F5
Linton Kent 31 G3
Linton N.Yorks. 101 F1
Linton Sc.Bord. 136 B4
Linton W.Yorks. 102 C3
Linton-on-Ouse 103 D1
Lintzford 120 A2
Linwood Hants. 14 A2
Linwood Lincs. 96 B4
Linwood Renf. 141 F3
Liphook 28 D4
Lipley 79 E4
Liscard 91 E3
Liscombe 22 B4
Liskeard 5 G3
L'islet 9 F4
Lismore 148 A1
Liss 28 C5
Liss Forest 28 C5
Lissett 104 D2
Lissington 96 B4
Liston 59 G3
Lisvane 38 A4
Liswerry 38 C4

Litcham **71** G1
Litchborough **56** B2
Litchfield **27** F2
Litherland **91** E3
Litlington *Cambs.* **58** B3
Litlington *E.Suss.* **18** A3
Little Abington **58** B3
Little Addington **69** E5
Little Alne **54** D1
Little Altcar **91** E2
Little Amwell **44** C1
Little Ann **27** E3
Little Asby **108** B2
Little Assynt **180** D2
Little Aston **66** C3
Little Atherfield **15** D5
Little Ayton **111** E1
Little Baddow **45** G2
Little Badminton **40** A4
Little Ballinluig **159** E4
Little Bampton **117** F1
Little Bardfield **59** E4
Little Barford **57** G2
Little Barningham **86** C2
Little Barrington **41** E1
Little Barrow **78** B1
Little Barugh **111** G5
Little Bavington **128** B4
Little Bealings **60** D3
Little Bedwyn **27** D1
Little Beeby **68** B2
Little Bentley **60** C5
Little Berkhamsted **44** B2
Little Billing **56** D1
Little Birch **53** E4
Little Bispham **99** G3
Little Blakenham **60** C3
Little Bloxwich **66** C2
Little Bollington **92** B4
Little Bookham **29** G2
Little Bourton **55** G3
Little Bowden **68** C4
Little Bradley **59** E2
Little Brampton **64** C4
Little Braxted **46** B1
Little Brechin **161** D3
Little Brickhill **57** E4
Little Bridgeford **79** F5
Little Brington **56** B1
Little Bromley **60** B5
Little Broughton **117** D3
Little Budworth **78** C1
Little Burdon **110** C1
Little Burstead **45** F3
Little Burton **104** D3
Little Bytham **69** F1
Little Canford **13** G3
Little Carlton *Lincs.*
  97 D4
Little Carlton *Notts.*
  82 C2
Little Casterton **69** F1
Little Catwick **104** D3
Little Catworth **69** F5
Little Cawthorpe **97** D4
Little Chalfield **25** F1
Little Chalfont **43** E3
Little Chart **32** B4
Little Chesterford **58** D3
Little Chesterton **56** A5
Little Cheverell **26** E2
Little Clacton **47** E1
Little Clanfield **41** E2
Little Clifton **117** D4
Little Coates **96** C2
Little Comberton **54** B3
Little Common **18** C3
Little Compton **55** E4
Little Corby **118** A2
Little Cornard **59** G4
Little Cowarne **53** F2
Little Coxwell **41** E3
Little Crakehall **110** B3
Little Cransley **68** D5
Little Crawley **57** E3
Little Creaton **68** C5
Little Creich **174** C1
Little Cressingham **71** G3
Little Crosby **91** E2
Little Crosthwaite **117** F4
Little Cubley **80** C4
Little Dalby **68** C1
Little Dens **179** F3
Little Dewchurch **53** E4
Little Doward **39** E1
Little Down **27** E2
Little Downham **70** D4
Little Drayton **79** D4

Little Driffield **104** C2
Little Dunham **71** G1
Little Dunkeld **159** F5
Little Dunmow **59** E5
Little Durnford **26** C4
Little Easton **59** E5
Little Eaton **81** E3
Little Eccleston **100** A4
Little Ellingham **72** B2
Little End **45** E2
Little Everdon **56** A2
Little Eversden **58** B2
Little Fakenham **72** A4
Little Faringdon **41** E2
Little Fencote **110** B3
Little Fenton **103** E4
Little Finborough **60** B2
Little Fransham **86** A4
Little Gaddesden **43** E1
Little Garway **52** D5
Little Gidding **69** G4
Little Glemham **61** E2
Little Glenshee **151** E1
Little Gorsley **53** F5
Little Gransden **58** A2
Little Green *Cambs.*
  58 A3
Little Green *Notts.* **82** C3
Little Green *Suff.* **72** B4
Little Green *Suff.* **72** B4
Little Green *Wrex.* **78** B3
Little Grimsby **99** D3
Little Gringley **95** E4
Little Gruinard **172** C1
Little Habton **111** G5
Little Hadham **58** C5
Little Hale **83** G3
Little Hallingbury **45** D1
Little Hampden **43** D2
Little Haresfield **40** A2
Little Harrowden **69** D5
Little Haseley **42** B2
Little Hatfield **105** D3
Little Hautbois **87** D3
Little Haven *Pembs.*
  34 B1
Little Haven *W.Suss.*
  29 G4
Little Hay **66** D2
Little Hayfield **93** E4
Little Haywood **80** B5
Little Heath **67** F4
Little Hereford **53** E1
Little Hockham **72** A3
Little Horkesley **60** A4
Little Hormead **58** C5
Little Horsted **17** G2
Little Horton **26** B1
Little Horwood **56** C4
Little Houghton **56** D2
Little Hucklow **93** F5
Little Hulton **92** B2
Little Hungerford **42** A5
Little Hutton **111** D5
Little Irchester **57** E1
Little Keyford **25** E3
Little Kimble **42** D2
Little Kineton **55** F2
Little Kingshill **43** D3
Little Langdale **107** E2
Little Langford **26** B4
Little Laver **45** E2
Little Lawford **67** G5
Little Leigh **92** A5
Little Leighs **45** G1
Little Lever **92** B2
Little Ley **169** D3
Little Linford **56** D3
Little Linton **59** D3
Little London *Bucks.*
  42 B1
Little London *E.Suss.*
  18 A2
Little London *Essex*
  58 C5
Little London *Hants.*
  27 E3
Little London *Hants.*
  28 B2
Little London *I.o.M.*
  98 B3
Little London *Lincs.*
  84 C5
Little London *Lincs.*
  84 A5
Little London *Lincs.*
  96 D5
Little London *Lincs.*
  96 B4

Little London *Norf.* **85** D5
Little London *Norf.* **71** F3
Little London *Oxon.*
  42 A2
Little London *Powys*
  63 G4
Little London *Suff.* **60** B2
Little London *W.Yorks.*
  102 B4
Little Longstone **93** F5
Little Lyth **65** D2
Little Malvern **53** G3
Little Maplestead **59** G4
Little Marcle **53** F4
Little Marland **21** F4
Little Marlow **43** D4
Little Marsden **101** E4
Little Massingham **85** F5
Little Melton **86** C5
Little Milford **34** C1
Little Milton **42** B2
Little Missenden **43** E3
Little Musgrave **108** C1
Little Ness **64** D1
Little Neston **91** D5
Little Newcastle **48** C5
Little Newsham **110** A1
Little Oakley *Essex* **60** D5
Little Oakley *Northants.*
  69 D4
Little Odell **57** E2
Little Offley **57** G5
Little Onn **66** A1
Little Orton *Cumb.*
  117 G1
Little Orton *Leics.* **67** F2
Little Ouse **71** E4
Little Ouseburn **102** D1
Little Overton **78** A3
Little Packington **67** E4
Little Parndon **44** D1
Little Paxton **57** G1
Little Petherick **4** D2
Little Plumpton **99** G4
Little Plumstead **87** E4
Little Ponton **83** E4
Little Posbrook **15** E2
Little Potheridge **21** F4
Little Preston **56** A2
Little Raveley **70** A4
Little Ribston **102** C2
Little Rissington **41** D1
Little Rogart **182** C4
Little Rollright **55** E4
Little Ryburgh **86** A3
Little Ryle **137** E5
Little Ryton **65** D2
Little Salkeld **118** B4
Little Sampford **59** E4
Little Saxham **59** G1
Little Scatwell **173** G4
Little Shelford **58** C2
Little Shrawardine **64** C1
Little Silver **10** C2
Little Singleton **99** G4
Little Smeaton *N.Yorks.*
  94 C1
Little Smeaton *N.Yorks.*
  110 C2
Little Snoring **86** A2
Little Sodbury **39** G4
Little Sodbury End **39** G4
Little Somborne **27** E4
Little Somerford **40** B4
Little Soudley **79** E5
Little Stainforth **101** E1
Little Stainton **110** C1
Little Stanney **91** F5
Little Staughton **57** G1
Little Steeping **84** C1
Little Stoke **79** G4
Little Stonham **60** C2
Little Street **70** D4
Little Stretton *Leics.*
  68 B2
Little Stretton *Shrop.*
  64 D3
Little Strickland **107** G1
Little Stukeley **70** A5
Little Sugnall **79** F4
Little Sutton **91** E5
Little Swinburne
  128 B4
Little Tarrington **53** F3
Little Tew **55** E4
Little Tey **59** G5
Little Thetford **70** D5
Little Thornage **86** B2

Little Thornton **99** G3
Little Thorpe **120** D3
Little Thurlow **59** E2
Little Thurlow Green
  59 E2
Little Thurrock **45** F5
Little Torboll **182** C5
Little Torrington **21** E4
Little Tosson **128** C1
Little Totham **46** B1
Little Town *Cumb.*
  117 F5
Little Town *Lancs.*
  100 C4
Little Town *Warr.* **92** A3
Little Twycross **67** F2
Little Urswick **107** F5
Little Wakering **46** C4
Little Walden **58** D3
Little Waldingfield **60** A3
Little Walsingham **86** A2
Little Waltham **45** G1
Little Warley **45** F3
Little Washbourne **54** B4
Little Weighton **104** B4
Little Welland **54** A4
Little Welnetham **59** G1
Little Wenham **60** C4
Little Wenlock **65** F2
Little Whittington **119** F1
Little Wilbraham **58** D2
Little Wishford **26** B4
Little Witcombe **40** B1
Little Witley **53** G1
Little Wittenham **42** A3
Little Wittingham Green
  73 D4
Little Wolford **55** E4
Little Woodcote **30** B2
Little Wratting **59** E3
Little Wymington **57** E1
Little Wymondley **58** A5
Little Wyrley **66** C2
Little Wytheford **65** E1
Little Yeldham **59** F4
Littlebeck **112** B2
Littleborough *Devon*
  10 B1
Littleborough *Gt.Man.*
  92 D1
Littleborough *Notts.*
  95 F4
Littlebourne **33** E3
Littlebredy **12** B4
Littlebury **58** D4
Littlebury Green **58** C4
Littledean **39** F1
Littleferry **182** D5
Littleham *Devon* **21** E3
Littleham *Devon* **10** D4
Littlehampton **16** C3
Littlehempston **9** E1
Littlehoughton **137** G5
Littlemill *E.Ayr.* **132** C4
Littlemill *High.* **175** F4
Littlemoor *Derbys.* **81** E1
Littlemoor *Dorset* **12** C4
Littlemore **42** A2
Littlemoss **92** D3
Littleover **81** E4
Littleport **71** D4
Littlestead Green **42** C5
Littlestone-on-Sea **19** F1
Littlethorpe **102** C1
Littleton *C. & W.Ches.*
  78 B1
Littleton *Hants.* **27** F4
Littleton *P. & K.* **152** A1
Littleton *Som.* **24** A4
Littleton *Surr.* **29** F1
Littleton Drew **40** A4
Littleton Panell **26** B2
Littleton-on-Severn
  39 E3
Littletown *Dur.* **120** C3
Littletown *I.o.W.* **15** E3
Littlewick Green **42** D5
Littlewindsor **12** A2
Littleworth *Glos.* **54** D4
Littleworth *Oxon.* **41** F3
Littleworth *S.Yorks.*
  94 D3
Littleworth *Staffs.* **66** C1
Littleworth *Worcs.* **54** A3
Littley Green **45** F1
Litton *Derbys.* **93** F5
Litton *N.Yorks.* **109** E5
Litton *Som.* **24** C2
Litton Cheney **12** B3

Liverpool **91** E3
Liverpool John Lennon
  Airport **91** F4
Liversedge **102** B5
Liverton *Devon* **10** B5
Liverton *R. & C.* **111** G1
Liverton Street **32** A4
Livingston **143** E3
Livingston Village **143** E3
Lixwm **90** C5
Lizard **3** E5
Liangarreglwyd **50** A2
Liaingoch **88** A4
Liaithddu **63** G4
Liampha **37** F5
Lian **63** D2
Lianaber **62** C1
Lianaelhaearn **74** C3
Lianaeron **50** A1
Lianafan **62** C5
Lianafan-fawr **51** F2
Lianafan-fechan **51** F2
Lianaligo **88** C4
Lianarmon **74** D4
Lianarmon Dyffryn Ceinog
  77 E4
Lianarmon-yn-Ial **77** E2
Lianarth *Cere.* **50** A2
Lianarth *Mon.* **38** C1
Lianarthney **50** B5
Lianasa **90** C4
Lianbabo **88** B4
Lianbadarn Fawr **62** B4
Lianbadarn Fynydd
  63 G5
Lianbadarn-y-garreg
  52 A3
Lianbadoc **38** C2
Lianbadrig **88** B3
Lianbeder **38** C3
Lianbedr *Gwyn.* **75** E5
Lianbedr *Powys* **52** B5
Lianbedr *Powys* **52** A3
Lianbedr-Dyffryn-Clwyd
  77 E2
Lianbedrgoch **88** D4
Lianbedrog **74** C4
Lianbedr-y-cennin **76** A1
Lianbenis **75** E2
Lianbethery **22** D1
Lianbister **64** A5
Lianblethian **37** F5
Lianboidy **49** F5
Lianbradach **38** A3
Lianbryn-mair **63** E2
Liancade **22** D1
Liancarfan **37** G5
Liancayo **38** C2
Liancynfelyn **62** C3
Liandafal **38** A2
Liandaff **38** A5
Liandaff North **38** A5
Liandanwg **75** E5
Liandawke **35** F3
Lianddaniel Fab **88** C5
Lianddarog **36** A1
Lianddeiniol **62** B5
Lianddeiniolen **75** E1
Liandderfel **76** C2
Lianddeusant *Carmar.*
  51 D5
Lianddeusant *I.o.A.*
  88 B4
Lianddew **51** G4
Lianddewi **36** A4
Lianddewi Rhydderch
  38 C1
Lianddewi Skirrid **38** C1
Lianddewi Velfrey **35** E1
Lianddewi Ystradenni
  52 A1
Lianddewi-Brefi **50** C2
Liandewi'r Cwm **51** G3
Lianddoged **76** B1
Liandona **89** D5
Liandowror **35** F1
Lianddulas **90** A5
Lianddwywe **75** E5
Lianddyfnan **88** D5
Liandefaelog Fach
  51 G4
Liandefaelog-tre'r-graig
  52 A5
Liandefalle **52** A4
Liandegfan **89** D5
Liandegla **77** E2
Liandegley **52** A1
Liandegveth **38** C3
Liandegwning **74** B4

Liandeilo **50** C5
Liandeilo Abercywyn
  35 G1
Liandeilo Graban **51** G3
Liandeilo'r-Fan **51** E4
Liandelog **48** B5
Liandenny **38** D2
Liandevaud **38** D3
Liandevenny **38** D4
Liandinabo **53** E5
Liandinam **63** G4
Liandissilio **49** E5
Liandogo **39** E2
Liandough *V. of Glam.*
  38 A5
Liandough *V. of Glam.*
  37 F5
Liandovery (Lianymddyfn)
  51 D4
Liandow **37** F5
Liandre *Carmar.* **50** C3
Liandre *Carmar.* **49** E5
Liandre *Cere.* **62** C4
Liandrillo **76** D4
Liandrindod Wells **51** G1
Liandrinio **64** B1
Liandudno **89** F4
Liandudno Junction
  89 F5
Liandwrog **75** D2
Liandybie **36** C1
Liandyfaelog **36** A1
Liandyfan **36** C1
Liandyfriog **49** G3
Liandyfrydog **88** C4
Liandygai **89** D5
Liandygwydd **49** F3
Liandyrnog **77** E1
Liandyry **36** A2
Liandysilio **64** B1
Liandysul **50** A3
Lianedeyrn **38** B4
Lianedy **36** B2
Lianeglwys **51** G4
Lianegryn **62** C2
Lianegwad **50** B5
Lianeilian **88** C3
Lianelian-yn-Rhos **89** G5
Lianelidan **77** E2
Lianelieu **52** A4
Lianellen **38** C1
Lianelli **36** B2
Lianelltyd **62** D1
Lianelly **38** B1
Lianelly Hill **38** B1
Lianelwedd **51** G2
Lianenddwyn **75** E5
Lianengan **74** B5
Lianerfyl **63** G2
Lianeuddog **88** C4
Lianfachraeth **88** B4
Lianfachreth **76** A5
Lianfaelog **88** B5
Lianfaelrhys **74** B5
Lianfaenor **38** D1
Lian-faes *I.o.A.* **89** E5
Lianfaes *Powys* **51** G5
Lianfaethlu **88** B3
Lianfaglan **75** D1
Lianfair **75** E5
Lianfair Caereinion **64** A2
Lianfair Clydogau **50** C2
Lianfair Dyffryn Clwyd
  77 E2
Lianfair Talhaiarn **90** A5
Lianfair Waterdine **64** B5
Lianfairfechan **89** E5
Lianfair-Nant-Gwyn
  49 E4
Lianfair-Orllwyn **49** G3
Lianfairpwllgwyngyll
  88 D5
Lianfairynghornwy **88** B3
Lianfair-yn-neubwll
  88 B5
Lianfallteg **35** E1
Lianfaredd **51** G2
Lianfarian **62** B5
Lianfechain **77** E5
Lianfechell **88** B3
Lianfendigaid **62** B2
Lianferres **77** E1
Lianfflewyn **88** B4
Lianfigael **88** B4
Lianfihangel Glyn Myfyr
  76 C3
Lianfihangel Nant Bran
  51 F4

Llanfihangel Rhydithon **52** A1
Llanfihangel Rogiet **38** D4
Llanfihangel Tal-y-llyn **52** A5
Llanfihangel-ar-arth **50** A3
Llanfihangel-nant-Melan **52** A2
Llanfihangel-uwch-Gwili **50** A5
Llanfihangel-y-Creuddyn **62** C5
Llanfihangel-yng-Ngwynfa **63** G1
Llanfihangel-yn-Nhywyn **88** B5
Llanfihangel-y-pennant *Gwyn.* **75** E3
Llanfihangel-y-pennant *Gwyn.* **62** C2
Llanfilo **52** A4
Llanfoist **38** B1
Llanfor **76** C4
Llanfrechfa **38** C3
Llanfrothen **75** F3
Llanfrynach **51** G5
Llanfwrog *Denb.* **77** E2
Llanfwrog *I.o.A.* **88** B4
Llanfyllin **64** A1
Llanfynydd *Carmar.* **50** B5
Llanfynydd *Flints.* **77** F2
Llanfyrnach **49** F4
Llangadfan **63** G1
Llangadog **50** D5
Llangadwaladr *I.o.A.* **74** C1
Llangadwaladr *Powys* **77** E4
Llangaffo **74** D1
Llangain **35** G1
Llangammarch Wells **51** F3
Llangan **37** F5
Llangarron **53** E5
Llangasty-Talyllyn **52** A5
Llangathen **50** B5
Llangattock **38** B1
Llangattock Lingoed **38** C1
Llangattock-Vibon-Avel **39** D1
Llangedwyn **77** E5
Llangefni **88** C5
Llangeinor **37** F4
Llangeitho **50** C2
Llangeler **49** G4
Llangelynin **62** B2
Llangendeirne **36** A1
Llangennech **36** B2
Llangennith **36** A3
Llangenny **38** B1
Llangernyw **76** B1
Llangian **74** B5
Llangiwg **36** D2
Llangloffan **48** C4
Llanglydwen **49** E5
Llangoed **89** E5
Llangoedmor **49** E3
Llangollen **77** F3
Llangolman **49** E5
Llangorse **52** A5
Llangorwen **62** C4
Llangovan **39** D2
Llangower **76** C4
Llangrannog **49** G2
Llangristiolus **88** C5
Llangrove **39** E1
Llangua **52** C5
Llangunllo **64** B5
Llangunnor **50** A5
Llangurig **63** E5
Llangwm *Conwy* **76** C3
Llangwm *Mon.* **38** D2
Llangwm *Pembs.* **34** C2
Llangwnnadl **74** B4
Llangwyfan **77** E1
Llangwyllog **88** C5
Llangwyryfon **62** C5
Llangybi *Cere.* **50** C2
Llangybi *Gwyn.* **74** D3
Llangybi *Mon.* **38** C2
Llangyfelach **36** C3
Llangynhafal **77** E1
Llangynidr **38** A1
Llangyniew **64** A2
Llangynin **35** F1
Llangynllo **49** G3

Llangynog *Carmar.* **35** G1
Llangynog *Powys* **77** D5
Llangynwyd **37** E4
Llanhamlach **51** G5
Llanharan **37** G4
Llanharry **37** G4
Llanhennock **38** C3
Llanhilleth **38** B2
Llanidloes **63** F4
Llaniestyn **74** B4
Llanigon **52** B4
Llanilid **37** F4
Llanishen *Cardiff* **38** A4
Llanishen *Mon.* **39** D2
Llanllawddog **50** A5
Llanllechid **75** F1
Llanlleonfel **51** F2
Llanlligan **63** G1
Llanllwch **35** G1
Llanllwchaiarn **64** A3
Llanllwni **50** A3
Llanllyfni **75** D2
Llanllywel **38** C3
Llanmadoc **36** A3
Llanmaes **22** C1
Llanmartin **38** C4
Llanmerewig **64** A3
Llanmihangel **37** F5
Llan-mill **35** E1
Llanmiloe **35** F2
Llanmorlais **36** B3
Llannefydd **90** A5
Llannerch Hall **90** B5
Llannerch-y-medd **88** C4
Llannerch-y-Môr **90** C5
Llannon *Carmar.* **36** B2
Llan-non *Cere.* **50** B1
Llannor **74** C4
Llanover **38** C2
Llanpumsaint **50** A5
Llanreithan **48** B4
Llanrhaeadr **77** D1
Llanrhaeadr-ym-Mochnant **77** E5
Llanrhian **48** B4
Llanrhidian **36** A3
Llanrhyddlad **88** B4
Llanrhystud **50** B1
Llanrothal **39** D1
Llanrug **75** E1
Llanrumney **38** B4
Llanrwst **76** A1
Llansadurnen **35** F1
Llansadwrn *Carmar.* **50** C4
Llansadwrn *I.o.A.* **89** D5
Llansaint **35** G2
Llansamlet **36** C3
Llansanffraid **88** B4
Llansanffraid Glan Conwy **89** G5
Llansannan **76** C1
Llansannor **37** F5
Llansantffraed **52** A5
Llansantffraed-Cwmdeuddwr **51** F1
Llansantffraed-in-Elwel **51** G2
Llansantffraid-ym-Mechain **77** F5
Llansawel **50** C4
Llansilin **77** F5
Llansoy **38** D2
Llanspyddid **51** G5
Llanstadwell **34** C2
Llansteffan **52** A3
Llanstephan **52** A3
Llantarnam **38** C3
Llanteg **35** E1
Llanthony **52** B5
Llantilio Crossenny **38** C1
Llantilio Pertholey **38** C1
Llantood **49** E3
Llantrisant *I.o.A.* **88** B4
Llantrisant *Mon.* **38** C3
Llantrisant *R.C.T.* **37** G4
Llantrithyd **37** G5
Llantwit Fardre **37** G4
Llantwit Major **22** C1
Llantysilio **77** E3
Llanuwchllyn **76** B5
Llanvaches **38** D3
Llanvair-Discoed **38** D3
Llanvapley **38** C1
Llanvetherine **38** C1
Llanveynoe **52** C4

Llanvihangel Crucorney (Llanfihangel Crucornau) **52** C5
Llanvihangel Gobion **38** C2
Llanvihangel-Ystern-Llewern **38** D1
Llanvithyn **37** G5
Llanwarne **53** E5
Llanwddyn **63** G1
Llanwenog **50** A3
Llanwern **38** C4
Llanwinio **49** F5
Llanwnda *Gwyn.* **75** D2
Llanwnda *Pembs.* **48** C4
Llanwnnen **50** B3
Llanwnog **63** G3
Llanwonno **37** G3
Llanwrda **50** D4
Llanwrin **63** F2
Llanwrthwl **51** F1
Llanwrtyd **51** E3
Llanwrtyd Wells **51** E3
Llanwyddelan **63** G2
Llanyblodwel **77** F5
Llanybri **35** G1
Llanybydder **50** B3
Llanycefn **49** E5
Llanychaer Bridge **48** C4
Llanycil **76** C4
Llanycrwys **50** C2
Llanymawddwy **63** E1
Llanymynech **77** F5
Llanynghenedl **88** B4
Llanynys **77** E1
Llan-y-pwll **78** A2
Llanyre **51** G1
Llanystumdwy **75** D4
Llanywern **52** A5
Llawhaden **35** D1
Llawndy **90** C4
Llawnt **77** F4
Llawr-y-dref **74** B5
Llawryglyn **63** F3
Llay **78** A2
Llechcynfarwy **88** B4
Llecheiddior **75** D3
Llechfaen **51** G5
Llechryd *Caerp.* **38** A2
Llechryd *Cere.* **49** F3
Llechrydau **77** F3
Lledrod *Cere.* **62** C5
Lledrod *Powys* **77** F5
Llethrid **36** B3
Llidiad-Nenog **50** A4
Llidiardau **76** B4
Llithfaen **74** C3
Lloc **90** C5
Llong **77** F1
Llowes **52** A3
Lloyney **64** B5
Llundain-fach **50** B2
Llwydcoed **37** F2
Llwydiarth **63** G1
Llwyn **64** B4
Llwyncelyn **50** A2
Llwyn-croes **50** A5
Llwyndafydd **49** G2
Llwynderw **64** A2
Llwyndyrys **74** C3
Llwyneinion **77** F3
Llwyngwril **62** B2
Llwynhendy **36** B3
Llwyn-Madoc **51** F2
Llwynmawr **77** F4
Llwyn-onn *Cere.* **50** A2
Llwyn-onn *M.Tyd.* **37** G1
Llwyn-y-brain *Carmar.* **35** E1
Llwyn-y-brain *Carmar.* **50** D4
Llwyn-y-groes **50** B2
Llwynypia **37** F3
Llynclys **77** F5
Llynfaes **88** C5
Llysfaen **89** G5
Llyswen **52** A4
Llysworney **37** F5
Llys-y-frân **48** D5
Llywel **51** E4
Load Brook **93** G4
Loandhu **173** G2
Loanhead *Aber.* **169** G1
Loanhead *Midloth.* **143** G3
Loans **78** A2
Lobb **21** E2
Lobhillcross **7** E2
Loch Choire Lodge **182** B1

Loch Eil Outward Bound **156** C2
Loch Head *D. & G.* **114** D2
Loch Head *D. & G.* **123** F1
Loch Sgioport **188** B3
Lochailort (Ceann Loch Ailleart) **155** G1
Lochaline (Loch Àlainn) **155** F5
Lochans **122** B5
Locharbriggs **125** D2
Lochawe (Loch Obha) **148** D2
Lochboisdale (Loch Baghasdail) **188** B4
Lochbuie **147** F2
Lochcarron (Loch Carrann) **172** B5
Lochdhu Hotel **186** C4
Lochdon **147** G2
Lochdrum **173** F2
Lochearnhead (Ceann Loch Èireann) **150** A2
Lochee **152** B1
Lochend *High.* **187** E2
Lochend (Ceann Loch) *High.* **165** G1
Lochfoot **124** D3
Lochgair **148** B5
Lochgarthside **165** G2
Lochgelly **151** G5
Lochgilphead (Ceann Loch Gilb) **139** G1
Lochgoilhead **149** E4
Lochgoyn **141** G5
Lochhill *E.Ayr.* **133** D4
Lochhill *Moray* **176** B3
Lochinch Castle **122** C4
Lochinver (An Lochan Inbhir) **180** C2
Lochlair **160** D5
Lochlane **150** D2
Lochlea **132** C2
Lochluichart **173** G3
Lochmaben **125** E2
Lochmaddy (Loch na Madadh) **188** C1
Lochore **151** G5
Lochranza **140** A4
Lochside *Aber.* **161** F3
Lochside *High.* **185** D3
Lochside *High.* **183** D1
Lochside *High.* **187** D2
Lochslin **175** E1
Lochton **123** D2
Lochty **152** D4
Lochuige **155** G4
Lochurr **124** B2
Lochussie **174** A4
Lochwinnoch **141** E4
Lockengate **5** E3
Lockerbie **125** F2
Lockeridge **26** C1
Lockerley **14** B3
Lockhills **118** B3
Locking **24** A2
Lockington *E.Riding* **104** B3
Lockington *Leics.* **81** F5
Lockleywood **79** D5
Locks Heath **15** E2
Locksbottom **30** D2
Locksgreen **14** D5
Lockton **112** B4
Loddington *Leics.* **68** C2
Loddington *Northants.* **68** D2
Loddiswell **8** D3
Loddon **73** E2
Lode **58** D1
Loders **12** A3
Lodsworth **29** E5
Lofthouse *N.Yorks.* **110** A5
Lofthouse *W.Yorks.* **102** C5
Loftus **111** G1
Logan *D. & G.* **114** A2
Logan *E.Ayr.* **133** D4
Loganlea **143** D3
Loggerheads **79** E4
Loggie (An Lagaidh) **180** D5
Logie *Angus* **161** G3
Logie *Angus* **160** B4
Logie *Fife* **152** C2
Logie *Moray* **175** G4

Logie Coldstone **168** B4
Logie Hill **175** D2
Logie Newton **169** D1
Logie Pert **161** E3
Logierait **159** E4
Login **49** E5
Lolworth **58** B1
Lonbain **171** F4
Londesborough **104** A3
London **44** C4
London Apprentice **5** E5
London Ashford Airport **19** F1
London Beach **32** A5
London Biggin Hill Airport **30** D2
London City Airport **44** D4
London Colney **44** A2
London Gatwick Airport **30** B4
London Heathrow Airport **43** F5
London Luton Airport **57** G5
London Minstead **14** B1
London Southend Airport **46** B4
London Stansted Airport **58** D5
Londonderry **110** B4
Londonthorpe **83** E4
Londubh **172** B1
Lonemore **175** D1
Long Ashton **39** E5
Long Bank **65** G5
Long Bennington **82** D3
Long Bredy **12** B3
Long Buckby **56** B1
Long Clawson **82** C5
Long Compton *Staffs.* **79** F5
Long Compton *Warks.* **55** E4
Long Crendon **42** B2
Long Crichel **13** F1
Long Dean **40** A5
Long Downs **3** E3
Long Drax **103** F5
Long Duckmanton **94** B5
Long Eaton **81** E2
Long Gill **101** D2
Long Green *C. & W.Ches.* **91** F5
Long Green *Essex* **60** A5
Long Green *Worcs.* **54** A4
Long Hanborough **41** G1
Long Itchington **55** G1
Long Lane **65** F1
Long Lawford **67** G5
Long Load **24** B5
Long Marston *Herts.* **43** D1
Long Marston *N.Yorks.* **103** E2
Long Marston *Warks.* **55** D3
Long Marton **118** C5
Long Meadowend **64** D4
Long Melford **59** G3
Long Newnton **40** B3
Long Preston **101** E3
Long Riston **104** D3
Long Stratton **72** C2
Long Street **56** C3
Long Sutton *Hants.* **28** C3
Long Sutton *Lincs.* **84** C5
Long Sutton *Som.* **24** B5
Long Thurlow **60** B1
Long Whatton **81** F5
Long Wittenham **42** A3
Longbenton **120** B1
Longborough **55** D5
Longbridge *Plym.* **8** B2
Longbridge *W.Mid.* **66** C5
Longbridge *Warks.* **55** E1
Longbridge Deverill **25** F3
Longburgh **117** G1
Longburton **12** C1
Longcliffe **80** D2
Longcombe **9** E2
Longcot **41** E3
Longcroft **142** B2
Longcross *Devon* **7** E3
Longcross *Surr.* **29** E1
Longden **80** D2
Longden Common **54** A4

Longdon Green **66** C1
Longdon upon Tern **65** F1
Longdown **10** B3
Longdrum **169** G3
Longfield **31** F2
Longfield Hill **31** F2
Longfleet **13** G3
Longford *Derbys.* **80** D4
Longford *Glos.* **54** A5
Longford *Gt.Lon.* **43** F5
Longford *Shrop.* **78** D4
Longford *Tel. & W.* **65** G1
Longford *W.Mid.* **67** F4
Longforgan **152** B2
Longformacus **145** D4
Longframlington **128** C3
Longham *Dorset* **13** G3
Longham *Norf.* **86** A4
Longhill **179** E2
Longhirst **129** E3
Longhope *Glos.* **39** F1
Longhope *Ork.* **190** A4
Longhorsley **128** C2
Longhoughton **137** G5
Longlands *Aber.* **168** B2
Longlands *Cumb.* **117** F3
Longlands *Gt.Lon.* **44** D5
Longlane *Derbys.* **81** D4
Longlane *W.Berks.* **41** G5
Longlevens **40** A1
Longley **93** F2
Longley Green **53** G2
Longmanhill **177** G3
Longmoor Camp **28** C4
Longmorn **176** B4
Longnewton *Sc.Bord.* **135** G3
Longnewton *Stock.* **110** C3
Longney **39** G1
Longniddry **144** B2
Longnor *Shrop.* **65** D2
Longnor *Staffs.* **80** B1
Longparish **27** F2
Longridge *Lancs.* **100** C4
Longridge *Staffs.* **66** B1
Longridge *W.Loth.* **143** D3
Longridge End **54** A5
Longridge Towers **145** G4
Longriggend **142** C2
Longrock **2** C3
Longsdon **79** G2
Longshaw **91** G2
Longside **179** F3
Longslow **79** D4
Longsowerby **117** G1
Longstanton **58** C1
Longstock **27** E4
Longstone **2** C5
Longstowe **58** B2
Longstreet **26** C2
Longthorpe **69** G3
Longton *Lancs.* **100** A5
Longton *Stoke* **79** G3
Longtown *Cumb.* **126** B3
Longtown *Here.* **52** C5
Longville in the Dale **65** E3
Longwell Green **39** F5
Longwick **42** C2
Longwitton **128** C3
Longworth **41** F3
Longyester **144** C3
Lonmay **179** F2
Lonmore **170** B5
Looe **5** G4
Loose **31** G3
Loosebeare **10** A2
Loosegate **84** B5
Loosley Row **42** D2
Lopcombe Corner **27** D4
Lopen **12** A1
Loppington **78** B5
Lorbottle **128** C1
Lorbottle Hall **128** C1
Lordington **15** E3
Lord's Hill **14** C1
Lorgill **170** A5
Lorn **141** E1
Lornty **159** G5
Loscoe **81** F3
Loscombe **12** A3
Lossiemouth **176** B2
Lossit **138** A4
Lostock Gralam **92** A5
Lostock Green **92** A5
Lostock Junction **92** A2
Lostwithiel **5** F4

Loth 190 C2
Lothbeg 183 E3
Lothersdale 101 F3
Lothmore 183 E3
Loudwater 43 E3
Loughborough 68 A1
Loughor 36 B3
Loughton Essex 44 D3
Loughton M.K. 56 D4
Loughton Shrop. 65 F4
Lound Lincs. 69 F1
Lound Notts. 95 D4
Lound Suff. 73 G2
Lount 67 F1
Lour 160 C5
Louth 96 D4
Love Clough 101 E5
Lovedean 15 F1
Lover 14 B1
Loversall 94 C3
Loves Green 45 F2
Lovesome Hill 110 C3
Loveston 35 D2
Lovington 24 C4
Low Ackworth 94 B1
Low Angerton 128 C3
Low Ballevain 130 B3
Low Barlay 123 G5
Low Barlings 96 A5
Low Bentham (Lower Bentham) 100 C1
Low Bolton 109 F3
Low Bradfield 93 G3
Low Bradley (Bradley) 101 G3
Low Braithwaite 118 A3
Low Brunton 128 B4
Low Burnham 95 E2
Low Burton 110 B4
Low Buston 129 E1
Low Catton 103 G2
Low Coniscliffe 110 B1
Low Craighead 132 A5
Low Dinsdale 110 C1
Low Ellington 110 B4
Low Entercommon 110 C2
Low Etherley 120 A5
Low Fell 120 B2
Low Gate 119 F1
Low Grantley 110 B5
Low Green 59 G1
Low Habberley 66 A5
Low Ham 24 B5
Low Hawsker 112 C2
Low Haygarth 108 B3
Low Hesket 118 A3
Low Hesleyhurst 128 C2
Low Hutton 103 G1
Low Kingthorpe 112 B4
Low Laithe 102 A1
Low Langton 96 B5
Low Leighton 93 E4
Low Lorton 117 E4
Low Marishes 112 B5
Low Marnham 82 D1
Low Middleton 137 F3
Low Mill 111 F3
Low Moor Lancs. 100 D3
Low Moor W.Yorks. 102 A5
Low Moorsley 120 C3
Low Moresby 116 C4
Low Newton-by-the-Sea 137 G4
Low Row Cumb. 118 B1
Low Row N.Yorks. 109 E3
Low Stillaig 140 A3
Low Street 86 B5
Low Tharston 72 C2
Low Torry 143 E1
Low Town 128 D1
Low Toynton 96 C5
Low Wood 107 E4
Low Worsall 110 C2
Lowbands 53 G4
Lowdham 82 B3
Lowe 78 C4
Lowe Hill 79 G2
Lower Achachenna 148 C2
Lower Aisholt 23 F4
Lower Apperley 54 A5
Lower Arncott 42 B1
Lower Ashtead 29 G2
Lower Ashton 10 B4
Lower Assendon 42 C4
Lower Auchalick 140 A2
Lower Ballam 99 G4

Lower Barewood 52 C2
Lower Bartle 100 A4
Lower Beeding 17 E1
Lower Benefield 69 E4
Lower Bentham (Low Bentham) 100 C1
Lower Bentley 54 B1
Lower Berry Hill 39 E1
Lower Birchwood 81 F2
Lower Boddington 55 G2
Lower Boscaswell 2 A3
Lower Bourne 28 D3
Lower Brailes 55 F4
Lower Breakish 163 E2
Lower Bredbury 92 F7
Lower Broadheath 54 A2
Lower Brynamman 38 C1
Lower Bullingham 53 E4
Lower Bullington 27 F3
Lower Burgate 14 A1
Lower Burrow 24 B5
Lower Burton 52 D2
Lower Caldecote 57 G3
Lower Cam 39 G2
Lower Cambourne 58 B2
Lower Camster 187 E4
Lower Chapel 51 G4
Lower Chenton 11 E2
Lower Chicksgrove 26 A4
Lower Chute 27 E2
Lower Clent 66 B4
Lower Creedy 10 B2
Lower Cumberworth 93 G2
Lower Darwen 100 C5
Lower Dean 57 F1
Lower Diabaig 172 A3
Lower Dicker 18 A2
Lower Dinchope 65 D4
Lower Down 64 C4
Lower Drift 2 B4
Lower Dunsforth 102 D1
Lower Earley 42 C5
Lower Edmonton 44 C3
Lower Elkstone 80 B2
Lower End Bucks. 42 B2
Lower End M.K. 57 E4
Lower End Northants. 57 D1
Lower Everleigh 26 C2
Lower Eythorne 33 E4
Lower Failand 39 E5
Lower Farrington 28 C4
Lower Fittleworth 16 C2
Lower Foxdale 98 A4
Lower Freystrop 34 C1
Lower Froyle 28 C3
Lower Gabwell 9 F1
Lower Gledfield 182 A5
Lower Godney 24 B3
Lower Gravenhurst 57 F4
Lower Green Essex 58 C4
Lower Green Herts. 57 G4
Lower Green Kent 31 F4
Lower Green Norf. 86 A2
Lower Green Staffs. 66 B2
Lower Green Bank 100 B2
Lower Halstock Leigh 12 B2
Lower Halstow 32 A2
Lower Hardres 32 D3
Lower Harpton 52 B1
Lower Hartshay 81 E2
Lower Hartwell 42 C1
Lower Hawthwaite 106 D4
Lower Haysden 31 E4
Lower Hayton 65 E4
Lower Heath 79 F1
Lower Hergest 52 B2
Lower Heyford 55 G5
Lower Higham 45 G5
Lower Holbrook 60 C4
Lower Hopton 93 G1
Lower Hordley 78 A5
Lower Horncroft 16 C2
Lower Horsebridge 18 A2
Lower Houses 93 F1
Lower Howsell 53 G3
Lower Kersal 92 C2
Lower Kilchattan 146 C5
Lower Kilcott 39 G4
Lower Killeyan 138 A5
Lower Kingcombe 12 B3
Lower Kingswood 30 B3
Lower Kinnerton 78 A1

Lower Langford 24 B1
Lower Largo 152 C4
Lower Leigh 80 B4
Lower Lemington 55 E4
Lower Lovacott 21 F3
Lower Loxhore 21 G2
Lower Lydbrook 39 E1
Lower Lye 52 D1
Lower Machen 38 B4
Lower Maes-coed 52 C4
Lower Mannington 13 G2
Lower Middleton Cheney 56 A3
Lower Milton 24 C3
Lower Moor 54 B3
Lower Morton 39 F3
Lower Nash 34 D2
Lower Nazeing 44 C2
Lower Netchwood 65 F3
Lower Nyland 25 E5
Lower Oddington 55 E5
Lower Ollach 162 D1
Lower Penarth 38 A5
Lower Penn 66 A3
Lower Pennington 14 C3
Lower Peover 92 B5
Lower Pollicott 42 C1
Lower Quinton 55 D3
Lower Race 38 B2
Lower Rainham 32 A2
Lower Roadwater 22 D4
Lower Sapey 53 F1
Lower Seagry 40 B4
Lower Shelton 57 E3
Lower Shiplake 42 C5
Lower Shuckburgh 55 G1
Lower Slaughter 55 D5
Lower Soothill 102 B5
Lower Stanton St. Quintin 40 B4
Lower Stoke 32 A1
Lower Stondon 57 G4
Lower Stone 39 F3
Lower Stonnall 66 C2
Lower Stow Bedon 72 A2
Lower Street Dorset 13 E3
Lower Street E.Suss. 18 C2
Lower Street Norf. 87 D2
Lower Street Norf. 86 C2
Lower Street Suff. 60 C2
Lower Stretton 92 A4
Lower Sundon 57 F5
Lower Swanwick 15 D2
Lower Swell 55 D5
Lower Tadmarton 55 G4
Lower Tale 11 D2
Lower Tean 80 B4
Lower Thurlton 73 F2
Lower Thurnham 100 A2
Lower Town Cornw. 3 D4
Lower Town Devon 10 A5
Lower Town I.o.S. 4 B1
Lower Town Pembs. 48 C4
Lower Trebullett 6 D3
Lower Tysoe 55 F3
Lower Upcott 10 B4
Lower Upham 15 E1
Lower Upnor 45 G5
Lower Vexford 23 E4
Lower Wallop 64 C2
Lower Walton 92 A4
Lower Waterhay 40 C3
Lower Weald 56 B4
Lower Wear 10 C4
Lower Weare 24 B2
Lower Welson 52 B2
Lower Whatley 25 E3
Lower Whitley 92 A5
Lower Wick 54 A2
Lower Wield 28 B3
Lower Winchendon (Nether Winchendon) 42 C1
Lower Withington 79 F1
Lower Woodend 42 D4
Lower Woodford 26 C4
Lower Wyche 53 G3
Lowerhouse 101 E4
Lowesby 68 C2
Lowestoft 73 G2
Loweswater 117 E4
Lowfield Heath 30 B4
Lowgill Cumb. 108 B3
Lowgill Lancs. 100 C1
Lowick Cumb. 107 D4
Lowick Northants. 69 E4

Lowick Northumb. 137 E3
Lowick Bridge 107 D4
Lowick Green 107 D4
Lownie Moor 160 C5
Lowsonford 55 D1
Lowther 118 B5
Lowther Castle 118 B5
Lowthorpe 104 C1
Lowton Devon 21 G5
Lowton Gt.Man. 92 A3
Lowton Som. 11 E1
Lowton Common 92 A3
Loxbeare 10 C1
Loxhill 39 F4
Loxhore 21 G2
Loxley 55 E2
Loxley Green 80 B4
Loxton 24 A2
Loxwood 29 F4
Lubachoinnich 181 G5
Lubcroy 181 F4
Lubenham 68 C4
Lubfearn 173 G2
Lubmore 173 D4
Lubreoch 157 G5
Luccombe 22 C3
Luccombe Village 15 E4
Lucker 137 F3
Luckett 7 D3
Luckington 40 A4
Lucklawhill 152 C2
Luckwell Bridge 22 C4
Lucton 52 D1
Lucy Cross 110 B1
Ludag 188 B4
Ludborough 96 C3
Ludbrook 8 C2
Ludchurch 35 E1
Luddenden 101 G5
Luddenden Foot 101 G5
Luddenham Court 32 B2
Luddesdown 31 F2
Luddington N.Lincs. 95 F1
Luddington Warks. 55 D2
Luddington in the Brook 69 G4
Ludford Lincs. 96 B4
Ludford Shrop. 65 E5
Ludgershall Bucks. 42 B1
Ludgershall Wilts. 27 D2
Ludgvan 2 C3
Ludham 87 E4
Ludlow 65 E5
Ludney 97 D3
Ludstock 53 F4
Ludstone 66 A3
Ludwell 26 A5
Ludworth 120 C3
Luffincott 6 D1
Luffness 144 B1
Lufton 12 B1
Lugar 133 D3
Luggate 144 C2
Luggate Burn 144 D2
Luggiebank 142 B2
Lugton 141 F4
Lugwardine 43 E3
Luib 163 D2
Luibeilt 157 E3
Luing 147 G3
Lulham 52 D3
Lullington Derbys. 67 E1
Lullington Som. 25 E2
Lulsgate Bottom 24 C1
Luisley 53 G2
Lulworth Camp 13 E4
Lumb Lancs. 101 E5
Lumb W.Yorks. 101 G5
Lumbutts 101 F5
Lumby 103 D4
Lumphanan 168 C4
Lumphinnans 151 G5
Lumsdaine 145 F3
Lumsdale 81 E1
Lumsden 168 B2
Lunan 161 E4
Lunanhead 160 C4
Luncarty 151 F2
Lund E.Riding 104 B3
Lund N.Yorks. 103 F4
Lundavra 156 C3
Lunderton 179 G3
Lundie Angus 152 A1
Lundie High. 164 C3
Lundin Links 152 C4
Lundwood 94 A2
Lundy 20 B1

Lunga 148 A4
Lunnon 36 B3
Lunsford's Cross 18 C2
Lunt 91 E2
Luntley 52 C2
Luppitt 11 E2
Lupset 94 A1
Lupton 107 G4
Lurgashall 29 E5
Lurgnich 156 B4
Lusby 84 B1
Luss 149 F5
Lussagiven 139 E1
Lusta 170 B4
Lustleigh 10 A4
Luston 53 D1
Luthermuir 161 E3
Luthrie 152 B3
Luton Devon 11 D2
Luton Devon 10 C5
Luton Luton 57 F5
Luton Med. 31 G2
Luton Airport 57 G5
Lutterworth 68 A4
Lutton Devon 8 B2
Lutton Dorset 13 F4
Lutton Lincs. 84 C5
Lutton Northants. 69 G4
Luxborough 22 C4
Luxulyan 5 E4
Lybster High. 186 C2
Lybster High. 187 E5
Lydacott 21 G2
Lydbury North 64 C4
Lydcott 21 G2
Lydd 19 F1
Lydden 33 E4
Lyddington 69 D3
Lydd-on-Sea 19 F1
Lyde Green 39 F5
Lydeard St. Lawrence 23 E4
Lydford 7 F2
Lydford-on-Fosse 24 C4
Lydgate Gt.Man. 93 D1
Lydgate Gt.Man. 93 D2
Lydgate W.Yorks. 101 F5
Lydham 64 C3
Lydiard Millicent 40 C4
Lydiard Tregoze 40 D4
Lydiate 91 E2
Lydlinch 12 D1
Lydney 39 F2
Lydstep 35 D3
Lye 66 B4
Lye Cross 24 B1
Lye Green Bucks. 43 E2
Lye Green E.Suss. 31 G5
Lye Green Warks. 55 D1
Lye's Green 25 F3
Lyford 41 F3
Lymbridge Green 32 D4
Lyme Regis 11 G3
Lymekilns 142 A4
Lyminge 33 D4
Lymington 14 C3
Lyminster 16 C3
Lymm 92 A4
Lympne 32 D5
Lympsham 24 A2
Lympstone 10 C4
Lynaberack 166 B5
Lynch 22 B3
Lynch Green 86 C5
Lynchat 166 B4
Lyndale House 170 C4
Lyndhurst 14 B4
Lyndon 69 E2
Lyne Aber. 169 E4
Lyne Sc.Bord. 143 G5
Lyne Surr. 29 F1
Lyne Down 53 F4
Lyne of Gorthleck 165 G2
Lyne of Skene 169 E3
Lyne Station 143 G5
Lyneal 78 B4
Lynegar 187 E3
Lyneham Oxon. 55 E5
Lyneham Wilts. 40 C5
Lyneholmeford 126 D4
Lynemore High. 167 E2
Lynemore Moray 167 F1
Lynemouth 129 E2
Lyness 190 A4
Lynford 71 G3
Lyng 86 B4
Lyngate 87 E3
Lynmouth 22 A3

Lynn 65 G1
Lynsted 32 B2
Lynstone 20 C5
Lynton 22 A3
Lyon's Gate 12 C2
Lyonshall 52 C2
Lyrabus 138 A3
Lytchett Matravers 13 F3
Lytchett Minster 13 F3
Lyth 187 E2
Lytham 99 G5
Lytham St. Anne's 99 G5
Lythe 112 B1
Lythe Hill 29 E4
Lythmore 186 C2

M

Mabe Burnthouse 3 E3
Mabie 125 D3
Mablethorpe 97 F4
Macclesfield 92 D5
Macclesfield Forest 93 D5
Macduff 177 G3
Macedonia 152 A4
Machan 142 B4
Machany 151 D3
Macharioch 130 C5
Machen 38 B4
Machie Arg. & B. 138 A3
Machrie Arg. & B. 138 B5
Machrie N.Ayr. 131 D2
Machrihanish 130 B3
Machrins 146 C5
Machynlleth 62 D2
McInroy's Point 140 D2
Mackerye End 44 A1
Mackworth 81 E4
Macmerry 144 B2
Macterry 177 G5
Madderty 151 E2
Maddiston 142 D2
Madehurst 16 B2
Madeley Staffs. 79 E3
Madeley Tel. & W. 65 G2
Madeley Heath 79 E3
Maders 6 D3
Madford 11 E1
Madingley 58 B1
Madjeston 25 F5
Madley 52 D4
Madresfield 54 A3
Madron 2 B3
Maenaddwyn 88 C4
Maenclochog 49 D5
Maendy Cardiff 38 A5
Maendy V. of Glam. 37 G5
Maenporth 3 E4
Maentwrog 75 F3
Maen-y-groes 49 G2
Maer Cornw. 20 C5
Maer Staffs. 79 E4
Maerdy Carmar. 50 C5
Maerdy Carmar. 50 C5
Maerdy Conwy 76 D3
Maerdy R.C.T. 37 F3
Maesbrook 77 F5
Maesbury Marsh 78 A5
Maes-glas 38 B4
Maesgwynne 49 F5
Maeshafn 77 F1
Maesllyn 49 G3
Maesmynis 51 G3
Maesteg 37 D3
Maes-Treylow 52 B1
Maesybont 36 B1
Maesycrugiau 50 A3
Maesycwmmer 38 A3
Magdalen Laver 45 E2
Maggieknockater 176 C5
Maggots End 58 C5
Magham Down 18 B2
Maghull 91 E2
Magna Park 68 A4
Magor 38 D4
Magpie Green 72 B4
Maiden Bradley 25 E4
Maiden Head 24 C1
Maiden Law 120 A3
Maiden Newton 12 B3
Maiden Wells 34 C3
Maidencombe 9 F1
Maidenhayne 11 F3
Maidenhead 43 D4
Maidens 132 A5
Maiden's Green 43 D5
Maidensgrove 42 C4
Maidenwell Cornw. 5 F2

Mai-Men

Maidenwell *Lincs.* **96** D5
Maidford **56** B2
Maids' Moreton **56** C4
Maidstone **31** G3
Maidwell **68** C5
Maindee **38** C4
Mainland *Ork.* **190** B3
Mainland *Shet.* **191** F3
Mains of Ardestie **152** D1
Mains of Balgavies
  160 D4
Mains of Balhall **160** D3
Mains of Ballindarg
  160 C4
Mains of Burgie **175** G4
Mains of Culsh **179** D3
Mains of Dillavaird
  161 F1
Mains of Drum **169** F4
Mains of Dudwick **169** G1
Mains of Faillie **166** B1
Mains of Fedderate
  179 D3
Mains of Glack **169** E2
Mains of Glassaugh
  177 E3
Mains of Glenbuchat
  168 A3
Mains of Linton **169** E3
Mains of Melgund **160** D4
Mains of Pitfour **179** E3
Mains of Pittrichie **169** F2
Mains of Sluie **175** G4
Mains of Tannachy
  176 C3
Mains of Thornton
  161 E2
Mains of Tig **122** C2
Mainsforth **120** C4
Mainsriddle **124** D5
Mainstone **64** B4
Maisemore **54** A5
Major's Green **66** D5
Makendon **128** A1
Makeney **81** E3
Makerstoun **136** A3
Malborough **8** D4
Malden Rushett **29** G1
Maldon **46** B2
Malham **101** F1
Maligar **171** D3
Malinbridge **94** A4
Mallaig (Malaig) **163** E5
Mallaigmore **163** E5
Mallaigvaig **163** E5
Malleny Mills **143** F3
Malletsheugh **141** G4
Malling **150** A4
Mallows Green **58** C5
Malltraeth **74** D1
Mallwyd **63** E1
Malmesbury **40** B4
Malmsmead **22** A3
Malpas *C. & W.Ches.*
  78 B3
Malpas *Cornw.* **4** C5
Malpas *Newport* **38** C3
Maltby *Lincs.* **96** B4
Maltby *S.Yorks.* **94** C3
Maltby *Stock.* **111** D1
Maltby le Marsh **97** E4
Malting End **59** F2
Malting Green **46** C1
Maltman's Hill **32** A4
Malton **111** G5
Malvern Link **53** G3
Malvern Wells **53** G3
Mambeg **140** D1
Mamble **65** F5
Mamhead **10** C4
Mamhilad **38** C2
Manaccan **3** E4
Manadon **8** A2
Manafon **64** A2
Manaton **10** A4
Manby **97** D4
Mancetter **67** F3
Manchester **92** C3
Manchester Airport **92** C4
Mancot Royal **78** A1
Mandally (Manndalaidh)
  165 D4
Manea **70** C4
Maneight **132** D5
Manfield **101** B1
Mangerton **12** A3
Mangotsfield **39** F5
Mangrove Green **57** G5

Mankinholes **101** F5
Manley **91** G5
Manmoel **38** A2
Mannal **154** A2
Manningford Abbots
  26 C2
Manningford Bohune
  26 C2
Manningford Bruce **26** C2
Manningham **102** A4
Mannings Heath **17** E1
Mannington **13** G2
Manningtree **60** C4
Mannofield **169** G4
Manor Park **43** E4
Manorbier **35** D3
Manorbier Newton **34** D2
Manordeifi **49** F3
Manordeilo **50** C5
Manorowen **48** C4
Mansell Gamage **52** C3
Mansell Lacy **52** D3
Mansergh **108** B4
Mansfield **81** G1
Mansfield Woodhouse
  81 G1
Manson Green **86** B5
Mansriggs **107** D4
Manston *Dorset* **13** E1
Manston *Kent* **33** F2
Manston *W.Yorks.* **102** C4
Manswood **13** F2
Manthorpe *Lincs.* **69** F1
Manthorpe *Lincs.* **83** E4
Manton *N.Lincs.* **95** G2
Manton *Notts.* **94** C5
Manton *Rut.* **69** D2
Manton *Wilts.* **26** C1
Manuden **58** C5
Manwood Green **45** E1
Maolachy **148** A3
Maperton **25** D5
Maple Cross **43** F3
Maplebeck **82** C1
Mapledurham **42** B5
Mapledurwell **28** B2
Maplehurst **29** G5
Maplescombe **31** E2
Mapleton **80** C3
Mapperley *Derbys.* **81** F3
Mapperley *Notts.* **81** G3
Mapperton *Dorset* **12** B3
Mapperton *Dorset* **13** F3
Mappleborough Green
  54 C1
Mappleton **105** E3
Mapplewell **94** A2
Mappowder **12** D2
Mar Lodge **167** E5
Marazion **2** C3
Marbury **78** C3
March **70** C3
Marcham **41** G3
Marchamley **78** C5
Marchamley Wood
  78 C4
Marchington **80** C4
Marchington Woodlands
  80 C5
Marchwiel **78** A3
Marchwood **14** C1
Marcross **22** C1
Marcus **160** D4
Marden *Here.* **53** E3
Marden *Kent* **31** G4
Marden *T. & W.* **129** F4
Marden *Wilts.* **26** B2
Marden Ash **45** E2
Marden Beech **31** G4
Marden Thorn **31** G4
Marden's Hill **31** D5
Mardon **136** D3
Mardy **38** C1
Mare Green **24** A5
Marefield **68** C2
Mareham le Fen **84** A1
Mareham on the Hill
  84 A1
Maresfield **17** G1
Marfleet **104** D4
Marford **78** A2
Margam **37** D4
Margaret Marsh **13** E1
Margaret Roding **45** E1
Margaretting **45** F2
Margaretting Tye **45** F2
Margate **33** F1
Margnaheglish **131** F2
Margreig **124** C3

Margrove Park **111** F1
Marham **71** F2
Marhamchurch **20** C5
Marholm **69** G2
Marian Cwm **90** B5
Mariandyrys **89** E4
Marian-glas **88** D4
Mariansleigh **22** A5
Marine Town **32** B1
Marishader **171** D3
Maristow House **8** A1
Mark **24** A3
Mark Causeway **24** A3
Mark Cross **31** E5
Markbeech **31** D4
Markby **97** E5
Markdhu **122** C3
Markeaton **81** E4
Market Bosworth **67** G2
Market Deeping **69** G1
Market Drayton **79** D4
Market Harborough **68** C4
Market Lavington **26** B2
Market Overton **69** D1
Market Rasen **96** B4
Market Stainton **96** C5
Market Street **87** D3
Market Warsop **81** G1
Market Weighton **104** A3
Market Weston **72** A4
Markethill **152** A1
Markfield **67** G1
Markham **38** A2
Markham Moor **95** E5
Markinch **152** A4
Markington **102** B1
Marks Gate **45** D3
Marks Tey **60** A5
Marksbury **25** D1
Markwell **7** D5
Markyate **43** F1
Marland **92** C1
Marlborough **26** C1
Marlbrook **66** B5
Marlcliff **54** C2
Marldon **9** E1
Marle Green **18** A2
Marlesford **61** E2
Marley Green **78** C3
Marley Hill **120** B2
Marlingford **86** C5
Marloes **34** A2
Marlow *Bucks.* **43** D4
Marlow *Here.* **64** D5
Marlpit Hill **30** D4
Marlpool **81** F3
Marnhull **13** D1
Marnoch **177** E4
Marple **93** D4
Marple Bridge **93** D4
Marr **94** C2
Marrel **183** F3
Marrick **109** F3
Marros **35** F2
Marsden *T. & W.* **120** C1
Marsden *W.Yorks.* **93** E1
Marsett **109** E4
Marsh **11** F1
Marsh Baldon **42** A3
Marsh Benham **27** F1
Marsh Gibbon **56** B5
Marsh Green *Devon*
  10 D3
Marsh Green *Gt.Man.*
  91 G2
Marsh Green *Kent* **30** D4
Marsh Green *Tel. & W.*
  65 F1
Marsh Lane **94** B5
Marsh Street **22** C3
Marshall Meadows
  145 G4
Marshalsea **11** G2
Marshalswick **44** A2
Marsham **86** C3
Marshaw **100** B2
Marshborough **33** F3
Marshbrook **64** A4
Marshchapel **97** D3
Marshfield *Newport*
  38 B4
Marshfield *S.Glos.* **39** G5
Marshgate **6** B1
Marshland St. James
  70 D2
Marshside **91** F1
Marshwood **11** G3
Marske **110** A2

Marske-by-the-Sea
  121 F5
Marsland Green **92** A3
Marston *C. & W.Ches.*
  92 A5
Marston *Here.* **52** C2
Marston *Lincs.* **83** D3
Marston *Oxon.* **42** A2
Marston *Staffs.* **79** G5
Marston *Staffs.* **66** A1
Marston *Warks.* **67** E3
Marston *Wilts.* **26** A2
Marston Doles **55** G2
Marston Green **67** D4
Marston Magna **24** C5
Marston Meysey **40** D3
Marston Montgomery
  80 C4
Marston Moretaine **57** E3
Marston on Dove **80** D5
Marston St. Lawrence
  56 A3
Marston Stannett **53** E2
Marston Trussell **68** B4
Marstow **39** E1
Marsworth **43** E1
Marten **27** D1
Marthall **92** B5
Martham **87** F4
Martin *Hants.* **13** G1
Martin *Lincs.* **83** G2
Martin *Lincs.* **84** A1
Martin Drove End **26** B5
Martin Hussingtree **54** A1
Martinhoe **21** E1
Martinscroft **92** A4
Martinstown **12** C4
Martlesham **60** D3
Martlesham Heath **60** D3
Martletwy **34** D1
Martley **53** G1
Martock **12** A1
Marton *Ches.E.* **79** F1
Marton *Cumb.* **106** D5
Marton *E.Riding* **105** D4
Marton *E.Riding* **105** E1
Marton *Lincs.* **95** E4
Marton *Middbro.* **111** E1
Marton *N.Yorks.* **102** D1
Marton *N.Yorks.* **111** G4
Marton *Shrop.* **64** B2
Marton *Shrop.* **78** B5
Marton *Warks.* **55** G1
Marton Abbey **103** E1
Marton-in-the-Forest
  103 E1
Marton-le-Moor **110** C5
Martyr Worthy **27** G4
Martyr's Green **29** F2
Marwood **21** F2
Mary Tavy **7** F3
Marybank (An Lagaidh)
  174 A4
Maryburgh (Baile Mairi)
  174 B4
Maryfield **8** A2
Marygold **145** F4
Maryhill *Aber.* **178** D3
Maryhill *Glas.* **141** G3
Marykirk **161** E4
Marylebone *Gt.Lon.*
  44 B4
Marylebone *Gt.Man.*
  91 G2
Marypark **167** F1
Maryport *Cumb.* **116** D3
Maryport *D. & G.* **114** B3
Marystow **7** E2
Maryton **161** E4
Marywell *Aber.* **169** G5
Marywell *Aber.* **168** C5
Marywell *Angus* **161** E5
Masham **110** B4
Mashbury **45** F1
Masongill **108** B5
Mastin Moor **94** B5
Mastrick **169** G4
Matchborough **54** C1
Matching **45** E1
Matching Green **45** E1
Matching Tye **45** E1
Matfen **128** C4
Matfield **31** F4
Mathern **39** E3
Mathon **53** G3
Mathry **48** B4
Matlaske **86** C2
Matlock **81** E1
Matlock Bank **81** E1

Matlock Bath **81** D2
Matson **40** A1
Matterdale End **117** G4
Mattersey **79** D5
Mattersey Thorpe **95** D4
Mattingley **28** C2
Mattishall **86** B3
Mattishall Burgh **86** B4
Mauchline **132** C3
Maud **179** E3
Maufant **4** C5
Maugersbury **55** D5
Maughold **98** C2
Mauld **165** E1
Maulden **57** F4
Maulds Meaburn **108** B1
Maunby **110** C4
Maund Bryan **53** E2
Maundown **23** D5
Mautby **87** F4
Mavesyn Ridware **66** C1
Mavis Enderby **84** B1
Maw Green **79** E2
Mawbray **117** D2
Mawdesley **91** F1
Mawdlam **37** E4
Mawgan **3** E4
Mawgan Porth **4** C3
Mawla **4** B5
Mawnan **3** E4
Mawnan Smith **3** E4
Mawsley **68** C5
Mawthorpe **97** E5
Maxey **69** G2
Maxstoke **67** E4
Maxted Street **32** D4
Maxton *Kent* **33** F4
Maxton *Sc.Bord.* **136** A3
Maxwellheugh **136** B3
Maxwellton **125** D3
Maxworthy **6** C1
May Hill **53** G5
Mayals **36** C3
Maybole **132** B5
Maybury **29** F2
Mayen **177** E5
Mayfair **44** B4
Mayfield *E.Suss.* **18** A1
Mayfield *Midloth.* **144** A3
Mayfield *Staffs.* **80** C3
Mayford **29** E2
Mayland **46** C2
Maylandsea **46** C2
Maynard's Green **18** A2
Maypole *I.o.S.* **4** B1
Maypole *Kent* **33** D2
Maypole *Mon.* **39** D1
Maypole Green *Essex*
  60 A5
Maypole Green *Norf.*
  73 F2
Maypole Green *Suff.*
  61 D1
Maypole Green *Suff.*
  60 A2
May's Green *N.Som.*
  24 A1
Mays Green *Oxon.* **42** C4
Mead **20** C4
Mead End **26** B5
Meadgate **25** D2
Meadle **42** D2
Meadow Green **53** G2
Meadowhall **94** A3
Meadowmill **144** B2
Meadowtown **64** C2
Meadwell **7** E2
Meaford **79** F4
Meal Bank **107** G3
Meals **97** E3
Mealsgate **117** F2
Meanley **100** D3
Meanwood **102** B4
Mearbeck **101** E1
Meare **24** B3
Meare Green **23** F5
Mearns **141** G4
Mears Ashby **56** D1
Measham **67** F1
Meathop **107** F4
Meavy **8** B1
Medbourne **68** D3
Meddon **20** C4
Meden Vale **81** G1
Medlar **100** A4
Medmenham **42** D4
Medomsley **120** A2
Medstead **28** B4
Meer Common **52** C2

Meer End **67** E5
Meerbrook **79** G1
Meesden **58** C4
Meeson **79** D5
Meeth **21** F5
Meeting House Hill **87** E3
Meggethead **134** C3
Meidrim **49** F5
Meifod *Denb.* **76** D2
Meifod *Powys* **64** A1
Meigle **160** A5
Meikle Earnock **142** B4
Meikle Grenach **140** B3
Meikle Kilmory **140** B3
Meikle Rahane **140** D1
Meikle Strath **161** E2
Meikle Tarty **169** G2
Meikle Wartle **169** F1
Meikleour **151** G1
Meikleyard **132** D2
Meinciau **36** A1
Meir **79** G3
Meirheath **79** G3
Melbourn **58** B3
Melbourne *Derbys.* **81** E5
Melbourne *E.Riding*
  103 G3
Melbury **21** D4
Melbury Abbas **13** E1
Melbury Bubb **12** B2
Melbury Osmond **12** B2
Melbury Sampford **12** B2
Melchbourne **57** F1
Melcombe Bingham
  13 D2
Melcombe Regis **12** C4
Meldon *Devon* **7** F1
Meldon *Northumb.*
  128 D3
Meldreth **58** B3
Meledor **4** D4
Melfort **148** A3
Melgarve **165** F5
Melgum **168** B4
Meliden (Gallt Melyd)
  90 B4
Melincourt **37** E2
Melin-y-coed **76** B1
Melin-y-ddol **63** G2
Melin-y-grug **63** G2
Melin-y-Wig **76** D3
Melkinthorpe **118** B5
Melkridge **118** D1
Melksham **26** A1
Melksham Forest **26** A1
Melldalloch **140** A2
Melling *Lancs.* **107** G5
Melling *Mersey.* **91** E2
Melling Mount **91** F2
Mellis **72** B4
Mellon Charles **180** A5
Mellon Udrigle **180** A5
Mellor *Gt.Man.* **93** D4
Mellor *Lancs.* **100** C4
Mellor Brook **100** C4
Mells **25** E3
Melmerby *Cumb.* **118** C4
Melmerby *N.Yorks.*
  109 F4
Melmerby *N.Yorks.*
  110 C5
Melplash **12** A3
Melrose *Aber.* **177** G3
Melrose *Sc.Bord.* **135** G2
Melsonby **110** A2
Meltham **93** E1
Melton *E.Riding* **104** B5
Melton *Suff.* **61** D2
Melton Constable **86** B2
Melton Mowbray **68** C1
Melton Ross **96** A1
Meltonby **103** G2
Melvaig **172** A1
Melverley **64** C1
Melverley Green **64** C1
Melvich **186** A2
Membury **11** F2
Memsie **179** E1
Memus **160** C4
Menabilly **5** E4
Menai Bridge
  (Porthaethwy) **89** D3
Mendham **73** D3
Mendlesham **60** C1
Mendlesham Green **60** B1
Menethorpe **103** G1
Menheniot **5** C4
Menie House **169** G2
Menithwood **53** G1

Mennock **133** G5
Menston **102** A3
Menstrie **150** D5
Mentmore **43** E1
Meoble **155** G1
Meole Brace **65** D1
Meon **15** E2
Meonstoke **15** F1
Meopham **31** F2
Meopham Green **31** F2
Mepal **70** C4
Meppershall **57** G4
Merbach **52** C3
Mercaston **81** D3
Mere *Ches.E.* **92** B4
Mere *Wilts.* **25** F4
Mere Brow **91** F1
Mere Green **66** D3
Mere Heath **92** A5
Mereclough **101** E4
Mereside **99** G4
Meretown **79** E5
Mereworth **31** F3
Mergie **161** F1
Meriden **67** E4
Merkadale **162** B1
Merkinch **174** C5
Merkland **124** B3
Merley **13** G3
Merlin's Bridge **34** C1
Merridge **23** F4
Merrifield **9** E3
Merrington **78** B5
Merrion **34** C3
Merriott **12** A1
Merrivale **7** F3
Merrow **29** F2
Merry Hill *Herts.* **44** A3
Merry Hill *W.Mid.* **66** B4
Merry Hill *W.Mid.* **66** A3
Merrymeet **5** G3
Mersea Island **46** D1
Mersham **32** C5
Merstham **30** B3
Merston **16** A3
Merstone **15** E4
Merther **4** C5
Merthyr **49** G5
Merthyr Cynog **51** F4
Merthyr Dyfan **23** E1
Merthyr Mawr **37** E5
Merthyr Tydfil **37** G2
Merthyr Vale **37** G3
Merton *Devon* **21** F4
Merton *Norf.* **72** A3
Merton *Oxon.* **42** A1
Mervinslaw **136** A5
Meshaw **10** A1
Messing **46** C1
Messingham **95** F2
Metcombe **11** D3
Metfield **73** D3
Metherell **8** A1
Metheringham **83** F1
Methlem **74** A4
Methley **102** C5
Methley Junction **102** C5
Methlick **169** F1
Methven **151** F2
Methwold **71** F3
Methwold Hythe **71** F3
MetroCentre **120** B1
Mettingham **73** E3
Metton **86** C2
Mevagissey **5** E5
Mewith Head **100** D1
Mexborough **94** B3
Mey **187** E1
Meysey Hampton **40** D2
Mial **172** A2
Miavaig **189** E2
Michaelchurch **53** E5
Michaelchurch Escley **52** C4
Michaelchurch-on-Arrow **52** B2
Michaelston-le-Pit **38** A5
Michaelston-super-Ely **38** A5
Michaelston-y-Fedw **38** B4
Michaelstow **5** E2
Michelcombe **8** C1
Micheldever **27** G4
Michelmersh **27** E5
Mickfield **60** C1
Mickle Trafford **78** B1
Micklebring **94** C3

Mickleby **112** B1
Micklefield **102** D4
Micklefield Green **43** F3
Mickleham **29** G2
Micklehurst **93** D2
Mickleover **81** E4
Micklethwaite *Cumb.* **117** F1
Micklethwaite *W.Yorks.* **101** G3
Mickleton *Dur.* **119** F5
Mickleton *Glos.* **55** D3
Mickletown **102** C5
Mickley *Derbys.* **94** A5
Mickley *N.Yorks.* **110** B5
Mickley Green **59** G2
Mickley Square **119** G1
Mid Ardlaw **179** F4
Mid Beltie **168** D4
Mid Calder **143** E3
Mid Clyth **187** E5
Mid Lambroak **12** A1
Mid Lavant **16** A3
Mid Letter **148** C4
Mid Lix **150** A1
Mid Mossdale **108** D3
Mid Yell **191** F2
Midbea **190** B1
Middle Assendon **42** C4
Middle Aston **55** G5
Middle Barton **55** G5
Middle Bickenhill **67** E4
Middle Bockhampton **14** A3
Middle Claydon **56** C5
Middle Drift **5** F3
Middle Drums **161** D4
Middle Duntisbourne **40** B2
Middle Handley **94** B5
Middle Harling **72** A3
Middle Kames **140** A1
Middle Littleton **54** C3
Middle Maes-coed **52** C4
Middle Marwood **21** F2
Middle Mill **48** B2
Middle Quarter **32** A5
Middle Rasen **96** A4
Middle Rigg **151** F4
Middle Salter **100** C1
Middle Sontley **78** A3
Middle Stoford **23** E5
Middle Taphouse **5** F3
Middle Town **4** B1
Middle Tysoe **55** F3
Middle Wallop **27** D4
Middle Winterslow **26** D4
Middle Woodford **26** C4
Middlebie **126** A4
Middlecliff **94** B2
Middlecott **21** E5
Middleham **110** A4
Middlehill *Aber.* **178** D3
Middlehill *Cornw.* **5** G3
Middlehope **65** E4
Middlemarsh **12** C2
Middlemoor **7** E3
Middlesbrough **121** D5
Middlesceugh **118** A3
Middleshaw **107** G4
Middlesmoor **109** F5
Middlestone **120** B4
Middlestone Moor **120** B4
Middlestown **93** G1
Middleton *Aber.* **169** F3
Middleton *Angus* **161** D5
Middleton *Cumb.* **108** B4
Middleton *Derbys.* **81** D4
Middleton *Derbys.* **80** C1
Middleton *Essex* **59** G3
Middleton *Gt.Man.* **92** C2
Middleton *Hants.* **27** F3
Middleton *Here.* **53** E1
Middleton *Lancs.* **100** A2
Middleton *Midloth.* **144** A4
Middleton *N.Yorks.* **111** G4
Middleton *Norf.* **71** G1
Middleton *Northants.* **68** D4
Middleton *Northumb.* **128** C3
Middleton *Northumb.* **137** E3
Middleton *P. & K.* **151** G4
Middleton *P. & K.* **159** G5
Middleton *Shrop.* **64** B3
Middleton *Shrop.* **65** E5

Middleton *Shrop.* **78** A5
Middleton *Suff.* **61** F1
Middleton *Swan.* **36** A4
Middleton *W.Yorks.* **102** A3
Middleton *W.Yorks.* **102** C5
Middleton *Warks.* **67** D3
Middleton Baggot **65** F3
Middleton Bank Top **128** C3
Middleton Cheney **55** G3
Middleton Green **79** G4
Middleton Hall **137** D4
Middleton Moor **61** F1
Middleton of Potterton **169** G3
Middleton on the Hill **53** E1
Middleton One Row **110** C1
Middleton Park **169** G3
Middleton Priors **65** F4
Middleton Quernhow **110** C5
Middleton St. George **110** C1
Middleton Scriven **65** F4
Middleton Stoney **56** B5
Middleton Tyas **110** B2
Middleton-in-Teesdale **119** F5
Middleton-on-Leven **111** D1
Middleton-on-Sea **16** B3
Middleton-on-the-Wolds **104** B3
Middletown *Cumb.* **106** A2
Middletown *Powys* **64** C1
Middlewich **79** E1
Middlewood *Ches.E.* **92** D4
Middlewood *S.Yorks.* **94** A3
Middlewood Green **60** B1
Middlezoy **24** A4
Middridge **120** B5
Midfield **185** E2
Midford **25** E1
Midge Hall **100** B5
Midgeholme **118** C2
Midgham **27** G1
Midgley *W.Yorks.* **93** G1
Midgley *W.Yorks.* **101** G5
Midhopestones **93** G3
Midhurst **29** D5
Midlem **135** G3
Midloe Grange **57** G1
Midpark **140** B4
Midsomer Norton **25** D2
Midthorpe **96** C3
Midtown *High.* **185** E2
Midtown *High.* **172** B1
Midtown of Barras **161** G1
Midville **84** B2
Midway **81** E5
Migdale **182** B5
Migvie **168** B4
Milarrochy **149** G5
Milber **10** B5
Milbethill **177** F4
Milborne Port **12** C1
Milborne St. Andrew **13** D3
Milborne Wick **25** D5
Milbourne *Northumb.* **128** D4
Milbourne *Wilts.* **40** B4
Milburn **118** C5
Milbury Heath **39** F3
Milcombe **55** G4
Milden **60** A3
Mildenhall *Suff.* **71** F5
Mildenhall *Wilts.* **26** D1
Mile Elm **26** A1
Mile End *Essex* **60** A5
Mile End *Glos.* **39** E1
Mile Oak **31** F4
Mile Town **32** B3
Milebrook **64** C5
Milebush **31** G2
Mileham **86** A4
Miles Green **79** F3
Miles Hope **53** E1
Miles's Green **27** G1
Milfield **136** D3

Milford *Derbys.* **81** E3
Milford *Devon* **20** C3
Milford *Shrop.* **78** B5
Milford *Staffs.* **79** G5
Milford *Surr.* **29** E3
Milford Haven (Aberdaugleddau) **34** B2
Milford on Sea **14** B3
Milkwall **39** E2
Mill Bank **101** G5
Mill Brow **93** D4
Mill End *Bucks.* **42** C4
Mill End *Cambs.* **59** E2
Mill End *Herts.* **58** B4
Mill End Green **59** E5
Mill Green *Cambs.* **59** E3
Mill Green *Essex* **45** E2
Mill Green *Herts.* **44** B2
Mill Green *Norf.* **72** C3
Mill Green *Shrop.* **79** D5
Mill Green *Staffs.* **80** B5
Mill Green *Suff.* **61** E1
Mill Green *Suff.* **60** C2
Mill Green *Suff.* **60** A3
Mill Green *W.Mid.* **66** C2
Mill Hill *B'burn.* **100** C5
Mill Hill *Cambs.* **58** A4
Mill Hill *Gt.Lon.* **44** B3
Mill Houses **100** C1
Mill Lane **28** C2
Mill of Camsail **141** D1
Mill of Colp **177** G5
Mill of Elrick **179** E3
Mill of Fortune **150** C2
Mill of Kingoodie **169** F2
Mill of Monquich **169** F5
Mill of Uras **161** G1
Mill Side **107** F4
Mill Street *Kent* **31** F3
Mill Street *Norf.* **86** B4
Milland **28** D5
Millbank **179** F3
Millbeck **117** F4
Millbreck **179** F3
Millbridge **28** D3
Millbrook *Beds.* **57** F4
Millbrook *Cornw.* **8** A2
Millbrook *Devon* **11** G3
Millbrook *S'ham.* **14** C3
Millburn *Aber.* **168** C2
Millburn *Aber.* **168** D1
Millcombe **9** E3
Millcorner **18** D1
Milldale **80** C2
Millden **165** E1
Milldens **160** D4
Millearne **151** E3
Millend **55** F5
Millenheath **78** C4
Millerhill **144** A3
Miller's Dale **93** F5
Millers Green *Derbys.* **81** D2
Miller's Green *Essex* **45** E2
Millgate **101** E5
Millhalf **52** B3
Millhayes *Devon* **11** E1
Millhayes *Devon* **11** F2
Millholme **107** G4
Millhouse *Arg. & B.* **140** A2
Millhouse *Cumb.* **117** G3
Millhouse Green **93** G2
Millhousebridge **125** F2
Millikenpark **141** F3
Millin Cross **34** C1
Millington **104** A2
Millington Green **81** D3
Millmeece **79** F4
Millness **165** E1
Millom **106** C4
Millow **59** F2
Millpool **5** F2
Millport **140** C4
Millthorpe **94** B5
Millthrop **108** B3
Milltimber **169** F4
Milltown *Aber.* **167** G4
Milltown *Cornw.* **5** F4
Milltown *D. & G.* **126** B4
Milltown *Derbys.* **81** E1
Milltown *Devon* **21** F2
Milltown *High.* **175** F5
Milltown of Aberdalgie **151** F2
Milltown of Auchindoun **168** A1

Milltown of Craigston **177** G4
Milltown of Edinvillie **176** B5
Milltown of Kildrummy **168** B3
Milltown of Rothiemay **177** E5
Milltown of Towie **168** B3
Milnathort **151** G4
Milners Heath **78** B1
Milngavie **141** G2
Milnrow **92** D1
Milnsbridge **93** F1
Milnthorpe **107** F4
Milovaig **170** A4
Milrig **132** D2
Milson **65** F5
Milstead **32** B3
Milston **26** C3
Milton *Angus* **160** B5
Milton *Cambs.* **58** C1
Milton *Cumb.* **118** B1
Milton *D. & G.* **124** C2
Milton *D. & G.* **124** C3
Milton *D. & G.* **122** D5
Milton *Derbys.* **81** D5
Milton *High.* **173** G4
Milton *High.* **175** D2
Milton *High.* **175** F4
Milton *High.* **172** A5
Milton *High.* **174** B5
Milton *High.* **187** F3
Milton (Baile a' Mhuilinn) *High.* **165** F1
Milton *Moray* **177** E3
Milton *N.Som.* **24** A1
Milton *Newport* **38** C4
Milton *Notts.* **95** E5
Milton *Oxon.* **56** A3
Milton *Oxon.* **41** G3
Milton *P. & K.* **151** E1
Milton *Pembs.* **34** D2
Milton *Ports.* **15** F3
Milton *Som.* **24** B5
Milton *Stir.* **150** A4
Milton *Stoke* **79** G2
Milton *W.Dun.* **141** F2
Milton Abbas **13** E2
Milton Abbot **7** E3
Milton Bridge **143** G3
Milton Bryan **57** E4
Milton Clevedon **25** D4
Milton Combe **8** A1
Milton Damerel **21** D4
Milton End **39** G1
Milton Ernest **57** F2
Milton Green **78** B2
Milton Hill **41** G3
Milton Keynes **57** D4
Milton Keynes Village **57** D4
Milton Lilbourne **26** C1
Milton Malsor **56** C2
Milton Morenish **150** B1
Milton of Auchinhove **168** C4
Milton of Balgonie **152** B4
Milton of Buchanan **149** G5
Milton of Cairnborrow **177** D5
Milton of Callander **150** A4
Milton of Campfield **169** D4
Milton of Campsie **142** A2
Milton of Coldwells **169** G1
Milton of Cullerlie **169** E4
Milton of Cushnie **168** C3
Milton of Dalcapon **159** E4
Milton of Inveramsay **169** E2
Milton of Noth **168** C2
Milton of Tullich **168** A5
Milton on Stour **25** E5
Milton Regis **32** A2
Milton Street **18** B3
Miltonduff **176** A3
Miltonhill **175** G3
Miltonise **122** C3
Milton-Lockhart **142** C5
Milton-under-Wychwood **41** E1
Milverton *Som.* **23** E5
Milverton *Warks.* **55** F1

Milwich **79** G5
Mimbridge **29** E1
Minard **148** B5
Minard Castle **148** B5
Minchington **13** F1
Minchinhampton **40** A2
Mindrum **136** C3
Mindrummill **136** C3
Minehead **22** C3
Minera **77** F2
Minety **40** C3
Minety Lower Moor **40** C3
Minffordd *Gwyn.* **62** D1
Minffordd *Gwyn.* **75** E4
Minffordd *Gwyn.* **89** D5
Miningsby **84** B1
Minions **5** G2
Minishant **132** B4
Minley Manor **28** D2
Minllyn **63** E1
Minnes **169** G2
Minnigaff **123** F4
Minnonie **177** G3
Minskip **102** C1
Minstead **14** B1
Minsted **29** D5
Minster *Kent* **32** B1
Minster *Kent* **33** F2
Minster Lovell **41** F1
Minsteracres **119** G2
Minsterley **64** C2
Minsterworth **39** G1
Minterne Magna **12** C2
Minterne Parva **12** C2
Minting **96** B5
Mintlaw **179** F3
Minto **135** G3
Minton **64** D3
Minwear **34** D1
Minworth **67** D3
Miodar **154** B2
Mirehouse **116** C5
Mireland **187** F2
Mirfield **102** B5
Miserden **40** B2
Miskin *R.C.T.* **37** G4
Miskin *R.C.T.* **37** G3
Misselfore **26** B5
Misson **95** D3
Misterton *Leics.* **68** A4
Misterton *Notts.* **95** E3
Misterton *Som.* **12** A2
Mistley **60** C4
Mitcham **30** B2
Mitchel Troy **39** D1
Mitcheldean **39** F1
Mitchell **4** C4
Mitchelland **107** F3
Mitcheltroy Common **39** D2
Mitford **129** D3
Mithian **4** B4
Mitton **66** A1
Mixbury **56** B5
Mixenden **101** G5
Moar **158** A5
Moat **126** C4
Moats Tye **60** B2
Mobberley *Ches.E.* **92** B5
Mobberley *Staffs.* **80** B3
Moccas **52** C3
Mochdre *Conwy* **89** G5
Mochdre *Powys* **63** G4
Mochrum **114** D2
Mockbeggar *Hants.* **14** A2
Mockbeggar *Kent* **31** G4
Mockerkin **117** D4
Modbury **8** C2
Moddershall **79** G4
Modsane **185** F2
Moelfre *I.o.A.* **88** D4
Moelfre *Powys* **77** E5
Moffat **134** B5
Mogerhanger **57** G3
Moin'a'choire **138** B3
Moine House **185** E3
Moira **67** F1
Molash **32** C3
Mol-chlach **162** C3
Mold (Yr Wyddgrug) **77** F1
Molehill Green *Essex* **59** D5
Molehill Green *Essex* **59** F5
Molescroft **104** C3
Molesden **128** D3
Molesworth **69** F5

Mollance 124 B4
Molland 22 B5
Mollington C. & W.Ches.
 91 E5
Mollinsburn 142 B2
Monach Islands (Heisker
 Islands) 188 A2
Monachty 50 B1
Monachyle 149 G3
Monevechadan 149 D4
Monewden 60 D2
Moneydie 151 F2
Moneyrow Green 43 D5
Moniaive 124 B1
Monifieth 152 D1
Monikie 152 D1
Monimail 152 A3
Monington 49 E3
Monk Bretton 94 A2
Monk Fryston 103 E5
Monk Hesleden 121 D4
Monk Sherborne 28 B2
Monk Soham 60 D1
Monk Soham Green
 60 D1
Monk Street 59 E5
Monken Hadley 44 B3
Monkerton 10 C3
Monkhide 53 F3
Monkhill 117 G1
Monkhopton 65 F3
Monkland 53 D2
Monkleigh 21 E3
Monknash 37 F5
Monkokehampton 21 F5
Monks Eleigh 60 A3
Monks Eleigh Tye 60 A3
Monk's Gate 17 E1
Monks' Heath 92 C5
Monk's Hill 32 A4
Monks Kirby 67 G4
Monks Risborough
 42 D2
Monkscross 7 D3
Monkseaton 129 F4
Monkshill 177 G5
Monksilver 23 D4
Monkswood 38 C2
Monkton Devon 11 E2
Monkton Kent 33 E2
Monkton Pembs. 34 C2
Monkton S.Ayr. 132 B3
Monkton T. & W. 120 C1
Monkton V. of Glam.
 37 F5
Monkton Combe 25 E1
Monkton Deverill 25 F4
Monkton Farleigh 25 F1
Monkton Heathfield
 23 F5
Monkton Up Wimborne
 13 G1
Monkton Wyld 11 G3
Monkwearmouth 120 C2
Monkwood 28 B4
Monmouth (Trefynwy)
 39 F1
Monnington Court 52 C4
Monnington on Wye
 52 C3
Monreith 115 D2
Montacute 12 B1
Monteach 179 D3
Montford 64 D1
Montford Bridge 64 D1
Montgarrie 168 C3
Montgomery (Trefaldwyn)
 64 B3
Montgreenan 141 E5
Montrave 152 B4
Montrose 161 F4
Monxton 27 E3
Monyash 80 C1
Monymusk 169 D3
Monzie 151 D2
Moodiesburn 142 A2
Moons Moat North 54 C1
Moonzie 152 B3
Moor Allerton 102 C4
Moor Cock 100 C1
Moor Crichel 13 F2
Moor End Beds. 57 F2
Moor End Beds. 57 E5
Moor End Cumb. 107 G5
Moor End E.Riding
 104 A4
Moor End Lancs. 99 G3

Moor End N.Yorks.
 103 E4
Moor End W.Yorks.
 101 G5
Moor Green W.Mid. 66 C4
Moor Green Wilts. 25 F1
Moor Head 102 A4
Moor Monkton 103 E2
Moor Row 116 D5
Moor Side Cumb. 106 D5
Moor Side Lancs. 100 A4
Moor Side Lancs. 100 A4
Moor Side Lincs. 84 A2
Moor Street 32 A2
Moorby 84 A1
Moorcot 52 C2
Moordown 13 G3
Moore 91 G4
Moorend 117 G1
Moorends 95 D1
Moorfield 93 E3
Moorgreen 81 F3
Moorhall 94 A5
Moorhampton 52 C3
Moorhouse Cumb.
 117 G1
Moorhouse Notts. 82 C1
Moorland (Northmoor
 Green) 24 A4
Moorlinch 24 A4
Moorsholm 111 F1
Moorside Dorset 13 D1
Moorside Gt.Man. 93 D2
Moorside W.Yorks.
 102 B4
Moorthorpe 94 B1
Moortown I.o.W. 14 D4
Moortown Lincs. 96 A3
Moortown Tel. & W.
 65 F1
Morangie 175 D1
Morar 163 E5
Morborne 69 G3
Morchard Bishop 10 A2
Morcombelake 12 A3
Morcott 69 E2
Morda 77 F5
Morden Dorset 13 F3
Morden Essex 45 E2
Morden Here. 53 E1
Morden Mersey. 91 D4
Morden Oxon. 42 B2
Moreton Staffs. 80 C4
Moreton Staffs. 65 G1
Moreton Corbet 78 C5
Moreton Jeffries 53 F3
Moreton Mill 78 C5
Moreton Morrell 55 F2
Moreton on Lugg 53 E3
Moreton Paddox 55 F2
Moreton Pinkney 56 A3
Moreton Say 78 D4
Moreton Valence 39 G2
Moretonhampstead
 10 A4
Moreton-in-Marsh 55 E4
Morfa Cere. 49 G2
Morfa Carmar. 36 B1
Morfa Glas 37 E2
Morfa Nefyn 74 B3
Morgan's Vale 26 C5
Morganstown 38 A4
Mork 39 E2
Morland 118 B5
Morley Derbys. 81 E3
Morley Dur. 120 A5
Morley W.Yorks. 102 B5
Morley Green 92 C4
Morley St. Botolph 72 B2
Mornick 6 B3
Morningside Edin.
 143 G2

Morningside N.Lan.
 142 C4
Morningthorpe 72 D2
Morpeth 129 E3
Morphie 161 F3
Morrey 66 D1
Morridge Side 80 B2
Morrilow Heath 79 G4
Morriston S.Ayr. 132 A5
Morriston Swan. 36 C3
Morristown 38 A5
Morroch 155 F1
Morston 86 B1
Mortehoe 21 E1
Morthen 94 B4
Mortimer 28 B1
Mortimer West End 28 B1
Mortimer's Cross 52 D1
Mortlake 44 B5
Morton Derbys. 81 F1
Morton Lincs. 83 F5
Morton Lincs. 95 F3
Morton Lincs. 83 D1
Morton Notts. 82 C1
Morton S.Glos. 39 F3
Morton Shrop. 77 F5
Morton Bagot 54 D1
Morton on the Hill 86 C4
Morton Tinmouth 120 A5
Morton-on-Swale 110 C3
Morvah 2 B3
Morval 5 G4
Morvich High. 182 C4
Morvich (A'Mhormhaich)
 High. 164 A2
Morvil 48 D4
Morville 65 F3
Morwellham 8 A1
Morwenstow 20 C4
Morwick Hall 129 E1
Mosborough 94 B4
Moscow 141 E5
Mosedale 117 G3
Moselden Height 93 E1
Moseley W.Mid. 66 C4
Moseley W.Mid. 66 B3
Moseley Worcs. 54 A2
Moses Gate 92 B2
Moss Arg. & B. 154 A2
Moss S.Yorks. 94 C1
Moss Wrex. 78 A2
Moss Bank 91 G3
Moss Houses 92 C4
Moss Nook 92 C4
Moss of Barmuckity
 176 B3
Moss Side Gt.Man. 92 C3
Moss Side Lancs. 99 G4
Moss Side Mersey. 91 E2
Mossat 168 B3
Mossblown 132 C3
Mossburnford 136 A5
Mossdale 124 A3
Mossend 142 B3
Mossgiel 132 C3
Mosshead 168 C1
Mossley Ches.E. 79 F1
Mossley Gt.Man. 93 D2
Mossley Hill 91 F4
Mosspaul Hotel 126 B2
Moss-side High. 175 E4
Moss-side Moray 177 E4
Mosstodloch 176 C3
Mosston 160 D5
Mossy Lea 91 G1
Mosterton 12 A2
Moston Gt.Man. 92 C2
Moston Shrop. 78 C5
Moston Green 79 E1
Mostyn 90 C4
Motcombe 25 F5
Mothecombe 8 C2
Motherby 118 A5
Motherwell 142 B4
Mottingham 44 D5
Mottisfont 27 E5
Mottistone 14 D4
Mottram in Longdendale
 93 D3
Mottram St. Andrew
 92 C5
Mouldsworth 91 G5
Moulin 159 E4
Moulsecoomb 17 F3
Moulsford 42 A4
Moulsham 45 G2
Moulsoe 57 E3

Moulton C. & W.Ches.
 79 D1
Moulton Lincs. 84 B5
Moulton N.Yorks. 110 B2
Moulton Northants.
 56 C1
Moulton Suff. 59 E1
Moulton V. of Glam.
 37 G5
Moulton Chapel 70 A1
Moulton St. Mary 87 F5
Moulton Seas End 84 B5
Mounie Castle 169 E2
Mount Cornw. 4 B4
Mount Cornw. 5 F3
Mount High. 175 F5
Mount Kent 33 D4
Mount W.Yorks. 93 F1
Mount Ambrose 4 B5
Mount Bures 60 A4
Mount Charles 5 E4
Mount Hawke 4 B5
Mount Manisty 91 E5
Mount Oliphant 132 B4
Mount Cornw. 5 F3
 79 F2
Mount Pleasant Derbys.
 81 E3
Mount Pleasant Derbys.
 67 E1
Mount Pleasant E.Suss.
 17 G2
Mount Pleasant Flints.
 90 D5
Mount Pleasant Gt.Lon.
 43 F3
Mount Pleasant Hants.
 14 C3
Mount Pleasant Norf.
 72 A2
Mount Pleasant Suff.
 59 F3
Mount Sorrel 26 B5
Mount Tabor 101 G5
Mountain 101 G4
Mountain Ash
 (Aberpennar) 37 G3
Mountain Cross 143 F5
Mountain Water 48 C3
Mountbenger 135 E3
Mountblairy 177 F4
Mountblow 141 G2
Mountfield 18 C1
Mountgerald 174 B3
Mountjoy 4 D3
Mountnessing 45 F3
Mounton 39 F3
Mountsorrel 68 A1
Mousa 191 F5
Mousehole 2 B4
Mouswald 125 E3
Mow Cop 79 F2
Mowden 110 B3
Mowhaugh 136 C4
Mowsley 68 B4
Mowtie 161 G1
Moxley 66 B3
Moy High. 157 D1
Moy High. 157 G1
Moy High. 166 B1
Moy House 175 E4
Moylgrove 49 E3
Muasdale 189 C4
Much Birch 53 E4
Much Cowarne 53 F3
Much Dewchurch 53 D4
Much Hadham 44 D1
Much Hoole 100 A5
Much Hoole Town 100 A5
Much Marcle 53 F4
Much Wenlock 65 F2
Muchalls 169 G5
Muchelney 24 B5
Muchelney Ham 24 B5
Muchlarnick 5 G4
Muchra 134 C4
Muchrachd 165 D1
Muck 154 D2
Mucking 45 F4
Muckle Roe 191 E3
Muckleford 12 C3
Mucklestone 79 E4
Muckleton 78 C5
Muckletown 168 C2
Muckley 65 F3
Muckley Corner 66 C2
Muckton 87 E4
Mudale 182 A1
Muddiford 21 F2

Muddles Green 18 A2
Muddleswood 17 E2
Mudeford 14 A3
Mudford 12 B1
Mudgley 24 B3
Mugdock 141 G2
Mugeary 162 C1
Mugginton 81 D3
Muggintonlane End
 81 D3
Muggleswick 119 G3
Mugswell 30 B3
Muie 182 B4
Muir 159 F1
Muir of Fowlis 168 C3
Muir of Lochs 176 C3
Muir of Ord (Am Blàr
 Dubh) 174 B4
Muirden 177 G4
Muirdrum 153 D1
Muiredge 152 B5
Muirhead Aber. 168 C3
Muirhead Angus 152 B1
Muirhead Fife 152 A4
Muirhead Moray 175 G3
Muirhead N.Lan. 142 A3
Muirhouses 143 E1
Muirkirk 133 E3
Muirmill 142 B1
Muirtack Aber. 169 G1
Muirtack Aber. 178 D3
Muirton High. 174 D3
Muirton P. & K. 151 E3
Muirton P. & K. 151 G2
Muirton of Ardblair
 159 G5
Muirton of Ballochy
 161 E2
Muirtown 175 F4
Muiryfold 177 G4
Muker 109 E3
Mulbarton 86 C5
Mulben 176 C4
Mull 147 E1
Mullacott Cross 21 F1
Mullion 3 D5
Mullion Cove 3 D5
Mumby 97 F5
Munderfield Row 53 F2
Munderfield Stocks 53 F2
Mundesley 87 E2
Mundford 71 G3
Mundham 73 E2
Mundon 46 B2
Mundurno 169 G3
Munerigie 165 D4
Mungasdale 180 B5
Mungoswells 144 B2
Mungrisdale 117 G3
Munlochy 174 C4
Munnoch 140 D5
Munsley 53 F2
Munslow 65 E4
Murchington 9 G2
Murcott Oxon. 42 A1
Murcott Wilts. 40 B3
Murdostoun 142 C4
Murieston 143 E3
Murkle 187 D2
Murlaganmore 150 A1
Murlaggan High. 164 B5
Murlaggan High. 157 F1
Murrell Green 28 C2
Murroes 152 C1
Murrow 70 B2
Mursley 56 D5
Murston 32 B2
Murthill 160 C4
Murthly 151 F1
Murton Cumb. 118 D5
Murton Dur. 120 C3
Murton Northumb.
 145 G5
Murton Swan. 36 B4
Murton York 103 E2
Musbury 11 F3
Muscliff 13 G3
Musdale (Musdàl) 148 B2
Musselburgh 144 A2
Mustard Hyrn 87 F4
Muston Leics. 82 D4
Muston N.Yorks. 113 D5
Mustow Green 66 A5
Mutford 73 F3
Muthill 151 D3
Mutley 8 A2
Mutterton 10 D2
Muxton 65 G1
Mybster 187 D3

Myddfai 51 D4
Myddle 78 B5
Myddlewood 78 B5
Mydroilyn 50 D2
Myerscough College
 100 A4
Myerscough Smithy
 100 C4
Mylor 3 F3
Mylor Bridge 3 F3
Mynachdy 38 B5
Mynachlog-ddu 49 E4
Myndtown 64 C4
Mynydd Llandygai 75 F1
Mynydd-bach Mon.
 39 D3
Mynydd-bach Swan.
 36 C3
Mynyddmechell 88 B4
Mynyddygarreg 36 A2
Mynytho 74 C2
Myrebird 169 E5
Mytchett 29 D2
Mytholm 101 F5
Mytholmroyd 101 G5
Mythop 99 G4
Myton-on-Swale 102 D1
Mytton 64 D1

N

Naast 172 B1
Nab's Head 100 C5
Naburn 103 E3
Nackington 33 D3
Nacton 60 D3
Nadderwater 10 B3
Nafferton 104 C2
Nailbridge 39 F1
Nailsbourne 23 F5
Nailsea 39 D5
Nailstone 67 G2
Nailsworth 40 A3
Nairn 135 E4
Nancegollan 2 D3
Nancekuke 4 A5
Nancledra 2 B3
Nanhoron 74 B4
Nannau 76 A5
Nannerch 77 E1
Nanpantan 68 A1
Nanpean 5 D4
Nanstallon 5 E3
Nant Peris 75 F2
Nant-ddu 37 G1
Nanternis 49 G2
Nantgaredig 50 A5
Nantgarw 38 A4
Nant-glas 51 F1
Nantglyn 76 D1
Nantgwyn 63 F5
Nantlle 75 E2
Nantmawr 77 F5
Nantmel 51 G1
Nantmor 75 F3
Nantwich 78 D2
Nantycaws 36 A1
Nant-y-derry 38 C2
Nant-y-dugoed 63 F1
Nantyffyllon 37 E3
Nantyglo 38 A1
Nant-y-Gollen 77 F5
Nant-y-groes 51 G1
Nant-y-moel 37 E3
Nant-y-Pandy 89 E5
Naphill 43 D3
Napley Heath 79 E4
Nappa 101 E2
Napton on the Hill 55 G1
Narberth (Arberth) 35 E1
Narborough Leics. 68 A3
Narborough Norf. 71 F1
Narkurs 6 D5
Narrachan 148 B3
Nasareth 75 D3
Naseby 68 B5
Nash Bucks. 56 C4
Nash Here. 52 C1
Nash Newport 38 C4
Nash Shrop. 65 F5
Nash V. of Glam. 37 F5
Nash Street 31 F2
Nassington 69 F3
Nasty 58 B5
Nateby Cumb. 108 C2
Nateby Lancs. 100 A3
Nately Scures 28 C2
Natland 107 G4
Naughton 60 B3

Naunton *Glos.* **54** D5
Naunton *Worcs.* **54** A4
Naunton Beauchamp **54** B2
Navenby **83** E2
Navestock **45** E3
Navestock Side **45** E3
Navidale **183** F3
Navity **175** D3
Nawton **111** F4
Nayland **60** A4
Nazeing **44** D2
Neacroft **14** A3
Neal's Green **67** F4
Neap House **95** F1
Near Sawrey **107** E3
Nearton End **56** D5
Neasden **44** B4
Neasham **110** C2
Neat Enstone **55** F5
Neath (Castell-nedd) **37** D3
Neatham **28** C3
Neatishead **87** E3
Nebo *Cere.* **50** B1
Nebo *Conwy* **76** B2
Nebo *Gwyn.* **75** D2
Nebo *I.o.A.* **88** C3
Necton **71** G2
Nedd **180** D1
Nedderton **129** E3
Nedging **60** A3
Nedging Tye **60** B3
Needham **72** D3
Needham Market **60** B2
Needham Street **59** F1
Needingworth **70** B5
Needwood **80** C5
Neen Savage **65** F5
Neen Sollars **65** F5
Neenton **65** F4
Nefyn **74** C3
Neighbourne **24** D3
Neilston **141** F4
Neithrop **55** G3
Nelson *Caerp.* **38** A3
Nelson *Lancs.* **101** E4
Nelson Village **129** E4
Nemphlar **142** C5
Nempnett Thrubwell **24** C1
Nenthall **119** D3
Nenthead **119** D3
Nenthorn **136** A3
Neopardy **10** A3
Nerabus **138** A4
Nercwys **77** F1
Nerbiy **138** B3
Nerston **142** A4
Nesbit **137** D3
Nesfield **101** G3
Ness **91** E5
Nesscliffe **64** C2
Neston *C. & W.Ches.* **91** D5
Neston *Wilts.* **25** F1
Nether Alderley **92** C5
Nether Auchendrane **132** B4
Nether Barr **119** D3
Nether Blainslie **144** C5
Nether Broughton **82** B5
Nether Burrow **108** B5
Nether Cerne **12** C3
Nether Compton **12** B1
Nether Crimond **169** F2
Nether Dalgliesh **135** D5
Nether Dallachy **176** C3
Nether Edge **94** A4
Nether End **93** G5
Nether Glasslaw **179** D2
Nether Handwick **160** B5
Nether Haugh **94** B3
Nether Heage **81** E2
Nether Heselden **109** D5
Nether Heyford **56** B2
Nether Kellet **100** B1
Nether Kinmundy **179** F3
Nether Langwith **94** C5
Nether Lenshie **177** F5
Nether Loads **81** E1
Nether Moor **81** E1
Nether Padley **93** G5
Nether Pitforthie **161** G2
Nether Poppleton **103** E2
Nether Silton **111** D3
Nether Skyborry **64** B5
Nether Stowey **23** E4

Nether Urquhart **151** G4
Nether Wallop **27** E4
Nether Wasdale **106** C2
Nether Wellwood **133** E3
Nether Welton **117** G2
Nether Westcote **55** E5
Nether Whitacre **67** E3
Nether Winchendon (Lower Winchendon) **42** C1
Nether Worton **55** G5
Netheravon **26** C3
Netherbrae **177** G4
Netherburn **142** C5
Netherbury **12** A3
Netherby *Cumb.* **126** B4
Netherby *N.Yorks.* **102** C2
Nethercott **55** G5
Netherfield *E.Suss.* **18** C2
Netherfield *Notts.* **82** B3
Netherfield *S.Lan.* **142** B5
Netherhall **140** D3
Netherhampton **26** C5
Netherhay **12** A2
Netherland Green **80** C4
Netherley **169** F5
Nethermill **125** E2
Nethermuir **179** E3
Netherseal **67** E1
Nethershield **133** D3
Netherstreet **26** A1
Netherthird *D. & G.* **124** B5
Netherthird *E.Ayr.* **133** D4
Netherthong **93** F2
Netherthorpe **94** C4
Netherton *Angus* **160** D4
Netherton *C. & W.Ches.* **91** G5
Netherton *Devon* **10** B5
Netherton *Hants.* **27** E2
Netherton *Mersey.* **91** E2
Netherton *N.Lan.* **142** B4
Netherton *Northumb.* **128** B1
Netherton *Oxon.* **41** G2
Netherton *P. & K.* **159** G4
Netherton *S.Lan.* **142** D4
Netherton *W.Mid.* **66** B4
Netherton *W.Yorks.* **93** G1
Netherton *W.Yorks.* **93** F1
Netherton *Worcs.* **54** B3
Netherton Burnfoot **128** B1
Netherton Northside **128** B1
Nethertown *Cumb.* **106** A2
Nethertown *Ork.* **187** F1
Nethertown *Staffs.* **66** D1
Netherwitton **128** D2
Netherwood *D. & G.* **125** D3
Netherwood *E.Ayr.* **133** E3
Nethy Bridge **167** E2
Netley Abbey **15** D2
Netley Marsh **14** C1
Nettlebed **42** B4
Nettlebridge **24** D3
Nettlecombe *Dorset* **12** B3
Nettlecombe *I.o.W.* **15** E5
Nettlecombe *Som.* **23** D4
Nettleden **43** F1
Nettleham **96** A5
Nettlestead *Kent* **31** F3
Nettlestead *Suff.* **60** B3
Nettlestead Green **31** F3
Nettlestone **15** E3
Nettlesworth **120** B3
Nettleton *Lincs.* **96** B2
Nettleton *Wilts.* **40** A5
Nettleton Hill **93** E1
Netton *Devon* **8** B3
Netton *Wilts.* **26** C4
Neuadd *Cere.* **50** A2
Neuadd *I.o.A.* **88** B3
Neuadd *Powys* **51** F3
Nevendon **45** G3
Nevern **49** D4
Nevill Holt **68** D3
New Abbey **125** D4
New Aberdour **179** D1
New Addington **30** C2
New Alresford **27** G4

New Alyth **160** A5
New Arley **67** E3
New Arram **104** C3
New Ash Green **31** F2
New Balderton **82** D2
New Barn **31** F2
New Belses **135** G3
New Bewick **137** E4
New Bolingbroke **84** B2
New Boultham **95** G5
New Bradwell **56** D3
New Brancepeth **120** B3
New Bridge *D. & G.* **124** D3
New Bridge *Devon* **10** A5
New Brighton *Flints.* **77** F1
New Brighton *Hants.* **15** G2
New Brighton *Mersey.* **91** E3
New Brighton *W.Yorks.* **102** B5
New Brighton *Wrex.* **77** F2
New Brinsley **81** D1
New Broughton **78** A2
New Buckenham **72** B2
New Byth **178** D2
New Cheriton **27** G5
New Cross *Cere.* **62** C5
New Cross *Gt.Lon.* **44** C5
New Cumnock **133** E4
New Deer **179** D3
New Duston **56** C1
New Earswick **103** F2
New Edlington **94** C3
New Elgin **176** B3
New Ellerby **105** D4
New Eltham **44** D5
New End **54** C1
New England **69** G2
New Farnley **102** B4
New Ferry **91** E4
New Galloway **124** A3
New Gilston **152** C4
New Greens **44** A2
New Grimsby **4** A1
New Hartley **129** F4
New Haw **29** F1
New Heaton **136** C3
New Hedges **35** E2
New Herrington **120** C2
New Hinksey **42** A2
New Holland **104** C5
New Houghton *Derbys.* **81** G1
New Houghton *Norf.* **85** F5
New Houses **108** D5
New Hunwick **120** A4
New Hutton **107** G3
New Hythe **31** G3
New Inn *Carmar.* **50** A4
New Inn *Fife* **152** A4
New Inn *Mon.* **39** D2
New Inn *Torfaen* **38** B3
New Invention *Shrop.* **64** B5
New Invention *W.Mid.* **66** B2
New Kelso **172** C5
New Lanark **142** C5
New Lane **91** F1
New Lane End **92** A3
New Leake **84** C2
New Leeds **179** E2
New Leslie **168** C2
New Lodge **94** A2
New Longton **100** B5
New Luce **122** C4
New Mains **133** G2
New Mains of Ury **161** G1
New Malden **30** B2
New Marske **121** F5
New Marton **78** A4
New Mill *Cornw.* **2** B3
New Mill *Herts.* **43** E1
New Mill *W.Yorks.* **93** F2
New Mill End **44** A1
New Mills *Cornw.* **4** C4
New Mills *Derbys.* **93** E4
New Mills *Glos.* **39** F2
New Mills *Mon.* **39** E2
New Mills (Y Felin Newydd) *Powys* **63** G2
New Milton **14** B3
New Mistley **60** C4
New Moat **49** D5

New Ollerton **82** B1
New Orleans **130** C4
New Oscott **66** C3
New Park *Cornw.* **5** F1
New Park *N.Yorks.* **102** B2
New Pitsligo **179** D2
New Polzeath **4** D2
New Quay (Ceinewydd) **49** G1
New Rackheath **87** D4
New Radnor (Maesyfed) **52** B1
New Rent **118** A4
New Ridley **119** G1
New Road Side **101** F3
New Romney **19** F1
New Rossington **94** D3
New Row *Cere.* **62** D5
New Row *Lancs.* **100** C4
New Sawley **81** F4
New Shoreston **137** F3
New Silksworth **120** C2
New Stevenston **142** B4
New Swannington **67** G1
New Totley **94** A5
New Town *Beds.* **57** G3
New Town *Cere.* **49** E5
New Town *Dorset* **13** F1
New Town *Dorset* **13** F2
New Town *E.Loth.* **144** B2
New Town *E.Suss.* **17** G1
New Town *Glos.* **54** C4
New Tredegar **38** A2
New Tupton **81** E1
New Ulva **139** F1
New Village **94** C2
New Walsoken **70** C2
New Waltham **96** C2
New Winton **144** B2
New World **70** B3
New Yatt **41** F1
New York *Lincs.* **84** A2
New York *T. & W.* **129** F4
Newall **102** B3
Newark **70** A2
Newark-on-Trent **82** D2
Newarthill **142** B4
Newball **96** A5
Newbarn **33** D5
Newbarns **106** D5
Newbattle **144** A3
Newbiggin *Cumb.* **118** A5
Newbiggin *Cumb.* **118** C5
Newbiggin *Cumb.* **118** B3
Newbiggin *Cumb.* **99** F1
Newbiggin *Cumb.* **106** B3
Newbiggin *Dur.* **119** F5
Newbiggin *N.Yorks.* **109** F4
Newbiggin *N.Yorks.* **109** E3
Newbiggin *Northumb.* **119** F1
Newbiggin-by-the-Sea **129** F3
Newbigging *Aber.* **169** F5
Newbigging *Aber.* **159** G1
Newbigging *Angus* **152** C1
Newbigging *Angus* **152** C1
Newbigging *Angus* **160** A5
Newbigging *S.Lan.* **143** E5
Newbiggin-on-Lune **108** C2
Newbold *Derbys.* **94** A5
Newbold *Leics.* **67** G1
Newbold on Avon **67** G5
Newbold on Stour **55** E3
Newbold Pacey **55** E2
Newbold Verdon **67** G2
Newborough (Niwbwrch) *I.o.A.* **74** D1
Newborough *Peter.* **70** A2
Newborough *Staffs.* **80** C5
Newbottle *Northants.* **56** A4
Newbottle *T. & W.* **120** C2
Newbourne **61** D3

Newbridge (Cefn Bychan) *Caerp.* **38** B3
Newbridge *Cornw.* **2** B3
Newbridge *Cornw.* **6** D4
Newbridge *E.Suss.* **31** D5
Newbridge *Edin.* **143** F2
Newbridge *Hants.* **14** B1
Newbridge *I.o.W.* **14** D4
Newbridge *N.Yorks.* **112** B4
Newbridge *Oxon.* **41** G2
Newbridge *Pembs.* **48** C4
Newbridge *Wrex.* **77** F3
Newbridge Green **54** A4
Newbridge on Wye **51** G2
Newbridge-on-Usk **38** C3
Newbrough **119** E1
Newbuildings **10** A2
Newburgh *Aber.* **179** E2
Newburgh *Aber.* **169** G2
Newburgh *Fife* **152** A3
Newburgh *Lancs.* **91** F1
Newburgh *Sc.Bord.* **135** E3
Newburn **120** A1
Newbury *Som.* **25** D2
Newbury *W.Berks.* **27** F1
Newbury *Wilts.* **25** F3
Newbury Park **44** D4
Newby *Cumb.* **118** B5
Newby *Lancs.* **101** E3
Newby *N.Yorks.* **111** E1
Newby *N.Yorks.* **100** D1
Newby *N.Yorks.* **112** D4
Newby Bridge **107** E4
Newby Cote **108** C5
Newby Cross **117** G1
Newby East **118** A2
Newby West **117** G1
Newby Wiske **110** D4
Newcastle *Bridgend* **37** E5
Newcastle *Mon.* **38** D1
Newcastle *Shrop.* **64** B4
Newcastle Emlyn (Castell Newydd Emlyn) **49** G3
Newcastle International Airport **129** D4
Newcastle upon Tyne **120** B1
Newcastleton **126** C3
Newcastle-under-Lyme **79** F3
Newchapel *Pembs.* **49** E5
Newchapel *Staffs.* **79** F2
Newchapel *Surr.* **30** C4
Newchurch *Carmar.* **49** G5
Newchurch *I.o.W.* **15** E4
Newchurch *Kent* **32** C5
Newchurch *Lancs.* **101** E5
Newchurch *Lancs.* **101** E4
Newchurch *Mon.* **39** D3
Newchurch *Powys* **52** B2
Newchurch *Staffs.* **80** C5
Newcott **11** F1
Newcraighall **144** A2
Newdigate **29** G3
Newell Green **43** D5
Newenden **18** D1
Newent **53** G5
Newerne **39** F2
Newfield *Dur.* **120** B4
Newfield *Dur.* **120** B2
Newfield *High.* **175** D2
Newfound **27** G2
Newgale **48** B5
Newgate **86** B1
Newgate Street **44** C2
Newhall *Ches.E.* **78** D3
Newhall *Derbys.* **81** D5
Newham **137** F4
Newham Hall **137** F4
Newhaven **17** G3
Newhey **92** D1
Newholm **112** B1
Newhouse **142** B3
Newick **17** G1
Newingreen **32** D5
Newington *Edin.* **143** G2
Newington *Kent* **33** D5
Newington *Kent* **32** A2
Newington *Notts.* **95** D3
Newington *Oxon.* **42** B3
Newington Bagpath **40** A3

Newland *Glos.* **39** E2
Newland *Hull* **104** C4
Newland *N.Yorks.* **103** F5
Newland *Oxon.* **41** F1
Newland *Worcs.* **53** G3
Newlandrig **144** A3
Newlands *Cumb.* **117** G3
Newlands *Essex* **46** B4
Newlands *Northumb.* **119** G2
Newlands *Sc.Bord.* **126** D2
Newland's Corner **29** F3
Newlands of Geise **186** C2
Newlands of Tynet **176** C3
Newlyn **2** B4
Newmachar **169** F3
Newmains **142** C4
Newman's End **45** E1
Newman's Green **59** G3
Newmarket *Suff.* **59** E1
Newmarket *W.Isles* **189** G2
Newmill *Aber.* **161** F1
Newmill *Aber.* **178** D3
Newmill *Aber.* **169** F2
Newmill *Moray* **176** D4
Newmill *Sc.Bord.* **135** F4
Newmill of Inshewan **160** C1
Newmillerdam **94** A1
Newmills **174** C3
Newmiln *P. & K.* **151** G1
Newmiln *P. & K.* **151** F2
Newmilns **132** D2
Newney Green **45** F2
Newnham *Glos.* **39** F1
Newnham *Hants.* **28** C2
Newnham *Herts.* **58** A4
Newnham *Kent* **32** B3
Newnham *Northants.* **56** A2
Newnham Bridge **53** F1
Newnham Paddox **67** G4
Newnoth **168** C1
Newport *Cornw.* **6** D2
Newport *Devon* **21** F2
Newport *E.Riding* **104** A4
Newport *Essex* **58** D4
Newport *Glos.* **39** F3
Newport *High.* **183** G2
Newport *I.o.W.* **15** E4
Newport (Casnewydd) *Newport* **38** C4
Newport *Norf.* **87** G4
Newport (Trefdraeth) *Pembs.* **49** D4
Newport *Som.* **24** A3
Newport *Tel. & W.* **65** G1
Newport Pagnell **57** D3
Newport-on-Tay **152** C2
Newpound Common **29** F5
Newquay **4** C3
Newquay Cornwall International Airport **4** C3
Newsbank **79** F1
Newseat **169** E1
Newsells **58** B4
Newsham *Lancs.* **100** B4
Newsham *N.Yorks.* **110** A1
Newsham *N.Yorks.* **110** C4
Newsham *Northumb.* **129** E4
Newsholme *E.Riding* **103** G5
Newsholme *Lancs.* **101** E2
Newsome **93** F1
Newstead *Northumb.* **137** F4
Newstead *Notts.* **81** G2
Newstead *Sc.Bord.* **135** G2
Newthorpe *N.Yorks.* **103** D4
Newthorpe *Notts.* **81** F3
Newtoft **96** A4
Newton *Aber.* **177** D5
Newton *Aber.* **179** F3
Newton *Arg. & B.* **148** C5
Newton *Bridgend* **37** E5
Newton *C. & W.Ches.* **78** C2

Newton C. & W.Ches. **91** G5
Newton Cambs. **70** C1
Newton Cambs. **58** A4
Newton Cardiff **38** B5
Newton Cumb. **106** D5
Newton Derbys. **81** F2
Newton Gt.Man. **93** D3
Newton Here. **52** D1
Newton Here. **53** E2
Newton Here. **52** C4
Newton High. **187** F3
Newton High. **174** D5
Newton High. **187** E3
Newton High. **181** E1
Newton High. **174** B4
Newton High. **175** D3
Newton Lancs. **100** C1
Newton Lancs. **107** G5
Newton Lancs. **99** G4
Newton Lincs. **83** F4
Newton Moray **176** D3
Newton N.Ayr. **104** A4
Newton Norf. **71** G1
Newton Northants.
69 D4
Newton Northumb.
119 G1
Newton Northumb.
128 B1
Newton Notts. **82** B3
Newton P. & K. **151** D1
Newton Pembs. **48** B5
Newton Pembs. **34** C2
Newton S.Glos. **39** F3
Newton S.Lan. **134** A2
Newton Sc.Bord. **136** A4
Newton Shrop. **78** B4
Newton Som. **23** E4
Newton Staffs. **80** B5
Newton Suff. **60** A3
Newton Swan. **36** C4
Newton W.Loth. **143** E2
Newton W.Yorks. **102** D5
Newton Warks. **68** A5
Newton Wilts. **26** D5
Newton Abbot **10** B5
Newton Arlosh **117** F1
Newton Aycliffe **120** B5
Newton Bewley **121** D5
Newton Blossomville
57 E2
Newton Bromswold **57** E1
Newton Burgoland **67** F2
Newton by Toft **96** A4
Newton Ferrers **8** B3
Newton Flotman **72** D2
Newton Green **39** E3
Newton Harcourt **68** B3
Newton Kyme **103** D3
Newton Longville **56** D4
Newton Mearns **141** G4
Newton Morrell N.Yorks.
110 B2
Newton Morrell Oxon.
56 B5
Newton Mountain **34** C2
Newton Mulgrave **111** G1
Newton of Affleck **152** C1
Newton of Ardtoe **155** F2
Newton of Balcanquhal
151 G3
Newton of Dalvey **175** G4
Newton of Falkland
152 A4
Newton of Leys **166** A1
Newton on the Hill **78** B5
Newton on Trent **95** F5
Newton Poppleford **11** D4
Newton Purcell **56** B4
Newton Regis **67** G2
Newton Reigny **118** A4
Newton St. Cyres **10** B3
Newton St. Faith **86** D4
Newton St. Loe **25** E1
Newton St. Petrock **21** E4
Newton Solney **81** D5
Newton Stacey **27** F3
Newton Stewart **123** F4
Newton Tony **26** D3
Newton Tracey **21** F3
Newton under Roseberry
111 E1
Newton Underwood
129 D3
Newton upon Derwent
103 G5
Newton Valence **28** C4

Newton with Scales
100 A4
Newtonairds **124** C2
Newtongrange **144** A3
Newtonhill **169** G5
Newton-le-Willows
Mersey. **91** A4
Newton-le-Willows
N.Yorks. **110** B4
Newtonmill **161** E3
Newtonmore
(Baile Ùr an t-Slèibh)
166 B5
Newton-on-Ouse
103 E2
Newton-on-Rawcliffe
112 B3
Newton-on-the-Moor
129 D1
Newtown Bucks. **43** E2
Newtown C. & W.Ches.
78 C2
Newtown Cornw. **5** G2
Newtown Cornw. **2** C4
Newtown Cumb. **118** B1
Newtown Derbys. **93** D4
Newtown Devon **22** A5
Newtown Devon **11** D3
Newtown Dorset **12** A1
Newtown Glos. **39** F2
Newtown Gt.Man. **91** G2
Newtown Gt.Man. **92** B2
Newtown Hants. **15** F1
Newtown Hants. **27** F1
Newtown Hants. **14** B1
Newtown Hants. **27** E5
Newtown Hants. **15** E1
Newtown Here. **53** F3
Newtown Here. **53** D2
Newtown High. **165** E4
Newtown I.o.M. **98** B4
Newtown I.o.W. **14** D3
Newtown Northumb.
128 C1
Newtown Northumb.
137 E4
Newtown Oxon. **42** C4
Newtown (Y Drenewydd)
Powys **64** A3
Newtown R.C.T. **37** G3
Newtown Shrop. **78** B4
Newtown Som. **23** F4
Newtown Som. **11** F1
Newtown Staffs. **79** G1
Newtown Staffs. **80** B1
Newtown Staffs. **66** B2
Newtown Wilts. **26** A5
Newtown Wilts. **27** E1
Newtown Linford **66** D2
Newtown St. Boswells
135 G2
Newtown Unthank **67** G2
Newtown-in-St-Martin
3 E4
Newtyle **160** A5
Newyears Green **43** F4
Neyland **34** C2
Nibley Glos. **39** F2
Nibley S.Glos. **39** F4
Nibley Green **39** G3
Nicholashayne **11** E1
Nicholaston **36** B4
Nidd **102** C1
Nigg Aberdeen **169** G4
Nigg High. **175** E2
Nightcott **22** B5
Nilig **76** D2
Nilston Rigg **119** E1
Nimlet **39** G5
Nine Ashes **45** E2
Nine Elms **40** D4
Nine Mile Burn **143** F4
Ninebanks **119** D2
Ninemile Bar (Crocketford)
124 C3
Nineveh **53** F1
Ninfield **18** C2
Ningwood **14** D4
Nisbet **136** A4
Niton **15** E5
Nitshill **141** G3
Nizels **31** E3
No Man's Heath
C. & W.Ches. **78** C3
No Man's Heath Warks.
67 E2
No Man's Land **5** G4
Noah's Ark **31** E3
Noak Hill **45** E3

Noblehill **125** D3
Noblethorpe **93** G2
Nobottle **56** B1
Nocton **83** F1
Noddsdale **140** D3
Nogdam End **87** E5
Noke **42** A1
Nolton **34** B1
Nolton Haven **34** B1
Nomansland Devon
10 B1
Nomansland Wilts. **14** B1
Noneley **78** B5
Nonington **33** E3
Nook Cumb. **126** C4
Nook Cumb. **107** G4
Noranside **160** C3
Norbreck **99** G3
Norbury Ches.E. **78** C3
Norbury Derbys. **80** C3
Norbury Gt.Lon. **44** C5
Norbury Shrop. **64** C3
Norbury Staffs. **79** E5
Norbury Common **78** C3
Norbury Junction **79** E5
Norchard **35** D3
Norcott Brook **92** A4
Nordelph **71** D2
Norden Dorset **13** F4
Norden Gt.Man. **92** C1
Nordley **65** F3
Norham **145** D2
Norland Town **101** G5
Norley **91** G5
Norleywood **14** C3
Norlington **17** G2
Norman Cross **69** G3
Normanby N.Lincs.
95 F1
Normanby N.Yorks.
111 G4
Normanby R. & C.
111 E1
Normanby by Stow **95** F4
Normanby le Wold **96** B3
Normanby-by-Spital
96 A4
Normandy **29** E2
Normann's Ruh **154** D5
Normanton Derby **81** E4
Normanton Leics. **82** D3
Normanton Lincs. **83** E3
Normanton Notts. **82** C2
Normanton Rut. **69** E2
Normanton W.Yorks.
102 C5
Normanton le Heath
67 F1
Normanton on Soar
81 G5
Normanton on Trent
82 C1
Normanton-on-the-Wolds
82 B4
Normoss **99** G4
Norrington Common
25 E1
Norris Green **8** A1
Norris Hill **67** F1
Norristhorpe **102** B5
North Acton **44** B4
North Anston **94** C4
North Ascot **29** E1
North Aston **55** G5
North Baddesley **14** C1
North Ballachulish
(Baile a' Chaolais a
Tuath) **156** C3
North Balloch **123** E1
North Barrow **24** D5
North Barsham **86** A2
North Benfleet **45** G4
North Berwick **144** C1
North Boarhunt **15** F1
North Bogbain **176** C4
North Bovey **10** A4
North Bradley **25** F2
North Brentor **7** E2
North Brewham **25** E4
North Bridge **29** E4
North Buckland **21** E1
North Burlingham **87** E4
North Cadbury **24** D5
North Cairn **122** A3
North Camp **29** D2

North Carlton Lincs.
95 G5
North Carlton Notts.
94 C4
North Cave **104** A4
North Cerney **40** C2
North Chailey **17** F1
North Charford **14** A1
North Charlton **137** F4
North Cheriton **25** D5
North Chideock **12** A3
North Cliffe **104** A4
North Clifton **95** F5
North Cockerington
97 D3
North Common S.Glos.
39 F5
North Common Suff.
72 A4
North Commonty **179** D3
North Connel **148** B1
North Coombe **10** B2
North Cornelly **37** E4
North Corner **39** F4
North Cotes **96** D2
North Cove **73** F3
North Cowton **110** B2
North Crawley **57** E3
North Cray **45** D5
North Creake **85** G4
North Curry **24** A5
North Dallens **156** B5
North Dalton **104** B2
North Deighton **102** C2
North Dell **189** G1
North Duffield **103** F4
North Elkington **96** C3
North Elmham **86** A3
North Elmsall **94** B1
North End Bucks. **56** D5
North End Dorset **25** F5
North End E.Riding
105 D2
North End E.Riding
105 D3
North End E.Riding
105 E4
North End Essex **45** F1
North End Hants. **25** F1
North End Hants. **14** A1
North End Leics. **48** A1
North End N.Som. **24** B1
North End Norf. **72** B2
North End Northumb.
128 D1
North End Ports. **15** F2
North End W.Suss. **16** D1
North End W.Suss. **16** B3
North Erradale **172** A1
North Essie **179** F2
North Fambridge **46** B3
North Ferriby **104** B5
North Frodingham
104 D2
North Gorley **14** A1
North Green Norf. **72** D3
North Green Suff. **73** E4
North Green Suff. **61** E1
North Green Suff. **61** E1
North Grimston **104** A1
North Halling **31** G2
North Harby **95** F5
North Hayling **15** G2
North Hazelrigg **137** E3
North Heasley **22** A4
North Heath W.Berks.
41 G5
North Heath W.Suss.
29 F5
North Hill **5** G2
North Hillingdon **43** F4
North Hinksey **41** G2
North Holmwood **29** G3
North Houghton **27** E4
North Huish **8** D2
North Hykeham **83** E1
North Johnston **34** C1
North Kelsey **96** A2
North Kessock **174** C5
North Killingholme **96** B3
North Kilvington **110** D4
North Kilworth **68** B4
North Kingston **14** A2
North Kyme **83** G2
North Lancing **17** D3
North Lee **42** D2
North Lees **110** C5
North Leigh **41** F1

North Leverton with
Habblesthorpe **95** E4
North Littleton **54** C3
North Lopham **72** B3
North Luffenham **69** E2
North Marden **16** A2
North Marston **56** C5
North Middleton Midloth.
144 A4
North Middleton
Northumb. **137** E4
North Millbrex **178** D3
North Molton **22** A5
North Moreton **42** A4
North Mundham **16** A3
North Muskham **82** C2
North Newbald **104** B4
North Newington **55** G4
North Newton **26** C2
North Newton **35** E4
North Nibley **39** G3
North Oakley **27** G2
North Ockendon **45** E4
North Ormesby **111** E1
North Ormsby **96** C3
North Otterington **110** C4
North Owersby **96** A3
North Perrott **12** A2
North Petherton **23** F4
North Petherwin **5** G1
North Pickenham **71** G2
North Piddle **54** B2
North Plain **125** F4
North Pool **9** D3
North Poorton **12** B3
North Quarme **22** C4
North Queensferry
143 F1
North Radworthy **22** A4
North Rauceby **83** F3
North Reston **97** D4
North Rigton **102** B3
North Rode **79** F1
North Roe **191** F2
North Ronaldsay **190** D1
North Runcton **71** E1
North Scale **99** E1
North Scarle **83** D1
North Seaton **129** E3
North Shian (Sithean a
Tuath) **156** B5
North Shields **121** E1
North Shoebury **46** C4
North Side **70** A3
North Skelton **111** F1
North Somercotes **97** E3
North Stainley **110** B5
North Stainmore **108** D1
North Stifford **45** F4
North Stoke B. & N.E.Som.
25 E1
North Stoke Oxon. **42** B4
North Stoke W.Suss.
16 C2
North Stoneham **14** D1
North Street Hants.
28 B4
North Street Kent **32** C3
North Street Med. **32** A1
North Street W.Berks.
42 B5
North Sunderland **137** G3
North Tamerton **6** D1
North Tarbothill **169** G3
North Tawton **21** G5
North Third **142** B1
North Thoresby **96** C3
North Tidworth **26** D3
North Togston **129** E1
North Town Devon **21** F5
North Town Hants.
29 D2
North Town W. & M.
43 D4
North Tuddenham **86** B4
North Uist (Uibhist a
Tuath) **188** B1
North Walsham **87** D2
North Waltham **27** G3
North Warnborough
28 C2
North Water Bridge
161 E3
North Watten **187** E3
North Weald Bassett
45 D2
North Wembley **44** A4
North Wheatley **95** E4
North Whilborough **9** E1

North Wick **24** C1
North Widcombe **24** C2
North Willingham **96** B4
North Wingfield **81** F1
North Witham **83** E1
North Wootton Dorset
12 C1
North Wootton Norf.
85 E5
North Wootton Som.
24 C3
North Wraxall **40** A5
North Wroughton **40** D4
North Yardhope **128** B1
Northacre **72** A2
Northall **57** E5
Northall Green **86** A4
Northallerton **110** C3
Northam Devon **21** E3
Northam S'ham. **14** D1
Northampton **56** C1
Northaw **44** B2
Northay Devon **11** G2
Northay Som. **11** F1
Northbeck **83** F3
Northborough **69** G2
Northbourne Kent **33** F3
Northbourne Oxon.
42 A4
Northbridge Street **18** C1
Northbrook Hants. **27** G4
Northbrook Oxon. **55** G5
Northburnhill **178** D3
Northchapel **29** E5
Northchurch **43** E2
Northcote Manor **21** G4
Northcott **7** F1
Northcourt **42** A3
Northedge **81** E1
Northend B. & N.E.Som.
25 E1
Northend Bucks. **42** C3
Northend Warks. **55** F2
Northfield Aber. **178** D3
Northfield Aberdeen
169 G4
Northfield High. **187** F4
Northfield Hull **104** C5
Northfield Sc.Bord.
145 G3
Northfield Som. **23** F4
Northfield W.Mid. **66** C5
Northfields **69** F2
Northfleet **45** F5
Northham **18** D1
Northill **57** G3
Northington Glos. **39** G2
Northington Hants.
27 G4
Northlands **84** B2
Northleach **40** D1
Northleigh Devon **11** E3
Northleigh Devon **21** G2
Northlew **7** F1
Northmoor **41** G2
Northmoor Green
(Moorland) **24** A4
Northmuir **160** B4
Northney **15** G2
Northolt **44** A4
Northop (Llaneurgain)
77 F1
Northop Hall **77** F1
Northorpe Lincs. **84** A4
Northorpe Lincs. **95** F3
Northorpe Lincs. **69** G1
Northover Som. **24** C5
Northover Som. **24** B4
Northowram **102** A5
Northport **13** F2
Northrepps **86** D2
Northton **189** E2
Northway Glos. **54** B4
Northway Swan. **23** E5
Northwich **92** A5
Northwick S.Glos. **39** E4
Northwick Som. **24** A3
Northwick Worcs. **54** A2
Northwold **71** G5
Northwood Gt.Lon. **43** F3
Northwood I.o.W. **15** D3
Northwood Kent **33** F2
Northwood Mersey.
91 F3
Northwood Shrop. **78** B4
Northwood Green **39** G1
Northwood Hills **44** A3
Norton Glos. **54** A5

Norton *Halton* **91** G4
Norton *Herts.* **58** A4
Norton *I.o.W.* **14** C4
Norton *Mon.* **52** D5
Norton *N.Som.* **24** A1
Norton *N.Yorks.* **111** G5
Norton *Northants.* **56** B1
Norton *Notts.* **94** C5
Norton *Powys* **52** C1
Norton *S.Yorks.* **94** C1
Norton *S.Yorks.* **94** A4
Norton *Shrop.* **65** E2
Norton *Shrop.* **65** G2
Norton *Shrop.* **65** D4
Norton *Stock.* **120** D5
Norton *Suff.* **60** A1
Norton *Swan.* **36** B3
Norton *V. of Glam.* **37** E5
Norton *W.Mid.* **40** A4
Norton *W.Suss.* **16** B3
Norton *W.Suss.* **16** A4
Norton *Wilts.* **40** A4
Norton *Worcs.* **54** A2
Norton *Worcs.* **54** C3
Norton Bavant **26** A3
Norton Bridge **79** F4
Norton Canes **66** C2
Norton Canon **52** C3
Norton Disney **83** D2
Norton Ferris **25** E4
Norton Fitzwarren **23** E5
Norton Green *Herts.*
  58 A5
Norton Green *I.o.W.*
  14 C4
Norton Green *Stoke*
  79 G2
Norton Hawkfield **24** C1
Norton Heath **45** F2
Norton in Hales **79** E4
Norton in the Moors
  79 F2
Norton Lindsey **55** E1
Norton Little Green **60** A1
Norton Malreward **24** D1
Norton Mandeville **45** E2
Norton St. Philip **25** E2
Norton Subcourse **73** F2
Norton Wood **54** C2
Norton Woodseats **94** A4
Norton-Juxta-Twycross
  67 F2
Norton-le-Clay **110** D5
Norton-sub-Hamdon
  12 A1
Norwell **82** C1
Norwell Woodhouse
  82 C1
Norwich **86** D5
Norwich International
  Airport **86** D4
Norwick **191** G1
Norwood End **45** E2
Norwood Green *Gt.Lon.*
  44 A5
Norwood Green *W.Yorks.*
  102 A5
Norwood Hill **30** B4
Norwood Park **24** C4
Noseley **68** C3
Noss Mayo **8** B3
Nosterfield **110** B4
Nosterfield End **59** E3
Nostie **163** G2
Notgrove **54** D5
Nottage **37** E5
Notting Hill **44** B4
Nottingham *High.*
  187 E5
Nottington **12** C4
Notton *W.Yorks.* **94** A1
Notton *Wilts.* **26** A1
Nottswood Hill **39** G1
Nounsley **45** G1
Noutard's Green **53** G1
Nowton **59** G1
Nox **64** D1
Noyadd Trefawr **49** F3
Nuffield **42** B4
Nun Monkton **103** E2
Nunburnholme **104** A3
Nuneaton **67** F4
Nuneham Courtenay
  42 A3
Nunney **25** E3
Nunnington *Here.* **53** E3
Nunnington *N.Yorks.*
  111 F5

Nunnington Park **23** D5
Nunnykirk **128** C2
Nunsthorpe **96** C2
Nunthorpe *Middbro.*
  111 E1
Nunthorpe *York* **103** E2
Nunton **26** C5
Nunwick *N.Yorks.* **110** C5
Nunwick *Northumb.*
  128 A4
Nup End **44** B1
Nupend **39** G2
Nursling **14** C1
Nursted **28** C5
Nurton **66** A3
Nutbourne *W.Suss.* **16** C2
Nutbourne *W.Suss.* **15** G2
Nutfield **30** C3
Nuthall **81** H1
Nuthampstead **58** C4
Nuthurst *W.Suss.* **29** G5
Nuthurst *Warks.* **67** D5
Nutley *E.Suss.* **17** G1
Nutley *Hants.* **28** B3
Nutwell **94** D2
Nyadd **150** C5
Nybster **187** F2
Nyetimber **16** A4
Nyewood **28** C5
Nymet Rowland **10** A2
Nymet Tracey **10** A2
Nympsfield **40** A2
Nynehead **23** E5
Nythe **24** B4
Nyton **16** B3

O

Oad Street **32** A2
Oadby **68** D2
Oak Cross **7** F1
Oak Tree **110** C1
Oakamoor **80** B3
Oakbank *Arg. & B.*
  147 G1
Oakbank *W.Loth.* **143** D3
Oakdale *Caerp.* **38** A3
Oakdale *Poole* **13** G3
Oake **23** E5
Oaken **66** A2
Oakenclough **100** B3
Oakengates **65** G1
Oakenhead **176** B3
Oakenholt **91** D5
Oakenshaw *Dur.* **120** B4
Oakenshaw *W.Yorks.*
  102 A5
Oakerthorpe **81** E2
Oakes **93** F1
Oakfield *I.o.W.* **15** E3
Oakfield *Torfaen* **38** B3
Oakford *Cere.* **50** A2
Oakford *Devon* **22** C5
Oakfordbridge **22** C5
Oakgrove **79** G1
Oakham **69** D2
Oakhanger **28** C4
Oakhill **24** D3
Oakington **58** C1
Oaklands *Conwy* **76** B2
Oaklands *Herts.* **44** B1
Oakle Street **39** G1
Oakley *Beds.* **57** F2
Oakley *Bucks.* **42** B1
Oakley *Fife* **143** E1
Oakley *Hants.* **27** G2
Oakley *Oxon.* **42** B2
Oakley *Poole* **13** G3
Oakley *Suff.* **72** C4
Oakley Green **43** E5
Oakridge Lynch **40** B2
Oaks **64** D2
Oaks Green **80** C4
Oaksey **40** B3
Oakshaw Ford **126** D4
Oakshott **28** C5
Oakthorpe **67** F1
Oaktree Hill **110** C3
Oakwoodhill **29** G4
Oakworth **101** G4
Oare *Kent* **32** C2
Oare *Som.* **22** B3
Oare *Wilts.* **26** C1
Oasby **83** F4
Oatfield **130** B4
Oath **24** A5
Oathlaw **160** C4
Oatlands **102** C2

Oban (An t-Òban)
  148 A2
Obley **54** C5
Oborne **12** C1
Obthorpe **69** F1
Occlestone Green **79** D1
Occold **72** C4
Occumster **187** E5
Ochiltree **132** D3
Ochr-y-foel **90** B5
Ochtertyre *P. & K.*
  150 D2
Ochtertyre *Stir.* **150** C5
Ockbrook **81** F4
Ockeridge **53** G1
Ockham **29** F2
Ockle **155** F2
Ockley **29** G4
Ocle Pychard **53** E3
Octon **112** B5
Odcombe **12** B1
Odd Down **25** E1
Oddendale **108** B1
Oddingley **54** B2
Oddington **42** A1
Oddsta **191** G2
Odell **57** E2
Odham **21** E5
Odiham **28** C2
Odsey **58** A4
Odstock **26** C5
Odstone **67** F2
Offchurch **55** F1
Offenham **54** C3
Offerton **92** D4
Offham *E.Suss.* **17** F2
Offham *Kent* **31** F3
Offham *W.Suss.* **16** C3
Offley Hoo **57** G5
Offleymarsh **79** E5
Offord Cluny **58** A1
Offord D'Arcy **58** A1
Offton **60** B3
Offwell **11** E3
Ogbourne Maizey **41** D5
Ogbourne St. Andrew
  41 D5
Ogbourne St. George
  41 D5
Ogil **160** C3
Ogle **128** D4
Oglet **91** F4
Ogmore **37** E5
Ogmore Vale **37** F3
Ogmore-by-Sea **37** E5
Okeford Fitzpaine **13** E1
Okehampton **7** F1
Okehampton Camp **7** F1
Olchard **10** B5
Olchfa **36** C3
Old **68** C5
Old Aberdeen **169** G4
Old Alresford **27** G4
Old Arley **67** E3
Old Basford **81** G3
Old Basing **28** B2
Old Belses **135** G3
Old Bewick **137** E4
Old Blair **159** D3
Old Bolingbroke **84** B1
Old Bramhope **102** B3
Old Brampton **94** A5
Old Bridge of Urr **124** B4
Old Buckenham **72** B2
Old Burdon **120** C2
Old Burghclere **27** F2
Old Byland **111** E4
Old Cassop **120** C4
Old Church Stoke **64** B3
Old Cleeve **22** D3
Old Clipstone **82** B1
Old Craig **169** G2
Old Craighall **144** A2
Old Crombie **177** E4
Old Dailly **122** D1
Old Dalby **82** B5
Old Dam **93** F5
Old Deer **179** E3
Old Dilton **25** F3
Old Down *S.Glos.* **39** F4
Old Down *Som.* **24** D2
Old Edlington **94** C3
Old Eldon **120** B5
Old Ellerby **105** D4
Old Felixstowe **61** E4
Old Fletton **69** G4
Old Ford **44** C4

Old Glossop **93** E3
Old Goginan **62** C4
Old Goole **103** G5
Old Gore **53** F5
Old Grimsby **4** A1
Old Hall **96** C1
Old Hall Green **58** B5
Old Hall Street **87** E2
Old Harlow **45** D1
Old Heath **60** B5
Old Heathfield **18** A1
Old Hill **66** B4
Old Hurst **70** B5
Old Hutton **107** G4
Old Kea **4** C5
Old Kilpatrick **141** F2
Old Kinnernie **169** E4
Old Knebworth **58** A5
Old Leake **84** C2
Old Leslie **168** C2
Old Malton **112** B5
Old Milton **14** B3
Old Milverton **55** E1
Old Montsale **46** D3
Old Netley **15** D1
Old Newton **60** B1
Old Philpstoun **143** E2
Old Poltalloch **148** A4
Old Radnor (Pencraig)
  52 B2
Old Rattray **179** F2
Old Rayne **169** D2
Old Romney **19** F1
Old Scone **151** G2
Old Shields **142** C2
Old Sodbury **39** G4
Old Somerby **83** E4
Old Stratford **56** C3
Old Sunderlandwick
  104 C2
Old Swarland **129** D1
Old Swinford **66** B4
Old Thirsk **110** D4
Old Town *Cumb.* **107** G4
Old Town *I.o.S.* **4** B1
Old Town Farm **128** A2
Old Tupton **81** E1
Old Warden **57** G3
Old Weston **69** F5
Old Windsor **43** E5
Old Wives Lees **32** C3
Old Woking **29** E2
Old Woodhall **84** A1
Old Woods **78** B5
Oldberrow **54** D1
Oldborough **10** A3
Oldbury *Kent* **31** E3
Oldbury *Shrop.* **65** G3
Oldbury *W.Mid.* **66** B4
Oldbury *Warks.* **67** F3
Oldbury Naite **39** F3
Oldbury on the Hill **40** A4
Oldbury-on-Severn **39** F3
Oldcastle *Bridgend* **37** F5
Oldcastle *Mon.* **52** C5
Oldcastle Heath **78** B3
Oldcotes **94** C4
Oldcroft **39** F2
Oldeamere **70** B3
Oldfield **54** B1
Oldford **25** E2
Oldhall *Aber.* **168** B5
Oldhall *High.* **187** E3
Oldham **92** D2
Oldham Edge **92** D2
Oldhamstocks **145** E2
Oldland **39** F4
Oldmeldrum **169** F2
Oldmill **168** C4
Oldpark **65** F2
Oldridge **10** B3
Oldshore Beg **184** A3
Oldshoremore **184** B3
Oldstead **111** E5
Oldtown **174** B1
Oldtown of Aigas **174** A5
Oldtown of Ord **177** E4
Oldwalls **36** A3
Oldways End **22** B5
Oldwhat **179** D2
Oldwich Lane **67** E5
Olgrinmore **186** D3
Oliver **134** C3
Oliver's Battery **27** F5
Ollaberry **191** F2
Ollerton *Ches.E.* **92** B5
Ollerton *Notts.* **82** B1
Ollerton *Shrop.* **78** D5
Olmstead Green **59** E3

Olney **57** D2
Olrig House **187** D2
Olton **66** D4
Olveston **39** F4
Ombersley **54** A1
Ompton **82** B1
Onchan **80** B3
Onecote **80** B2
Onehouse **60** B2
Ongar Hill **85** D5
Ongar Street **52** C1
Onibury **65** D5
Onich (Omhanaich)
  156 C3
Onllwyn **37** E1
Onneley **79** E3
Onslow Green **45** F1
Onslow Village **29** E3
Opinan *High.* **180** A5
Opinan *High.* **172** A2
Orange Lane **145** E5
Orbliston **176** C4
Orbost **170** B5
Orby **84** C1
Orcadia **140** C3
Orchard **140** C3
Orchard Portman **23** F5
Orcheston **26** B3
Orcop **53** D5
Orcop Hill **53** D5
Ord **163** F2
Ordhead **169** D3
Ordie **168** B4
Ordiequish **176** C4
Ordsall **95** D5
Ore **18** D2
Oreham Common **17** E2
Oreston **8** B2
Oreton **65** F5
Orford *Suff.* **61** F3
Orford *Warr.* **92** A3
Organford **13** F3
Orgreave **66** D1
Orkney Islands **190** B3
Orlestone **32** B5
Orleton *Here.* **53** F1
Orleton *Worcs.* **53** F1
Orleton Common **53** D1
Orlingbury **69** D5
Ormesby **111** E1
Ormesby St. Margaret
  87 F3
Ormesby St. Michael
  87 F4
Ormidale **140** B1
Ormiscaig **180** A5
Ormiston **144** B3
Ormlie **186** D2
Ormsaigmore **155** D3
Ormsary **139** F2
Ormskirk **91** F2
Oronsay **138** B1
Orpington **31** D2
Orrell *Gt.Man.* **91** G2
Orrell *Mersey.* **91** F3
Orrisdale **98** B2
Orrok House **169** G3
Orroland **116** A2
Orsett **45** F4
Orsett Heath **45** F4
Orslow **66** A1
Orston **82** C3
Orton *Cumb.* **108** B2
Orton *Northants.* **68** D5
Orton Longueville **69** G3
Orton Rigg **117** G1
Orton Waterville **69** G3
Orton-on-the-Hill **67** F2
Orwell **58** B2
Osbaldeston **100** C4
Osbaldwick **103** F2
Osbaston *Leics.* **67** G2
Osbaston *Shrop.* **78** A5
Osbaston *Tel. & W.* **65** E1
Osbaston Hollow **67** G2
Osborne **15** E3
Osbournby **83** F4
Oscroft **78** C1
Ose **170** C5
Osgathorpe **67** G1
Osgodby *Lincs.* **96** A3
Osgodby *N.Yorks.* **103** F3
Osgodby *N.Yorks.* **113** D4
Oskaig **162** D1
Osleston **80** D4
Osmaston *Derby* **81** E4
Osmaston *Derbys.* **80** C3
Osmington **12** D4
Osmington Mills **12** D4

Osmondthorpe **102** C4
Osmotherley **111** D3
Osnaburgh (Dairsie)
  152 C3
Ospringe **32** C2
Ossett **102** B5
Ossett Street Side **102** B5
Ossington **82** C1
Ostend **46** C3
Osterley **44** A5
Oswaldkirk **111** F5
Oswaldtwistle **100** D5
Oswestry **77** F5
Oteley **78** B4
Otford **31** E3
Otham **31** G3
Otherton **66** B1
Othery **24** A4
Otley *Suff.* **60** D2
Otley *W.Yorks.* **102** B3
Otter **140** A2
Otterbourne **27** F5
Otterburn *N.Yorks.*
  101 E2
Otterburn *Northumb.*
  128 A2
Otterburn Camp **128** A2
Otterden Place **32** B3
Otterham **6** B1
Otterham Quay **32** A2
Otterhampton **23** F3
Ottershaw **29** F1
Otterswick **191** G2
Otterton **11** D4
Otterwood **14** D2
Ottery St. Mary **11** D3
Ottinge **33** D4
Ottringham **105** E5
Oughterby **117** F1
Oughtershaw **109** D4
Oughterside **117** E2
Oughtibridge **94** A3
Oulston **111** E5
Oulton *Cumb.* **117** F1
Oulton *Norf.* **86** C3
Oulton *Staffs.* **79** G4
Oulton *Staffs.* **79** E5
Oulton *Suff.* **73** G2
Oulton *W.Yorks.* **102** C5
Oulton Broad **73** G2
Oulton Grange **79** G4
Oulton Street **86** C3
Oultoncross **79** G4
Oundle **69** F4
Ousby **118** C4
Ousdale **183** F2
Ousden **59** F2
Ousefleet **104** A5
Ouston *Dur.* **120** B2
Ouston *Northumb.*
  128 C4
Out Newton **105** F5
Out Rawcliffe **100** A3
Outcast **107** E5
Outchester **137** F3
Outgate **107** E3
Outhgill **108** C2
Outlands **79** E5
Outlane **93** E1
Outwell **70** C1
Outwood *Surr.* **30** C4
Outwood *W.Yorks.*
  102 C5
Outwoods **65** G1
Ouzlewell Green **102** C5
Ovenden **101** G5
Over *C. & W.Ches.* **78** D1
Over *Cambs.* **70** B5
Over *Glos.* **40** A1
Over *S.Glos.* **39** G4
Over Burrows **81** D4
Over Compton **12** B1
Over Dinsdale **110** C1
Over End **93** G5
Over Green **67** D3
Over Haddon **80** D1
Over Hulton **92** A2
Over Kellet **100** B3
Over Kiddington **55** G5
Over Monnow **39** D2
Over Norton **55** F5
Over Peover **92** B5
Over Rankeilour **152** B3
Over Silton **111** D3
Over Stowey **23** E4
Over Stratton **12** A1
Over Tabley **92** B4
Over Wallop **27** D4

Over Whitacre 67 E3
Over Winchendon (Upper Winchendon) 42 C1
Over Worton 55 G5
Overbister 190 C2
Overbrae 178 D2
Overbury 54 B4
Overcombe 12 C4
Overgreen 94 A5
Overleigh 24 B4
Overpool 91 E5
Overscaig Hotel 181 G2
Overseal 67 E1
Overslade 67 G5
Oversland 32 C3
Oversley Green 54 C2
Overstone 56 D1
Overstrand 86 D1
Overthorpe 55 G3
Overton Aber. 169 E3
Overton Aberdeen 169 F3
Overton C. & W.Ches. 91 G5
Overton Hants. 27 G3
Overton Lancs. 100 A2
Overton N.Yorks. 103 E2
Overton Shrop. 65 E5
Overton Swan. 36 A4
Overton W.Yorks. 93 G1
Overton (Owrtyn) Wrex. 78 A3
Overton Bridge 78 A3
Overtown Lancs. 108 B5
Overtown N.Lan. 142 C4
Overtown Swin. 41 D5
Overy 42 A1
Oving Bucks. 56 C5
Oving W.Suss. 16 B3
Ovingdean 17 F3
Ovingham 119 G1
Ovington Dur. 110 A1
Ovington Essex 59 F3
Ovington Hants. 27 G4
Ovington Norf. 86 A5
Ovington Northumb. 119 G1
Ower Hants. 14 C1
Ower Hants. 15 D2
Owermoigne 13 D4
Owlpen 39 G3
Owl's Green 61 D1
Owlswick 42 C2
Owmby 96 A2
Owmby-by-Spital 96 A4
Owslebury 27 G5
Owston 68 C2
Owston Ferry 95 F3
Owstwick 105 E4
Owthorpe 82 B4
Oxborough 71 F2
Oxcliffe Hill 100 A1
Oxcombe 96 D5
Oxen End 59 E5
Oxen Park 107 E4
Oxencombe 10 B4
Oxenhall 53 G5
Oxenholme 107 G3
Oxenhope 101 G4
Oxenpill 24 B3
Oxenton 54 B4
Oxenwood 27 E2
Oxford 42 A2
Oxhey 44 A3
Oxhill 55 F3
Oxley 66 B2
Oxley Green 46 C1
Oxley's Green 18 B1
Oxnam 136 B5
Oxnead 86 D3
Oxnop Ghyll 109 E3
Oxshott 29 G1
Oxspring 93 G2
Oxted 30 C3
Oxton Mersey. 91 E4
Oxton Notts. 82 B2
Oxton Sc.Bord. 144 B4
Oxwich 36 A4
Oxwich Green 36 A4
Oxwick 86 A3
Oykel Bridge 181 F4
Oyne 169 D2
Ozleworth 39 G3

P
Pabbay 188 B1
Packington 67 F1

Packwood 67 D5
Padanaram 160 C4
Padbury 56 C4
Paddington 44 B4
Paddlesworth 33 D4
Paddock 32 B3
Paddock Wood 31 F4
Paddockhaugh 176 B4
Paddockhole 126 A3
Paddolgreen 78 C4
Padeswood 77 F1
Padfield 93 E3
Padiham 101 D4
Padside 102 A2
Padstow 4 D2
Padworth 28 B1
Paganhill 40 A2
Pagham 16 A4
Paglesham Churchend 46 C3
Paglesham Eastend 46 C3
Paignton 9 E1
Pailton 67 G4
Paine's Corner 18 B1
Painscastle 52 A3
Painshawfield 119 G1
Painswick 40 A2
Paisley 141 F3
Pakefield 73 G2
Pakenham 60 A1
Pale 76 C1
Palehouse Common 17 G2
Palestine 27 D3
Paley Street 43 D5
Palgowan 123 F2
Palgrave 72 C4
Pallinsburn House 136 C3
Palmarsh 32 D5
Palmers Cross 29 F3
Palmers Green 44 C3
Palmerscross 176 B3
Palmerston 38 A5
Palnackie 124 C5
Palnure 123 F4
Palterton 81 F1
Pamber End 28 B2
Pamber Green 28 B2
Pamber Heath 28 B1
Pamington 54 B4
Pamphill 13 F2
Pampisford 58 C3
Panborough 24 B3
Panbride 153 D1
Pancrasweek 20 C5
Pancross 22 D1
Pandy Gwyn. 62 C2
Pandy Mon. 52 C5
Pandy Powys 63 F2
Pandy Wrex. 77 E4
Pandy Tudur 76 B1
Pandy'r Capel 77 F2
Panfield 59 F5
Pangbourne 42 B5
Pannal 92 B3
Pannal Ash 102 B2
Panshanger 44 B1
Pant 77 F5
Pant Glas 75 D3
Pant Gwyn 76 B5
Pant Mawr 63 E4
Pantasaph 90 C5
Panteg 38 C3
Pantglas 63 D3
Pantgwyn Carmar. 50 B5
Pantgwyn Cere. 49 F3
Pant-lasau 36 C2
Panton 96 B5
Pant-pastynog 76 D1
Pantperthog 62 D2
Pant-y-dwr 63 F5
Pantyffordd 77 F2
Pant-y-ffridd 64 A2
Pantyffynnon 36 C1
Pantygasseg 38 B3
Pantygelli 38 C1
Pantymwyn 77 E1
Panxworth 87 E4
Papa Stour 191 E3
Papa Westray 190 B1
Papcastle 117 E3
Papple 5 E4
Papplewick 81 G2
Par 5 E4
Parbold 91 F1

Parbrook Som. 24 C4
Parbrook W.Suss. 29 F5
Parc 76 B4
Parcllyn 49 F2
Parcrhydderch 50 C2
Parc-Seymour 38 D3
Parc-y-rhôs 50 B3
Pardshaw 117 D4
Parham 61 E1
Parish Holm 133 F3
Park 177 E4
Park Close 101 E3
Park Corner E.Suss. 31 E5
Park Corner Oxon. 42 B4
Park End Northumb. 128 A4
Park End Staffs. 79 E2
Park End Worcs. 65 G5
Park Gate Hants. 15 E2
Park Gate W.Yorks. 102 A3
Park Gate W.Yorks. 93 G1
Park Gate Worcs. 66 B5
Park Green 60 C1
Park Hill 94 A4
Park Lane 78 B3
Park Langley 30 C2
Park Street 44 A2
Parkend Cumb. 117 G3
Parkend Glos. 39 F2
Parker's Green 31 F4
Parkeston 60 D4
Parkfield Cornw. 6 D4
Parkfield S.Glos. 39 F5
Parkfield W.Mid. 66 B3
Parkford 160 C4
Parkgate C. & W.Ches. 91 D5
Parkgate D. & G. 125 E2
Parkgate Kent 32 A5
Parkgate S.Yorks. 94 B3
Parkgate Surr. 30 B4
Parkham 21 D3
Parkham Ash 21 D3
Parkhead 142 A3
Parkhill Angus 161 E5
Parkhill P. & K. 159 G5
Parkhouse 39 D2
Parkhurst 15 D3
Parkmill 36 B4
Parkmore 176 C5
Parkneuk 161 F2
Parkside 78 A2
Parkstone 13 G3
Parkway 24 C5
Parley Cross 13 G3
Parley Green 14 A3
Parlington 102 D4
Parracombe 21 G1
Parrog 44 A3
Parson Cross 94 A3
Parson Drove 70 B2
Parsonage Green 45 F1
Parsonby 117 E3
Partick 141 G3
Partington 92 B3
Partney 84 C1
Parton Cumb. 116 C4
Parton D. & G. 124 A3
Partridge Green 17 D2
Parwich 80 C2
Paslow Wood Common 45 E2
Passenham 56 C4
Passfield 28 D4
Passingford Bridge 45 E3
Paston 87 E2
Paston Street 87 E2
Pasturefields 79 G5
Patchacott 7 E1
Patcham 17 F3
Patchetts Green 44 A3
Patching 16 C3
Patchole 21 G1
Patchway 39 F4
Pateley Bridge 102 A1
Path of Condie 151 F3
Pathe 24 A4
Pathfinder Village 10 B3
Pathhead Aber. 161 E1
Pathhead E.Ayr. 133 E4
Pathhead Fife 152 A5
Pathhead Midloth. 144 A3
Pathlow 55 D2
Patmore Heath 58 C5
Patna 132 C4
Patney 26 B2
Patrick 98 A3

Patrick Brompton 110 B3
Patrington 105 F5
Patrington Haven 105 F5
Patrishow 52 B5
Patrixbourne 33 D3
Patterdale 117 G5
Pattingham 66 A3
Pattishall 56 B2
Pattiswick 59 G5
Paul 2 B4
Paulerspury 56 C3
Paull 105 D5
Paull Holme 105 D5
Paul's Green 2 D3
Paulton 25 D2
Pauperhaugh 128 C2
Pave Lane 65 G1
Pavenham 57 E2
Pawlett 24 A3
Pawston 136 C3
Paxford 55 D4
Paxhill Park 17 F1
Paxton 145 G4
Payden Street 32 B3
Payhembury 11 D2
Paythorne 101 E2
Peacehaven 17 G3
Peacemarsh 25 F5
Peachley 54 A2
Peak Dale 93 E5
Peak Forest 93 F5
Peakirk 69 G2
Pean Hill 32 D2
Pear Tree 81 E4
Pearsie 160 C4
Pearson's Green 31 F4
Peartree 44 B1
Peartree Green Essex 45 E3
Peartree Green Here. 53 F4
Pease Pottage 30 B5
Peasedown St. John 25 E2
Peasehill 81 F3
Peaseland Green 86 B4
Peasemore 41 G5
Peasenhall 61 E1
Peaslake 29 F3
Peasley Cross 91 G3
Peasmarsh E.Suss. 19 D1
Peasmarsh Surr. 29 E3
Peaston 144 B3
Peastonbank 144 B3
Peat Inn 152 C4
Peathill 179 E1
Peatling Magna 68 A3
Peatling Parva 68 A4
Peaton 65 E4
Pebble Coombe 30 B3
Pebmarsh 59 G4
Pebworth 54 D3
Pecket Well 101 F5
Peckforton 78 C2
Peckham 44 C5
Peckleton 67 G2
Pedham 87 E4
Pedmore 66 B4
Pedwell 24 B4
Peebles 143 G5
Peel I.o.M. 98 A3
Peel Lancs. 99 G4
Peening Quarter 19 D1
Peggs Green 67 G1
Pegsdon 57 G4
Pegswood 129 E2
Pegwell 33 F2
Peinchorran 162 D1
Peinlich 170 B4
Pelcomb 34 C1
Pelcomb Bridge 34 C1
Pelcomb Cross 34 C1
Peldon 46 C1
Pellon 101 G5
Pelsall 66 C2
Pelton 120 B2
Pelutho 117 F2
Pelynt 5 G4
Pemberton 91 G2
Pembrey (Pen-bre) 36 A2
Pembridge 52 C2
Pembroke (Penfro) 34 C2
Pembroke Dock (Doc Penfro) 34 C2
Pembury 31 F4
Penallt 39 E1
Penally 35 E3

Penalt 53 E5
Penare 5 D5
Penarran 64 A4
Penarth 38 A5
Pen-bont Rhydybeddau 62 C4
Penboyr 49 G4
Penbryn 49 F2
Pencader 50 A4
Pen-cae 50 A2
Pen-cae-cwm 76 C1
Pencaenewydd 74 D3
Pencaitland 144 B3
Pencarnisiog 88 B5
Pencarreg 50 B3
Pencarrow 5 F1
Pencelli 51 G5
Pen-clawdd 36 B3
Pencoed 37 F4
Pencombe 53 E2
Pencoyd 53 E5
Pencraig Here. 53 E5
Pencraig Powys 76 D5
Pendeen 2 A3
Penderyn 37 F2
Pendine (Pentywyn) 35 F2
Pendlebury 92 B2
Pendleton 101 D4
Pendock 53 G4
Pendoggett 5 E2
Pendomer 12 B1
Pendoylan 37 G5
Penegoes 63 D2
Penelewey 4 C5
Pen-ffordd 49 D5
Pengam 38 A3
Penge 44 C5
Pengenffordd 52 A5
Pengorffwysfa 88 C3
Pengover Green 5 G3
Pen-groes-oped 38 C2
Pengwern 90 B5
Penhale 3 D5
Penhallow 4 B4
Penhalvean 3 E3
Penhe.g 62 C3
Penhill 41 D4
Penhow 38 D3
Penhurst 18 B2
Peniarth 62 C2
Penicuik 143 G3
Peniel 50 A5
Penifiler 171 D5
Peninver 130 C3
Penisa'r Waun 75 E1
Penisarcwm 63 G1
Penishawain 51 G4
Penistone 93 G2
Penjerrick 3 E3
Penketh 91 G4
Penkill 122 D1
Penkridge 66 B1
Penlean 6 C1
Penley 78 B4
Penllech 74 B4
Penllergaer 36 C3
Pen-llyn I.o.A. 88 B4
Penllyn V. of Glam. 37 F5
Pen-lôn 74 D1
Penmachno 76 A2
Penmaen 36 B4
Penmaenan 89 F5
Penmaenmawr 89 F5
Penmaenpool (Llyn Penmaen) 62 C1
Penmaen-Rhôs 89 G5
Penmark 23 D1
Penmon 89 E4
Penmorfa 75 E3
Penmynydd 88 D5
Penn Bucks. 43 E3
Penn W.Mid. 66 B3
Penn Street 43 E3
Pennal 62 C2
Pennal-isaf 62 D2
Pennan 178 D1
Pennance 4 B5
Pennant Cere. 50 B1
Pennant Powys 63 E3
Pennant Melangell 76 D5
Pennar 34 C2
Pennard 36 B4
Pennerley 64 C3
Penninghame 123 E4
Pennington Cumb. 107 D5
Pennington Hants. 14 C3
Pennington Green 92 A2

Pennorth 52 A5
Pennsylvania 39 G5
Penny Bridge 107 E4
Pennycross 8 A2
Pennyfuir 148 A1
Pennygate 87 E3
Pennyghael 147 E2
Pennyglen 132 A4
Pennygown 155 F5
Pennymoor 10 B1
Penny's Green 72 C2
Pennyvenie 132 C5
Penparc Cere. 49 F3
Penparc Pembs. 48 B3
Penparcau 62 B4
Penpedairheol 38 C2
Penpethy 5 E1
Penpillick 5 G4
Penpol 3 F3
Penpoll 5 F4
Penponds 2 D3
Penpont D. & G. 124 C1
Penpont Powys 51 F3
Penprysg 37 F4
Penquit 8 C2
Penrherber 49 F4
Penrhiw 49 F3
Penrhiwceiber 37 G3
Penrhiwgoch 36 B1
Penrhiw-llan 49 G3
Penrhiw-pâl 49 G3
Penrhiwtyn 36 D3
Penrhos Gwyn. 74 C4
Penrhos I.o.A. 88 A4
Penrhos Mon. 38 D1
Penrhos Powys 37 E1
Penrhos-garnedd 89 D5
Penrhyn Bay (Bae Penrhyn) 89 G4
Penrhyn-coch 62 C4
Penrhyndeudraeth 75 F4
Penrhyn-side 89 G4
Penrhys 37 G3
Penrice 36 A4
Penrith 118 B5
Penrose Cornw. 4 C2
Penrose Cornw. 5 G1
Penruddock 118 A5
Penryn 3 E3
Pensarn Carmar. 36 A1
Pensarn Conwy 90 A5
Pen-sarn Gwyn. 75 E5
Pen-sarn Gwyn. 74 D3
Pensax 53 G1
Pensby 91 D4
Penselwood 25 E4
Pensford 24 D1
Pensham 54 B3
Penshaw 120 C2
Penshurst 31 E4
Pensilva 5 G3
Pensnett 66 B4
Penston 144 B2
Pentewan 5 E5
Pentir 75 E1
Pentire 4 B3
Pentireglaze 4 D2
Pentlepoir 35 E2
Pentlow 59 G3
Pentlow Street 59 G3
Pentney 71 F1
Penton Mewsey 27 E3
Pentonville 44 C4
Pentraeth 88 D5
Pentre Powys 75 D3
Pentre Powys 63 G4
Pentre Powys 52 B5
Pentre Powys 64 B3
Pentre Powys 64 A4
Pentre R.C.T. 37 F3
Pentre Shrop. 64 C1
Pentre Shrop. 64 C5
Pentre Wrex. 77 F3
Pentre Wrex. 78 A3
Pentre Berw 88 C5
Pentre Ffwrndan 91 E5
Pentre Galar 49 E4
Pentre Gwenlais 36 C1
Pentre Gwynfryn 75 E5
Pentre Halkyn 90 D5
Pentre Isaf 76 B1
Pentre Llanrhaeadr 77 D1
Pentre Maelor 78 A3
Pentre Meyrick 37 F5
Pentre Poeth 37 C3
Pentre Saron 76 D1
Pentre-bach Cere. 50 B3
Pentrebach M.Tyd. 37 G2

Pentre-bach *Powys* 51 F4
Pentrebach *R.C.T.* 37 G4
Pentrebach *Swan.* 36 B2
Pentre-bont 76 A2
Pentre-bwlch 77 E3
Pentrecagal 49 G3
Pentre-celyn *Denb.* 77 E2
Pentre-celyn *Powys* 63 E2
Pentre-chwyth 36 C3
Pentreclwydau 37 E2
Pentre-cwrt 49 G4
Pentre-Dolau-Honddu 51 F3
Pentredwr *Denb.* 77 E3
Pentre-dwr *Swan.* 36 C3
Pentrefelin *Carmar.* 50 C5
Pentrefelin *Cere.* 50 C3
Pentrefelin *Conwy* 89 G5
Pentrefelin *Gwyn.* 75 E4
Pentrefelin *Powys* 77 E5
Pentrefoelas 76 B2
Pentregat 49 G2
Pentreheyling 64 B3
Pentre-llwyn-llŵyd 51 F2
Pentre-llyn 62 C5
Pentre-llyn-cymmer 76 C2
Pentre-piod 76 B4
Pentre-poeth 38 B4
Pentre'r beirdd 64 A1
Pentre'r Felin 76 B1
Pentre'r-felin 51 F4
Pentre-tafarn-y-fedw 76 B1
Pentre-ty-gwyn 51 E4
Pentrich 81 E2
Pentridge 13 G1
Pentwyn *Caerp.* 38 A2
Pen-twyn *Caerp.* 38 B2
Pentwyn *Cardiff* 38 B4
Pen-twyn *Mon.* 39 E2
Pentwyn-mawr 38 A3
Pentyrch 38 A4
Penuwch 50 B1
Penwithick 5 E4
Penwood 27 F1
Penwortham 100 B5
Penwortham Lane 100 B5
Penwyllt 37 E1
Pen-y-banc 50 C5
Pen-y-bont *Carmar.* 51 D4
Pen-y-bont *Carmar.* 49 G5
Pen-y-bont *Powys* 63 G1
Pen-y-bont *Powys* 77 F5
Penybont *Powys* 52 A1
Penybontfawr 77 D5
Penybryn *Caerp.* 38 A3
Pen-y-bryn *Gwyn.* 62 C1
Pen-y-bryn *Pembs.* 49 E3
Pen-y-bryn *Wrex.* 77 F3
Pen-y-cae *Powys* 37 E1
Penycae *Wrex.* 77 F3
Pen-y-cae-mawr 38 D3
Pen-y-cefn 90 C5
Pen-y-clawdd 38 D2
Pen-y-coedcae 37 G4
Penycwm 48 B5
Pen-y-Darren 37 G2
Pen-y-fai 37 E4
Penyffordd *Flints.* 78 A1
Penyffordd *Flints.* 90 C4
Penyffridd 75 E2
Pen-y-gaer 52 A5
Pen-y-garn *Carmar.* 50 B4
Pen-y-garn *Cere.* 62 C4
Penygarn *Torfaen* 38 B2
Penygarnedd 77 E5
Pen-y-garreg 51 G3
Pen-y-Graig *Gwyn.* 74 B4
Penygraig *R.C.T.* 37 G3
Penygroes *Carmar.* 36 B1
Penygroes *Gwyn.* 75 D2
Pen-y-Gwryd Hotel 75 F2
Pen-y-lan 38 C2
Pen-y-Mynydd *Carmar.* 36 A2
Penymynydd *Flints.* 78 A1
Pen-y-park 77 F1
Pen-y-Parc 52 B3
Pen-yr-englyn 37 F3
Pickering Nook 120 A2
Penyrheol *Swan.* 36 B3
Penyrheol *Mon.* 38 D1
Penywaun 37 F2
Penzance 2 B3
Penzance Heliport 2 B3
Peopleton 54 B2
Peover Heath 92 B5
Peper Harow 29 E2
Peplow 78 D5
Pepper Arden 110 B2
Pepper's Green 45 F1
Perceton 141 E5
Percie 168 C2
Percyhorner 179 E1
Perham Down 27 D3
Periton 22 C3
Perivale 44 A4
Perkhill 168 C4
Perkins Beach 64 C2
Perkin's Village 10 D3
Perlethorpe 94 D5
Perran Downs 2 C3
Perranarworthal 3 E3
Perranporth 4 B4
Perranuthnoe 2 C4
Perranzabuloe 4 B4
Perrott's Brook 40 C2
Perry Barr 66 C3
Perry Crofts 67 E2
Perry Green *Essex* 59 G5
Perry Green *Herts.* 44 D1
Perry Green *Wilts.* 40 B4
Perry Street 45 F5
Perrymead 25 E1
Pershall 79 F5
Pershore 54 B3
Persie House 159 G4
Pert 161 E3
Pertenhall 57 F1
Perth (Peairt) 151 G2
Perthcelyn 37 G3
Perthy 78 A4
Perton 66 A3
Pestalozzi Children's Village 18 C2
Peter Tavy 7 F3
Peterborough 69 G3
Peterburn 172 A1
Peterchurch 52 C4
Peterculter 169 F4
Peterhead 179 G3
Peterlee 120 D3
Peter's Green 44 A1
Peters Marland 21 E4
Petersfield 28 C5
Petersfinger 26 C5
Peterstone Wentlooge 38 B4
Peterston-super-Ely 37 G5
Peterstow 53 E5
Petham 32 D3
Petrockstowe 21 F5
Pett 19 D2
Pettaugh 60 C2
Pettenil Green 118 A3
Pettinain 143 D5
Pettistree 61 D2
Petton *Devon* 22 D5
Petton *Shrop.* 78 B5
Petts Wood 30 D2
Petty 169 E1
Petty France 39 E2
Pettycur 143 G1
Pettymuick 169 G2
Petworth 29 E5
Pevensey 18 B3
Pevensey Bay 18 B3
Peverell 8 A2
Pewsey 26 C1
Pheasant's Hill 42 C4
Phesdo 161 E2
Philham 20 C3
Philiphaugh 135 F3
Phillack 2 C3
Philleigh 3 F2
Philpstoun 143 E2
Phocle Green 53 F5
Phoenix Green 28 C2
Phones 166 B5
Phorp 175 G4
Pibsbury 24 B5
Pica 116 D4
Piccadilly Corner 73 D3
Pickerells 45 E2
Pickering 111 G4
Pickering Nook 120 A2
Picket Piece 27 E1
Picket Post 14 A2
Pickford Green 67 E4
Pickhill 110 C3
Picklescott 64 D3
Pickletillem 152 C2
Pickmere 92 A5
Pickney 23 E5
Pickston 151 E2
Pickup Bank 100 D5
Pickwell *Devon* 21 E1
Pickwell *Leics.* 68 C1
Pickworth *Lincs.* 83 F4
Pickworth *Rut.* 69 E1
Picton *C. & W.Ches.* 91 F5
Picton *N.Yorks.* 110 D2
Piddinghoe 17 G3
Piddington *Bucks.* 42 D3
Piddington *Northants.* 56 D2
Piddington *Oxon.* 42 B1
Piddlehinton 12 D3
Piddletrenthide 12 D3
Pidley 70 B5
Piercebridge 110 B1
Pierowall 190 B1
Pigdon 121 D3
Pike Hill 101 E4
Pikehall 80 C2
Pikeshill 14 B2
Pilgrims Hatch 45 E3
Pilham 95 F3
Pill 39 E5
Pillaton *Cornw.* 7 D4
Pillaton *Staffs.* 66 B1
Pillerton Hersey 55 E3
Pillerton Priors 55 E3
Pilleth 52 B1
Pilley *Hants.* 14 C3
Pilley *S.Yorks.* 94 A2
Pilling 100 A3
Pilling Lane 99 G3
Pillowell 39 F2
Pilning 39 E4
Pilsbury 80 C1
Pilsdon 12 A3
Pilsgate 69 F2
Pilsley *Derbys.* 81 F1
Pilsley *Derbys.* 93 G5
Pilson Green 87 E4
Piltdown 17 G1
Pilton *Devon* 21 F2
Pilton *Northants.* 69 F4
Pilton *Rut.* 69 E2
Pilton *Som.* 24 C3
Pilton *Swan.* 36 A4
Pilton Green 36 A4
Pimhole 92 C1
Pimlico 43 F2
Pimperne 13 F2
Pin Mill 60 D4
Pinchbeck 84 A5
Pinchbeck Bars 84 A5
Pinchbeck West 84 A5
Pincheon Green 95 D1
Pinchinthorpe 111 E1
Pindon End 56 C3
Pinehurst 40 D4
Pinfold 91 E1
Pinged 36 A2
Pinhay 11 G3
Pinhoe 10 C3
Pinkneys Green 43 D4
Pinley Green 55 E1
Pinminnoch 122 C1
Pinmore 122 D1
Pinn 11 E4
Pinner 44 A4
Pinner Green 44 A3
Pinvin 54 B3
Pinwherry 122 C2
Pinxton 81 F2
Pipe & Lyde 53 E3
Pipe Gate 79 E3
Pipe Ridware 66 C1
Pipehill 66 C2
Piperhall 140 B4
Piperhill 175 E4
Pipers Pool 5 G1
Pipewell 68 D4
Pippacott 21 F2
Pipton 52 A4
Pirbright 29 E2
Pirnmill 139 G5
Pirton *Herts.* 57 G4
Pirton *Worcs.* 54 A3
Pisgah 150 C4
Pishill 42 C4
Pistyll 74 C3
Pitagowan 158 D3
Pitblae 179 E1
Pitcairngreen 151 F2
Pitcairns 151 F3
Pitcaple 169 E2
Pitch Green 42 C2
Pitch Place *Surr.* 29 E2
Pitch Place *Surr.* 29 D4
Pitchcombe 40 A2
Pitchcott 56 C5
Pitchford 65 E2
Pitcombe 25 D4
Pitcot 37 E5
Pitcox 144 D2
Pitcur 152 A1
Pitfichie 169 D3
Pitgrudy 182 C1
Pitinnan 169 E1
Pitkennedy 160 D4
Pitkevy 152 A4
Pitlessie 152 B4
Pitlochry 159 E4
Pitman's Corner 60 C1
Pitmedden 169 F2
Pitminster 11 F1
Pitmuies 160 D4
Pitmunie 169 D3
Pitnacree 159 E4
Pitney 24 B5
Pitroddie 152 A2
Pitscottie 152 C3
Pitsea 45 G4
Pitsford 56 B1
Pitsford Hill 23 D4
Pitstone 43 E1
Pitt *Devon* 10 D1
Pitt *Hants.* 27 F5
Pittendreich 176 A3
Pittentrail 182 C4
Pittenweem 152 D4
Pitteuchar 152 A5
Pittington 120 C3
Pittodrie House 169 D2
Pitton *Swan.* 36 A4
Pitton *Wilts.* 26 D5
Pittulie 179 E1
Pittville 54 B5
Pity Me 120 B3
Pityme 4 D2
Pixey Green 72 D4
Pixley 53 F4
Place Newton 112 B5
Plaidy 177 G4
Plain Dealings 35 D4
Plainfield 128 B1
Plains 142 B3
Plainsfield 23 E4
Plaish 65 E2
Plaistow *Gt.Lon.* 44 C4
Plaistow *W.Suss.* 29 F4
Plaitford 14 B1
Plaitford Green 27 D5
Plas 38 A2
Plas Gwynant 75 F2
Plas Isaf 77 D3
Plas Llwyd 90 A5
Plas Llwyngwern 63 D2
Plas Llysyn 63 F3
Plas Nantyr 77 E4
Plashett 35 F2
Plasisaf 76 C1
Plas-rhiw-Saeson 63 F2
Plastow Green 27 G1
Plas-yn-Cefn 90 B5
Platt 31 F3
Platt Bridge 92 A2
Platt Lane 78 C4
Platt's Heath 32 A3
Plawsworth 120 B3
Plaxtol 31 F3
Play Hatch 42 C5
Playden 19 E1
Playford 60 D3
Playing Place 4 C5
Playley Green 53 G4
Plealey 64 D2
Plean 142 C1
Pleasance 152 A3
Pleasant Valley 58 D4
Pleasington 100 C5
Pleasley 81 G1
Pleasleyhill 81 G1
Pleck *Dorset* 12 D1
Pleck *W.Mid.* 66 B3
Pledgdon Green 59 D5
Pledwick 94 A1
Plemstall 91 F5
Plenmeller 118 D1
Pleshey 45 F1
Plockton (Am Ploc) 163 G1
Plomer's Hill 43 D3
Plot Gate 24 C4
Plough Hill 67 F3
Plowden 64 C4
Ploxgreen 64 C2
Pluckley 32 B4
Pluckley Thorne 32 B4
Plucks Gutter 33 E2
Plumbland 117 E3
Plumbley 94 B4
Plumley 92 B5
Plumpton *Cumb.* 118 A4
Plumpton *E.Suss.* 17 F2
Plumpton *Northants.* 56 B3
Plumpton Green 17 F2
Plumpton Head 118 B4
Plumstead *Gt.Lon.* 45 D5
Plumstead *Norf.* 86 C2
Plumtree 82 B4
Plungar 82 C4
Plush 12 D2
Plusha 5 G1
Plushabridge 6 D3
Plwmp 49 G2
Plym Bridge 8 B2
Plymouth 8 A2
Plymouth City Airport 8 B1
Plympton 8 B2
Plymstock 8 B2
Plymtree 11 D2
Pockley 111 F4
Pocklington 104 A3
Pockthorpe 86 B3
Pocombe Bridge 10 B3
Pode Hole 84 A5
Podimore 24 C5
Podington 57 E1
Podmore 79 E4
Podsmead 40 A2
Poffley End 41 F1
Point Clear 47 D1
Pointon 83 G4
Polanach 156 B4
Polapit Tamar 6 D2
Polbae 123 D3
Polbain 180 B3
Polbathic 6 D5
Polbeth 143 E3
Poldean 125 F1
Pole Moor 93 E1
Polebrook 69 F4
Polegate 18 A3
Poles 182 C5
Polesworth 67 E2
Polglass 180 C4
Polgooth 5 D4
Polgown 133 F5
Poling 16 C3
Poling Corner 16 C3
Polkerns 5 E4
Polla 184 C3
Pollardras 2 D3
Polldubh 156 D3
Pollie 182 C1
Pollington 94 D1
Polloch 155 G3
Pollok 141 G3
Pollokshaws 141 G3
Pollokshields 141 G3
Polmassick 5 D5
Polmont 142 D2
Polnoon 141 G4
Polperro 5 G4
Polruan 5 F4
Polsham 24 C3
Polstead 60 A4
Polstead Heath 60 A3
Poltalloch 148 A5
Poltimore 10 C3
Polton 143 G3
Polwarth 145 E4
Polyphant 5 G1
Polzeath 4 D2
Pomphlett 8 B2
Pond Street 58 C4
Ponders End 44 C3
Pondersbridge 70 A3
Ponsanooth 3 E3
Ponsonby 106 B2
Ponsongath 3 E5
Ponsworthy 10 A5
Pont Aber 50 D3
Pont Aberglaslyn 75 E3
Pont ar Hydfer 51 E5
Pont Crugnant 63 E3
Pont Cyfyng 76 B2
Pont Dolgarrog 76 A1
Pont Pen-y-benglog 75 F1
Pont Rhyd-sarn 76 B5
Pont Rhyd-y-cyff 37 E4
Pont Walby 37 E2
Pont yr Alwen 76 C2
Pontamman 36 C1
Pontantwn 36 A1
Pontardawe 36 D2
Pontarddulais 36 B2
Pontargothi 50 B5
Pont-ar-llechau 50 D5
Pontarsais 50 A5
Pontblyddyn 77 F1
Pontbren Llwyd 37 F2
Pontefract 103 D5
Ponteland 129 D4
Ponterwyd 62 D4
Pontesbury 64 D2
Pontesbury Hill 64 C2
Pontesford 64 D2
Pontfadog 77 F4
Pontfaen *Pembs.* 48 D4
Pont-faen *Powys* 51 F4
Pontgarreg 49 G2
Pont-Henri 36 A2
Ponthir 38 C3
Ponthirwaun 49 F3
Pontllanfraith 38 A3
Pontlliw 36 C2
Pontllyfni 74 D2
Pontlottyn 38 A2
Pontneddfechan 37 F2
Pontrhydfendigaid 50 D1
Pontrhydyfen 37 D3
Pont-rhyd-y-groes 62 D3
Pontrhydyrun 38 B3
Pontrilas 52 C5
Pontrobert 64 A1
Pont-rug 75 E1
Ponts Green 18 B2
Pontshill 53 F5
Pont-siân 50 A3
Pontsticill 37 G1
Pontwelly 50 A4
Pontyates (Pont-iets) 36 A2
Pontyberem 36 B1
Pont-y-blew 78 A4
Pontybodkin 77 F2
Pontyclun 37 G4
Pontycymer 37 F3
Pontygwaith 37 G3
Pontymister 38 B3
Pontymoel 38 B2
Pont-y-pant 76 A2
Pontypool 38 B2
Pontypridd 37 G3
Pont-y-rhyl 37 F4
Pontywaun 38 B3
Pooksgreen 14 C1
Pool *Cornw.* 4 A5
Pool *W.Yorks.* 102 B3
Pool Bank 107 F4
Pool Green 66 C2
Pool Head 53 E2
Pool of Muckhart 151 F4
Pool Quay 64 B1
Pool Street 59 F4
Poole 13 G3
Poole Keynes 40 B3
Poolend 79 G2
Poolewe 172 A1
Pooley Bridge 118 A3
Pooley Street 72 B3
Poolfold 79 F2
Poolhill 53 G5
Poolsbrook 94 B5
Poolthorne Farm 96 A2
Pope Hill 34 C1
Popeswood 28 D1
Popham 27 F3
Poplar 44 C4
Porchfield 14 D3
Porin 173 G4
Poringland 87 D5
Porkellis 3 D3
Porlock 22 B3
Porlock Weir 22 B3
Port Allen 152 A2

Port Appin (Port na h-
Apainn) 156 B5
Port Askaig 138 C3
Port Bannatyne 140 B3
Port Carlisle 126 A5
Port Charlotte 138 A4
Port Clarence 121 E5
Port Driseach 140 A2
Port e Vullen 98 C2
Port Ellen 138 B5
Port Elphinstone 169 E3
Port Erin 98 A5
Port Erroll 179 F4
Port Eynon 36 A4
Port Gaverne 5 E2
Port Glasgow 141 E2
Port Henderson 172 A2
Port Isaac 5 D1
Port Logan 114 A2
Port Mòr 154 D2
Port Mulgrave 111 G1
Port na Craig 159 E4
Port nan Long 188 B1
Port of Menteith 150 A4
Port of Ness 189 G1
Port o'Warren 124 C5
Port Penrhyn 89 D5
Port Quin 5 D1
Port Ramsay 156 A5
Port St. Mary 98 A5
Port Solent 15 F2
Port Sunlight 91 E4
Port Talbot 37 D4
Port Wemyss 138 A4
Port William 114 D2
Portachoillan 139 F4
Portavadie 140 A3
Portbury 39 E5
Portchester 15 F2
Portencross 140 C5
Portesham 12 C4
Portessie 176 D3
Portfield Arg. & B.
147 G2
Portfield W.Suss. 16 A3
Portfield Gate 34 C1
Portgate 7 E2
Portgordon 176 C3
Portgower 183 F3
Porth Cornw. 4 C3
Porth R.C.T. 30 E3
Porth Colmon 74 A4
Porth Navas 3 E4
Porthallow Cornw. 3 E4
Porthallow Cornw. 5 G4
Porthcawl 37 E5
Porthcothan 4 C2
Porthcurno 2 A4
Porthgain 48 B4
Porthill 79 F3
Porthkerry 23 D1
Porthleven 2 D4
Porthmadog 75 E4
Porthmeor 2 B3
Portholland 5 D5
Porthoustock 3 F4
Porthpean 5 E4
Porthtowan 4 A5
Porthyrhyd Carmar.
50 D4
Porthyrhyd Carmar.
36 B1
Porth-y-waen 77 F5
Portincaple 149 E5
Portington 103 G4
Portinnisherrich 148 B3
Portinscale 117 F4
Portishead 39 E5
Portknockie 177 D3
Portlethen 169 G5
Portlethen Village 169 G5
Portloe 3 E3
Portlooe 5 G4
Portmahomack 175 F1
Portmeirion 75 E4
Portmellon 5 E5
Portmore 14 C3
Port-na-Con 184 D2
Portnacroish (Port na
Croise) 156 B5
Portnaguran 189 G2
Portnahaven 138 A4
Portnalong 162 B1
Portnaluchaig 155 F1
Portobello 144 A2
Porton 26 C4
Portpatrick 122 B5
Portreath 4 A5

Portree (Port Righ)
171 D5
Portscatho 3 F3
Portsea 15 F2
Portskerra 186 A2
Portskewett 39 E4
Portslade 17 E3
Portslade-by-Sea 17 E3
Portslogan 122 A5
Portsmouth 15 F3
Portsonachan 148 C2
Portsoy 177 E3
Portuairk 154 D3
Portway Here. 52 C3
Portway Here. 53 E1
Portway Here. 53 D4
Portway Worcs. 66 C5
Portwrinkle 7 D5
Portyerrock 115 E3
Posenhall 65 F2
Poslingford 59 F3
Postbridge 7 G3
Postcombe 42 C3
Postling 32 D5
Postwick 87 D5
Potarch 168 C5
Potsgrove 57 E5
Pott Row 85 F5
Pott Shrigley 92 D5
Potten End 43 F2
Potter Brompton 112 C5
Potter Heigham 87 F4
Potter Street 45 D2
Pottergate Street 72 C2
Potterhanworth 83 F1
Potterhanworth Booths
83 F1
Potterne 26 A2
Potterne Wick 26 B2
Potternewton 102 C4
Potters Bar 44 B2
Potters Crouch 44 A2
Potter's Green 67 F4
Potters Marston 67 G3
Potterspury 56 C3
Potterton Aber. 169 G3
Potterton W.Yorks.
102 D4
Pottle Street 25 F3
Potto 111 D2
Potton 58 A3
Pott's Green 60 A5
Poughill Cornw. 20 C5
Poughill Devon 10 B2
Poulshot 26 A2
Poulton 40 D2
Poulton-le-Fylde 99 G4
Pound Bank 53 G3
Pound Green E.Suss.
18 A1
Pound Green Suff. 59 F2
Pound Green Worcs.
65 G5
Pound Hill 30 B5
Pound Street 27 F1
Poundbury 12 C3
Poundffald 36 B3
Poundfield 31 G5
Poundgate 17 G1
Poundland 122 C2
Poundon 56 B5
Poundsbridge 31 E4
Poundsgate 10 A5
Poundstock 6 C1
Povey Cross 30 B4
Pow Green 53 G3
Powburn 137 E5
Powderham 10 C4
Powerstock 12 B3
Powfoot 125 F4
Powick 54 A2
Powler's Piece 21 D4
Powmill 151 F5
Poxwell 12 D4
Poyle 43 F5
Poynings 17 E2
Poyntington 25 D5
Poynton Ches.E. 92 D4
Poynton Tel. & W. 65 E1
Poynton Green 65 E1
Poyntzfield 174 D3
Poys Street 73 E4
Poyston 34 C1
Poyston Cross 34 C1
Praa Sands 2 A4
Pratis 152 B4
Pratt's Bottom 31 D2
Praze-an-Beeble 2 D3

Predannack Wollas 3 D5
Prees 78 A4
Prees Green 78 C4
Prees Heath 78 C4
Prees Higher Heath 78 C4
Prees Lower Heath 78 C4
Preesall 99 G3
Preesgweene 77 F4
Prenbrigog 77 F1
Prendergast 34 C1
Prendwick 137 E5
Pren-gwyn 50 A3
Prenteg 75 E3
Prenton 91 E4
Prescot 91 F3
Prescott Devon 11 D1
Prescott Shrop. 78 B5
Presley 175 G4
Pressen 136 C3
Prestatyn 90 B4
Prestbury Ches.E. 92 D5
Prestbury Glos. 54 B5
Presteigne (Llanandras)
52 C1
Presthope 65 E3
Prestleigh 24 D3
Prestolee 92 B2
Preston B. & H. 17 F3
Preston Devon 10 B5
Preston Dorset 12 D4
Preston E.Loth. 144 C2
Preston E.Riding 105 D4
Preston Glos. 53 F4
Preston Glos. 40 C2
Preston Herts. 57 G5
Preston Kent 32 C2
Preston Kent 33 E2
Preston Lancs. 100 B5
Preston Northumb.
137 F4
Preston Rut. 69 D2
Preston Sc.Bord. 145 E4
Preston Shrop. 65 E1
Preston Som. 23 D4
Preston Suff. 60 A2
Preston Torbay 9 E1
Preston Wilts. 40 C5
Preston Bagot 55 D1
Preston Bissett 56 B4
Preston Bowyer 23 E5
Preston Brockhurst 78 C5
Preston Brook 91 G4
Preston Candover 28 B3
Preston Capes 56 A2
Preston Deanery 56 C2
Preston Gubbals 65 D1
Preston on Stour 55 E2
Preston on the Hill 91 G4
Preston on Wye 52 C3
Preston Plucknett 12 B1
Preston upon the Weald
Moors 65 F1
Preston Wynne 53 E3
Preston-le-Skerne 120 C5
Prestonpans 144 A2
Preston-under-Scar
109 F3
Prestwich 92 C2
Prestwick Northumb.
129 D4
Prestwick S.Ayr. 132 B3
Prestwold 81 G5
Prestwood Bucks. 43 D2
Prestwood Staffs. 80 C3
Price Town 37 F3
Prickwillow 71 D4
Priddy 24 C1
Priest Hill 100 C4
Priest Hutton 107 G5
Priest Weston 64 B3
Priestcliffe 93 F5
Priestland 133 D2
Priestwood 31 F2
Primethorpe 68 A3
Primrose Green 86 B4
Primrose Hill 44 B4
Princes End 66 B3
Princes Gate 35 E1
Princes Risborough 42 D2
Princethorpe 67 G5
Princetown Caerp. 38 A1
Princetown Devon 7 E3
Prior Muir 152 D1
Prior's Frome 53 E4
Priors Halton 65 D5
Priors Hardwick 55 G2
Priors Marston 55 G2
Prior's Norton 54 A5
Priors Park 54 A4

Priorslee 65 G1
Priory Wood 52 B3
Priston 25 D1
Pristow Green 72 C3
Prittlewell 46 B4
Privett 28 B5
Proaig 138 C4
Probus 4 C5
Protstonhill 178 D1
Prudhoe 119 E1
Prussia Cove 2 C4
Pubil 157 G5
Publow 24 D1
Puckeridge 58 B5
Puckington 11 G1
Pucklechurch 39 F5
Pucknall 27 E5
Puckrup 54 A4
Puddinglake 79 E1
Puddington C. & W.Ches.
91 E5
Puddington Devon 10 B1
Puddlebrook 39 F1
Puddledock 72 B2
Puddletown 13 D3
Pudleston 65 E2
Pudsey 102 B4
Pulborough 16 C2
Puldagon 187 F4
Puleston 79 E5
Pulford 78 A2
Pulham 12 D2
Pulham Market 72 C3
Pulham St. Mary 72 D3
Pulley 65 D2
Pulloxhill 57 F4
Pulrossie 174 D1
Pulverbatch 64 D2
Pumpherston 143 E3
Pumsaint 50 C3
Puncheston 48 D5
Puncknowle 12 B4
Punnett's Town 18 B1
Purbrook 15 F2
Purfleet 45 E5
Puriton 24 A3
Purleigh 46 B2
Purley 30 C2
Purley on Thames 42 B5
Purlogue 64 B5
Purlpit 25 F1
Purls Bridge 70 C4
Purse Caundle 12 C1
Purslow 64 C4
Purston Jaglin 94 B1
Purtington 11 G2
Purton Glos. 39 F2
Purton Glos. 39 F2
Purton Wilts. 40 C3
Purton Stoke 40 C3
Purves Hall 145 E5
Pury End 56 C3
Pusey 41 F3
Putley 53 F4
Putley Green 53 F4
Putney 44 B3
Putsborough 21 E1
Puttenham Herts. 43 D1
Puttenham Surr. 22 C3
Puttock End 59 E3
Putts Corner 11 E3
Puxton 24 B1
Pwll 36 A2
Pwll-crochan 34 C2
Pwlldefaid 74 A5
Pwll-glas 77 E2
Pwllgloyw 51 G4
Pwllheli 74 C3
Pwll-Mawr 38 B5
Pwllmeyric 39 E3
Pwll-trap 35 F1
Pwll-y-glaw 37 E4
Pye Corner Herts. 45 D1
Pye Corner Kent 32 A4
Pye Corner Newport
38 C4
Pye Green 66 B1
Pyecombe 17 E2
Pye Bridgend 37 E4
Pyle I.o.W. 15 D5
Pyleigh 23 E4
Pylle 24 D4
Pymoor (Pymore) 70 C4
Pymore (Pymoor) Cambs.
70 C4
Pymore Dorset 12 A3
Pyrford 29 F2

Pyrford Green 29 F2
Pyrton 42 B3
Pytchley 69 D5
Pyworthy 20 D5

Q

Quabbs 64 B4
Quadring 84 A4
Quadring Eaudike 84 A4
Quainton 56 C5
Quarff 191 F6
Quarley 27 D3
Quarndon 81 E3
Quarr Hill 15 E3
Quarrier's Village 141 E3
Quarrington 83 F3
Quarrington Hill 120 C4
Quarry Bank 66 B4
Quarrybank 78 C1
Quarrywood 176 A3
Quarter 142 B3
Quatford 65 G4
Quatt 65 G4
Quebec 120 A3
Quedgeley 40 A1
Queen Adelaide 71 D4
Queen Camel 24 C5
Queen Charlton 24 D1
Queen Dart 10 B1
Queen Oak 25 E4
Queen Street 31 F4
Queenborough 32 B1
Queen's Bower 15 E4
Queen's Head 78 A5
Queensbury Gt.Lon.
44 A4
Queensbury W.Yorks.
102 A4
Queensferry
(South Queensferry)
Edin. 143 F2
Queensferry Flints. 78 A1
Queenzieburn 142 A2
Quemerford 26 B1
Quendale 191 F6
Quendon 58 D4
Queniborough 68 B1
Quenington 40 D2
Quernmore 100 B1
Queslett 66 C3
Quethiock 4 D4
Quick's Green 42 A5
Quidenham 72 B3
Quidhampton 27 G2
Quilquox 169 G1
Quina Brook 78 C4
Quine's Hill 98 B4
Quinhill 139 F4
Quinton Northants.
56 C2
Quinton W.Mid. 66 B4
Quinton Green 56 C2
Quintrell Downs 4 C3
Quixhill 80 C3
Quoditch 7 E1
Quoig 150 D2
Quoigs 78 C3
Quoiggs House 150 D4
Quoisley 78 C3
Quorn (Quorndon) 68 A1
Quorndon (Quorn) 68 A1
Quothquan 143 A2
Quoys of Reiss 187 F3

R

Raasay 171 E5
Raby 91 E5
Rachan 134 C2
Rachub 75 F1
Rackenford 10 B1
Rackham 16 C2
Rackheath 87 D4
Racks 125 E3
Radbourne 81 D4
Radcliffe Gt.Man. 92 B2
Radcliffe Northumb.
129 E1
Radcliffe on Trent 82 B4
Radclive 56 B4
Radcot 41 E3
Raddington 22 D5
Radernie 152 C4
Radford B. & N.E.Som.
25 D2
Radford Nott. 81 G3
Radford Oxon. 55 G5
Radford W.Mid. 67 F4
Radford Semele 55 F1
Radipole 12 C4

Radlett 44 A2
Radley 42 A3
Radley Green 45 F2
Radmore Green 78 C2
Radnage 42 C3
Radstock 25 D2
Radstone 56 A3
Radway 55 F3
Radway Green 79 E2
Radwell Beds. 57 F2
Radwell Herts. 58 A4
Radwinter 59 E4
Radyr 38 A4
Raechester 128 B3
Raemoir House 169 D5
Raffin 180 C1
Rafford 175 G4
Ragdale 68 B1
Ragged Appleshaw 27 E3
Raglan 38 D2
Ragnall 95 F5
Rahoy 155 F4
Rain Shore 92 C1
Rainford 91 F2
Rainham Gt.Lon. 45 E4
Rainham Med. 32 A2
Rainhill 91 F3
Rainhill Stoops 91 G3
Rainow 92 B2
Rainsough 92 B2
Rainton 110 C5
Rainworth 81 G2
Raisbeck 108 B2
Raise 118 D3
Rait 152 A2
Raithby Lincs. 84 B1
Raithby Lincs. 96 D4
Rake 28 D5
Raleigh's Cross 22 D4
Ram 50 B3
Ram Alley 26 D1
Ram Lane 32 B4
Ramasaig 170 A5
Rame Cornw. 3 E3
Rame Cornw. 8 A3
Rampisham 12 B2
Rampside 99 F1
Rampton Cambs. 58 C1
Rampton Notts. 95 F5
Ramsbottom 92 B1
Ramsbury 41 E5
Ramscraigs 183 G2
Ramsdean 28 C5
Ramsdell 27 G2
Ramsden 41 F1
Ramsden Bellhouse
45 G3
Ramsden Heath 45 G3
Ramsey Cambs. 70 A4
Ramsey Essex 60 D4
Ramsey I.o.M. 98 C2
Ramsey Forty Foot 70 B4
Ramsey Heights 70 A4
Ramsey Island Essex
46 C2
Ramsey Island Pembs.
48 A5
Ramsey Mereside 70 A4
Ramsey St. Mary's 70 A4
Ramsgate 33 F2
Ramsgate Street 86 B2
Ramsgill 110 A5
Ramsholt 61 E3
Ramshorn 80 B3
Ramsnest Common 29 E4
Ranachan 155 F3
Ranby Lincs. 96 C5
Ranby Notts. 95 D4
Rand 96 B5
Randwick 40 A2
Rangemore 80 C5
Rangeworthy 39 F4
Rankinston 132 C4
Rank's Green 45 G1
Ranmoor 94 A4
Rannoch School 158 A4
Ranochan 156 A1
Ranscombe 22 C3
Ranskill 95 D4
Ranton 79 F5
Ranton Green 79 F5
Ranworth 87 E4
Rapps 11 G1
Rascarrel 116 A2
Rash 108 A4
Rashwood 54 B1
Raskelf 111 D5
Rassau 38 A1
Rastrick 102 A5

Ratagan **164** A3
Ratby **68** A2
Ratcliffe Culey **67** F3
Ratcliffe on Soar **81** F5
Ratcliffe on the Wreake **68** B1
Ratfyn **26** C3
Rathen **179** E1
Rathillet **152** B2
Rathliesbeag **157** E1
Ratho **143** F2
Ratho Station **143** F2
Rathven **176** D3
Ratley **55** F3
Ratling **33** E3
Ratlinghope **64** D3
Ratsloe **10** C3
Rattar **187** E1
Ratten Row *Cumb.* **117** G2
Ratten Row *Lancs.* **100** A3
Rattery **8** D1
Rattlesden **60** A2
Rattray **159** G5
Raughton Head **117** G2
Raunds **69** E5
Ravenfield **94** B3
Ravenglass **106** B3
Raveningham **73** E2
Raven's Green **60** C5
Ravenscar **112** C2
Ravensdale **98** B2
Ravensden **57** F2
Ravenshaw **101** F3
Ravenshayes **10** C2
Ravenshead **81** G4
Ravensmoor **78** D2
Ravensthorpe *Northants.* **68** B5
Ravensthorpe *W.Yorks.* **102** B5
Ravenstone *Leics.* **67** G1
Ravenstone *M.K.* **57** D2
Ravenstonedale **108** C2
Ravenstruther **142** D5
Ravensworth **110** A2
Raw **112** C2
Rawcliffe *E.Riding* **103** F5
Rawcliffe *York* **103** E2
Rawcliffe Bridge **103** F5
Rawdon **102** B4
Rawmarsh **94** B3
Rawnsley **66** C1
Rawreth **45** G3
Rawridge **11** F2
Rawson Green **81** E3
Rawtenstall **101** E5
Rawyards **142** B3
Raxton **169** F1
Raydon **60** B4
Raylees **128** B2
Rayleigh **46** B3
Raymond's Hill **11** G3
Rayne **59** F5
Rayners Lane **44** A4
Raynes Park **30** B2
Reach **59** G1
Read **101** D4
Reading **42** C5
Reading Green **72** C4
Reading Street **32** B5
Reagill **108** B1
Rearquhar **182** C5
Rearsby **68** B1
Rease Heath **78** D2
Reaster **187** E2
Reaveley **137** E5
Reay **186** B2
Reculver **33** E2
Red Ball **11** D1
Red Bull **79** F2
Red Dial **117** F2
Red Hill *Hants.* **15** G1
Red Hill *Warks.* **54** D2
Red Lodge **71** F5
Red Lumb **92** C1
Red Oaks Hill **59** D4
Red Point **172** A3
Red Post *Cornw.* **20** C5
Red Post *Devon* **9** E1
Red Rail **53** E5
Red Rock **92** G2
Red Roses **35** F1
Red Row **129** E2
Red Street **79** F2

Red Wharf Bay (Traeth Coch) **88** D4
Redberth **35** D2
Redbourn **44** A1
Redbourne **95** G3
Redbrook *Glos.* **39** E1
Redbrook *Wrex.* **78** C3
Redbrook Street **32** B5
Redburn *High.* **174** B3
Redburn *High.* **175** F5
Redburn *Northumb.* **119** D1
Redcar **121** F5
Redcastle *Angus* **161** E4
Redcastle *High.* **174** B5
Redcliff Bay **38** D5
Redcloak **161** G1
Reddingmuirhead **142** D2
Reddish **92** C3
Redditch **54** C1
Rede **59** G2
Redenhall **73** D3
Redesmouth **128** A3
Redford *Aber.* **161** F2
Redford *Angus* **161** D5
Redford *Dur.* **119** G4
Redford *W.Suss.* **29** D5
Redgrave **72** B4
Redheugh **160** C3
Redhill *Aber.* **169** D1
Redhill *Aber.* **169** E4
Redhill *Moray* **177** E5
Redhill *N.Som.* **24** B1
Redhill *Notts.* **81** G3
Redhill *Surr.* **30** B3
Redhill Aerodrome & Heliport **30** B3
Redhouse *Aber.* **168** C2
Redhouse *Arg. & B.* **139** G3
Redhouses **138** B3
Redisham **73** F3
Redland **39** E5
Redlingfield **72** C4
Redlynch *Som.* **25** E4
Redlynch *Wilts.* **26** D5
Redmarley D'Abitot **53** G4
Redmarshall **120** C5
Redmile **82** C4
Redmire **109** F3
Redmoor **5** E3
Rednal **78** A5
Redpath **135** G2
Redruth **4** A5
Redscarhead **143** G5
Redshaw **133** G3
Redstone Bank **35** E1
Redwick *Newport* **38** D4
Redwick *S.Glos.* **39** E4
Redworth **120** B5
Reed **58** B4
Reed End **58** B4
Reedham **87** F5
Reedley **101** E4
Reedness **103** G5
Reepham *Lincs.* **96** A5
Reepham *Norf.* **86** B3
Reeth **109** F3
Regaby **98** C2
Regil **24** C1
Regoul **175** E4
Reiff **180** B3
Reigate **30** B3
Reighton **113** E5
Reisgill **187** E5
Reiss **187** F3
Rejerrah **4** C4
Releath **3** D3
Relubbus **2** C5
Relugas **175** F5
Remenham **42** C4
Remenham Hill **42** C4
Remony **158** C5
Rempstone **81** G5
Rendcomb **40** C1
Rendham **61** E1
Rendlesham **61** E2
Renfrew **141** G3
Renhold **57** F2
Renishaw **94** B5
Rennington **137** G5
Renton **141** E2
Renwick **118** B3
Repps **87** F4
Repton **81** E5
Rescobie **160** D4
Rescorla **5** E4
Resipole **155** D3

Resolis **174** C3
Resolven **37** E2
Resourie **156** A2
Respryn **5** F3
Reston **145** F3
Restormel **5** F3
Reterth **4** D3
Retew **4** D4
Retford (East Retford) **95** E4
Rettendon **45** G3
Rettendon Place **45** G3
Retyn **4** C4
Revesby **84** A1
Revesby Bridge **84** B1
Rew **10** A5
Rew Street **15** D3
Rewe *Devon* **10** C3
Rewe *Devon* **10** B3
Reybridge **26** A1
Reydon **73** G4
Reydon Smear **73** G4
Reymerston **86** B5
Reynalton **35** D2
Reynoldston **36** A4
Rezare **7** D3
Rhadyr **38** C2
Rhandirmwyn **51** D3
Rhaoine **182** B4
Rhayader (Rhaeadr Gwy) **51** F1
Rhedyn **74** B3
Rhegreanoch **180** C3
Rheindown **174** B5
Rhelonie **182** A5
Rhemore **155** E4
Rheola **37** E2
Rhes-y-cae **77** E1
Rhewl *Denb.* **77** E2
Rhewl *Denb.* **77** E1
Rhewl *Shrop.* **78** A4
Rhian **182** A4
Rhicarn **180** C2
Rhiconich **184** B3
Rhicullen **174** C2
Rhidorroch **181** D5
Rhifail **185** G4
Rhigos **37** F2
Rhilochan **182** C4
Rhinduie **174** B5
Rhireavach **180** C5
Rhiroy **173** E1
Rhiston **64** B3
Rhiw **74** B5
Rhiwargor **76** C2
Rhiwbina **38** A4
Rhiwbryfdir **75** F3
Rhiwderin **38** B4
Rhiwinder **37** G4
Rhiwlas *Gwyn.* **75** E1
Rhiwlas *Gwyn.* **76** C4
Rhiwlas *Powys* **77** F4
Rhode **23** F4
Rhodes Minnis **32** D4
Rhodesia **94** C5
Rhodiad-y-brenin **48** A5
Rhodmad **62** B5
Rhonadale **130** C2
Rhonehouse (Kelton Hill) **124** B5
Rhoose **23** D1
Rhos *Carmar.* **49** G4
Rhos *N.P.T.* **36** D2
Rhos Common **64** B1
Rhosaman **36** D1
Rhoscolyn **88** A5
Rhoscrowther **34** C2
Rhosesmor **77** F1
Rhos-fawr **74** C4
Rhosgadfan **75** E2
Rhos-goch *I.o.A.* **88** C4
Rhosgoch *Powys* **52** A3
Rhos-hill **49** E3
Rhoshirwaun **74** A5
Rhoslan **75** D3
Rhoslefain **62** B2
Rhosllanerchrugog **77** F3
Rhoslligwy **88** C4
Rhosmaen **50** C5
Rhosmeirch **88** C5
Rhosneigr **88** B5
Rhosnesni **78** A2
Rhôs-on-Sea **89** G4
Rhossili **36** A4
Rhosson **48** A5
Rhostrehwfa **88** C5
Rhostryfan **75** D2
Rhostyllen **78** A3

Rhos-y-bol **88** C4
Rhos-y-brithdir **77** E5
Rhosycaerau **48** C4
Rhos-y-garth **62** C5
Rhos-y-gwaliau **76** C4
Rhos-y-llan **74** B4
Rhos-y-mawn **76** B1
Rhos-y-Meirch **52** B1
Rhu **141** D1
Rhualt **90** B5
Rhubodach **140** B2
Rhuddall Heath **78** C1
Rhuddlan **90** B5
Rhue **180** D5
Rhulen **52** A3
Rhumach **155** F1
Rhunahaonne **139** F5
Rhyd *Gwyn.* **75** F3
Rhyd *Powys* **62** B2
Rhydargaeau **50** A5
Rhydcymerau **50** B4
Rhyd-Ddu **75** E2
Rhydding **36** D3
Rhydgaled **76** C1
Rhydlanfair **76** B2
Rhydlewis **49** G3
Rhydlios **74** A4
Rhyd-Rosser **50** B1
Rhydspence **52** B3
Rhydtalog **77** F2
Rhyd-uchaf **76** B4
Rhyd-wen **76** C5
Rhyd-wyn **88** B4
Rhyd-y-ceirw **77** F2
Rhyd-y-clafdy **74** C4
Rhydycroesau **77** F4
Rhydyfelin *Cere.* **62** B5
Rhydyfelin *R.C.T.* **37** G4
Rhyd-y-foel **90** B5
Rhyd-y-fro **36** D2
Rhyd-y-groes **75** E1
Rhydymain **76** B5
Rhydymwyn **77** F1
Rhyd-yr-onnen **62** C2
Rhyd-y-sarn **75** F3
Rhydywrach **35** E1
Rhyl **90** B4
Rhymney **38** A2
Rhynd **78** A4
Rhynie *Aber.* **168** B2
Rhynie *High.* **175** D2
Ribbesford **65** G5
Ribchester **100** C4
Ribigill **185** E3
Riby **96** B2
Riccall **103** F4
Riccarton **132** C2
Richards Castle **53** D1
Richings Park **43** F5
Richmond *Gt.Lon.* **44** A5
Richmond *N.Yorks.* **110** A2
Richmond *S.Yorks.* **94** B4
Rich's Holford **23** E4
Rickarton **161** G1
Rickerscote **79** G5
Rickford **24** B2
Rickinghall **72** B4
Rickleton **120** B2
Rickling **58** D4
Rickling Green **58** D5
Rickmansworth **43** F3
Riddell **135** G3
Riddings **81** F2
Riddlecombe **21** G4
Riddlesden **101** G3
Ridge *Dorset* **13** F4
Ridge *Herts.* **44** B2
Ridge *Wilts.* **26** B5
Ridge Green **30** C4
Ridge Lane **67** E3
Ridgebourne **51** D2
Ridgeway **94** B4
Ridgeway Cross **53** G3
Ridgeway Moor **94** B4
Ridgewell **59** F3
Ridgewood **17** G1
Ridgmont **57** E4
Ridham Dock **32** B2
Riding Gate **25** E5
Riding Mill **119** D1
Ridley **31** F2
Ridleywood **78** A2
Ridlington *Norf.* **87** E2

Ridlington *Rut.* **68** D2
Ridsdale **128** B3
Riechip **159** F5
Rievaulx **111** E4
Rift House **121** D4
Rigg *D. & G.* **126** A5
Rigg *High.* **171** E4
Riggend **142** B3
Rigifa **187** F1
Rigmaden Park **108** B4
Rigsby **97** E5
Rigside **131** G2
Riley Green **100** C5
Rileyhill **66** D1
Rilla Mill **5** G2
Rillaton **5** G2
Rillington **112** B5
Rimington **101** E3
Rimpton **24** D5
Rimswell **105** F5
Rinaston **48** C5
Ring o' Bells **91** F1
Ringford **124** A5
Ringinglow **93** G4
Ringland **86** C4
Ringles Cross **17** G1
Ringmer **17** G2
Ringmore *Devon* **8** C3
Ringmore *Devon* **10** C5
Ringorm **176** B5
Ring's End **70** B2
Ringsfield **73** F3
Ringsfield Corner **73** F3
Ringshall *Herts.* **43** E1
Ringshall *Suff.* **60** B2
Ringshall Stocks **60** B2
Ringstead *Norf.* **85** F3
Ringstead *Northants.* **69** E5
Ringwood **14** A2
Ringwould **33** F4
Rinloan **167** G4
Rinmore **168** B3
Rinsey **2** C4
Ripe **18** A3
Ripley *Derbys.* **81** E2
Ripley *Hants.* **14** A3
Ripley *N.Yorks.* **102** B1
Ripley *Surr.* **29** F2
Riplingham **104** B4
Ripon **110** C5
Rippingale **83** G5
Ripple *Kent* **33** F4
Ripple *Worcs.* **54** A4
Ripponden **93** G1
Risabus **138** B5
Risbury **53** E2
Risby *E.Riding* **104** C4
Risby *Suff.* **59** F1
Risca **38** B3
Rise **105** D3
Riseden **31** G5
Risegate **84** A5
Riseholme **95** G5
Riseley *Beds.* **57** F1
Riseley *W'ham* **28** C1
Rishangles **60** C1
Rishton **100** D4
Rishworth **93** E1
Risinghurst **42** A2
Risley *Derbys.* **81** F4
Risley *Warr.* **92** A3
Risplith **102** B1
Rispond **185** D2
Rivar **27** E1
Rivenhall **46** B1
Rivenhall End **46** B1
River *Kent* **33** E4
River *W.Suss.* **28** D5
River Bank **58** D1
River Bridge **24** A3
Riverford Bridge **9** D1
Riverhead **31** E3
Riverside **38** A5
Riverton **21** G2
Riverview Park **45** F5
Rivington **92** A1
Roa Island **99** F1
Roach Bridge **100** B5
Road Green **73** D2
Road Weedon **56** B2
Roade **56** C2
Roadhead **126** D4
Roadside **187** D2
Roadside of Kinneff **161** G2
Roadwater **22** D4
Roag **170** B5
Roast Green **58** C4

Roath **38** A5
Roberton *S.Lan.* **134** A3
Roberton *Sc.Bord.* **135** F4
Robertsbridge **18** C3
Robertstown *Moray* **176** B5
Robertstown *R.C.T.* **37** G2
Roberttown **102** A5
Robeston Cross **34** B2
Robeston Wathen **35** D1
Robeston West **34** B2
Robin Hood *Derbys.* **93** G5
Robin Hood *Lancs.* **91** G1
Robin Hood *W.Yorks.* **102** C5
Robin Hood Doncaster Sheffield Airport **95** D3
Robin Hood's Bay **112** C2
Robinhood End **59** F4
Robins **28** D5
Roborough *Devon* **21** F4
Roborough *Plym.* **8** B1
Roby **91** F3
Roby Mill **91** G2
Rocester **80** C4
Roch **48** B5
Roch Bridge **48** B5
Roch Gate **48** B5
Rochallie **159** G4
Rochdale **92** C1
Roche **5** D3
Rochester *Med.* **31** G2
Rochester *Northumb.* **128** A2
Rochford *Essex* **46** B3
Rochford *Worcs.* **53** F1
Rock *Cornw.* **4** D2
Rock *Northumb.* **137** G5
Rock *Worcs.* **65** G5
Rock Ferry **91** F4
Rockbeare **10** D3
Rockbourne **14** A1
Rockcliffe *Cumb.* **126** B5
Rockcliffe *D. & G.* **124** C5
Rockcliffe Cross **126** B5
Rockfield *Arg. & B.* **139** G4
Rockfield *High.* **175** F1
Rockfield *Mon.* **39** D1
Rockford **14** A2
Rockhampton **39** F3
Rockhead **5** E1
Rockingham **69** D3
Rockland All Saints **72** A2
Rockland St. Mary **87** E5
Rockland St. Peter **72** A2
Rockley **41** D5
Rockside **138** A3
Rockwell End **42** C4
Rockwell Green **11** E1
Rodborough **40** A2
Rodbourne **40** B4
Rodbridge Corner **59** G3
Rodd **52** C1
Roddam **137** E4
Rodden **12** C4
Rode **25** F2
Rode Heath **79** F2
Rodeheath **79** F1
Rodel **189** D1
Roden **65** D1
Rodhuish **22** D4
Rodington **65** E1
Rodington Heath **65** E1
Rodley **39** G1
Rodmarton **40** B3
Rodmell **17** G3
Rodmersham **32** B2
Rodmersham Green **32** B2
Rodney Stoke **24** B2
Rodsley **80** D3
Rodway **23** F3
Roe Cross **93** D3
Roe Green **58** B4
Roecliffe **102** C1
Roehampton **44** B5
Roffey **29** G4
Rogart **182** C4
Rogate **28** D5
Rogerstone **38** B4
Rogiet **39** D4
Rokemarsh **42** B3
Roker **120** D2
Rollesby **87** F4
Rolleston *Leics.* **68** C2
Rolleston *Notts.* **82** C2
Rollestone **26** B3

Rolleston-on-Dove **80** D5
Rolston **105** E3
Rolstone **24** A1
Rolvenden **32** A5
Rolvenden Layne **32** A5
Romaldkirk **119** F5
Romanby **110** C3
Romannobridge **143** F5
Romansleigh **22** A5
Romesdal **170** D4
Romford *Dorset* **13** G2
Romford *Gt.Lon.* **45** E4
Romiley **92** D3
Romney Street **31** E2
Romsey **27** E5
Romsley *Shrop.* **65** G4
Romsley *Worcs.* **66** B5
Rona **171** F4
Ronachan **139** F4
Ronague **98** A4
Ronnachmore **138** B4
Rood End **66** C4
Rookhope **119** F3
Rookley **15** E4
Rookley Green **15** E4
Rooks Bridge **24** A2
Rook's Nest **23** D4
Rookwith **110** B4
Roos **105** E4
Roose **99** F1
Roosebeck **99** F1
Roosecote **99** F1
Rootham's Green **57** F2
Rootpark **143** D4
Ropley **28** B4
Ropley Dean **28** B4
Ropley Soke **28** B4
Ropsley **83** E4
Rora **179** F2
Rorandle **169** D3
Rorrington **64** C2
Rosarie **176** C5
Rose **4** B4
Rose Ash **22** A5
Rose Green *Essex* **60** A5
Rose Green *W.Suss.* **16** B4
Rose Hill **17** G2
Roseacre *Kent* **31** G3
Roseacre *Lancs.* **100** A4
Rosebank **142** C5
Rosebrough **137** F4
Rosebush **49** D5
Rosecare **6** B1
Rosecliston **4** C4
Rosedale Abbey **111** G3
Roseden **137** E4
Rosehall **181** G4
Rosehearty **179** E1
Rosehill *Aber.* **168** C5
Rosehill *Shrop.* **65** D1
Roseisle **176** A3
Roselands **18** B3
Rosemarket **34** C2
Rosemarkie **174** D4
Rosemary Lane **11** E1
Rosemount *P. & K.* **159** G3
Rosemount *S.Ayr.* **132** B3
Rosenannon **5** D3
Rosenithon **3** F4
Rosepool **34** B1
Rosevean **5** E4
Roseville **66** B3
Rosewell **143** G3
Roseworth **120** D5
Rosgill **107** G1
Roshven **155** G2
Roskhill **170** B5
Roskorwell **3** E4
Rosley **117** G2
Roslin **143** G3
Rosliston **67** E1
Rosneath **141** D1
Ross *D. & G.* **115** G2
Ross *Northumb.* **137** F3
Ross *P. & K.* **150** C2
Ross Priory **141** F1
Rossdhu House **141** E1
Rossett **78** A2
Rossett Green **102** C2
Rosside **107** D5
Rossie Farm School **161** E4
Rossie Ochill **151** F3
Rossie Priory **152** A1
Rossington **94** D3

Rosskeen **174** C3
Rossmore **13** G3
Ross-on-Wye **53** F5
Roster **187** E5
Rostherne **92** B4
Rosthwaite *Cumb.* **117** F5
Rosthwaite *Cumb.* **106** D4
Roston **80** D2
Rosudgeon **2** C4
Rosyth **143** F1
Rothbury **128** C1
Rotherby **68** B1
Rotherfield **31** E5
Rotherfield Greys **42** C4
Rotherfield Peppard **42** C4
Rotherham **94** B3
Rothersthorpe **56** C2
Rotherwick **28** C2
Rothes **176** B5
Rothesay **140** B3
Rothiebrisbane **169** E1
Rothienorman **169** E1
Rothiesholm **190** C2
Rothley *Leics.* **68** A1
Rothley *Northumb.* **128** C3
Rothney **168** D2
Rothwell *Lincs.* **96** B3
Rothwell *Norf.* **85** F5
Rothwell *Northants.* **68** D4
Rothwell *W.Yorks.* **102** C5
Rotsea **104** C2
Rottal **160** B3
Rotten Row *Bucks.* **42** C4
Rotten Row *W.Mid.* **67** D5
Rottingdean **17** F3
Rottington **116** C5
Roud **15** E4
Roudham **72** A3
Rough Close **79** G4
Rough Common **32** D3
Rougham *Norf.* **85** G5
Rougham *Suff.* **60** A1
Rougham Green **60** A1
Roughburn **157** F1
Roughlee **101** E4
Roughley **66** D3
Roughton *Lincs.* **84** A1
Roughton *Norf.* **86** D2
Roughton *Shrop.* **65** G3
Round Bush **44** A3
Roundbush Green **45** E1
Roundham **12** A2
Roundhay **102** C4
Roundstreet Common **29** F5
Roundway **26** B1
Rous Lench **54** C2
Rousay **190** B2
Rousdon **11** F3
Rousham **55** G5
Rousham Gap **55** G5
Routenburn **140** C3
Routh **104** C3
Rout's Green **42** C3
Row *Cornw.* **5** E2
Row *Cumb.* **107** F4
Row *Cumb.* **118** C4
Row Heath **47** E1
Row Town **29** F1
Rowanburn **126** C4
Rowardennan Lodge **149** F5
Rowarth **93** E4
Rowbarton **23** F5
Rowberrow **24** B2
Rowchoish **149** F4
Rowde **26** A1
Rowden **7** G1
Rowen **89** F5
Rowfields **80** C3
Rowfoot **118** C1
Rowhedge **60** B5
Rowhook **29** G4
Rowington **55** E1
Rowland **93** G5
Rowland's Castle **15** G1
Rowlands Gill **120** A2
Rowledge **28** D3
Rowlestone **52** C5
Rowley *Devon* **10** A1
Rowley *Dur.* **119** E3
Rowley *Shrop.* **64** C2
Rowley Park **79** G5
Rowley Regis **66** B4

Rowly **29** F3
Rowner **15** E2
Rowney Green **66** C5
Rownhams **14** C1
Rowrah **117** D5
Rowsham **43** E1
Rowsley **81** D1
Rowstock **41** G4
Rowston **83** F2
Rowthorne **81** E1
Rowton *C. & W.Ches.* **78** B1
Rowton *Shrop.* **64** C1
Rowton *Tel. & W.* **65** F1
Roxburgh **136** B3
Roxby *N.Lincs.* **95** G1
Roxby *N.Yorks.* **111** G1
Roxton **57** G2
Roxwell **45** F2
Royal British Legion Village **31** G3
Royal Leamington Spa **55** F1
Royal Oak **91** F2
Royal Tunbridge Wells **31** E5
Roybridge (Drochaid Ruaidh) **157** F2
Roydon *Essex* **44** D1
Roydon *Norf.* **72** B3
Roydon *Norf.* **85** F5
Roydon Hamlet **44** D2
Royston *Herts.* **58** B3
Royston *S.Yorks.* **94** A1
Royton **92** D2
Rozel **8** C5
Ruabon (Rhiwabon) **78** A3
Ruaig **154** B2
Ruan Lanihorne **4** C5
Ruan Major **3** D5
Ruan Minor **3** E5
Ruanaich **146** B2
Ruardean **39** F1
Ruardean Hill **39** F1
Ruardean Woodside **39** F1
Rubery **66** B5
Ruckcroft **118** B3
Ruckinge **32** D3
Ruckland **96** D5
Rucklers Lane **43** F2
Ruckley **65** E2
Rudbaxton **48** C5
Rudby **111** D2
Rudchester **120** A1
Ruddington **81** G4
Ruddlemoor **5** E4
Rudford **53** G5
Rudge **25** F2
Rudgeway **39** F4
Rudgwick **29** F4
Rudhall **53** F5
Rudheath **92** A5
Rudley Green **46** B2
Rudloe **25** F1
Rudry **38** A4
Rudston **79** G2
Rufford **91** F1
Rufforth **103** E2
Ruffside **119** F2
Rugby **68** A5
Rugeley **66** C1
Ruilick **174** B5
Ruishton **23** F5
Ruislip **43** F4
Ruislip Gardens **43** F4
Ruislip Manor **44** A4
Rum **162** B5
Rumbling Bridge **151** F5
Rumburgh **73** E3
Rumford **4** C2
Rumleigh **8** A1
Rumney **38** B5
Rumwell **23** E5
Runacraig **150** A3
Runcorn **91** G4
Runcton **16** A3
Runcton Holme **71** E2
Rundlestone **7** F3
Runfold **29** D3
Runhall **86** B5
Runham *Norf.* **87** F4
Runham *Norf.* **87** G5
Runnington **23** E5
Runsell Green **45** G2
Runshaw Moor **91** G1
Runswick Bay **112** B1

Runtaleave **160** A3
Runwell **45** G3
Ruscombe *Glos.* **40** A2
Ruscombe *W'ham* **42** C5
Rush Green *Gt.Lon.* **45** E4
Rush Green *Herts.* **58** A5
Rushall *Here.* **53** F4
Rushall *Norf.* **72** C3
Rushall *W.Mid.* **66** C2
Rushall *Wilts.* **26** C2
Rushbrooke **59** G1
Rushbury **65** E3
Rushden *Herts.* **58** B4
Rushden *Northants.* **57** E1
Rushford *Devon* **7** E3
Rushford *Norf.* **72** A3
Rushgreen **92** A4
Rushlake Green **18** B2
Rushmere **73** F3
Rushmere St. Andrew **60** D3
Rushmoor **29** D3
Rushock **66** A5
Rusholme **92** C3
Rushton *C. & W.Ches.* **78** C1
Rushton *Northants.* **68** D4
Rushton *Shrop.* **65** F2
Rushton Spencer **79** G1
Rushwick **54** A2
Rushy Green **17** G2
Rushyford **120** B5
Ruskie **150** B4
Rusko **123** G5
Rusland **107** E4
Rusper **30** B5
Ruspidge **39** F1
Russ Hill **30** B4
Russel **172** B5
Russell Green **45** G1
Russell's Green **18** C3
Russell's Water **42** C3
Russel's Green **73** D4
Rusthall **31** E5
Rustington **16** C3
Ruston **112** C4
Ruston Parva **104** C1
Ruswarp **112** B2
Rutherend **142** A4
Rutherford **136** A3
Rutherglen **142** A3
Ruthernbridge **5** E3
Ruthers of Howe **187** F2
Ruthin (Rhuthun) *Denb.* **77** E2
Ruthin *V. of Glam.* **37** F5
Ruthrieston **169** G4
Ruthven *Aber.* **177** E5
Ruthven *Angus* **160** A5
Ruthven *High.* **166** C1
Ruthven *High.* **166** B5
Ruthvoes **4** D3
Ruthwaite **117** F3
Ruthwell **125** E4
Ruyton-XI-Towns **78** A5
Ryal **128** C2
Ryal Fold **100** C5
Ryall *Dorset* **12** A3
Ryall *Worcs.* **54** A3
Ryarsh **31** F3
Rydal **107** E2
Ryde **15** E3
Rydon **20** D5
Rye **19** E1
Rye Foreign **19** D1
Rye Harbour **19** E2
Rye Park **44** C2
Rye Street **53** G4
Ryebank **78** C4
Ryeford **53** F5
Ryehill *Aber.* **169** D2
Ryehill *E.Riding* **105** E5
Ryhall **68** F1
Ryhill **94** A1
Ryhope **120** D2
Rylands **81** G4
Rylstone **101** F2
Ryme Intrinseca **12** B1
Ryther **103** E4
Ryton *Glos.* **53** G4
Ryton *N.Yorks.* **111** G5
Ryton *Shrop.* **65** G2
Ryton *T. & W.* **120** A1

Ryton-on-Dunsmore **67** F5

S

Saasaig **163** E4
Sabden **101** E4
Sabden Fold **101** E4
Sackers Green **60** A4
Sacombe **44** C1
Sacombe Green **44** C1
Sacriston **120** B3
Sadberge **110** C1
Saddell **130** C2
Saddington **68** B3
Saddle Bow **71** E1
Sadgill **107** F2
Saffron Walden **58** D4
Sageston **35** D2
Saham Hills **86** A5
Saham Toney **71** G2
Saighdinis **188** B2
Saighton **78** B1
St. Abbs **145** G3
St. Agnes **4** B4
St. Albans **44** A2
St. Allen **4** C4
St. Andrews **152** D3
St. Andrews Major **38** A5
St. Anne **9** G4
St. Anne's **99** G5
St. Ann's **125** E1
St. Ann's Chapel *Cornw.* **7** E3
St. Ann's Chapel *Devon* **8** C3
St. Anthony **3** F3
St. Anthony-in-Meneage **3** E4
St. Anthony's Hill **18** B3
St. Arvans **39** E3
St. Asaph (Llanelwy) **90** B5
St. Athan **22** D1
St. Aubin **8** C5
St. Audries **23** E3
St. Austell **5** E4
St. Bees **116** C5
St. Blazey **5** E4
St. Blazey Gate **5** E4
St. Boswells **135** G2
St. Brelade **8** B5
St. Breock **5** D2
St. Breward **5** E2
St. Briavels **39** E2
St. Brides **34** B1
St. Brides Major **37** E5
St. Bride's Netherwent **38** D4
St. Brides Wentlooge **38** B4
St. Bride's-super-Ely **37** G5
St. Budeaux **8** A2
St. Buryan **2** B4
St. Catherine **25** E1
St. Catherines **148** D4
St. Clears (Sanclêr) **35** F1
St. Cleer **5** G3
St. Clement *Chan.I.* **8** C5
St. Clement *Cornw.* **4** C5
St. Clether **5** G1
St. Colmac **140** B3
St. Columb Major **4** D3
St. Columb Minor **4** C3
St. Columb Road **4** D4
St. Combs **179** F1
St. Cross South Elmham **73** D3
St. Cyrus **161** F3
St. Davids *Fife* **143** F1
St. David's *P. & K.* **151** E2
St. David's (Tyddewi) *Pembs.* **48** A5
St. Day **4** B5
St. Decumans **23** E3
St. Dennis **5** D4
St. Denys **14** C3
St. Dogmaels (Llandudoch) **49** E3
St. Dogwells **48** C5
St. Dominick **8** A1
St. Donats **22** C1
St. Edith's Marsh **26** A1
St. Endellion **5** D2
St. Enoder **4** C4
St. Erme **4** C5
St. Erney **7** D5

Ryton-on-Dunsmore **67** F5

St. Erth **2** C3
St. Erth Praze **2** C3
St. Ervan **4** C2
St. Eval **4** C3
St. Ewe **5** D5
St. Fagans **38** A5
St. Fergus **179** F2
St. Fillans **150** B2
St. Florence **35** D2
St. Gennys **6** B1
St. George *Bristol* **39** F5
St. George *Conwy* **90** A5
St. Georges *N.Som.* **24** A1
St. George's *Tel. & W.* **65** G1
St. George's *V. of Glam.* **37** G5
St. Germans **7** D5
St. Giles in the Wood **21** F4
St. Giles on the Heath **7** D1
St. Harmon **63** F5
St. Helen Auckland **120** A5
St. Helena **86** C4
St. Helen's *E.Suss.* **18** D2
St. Helens *I.o.W.* **15** F4
St. Helens *Mersey.* **91** G3
St. Helier *Chan.I.* **8** C5
St. Helier *Gt.Lon.* **30** B2
St. Hilary *Cornw.* **2** C3
St. Hilary *V. of Glam.* **37** G5
St. Hill **30** C5
St. Ibbs **57** G5
St. Illtyd **38** B2
St. Ippollitts **57** G5
St. Ishmael **35** G2
St. Ishmael's **34** B2
St. Issey **4** D2
St. Ive **6** D4
St. Ives *Cambs.* **70** B5
St. Ives *Cornw.* **2** C2
St. Ives *Dorset* **14** A2
St. James South Elmham **73** E3
St. John *Chan.I.* **8** C4
St. John *Cornw.* **8** A2
St. John's *Gt.Lon.* **44** C5
St. John's *I.o.M.* **98** A3
St. John's *Surr.* **29** E2
St. John's *Worcs.* **54** A2
St. John's Chapel *Devon* **21** F3
St. John's Chapel *Dur.* **119** E4
St. John's Fen End **70** D1
St. John's Hall **119** G4
St. John's Highway **70** D1
St. John's Kirk **134** A2
St. John's Town of Dalry **124** A2
St. Judes **98** B2
St. Just **2** A3
St. Just in Roseland **3** F3
St. Katherines **169** E1
St. Keverne **3** E4
St. Kew **5** E2
St. Kew Highway **5** E2
St. Keyne **5** G3
St. Lawrence *Cornw.* **5** E3
St. Lawrence *Essex* **46** C2
St. Lawrence *I.o.W.* **15** E5
St. Leonards *Bucks.* **43** E2
St. Leonards *Dorset* **14** A2
St. Leonards *E.Suss.* **18** D3
St. Leonards Grange **14** D3
St. Leonard's Street **31** F3
St. Levan **2** A4
St. Lythans **38** A5
St. Mabyn **5** E2
St. Madoes **151** G2
St. Margaret South Elmham **73** E3
St. Margarets *Here.* **52** C4
St. Margarets *Herts.* **44** C1
St. Margarets *Wilts.* **26** D1

St. Margaret's at Cliffe 33 F4
St. Margaret's Hope 190 B4
St. Mark's 98 A4
St. Martin Chan.I. 9 F5
St. Martin Chan.I. 8 C5
St. Martin Cornw. 5 G4
St. Martin Cornw. 3 E4
St. Martin's I.o.S. 4 B1
St. Martins P. & K. 151 G1
St. Martin's Shrop. 78 A4
St. Mary 8 C5
St. Mary Bourne 27 F2
St. Mary Church 37 G5
St. Mary Cray 31 D2
St. Mary Hill 37 F5
St. Mary Hoo 45 G5
St. Mary in the Marsh 19 F1
St. Marychurch 9 F1
St. Mary's I.o.S. 4 B1
St. Mary's Ork. 190 B3
St. Mary's Airport 4 B1
St. Mary's Bay 19 F1
St. Mary's Croft 122 B4
St. Mary's Grove 24 B1
St. Maughans Green 39 F1
St. Mawes 3 F3
St. Mawgan 4 C3
St. Mellion 7 D4
St. Mellons 38 B4
St. Merryn 4 C2
St. Mewan 5 D4
St. Michael Caerhays 5 D5
St. Michael Church 24 A4
St. Michael Penkevil 4 C5
St. Michael South Elmham 73 E3
St. Michaels Fife 152 C2
St. Michaels Kent 32 A5
St. Michaels Worcs. 53 E1
St. Michael's on Wyre 100 A3
St. Minver 5 D2
St. Monans 152 D4
St. Neot 5 F3
St. Neots 67 E3
St. Newlyn East 4 C4
St. Nicholas Pembs. 48 C4
St. Nicholas V. of Glam. 37 G5
St. Nicholas at Wade 33 E2
St. Ninians 150 C5
St. Osyth 47 E1
St. Owen's Cross 53 E5
St. Paul's Cray 31 D2
St. Paul's Walden 57 G5
St. Peter 8 C5
St. Peter Port 9 F5
St. Peter's 32 F2
St. Petrox 34 C3
St. Pinnock 5 F3
St. Quivox 132 B3
St. Ruan 3 E5
St. Sampson 9 F4
St. Saviour Chan.I. 9 E5
St. Saviour Chan.I. 8 C5
St. Stephen 4 D4
St. Stephens Cornw. 8 A2
St. Stephens Cornw. 6 D2
St. Stephens Herts. 44 A2
St. Teath 5 E1
St. Thomas 10 C3
St. Tudy 5 E2
St. Twynnells 34 C3
St. Veep 5 F4
St. Vigeans 161 E5
St. Wenn 5 D3
St. Weonards 53 D5
St. Winnow 5 F4
Saintbury 34 F4
Salachail 156 C4
Salcombe 8 D4
Salcombe Regis 11 E4
Salcott 46 C1
Sale 92 B3
Sale Green 54 B2
Saleby 97 E5
Salehurst 18 C1
Salem Carmar. 50 C5
Salem Cere. 62 C4

Salem Gwyn. 75 E2
Salen Arg. & B. 155 E5
Salen High. 155 F3
Salendine Nook 93 F1
Salesbury 100 C4
Saleway 54 B2
Salford Beds. 57 E4
Salford Gt.Man. 92 C3
Salford Oxon. 55 E5
Salford Priors 54 C2
Salfords 30 B4
Salhouse 87 E4
Saline 151 F5
Salisbury 26 C5
Salkeld Dykes 118 B4
Sallachan 156 B3
Sallachy 148 C3
Sallachy High. 182 A4
Sallachy High. 164 A1
Salle 86 C3
Salmonby 96 D5
Salmond's Muir 153 D1
Salperton 42 C5
Salph End 57 F2
Salsburgh 142 C3
Salt 79 G5
Salt Hill 43 E4
Salt Holme 121 D5
Saltaire 102 A4
Saltburn 174 D2
Saltburn-by-the-Sea 121 F5
Saltby 83 D5
Saltcoats Cumb. 106 B3
Saltcoats N.Ayr. 140 D5
Saltcotes 99 G5
Saltdean 17 F3
Salterbeck 116 C4
Salterforth 101 E3
Saltergate 112 B3
Salterhill 176 B3
Salterswall 78 D1
Saltfleet 87 F3
Saltfleetby All Saints 97 E3
Saltfleetby St. Clements 97 E3
Saltfleetby St. Peter 97 E4
Saltford 25 D1
Salthaugh Grange 105 E5
Salthouse 86 B1
Saltley 66 C4
Saltmarshe 103 G5
Saltney 78 A1
Salton 111 G4
Saltrens 21 E3
Saltwick 129 D4
Saltwood 33 D5
Salum 154 B2
Salvington 16 D3
Salwarpe 54 A1
Salwayash 12 A3
Sambrook 79 E5
Samlesbury 100 C4
Sampford Arundel 11 E1
Sampford Brett 23 D3
Sampford Courtenay 21 G5
Sampford Moor 11 E1
Sampford Peverell 10 D1
Sampford Spiney 7 F3
Samuelston 44 B2
Sanaigmore 138 A2
Sancreed 2 B4
Sancton 104 B4
Sand 24 B3
Sand Hutton 103 F2
Sandaig Arg. & B. 154 A2
Sandaig High. 163 F3
Sandaig High. 163 F3
Sandal Magna 94 A1
Sanday 190 C2
Sandbach 79 E1
Sandbank 140 C1
Sandbanks 13 G4
Sandend 177 E3
Sanderstead 30 C2
Sandford Cumb. 108 C1
Sandford Devon 10 B2
Sandford Dorset 18 F3
Sandford I.o.W. 15 E4
Sandford N.Som. 24 B2
Sandford S.Lan. 142 B5
Sandford Shrop. 78 C4
Sandford Shrop. 78 A5
Sandford Orcas 24 D5

Sandford St. Martin 55 G5
Sandfordhill 179 G3
Sandford-on-Thames 42 A2
Sandgarth 190 B3
Sandgate 33 E5
Sandgreen 123 G5
Sandhaven 179 E1
Sandhead 122 B5
Sandhills Dorset 12 C1
Sandhills Dorset 12 B3
Sandhills Surr. 29 E4
Sandhills W.Yorks. 102 C4
Sandhoe 119 F1
Sandholme E.Riding 104 A4
Sandholme Lincs. 84 B4
Sandhurst Brack.F. 28 D1
Sandhurst Glos. 54 A5
Sandhurst Kent 18 C1
Sandhurst Cross 18 C1
Sandhutton 110 C4
Sandiacre 81 F4
Sandilands 88 F4
Sandiway 92 A5
Sandleheath 14 A1
Sandleigh 41 G2
Sandling 31 G3
Sandlow Green 79 E1
Sandness 191 E3
Sandon Essex 45 G2
Sandon Herts. 58 B4
Sandon Staffs. 79 G5
Sandown 15 F4
Sandplace 5 G4
Sandridge Devon 9 E2
Sandridge Herts. 44 A1
Sandridge Wilts. 26 A1
Sandringham 85 E3
Sandrocks 17 F1
Sandsend 112 B1
Sandside 107 F4
Sandside House 186 B2
Sandsound 191 E4
Sandtoft 95 E2
Sanduck 10 A4
Sandway 32 A3
Sandwell 86 C4
Sandwich 33 F3
Sandwick Cumb. 107 F1
Sandwick Shet. 191 F5
Sandwith 116 C5
Sandy Beds. 57 G3
Sandy Carmar. 36 A2
Sandy Bank 84 A2
Sandy Haven 34 B2
Sandy Lane W.Yorks. 102 A4
Sandy Lane Wilts. 26 A1
Sandy Lane Wrex. 78 B3
Sandy Way 15 D4
Sandycroft 78 A1
Sandygate Devon 10 B5
Sandygate I.o.M. 98 B2
Sandyhills 124 C5
Sandylands 100 A1
Sandypark 10 A4
Sandyway 53 D5
Sangobeg 184 D2
Sankyn's Green 53 G1
Sanna 155 D3
Sannaig 138 D3
Sannox 140 B5
Sanquhar 133 F5
Santon Bridge 106 C2
Santon Downham 71 G4
Sant-y-Nyll 37 G5
Sapcote 67 G3
Sapiston 72 A4
Sapley 15 E2
Sapperton Derbys. 80 C4
Sapperton Glos. 40 B2
Sapperton Lincs. 83 F4
Saracen's Head 84 B5
Sarclet 187 F4
Sardis 34 C2
Sarisbury 15 E2
Sark 9 E5
Sarn Bridgend 37 F4
Sarn Powys 64 B3
Sarn Bach 74 C5
Sarn Meyllteyrn 74 B4
Sarnau Carmar. 35 G1
Sarnau Cere. 49 G2
Sarnau Gwyn. 76 C2
Sarnau Powys 64 B1
Sarnau Powys 51 G4
Sarnesfield 52 C2
Saron Carmar. 36 C1
Saron Carmar. 49 G4

Saron Gwyn. 75 E1
Saron Gwyn. 75 D2
Sarratt 43 F3
Sarre 33 E2
Sarsden 55 E5
Sarsgrum 184 C2
Sartfield 98 B2
Satley 120 A3
Satron 109 E3
Satterleigh 21 G3
Satterthwaite 107 E3
Sauchen 169 D3
Saucher 151 G1
Sauchie 151 D5
Sauchieburn 161 E3
Sauchnie 132 B4
Saughall 91 D5
Saughall Massie 91 D4
Saughtree 127 D2
Saul 39 G2
Saundby 95 E4
Saundersfoot 35 E2
Saunderton 42 C2
Saunton 21 E2
Sausthorpe 84 B5
Saval 182 A4
Savalbeg 182 A4
Saverley Green 79 G4
Savile Town 102 B5
Sawbridge 56 A1
Sawbridgeworth 45 D1
Sawdon 112 C4
Sawley Derbys. 81 F4
Sawley Lancs. 101 D3
Sawley N.Yorks. 102 B1
Sawston 58 C3
Sawtry 69 G4
Saxby Leics. 68 D1
Saxby Lincs. 96 A4
Saxby All Saints 95 G1
Saxelbye 82 B5
Saxham Street 60 B1
Saxilby 95 F5
Saxlingham 86 B2
Saxlingham Green 72 D2
Saxlingham Nethergate 72 D2
Saxlingham Thorpe 72 D2
Saxmundham 61 E1
Saxon Street 59 E2
Saxondale 82 B4
Saxtead 61 D1
Saxtead Green 61 D1
Saxtead Little Green 61 D1
Saxthorpe 86 C2
Saxton 103 D4
Sayers Common 17 E2
Scackleton 111 F5
Scaftworth 95 D3
Scagglethorpe 112 B5
Scaitcliffe 101 D5
Scalasaig 146 C5
Scalby E.Riding 104 A5
Scalby N.Yorks. 112 D3
Scaldwell 68 C5
Scale Houses 118 B3
Scaleby 118 A1
Scalebyhill 118 A1
Scales Cumb. 117 G4
Scales Cumb. 107 D5
Scalford 82 C5
Scaling 111 G1
Scallasaig 163 G3
Scallastle 147 G1
Scalloway 191 F4
Scalpay (Eilean Scalpaigh) 189 G2
Scamblesby 96 C5
Scammadale 148 C2
Scamodale 156 A2
Scampston 112 B5
Scampton 95 G5
Scaniport 166 A1
Scapa 190 B3
Scapegoat Hill 101 F1
Scarborough 112 D4
Scarcewater 4 D4
Scarcliffe 81 F1
Scarcroft 102 C3
Scardroy 173 F4
Scarfskerry 187 E1
Scargill 109 F1
Scarinish 154 B2
Scarisbrick 91 E1
Scarning 86 A4
Scarrington 82 C3
Scarrowhill 118 B2
Scarth Hill 91 F2

Scarthingwell 103 D4
Scartho 96 C2
Scatraig 166 B1
Scaur D. & G. 124 C3
Scaur (Kippford) D. & G. 124 C5
Scawby 95 G2
Scawby Brook 95 G2
Scawton 111 E4
Scayne's Hill 17 F1
Scethrog 52 A5
Schaw 132 C3
Scholar Green 79 F2
Scholes S.Yorks. 94 A3
Scholes W.Yorks. 102 C4
Scholes W.Yorks. 93 F2
Scholes W.Yorks. 102 A5
School Green 78 D1
School House 11 G2
Schoose 116 D4
Sciberscross 182 C4
Scilly Isles (Isles of Scilly) 4 B1
Scissett 93 G1
Scleddau 48 C4
Sco Ruston 87 D3
Scofton 94 D2
Scole 72 C4
Scone 151 G2
Scones Lethendy 151 G2
Sconser 52 D1
Scoor 146 D3
Scopwick 83 F2
Scoraig 180 C5
Scorborough 104 C3
Scorrier 4 B5
Scorriton 8 D1
Scorton Lancs. 100 B3
Scorton N.Yorks. 110 B2
Scot Hay 79 E3
Scotby 118 A2
Scotch Corner 110 B2
Scotforth 100 A2
Scothern 96 A5
Scotland 83 F4
Scotland End 55 F4
Scotland Street 60 A4
Scotlandwell 151 G4
Scotnish 139 F1
Scots' Gap 128 C3
Scotsburn 174 D2
Scotston Aber. 161 F2
Scotston P. & K. 159 E5
Scotstoun 141 G3
Scotstown 156 A3
Scott Willoughby 83 F4
Scotter 95 F2
Scotterthorpe 95 F2
Scottlethorpe 83 F5
Scotton Lincs. 95 F3
Scotton N.Yorks. 110 A3
Scotton N.Yorks. 102 C3
Scottow 87 D3
Scoughall 144 D1
Scoulton 86 A5
Scounslow Green 80 B5
Scourie 184 A4
Scourie More 184 A4
Scousburgh 191 F5
Scouthead 93 D2
Scrabster 186 D1
Scrafield 84 B3
Scrainwood 128 B1
Scrane End 84 B3
Scraptoft 68 B2
Scratby 87 G4
Scrayingham 103 G2
Scredington 83 F3
Scremby 84 C1
Scremerston 137 G2
Screveton 82 C3
Scriven 102 C2
Scronkey 100 A3
Scrooby 95 D3
Scropton 80 C4
Scrub Hill 84 A2
Scruton 110 C3
Sculthorpe 85 G4
Scunthorpe 95 F1
Scurlage 36 A4
Sea 11 G1
Sea Mills 39 G4
Sea Palling 87 F3
Seabank 156 B5
Seaborough 12 A2
Seaburn 120 D1
Seacombe 91 D3
Seacroft Lincs. 85 D1
Seacroft W.Yorks. 102 C4

Seadyke 84 B4
Seafield Arg. & B. 139 F1
Seafield S.Ayr. 132 B3
Seafield W.Loth. 143 E3
Seaford 17 G4
Seaforth 91 E3
Seagrave 68 B3
Seagry Heath 40 B4
Seaham 120 D3
Seaham Grange 120 D2
Seahouses 137 G3
Seal 31 E3
Sealand 78 A1
Seale 29 D3
Sealyham 48 C5
Seamer N.Yorks. 111 D1
Seamer N.Yorks. 112 D4
Seamill 140 C5
Searby 96 A2
Seasalter 32 C2
Seascale 106 B2
Seathorne 85 D1
Seathwaite Cumb. 117 F5
Seathwaite Cumb. 106 D3
Seatle 107 E4
Seatoller 117 F5
Seaton Cornw. 6 D5
Seaton Cumb. 116 D3
Seaton Devon 11 F3
Seaton Dur. 120 C2
Seaton E.Riding 105 D3
Seaton Northumb. 129 F4
Seaton Rut. 69 E3
Seaton Burn 129 E4
Seaton Carew 121 E5
Seaton Delaval 129 F4
Seaton Junction 11 F3
Seaton Ross 103 G3
Seaton Sluice 129 F4
Seatown Aber. 179 G2
Seatown Dorset 12 A3
Seatown Moray 177 D1
Seave Green 111 E3
Seaview 15 F3
Seaville 117 E1
Seavington St. Mary 12 A1
Seavington St. Michael 12 A1
Seawick 47 E1
Sebastopol 38 B3
Sebergham 117 G2
Seckington 67 E2
Second Coast 180 B5
Sedbergh 108 B3
Sedbury 39 E3
Sedbusk 109 D3
Seddington 57 G3
Sedgeberrow 54 C4
Sedgebrook 83 D4
Sedgefield 120 C5
Sedgeford 85 F3
Sedgehill 25 F5
Sedgemere 67 E5
Sedgley 66 B3
Sedlescombe 18 C2
Sedlescombe Street 18 C2
Seend 26 A1
Seend Cleeve 26 A1
Seer Green 43 E3
Seething 73 E2
Sefton 91 E2
Seghill 129 E4
Seifton 65 D4
Seighford 79 F5
Seil 147 G2
Seion 75 E1
Seisdon 66 B3
Selattyn 77 F4
Selborne 28 C4
Selby 103 E4
Selham 29 E5
Selhurst 30 C2
Selkirk 135 F3
Sellack 53 E5
Sellafield 106 B2
Sellafirth 191 F1
Sellindge 32 D5
Selling 32 C3
Sells Green 26 A1
Selly Oak 66 C4
Selmeston 18 A3
Selsdon 30 C2
Selsey 16 A4
Selsfield Common 30 C5

Selside *Cumb.* 107 G3
Selside *N.Yorks.* 108 C5
Selsley 40 A2
Selstead 33 E4
Selston 81 F2
Selworthy 22 C3
Semer 60 A3
Semington 25 F1
Semley 25 F5
Send 29 F2
Send Marsh 29 F2
Senghenydd 38 A3
Sennen 2 A4
Sennen Cove 2 A4
Sennybridge 51 F5
Senwick 115 G2
Sequer's Bridge 8 C2
Serlby 94 D4
Serrington 26 B4
Sessay 111 D5
Setchey 71 E1
Setley 14 C2
Setter 191 F3
Settle 101 E1
Settrington 112 B5
Seven Ash 23 E4
Seven Bridges 40 D3
Seven Kings 45 D4
Seven Sisters 37 E2
Seven Springs 40 B1
Sevenhampton *Glos.* 54 C5
Sevenhampton *Swin.* 41 E3
Sevenoaks 31 E3
Sevenoaks Weald 31 E3
Severn Beach 39 E4
Severn Stoke 54 A3
Sevick End 57 F2
Sevington 32 C4
Sewards End 59 D4
Sewardstone 44 C3
Sewerby 105 D1
Seworgan 3 E3
Sewstern 83 D5
Seymour Villas 21 E1
Sezincote 55 D4
Sgiogarstaigh 189 G1
Sgodachail 181 G5
Shabbington 42 B2
Shackerley 66 A2
Shackerstone 67 F2
Shackleford 29 E3
Shadfen 128 E3
Shadforth 120 C3
Shadingfield 73 F3
Shadoxhurst 32 B5
Shadsworth 100 D5
Shadwell *Norf.* 72 A3
Shadwell *W.Yorks.* 102 A4
Shaftenhoe End 58 C4
Shaftesbury 25 F5
Shafton 94 A1
Shalbourne 27 E1
Shalcombe 14 C4
Shalden 28 B3
Shalden Green 28 C3
Shaldon 10 C5
Shalfleet 14 C4
Shalford *Essex* 59 F5
Shalford *Surr.* 29 F3
Shalford Green 59 F5
Shallowford *Devon* 22 A3
Shallowford *Staffs.* 79 F5
Shalmsford Street 32 C3
Shalmstry 186 D2
Shalstone 56 B4
Shalunt 140 B2
Shambellie 125 D4
Shamley Green 29 F3
Shandon 141 D1
Shandwick 175 E2
Shangton 68 C3
Shankend 135 G5
Shankhouse 129 E4
Shanklin 15 E4
Shannochie 131 E3
Shantron 141 E1
Shantullich 174 C4
Shanzie 160 A4
Shap 107 G1
Shapinsay 190 B3
Shapwick *Dorset* 13 F2
Shapwick *Som.* 24 B4
Sharcott 26 C2
Shard End 67 D4
Shardlow 81 F4
Shareshill 66 B2
Sharlston 94 A1

Sharlston Common 94 A1
Sharnal Street 45 G5
Sharnbrook 57 E2
Sharneyford 101 E5
Sharnford 67 G3
Sharnhill Green 12 D2
Sharow 110 C5
Sharp Street 87 E3
Sharpenhoe 57 F4
Sharperton 128 B4
Sharpham House 9 E2
Sharpness 39 F2
Sharpthorne 30 C5
Sharrington 86 B2
Shatterford 65 G4
Shatterling 33 E3
Shaugh Prior 8 B1
Shave Cross 12 A3
Shavington 79 E2
Shaw *Gt.Man.* 92 D2
Shaw *Swin.* 40 D4
Shaw *W.Berks.* 27 F1
Shaw *Wilts.* 25 F1
Shaw Green *Herts.* 58 A4
Shaw Green *N.Yorks.* 102 B2
Shaw Mills 102 B1
Shaw Side 92 D2
Shawbost 189 F2
Shawbury 78 C5
Shawell 68 A4
Shawfield *Gt.Man.* 92 C1
Shawfield *Staffs.* 80 B1
Shawford 27 F5
Shawforth 101 E5
Shawhead 124 C3
Shawtonhill 142 A5
Sheanachie 130 C4
Sheandow 167 G1
Shearington 125 E4
Shearsby 68 B3
Shebbear 21 E5
Shebdon 79 E5
Shebster 186 C2
Shedfield 15 E1
Sheen 80 C1
Sheepridge 93 F1
Sheepscombe 40 A1
Sheepstor 8 B1
Sheepwash *Devon* 21 E5
Sheepwash *Northumb.* 129 E3
Sheepway 39 D5
Sheepy Magna 67 F2
Sheepy Parva 67 F2
Sheering 45 E1
Sheerness 32 B1
Sheet 28 C5
Sheffield 94 A4
Sheffield Bottom 28 B1
Sheffield City Airport 94 B4
Sheffield Green 17 G1
Shefford 57 G4
Shefford Woodlands 41 F5
Sheigra 184 A2
Sheinton 65 F2
Shelderton 64 D5
Sheldon *Derbys.* 80 C1
Sheldon *Devon* 11 E2
Sheldon *W.Mid.* 66 D4
Sheldwich 32 C3
Sheldwich Lees 32 C3
Shelf *Bridgend* 37 F4
Shelf *W.Yorks.* 102 A5
Shelfanger 72 C3
Shelfield *W.Mid.* 66 C2
Shelfield *Warks.* 54 D1
Shelfield Green 54 D1
Shelford 82 B3
Shellachan *Arg. & B.* 148 A2
Shellachan *Arg. & B.* 148 C2
Shellbrook 67 F1
Shellbrook Hill 78 A3
Shelley *Essex* 45 E2
Shelley *Suff.* 60 B4
Shelley *W.Yorks.* 93 G1
Shellingford 41 F3
Shellow Bowells 45 F2
Shelsley Beauchamp 53 G1

Shelsley Walsh 53 G1
Shelswell 56 B4
Shelthorpe 68 A1
Shelton *Beds.* 57 F1

Shelton *Norf.* 72 D2
Shelton *Notts.* 82 C3
Shelton *Shrop.* 65 D1
Shelve 64 C3
Shelwick 53 E3
Shelwick Green 53 E3
Shenfield 45 F3
Shenington 55 F3
Shenley 44 A2
Shenley Brook End 56 D4
Shenley Church End 56 D4
Shenleybury 44 A2
Shenmore 52 C4
Shennanton 123 E4
Shenstone *Staffs.* 66 D2
Shenstone *Worcs.* 66 A5
Shenstone Woodend 66 D2
Shenton 67 F2
Shenval 167 G2
Shepeau Stow 70 B1
Shephall 58 A5
Shepherd's Bush 44 B5
Shepherd's Green 42 C4
Shepherd's Patch 39 G2
Shepherdswell (Sibertswold) 33 E4
Shepley 93 F2
Sheppardstown 187 E5
Shepperdine 39 F3
Shepperton 29 F1
Shepreth 58 B3
Shepshed 67 G1
Shepton Beauchamp 12 A1
Shepton Mallet 24 D3
Shepton Montague 25 D4
Shepway 31 G3
Sheraton 120 D4
Sherborne *Dorset* 12 C1
Sherborne *Glos.* 41 D1
Sherborne St. John 28 B2
Sherbourne 55 E1
Sherbourne Street 60 A3
Sherburn *Dur.* 120 C3
Sherburn *N.Yorks.* 112 C5
Sherburn Hill 120 C3
Sherburn in Elmet 103 D4
Shere 29 F3
Shereford 85 G5
Sherfield English 27 D5
Sherfield on Loddon 28 B2
Sherford *Devon* 9 D3
Sherford *Som.* 23 F5
Sheriff Hutton 103 F1
Sheriffhales 65 G1
Sheringham 86 C1
Sherington 57 D3
Shernal Green 54 B1
Shernborne 85 F4
Sherramore 165 G5
Sherrington 26 A4
Sherston 40 A4
Sherwood 81 G3
Sherwood Green 21 F3
Shetland Islands 191 F3
Shettleston 142 A3
Shevington 91 G2
Shevington Moor 91 G1
Sheviock 7 D5
Shide 15 E4
Shiel Bridge (Drochaid Sheile) 164 A3
Shieldaig *High.* 172 B4
Shieldaig *High.* 172 B2
Shieldhill 142 C2
Shielfoot 155 F2
Shielhill 160 C4
Shiels 169 D4
Shifford 41 F2
Shifnal 65 G2
Shilbottle 129 E1
Shildon 120 B5
Shillingford *Devon* 22 C5
Shillingford *Oxon.* 42 A3
Shillingford Abbot 10 C4
Shillingford St. George 10 C4
Shillingstone 13 E1
Shillington 57 G4
Shillmoor 128 A1
Shilstone 21 F5
Shilton *Oxon.* 41 E2
Shilton *Warks.* 67 G4
Shimpling *Norf.* 72 C3
Shimpling *Suff.* 59 G2
Shimpling Street 59 G2

Shincliffe 120 B3
Shiney Row 120 C2
Shinfield 28 C1
Shingay 58 B3
Shingham 71 F2
Shingle Street 61 E3
Shinness Lodge 182 A3
Shipbourne 31 E3
Shipbrookhill 92 A5
Shipdham 86 A5
Shipham 24 B2
Shiphay 9 E1
Shiplake 42 C5
Shiplake Row 42 C5
Shipley *Northumb.* 137 F5
Shipley *Shrop.* 66 A3
Shipley *W.Suss.* 29 G5
Shipley *W.Yorks.* 102 A4
Shipley Bridge *Devon* 8 C1
Shipley Bridge *Surr.* 30 C4
Shipley Common 81 F3
Shipmeadow 73 E2
Shippea Hill 71 E4
Shippon 41 G3
Shipston on Stour 55 E3
Shipton *Glos.* 40 C1
Shipton *N.Yorks.* 103 E1
Shipton *Shrop.* 65 E3
Shipton Bellinger 26 D3
Shipton Gorge 12 A3
Shipton Green 16 A3
Shipton Moyne 40 A4
Shipton Oliffe 40 C1
Shipton Solers 40 C1
Shipton-on-Cherwell 41 G1
Shiptonthorpe 104 A3
Shipton-under-Wychwood 41 E1
Shira 149 D3
Shirburn 42 B3
Shirdley Hill 91 E1
Shire Oak 66 C2
Shirebrook 81 G1
Shirecliffe 94 A3
Shiregreen 94 A3
Shirehampton 39 E5
Shiremoor 129 F4
Shirenewton 39 D3
Shireoaks 94 C4
Shirl Heath 52 D2
Shirland 81 E2
Shirley *Derbys.* 80 D3
Shirley *Gt.Lon.* 30 C2
Shirley *Hants.* 14 A3
Shirley *S'ham.* 14 D1
Shirley *W.Mid.* 66 D5
Shirley Heath 66 D5
Shirley Warren 14 C1
Shirleywich 79 G5
Shirrell Heath 15 E1
Shirwell 21 F2
Shirwell Cross 21 F2
Shiskine 131 E3
Shittlehope 119 G4
Shobdon 52 C1
Shobley 14 A2
Shobrooke 10 B2
Shocklach 78 B3
Shocklach Green 78 B3
Shoeburyness 46 C4
Sholden 33 F3
Sholing 15 D1
Shoot Hill 64 D1
Shooter's Hill 44 D5
Shop *Cornw.* 4 C2
Shop *Cornw.* 20 C4
Shop Corner 60 D4
Shopnoller 23 E4
Shore 92 D1
Shoreditch 44 C4
Shoreham 31 E2
Shoreham Airport 17 D3
Shoreham-by-Sea 17 E3
Shoremill 174 D3
Shoresdean 145 G5
Shoreswood 145 G5
Shoreton 174 C3
Shorley 27 G5
Shorncote 40 C3
Shorne 45 F5
Shorne Ridgeway 45 F5
Short Cross 64 B2
Short Green 72 B3
Short Heath *Derbys.* 67 F1

Short Heath *W.Mid.* 66 C3
Shortacombe 7 F2
Shortbridge 17 G1
Shortfield Common 28 D3
Shortgate 17 G2
Shortgrove 58 D4
Shorthampton 55 F5
Shortlands 30 C2
Shortlanesend 4 C5
Shorton 9 E1
Shorwell 15 D4
Shoscombe 25 E2
Shotatton 78 A5
Shoteham 57 D2
Shotgate 45 G3
Shotley *Northants.* 69 E3
Shotley *Suff.* 60 D4
Shotley Bridge 119 G2
Shotley Gate 60 D4
Shotleyfield 119 G2
Shottenden 32 C3
Shottermill 29 D4
Shottery 55 D2
Shotteswell 55 G3
Shottisham 61 E3
Shottle 81 E3
Shottlegate 81 E3
Shotton *Dur.* 120 D4
Shotton *Dur.* 120 C5
Shotton *Flints.* 78 A1
Shotton *Northumb.* 129 E4
Shotton Colliery 120 C3
Shotts 142 C3
Shotwick 91 F5
Shouldham 71 E2
Shouldham Thorpe 71 E2
Shoulton 54 A1
Shover's Green 31 F5
Shrawardine 64 C1
Shrawley 54 A1
Shreding Green 43 F4
Shrewley 55 E1
Shrewsbury 65 D1
Shrewton 26 B3
Shripney 16 B3
Shrivenham 41 E4
Shropham 72 A2
Shrub End 60 A5
Shucknall 53 E3
Shudy Camps 59 E3
Shurdington 40 B1
Shurlock Row 42 D5
Shurnock 54 C1
Shurrery 186 C3
Shurrery Lodge 186 C3
Shurton 23 F3
Shustoke 67 E3
Shut Heath 79 F5
Shutford 55 F3
Shuthonger 54 A4
Shutlanger 56 C3
Shutt Green 66 A2
Shuttington 67 E2
Shuttlewood 94 B5
Shuttleworth 92 B1
Sibbaldbie 125 F2
Sibbertoft 68 B4
Sibdon Carwood 64 D4
Sibertswold (Shepherdswell) 33 E4
Sibford Ferris 55 F4
Sibford Gower 55 F4
Sible Hedingham 59 F4
Sibley's Green 59 E5
Sibsey 84 B2
Sibson *Cambs.* 69 F3
Sibson *Leics.* 67 F2
Sibster 187 F3
Sibthorpe 82 C3
Sibton 61 E1
Sibton Green 73 E4
Sicklesmere 59 G1
Sicklinghall 102 C3
Sidbury *Devon* 11 E3
Sidbury *Shrop.* 65 F4
Sidcot 24 B2
Sidcup 45 D5
Siddal 102 A5
Siddington *Ches.E.* 92 C5
Siddington *Glos.* 40 C3
Sidemoor 66 B5
Sidestrand 87 D2
Sidford 11 E3

Sidlesham 16 A4
Sidley 18 C3
Sidlow 30 B4
Sidmouth 11 E4
Sigford 10 A5
Sigglesthorne 105 D3
Sigingstone 37 F5
Signet 41 E1
Silchester 28 B1
Sileby 68 B1
Silecroft 106 C1
Silfield 72 C2
Silian 50 B2
Silk Willoughby 83 F3
Silkstead 27 F5
Silkstone 93 G2
Silkstone Common 93 G2
Sill Field 107 G2
Silloth 117 E1
Sills 128 A1
Sillyearn 177 E4
Silpho 112 C3
Silsden 101 G3
Silsoe 57 F4
Silver End *Beds.* 57 G3
Silver End *Essex* 59 G5
Silver Green 73 D2
Silver Street *Kent* 32 A2
Silver Street *Som.* 24 C4
Silverburn 143 G3
Silvercraigs 139 G1
Silverdale *Lancs.* 107 F5
Silverdale *Staffs.* 79 F3
Silvergate 86 C3
Silverhill 18 C2
Silverlace Green 61 E2
Silverley's Green 73 D4
Silvermoss 169 F1
Silverstone 56 B3
Silverton 10 C2
Silvington 65 F5
Simister 92 C2
Simmondley 93 E3
Simonburn 128 A4
Simonsbath 22 A4
Simonside 120 C1
Simonstone *Bridgend* 37 F4
Simonstone *Lancs.* 101 D4
Simprim 145 F5
Simpson 57 D4
Sinclair's Hill 145 F4
Sinclairston 132 C4
Sinderby 110 C3
Sinderhope 119 E2
Sindlesham 28 C1
Sinfin 81 E4
Singdean 135 G5
Singleton *Lancs.* 99 G4
Singleton *W.Suss.* 16 A2
Singlewell 45 F5
Singret 78 A2
Sinkhurst Green 32 A4
Sinnahard 168 B3
Sinnington 111 G4
Sinton Green 54 A1
Sipson 43 F5
Sirhowy 38 A1
Sisland 73 E2
Sissinghurst 31 G5
Siston 39 F5
Sithney 2 D4
Sittingbourne 32 B2
Siulaisiadar 189 G2
Six Ashes 65 G4
Six Hills 82 B5
Six Mile Bottom 59 D2
Six Roads End 80 C5
Sixhills 96 B4
Sixmile 96 B4
Sixpenny Handley 13 G1
Sizewell 61 F1
Skail 185 G4
Skaill *Ork.* 190 A3
Skaill *Ork.* 190 C3
Skares *Aber.* 168 D1
Skares *E.Ayr.* 132 D4
Skateraw 145 E2
Skaw 191 G3
Skeabost 170 D5
Skeeby 110 B2
Skeffington 68 C2
Skeffling 97 D1
Skegby 81 G1
Skegness 85 D1
Skelbo 182 C5
Skelbo Street 182 C5
Skelbrooke 94 C1

Skeldon 132 B4
Skeldyke 84 B4
Skellingthorpe 95 G5
Skellow 94 C1
Skelmanthorpe 93 G1
Skelmersdale 91 F2
Skelmorlie 140 C3
Skelmuir 179 E3
Skelpick 185 G3
Skelton Cumb. 118 A4
Skelton E.Riding 103 G5
Skelton N.Yorks. 109 F2
Skelton (Skelton-in-Cleveland) R. & C. 111 F1
Skelton York 103 G2
Skelton-in-Cleveland (Skelton) 111 F1
Skelton-on-Ure 102 C1
Skelwick 190 B1
Skelwith Bridge 107 E2
Skendleby 84 C1
Skendleby Psalter 97 E5
Skenfrith 53 D5
Skerne 104 C2
Skeroblingarry 130 C3
Skerray 185 F2
Skerton 100 A1
Sketchley 67 G3
Sketty 36 C3
Skewen 36 D3
Skewsby 111 F5
Skeyton 86 D3
Skeyton Corner 87 D3
Skidbrooke 97 E3
Skidbrooke North End 97 E3
Skidby 104 C4
Skilgate 22 C5
Skillington 83 D5
Skinburness 117 E1
Skinflats 142 D1
Skinidin 170 B5
Skinnet 186 D2
Skinningrove 111 G1
Skipness 139 G4
Skippool 99 G3
Skipsea 105 D2
Skipsea Brough 105 D2
Skipton 101 F2
Skipton-on-Swale 110 C5
Skipwith 103 F4
Skirbeck 84 B3
Skirbeck Quarter 84 B3
Skirethorns 101 F1
Skirlaugh 104 D4
Skirling 134 B2
Skirmett 42 C4
Skirpenbeck 103 G2
Skirwith Cumb. 118 C4
Skirwith N.Yorks. 108 C5
Skirza 187 F2
Skittle Green 42 C2
Skomer Island 34 A2
Skulamus 163 E2
Skullomie 185 F2
Skyborry Green 64 B5
Skye 162 C1
Skye Green 59 G5
Skye of Curr 167 D2
Skyreholme 101 G1
Slack Aber. 168 C1
Slack Derbys. 81 E1
Slack W.Yorks. 101 F5
Slackhall 93 E4
Slackhead 176 D3
Slad 40 A2
Slade Devon 21 F1
Slade Devon 11 E2
Slade Pembs. 34 C1
Slade Swan. 36 A4
Slade Green 45 E5
Slade Hooton 94 C4
Sladesbridge 5 E2
Slaggyford 118 C2
Slaidburn 100 D2
Slains Park 161 G2
Slaithwaite 93 E1
Slaley 119 F2
Slamannan 142 C2
Slapton Bucks. 57 E5
Slapton Devon 9 E3
Slapton Northants. 56 B3
Slate Haugh 177 D3
Slatepit Dale 81 F1
Slattadale 172 B2
Slaugham 17 E1
Slaughden 61 F2

Slaughterford 40 A5
Slawston 68 C3
Sleaford Hants. 28 D4
Sleaford Lincs. 83 F3
Sleagill 107 G1
Sleap 78 B5
Sledge Green 54 A4
Sledmere 104 B1
Sleights 112 B2
Slepe 13 F3
Slerra 20 D3
Slickly 187 E2
Sliddery 131 E3
Sliemore 167 E2
Sligachan 162 C2
Slimbridge 39 G2
Slindon Staffs. 79 F5
Slindon W.Suss. 16 B3
Slinfold 29 G4
Sling 39 E2
Slingsby 111 F5
Slioch 168 C1
Slip End Beds. 43 F1
Slip End Herts. 58 A4
Slipton 69 E5
Slitting Mill 66 C1
Slochd 166 C2
Slockavullin 148 A5
Sloganie 124 A4
Sloley 87 E3
Slongaber 124 C3
Sloothby 97 E5
Slough 43 E4
Slough Green Som. 23 F5
Slough Green W.Suss. 17 E1
Sluggan 166 C2
Slyne 100 A1
Smailholm 136 A3
Small Dole 17 E2
Small Hythe 32 A5
Smallbridge 92 D1
Smallbrook 10 B3
Smallburgh 87 E3
Smallburn Aber. 179 F3
Smallburn E.Ayr. 133 E3
Smalldale 93 E5
Smalley 81 F3
Smallfield 30 C4
Smallford 44 A2
Smallridge 11 F2
Smallthorne 79 F2
Smallworth 72 B3
Smannell 27 E3
Smardale 108 C2
Smarden 32 A4
Smaull 138 A3
Smeatharpe 11 E1
Smeeth 32 C5
Smeeton Westerby 68 B3
Smerral 183 G1
Smestow 66 A3
Smethwick 66 C4
Smethwick Green 79 F1
Sminsary 155 F2
Smisby 67 F1
Smith End Green 53 G2
Smithfield 118 A1
Smithies 94 A2
Smithincott 11 D1
Smith's End 58 B4
Smith's Green Essex 59 D5
Smith's Green Essex 59 E3
Smithstown 172 A2
Smithton 174 D5
Smithy Green 92 B5
Smockington 67 G4
Smyrton 122 C2
Smythe's Green 46 C1
Snailbeach 64 C2
Snailwell 59 E1
Snainton 112 C4
Snaith 103 F3
Snape N.Yorks. 110 B4
Snape Suff. 61 E2
Snape Green 91 E1
Snape Watering 61 E2
Snarestone 67 F2
Snarford 96 A4
Snargate 19 E1
Snave 19 F1
Sneachill 54 B2
Snead 64 C3
Snead's Green 54 A1
Sneath Common 72 C3
Sneaton 112 B2
Sneatonthorpe 112 C2

Snelland 96 A4
Snellings 106 A2
Snelston 80 C3
Snetterton 72 A2
Snettisham 85 E4
Snipeshill 32 B2
Snitter 128 C1
Snitterby 95 G3
Snitterfield 55 E2
Snitterton 81 D1
Snittlegarth 117 F3
Snitton 65 E5
Snodhill 52 C3
Snodland 31 G2
Snow End 58 C4
Snow Street 72 B3
Snowden Hill 93 G2
Snowshill 54 C4
Soar Cardiff 37 G4
Soar Carmar. 50 C5
Soar Devon 8 D4
Soay 162 C3
Soberton 15 F1
Soberton Heath 15 F1
Sockbridge 118 B5
Sockburn 110 C2
Sodom 90 B5
Sodylt Bank 78 A4
Softley 119 G5
Soham 71 E5
Soham Cotes 71 D5
Soldon 20 D4
Soldon Cross 20 D4
Soldridge 28 B4
Sole Street Kent 32 C4
Sole Street Kent 31 F2
Soleburn 122 B4
Solihull 67 D5
Solihull Lodge 66 C5
Sollas 188 B1
Sollers Dilwyn 52 D2
Sollers Hope 53 F4
Sollom 91 F1
Solomon's Tump 39 G1
Solsgirth 151 E5
Solva 48 A5
Solwaybank 126 B4
Somerby Leics. 68 C1
Somerby Lincs. 96 A2
Somercotes 81 F2
Somerford 66 B2
Somerford Keynes 40 C3
Somerley 16 A4
Somerleyton 73 F2
Somersal Herbert 80 C4
Somersby 96 D5
Somersham Cambs. 70 B5
Somersham Suff. 60 B3
Somerton Newport 38 C4
Somerton Oxon. 55 G5
Somerton Som. 24 B5
Somerton Suff. 59 G2
Sompting 17 D3
Sompting Abbotts 17 D3
Sonning 42 C5
Sonning Common 42 C4
Sonning Eye 42 C5
Sontley 78 A3
Sookholme 81 G1
Sopley 14 A3
Sopworth 40 A4
Sorbie 115 E2
Sordale 186 D2
Sorisdale 154 B3
Sorn 133 D3
Sornhill 132 D2
Soroba 148 A2
Sortat 187 E2
Sotby 96 C5
Sots Hole 83 G1
Sotterley 73 F3
Soudley 79 E5
Soughton 77 F1
Soulbury 57 D5
Soulby 108 C1
Souldern 56 A4
Souldrop 57 E1
Sound 78 D3
Sourhope 136 C4
Sourton 7 F1
Soutergate 106 D4
South Acre 71 G1
South Acton 44 A5
South Alkham 33 E4
South Allington 9 E4
South Alloa 151 D5
South Ambersham 29 E5
South Anston 94 C4

South Ascot 29 E1
South Baddesley 14 C3
South Ballachulish (Baile a' Chaolais a Deas) 156 C4
South Balloch 123 E1
South Bank 121 E5
South Barrow 24 D5
South Bellsdyke 142 D1
South Benfleet 45 G4
South Bersted 16 B3
South Blackbog 169 E1
South Bockhampton 14 A3
South Bowood 12 A3
South Brent 8 C1
South Brentor 7 E2
South Brewham 25 E4
South Broomhill 129 E2
South Burlingham 87 E5
South Cadbury 24 D5
South Cairn 32 A4
South Carlton 95 G5
South Cave 104 B4
South Cerney 40 C3
South Chard 11 G2
South Charlton 137 F4
South Cheriton 25 D5
South Church 120 B5
South Cliffe 104 A4
South Clifton 95 F5
South Cockerington 97 D4
South Common 17 F2
South Cornelly 37 E4
South Corriegills 131 F2
South Cove 73 F3
South Creagan 156 B5
South Creake 85 G4
South Crosland 93 F1
South Croxton 68 B1
South Croydon 30 C2
South Dalton 104 B3
South Darenth 45 E5
South Duffield 103 F4
South Elkington 96 C4
South Elmsall 94 B1
South Erradale 172 A2
South Fambridge 46 B3
South Fawley 41 F4
South Ferriby 104 B5
South Field 104 C5
South Flobbets 169 E1
South Godstone 30 C4
South Gorley 14 A1
South Green Essex 45 F3
South Green Essex 46 D1
South Green Norf. 86 B4
South Green Suff. 72 C4
South Gyle 143 F2
South Hall 140 B2
South Hanningfield 45 G3
South Harefield 43 F4
South Harting 15 G1
South Hayling 15 G3
South Hazelrigg 137 E3
South Heath 43 E2
South Heighton 17 G3
South Hetton 120 C3
South Hiendley 94 A1
South Hill 6 D3
South Hinksey 42 C2
South Hole 20 C4
South Holme 111 F5
South Holmwood 29 G3
South Hornchurch 45 E4
South Hourat 141 D4
South Huish 8 C3
South Hykeham 83 E1
South Hylton 120 C2
South Kelsey 96 A3
South Kessock (Ceasag a Deas) 174 C5
South Killingholme 96 B1
South Kilvington 110 D4
South Kilworth 88 C5
South Kirkby 94 B1
South Kirkton 169 E4
South Knighton 10 B5
South Kyme 83 G3
South Lancing 17 D3
South Ledaig 148 B1
South Leigh 41 F2
South Leverton 95 E4

South Littleton 54 C3
South Lopham 72 B3
South Luffenham 69 E2
South Malling 17 G2
South Marston 41 D4
South Middleton 137 D4
South Milford 103 D3
South Milton 8 C3
South Mimms 44 B2
South Molton 22 A5
South Moor 120 A2
South Moreton 42 A4
South Mundham 16 A3
South Muskham 82 C2
South Newbald 104 B4
South Newington 55 G4
South Newton 26 B4
South Normanton 81 F2
South Norwood 30 C2
South Nutfield 30 C4
South Ockendon 45 E4
South Ormsby 97 D5
South Ossett 93 G1
South Otterington 110 C4
South Owersby 96 A3
South Oxhey 44 A3
South Park 30 B4
South Parks 152 A4
South Perrott 12 A2
South Petherton 12 A1
South Petherwin 6 D2
South Pickenham 71 G2
South Pool 9 D3
South Queensferry (Queensferry) 143 F2
South Radworthy 22 A4
South Rauceby 83 F3
South Raynham 85 G5
South Redbriggs 177 G5
South Reston 97 E4
South Ronaldsay 190 B4
South Ruislip 44 A4
South Runcton 71 E2
South Scarle 82 D1
South Shian (Sithean a Deas) 156 B5
South Shields 120 C1
South Somercotes 97 E3
South Somercotes Fen Houses 97 E3
South Stainley 102 C1
South Stoke Oxon. 42 B4
South Stoke W.Suss. 16 C3
South Street E.Suss. 17 F2
South Street Gt.Lon. 30 D3
South Street Kent 31 F2
South Street Kent 32 D2
South Street Kent 32 A2
South Tawton 7 G1
South Thoresby 97 E5
South Tidworth 26 D3
South Tottenham 44 C4
South Town Devon 10 C4
South Town Hants. 28 B4
South Uist (Uibhist a Deas) 188 B3
South Upper Barrack 179 E3
South View 28 B2
South Walsham 87 E4
South Warnborough 28 C3
South Weald 45 E3
South Weston 42 C3
South Wheatley Cornw. 6 C1
South Wheatley Notts. 95 E4
South Wigston 68 A3
South Willingham 96 B4
South Wingfield 81 E2
South Witham 69 E1
South Wonston 27 F4
South Woodham Ferrers 46 B3
South Wootton 85 E5
South Wraxall 25 D1
South Yardle 66 D4
South Zeal 7 G1
Southall 44 A4
Southam Glos. 54 B5
Southam Warks. 55 G1
Southampton 14 D1
Southampton Airport 15 D1

Southbar 141 F3
Southborough Gt.Lon. 30 D2
Southborough Kent 31 E4
Southbourne Bourne. 14 A3
Southbourne W.Suss. 15 G2
Southbrook 10 D3
Southburgh 86 B5
Southburn 104 B2
Southchurch 46 C4
Southcott Devon 7 F1
Southcott Wilts. 26 C2
Southcourt 42 D1
Southdean 127 E1
Southdene 91 F3
Southease 17 G3
Southend Aber. 177 G5
Southend Arg. & B. 130 B5
Southend Bucks. 42 C4
Southend W.Berks. 42 A5
Southend Wilts. 41 D5
Southend Airport 46 B4
Southend-on-Sea 46 B4
Southerfield 117 E2
Southerly 7 F2
Southern Green 58 B4
Southerndown 37 E5
Southerness 125 D5
Southery 71 E3
Southfield 152 A5
Southfields 44 B5
Southfleet 45 F5
Southgate Cere. 62 B4
Southgate Gt.Lon. 44 C3
Southgate Norf. 86 C3
Southgate Norf. 85 E4
Southgate Swan. 36 B4
Southill 57 G3
Southington 27 E2
Southleigh 11 F3
Southmarsh 25 E4
Southminster 46 C3
Southmoor 41 F3
Southmuir 160 B4
Southoe 57 G1
Southolt 60 C1
Southorpe 69 F2
Southowram 102 A5
Southport 91 E1
Southrepps 87 D2
Southrey 83 G1
Southrop 41 D2
Southrope 28 B3
Southsea Ports. 15 F3
Southsea Wrex. 77 F2
Southstoke 25 E1
Southtown 87 G5
Southwaite Cumb. 108 C2
Southwaite Cumb. 118 A3
Southwater 29 G5
Southwater Street 29 G5
Southway 24 C3
Southwell Dorset 12 C5
Southwell Notts. 82 B2
Southwick D. & G. 124 D5
Southwick Hants. 15 F2
Southwick Northants. 69 F3
Southwick Som. 24 A3
Southwick T. & W. 120 C2
Southwick W.Suss. 17 E3
Southwick Wilts. 25 F2
Southwold 73 G4
Southwood 24 C4
Sowden 10 C4
Sower Carr 99 G3
Sowerby N.Yorks. 110 D4
Sowerby W.Yorks. 101 G5
Sowerby Bridge 101 G5
Sowerby Row 117 F2
Sowerhill 22 B5
Sowley Green 59 F2
Sowood 93 E1
Sowton 10 C3
Soyal 182 A5
Spa Common 87 D2
Spadeadam 127 D4
Spalding 84 A5
Spaldington 103 G4
Spaldwick 69 G5
Spalefield 153 D4
Spalford 82 D1

Spanby 83 F4
Sparham 86 B4
Spark Bridge 107 E4
Sparkford 24 D5
Sparkhill 66 C4
Sparkwell 8 B2
Sparrow Green 86 A4
Sparrowpit 93 E4
Sparrow's Green 31 F5
Sparsholt Hants. 27 F4
Sparsholt Oxon. 41 F4
Spartylea 119 E3
Spath 80 B4
Spaunton 111 G4
Spaxton 23 F4
Spean Bridge (Drochaid an Aonachain) 157 E1
Spear Hill 16 D2
Speddoch 124 C2
Speedwell 39 F5
Speen Bucks. 42 D2
Speen W.Berks. 27 F1
Speeton 113 E5
Speke 91 F4
Speldhurst 31 E4
Spellbrook 45 D1
Spelsbury 55 F5
Spen Green 79 F1
Spencers Wood 28 C1
Spennithorne 110 A4
Spennymoor 120 B4
Spernall 54 C1
Spetchley 54 A2
Spetisbury 13 F2
Spexhall 73 E3
Spey Bay 176 C3
Speyview 176 B5
Spilsby 84 B1
Spindlestone 137 F3
Spinkhill 94 B5
Spinningdale 174 C1
Spirthill 40 B5
Spital High. 187 D3
Spital W. & M. 43 E5
Spital in the Street 95 G3
Spitalbrook 44 C2
Spithurst 17 G2
Spittal D. & G. 123 F4
Spittal D. & G. 123 E5
Spittal E.Loth. 144 B2
Spittal Northumb. 137 E1
Spittal Pembs. 48 C5
Spittal of Glenmuick 160 B1
Spittal of Glenshee 159 G3
Spittalfield 159 G5
Spixworth 86 D4
Splayne's Green 17 G1
Splott 38 B5
Spofforth 102 C2
Spondon 81 F4
Spooner Row 72 B2
Spoonley 79 D4
Sporle 71 G1
Sportsman's Arms 76 C2
Spott 145 D2
Spratton 68 C5
Spreakley 28 D3
Spreyton 7 G1
Spriddlestone 8 B2
Spridlington 96 A4
Spring Grove 44 A5
Spring Vale 15 F3
Springburn 142 A3
Springfield Arg. & B. 140 B2
Springfield D. & G. 126 B5
Springfield Fife 152 B3
Springfield Moray 175 G4
Springfield P. & K. 151 G1
Springfield W.Mid. 66 C4
Springhill Staffs. 66 C2
Springhill Staffs. 66 B2
Springholm 124 C4
Springkell 126 A4
Springleys 169 E1
Springside 132 B2
Springthorpe 95 F4
Springwell 120 B2
Sproatley 105 D4
Sproston Green 79 E1
Sprotbrough 94 C2
Sproughton 60 C3

Sprouston 136 B3
Sprowston 86 D4
Sproxton Leics. 83 D5
Sproxton N.Yorks. 111 F4
Sprytown 7 E2
Spurlands End 43 D3
Spurstow 78 C2
Spyway 12 B3
Square Point 124 B3
Squires Gate 99 G4
Sròndoire 139 G2
Sronphadruig Lodge 158 C2
Stableford Shrop. 65 G3
Stableford Staffs. 79 F4
Stacey Bank 93 G3
Stackhouse 101 E1
Stackpole 34 C3
Stacksteads 101 E5
Staddiscombe 8 B2
Staddlethorpe 104 A5
Staden 93 E5
Stadhampton 42 B3
Staffield 118 B3
Staffin 171 D3
Stafford 79 G5
Stagden Cross 45 F1
Stagsden 57 E3
Stagshaw Bank 119 F1
Stain 187 F2
Stainburn Cumb. 116 D4
Stainburn N.Yorks. 102 B3
Stainby 83 E5
Staincross 94 A1
Staindrop 120 A5
Staines 41 G5
Stainfield Lincs. 83 F5
Stainfield Lincs. 96 B5
Stainforth N.Yorks. 101 E1
Stainforth S.Yorks. 94 D1
Staining 99 G4
Stainland 93 E1
Stainsacre 112 C2
Stainsby Derbys. 81 F1
Stainsby Lincs. 96 D5
Stainton Cumb. 107 G4
Stainton Cumb. 118 A5
Stainton Dur. 109 F1
Stainton Middbro. 111 D1
Stainton N.Yorks. 110 A3
Stainton S.Yorks. 94 C3
Stainton by Langworth 96 A5
Stainton le Vale 96 B3
Stainton with Adgarley 106 D5
Staintondale 112 C3
Stair Cumb. 117 F4
Stair E.Ayr. 132 C3
Stairfoot 94 A2
Staithes 111 G2
Stake Pool 100 A3
Stakeford 129 E3
Stakes 15 F2
Stalbridge 12 D1
Stalbridge Weston 12 D1
Stalham 87 E3
Stalham Green 87 E3
Stalisfield Green 32 B3
Stalling Busk 109 E4
Stallingborough 96 B1
Stallington 79 G4
Stalmine 99 G3
Stalybridge 93 D3
Stambourne 59 F4
Stamford Lincs. 69 F2
Stamford Northumb. 137 G5
Stamford Bridge C. & W.Ches. 78 B1
Stamford Bridge E.Riding 103 G2
Stamfordham 128 C4
Stanah 99 G3
Stanborough 44 B1
Stanbridge Beds. 58 E5
Stanbridge Dorset 13 G2
Stanbridge Earls 27 E5
Stanbury 101 G4
Stand 142 B3
Standburn 142 D2
Standeford 66 B2
Standen 32 A5
Standen Street 32 A5
Standerwick 25 F2
Standford 28 D4

Standford Bridge 79 E5
Standish Glos. 40 A2
Standish Gt.Man. 91 G1
Standlake 41 F2
Standon Hants. 27 F5
Standon Herts. 58 B5
Standon Staffs. 79 F4
Standon Green End 44 C1
Stane 142 C4
Stanecastle 132 B2
Stanfield 86 A3
Stanford Beds. 57 G3
Stanford Kent 32 D5
Stanford Shrop. 64 C1
Stanford Bishop 53 F2
Stanford Bridge 53 G1
Stanford Dingley 42 A5
Stanford End 28 C1
Stanford in the Vale 41 F3
Stanford on Avon 68 A5
Stanford on Soar 81 G5
Stanford on Teme 53 G1
Stanford Rivers 45 E2
Stanford-le-Hope 45 F4
Stanfree 94 B5
Stanghow 111 F1
Stanground 70 A3
Stanhoe 85 G4
Stanhope Dur. 119 F4
Stanhope Sc.Bord. 134 C3
Stanion 69 E4
Stanklyn 86 B5
Stanley Derbys. 81 F3
Stanley Dur. 120 A2
Stanley Notts. 81 F1
Stanley P. & K. 151 G1
Stanley Staffs. 79 G2
Stanley W.Yorks. 102 C5
Stanley Wilts. 40 B5
Stanley Common 81 F3
Stanley Crook 120 A4
Stanley Gate 91 F2
Stanley Green 13 G3
Stanley Hill 53 F3
Stanleygreen 78 C2
Stanlow C. & W.Ches. 91 F5
Stanlow Shrop. 65 G3
Stanmer 17 F2
Stanmore Gt.Lon. 44 A3
Stanmore W.Berks. 41 G5
Stannersburn 127 F3
Stanningfield 59 G2
Stannington Northumb. 129 E4
Stannington S.Yorks. 94 A4
Stansbatch 52 C1
Stansfield 59 F2
Stanshope 80 C2
Stanstead 59 G3
Stanstead Abbotts 44 C1
Stansted 31 F2
Stansted Airport 58 D5
Stansted Mountfitchet 58 D5
Stanton Derbys. 67 E1
Stanton Glos. 54 C4
Stanton Northumb. 128 D2
Stanton Staffs. 80 C3
Stanton Suff. 72 A4
Stanton by Bridge 81 E5
Stanton by Dale 81 F4
Stanton Drew 24 C1
Stanton Fitzwarren 41 D3
Stanton Harcourt 41 G2
Stanton Hill 81 F1
Stanton in Peak 80 D1
Stanton Lacy 65 D5
Stanton Lees 81 D1
Stanton Long 65 E3
Stanton Prior 25 D1
Stanton St. Bernard 26 B1
Stanton St. John 42 A2
Stanton St. Quintin 40 B5
Stanton Street 60 A1
Stanton under Bardon 67 G1
Stanton upon Hine Heath 78 C5
Stanton Wick 24 D1
Stanton-on-the-Wolds 82 A4
Stanwardine in the Fields 78 B5

Stanwardine in the Wood 78 B5
Stanway Essex 60 A5
Stanway Glos. 54 C4
Stanway Green Essex 60 A5
Stanway Green Suff. 72 D4
Stanwell 43 F5
Stanwell Moor 43 F5
Stanwick 69 E5
Stanwix 118 A2
Stapeley 79 D3
Stapenhill 81 D5
Staple Kent 33 E3
Staple Som. 23 E3
Staple Cross 22 D5
Staple Fitzpaine 11 F1
Staplecross 18 C1
Staplefield 17 E1
Stapleford Cambs. 58 C2
Stapleford Herts. 44 C1
Stapleford Leics. 68 D1
Stapleford Lincs. 83 D5
Stapleford Notts. 81 F4
Stapleford Wilts. 26 B4
Stapleford Abbotts 45 D2
Stapleford Tawney 45 E3
Staplegrove 23 F5
Staplehay 23 F5
Staplehurst 31 G4
Staplers 15 E4
Staplestreet 32 C2
Stapleton Cumb. 126 D4
Stapleton Here. 52 C1
Stapleton Leics. 67 G3
Stapleton N.Yorks. 110 B1
Stapleton Shrop. 65 D2
Stapleton Som. 24 B5
Stapley 11 E1
Staploe 57 G1
Staplow 57 F3
Star Fife 152 B4
Star Pembs. 49 F4
Star Som. 24 B2
Starbotton 109 E5
Starcross 10 C4
Stareton 67 F5
Starkholmes 81 E2
Starling 92 B1
Starling's Green 58 C4
Starr 123 F1
Starston 72 D3
Startforth 109 F1
Startley 40 B4
Statham 92 A4
Stathe 24 A5
Stathern 82 D4
Station Town 120 D4
Staughton Green 57 G1
Staughton Highway 57 G1
Staunton Glos. 39 E1
Staunton Glos. 53 G5
Staunton Harold Hall 81 E5
Staunton in the Vale 82 D3
Staunton on Arrow 52 C1
Staunton on Wye 52 C3
Staveley Cumb. 107 F3
Staveley Derbys. 94 B5
Staveley N.Yorks. 102 C1
Staveley-in-Cartmel 107 E4
Staverton Devon 9 D1
Staverton Glos. 54 A5
Staverton Northants. 56 A1
Staverton Wilts. 25 F1
Staverton Bridge 54 A5
Stawell 24 A4
Stawley 23 D5
Staxigoe 187 F3
Staxton 112 D5
Staylittle (Penffordd-las) 63 E3
Staynall 101 F2
Staythorpe 82 C2
Stean 109 F5
Steane 56 A4
Stearsby 111 F5
Steart 23 F3
Stebbing 59 E5
Stebbing Green 59 E5
Stechford 66 D4
Stedham 29 D5
Steel Cross 31 E5

Steel Green 106 C5
Steele Road 126 C2
Steen's Bridge 53 E2
Steep 28 C5
Steep Marsh 28 C5
Steeple Dorset 13 F4
Steeple Essex 46 C2
Steeple Ashton 26 A2
Steeple Aston 55 G5
Steeple Barton 55 G5
Steeple Bumpstead 59 E3
Steeple Claydon 56 B5
Steeple Gidding 69 G2
Steeple Langford 26 B4
Steeple Morden 58 A3
Steeraway 65 F2
Steeton 101 G3
Stein 170 B4
Steinmanhill 177 G5
Stella 100 A1
Stelling Minnis 32 D4
Stembridge 24 B5
Stemster High. 187 D2
Stemster High. 187 D4
Stemster House 187 D2
Stenalees 5 E4
Stenhill 11 E1
Stenhousemuir 142 C1
Stenigot 96 C4
Stenness 191 E3
Stenscholl 171 D3
Stenson 81 E5
Stenton E.Loth. 144 D2
Stenton P. & K. 159 F5
Stepaside Pembs. 35 E2
Stepaside Powys 63 G4
Stepney 44 C4
Steppingley 57 F4
Stepps 142 A3
Sternfield 61 E1
Sterridge 21 F1
Stert 26 B2
Stetchworth 59 E2
Stevenage 58 A5
Stevenston 141 D5
Steventon Hants. 27 G3
Steventon Oxon. 41 G3
Steventon End 59 E3
Stevington 57 E2
Stewartby 57 E2
Stewarton D. & G. 115 E2
Stewarton E.Ayr. 141 F5
Stewkley 57 D5
Stewley 11 G1
Stewton 97 D4
Steyning 17 D2
Steynton 34 C2
Stibb 20 C4
Stibb Cross 21 E4
Stibb Green 26 D1
Stibbard 86 A3
Stibbington 69 F3
Stichill 136 B3
Sticker 5 D4
Stickford 84 B1
Sticklepath Devon 7 G1
Sticklepath Som. 11 G1
Stickling Green 58 C4
Stickney 84 B2
Stiff Street 32 A2
Stifford's Bridge 53 G3
Stileway 24 B3
Stilligarry 188 B3
Stillingfleet 103 E3
Stillington N.Yorks. 103 E1
Stillington Stock. 120 C5
Stilton 69 G3
Stinchcombe 39 G3
Stinsford 12 D3
Stirchley Tel. & W. 65 G2
Stirchley W.Mid. 66 C4
Stirkoke House 187 F3
Stirling Aber. 179 G3
Stirling (Sruighlea) Stir. 150 C5
Stirton 101 F2
Stisted 59 G5
Stitchcombe 26 D1
Stithians 3 E3
Stittenham 174 C2
Stivichall 67 F5
Stix 158 C5
Stixwould 83 G1
Stoak 91 F5
Stobo 134 C2
Stoborough 13 F4

Stoborough Green 13 F4
Stobwood 143 D4
Stock 45 F3
Stock Green 54 B2
Stock Lane 41 E5
Stock Wood 54 C2
Stockbridge Hants. 27 E4
Stockbridge Stir. 150 C4
Stockbridge W.Suss. 16 A3
Stockbury 32 A2
Stockcross 27 F1
Stockdale 3 E3
Stockdalewath 117 G2
Stockerston 68 D3
Stocking Green Essex 59 D4
Stocking Green M.K. 56 D3
Stocking Pelham 58 C5
Stockingford 67 F3
Stockland Cardiff 38 A5
Stockland Devon 11 F2
Stockland Bristol 23 F3
Stockleigh English 10 B2
Stockleigh Pomeroy 10 B2
Stockley 26 B1
Stocklinch 11 G1
Stockport 92 C3
Stocksbridge 93 G3
Stocksfield 119 G1
Stockton Here. 53 E1
Stockton Norf. 73 E2
Stockton Shrop. 65 G3
Stockton Shrop. 64 B2
Stockton Tel. & W. 65 G1
Stockton Warks. 55 G1
Stockton Wilts. 26 A4
Stockton Heath 92 A4
Stockton on Teme 53 G1
Stockton on the Forest 103 F2
Stockton-on-Tees 110 D1
Stockwell 40 B1
Stockwell Heath 80 B5
Stockwood Bristol 24 D1
Stockwood Dorset 12 B2
Stoddday 100 A2
Stodmarsh 33 E2
Stody 86 B2
Stoer 180 C2
Stoford Som. 12 B1
Stoford Wilts. 26 B4
Stogumber 23 D4
Stogursey 23 F3
Stoke Devon 20 C3
Stoke Hants. 27 F2
Stoke Hants. 15 G2
Stoke Med. 32 A1
Stoke Plym. 8 A2
Stoke W.Mid. 67 F5
Stoke Abbott 12 A2
Stoke Albany 68 D4
Stoke Ash 72 C4
Stoke Bardolph 82 B3
Stoke Bishop 39 E5
Stoke Bliss 53 F1
Stoke Bruerne 56 C2
Stoke by Clare 59 F3
Stoke Canon 10 C5
Stoke Charity 27 F4
Stoke Climsland 7 D3
Stoke D'Abernon 29 G2
Stoke Doyle 69 F4
Stoke Dry 69 D3
Stoke Edith 53 F3
Stoke Farthing 26 B5
Stoke Ferry 71 F3
Stoke Fleming 9 E3
Stoke Gabriel 9 E2
Stoke Gifford 39 F5
Stoke Golding 67 F3
Stoke Goldington 56 D3
Stoke Green 43 E4
Stoke Hammond 57 D5
Stoke Heath Shrop. 79 D5
Stoke Heath Worcs. 54 B1
Stoke Holy Cross 86 D5
Stoke Lacy 53 F3
Stoke Lyne 56 A5
Stoke Mandeville 42 D1
Stoke Newington 44 C4
Stoke on Tern 78 D5
Stoke Orchard 54 B5
Stoke Pero 22 B3
Stoke Poges 43 E4

Stoke Pound **54** B1
Stoke Prior *Here.* **53** E2
Stoke Prior *Worcs.* **54** B1
Stoke Rivers **21** G2
Stoke Rochford **83** E5
Stoke Row **42** E4
Stoke St. Gregory **24** A5
Stoke St. Mary **23** F5
Stoke St. Michael **25** D3
Stoke St. Milborough **65** E4
Stoke sub Hamdon **12** A1
Stoke Talmage **42** B3
Stoke Villice **24** C1
Stoke Wake **13** D2
Stokeford **13** E4
Stokeham **95** E5
Stokeinteignhead **10** C5
Stokenchurch **42** C3
Stokenham **9** E3
Stoke-on-Trent **79** F3
Stokesay **64** D4
Stokesby **87** F4
Stokesley **111** E2
Stolford **23** F3
Ston Easton **24** D2
Stonar Cut **33** F2
Stondon Massey **45** E2
Stone *Bucks.* **42** C1
Stone *Glos.* **39** F3
Stone *Kent* **45** E5
Stone *Kent* **19** E1
Stone *S.Yorks.* **94** C4
Stone *Som.* **24** C1
Stone *Staffs.* **79** G4
Stone *Worcs.* **66** A5
Stone Allerton **24** B2
Stone Cross *Dur.* **109** F1
Stone Cross *E.Suss.* **18** B3
Stone Cross *E.Suss.* **18** A1
Stone Cross *Kent* **32** C5
Stone Cross *Kent* **31** E5
Stone House **108** C4
Stone Street *Kent* **31** E3
Stone Street *Suff.* **73** E3
Stone Street *Suff.* **60** A4
Stonea **70** C3
Stonebridge *E.Suss.* **18** A1
Stonebridge *N.Som.* **24** A2
Stonebridge *Warks.* **67** E4
Stonebroom **81** F2
Stonecross Green **59** G2
Stonefield *Arg. & B.* **139** G2
Stonefield *Staffs.* **79** G4
Stonegate *E.Suss.* **18** B1
Stonegate *N.Yorks.* **111** E2
Stonegrave **111** F5
Stonehaugh **127** F4
Stonehaven **161** G1
Stonehill **29** E1
Stonehouse *C. & W.Ches.* **91** G5
Stonehouse *D. & G.* **124** C4
Stonehouse *Glos.* **40** A2
Stonehouse *Northumb.* **118** C2
Stonehouse *Plym.* **8** A2
Stonehouse *S.Lan.* **142** B5
Stoneleigh *Surr.* **30** B2
Stoneleigh *Warks.* **67** F5
Stoneley Green **78** D2
Stonely **57** G1
Stoner Hill **28** C5
Stones **101** F5
Stones Green **60** C5
Stonesby **82** D5
Stonesfield **41** F1
Stonestreet Green **32** C5
Stonethwaite **117** F5
Stoney Cross **14** B1
Stoney Middleton **93** G5
Stoney Stanton **67** G3
Stoney Stoke **25** E4
Stoney Stratton **25** D4
Stoney Stretton **64** C2
Stoneyburn **143** D2
Stoneyford **11** D4
Stoneygate **68** B2

Stoneyhills **46** C3
Stoneykirk **122** B5
Stoneywood **169** F3
Stonham Aspal **60** C2
Stonnall **66** C2
Stonor **42** C4
Stonton Wyville **68** C3
Stony Houghton **81** F1
Stony Stratford **56** C3
Stonybreck **191** E5
Stoodleigh *Devon* **10** C1
Stoodleigh *Devon* **21** G2
Stopham **16** C2
Stopsley **57** G5
Stoptide **4** D2
Storeton **91** E4
Stormontfield **151** G2
Stornoway (Steornabhagh) **189** G2
Stornoway Airport **189** G2
Storridge **53** G3
Storrington **16** C2
Storrs **93** G4
Storth **107** F4
Storwood **103** G3
Stotfield **176** B2
Stotfold **58** A4
Stottesdon **65** F4
Stoughton *Leics.* **68** B2
Stoughton *Surr.* **29** E2
Stoughton *W.Suss.* **15** G1
Stoughton Cross **24** B3
Stoul **163** F5
Stoulton **54** B3
Stour Provost **25** E5
Stour Row **25** F5
Stourbridge **66** A4
Stourpaine **13** E2
Stourport-on-Severn **66** A5
Stourton *Staffs.* **66** A4
Stourton *Warks.* **56** B4
Stourton *Wilts.* **25** E4
Stourton Caundle **12** D1
Stoven **73** F3
Stow *Lincs.* **95** F4
Stow *Sc.Bord.* **144** B5
Stow Bardolph **71** E2
Stow Bedon **72** A2
Stow cum Quy **58** D1
Stow Longa **69** G5
Stow Maries **46** B3
Stow Pasture **95** F4
Stowbridge **71** D2
Stowe *Glos.* **39** E2
Stowe *Shrop.* **64** C1
Stowe *Staffs.* **66** D1
Stowe-by-Chartley **80** B5
Stowehill **56** B2
Stowell *Glos.* **40** C1
Stowell *Som.* **25** D5
Stowey **24** C2
Stowford *Devon* **7** E2
Stowford *Devon* **21** G3
Stowford *Devon* **11** E4
Stowlangtoft **60** A1
Stowmarket **60** B2
Stow-on-the-Wold **55** D5
Stowting **32** D4
Stowupland **60** B2
Straad **140** B3
Stracathro **161** E3
Strachan **169** D5
Strachur (Clachan Strachur) **148** C4
Stradbroke **72** D4
Stradishall **59** F2
Stradsett **71** E2
Stragglethorpe **83** E2
Straight Soley **41** F5
Straiton *Edin.* **143** G3
Straiton *S.Ayr.* **132** B5
Straloch *Aber.* **169** F2
Straloch *P. & K.* **159** F3
Stramshall **80** B4
Strands **106** C4
Strang **98** B4
Strangford **53** E2
Stranraer **122** B4
Strata Florida **50** D1
Stratfield Mortimer **28** B1
Stratfield Saye **28** B1
Stratfield Turgis **28** B2
Stratford *Beds.* **57** G3
Stratford *Glos.* **54** B4
Stratford *Gt.Lon.* **44** C4
Stratford St. Andrew **61** E2

Stratford St. Mary **60** B4
Stratford sub Castle **26** C4
Stratford Tony **26** B5
Stratford-upon-Avon **55** E2
Strath *High.* **180** C2
Strath *High.* **164** A5
Strathaven **142** B5
Strathblane **141** G2
Strathcanaird **181** D4
Strathcarron **172** C5
Strathdon **168** A3
Strathgirnock **168** A5
Strathkinness **152** C3
Strathmiglo **152** B3
Strathpeffer (Strath Pheofhair) **174** A4
Strathrannoch **173** G2
Strathtay **159** E4
Strathwhillan **131** F2
Strathy **186** A2
Strathyre **150** A3
Stratton *Cornw.* **20** C5
Stratton *Dorset* **12** C3
Stratton *Glos.* **40** C2
Stratton Audley **56** B5
Stratton Hall **60** D4
Stratton St. Margaret **41** D4
Stratton St. Michael **72** D2
Stratton Strawless **86** D3
Stratton-on-the-Fosse **25** D2
Stravanan **140** B4
Stravithie **152** D3
Strawberry Hill **44** A5
Stream **23** D4
Streat **17** F2
Streatham **44** B5
Streatham Vale **44** B5
Streatley *Beds.* **57** F5
Streatley *W.Berks.* **42** A4
Street *Devon* **11** F2
Street *Lancs.* **100** B2
Street *N.Yorks.* **111** G2
Street *Som.* **24** B4
Street *Som.* **11** G2
Street Ashton **67** G4
Street Dinas **78** A4
Street End **16** A4
Street Gate **120** D2
Street Houses **103** E3
Street Lane **81** E3
Street on the Fosse **24** D4
Streethay **66** D1
Streethouse **102** C5
Streetlam **110** C3
Streetly **66** C3
Streetly End **59** E3
Strefford **64** D4
Strelley **81** G3
Strensall **103** F1
Strensham **54** B3
Stretcholt **23** F3
Strete **9** E3
Stretford *Gt.Man.* **92** B3
Stretford *Here.* **52** D2
Stretford *Here.* **53** E1
Strethall **58** C4
Stretham **70** D5
Strettington **16** A3
Stretton *C. & W.Ches.* **78** D2
Stretton *Derbys.* **81** E1
Stretton *Rut.* **69** E1
Stretton *Staffs.* **66** A1
Stretton *Staffs.* **81** D5
Stretton *Warr.* **92** A4
Stretton en le Field **67** F1
Stretton Grandison **53** F3
Stretton Heath **64** C1
Stretton Sugwas **53** D3
Stretton under Fosse **67** G4
Stretton Westwood **65** E3
Stretton-on-Dunsmore **67** G5
Stretton-on-Fosse **55** E4
Stribers **107** E4
Strichen **179** E2
Strines **93** D4
Stringston **23** E3
Strixton **57** E1
Stroat **39** E3
Stromeferry **163** G1
Stromemore **163** G1

Stromness **190** A3
Stronaba **157** E1
Stronachlachar **149** G3
Strone *Arg. & B.* **140** C1
Strone *High.* **165** G2
Strone *High.* **156** D1
Strone *Stir.* **149** G3
Stronechrubie **181** E3
Stronlonag **140** C1
Stronmilchan (Sròn nam Mialchon) **149** D2
Stronsay **190** G2
Strontian (Sròn an t-Sithein) **156** A3
Strontoiller **148** B2
Stronvar **150** A2
Strood **31** G2
Strood Green *Surr.* **30** B4
Strood Green *W.Suss.* **29** F5
Strood Green *W.Suss.* **29** G4
Stroquhan **124** C2
Stroud *Glos.* **40** A2
Stroud *Hants.* **28** C5
Stroud Common **29** F3
Stroud Green *Essex* **46** B3
Stroud Green *Glos.* **40** A2
Stroude **29** F1
Stroul **140** D1
Stroxton **83** E4
Struan *High.* **162** B1
Struan *P. & K.* **158** C3
Strubby *Lincs.* **97** E4
Strubby *Lincs.* **96** B5
Strumpshaw **87** E5
Struthers **152** B3
Struy **165** F1
Stryd y Facsen **88** B4
Stryt-cae-rhedyn **77** F1
Stryt-issa **77** F3
Stuartfield **179** E3
Stub Place **106** B3
Stubber's Green **66** C2
Stubbington **15** E2
Stubbins **92** B5
Stubbs Green **73** E2
Stubhampton **13** F1
Stubley **94** A5
Stubshaw Cross **91** G2
Stubton **83** D3
Stuck *Arg. & B.* **140** B3
Stuck *Arg. & B.* **148** D5
Stuckbeg **149** E5
Stuckgowan **149** F4
Stuckindroin **149** F3
Stuckreoch **148** C5
Stuckton **14** A1
Stud Green **43** D5
Studdon **119** E2
Studfold **108** D5
Studham **43** F1
Studholme **117** F1
Studland **13** G4
Studley *Warks.* **54** C1
Studley *Wilts.* **40** B5
Studley Common **54** C1
Studley Green **42** C3
Studley Roger **110** B5
Stuggadhoo **98** B4
Stump Cross *Essex* **58** D3
Stump Cross *Lancs.* **100** B4
Stuntney **71** D5
Stunts Green **18** B2
Sturbridge **79** F4
Sturgate **95** F4
Sturmer **59** E3
Sturminster Common **13** D1
Sturminster Marshall **13** F2
Sturminster Newton **13** D1
Sturry **33** D2
Sturton **72** C4
Sturton *N.Yorks.* **103** D3
Sturton *Suff.* **60** C4
Styal **92** C4
Styrrup **94** D3
Succoth *Aber.* **168** B1
Succoth *Arg. & B.* **149** E4
Succothmore **148** D4
Suckley **53** G2
Suckley Green **53** G2
Suckley Knowl **53** G2

Sudborough **69** E4
Sudbourne **61** F2
Sudbrook *Lincs.* **83** E3
Sudbrook *Mon.* **39** E4
Sudbrooke **96** A5
Sudbury *Derbys.* **80** C4
Sudbury *Gt.Lon.* **44** A4
Sudbury *Suff.* **59** G3
Sudden **92** C1
Sudgrove **40** B2
Suffield *N.Yorks.* **112** C3
Suffield *Norf.* **86** D2
Sugarloaf **32** B5
Sugnall **79** E4
Sugwas Pool **53** D3
Suie Lodge Hotel **149** G2
Suisnish **163** D3
Sulby *I.o.M.* **98** C3
Sulby *I.o.M.* **98** B4
Sulgrave **56** B3
Sulham **42** B5
Sulhamstead **28** B1
Sullington **16** C2
Sully **23** E1
Sumburgh **191** F5
Sumburgh Airport **191** F5
Summer Bridge **102** B1
Summer Isles **180** B4
Summer Lodge **109** E3
Summercourt **4** C1
Summerfield *Norf.* **85** F4
Summerfield *Worcs.* **66** A5
Summerhill **78** A2
Summerhouse **110** B1
Summerlands **107** G4
Summerleaze **38** D4
Summertown **42** A2
Summit **92** C1
Sun Green **93** D3
Sunadale **139** G5
Sunbiggin **108** B2
Sunbury **29** G1
Sundaywell **124** C2
Sunderland *Cumb.* **117** E3
Sunderland *Lancs.* **100** A2
Sunderland *T. & W.* **120** C2
Sunderland Bridge **120** B4
Sundhope **135** E3
Sundon Park **57** F5
Sundridge **31** D3
Sundrum Mains **132** C3
Sunhill **40** D2
Sunipol **154** C4
Sunk Island **96** D1
Sunningdale **29** E1
Sunninghill **29** E1
Sunningwell **41** G2
Sunniside *Dur.* **120** A4
Sunniside *T. & W.* **120** B2
Sunny Bank **107** D3
Sunny Brow **120** A4
Sunnylaw **150** C5
Sunnyside *Aber.* **169** F5
Sunnyside *Northumb.* **119** F1
Sunnyside *S.Yorks.* **94** B3
Sunnyside *W.Suss.* **30** C5
Sunton **26** D2
Sunwick **145** F4
Surbiton **29** G1
Surfleet **84** A5
Surfleet Seas End **84** A5
Surlingham **87** E5
Sustead **86** C2
Susworth **95** F2
Sutcombe **20** D4
Sutcombemill **20** D4
Suton **72** B2
Sutors of Cromarty **175** E3
Sutterby **97** D5
Sutterton **84** A4
Sutton *Beds.* **58** A3
Sutton *Cambs.* **70** C5
Sutton *Devon* **10** A2
Sutton *Devon* **8** D5
Sutton *Gt.Lon.* **30** B2
Sutton *Kent* **33** F4
Sutton *Lincs.* **83** D2
Sutton *Norf.* **87** E3
Sutton *Notts.* **82** C4
Sutton *Notts.* **95** D4
Sutton *Oxon.* **41** G2
Sutton *Pembs.* **34** C1

Sutton *Peter.* **69** F3
Sutton *S.Yorks.* **94** C1
Sutton *Shrop.* **65** G4
Sutton *Shrop.* **79** D4
Sutton *Shrop.* **65** E1
Sutton *Shrop.* **78** B5
Sutton *Staffs.* **79** E5
Sutton *Suff.* **61** E3
Sutton *W.Suss.* **16** B2
Sutton Abinger **29** G3
Sutton at Hone **45** E5
Sutton Bassett **68** C4
Sutton Benger **40** B5
Sutton Bingham **12** B1
Sutton Bonington **81** G5
Sutton Bridge **84** C5
Sutton Cheney **67** G2
Sutton Coldfield **66** D3
Sutton Courtenay **42** A3
Sutton Crosses **84** C5
Sutton Grange **110** B5
Sutton Green *Oxon.* **41** E2
Sutton Green *Surr.* **29** F2
Sutton Green *Wrex.* **78** B3
Sutton Holms **13** G2
Sutton Howgrave **110** C5
Sutton in Ashfield **81** F2
Sutton in the Elms **68** A3
Sutton Ings **104** D4
Sutton Lane Ends **92** D5
Sutton le Marsh **97** F4
Sutton Leach **91** G3
Sutton Maddock **65** G2
Sutton Mallet **24** A4
Sutton Mandeville **26** A5
Sutton Montis **24** D5
Sutton on Sea **97** F4
Sutton on the Hill **80** D4
Sutton on Trent **82** C1
Sutton Poyntz **12** B1
Sutton St. Edmund **70** B1
Sutton St. James **70** C1
Sutton St. Nicholas **53** E2
Sutton Scarsdale **81** F1
Sutton Scotney **27** F4
Sutton upon Derwent **103** G3
Sutton Valence **32** A4
Sutton Veny **25** F3
Sutton Waldron **13** E1
Sutton Weaver **91** G5
Sutton Wick *B. & N.E.Som.* **24** C2
Sutton Wick *Oxon.* **41** G3
Sutton-in-Craven **101** G3
Sutton-on-Hull **104** D4
Sutton-on-the-Forest **103** E1
Sutton-under-Brailes **55** F4
Sutton-under-Whitestonecliffe **111** D4
Swaby **97** D5
Swadlincote **67** F1
Swaffham **71** G2
Swaffham Bulbeck **59** D1
Swaffham Prior **59** D1
Swafield **87** D2
Swainby **111** D2
Swainshill **53** D3
Swainswick **25** E1
Swalcliffe **55** F4
Swalecliffe **32** D2
Swallow **96** B2
Swallow Beck **83** E1
Swallowcliffe **26** A5
Swallowfield **28** C1
Swallows Cross **45** F3
Swampton **27** F2
Swan Green *C. & W.Ches.* **92** B5
Swan Green *Suff.* **73** D4
Swan Street **59** G5
Swanage **13** G5
Swanbach **79** D3
Swanbourne **56** D5
Swanbridge **23** E1
Swancote **65** G3
Swanland **104** B5
Swanlaws **136** B5
Swanley **31** E2
Swanley Village **31** E2
Swanmore *Hants.* **15** E1
Swanmore *I.o.W.* **15** E3
Swannington *Leics.* **67** G1
Swannington *Norf.* **86** C4

Swanscombe **45** F5
Swansea (Abertawe)
  36 C3
Swanston **143** G3
Swanton Abbot **87** D3
Swanton Morley **86** B4
Swanton Novers **86** B2
Swanton Street **32** A3
Swanwick *Derbys.* **81** F2
Swanwick *Hants.* **15** F2
Swanwick Green **78** C3
Swarby **83** F3
Swardeston **86** D5
Swarkestone **81** E5
Swarland **129** D1
Swarraton **27** G4
Swarthmoor **107** D5
Swaton **83** G4
Swavesey **58** B1
Sway **14** B3
Swayfield **83** E5
Swaythling **14** D1
Swaythorpe **104** C1
Sweetham **10** B3
Sweethay **23** F5
Sweetshouse **5** E3
Sweffling **61** E1
Swell **24** A5
Swepstone **67** F1
Swerford **55** F4
Swettenham **79** F1
Swffryd **38** B3
Swift's Green **32** A4
Swiftsden **18** C1
Swilland **60** C2
Swillington **102** C4
Swimbridge **21** G4
Swimbridge Newland
  21 F2
Swinbrook **41** E1
Swincliffe **102** B2
Swincombe **21** G1
Swinden **101** E2
Swinderby **83** D1
Swindon *Staffs.* **66** A3
Swindon *Swin.* **41** D4
Swindon Village **54** B5
Swine **104** D4
Swinefleet **103** G5
Swineford **25** D1
Swineshead *Beds.* **57** F1
Swineshead *Lincs.* **84** A3
Swineshead Bridge **84** A3
Swineside **109** F4
Swiney **187** E5
Swinford *Leics.* **68** A5
Swinford *Oxon.* **41** G2
Swingate **81** G3
Swingfield Minnis **33** G4
Swingleton Green **60** A3
Swinhoe **137** G4
Swinhope **96** C3
Swinithwaite **109** F4
Swinscoe **80** C3
Swinside Hall **136** B5
Swinstead **83** F5
Swinton *Gt.Man.* **92** B2
Swinton *N.Yorks.* **111** G5
Swinton *N.Yorks.* **111** F3
Swinton *S.Yorks.* **94** B3
Swinton *Sc.Bord.* **145** F5
Swinton Quarter **145** F5
Swintonmill **145** F5
Swithland **68** A1
Swordale **174** B3
Swordland **163** F5
Swordle **155** E2
Swordly **185** G2
Sworton Heath **92** A4
Swyddffynnon **50** C1
Swyncombe **42** B3
Swynnerton **79** F4
Swyre **12** B4
Sychant **63** F5
Syde **40** B1
Sydenham *Gt.Lon.* **44** C5
Sydenham *Oxon.* **30** D1
Sydenham Damerel **7** E3
Syderstone **85** G4
Sydling St. Nicholas
  12 C3
Sydmonton **27** F2
Sydney **79** E2
Syerston **82** C3
Sykehouse **94** D1
Sykes **100** C2
Sylen **36** B2
Symbister **191** F3
Symington *S.Ayr.* **132** B2

Symington *S.Lan.* **134** A2
Symonds Yat **39** E1
Symondsbury **12** A3
Synod Inn (Post-mawr)
  50 A2
Syre **185** F4
Syreford **54** C5
Syresham **56** B3
Syston *Leics.* **68** B1
Syston *Lincs.* **83** E3
Sytchampton **54** A1
Sywell **56** D1

T

Taagan **172** D3
Tableyhill **92** B5
Tachbrook Mallory **55** F1
Tacher **187** D4
Tackley **55** G5
Tacolneston **72** C2
Tadcaster **103** D3
Tadden **13** F2
Taddington *Derbys.*
  93 F5
Taddington *Glos.* **54** C4
Taddiport **21** E4
Tadley **28** B1
Tadlow **58** A3
Tadmarton **55** F4
Tadpole Bridge **41** F2
Tadworth **30** B3
Tafarnaubach **38** A1
Tafarn-y-bwlch **49** D2
Tafarn-y-Gelyn **77** E1
Taff Merthyr Garden
  Village **38** A3
Taff's Well (Ffynnon Taf)
  38 A4
Tafolwern **63** E2
Taibach *N.P.T.* **37** D4
Tai-bach *Powys* **77** E5
Taicynhaeaf **62** C1
Tain *High.* **187** E2
Tain *High.* **175** D1
Tai'n Lôn **74** D3
Tai'r Bull **51** F5
Tairgwaith **36** D1
Tai'r-heol **38** A3
Tairlaw **132** C5
Tai'r-ysgol **36** C3
Takeley **59** D5
Takeley Street **58** D5
Talachddu **51** G4
Talacre **90** C4
Talardd **76** B5
Talaton **11** D3
Talbenny **34** B1
Talbot Green **37** G4
Talbot Village **13** G3
Talerddig **63** F2
Talgarreg **50** A2
Talgarth **52** A4
Taliesin **62** C1
Talisker **162** B1
Talke Pits **79** F2
Talkin **118** B2
Talla Linnfoots **134** C3
Talladale **172** C2
Talladh-a-Bheithe **158** A4
Talland **5** G4
Tallarn Green **78** B3
Tallentire **117** E3
Talley (Talyllychau)
  50 C4
Tallington **69** F2
Talmine **185** E2
Talog **49** G5
Tal-sarn **50** B2
Talsarnau **75** F4
Talskiddy **4** D3
Talwrn *I.o.A.* **88** C5
Talwrn *Wrex.* **77** F3
Talwrn *Wrex.* **78** A3
Talybont *Cere.* **62** C4
Tal-y-bont *Conwy* **76** A1
Tal-y-bont *Gwyn.* **75** E5
Tal-y-bont *Gwyn.* **89** E5
Talybont-on-Usk **52** A5
Tal-y-Cae **75** F1
Tal-y-coed **38** D1
Talygarn **37** F3
Tal-y-llyn *Gwyn.* **62** D2
Talyllyn *Powys* **52** A5
Talysarn **75** D2
Tal-y-wern **63** E2
Tamavoid **150** A5
Tamerton Foliot **8** A1

Tamworth **67** E2
Tamworth Green **84** B3
Tan Office Green **59** F2
Tandem **93** F1
Tandridge **30** C3
Tanerdy **50** A5
Tanfield **120** A2
Tanfield Lea **120** A2
Tang **102** B2
Tang Hall **103** F2
Tangiers **34** C1
Tanglandford **169** F1
Tangley **27** E2
Tangmere **16** B3
Tangy **130** B3
Tankersley **94** A2
Tankerton **32** D2
Tan-lan **75** F3
Tannach **187** F4
Tannachie **161** F1
Tannach *182* C4
Tannadice **160** C4
Tannington **60** D1
Tannochside **142** A3
Tansley **81** E2
Tansley Knoll **81** E2
Tansor **79** F3
Tantobie **120** A2
Tanton **111** E1
Tanworth in Arden **66** D5
Tan-y-fron **76** C1
Tan-y-graig **74** C4
Tanygrisiau **75** F3
Tan-y-groes **49** F3
Tan-y-pistyll **77** D5
Tan-yr-allt **90** B4
Tapeley **21** E3
Taplow **43** E4
Tapton Grove **94** B5
Taransay (Tarasaigh)
  189 E4
Taraphocain **156** C5
Tarbat House **175** D2
Tarbert *Arg. & B.* **139** G3
Tarbert *Arg. & B.* **139** E4
Tarbert *Arg. & B.* **139** E1
Tarbert *High.* **155** F3
Tarbert (An Tairbeart)
  W.Isles **189** F4
Tarbet (An Tairbeart)
  Arg. & B. **149** F4
Tarbet *High.* **163** F5
Tarbet *High.* **184** A4
Tarbock Green **91** F4
Tarbolton **132** C3
Tarbrax **143** G4
Tardebigge **54** B1
Tardy Gate **100** B5
Tarfside **160** C2
Tarland **168** B4
Tarleton **100** A5
Tarlscough **91** F1
Tarlton **40** B3
Tarnbrook **100** B2
Tarnock **24** A2
Tarporley **78** C1
Tarr **23** E4
Tarrant Crawford **13** F2
Tarrant Gunville **13** F1
Tarrant Hinton **13** F1
Tarrant Keyneston **13** F2
Tarrant Launceston **13** F2
Tarrant Monkton **13** F2
Tarrant Rawston **13** F2
Tarrant Rushton **13** F2
Tarrel **175** E1
Tarring Neville **17** G3
Tarrington **53** F3
Tarrnacraig **131** E2
Tarsappie **151** G2
Tarskavaig **163** D4
Tarves **169** E2
Tarvie *P. & K.* **159** F3
Tarvin **78** B1
Tarvin Sands **78** B1
Tasburgh **72** D2
Tasley **65** F3
Taston **55** F5
Tatenhill **80** D5
Tathall End **56** D3
Tatham **100** C1
Tathwell **96** D4
Tatsfield **30** D3
Tattenhall **78** B2
Tattenhoe **56** D4
Tatterford **85** G5
Tattersett **85** G4

Tattershall **84** A2
Tattershall Bridge **83** G2
Tattershall Thorpe **84** A2
Tattingstone **60** C4
Tatworth **11** G2
Tauchers **176** C5
Taunton **23** F5
Tavelty **169** E3
Taverham **42** D2
Tavernspite **35** E1
Tavistock **7** E3
Taw Bridge **21** G5
Taw Green **7** G1
Tawstock **21** F3
Taxal **93** E5
Tayburn **141** G5
Taychreggan **148** C2
Tayinloan **139** E5
Taylors Cross **20** C4
Taynafead **148** C3
Taynish **139** F1
Taynton *Glos.* **53** G5
Taynton *Oxon.* **41** E1
Taynuilt (Taigh an Uillt)
  148 C1
Tayock **161** E4
Tayovullin **138** A2
Tayport **152** C2
Tayvallich **139** F1
Tea Green **57** G5
Tealby **96** B3
Tealing **152** C1
Team Valley **120** B1
Teangue **163** E4
Teasses **152** C4
Tebay **108** B2
Tebworth **57** E5
Tedburn St. Mary **10** B3
Teddington *Glos.* **54** B4
Teddington *Gt.Lon.*
  44 A5
Tedstone Delamere **53** F2
Tedstone Wafre **53** F2
Teeton **68** B5
Teffont Evias **26** A4
Teffont Magna **26** A4
Tegryn **49** F4
Teigh **69** D1
Teign Village **10** B4
Teigncrace **10** B5
Teignmouth **10** C5
Telford **65** F2
Telham **18** C2
Tellisford **25** F2
Telscombe **17** G3
Telscombe Cliffs **17** G3
Tempar **158** B4
Templand **125** G2
Temple *Cornw.* **5** F2
Temple *Midloth.* **144** A4
Temple Balsall **67** E5
Temple Bar **50** B2
Temple Cloud **24** D2
Temple End **59** E2
Temple Ewell **33** E4
Temple Grafton **54** D2
Temple Guiting **54** C5
Temple Herdewyke **55** F2
Temple Hirst **103** F5
Temple Normanton **81** F1
Temple Sowerby **118** C5
Templecombe **25** E5
Templeton *Devon* **10** B1
Templeton *Pembs.* **35** E1
Templeton Bridge **10** B1
Templewood **161** E3
Tempsford **57** G2
Ten Mile Bank **71** E3
Tenbury Wells **53** E1
Tenby (Dinbych-y-pysgod)
  35 E2
Tendring **60** C5
Tendring Green **60** C5
Tenga **155** E5
Tenterden **32** A5
Tepersie Castle **168** C2
Terally **114** B2
Terling **45** G1
Tern **65** F1
Ternhill **78** D4
Terregles **124** D3
Terriers **43** D3
Terrington **111** F5
Terrington St. Clement
  85 D5

Terrington St. John **70** D1
Terry's Green **66** D5
Tervieside **167** G1
Teston **31** G3

Testwood **14** C1
Tetbury **40** A3
Tetbury Upton **40** A3
Tetchill **78** A4
Tetcott **6** D1
Tetford **96** D5
Tetney **96** D2
Tetney Lock **96** D2
Tetsworth **42** B2
Tettenhall **66** A2
Tettenhall Wood **66** A3
Tetworth **42** C1
Teuchan **179** F4
Teversal **81** F1
Teversham **58** C2
Teviothead **135** F5
Tewel **161** G1
Tewin **43** F1
Tewkesbury **54** A4
Teynham **32** B2
Thackley **102** A4
Thainston **161** E2
Thainstone **169** E3
Thakeham **16** D2
Thame **42** C2
Thames Ditton **29** G1
Thames Haven **45** G4
Thamesmead **45** D4
Thanington **32** D3
Thankerton **134** A2
Tharston **72** C2
Thatcham **27** G1
Thatto Heath **91** G3
Thaxted **59** E4
The Apes Hall **71** D3
The Bage **52** B3
The Balloch **150** D3
The Banking **169** E1
The Bar **29** G5
The Birks **169** E4
The Bog **64** C3
The Bourne **28** D3
The Bratch **86** A3
The Broad **53** D1
The Bryn **38** C2
The Burf **54** A1
The Burn **161** D2
The Butts **25** E3
The Camp **40** B2
The Chequer **78** B3
The City *Bucks.* **42** C3
The City *Suff.* **73** E3
The Common *Wilts.*
  26 D4
The Common *Wilts.*
  40 C4
The Craigs **181** G5
The Cronk **98** B2
The Delves **66** C3
The Den **141** E4
The Dicker **18** A3
The Down **65** F3
The Drums **160** B3
The Eaves **39** F2
The Flatt **127** D4
The Folly **44** A1
The Forge **52** C2
The Forstal *E.Suss.* **31** E5
The Forstal *Kent* **32** C5
The Grange *Lincs.* **97** F5
The Grange *Shrop.* **78** A4
The Grange *Surr.* **30** C4
The Green *Arg. & B.*
  154 A2
The Green *Cumb.* **106** C4
The Green *Essex* **45** G1
The Green *Flints.* **77** F1
The Green *Wilts.* **25** F4
The Grove **54** A3
The Haven **29** F4
The Headland **121** E4
The Heath **80** B4
The Herberts **37** F5
The Hermitage **30** B3
The Hill **106** C4
The Holme **102** B2
The Howe **98** A5
The Isle **65** D1
The Laurels **73** E2
The Leacon **32** B5
The Lee **43** D2
The Leigh **54** A5
The Lhen **98** B1
The Lodge **149** D5
The Marsh **64** C3
The Moor *E.Suss.* **18** D2
The Moor *Kent* **18** C1
The Mumbles **36** C4
The Murray **142** A4

The Mythe **54** A4
The Narth **39** E2
The Neuk **169** E5
The Node **44** B1
The Oval **25** E1
The Polchar **166** D4
The Quarter **32** A4
The Reddings **54** B5
The Rhos **34** D1
The Rookery **79** F2
The Rowe **79** F4
The Sale **67** D1
The Sands **30** D3
The Shoe **40** A5
The Slade **42** A5
The Smithies **65** F3
The Stocks **19** E1
The Swillett **43** F3
The Thrift **58** B4
The Vauld **53** E3
The Wern **77** F2
The Wyke **65** G2
Theakston **110** C4
Thealby **95** F1
Theale *Som.* **24** B3
Theale *W.Berks.* **42** B5
Thearne **104** C4
Theberton **61** F1
Thedden Grange **28** B4
Theddingworth **68** B4
Theddlethorpe All Saints
  97 E4
Theddlethorpe St. Helen
  97 E4
Thelbridge Barton **10** A1
Thelbridge Cross **10** A1
Thelnetham **72** B4
Thelveton **72** C3
Thelwall **92** A4
Themelthorpe **86** B3
Thenford **56** A3
Therfield **58** B4
Thetford *Lincs.* **69** G1
Thetford *Norf.* **71** G4
Thethwaite **117** G2
Theydon Bois **44** D3
Theydon Garnon **45** D3
Theydon Mount **45** D3
Thickwood **40** A5
Thimbleby *Lincs.* **84** A1
Thimbleby *N.Yorks.*
  110 D3
Thingley **25** F1
Thirkleby **111** D5
Thirlby **111** D4
Thirlestane **144** C5
Thirn **110** B4
Thirsk **110** D4
Thirston New Houses
  129 D2
Thirtleby **105** D4
Thistleton *Lancs.* **100** A4
Thistleton *Rut.* **69** E1
Thistley Green **71** F5
Thixendale **104** A1
Thockrington **128** B4
Tholomas Drove **70** B2
Tholthorpe **103** D1
Thomas Chapel **35** E2
Thomas Close **118** A3
Thomastown **168** C1
Thompson **72** A2
Thomshill **176** B4
Thong **45** F5
Thongsbridge **93** F2
Thoralby **109** F4
Thoresby **94** D5
Thoresthorpe **97** E5
Thoresway **96** C3
Thorganby *Lincs.* **96** C3
Thorganby *N.Yorks.*
  103 F3
Thorgill **111** G3
Thorington **73** F4
Thorington Street **60** B4
Thorley **45** D2
Thorley Houses **58** C5
Thorley Street *Herts.*
  45 D1
Thorley Street *I.o.W.*
  14 C4
Thormanby **111** D5
Thornaby-on-Tees
  111 D1
Thornage **86** B2
Thornborough *Bucks.*
  56 C4
Thornborough *N.Yorks.*
  110 B5

Thornbury *Devon* 21 D5
Thornbury *Here.* 53 F2
Thornbury *S.Glos.* 39 F3
Thornbury *W.Yorks.* 102 A4
Thornby 68 B5
Thorncliff 93 G1
Thorncliffe 80 B2
Thorncombe 11 G2
Thorncombe Street 29 F3
Thorncote Green 57 G3
Thorncross 14 D4
Thorndon 60 C1
Thorndon Cross 7 F1
Thorne 95 D1
Thorne St. Margaret 23 D5
Thorner 102 C4
Thorney *Bucks.* 43 F5
Thorney *Notts.* 95 F5
Thorney *Peter.* 70 A2
Thorney *Som.* 24 B5
Thorney Hill 14 B3
Thornfalcon 23 F5
Thornford 12 C1
Thorngrafton 119 D1
Thorngrove 24 A4
Thorngumbald 105 E5
Thornham 85 F3
Thornham Magna 72 C4
Thornham Parva 72 C4
Thornhaugh 69 F2
Thornhill *Cardiff* 38 A4
Thornhill *Cumb.* 106 B2
Thornhill *D. & G.* 124 C1
Thornhill *Derbys.* 93 F4
Thornhill *S'ham.* 15 D5
Thornhill *Stir.* 150 B4
Thornhill *W.Yorks.* 93 G1
Thornhill Lees 93 G1
Thornholme 104 D1
Thornicombe 13 E2
Thornley *Dur.* 120 C4
Thornley *Dur.* 120 A4
Thornley Gate 119 E2
Thornliebank 141 G4
Thornroan 169 E1
Thorns 59 F2
Thorns Green 92 B4
Thornsett 93 E4
Thornthwaite *Cumb.* 117 F4
Thornthwaite *N.Yorks.* 102 A4
Thornton *Angus* 160 B5
Thornton *Bucks.* 56 C4
Thornton *E.Riding* 103 G3
Thornton *Fife* 152 A5
Thornton *Lancs.* 99 G3
Thornton *Leics.* 67 G2
Thornton *Lincs.* 84 A1
Thornton *Mersey.* 91 F4
Thornton *Middbro.* 111 D1
Thornton *Northumb.* 145 G5
Thornton *P. & K.* 159 F5
Thornton *Pembs.* 34 C2
Thornton *W.Yorks.* 102 A4
Thornton Bridge 110 D5
Thornton Curtis 96 A1
Thornton Heath 30 C2
Thornton Hough 91 E4
Thornton in Lonsdale 108 B5
Thornton le Moor 96 A3
Thornton Park 145 G5
Thornton Rust 109 E4
Thornton Steward 110 A4
Thornton Watlass 110 B4
Thorntonhall 141 G4
Thornton-in-Craven 101 F3
Thornton-le-Beans 110 D3
Thornton-le-Clay 103 F1
Thornton-le-Dale 112 B4
Thornton-le-Moor 110 C4
Thornton-le-Moors 91 F4
Thornton-le-Street 110 D4
Thorntonloch 145 E2
Thornwood 45 D2
Thornyhill 161 E2
Thornylee 135 F2
Thoroton 82 C3

Thorp Arch 102 D3
Thorpe *Derbys.* 80 C2
Thorpe *E.Riding* 104 B3
Thorpe *Lincs.* 97 E4
Thorpe *N.Yorks.* 101 G1
Thorpe *Norf.* 73 F2
Thorpe *Notts.* 82 C2
Thorpe *Surr.* 29 F1
Thorpe Abbotts 72 C3
Thorpe Acre 81 G5
Thorpe Arnold 82 C5
Thorpe Audlin 94 B1
Thorpe Bassett 112 B5
Thorpe Bay 46 C1
Thorpe by Water 69 D3
Thorpe Constantine 67 E2
Thorpe Culvert 84 C1
Thorpe End 87 D4
Thorpe Green *Essex* 60 C5
Thorpe Green *Lancs.* 100 B5
Thorpe Green *Suff.* 60 A2
Thorpe Hall 111 E5
Thorpe Hesley 94 A3
Thorpe in Balne 94 C1
Thorpe in the Fallows 95 G4
Thorpe Langton 68 C3
Thorpe Larches 120 C5
Thorpe le Street 104 A3
Thorpe Malsor 68 D5
Thorpe Mandeville 56 A3
Thorpe Market 86 D2
Thorpe Morieux 60 A2
Thorpe on the Hill *Lincs.* 83 E1
Thorpe on the Hill *W.Yorks.* 102 C5
Thorpe Row 86 A5
Thorpe St. Andrew 87 D5
Thorpe St. Peter 84 C1
Thorpe Salvin 94 C2
Thorpe Satchville 68 C1
Thorpe Street 72 B4
Thorpe Thewles 120 D5
Thorpe Tilney Dales 83 G2
Thorpe Underwood *N.Yorks.* 103 D2
Thorpe Underwood *Northants.* 68 C4
Thorpe Waterville 69 F4
Thorpe Willoughby 103 E4
Thorpefield 110 D5
Thorpe-le-Soken 60 C5
Thorpeness 61 F1
Thorpland 71 E2
Thorrington 60 B5
Thorverton 10 C2
Thrandeston 72 C4
Thrapston 69 E5
Threapland 101 F1
Threapwood 78 B3
Threapwood Head 80 B3
Three Ashes 25 D3
Three Bridges 30 B5
Three Burrows 4 B5
Three Chimneys 32 A5
Three Cocks (Aberllynfi) 52 A4
Three Crosses 36 B3
Three Cups Corner 18 B1
Three Hammers 5 G1
Three Holes 70 D2
Three Leg Cross 31 F5
Three Legged Cross 13 G2
Three Mile Cross 28 C1
Three Oaks 18 D2
Threehammer Common 87 E4
Threekingham 83 F4
Threemilestone 4 B5
Threlkeld 117 G4
Threshfield 101 F1
Threxton Hill 71 G2
Thrigby 87 F4
Thringarth 119 F5
Thringstone 67 G1
Thrintoft 110 C3
Thriplow 58 C3
Throapham 94 C4
Throckenholt 70 B2
Throcking 58 B4
Throckley 120 A1
Throckmorton 54 B3
Throop 13 E3

Throphill 128 D3
Thropton 128 C1
Througham 40 B2
Throwleigh 7 G1
Throwley 32 B3
Throws 59 E5
Thrumpton *Notts.* 81 G4
Thrumpton *Notts.* 95 E5
Thrumster 187 F4
Thrunton 137 E5
Thrupp *Glos.* 40 A2
Thrupp *Oxon.* 41 E3
Thrupp *Oxon.* 41 E3
Thruscross 102 A2
Thrushelton 7 E2
Thrussington 68 B1
Thruxton *Hants.* 27 D3
Thruxton *Here.* 52 D4
Thrybergh 94 B3
Thulston 81 F4
Thunder Bridge 93 F1
Thundergay 139 G5
Thundersley 46 B4
Thunderton 179 F3
Thundridge 44 C1
Thurcaston 68 A1
Thurcroft 94 B4
Thurdistoft 187 E2
Thurdon 20 C4
Thurgarton *Norf.* 86 C2
Thurgarton *Notts.* 82 B3
Thurgoland 93 G2
Thurlaston *Leics.* 68 A3
Thurlaston *Warks.* 67 G5
Thurlbear 23 F5
Thurlby *Lincs.* 69 G1
Thurlby *Lincs.* 83 E1
Thurlby *Lincs.* 97 E5
Thurleigh 57 F2
Thurlestone 8 C3
Thurloxton 23 F4
Thurlstone 93 G2
Thurlton 73 F2
Thurlwood 79 F2
Thurmaston 68 B2
Thurnby 87 F4
Thurne 87 F4
Thurnham 32 A3
Thurning *Norf.* 86 B3
Thurning *Northants.* 69 F4
Thurnscoe 94 B2
Thursby 117 G1
Thursden 101 F4
Thursford 86 A2
Thursley 29 E4
Thurso (Inbhir Theòrsa) 186 D2
Thurstaston 90 D4
Thurston 60 A1
Thurston Clough 93 D2
Thurstonfield 117 G1
Thurstonland 93 F1
Thurton 87 E5
Thurvaston *Derbys.* 80 D4
Thurvaston *Derbys.* 80 C4
Thuster 187 E3
Thuxton 86 B5
Thwaite *N.Yorks.* 109 D3
Thwaite *Suff.* 60 C1
Thwaite Head 107 E3
Thwaite St. Mary 73 E2
Thwaites 101 G3
Thwaites Brow 101 G3
Thwing 113 D5
Tibberton *Glos.* 53 G5
Tibberton *Tel. & W.* 79 D5
Tibberton *Worcs.* 54 B2
Tibbie Shiels Inn 134 D3
Tibenham 72 C2
Tibertich 148 A4
Tibshelf 81 F1
Tibthorpe 104 B2
Ticehurst 31 F5
Tichborne 27 G4
Tickencote 69 E2
Tickenham 39 D5
Tickford End 57 D3
Tickhill 94 C3
Ticklerton 65 D3
Ticknall 81 E5
Tickton 104 C3
Tidbury Green 66 D5
Tidcombe 27 D2
Tiddington *Oxon.* 42 B2

Tiddington *Warks.* 55 E2
Tiddleywink 40 A5
Tidebrook 18 B1
Tideford 6 D5
Tideford Cross 6 D4
Tidenham 39 E3
Tidenham Chase 39 E3
Tideswell 93 F5
Tidmarsh 42 B5
Tidmington 55 E4
Tidpit 13 G1
Tidworth 26 D3
Tiers Cross 34 C1
Tiffield 56 B2
Tifty 177 G5
Tigerton 160 D3
Tighachnoic 155 F5
Tighnablair 150 C3
Tighnabruaich 140 A2
Tighnacomaire 156 B3
Tigley 9 D1
Tilbrook 57 F1
Tilbury 45 F5
Tilbury Green 59 F3
Tile Hill 67 E5
Tilehurst 42 B5
Tilford 29 D3
Tilgate 30 B5
Tilgate Forest Row 30 B5
Tillathrowie 168 B1
Tillers' Green 53 F4
Tillery 169 G2
Tilley 78 C5
Tillicoultry 151 E5
Tillingham 46 C2
Tillington *Here.* 53 D3
Tillington *W.Suss.* 29 E5
Tillington Common 53 D3
Tillyarblet 160 D3
Tillybirloch 169 D4
Tillycairn Castle 169 D3
Tillycorthie 169 G2
Tillydrine 168 D4
Tillyfar 179 D3
Tillyfour 168 C3
Tillyfourie 168 D3
Tillygreig 169 F2
Tillypronie 168 B4
Tilmanstone 33 F3
Tiln 95 E4
Tilney All Saints 71 D1
Tilney Fen End 70 D1
Tilney High End 71 D1
Tilney St. Lawrence 70 D1
Tilshead 26 B3
Tilstock 78 C2
Tilston 78 B2
Tilstone Fearnall 78 C1
Tilsworth 57 E5
Tilton on the Hill 68 C2
Tiltups End 40 A3
Timberland 83 G2
Timberland Dales 83 G1
Timbersbrook 79 F1
Timberscombe 22 C3
Timble 102 A2
Timewell 22 C5
Timperley 92 B4
Timsbury *B. & N.E.Som.* 25 D2
Timsbury *Hants.* 27 E5
Timsgearraidh 189 E2
Timworth 59 G1
Timworth Green 59 G1
Tincleton 13 F1
Tindale 118 C2
Tindon End 59 E4
Tingewick 56 B4
Tingley 102 B5
Tingrith 57 F4
Tingwall 190 B2
Tingwall (Lerwick) Airport 191 F4
Tinhay 7 D2
Tinney 6 C1
Tinshill 102 B4
Tinsley 94 B3
Tinsley Green 30 B5
Tintagel 5 E1
Tintern Parva 39 E2
Tintinhull 12 A1
Tintwistle 93 E3
Tinwald 125 E2
Tinwell 69 F2
Tippacott 22 A3
Tipperty *Aber.* 161 F1
Tipperty *Aber.* 169 G2
Tipps End 70 C3
Tiptoe 14 B3

Tipton 66 B3
Tipton St. John 11 D3
Tiptree 46 B1
Tiptree Heath 46 B1
Tirabad 51 E3
Tiree 154 A2
Tiree Airport 154 B2
Tirindrish 157 E1
Tirley 54 A5
Tirphil 38 A2
Tirril 118 B5
Tir-y-dail 36 C1
Tisbury 26 A5
Tisman's Common 29 F4
Tissington 80 C2
Tister 187 D2
Titchberry 20 C3
Titchfield 15 E2
Titchmarsh 69 F5
Titchwell 85 G3
Tithby 82 B4
Titley 52 C1
Titlington 137 F5
Titmore Green 58 A5
Titsey 30 D3
Titson 20 C5
Tittensor 79 F4
Tittleshall 85 G5
Tiverton *C. & W.Ches.* 78 C1
Tiverton *Devon* 10 C1
Tivetshall St. Margaret 72 C3
Tivetshall St. Mary 72 C3
Tivington 22 C3
Tixall 79 G5
Tixover 69 E2
Toab 191 F5
Tobermory 155 E4
Toberonochy 147 G4
Tocher 169 D1
Tockenham 40 C5
Tockenham Wick 40 C5
Tockholes 100 C5
Tockington 39 F4
Tockwith 103 D2
Todber 25 E5
Toddington *Beds.* 57 F5
Toddington *Glos.* 54 C4
Todenham 55 E4
Todhills *Angus* 152 C1
Todhills *Cumb.* 126 B5
Todlachie 169 D3
Todmorden 101 F5
Todwick 94 B4
Toft *Cambs.* 58 B2
Toft *Lincs.* 69 F1
Toft *Shet.* 191 F2
Toft Hill 120 A5
Toft Monks 73 F2
Toft next Newton 96 A4
Toftcarl 187 F4
Toftrees 85 G5
Tofts 187 F2
Toftwood 86 A4
Togston 129 E1
Tokavaig 163 E3
Tokers Green 42 B5
Tolastadh a'Chaolais 189 E2
Tolastadh Ùr 189 G1
Toll Bar 94 C2
Toll of Birness 179 F4
Tolland 23 E4
Tollard Farnham 13 F1
Tollard Royal 13 F1
Tollcross 142 A3
Toller Down Gate 12 B1
Toller Fratrum 12 B3
Toller Porcorum 12 B3
Toller Whelme 12 B2
Tollerton *N.Yorks.* 103 E1
Tollerton *Notts.* 82 B4
Tollesbury 46 C1
Tollesby 111 E1
Tolleshunt D'Arcy 46 C1
Tolleshunt Knights 46 C1
Tolleshunt Major 46 B1
Tolpuddle 13 E2
Tolvah 166 C5
Tolworth 29 G1
Tomatin 166 C2
Tombreck 166 A1
Tomchrasky (Tom Chrasgaidh) 165 D3
Tomdoun 164 C4
Tomdow 175 G5
Tomich *High.* 165 E2
Tomich *High.* 174 D2

Tomich *High.* 182 B4
Tomintoul 167 F3
Tomnacross 174 B5
Tomnamoon 175 G4
Tomnaven 168 B1
Tomnavoulin 167 G2
Tomvaich 167 E1
Ton Pentre 37 F3
Tonbridge 31 E4
Tondu 37 E4
Tonedale 23 E5
Tonfanau 62 B2
Tong *Kent* 32 A4
Tong *Shrop.* 65 G2
Tong *W.Yorks.* 102 B4
Tong Norton 65 G2
Tong Street 102 A4
Tonge 81 F5
Tongham 29 D3
Tongland 124 A5
Tongue 185 E3
Tongue House 185 E3
Tongwynlais 38 A4
Tonmawr 37 E3
Tonna 37 D3
Tonwell 44 C1
Tonypandy 37 F3
Tonyrefail 37 G4
Toot Baldon 42 A2
Toot Hill 45 E2
Toothill *Hants.* 14 C1
Toothill *Swin.* 40 D4
Tooting Graveney 44 B5
Top End 57 F1
Top of Hebers 92 C2
Topcliffe 110 D5
Topcroft 73 D2
Topcroft Street 73 D2
Toppesfield 59 F4
Toppings 92 B1
Toprow 72 C2
Topsham 10 C4
Topsham Bridge 8 C2
Torastan 154 B3
Torbain 167 F3
Torbeg *Aber.* 168 A5
Torbeg *N.Ayr.* 131 E3
Torbothie 142 C4
Torbryan 9 E1
Torcastle 156 D2
Torcross 9 E3
Tordarroch 166 A1
Tore (An Todhar) 174 C4
Toreduff 176 A3
Toremore *High.* 167 F1
Toremore *High.* 183 G1
Torfrey 5 E2
Torgyle 165 E3
Torksey 95 F5
Torlundy (Tòrr Lunndaidh) 156 D2
Tormarton 39 G5
Tormisdale 138 A4
Tormore 131 E2
Tormsdale 186 D3
Tornagrain 175 D4
Tornahaish 167 G4
Tornaveen 168 D4
Torness 165 G2
Toronto 120 A4
Torpenhow 117 F3
Torphichen 143 D2
Torphins 168 D4
Torpoint 8 A2
Torquay 9 F1
Torquhan 144 B5
Torr 8 B2
Torran *Arg. & B.* 148 A4
Torran *High.* 174 D2
Torran *High.* 171 E5
Torrance 142 A2
Torrance House 142 A4
Torrancroy 168 A3
Torre *Som.* 22 D3
Torre *Torbay* 9 F1
Torrich 175 E4
Torridon 172 B4
Torrin 163 D2
Torrisdale *Arg. & B.* 130 C2
Torrisdale *High.* 185 F2
Torrish 183 E3
Torrisholme 100 A1
Torroble 182 A4
Torry *Aber.* 176 D5
Torry *Aberdeen* 169 G4
Torryburn 143 E1
Torsonce 144 B5
Torterston 179 F3

Torthorwald **125** E3
Tortington **16** B3
Torton **66** A5
Tortworth **39** G3
Torvaig **171** D5
Torver **107** D3
Torwood **142** C1
Torworth **95** D4
Tosberry **20** C3
Toscaig **163** F1
Toseland **58** A1
Tosside **101** D2
Tostarie **154** C5
Tostock **60** A1
Totaig **170** A4
Totamore **154** A4
Tote **170** D5
Tote Hill **29** D5
Totegan **186** A2
Totford **27** G4
Totham Hill **46** B1
Tothill **97** E4
Totland **14** C4
Totley **94** A5
Totnes **9** E1
Toton **81** G4
Totronald **154** C5
Totscore **170** C3
Tottenham **44** C3
Tottenhill **71** E1
Tottenhill Row **71** E1
Totteridge *Bucks.* **43** D3
Totteridge *Gt.Lon.* **44** B3
Totternhoe **57** E5
Tottington *Gt.Man.* **92** B1
Tottington *Norf.* **71** G3
Totton **14** C1
Toulton **23** E4
Tournaig **182** B1
Toux **179** E2
Tovil **31** G3
Tow Law **120** A4
Towan Cross **4** B5
Toward **140** C3
Towcester **56** B3
Towednack **2** B3
Tower End **71** E1
Towersey **42** C2
Towie *Aber.* **179** D1
Towie *Aber.* **168** C2
Towie *Aber.* **168** B3
Towiemore **176** C5
Town End *Cambs.* **70** C3
Town End *Cumb.* **107** F4
Town End *Mersey.* **91** F4
Town Green *Lancs.* **91** F2
Town Green *Norf.* **87** B4
Town of Lowton **92** A3
Town Row **31** E5
Town Street **71** F4
Town Yetholm **136** C4
Townfield **119** F3
Townhead *D. & G.* **115** G2
Townhead *S.Yorks.* **93** F2
Townhead of Greenlaw **124** B4
Townhill *Fife* **143** F1
Townhill *Swan.* **36** C3
Towns End **27** G2
Towns Green **78** D1
Townshend **2** C3
Towthorpe *E.Riding* **104** B1
Towthorpe *York* **103** F2
Towton **103** D4
Towyn **90** A5
Toynton All Saints **84** B1
Toynton Fen Side **84** B1
Toynton St. Peter **84** C1
Toy's Hill **31** D3
Trabboch **132** C3
Traboe **3** E4
Tradespark **175** E4
Trafford Centre **92** B3
Trafford Park **92** B3
Trallong **51** F5
Trallwn **36** C3
Tram Inn **53** D4
Tranent **144** B2
Tranmere **91** E4
Trantlebeg **186** A3
Trantlemore **186** A3
Tranwell **129** D3
Trap **36** C1
Trap Street **79** F1
Traprain **144** C2
Trap's Green **54** D1

Traquair **135** E2
Trawden **101** F4
Trawscoed (Crosswood) **62** C5
Trawsfynydd **76** A4
Trealaw **37** G3
Treales **100** A4
Trearddur **88** A5
Treaslane **170** C4
Tre-Aubrey **37** G5
Trebanog **37** G3
Trebanos **36** D2
Trebarrow **6** C1
Trebartha **5** G2
Trebarvah **3** E3
Trebarwith **5** E1
Trebeath **5** G1
Trebetherick **4** C4
Tre-boeth **36** C3
Treborough **22** D4
Trebudannon **4** C3
Trebullett **6** D3
Treburley **6** D3
Treburrick **4** C2
Trebyan **5** E3
Trecastle **51** E5
Trecott **21** G5
Trecrogo **6** D2
Trecwn **48** C4
Trecynon **37** F2
Tredaule **5** G1
Tredavoe **2** B4
Treddiog **48** B5
Tredegar **38** A2
Tredington *Glos.* **54** B5
Tredington *Warks.* **55** E3
Tredinnick *Cornw.* **4** D3
Tredinnick *Cornw.* **5** G4
Tredogan **23** D1
Tredomen **52** A4
Tredrissi **49** D3
Tredunnock **38** C3
Tredustan **52** A4
Tredworth **40** A1
Treen *Cornw.* **2** A4
Treen *Cornw.* **2** B3
Treesmill **5** E4
Treeton **94** B4
Trefasser **48** B4
Trefdraeth **88** C5
Trefecca **52** A4
Trefechan **37** G2
Trefeglwys **63** F3
Trefenter **50** C1
Treffgarne **48** C5
Treffynnon **48** B5
Trefgarn Owen **48** B5
Trefil **38** A1
Trefilan **50** B2
Trefin **48** B4
Treflach **77** F5
Trefnanney **64** B1
Trefnant **90** B5
Trefonen **77** F5
Trefor *Gwyn.* **74** C3
Trefor *I.o.A.* **88** B4
Treforest **37** G4
Treforest Industrial Estate **38** A4
Trefriw **76** A1
Tregadillett **5** G1
Tregaian **88** C5
Tregare **38** D1
Tregarland **5** G4
Tregarne **3** E4
Tregaron **50** C2
Tregarth **75** F1
Tregaswith **4** C3
Tregavethan **4** B5
Tregear **4** C4
Tregeare **5** G1
Tregeiriog **77** E4
Tregele **88** B3
Tregidden **3** E4
Tregiskey **5** E5
Treglemais **48** B5
Tregole **6** B1
Tregonetha **5** F3
Tregony **4** D5
Tregoodwell **5** F1
Tregoss **5** D3
Tregowris **3** E4
Tregoyd **52** A4
Tregrehan Mills **5** E4
Tre-groes **50** A3
Treguff **37** G5
Tregullon **5** E3
Tregunnon **5** G1

Tregurrian **4** C3
Tregynon **63** G3
Trehafod **37** G3
Trehan **8** A2
Treharris **37** G3
Treherbert **37** F3
Tre-hill **37** G5
Trekenner **6** D3
Treknow **5** E1
Trelan **3** E5
Trelash **6** B1
Trelassick **4** C4
Trelawnyd **90** B5
Trelech **49** F4
Treleddyd-fawr **48** A5
Trelewis **38** A3
Treligga **5** E1
Trelights **5** D2
Trelill **5** E2
Trelissick **3** F3
Trellech **39** E2
Trelleck Grange **39** D2
Trelogan **90** C4
Trelowla **5** G4
Trelystan **64** B2
Tremadog **75** E3
Tremail **5** F1
Tremain **49** F3
Tremaine **5** G1
Tremar **5** G3
Trematon **7** D5
Tremeirchion **90** B5
Tremethick Cross **2** B3
Tremore **5** E3
Trenance *Cornw.* **4** C3
Trenance *Cornw.* **4** C2
Trenarren **5** E5
Trench *Tel. & W.* **65** F1
Trench *Wrex.* **78** A4
Trencreek **4** C3
Trenear **3** D3
Treneglos **5** G1
Trenewan **5** F4
Trengune **6** B1
Trent **12** B1
Trent Port **95** E4
Trent Vale **79** F3
Trentham **79** F3
Trentishoe **21** G1
Trenwheal **2** D3
Treoes **37** F5
Treorchy **37** F3
Treowen **38** B3
Trequite **5** E2
Tre'r-ddol **62** C3
Trerhyngyll **37** G5
Tre-Rhys **48** B5
Trerulefoot **6** D5
Tresaith **49** F2
Tresco **4** A1
Trescott **66** A3
Trescowe **2** C3
Tresean **4** B4
Tresham **39** G3
Treshnish **154** C5
Tresillian **4** C5
Tresinney **5** F1
Treskinnick Cross **6** C1
Treslea **5** F3
Tresmeer **5** G1
Tresowes Green **2** D4
Tresparrett **6** B1
Tresparrett Posts **6** B1
Tressait **158** D3
Treswell **95** E5
Trethewey **2** A4
Trethomas **38** A4
Trethurgy **5** E4
Tretio **48** A5
Tretire **53** E5
Tretower **52** A5
Treuddyn **77** F2
Trevadlock **5** G2
Trevalga **6** A1
Trevalyn **78** A2
Trevanson **5** D2
Trevarnon **2** C3
Trevarrack **2** B3
Trevarren **4** D3
Trevarrian **4** C3
Trevarrick **5** D5
Tre-vaughan *Carmar.* **49** G5
Trevaughan *Carmar.* **35** E1
Treveighan **5** E2
Trevellas **4** B4
Trevelmond **5** G3

Trevenen **3** D4
Treverva **3** E3
Trevescan **2** A4
Trevethin **38** B2
Trevigro **6** D4
Trevine **148** C2
Treviscoe **4** D4
Trevivian **5** F1
Trevone **4** C2
Trevor **77** F3
Trewalder **5** E1
Trewarmett **5** E1
Trewarthenick **4** D5
Trewassa **5** F1
Trewellard **2** A3
Trewen *Cornw.* **5** G1
Trewen *Here.* **39** E1
Trewennack **3** D4
Trewent **34** D3
Trewern **64** B1
Trewethern **5** E1
Trewidland **5** G4
Trewilym **49** E3
Trewint *Cornw.* **6** B1
Trewint *Cornw.* **5** G1
Trewithian **3** F3
Trewoon **5** D2
Treworga **4** C5
Treworlas **3** F3
Trewornan **5** D2
Treworthal **3** F3
Tre-wyn **52** C5
Treyarnon **4** C2
Treyford **16** A2
Trezaise **5** D4
Triangle **101** G5
Trickett's Cross **13** G2
Triermain **118** B1
Trimdon **120** C4
Trimdon Colliery **120** C4
Trimdon Grange **120** C4
Trimingham **87** D2
Trimley Lower Street **61** D4
Trimley St. Martin **61** D4
Trimley St. Mary **61** D4
Trimpley **65** G3
Trimsaran **36** A2
Trimstone **21** E1
Trinafour **158** C3
Trinant **38** B3
Tring **43** E1
Trinity *Angus* **161** E3
Trinity *Chan.I.* **8** C5
Trinity *Edin.* **143** G2
Trisant **62** D5
Triscombe *Som.* **22** C4
Triscombe *Som.* **23** E4
Trislaig **156** C2
Trispen **4** C4
Tritlington **129** E2
Trochry **151** E1
Troedyraur **49** G3
Troedyrhiw **37** G2
Trofarth **89** G5
Troon *Cornw.* **3** D3
Troon *S.Ayr.* **132** B2
Troston **71** G5
Troswell **6** C1
Trottick **152** C1
Trottiscliffe **31** F2
Trotton **28** D5
Trough Gate **101** E5
Troughend **128** A2
Troustan **140** B2
Troutbeck *Cumb.* **107** F2
Troutbeck *Cumb.* **117** G4
Troutbeck Bridge **107** F2
Trow Green **39** E2
Troway **94** A5
Trowbridge *Cardiff* **38** B4
Trowbridge *Wilts.* **25** F2
Trowell **81** F4
Trowle Common **25** F2
Trowley Bottom **43** F1
Trows **136** A3
Trowse Newton **86** D5
Troy **102** B4
Trudernish **138** C4
Trudoxhill **25** E3
Trull **23** F5
Trumpan **170** B3
Trumpet **53** F4
Trumpington **58** C2
Trumps Green **29** E1
Trunch **12** D4
Trunnah **99** G3
Truro **4** C5
Truscott **6** D2

Trusham **10** B4
Trusley **81** D4
Trusthorpe **97** F4
Truthan **4** C4
Trysull **66** A3
Tubney **41** G3
Tuckhill **65** G4
Tuckingmill **4** A5
Tuddenham *Suff.* **60** C3
Tuddenham *Suff.* **71** F5
Tudeley **31** G2
Tudeley Hale **31** F4
Tudhoe **120** B4
Tudweiliog **74** B4
Tuesley **29** E3
Tuffley **40** A1
Tufton *Hants.* **27** F3
Tufton *Pembs.* **48** D5
Tugby **60** C2
Tugford **65** E4
Tughall **137** G4
Tulchan **151** E2
Tullibody **150** A1
Tullich *Arg. & B.* **148** C3
Tullich *Arg. & B.* **148** A3
Tullich *High.* **175** E2
Tullich *High.* **166** A2
Tullich *Moray* **176** C5
Tullich *Stir.* **150** A1
Tullich *Muir* **174** D2
Tulliemet **159** F4
Tulloch *Aber.* **169** F1
Tulloch *Aber.* **168** C4
Tulloch *High.* **182** B5
Tulloch *Moray* **175** G4
Tullochgorm **148** B5
Tullochgribban High **166** D2
Tullochvenus **168** C4
Tulloes **160** D5
Tullybannocher **150** C2
Tullybelton **151** F1
Tullyfergus **160** A5
Tullymurdoch **159** G4
Tullynessle **168** C3
Tulse Hill **44** C5
Tumble (Y Tymbl) **36** B1
Tumby **84** A2
Tumby Woodside **84** A2
Tummel Bridge **158** C4
Tunbridge Wells **31** E5
Tundergarth Mains **125** F2
Tunga **189** G2
Tungate **87** D3
Tunley **25** D2
Tunstall *E.Riding* **105** F4
Tunstall *Kent* **32** A2
Tunstall *Lancs.* **108** B5
Tunstall *N.Yorks.* **110** B3
Tunstall *Norf.* **87** F5
Tunstall *Stoke* **79** F2
Tunstall *Suff.* **61** E2
Tunstall *T. & W.* **120** D2
Tunstead *Gt.Man.* **93** E2
Tunstead *Norf.* **87** E3
Tunstead Milton **93** E4
Tunworth **28** B3
Tupholme **83** G1
Tupsley **53** E4
Tupton **81** D3
Tur Langton **68** C3
Turbiskill **139** F1
Turclossie **179** D2
Turgis Green **28** B2
Turin **160** D4
Turkdean **40** D1
Turleigh **25** F1
Turn **91** C1
Turnastone **52** C4
Turnberry **132** A5
Turnchapel **8** A2
Turnditch **81** D3
Turner's Green **55** D1
Turners Hill **30** C5
Turners Puddle **13** E4
Turnford **44** C2
Turnworth **13** E2
Turret Bridge **165** E5
Turriff **177** G5
Turton Bottoms **92** B1
Turvey **57** E2
Turville **42** C3
Turville Heath **42** C3
Turweston **56** B4
Tutbury **80** D5
Tutnall **66** B5
Tutshill **39** E3
Tuttington **86** D3

Tutts Clump **42** A5
Tutwell **7** D3
Tuxford **95** E5
Twatt **190** A2
Twechar **142** C2
Tweedmouth **145** G4
Tweedsmuir **134** B3
Twelve Oaks **18** B1
Twelveheads **4** B5
Twemlow Green **79** E1
Twenty **83** G5
Twickenham **44** A5
Twigworth **54** A5
Twineham **17** E1
Twineham Green **17** E1
Twinhoe **25** E2
Twinstead **59** G4
Twiss Green **92** A3
Twiston **101** E3
Twitchen *Devon* **22** A4
Twitchen *Shrop.* **64** C5
Twitton **31** F3
Twizell House **137** F4
Two Bridges *Devon* **7** G3
Two Bridges *Glos.* **39** F2
Two Dales **81** D1
Two Gates **67** E2
Two Mills **91** E5
Twycross **67** F2
Twyford *Bucks.* **56** B5
Twyford *Derbys.* **81** E5
Twyford *Dorset* **13** E1
Twyford *Hants.* **27** F5
Twyford *Leics.* **68** C1
Twyford *Norf.* **86** B3
Twyford *Oxon.* **55** G4
Twyford Common **53** E4
Twyn Shôn-Ifan **38** A3
Twynholm **124** A5
Twyning **54** A4
Twynllanan **51** D5
Twyn-yr-odyn **38** A4
Twyn-y-Sheriff **38** D2
Twywell **69** E5
Ty Croes **88** B5
Tycroes **36** C1
Tycrwyn **64** A1
Tydd Gote **70** C1
Tydd St. Giles **70** C1
Tydd St. Mary **70** C1
Tye Common **45** F3
Tye Green *Essex* **59** F5
Tye Green *Essex* **58** D5
Tye Green *Essex* **45** F1
Tye Green *Essex* **44** D2
Tyersal **102** A2
Ty-hen **74** A4
Tyldesley **92** A2
Tyle-garw **37** G4
Tyler Hill **32** D2
Tylers Green *Bucks.* **43** E3
Tyler's Green *Essex* **45** E2
Tylorstown **37** G3
Tylwch **63** F2
Ty-Mawr *Conwy* **76** C3
Ty-mawr *Denb.* **77** E3
Ty-nant *Conwy* **76** C3
Ty-nant *Gwyn.* **76** C5
Tyndrum (Taigh an Droma) **149** F1
Tyneham **13** E4
Tynehead **144** A4
Tynemouth **120** C1
Tynewydd **37** F3
Tyninghame **144** D2
Tynron **124** C1
Tyntesfield **39** E5
Tyn-y-cefn **77** D3
Ty'n-y-coedcae **38** A4
Tyn-y-cwm **51** E2
Tyn-y-ffridd **77** E4
Ty'n-y-garn **37** E4
Tyn-y-gongl **88** D4
Tynygraig *Cere.* **50** C1
Tyn-y-graig *Powys* **51** G3
Ty'n-y-groes **89** F5
Tyrie **179** E1
Tyringham **57** D3
Tyseley **66** D4
Tythegston **37** E5
Tytherington *Ches.E.* **92** D5
Tytherington *S.Glos.* **39** F4
Tytherington *Som.* **25** E3

Tytherington *Wilts.* **26** A3
Tytherton Lucas **40** B5
Tyttenhanger **44** A2
Ty-uchaf **76** C5
Tywardreath **5** E4
Tywardreath Highway **5** E4
Tywyn **62** B2

U

Uachdar **188** B2
Uags **163** F1
Ubberley **79** G3
Ubbeston Green **73** E4
Ubley **24** C2
Uckerby **110** B2
Uckfield **17** G1
Uckinghall **54** A4
Uckington **54** B5
Uddingston **142** A3
Uddington **133** G2
Udimore **19** D2
Udley **24** B1
Udny Green **169** F2
Udny Station **169** G2
Udston **142** B4
Udstonhead **142** B5
Uffcott **40** D5
Uffculme **11** D1
Uffington *Lincs.* **69** F2
Uffington *Oxon.* **41** E4
Uffington *Shrop.* **65** E1
Ufford *Peter.* **69** F2
Ufford *Suff.* **61** D2
Ufton **55** F1
Ufton Green **28** B1
Ufton Nervet **28** B1
Ugborough **8** C2
Ugford **26** B4
Uggeshall **73** F3
Ugglebarnby **112** B2
Ugley **58** D5
Ugley Green **58** D5
Ugthorpe **111** G1
Uig *Arg. & B.* **154** A4
Uig *Arg. & B.* **140** C1
Uig *High.* **170** A4
Uig (Uige) *High.* **170** C3
Uiginish **170** B5
Uigshader **170** D5
Uisken **146** A1
Uis010 **187** F4
Ulcat Row **118** A5
Ulceby *Lincs.* **97** E5
Ulceby *N.Lincs.* **96** B1
Ulceby Cross **97** E5
Ulceby Skitter **96** B1
Ulcombe **32** A4
Uldale **117** F3
Uldale House **108** C3
Uley **39** G3
Ulgham **129** E2
Ullapool (Ullapul) **180** D5
Ullenhall **54** D1
Ullenwood **40** B1
Ulleskelf **103** E4
Ullesthorpe **68** A4
Ulley **94** B2
Ullingswick **53** E3
Ullinish **162** B1
Ullock **117** D4
Ulpha *Cumb.* **106** C3
Ulpha *Cumb.* **107** F4
Ulrome **105** D2
Ulsta **191** F2
Ulting **46** B2
Uluvalt **147** E1
Ulva **146** D1
Ulverston **107** D5
Ulwell **13** G4
Ulzieside **133** F5
Umberleigh **21** G3
Unapool **181** E1
Underbarrow **107** F3
Undercliffe **102** A4
Underhill **44** B3
Underling Green **31** G4
Underriver **31** E3
Underwood *Newport* **38** C4
Underwood *Notts.* **81** F2
Underwood *Plym.* **8** B2
Undley **71** E4
Undy **38** D4
Union Croft **169** F5
Union Mills **98** B4
Union Street **31** G5

Unst **191** G1
Unstone **94** A5
Unstone Green **94** A5
Unsworth **92** C2
Unthank *Cumb.* **118** A4
Unthank *Derbys.* **94** A5
Up Cerne **12** C2
Up Exe **10** C2
Up Hatherley **54** B5
Up Holland **91** G2
Up Marden **15** G1
Up Mudford **12** B1
Up Nately **28** B2
Up Somborne **27** E4
Up Sydling **12** C2
Upavon **26** C2
Upchurch **32** A2
Upcott *Devon* **7** E1
Upcott *Devon* **21** F2
Upcott *Here.* **52** C2
Upcott *Som.* **22** C5
Upend **59** E2
Upgate **86** C4
Upgate Street *Norf.* **72** B2
Upgate Street *Norf.* **73** D2
Uphall *Dorset* **12** B2
Uphall *W.Loth.* **143** E2
Uphall Station **143** E3
Upham *Devon* **10** B2
Upham *Hants.* **27** G5
Uphampton *Here.* **52** C1
Uphampton *Worcs.* **54** A1
Uphempston **9** E1
Uphill **24** A2
Uplands *Glos.* **40** A2
Uplands *Swan.* **36** C3
Uplawmoor **141** F4
Upleadon **53** G5
Upleatham **111** F1
Uplees **32** C2
Uploders **12** B3
Uplowman **10** D1
Uplyme **11** G3
Upminster **45** E4
Upottery **11** F2
Upper Affcot **64** D4
Upper Ardroscadale **140** B3
Upper Arley **65** G4
Upper Arncott **42** B1
Upper Astley **65** E1
Upper Aston **66** A3
Upper Astrop **56** A4
Upper Basildon **42** B5
Upper Benefield **69** E4
Upper Bentley **54** B1
Upper Berwick **65** D1
Upper Bighouse **186** A3
Upper Boat **38** A4
Upper Boddam **168** D1
Upper Boddington **55** G2
Upper Borth **62** C4
Upper Boyndlie **179** E1
Upper Brailes **55** F4
Upper Breakish **163** E2
Upper Breinton **65** D3
Upper Broadheath **54** A2
Upper Broughton **82** B5
Upper Brynamman **36** D1
Upper Bucklebury **27** G1
Upper Burgate **14** A1
Upper Burnhaugh **169** F5
Upper Caldecote **57** G2
Upper Camster **187** E4
Upper Canada **24** A2
Upper Catesby **56** A2
Upper Catshill **66** B5
Upper Chapel **51** G3
Upper Cheddon **23** F5
Upper Chicksgrove **26** A4
Upper Chute **27** D2
Upper Clatford **27** E2
Upper Coberley **40** B1
Upper Colwall **53** G3
Upper Cotton **80** B3
Upper Cound **65** E2
Upper Cumberworth **93** G2
Upper Cwmbran **38** B3
Upper Dallachy **176** C3
Upper Dean **57** F1
Upper Denby **93** G2
Upper Denton **118** C1
Upper Derraid **167** E1
Upper Diabaig **172** B3

Upper Dicker **18** A2
Upper Dovercourt **60** D4
Upper Dunsforth **102** D1
Upper Dunsley **43** E1
Upper Eastern Green **67** E4
Upper Eathie **175** D3
Upper Egleton **53** F3
Upper Elkstone **80** B2
Upper End **93** E5
Upper Enham **27** E3
Upper Farringdon **28** C4
Upper Framilode **39** G1
Upper Froyle **28** C3
Upper Gills **187** F1
Upper Glendessarry **164** A5
Upper Godney **24** B3
Upper Gornal **66** B3
Upper Gravenhurst **57** G4
Upper Green *Essex* **58** C4
Upper Green *Essex* **59** D4
Upper Green *Mon.* **38** C1
Upper Green *W.Berks.* **27** E1
Upper Grove Common **53** E5
Upper Gylen **148** A2
Upper Hackney **80** D1
Upper Halliford **29** F1
Upper Halling **31** F2
Upper Hambleton **69** E2
Upper Harbledown **32** D3
Upper Hardres Court **33** D3
Upper Hartfield **31** D5
Upper Hatton **79** F4
Upper Hawkhillock **179** F4
Upper Hayesden **31** E4
Upper Hayton **65** E4
Upper Heath **65** E4
Upper Heaton **93** F1
Upper Hellesdon **86** D4
Upper Helmsley **103** F2
Upper Hengoed **77** F4
Upper Hergest **62** B2
Upper Heyford *Northants.* **56** B2
Upper Heyford *Oxon.* **55** G5
Upper Hill *Here.* **53** D2
Upper Hill *S.Glos.* **39** F3
Upper Horsebridge **18** A2
Upper Howsell **53** G3
Upper Hulme **80** B1
Upper Inglesham **41** E3
Upper Kilchattan **146** C5
Upper Killay **36** B3
Upper Knockando **176** A5
Upper Lambourn **41** F4
Upper Langford **24** B2
Upper Langwith **81** G1
Upper Largo **152** C4
Upper Leigh **80** B4
Upper Ley **39** G1
Upper Loads **81** E2
Upper Lochton **169** D5
Upper London **66** C1
Upper Longwood **65** F2
Upper Ludstone **66** A3
Upper Lybster **187** F5
Upper Lydbrook **39** F1
Upper Lyde **53** D3
Upper Lye **52** C1
Upper Maes-coed **52** C4
Upper Midhope **93** G3
Upper Milovaig **170** A5
Upper Milton **41** F3
Upper Minety **40** C3
Upper Moor **54** B3
Upper Morton **39** F3
Upper Muirskie **169** F5
Upper Nash **34** D2
Upper Newbold **94** A5
Upper North Dean **43** D3
Upper Norwood **44** C5
Upper Obney **151** F1
Upper Oddington **55** E5
Upper Ollach **162** D1
Upper Padley **93** G5
Upper Pennington **14** B3
Upper Pollicott **42** C1
Upper Poppleton **103** E2
Upper Quinton **55** D3
Upper Ratley **27** E5
Upper Ridinghill **179** F2
Upper Rissington **55** E5
Upper Rochford **53** F1

Upper Sapey **53** F1
Upper Scolton **48** C5
Upper Seagry **40** B4
Upper Shelton **57** E3
Upper Sheringham **86** C1
Upper Shuckburgh **55** G2
Upper Siddington **40** C3
Upper Skelmorlie **140** D3
Upper Slaughter **55** D5
Upper Sonachan **148** C2
Upper Soudley **39** F1
Upper Staploe **57** G2
Upper Stoke **87** D5
Upper Stondon **57** G4
Upper Stowe **56** B2
Upper Street *Hants.* **14** A1
Upper Street *Norf.* **87** E4
Upper Street *Norf.* **72** C4
Upper Street *Suff.* **60** C4
Upper Street *Suff.* **60** C2
Upper Strensham **54** B4
Upper Sundon **57** F5
Upper Swanmore **15** E1
Upper Swell **55** D5
Upper Tean **80** B4
Upper Thurnham **100** A2
Upper Tillyrie **151** G4
Upper Tooting **44** B5
Upper Town *Derbys.* **80** D1
Upper Town *Derbys.* **81** D2
Upper Town *Derbys.* **80** D2
Upper Town *Here.* **53** E3
Upper Town *N.Som.* **24** C1
Upper Tysoe **55** F3
Upper Upham **41** E5
Upper Upnor **45** G5
Upper Victoria **152** D1
Upper Vobster **25** E3
Upper Wardington **55** G3
Upper Waterhay **40** C3
Upper Weald **56** C4
Upper Weedon **56** B2
Upper Welson **52** B2
Upper Weston **25** E1
Upper Whiston **94** B4
Upper Wick **54** A2
Upper Wield **28** C3
Upper Winchendon (Over Winchendon) **42** C1
Upper Witton **66** C3
Upper Woodford **26** C4
Upper Woolhampton **27** G1
Upper Wootton **27** G2
Upper Wraxall **40** A5
Upper Wyche **53** G3
Upperby **118** A2
Uppermill **93** D2
Upperthong **93** F2
Upperton **29** E5
Uppertown *Derbys.* **81** E1
Uppertown *Ork.* **187** F1
Uppingham **69** D2
Uppington **65** E2
Upsall **111** D4
Upsettlington **145** F5
Upshire **44** D2
Upstreet **33** E2
Upthorpe **72** A4
Upton *Bucks.* **42** C1
Upton *C. & W.Ches.* **78** B1
Upton *Cambs.* **69** G5
Upton *Cornw.* **5** G2
Upton *Cornw.* **20** C5
Upton *Devon* **11** D2
Upton *Devon* **8** D3
Upton *Dorset* **13** F5
Upton *Dorset* **12** D4
Upton *E.Riding* **104** D2
Upton *Hants.* **27** E2
Upton *Hants.* **14** C1
Upton *Leics.* **67** F3
Upton *Lincs.* **95** F4
Upton *Mersey.* **91** D4
Upton *Norf.* **87** E4
Upton *Northants.* **56** C1
Upton *Notts.* **95** E5
Upton *Notts.* **82** C2
Upton *Oxon.* **42** A4
Upton *Oxon.* **41** E1
Upton *Pembs.* **34** D2
Upton *Peter.* **69** G2

Upton *Slo.* **43** E5
Upton *Som.* **22** C5
Upton *Som.* **24** B5
Upton *W.Yorks.* **94** B1
Upton *Wilts.* **25** F4
Upton Bishop **53** F5
Upton Cheyney **25** D1
Upton Cressett **65** F3
Upton Crews **53** F5
Upton Cross **5** G2
Upton End **57** G4
Upton Grey **28** B3
Upton Hellions **10** B2
Upton Lovell **26** A3
Upton Magna **65** E1
Upton Noble **25** E4
Upton Park **44** D4
Upton Pyne **10** C3
Upton St. Leonards **40** A1
Upton Scudamore **25** F3
Upton Snodsbury **54** B2
Upton upon Severn **54** A3
Upton Warren **54** B1
Upwaltham **16** B2
Upware **70** B5
Upwell **70** D2
Upwey **12** C4
Upwick Green **58** C5
Upwood **70** A4
Urafirth **191** E2
Urchany **175** E5
Urchfont **26** B2
Urdimarsh **53** E2
Urlay Nook **110** D1
Urmston **92** B3
Urpeth **120** B2
Urquhart *High.* **174** B4
Urquhart *Moray* **176** B3
Urra **111** E2
Urray **174** B4
Ushaw Moor **120** B3
Usk (Brynbuga) **38** C2
Usselby **96** A3
Usworth **120** C2
Utley **101** G3
Uton **10** B3
Utterby **96** D3
Uttoxeter **80** B4
Uwchmynydd **74** A5
Uxbridge **43** F4
Uyeasound **191** G1
Uzmaston **34** C1

V

Valley (Y Fali) **88** A3
Valley Truckle **5** F1
Valleyfield *D. & G.* **124** A5
Valleyfield *Fife* **143** E1
Valsgarth **191** G1
Vange **45** G4
Vardre **36** C2
Varteg **38** B2
Vatersay (Bhatarsaigh) **188** A5
Vatten **170** B5
Vaul **154** B2
Vaynor **37** G1
Vaynor Park **64** A2
Veaullt **52** A2
Veensgarth **191** F4
Velindre *Pembs.* **49** D4
Velindre *Powys* **52** A4
Vellow **23** D4
Venn **8** D3
Venn Ottery **11** D3
Venngreen **21** D4
Vennington **64** C2
Venny Tedburn **10** B3
Venterdon **7** D3
Ventnor **15** E5
Venton **8** B2
Vernham Dean **27** E2
Vernham Street **27** E2
Vernolds Common **65** D4
Verwood **13** G2
Veryan **3** G3
Veryan Green **4** D5
Vickerstown **99** E1
Victoria **5** D3
Vidlin **191** F3
Viewfield **186** C2
Viewpark **142** B3
Vigo **66** C2
Vigo Village **31** F2
Villavin **21** F4
Vinehall Street **18** C1
Vine's Cross **18** A2

Viney Hill **39** F2
Virginia Water **29** E1
Virginstow **7** D1
Virley **46** C1
Vobster **25** E3
Voe **191** F3
Vowchurch **52** C4
Vron Gate **64** C2

W

Waberthwaite **106** C3
Wackerfield **120** A5
Wacton **72** C2
Wadborough **54** B3
Waddesdon **42** C1
Waddeton **9** E2
Waddicar **91** E3
Waddingham **95** G3
Waddington *Lancs.* **100** D3
Waddington *Lincs.* **83** E1
Waddingworth **96** B5
Waddon *Devon* **10** B4
Waddon *Gt.Lon.* **30** C2
Wadebridge **5** D2
Wadeford **11** G1
Wadenhoe **69** F4
Wadesmill **44** C1
Wadhurst **31** F5
Wadshelf **94** A5
Wadworth **94** C3
Wadworth Hill **105** E5
Waen *Denb.* **77** E1
Waen *Denb.* **76** C1
Waen Aberwheeler **77** D1
Waen-fâch **64** B1
Waen-wen **75** E1
Wag **183** E2
Wainfleet All Saints **84** C2
Wainfleet Bank **84** C2
Wainfleet St. Mary **84** C2
Wainford **73** E2
Waingroves **81** F3
Wainhouse Corner **6** B1
Wainscott **45** G5
Wainstalls **101** G5
Waitby **108** C2
Wakefield **102** C5
Wakerley **69** E3
Wakes Colne **59** G5
Walberswick **73** F4
Walberton **16** B3
Walbottle **120** A1
Walcot *Lincs.* **83** F4
Walcot *Lincs.* **83** G2
Walcot *N.Lincs.* **104** A5
Walcot *Shrop.* **64** C4
Walcot *Tel. & W.* **65** E1
Walcot Green **72** C3
Walcote *Leics.* **68** A4
Walcote *Warks.* **54** D2
Walcott **87** E2
Walcott Dales **83** G2
Walden **109** F4
Walden Head **109** E4
Walden Stubbs **94** C1
Walderslade **31** G2
Walderton **15** G1
Walditch **12** A3
Waldley **80** C4
Waldridge **120** B3
Waldringfield **61** D2
Waldron **18** A2
Wales **94** B4
Walesby *Lincs.* **96** B3
Walesby *Notts.* **95** D5
Waleswood **94** B4
Walford *Here.* **64** D5
Walford *Here.* **53** E5
Walford *Shrop.* **78** B5
Walford *Staffs.* **79** F5
Walford Heath **64** D1
Walgherton **79** D3
Walgrave **68** D5
Walhampton **14** C3
Walk Mill **101** E4
Walkden **92** B2
Walker **120** B1
Walker Fold **100** C3
Walkerburn **135** E2
Walkeringham **95** E3
Walkenith **95** E3
Walkern **58** A5
Walker's Green **53** E3
Walkford **14** B3
Walkhampton **8** B1
Walkingham Hill **102** C1
Walkington **104** B4

Walkwood 54 C1
Wall Cornw. 2 D3
Wall Northumb. 119 F1
Wall Staffs. 66 D2
Wall End 106 D4
Wall Heath 66 A4
Wall Houses 119 G1
Wall under Heywood 65 E3
Wallacehall 126 A4
Wallacetown 132 A5
Wallasey 91 D3
Wallaston Green 34 C2
Wallend 32 A1
Waller's Green 53 F4
Wallingford 42 B4
Wallington Gt.Lon. 30 B2
Wallington Hants. 15 E2
Wallington Wrex. 78 B3
Wallingwells 94 C4
Wallis 48 D5
Wallisdown 13 G3
Walliswood 29 G4
Walls 191 E4
Wallsend 120 C1
Wallyford 144 A2
Walmer 33 F3
Walmer Bridge 100 A5
Walmersley 92 C1
Walmley 66 D3
Walmsgate 97 D5
Walpole 73 E4
Walpole Cross Keys 70 D1
Walpole Highway 70 D1
Walpole Marsh 70 C1
Walpole St. Andrew 70 D1
Walpole St. Peter 70 D1
Walrond's Park 24 A5
Walrow 24 A3
Walsall 66 C3
Walsall Wood 66 C2
Walsden 101 F5
Walsgrave on Sowe 67 F4
Walsham le Willows 72 B4
Walshford 102 D2
Walsoken 70 C1
Walston 143 E5
Walsworth 57 G4
Walter's Ash 42 D3
Walterston 37 G5
Walterstone 52 C5
Waltham Kent 32 D4
Waltham N.E.Lincs. 96 C2
Waltham Abbey 44 C2
Waltham Chase 15 E1
Waltham Cross 44 C2
Waltham on the Wolds 82 C5
Waltham St. Lawrence 42 D5
Walthamstow 44 C4
Walton Bucks. 42 D1
Walton Cumb. 118 B5
Walton Derbys. 81 E1
Walton Leics. 68 A4
Walton M.K. 57 D4
Walton Mersey. 91 E3
Walton Peter. 69 G2
Walton Powys 52 B2
Walton Shrop. 65 D5
Walton Som. 24 B4
Walton Staffs. 79 F4
Walton Suff. 61 E4
Walton Tel. & W. 65 E1
Walton W.Yorks. 94 A1
Walton W.Yorks. 102 D3
Walton Warks. 55 F1
Walton Cardiff 54 B4
Walton East 48 D5
Walton Elm 13 D1
Walton Highway 70 C1
Walton Lower Street 61 D4
Walton on the Hill 30 B3
Walton on the Naze 61 D5
Walton on the Wolds 68 A1
Walton Park D. & G. 124 B3
Walton Park N.Som. 38 D5
Walton West 34 B1
Walton-in-Gordano 38 D5
Walton-le-Dale 100 B5
Walton-on-Thames 29 G1

Walton-on-the-Hill 79 G5
Walton-on-Trent 67 E1
Walwen Flints. 90 C5
Walwen Flints. 90 C5
Walwick 128 B4
Walworth 110 B1
Walworth Gate 120 B5
Walwyn's Castle 34 B1
Wambrook 11 F2
Wanborough Surr. 29 E3
Wanborough Swin. 41 E4
Wandel 134 A3
Wandon 137 E4
Wandon End 57 G5
Wandsworth 44 B5
Wandylaw 137 F4
Wangford Suff. 73 F4
Wangford Suff. 71 F4
Wanlip 68 A1
Wanlockhead 133 G4
Wannock 18 A3
Wansford E.Riding 104 C2
Wansford Peter. 69 F3
Wanshurst Green 31 G4
Wanstrow 25 E3
Wanswell 39 F2
Wantage 41 F4
Wapley 39 G5
Wappenbury 55 F1
Wappenham 56 B3
Warblebank 117 F2
Warbleton 18 B2
Warblington 15 G2
Warborough 42 A3
Warboys 70 B4
Warbreck 99 G4
Warbstow 6 C1
Warburton 92 A4
Warcop 108 C1
Ward End 66 D4
Ward Green 60 B1
Warden Kent 32 C1
Warden Northumb. 119 F1
Warden Hill 54 B5
Warden Street 57 G3
Wardhouse 168 C1
Wardington 55 G3
Wardle Ches.E. 78 D2
Wardle Gt.Man. 92 D1
Wardley Gt.Man. 92 B2
Wardley Rut. 68 D2
Wardley T. & W. 120 C1
Wardlow 93 F5
Wardsend 92 D4
Wardy Hill 70 C4
Ware Herts. 44 C1
Ware Kent 33 E2
Wareham 13 F4
Warehorne 32 B5
Waren Mill 137 F3
Warenford 137 F4
Warenton 137 F3
Wareside 44 C1
Waresley Cambs. 58 A2
Waresley Worcs. 66 A5
Warfield 43 D5
Wargrave Mersey. 91 G3
Wargrave W'ham 42 C5
Warham Here. 53 D4
Warham Norf. 86 A1
Wark Northumb. 128 A4
Wark Northumb. 136 C3
Warkleigh 21 G3
Warkton 69 D5
Warkworth Northants. 55 G3
Warkworth Northumb. 129 E1
Warland 101 F5
Warleggan 5 F3
Warley Essex 45 E3
Warley W.Mid. 66 C4
Warley Town 101 G5
Warlingham 30 C3
Warmfield 102 C5
Warmingham 79 E1
Warminghurst 16 B2
Warmington Northants. 69 F3
Warmington Warks. 55 G3
Warminster 25 F3
Warmlake 32 A4
Warmley 39 F5
Warmley Hill 39 F5
Warmsworth 94 C2
Warmwell 13 D4

Warndon 54 A2
Warners End 43 F2
Warnford 28 B5
Warnham 29 G4
Warningcamp 16 C3
Warninglid 17 E1
Warren Ches.E. 92 C5
Warren Pembs. 34 C3
Warren House 7 G2
Warren Row 42 D4
Warren Street 32 B3
Warrenby 121 E5
Warren's Green 58 A5
Warrington M.K. 57 D2
Warrington Warr. 92 A4
Warroch 151 E4
Warsash 15 D2
Warslow 80 B2
Warsop Vale 81 G1
Warter 104 A2
Warthill 103 F2
Wartle 168 C4
Wartling 18 B3
Wartnaby 82 C5
Warton Lancs. 107 G5
Warton Lancs. 100 A5
Warton Northumb. 128 C1
Warton Warks. 67 E2
Warton Bank 100 A5
Warwick 55 E1
Warwick Bridge 118 A2
Warwick Wold 30 C3
Warwick-on-Eden 118 A2
Wasbister 190 B2
Wasdale Head 106 C2
Wash 93 E4
Wash Common 27 F1
Washall Green 58 C4
Washaway 5 E3
Washbourne 9 D2
Washbrook 24 B3
Washfield 10 C1
Washfold 87 F2
Washford Som. 22 D3
Washford Pyne 10 B1
Washingborough 96 A5
Washington T. & W. 120 C2
Washington W.Suss. 16 D2
Washmere Green 60 A3
Wasing 27 G1
Waskerley 119 G3
Wasperton 55 E2
Wasps Nest 83 F1
Wass 111 E5
Watchet 23 D3
Watchfield Oxon. 41 E3
Watchfield Som. 24 A3
Watchgate 107 G3
Watcombe 9 F1
Watendlath 117 F5
Water 101 E5
Water Eaton M.K. 57 D4
Water Eaton Oxon. 42 A1
Water End Beds. 57 G3
Water End Beds. 57 F4
Water End E.Riding 103 G4
Water End Essex 59 D3
Water End Herts. 44 B3
Water End Herts. 43 F1
Water Newton 69 G3
Water Orton 67 D3
Water Stratford 56 B4
Water Yeat 107 D4
Waterbeach 58 C1
Waterbeck 126 A4
Watercombe 13 D4
Waterend 42 C3
Waterfall 80 B2
Waterfoot E.Renf. 141 G4
Waterfoot Lancs. 101 E5
Waterford 44 C1
Watergate 5 F1
Waterhead Cumb. 107 F2
Waterhead D. & G. 124 B3
Waterheath 73 F2
Waterhill of Bruxie 179 E5
Waterhouses Dur. 120 A3
Waterhouses Staffs. 80 B2

Wateringbury 31 F3
Waterlane 40 B2
Waterloo Aber. 179 F4
Waterloo Derbys. 81 F1
Waterloo Gt.Man. 92 D2
Waterloo High. 163 E2
Waterloo Mersey. 91 E3
Waterloo N.Lan. 142 C4
Waterloo Norf. 86 D4
Waterloo P. & K. 151 F1
Waterloo Pembs. 34 C2
Waterloo Poole 13 G3
Waterloo Cross 11 D1
Waterloo Port 75 D1
Waterlooville 15 F1
Watermeetings 134 A4
Watermillock 118 A5
Waterperry 42 B2
Waterrow 23 D5
Waters Upton 65 F1
Watersfield 16 C2
Watersheddings 92 D2
Waterside Aber. 168 A3
Waterside Aber. 179 F5
Waterside B'burn. 100 D5
Waterside Bucks. 43 E2
Waterside E.Ayr. 132 C5
Waterside E.Ayr. 141 F5
Waterside E.Dun. 142 A2
Waterstock 42 B2
Waterston 34 C2
Waterthorpe 94 B2
Watford Herts. 44 A3
Watford Northants. 56 B1
Watford Park 38 A4
Wath N.Yorks. 110 C5
Wath N.Yorks. 102 A1
Wath Brow 116 D5
Wath upon Dearne 94 B2
Watley's End 39 F4
Watlington Norf. 71 E1
Watlington Oxon. 42 B3
Watnall 81 G3
Watten 187 E3
Wattisfield 72 B4
Wattisham 60 B2
Watton Dorset 12 A3
Watton E.Riding 104 C3
Watton Norf. 86 A5
Watton at Stone 44 C1
Watton Green 86 A5
Watton's Green 45 E3
Wattston 142 B3
Wattstown 37 G3
Wattsville 38 B3
Waughtonhill 179 E2
Waun Fawr 62 C4
Waun y Clyn 36 A2
Waunarlwydd 36 C3
Waunclunda 50 C4
Waunfawr 75 E2
Wavendon 57 E4
Waverbridge 117 F2
Waverton C. & W.Ches. 78 B1
Waverton Cumb. 117 F2
Wavertree 91 E4
Wawne 104 C4
Waxham 87 F3
Waxholme 105 F5
Way Gill 101 F1
Way Village 10 B1
Way Wick 24 A1
Wayford 12 A2
Waytown 12 A3
Weachyburn 177 F4
Weacombe 23 E3
Weald 41 E2
Wealdstone 44 A3
Weardley 102 B3
Weare 24 B2
Weare Giffard 21 E3
Wearhead 119 E4
Wearne 24 B5
Weasenham All Saints 85 G5
Weasenham St. Peter 85 G5
Weathercote 108 C5
Weatheroak Hill 66 C5
Weaverham 92 A5
Weaverthorpe 112 C5
Webheath 54 C1
Webton 52 D4
Wedderlairs 169 F1
Weddington 67 F3

Wedhampton 26 B2
Wedmore 24 B3
Wednesbury 66 B3
Wednesfield 66 B3
Weedon 42 D1
Weedon Bec 56 B3
Weedon Lois 56 B3
Weeford 66 D2
Week Devon 10 A1
Week Devon 9 D1
Week Som. 22 C4
Week Orchard 20 C5
Week St. Mary 6 C1
Weeke 27 F4
Weekley 69 D4
Weel 104 C4
Weeley 60 C5
Weeley Heath 60 C5
Weem 158 D4
Weeping Cross 79 G3
Weethley 54 C2
Weeting 71 F4
Weeton E.Riding 105 F3
Weeton Lancs. 99 G4
Weeton N.Yorks. 102 B3
Weetwood 102 B4
Weir Essex 46 B4
Weir Lancs. 101 E5
Weir Quay 8 A1
Weirbrook 78 A5
Welbeck Abbey 94 C5
Welborne 86 B5
Welbourn 83 E2
Welburn N.Yorks. 103 G1
Welburn N.Yorks. 111 F4
Welbury 110 C2
Welby 83 E2
Welches Dam 70 C4
Welcombe 20 C4
Weldon 69 E4
Welford Northants. 68 B4
Welford W.Berks. 41 G5
Welford-on-Avon 54 D2
Welham Leics. 68 C3
Welham Green 44 B2
Welham Notts. 95 E4
Well Hants. 28 C3
Well Lincs. 97 E5
Well N.Yorks. 110 B4
Well End Bucks. 43 D4
Well End Herts. 44 B3
Well Hill 31 D2
Well Street 31 F3
Well Town 10 C2
Welland 53 G3
Wellbank 152 C1
Wellesbourne 55 E2
Wellhill 175 F3
Wellhouse W.Berks. 42 A5
Wellhouse W.Yorks. 93 E1
Welling 45 D5
Wellingborough 57 D1
Wellingham 85 G5
Wellingore 83 E2
Wellington Cumb. 106 B2
Wellington Here. 53 D3
Wellington Som. 23 E5
Wellington Tel. & W. 65 F1
Wellington Heath 53 G3
Wellington Marsh 53 D3
Wellow B. & N.E.Som. 25 E2
Wellow I.o.W. 14 C4
Wellow Notts. 82 B1
Wells 24 C3
Wells Green 66 D4
Wellsborough 67 F2
Wells-next-the-Sea 86 A1
Wellstye Green 45 F1
Wellwood 143 E1
Welney 70 D3
Welsh Bicknor 39 E1
Welsh End 78 C4
Welsh Frankton 78 A4
Welsh Hook 48 C5
Welsh Newton 39 D1
Welsh St. Donats 37 G2
Welshampton 78 B4
Welshpool (Y Trallwng) 64 B2
Welton B. & N.E.Som. 25 D2
Welton Cumb. 117 G2
Welton E.Riding 104 B5
Welton Lincs. 96 A4

Welton Northants. 56 A1
Welton le Marsh 84 C1
Welton le Wold 96 C4
Welwick 105 F5
Welwyn 44 B1
Welwyn Garden City 44 B1
Wem 78 C5
Wembdon 23 F4
Wembley 44 A4
Wembley Park 44 A4
Wembury 8 B3
Wembworthy 21 G4
Wemyss Bay 140 C3
Wenallt Cere. 62 C5
Wenallt Gwyn. 76 C3
Wendens Ambo 58 D4
Wendlebury 42 A1
Wendling 86 A4
Wendover 43 D2
Wendover Dean 43 D2
Wendron 3 D3
Wendy 58 B3
Wenfordbridge 5 E2
Wenhaston 73 F4
Wenlli 76 B1
Wennington Cambs. 70 A5
Wennington Gt.Lon. 45 E4
Wennington Lancs. 108 B5
Wensley Derbys. 81 D1
Wensley N.Yorks. 109 F4
Wentbridge 94 B1
Wentnor 64 C3
Wentworth Cambs. 70 C5
Wentworth S.Yorks. 94 A3
Wenvoe 38 A5
Weobley 52 C2
Weobley Marsh 52 D2
Weoley Castle 66 C4
Wepham 16 C3
Wepre 77 F1
Wereham 71 E2
Wergs 66 B2
Wern Gwyn. 75 E4
Wern Powys 64 B1
Wern Powys 38 A1
Wern Shrop. 77 F2
Wernffrwd 36 B3
Wern-olau 36 B3
Wernrheolydd 38 C1
Wern-y-cwrt 38 C2
Werrington Cornw. 6 D2
Werrington Peter. 69 G2
Werrington Staffs. 79 G3
Wervil Grange 49 G2
Wervin 91 F5
Wesham 100 A4
Wessington 81 E2
West Aberthaw 22 D1
West Acre 71 F1
West Acton 44 A4
West Allerdean 145 E3
West Alvington 8 D3
West Amesbury 26 A1
West Anstey 22 B5
West Ashby 96 C5
West Ashford 21 F2
West Ashling 16 A3
West Ashton 25 F2
West Auckland 120 A5
West Ayton 112 C4
West Bagborough 23 E4
West Barkwith 96 B4
West Barnby 112 B1
West Barns 145 D2
West Barsham 86 A2
West Bay 12 A3
West Beckham 86 C2
West Benhar 142 C3
West Bergholt 60 A5
West Bexington 12 B4
West Bilney 71 F1
West Blatchington 17 E3
West Boldon 120 C1
West Bourton 25 E5
West Bowling 102 A4
West Brabourne 32 C4
West Bradford 100 D3
West Bradley 24 C4
West Bretton 93 G1
West Bridgford 81 G4
West Bromwich 66 C3
West Buckland Devon 21 G2

West Buckland *Som.* 23 E5
West Burton *N.Yorks.* 109 F4
West Burton *W.Suss.* 16 B2
West Butsfield 119 G3
West Butterwick 95 F2
West Byfleet 29 F1
West Cairncake 178 D3
West Caister 87 G4
West Calder 143 E3
West Camel 24 C5
West Carbeth 141 G2
West Carr Houses 95 E2
West Cauldcoats 142 A5
West Chaldon 13 D4
West Challow 41 F4
West Charleton 9 D3
West Chevington 129 G2
West Chiltington 16 C2
West Chiltington Common 16 C2
West Chinnock 12 A1
West Chisenbury 26 C1
West Clandon 29 F2
West Cliffe 33 F4
West Clyne 183 D4
West Coker 12 A1
West Compton *Dorset* 12 B3
West Compton *Som.* 24 C3
West Cowick 103 F5
West Cross 36 C4
West Crudwell 40 B3
West Curry 6 C1
West Curthwaite 117 G2
West Dean *W.Suss.* 16 A2
West Dean *Wilts.* 27 D5
West Deeping 69 G2
West Derby 91 E3
West Dereham 71 E2
West Ditchburn 137 F4
West Down 21 F1
West Drayton *Gt.Lon.* 43 F5
West Drayton *Notts.* 95 E4
West Dullater 150 A4
West Dunnet 187 E1
West Edington 129 D3
West Ella 104 C5
West End *Beds.* 57 E2
West End *Brack.F.* 43 D5
West End *Caerp.* 38 B3
West End *Cambs.* 70 C3
West End *E.Riding* 104 C1
West End *Hants.* 15 D1
West End *Herts.* 44 B2
West End *Kent* 33 D2
West End *Lancs.* 100 A1
West End *Lincs.* 97 D3
West End *N.Yorks.* 102 A2
West End *Norf.* 87 F4
West End *Norf.* 86 A5
West End *Oxon.* 41 E3
West End *Oxon.* 42 A4
West End *S.Lan.* 143 D5
West End *Suff.* 73 F3
West End *Surr.* 29 G1
West End *Surr.* 29 E1
West End *Wilts.* 40 B5
West End *Wilts.* 26 A5
West End *Wilts.* 26 A5
West End Green 28 B1
West Farleigh 31 G3
West Farndon 56 A2
West Felton 78 A5
West Firle 17 G3
West Fleetham 137 F4
West Flotmanby 113 D5
West Garforth 102 C4
West Ginge 41 G4
West Glen 140 A2
West Grafton 26 D1
West Green *Gt.Lon.* 44 C4
West Green *Hants.* 28 C2
West Grimstead 26 D5
West Grinstead 29 G5
West Haddlesey 103 E5
West Haddon 68 B5
West Hagbourne 42 A4
West Hagley 66 B4
West Hall 118 B1

West Hallam 81 F3
West Halton 104 B5
West Ham 44 C4
West Handley 94 A5
West Hanney 41 G3
West Hanningfield 45 G3
West Hardwick 94 B1
West Harnham 26 C5
West Harptree 24 C2
West Harrow 44 A4
West Harting 28 C5
West Hatch *Som.* 23 F5
West Hatch *Wilts.* 26 A5
West Head 71 D2
West Heath *Ches.E.* 79 F1
West Heath *Gt.Lon.* 45 D5
West Heath *Hants.* 29 D2
West Heath *Hants.* 27 G2
West Heath *W.Mid.* 66 C5
West Helmsdale 183 F3
West Hendon 44 B4
West Hendred 41 G4
West Heslerton 112 C5
West Hewish 24 A1
West Hill *Devon* 11 D3
West Hill *E.Riding* 105 D1
West Hill *N.Som.* 39 D5
West Hoathly 30 C5
West Holme 13 E4
West Horndon 45 F4
West Horrington 24 C3
West Horsley 29 F2
West Horton 137 E3
West Hougham 33 E5
West Howe 15 G3
West Howetown 22 C4
West Huntspill 24 A3
West Hyde 43 F3
West Hythe 32 D5
West Ilsley 41 G4
West Itchenor 15 G2
West Keal 84 B1
West Kennett 26 C1
West Kilbride 140 D5
West Kingsdown 31 E2
West Kington 40 A5
West Kington Wick 40 A5
West Kirby 90 B1
West Knapton 112 B5
West Knighton 12 D4
West Knoyle 25 F4
West Kyloe 137 E2
West Lambrook 12 A1
West Langdon 33 F4
West Langwell 182 B4
West Lavington *W.Suss.* 29 D5
West Lavington *Wilts.* 26 B2
West Layton 110 A2
West Leake 81 G5
West Learmonth 136 C3
West Lees 111 D2
West Leigh *Devon* 21 G5
West Leigh *Devon* 9 D2
West Leigh *Som.* 23 E4
West Leith 43 E1
West Lexham 71 G1
West Lilling 103 F1
West Lingo 152 C4
West Linton 143 F4
West Liss 28 C5
West Littleton 39 G5
West Lockinge 41 G4
West Looe 5 G4
West Lulworth 13 E4
West Lutton 104 B1
West Lydford 24 C4
West Lyn 22 A5
West Lyng 24 A5
West Lynn 71 E1
West Mains 137 E2
West Malling 31 F3
West Malvern 53 G3
West Marden 15 G1
West Markham 95 E5
West Marsh 96 C2
West Marton 101 E2
West Melbury 25 F5
West Melton 94 B2
West Meon 28 B5
West Meon Hut 28 B5
West Mersea 46 D1
West Milton 12 A3

West Minster 32 B1
West Molesey 29 G1
West Monkton 23 F5
West Moors 13 G2
West Morden 13 F3
West Morriston 144 D5
West Morton 101 G3
West Mostard 108 C3
West Mudford 24 C5
West Muir 161 D3
West Ness 111 F5
West Newbiggin 110 C2
West Newton *E.Riding* 105 D4
West Newton *Norf.* 85 E5
West Norwood 44 C5
West Ogwell 9 E1
West Orchard 13 E1
West Overton 26 C1
West Panson 6 C1
West Park *Aber.* 169 E5
West Park *Mersey.* 91 G3
West Parley 13 G3
West Peckham 31 F3
West Pelton 120 B2
West Pennard 24 C4
West Pentire 4 B3
West Perry 57 G1
West Porlock 22 B3
West Prawle 9 D4
West Preston 16 C3
West Pulham 12 D2
West Putford 21 F4
West Quantoxhead 23 E3
West Raddon 10 B2
West Rainton 120 C3
West Rasen 96 A4
West Raynham 85 G5
West Retford 95 D4
West Rounton 110 D2
West Row 71 E5
West Rudham 85 G5
West Runton 86 C1
West Saltoun 144 B3
West Sandford 10 B3
West Scrafton 109 F4
West Shepton 24 D3
West Shinness Lodge 182 A3
West Somerton 87 F4
West Stafford 12 D4
West Stockwith 95 E3
West Stoke 16 A3
West Stonesdale 109 D2
West Stoughton 24 B3
West Stour 25 E5
West Stourmouth 33 E2
West Stow 71 G5
West Stowell 26 C1
West Stratton 27 G3
West Street *Kent* 32 B3
West Street *Kent* 33 D2
West Street *Med.* 45 G5
West Street *Suff.* 72 A4
West Tanfield 110 B5
West Taphouse 5 F3
West Tarbert 139 G3
West Tarring 16 D3
West Thirston 129 D1
West Thorney 15 G2
West Thurrock 45 E5
West Tilbury 45 F5
West Tisted 28 B5
West Tofts *Norf.* 71 G3
West Tofts *P.& K.* 151 G1
West Torrington 96 B5
West Town *B.& N.E.Som.* 24 C1
West Town *Hants.* 15 G3
West Town *N.Som.* 24 B1
West Town *Som.* 24 C1
West Tytherley 27 D5
West Walton 70 C1
West Wellow 14 B1
West Wembury 8 B3
West Wemyss 152 B5
West Wick 24 A1
West Wickham *Cambs.* 59 E3
West Wickham *Gt.Lon.* 30 C2
West Williamston 34 D2
West Winch 71 E1
West Winterslow 26 D4
West Wittering 15 G3
West Witton 109 F4
West Woodburn 128 A3
West Woodhay 27 E1
West Woodlands 25 E3
West Worldham 28 C4

West Worlington 10 A1
West Worthing 16 D3
West Wratting 59 E2
West Wycombe 42 D3
West Yatton 40 A5
West Yell 191 E1
West Youlstone 20 C4
Westbere 33 D2
Westborough 82 D3
Westbourne *Bourne.* 13 G3
Westbourne *W.Suss.* 15 G2
Westbourne Green 44 B4
Westbrook *Kent* 33 F1
Westbrook *W.Berks.* 41 G5
Westbrook *Wilts.* 26 A1
Westbury *Bucks.* 56 B4
Westbury *Shrop.* 64 C2
Westbury *Wilts.* 25 F2
Westbury Leigh 25 F2
Westbury on Trym 39 E5
Westbury-on-Severn 39 G1
Westbury-sub-Mendip 24 C3
Westby *Lancs.* 99 G4
Westby *Lincs.* 83 E5
Westcliff-on-Sea 46 B4
Westcombe 25 D4
Westcot 41 F4
Westcott *Bucks.* 42 C1
Westcott *Devon* 10 D2
Westcott *Surr.* 29 G3
Westcott Barton 55 G5
Westcourt 26 D1
Westcroft 56 D4
Westdean 18 A4
Westdowns 5 E1
Westend Town 39 G5
Wester Aberchalder 165 G2
Wester Badentyre 177 G4
Wester Balgedie 151 G4
Wester Culbeuchly 177 F3
Wester Dechmont 143 E2
Wester Fintray 169 F3
Wester Foffarty 160 C3
Wester Greenskares 177 G3
Wester Gruinards 182 A5
Wester Hailes 143 G3
Wester Lealty 174 C2
Wester Lonvine 174 D2
Wester Newburn 152 C4
Wester Ord 169 F4
Westerdale *High.* 186 D3
Westerdale *N.Yorks.* 111 F2
Westerfield 60 C3
Westergate 16 B3
Westerham 30 D3
Westerhope 120 A1
Westerleigh 39 F5
Westerloch 187 F3
Westerton *Aber.* 169 E5
Westerton *Angus* 161 E4
Westerton *Dur.* 120 B4
Westerton *P.& K.* 151 D3
Westfield *Cumb.* 116 C4
Westfield *E.Suss.* 18 D2
Westfield *High.* 186 C2
Westfield *N.Lan.* 142 B2
Westfield *Norf.* 86 A5
Westfield *W.Loth.* 142 D2
Westfield *W.Yorks.* 102 B5
Westfield Sole 31 G2
Westgate *Dur.* 119 F4
Westgate *N.Lincs.* 95 E2
Westgate *Norf.* 86 A1
Westgate *Northumb.* 128 D4
Westgate Hill 102 B5
Westgate on Sea 33 F1
Westhall *Aber.* 169 E5
Westhall *Suff.* 73 F3
Westham *Dorset* 12 C5
Westham *E.Suss.* 18 B3
Westham *Som.* 24 B3
Westhampnett 16 A3
Westhay *Devon* 11 G2
Westhay *Som.* 24 B3
Westhead 91 F2
Westhide 53 E3
Westhill *Aber.* 169 F4
Westhill *High.* 174 D5

Westhope *Here.* 53 D2
Westhope *Shrop.* 65 D3
Westhorp 56 A2
Westhorpe *Lincs.* 84 A4
Westhorpe *Notts.* 82 B2
Westhorpe *Suff.* 60 B1
Westhoughton 92 A2
Westhouse 108 B5
Westhouses 81 F2
Westhumble 29 G2
Westlake 8 C2
Westlands 79 F3
Westlea 40 D4
Westleigh *Devon* 21 E3
Westleigh *Devon* 11 D1
Westleigh *Gt.Man.* 92 A2
Westleton 61 F1
Westley *Shrop.* 64 C2
Westley *Suff.* 59 G1
Westley Heights 45 F4
Westley Waterless 59 E2
Westlington 42 C1
Westlinton 126 B5
Westloch 143 G4
Westmancote 54 B4
Westmarsh 33 E2
Westmeston 17 F2
Westmill 58 B5
Westminster 44 B5
Westmuir 160 B4
Westness 190 B2
Westnewton *Cumb.* 117 D2
Westnewton *Northumb.* 136 D3
Westoe 120 C1
Weston *B.& N.E.Som.* 25 E1
Weston *Ches.E.* 79 E2
Weston *Devon* 11 E4
Weston *Devon* 11 E4
Weston *Dorset* 12 C5
Weston *Halton* 91 G4
Weston *Hants.* 28 C5
Weston *Here.* 52 C2
Weston *Herts.* 58 A4
Weston *Lincs.* 84 A5
Weston *Moray* 177 D3
Weston *N.Yorks.* 102 A3
Weston *Northants.* 56 A3
Weston *Notts.* 82 C1
Weston *S'ham.* 15 D1
Weston *Shrop.* 78 C5
Weston *Shrop.* 65 E3
Weston *Shrop.* 64 C5
Weston *Staffs.* 79 F5
Weston *W.Berks.* 41 G5
Weston Bampfylde 24 D5
Weston Beggard 53 E3
Weston by Welland 68 C3
Weston Colville 59 E2
Weston Corbett 28 B3
Weston Coyney 79 G3
Weston Favell 56 C1
Weston Green *Cambs.* 59 E2
Weston Green *Norf.* 86 C4
Weston Heath 65 G1
Weston Hills 84 A5
Weston in Arden 67 F4
Weston Jones 79 E5
Weston Longville 86 C4
Weston Lullingfields 78 B5
Weston Patrick 28 B3
Weston Point 91 F4
Weston Rhyn 77 F4
Weston Subedge 54 D3
Weston Town 25 E3
Weston Turville 43 D1
Weston under Penyard 53 F5
Weston under Wetherley 55 F1
Weston Underwood *Derbys.* 81 D1
Weston Underwood *M.K.* 57 D2
Westonbirt 40 A4
Westoning 57 F4
Weston-in-Gordano 39 D5
Weston-on-Avon 55 D2
Weston-on-the-Green 42 A1
Weston-on-Trent 81 F5
Weston-super-Mare 24 A1

Weston-under-Lizard 66 A1
Westonzoyland 24 A4
Westow 103 G1
Westport *Arg.& B.* 130 D3
Westport *Som.* 24 A5
Westra 38 A5
Westray 190 B1
Westridge Green 42 A5
Westrigg 142 D3
Westruther 144 D5
Westry 70 B2
Westside 169 F5
Westvale 91 F3
Westville 81 G3
Westward 117 F2
Westward Ho! 21 E3
Westwell *Kent* 32 B4
Westwell *Oxon.* 41 E2
Westwell Leacon 32 B4
Westwick *Cambs.* 58 C1
Westwick *Dur.* 109 F1
Westwick *N.Yorks.* 102 A5
Westwick *Norf.* 87 D3
Westwood *Devon* 10 D3
Westwood *Peter.* 69 G3
Westwood *S.Lan.* 142 A4
Westwood *Wilts.* 25 F2
Westwood Heath 67 E5
Westwoodside 95 E3
Wetham Green 32 A2
Wetheral 118 A2
Wetherby 102 D3
Wetherden 60 B1
Wetherden Upper Town 60 B1
Wetheringsett 60 C1
Wethersfield 59 F4
Wetherup Street 60 C1
Wetley Abbey 79 G3
Wetley Rocks 79 G3
Wettenhall 78 D1
Wettenhall Green 78 D1
Wetton 80 C2
Wetwang 104 B2
Wetwood 79 E4
Wexcombe 27 D2
Wexham Street 43 E4
Weybourne *Norf.* 86 C1
Weybourne *Surr.* 29 D3
Weybread 29 E2
Weybread Street 73 D4
Weybridge 29 F1
Weycroft 11 G2
Weydale 186 D2
Weyhill 27 E3
Weymouth 12 C5
Whaddon *Bucks.* 56 D4
Whaddon *Cambs.* 58 B3
Whaddon *Glos.* 40 A3
Whaddon *Glos.* 54 B5
Whaddon *Wilts.* 26 C5
Whaddon *Wilts.* 25 F1
Whaddon Gap 58 B3
Whale 118 B5
Whaley 94 C5
Whaley Bridge 93 E4
Whaley Thorns 94 C5
Whaligoe 187 F3
Whalley 100 D4
Whalsay 191 G3
Whalton 128 D3
Wham 101 D1
Whaplode 84 B5
Whaplode Drove 70 B1
Whaplode St. Catherine 70 B1
Wharfe 101 D1
Wharles 100 A4
Wharley End 57 E3
Wharncliffe Side 93 G3
Wharram le Street 104 A1
Wharram Percy 104 A1
Wharton *C.& W.Ches.* 79 D1
Wharton *Here.* 53 E2
Whashton 110 A2
Whatcote 55 F3
Whateley 67 E3
Whatfield 60 B3
Whatley 25 E3
Whatlington 18 C2
Whatsole Street 32 D4
Whatstandwell 81 E2
Whatton 82 C4
Whauphill 115 E2
Whaw 109 E2

Wheatacre 73 F2
Wheatcroft 81 E2
Wheatenhurst 39 G2
Wheatfield 42 B3
Wheathampstead 44 A1
Wheathill Shrop. 65 F4
Wheathill Som. 24 C4
Wheatley Hants. 28 C4
Wheatley Lane 101 E4
Wheatley Oxon. 42 B2
Wheatley W.Yorks. 101 G5
Wheatley Hill 120 C4
Wheatley Lane 101 E4
Wheatley Park 94 C2
Wheaton Aston 66 A1
Wheddon Cross 22 C4
Wheedlemont 168 B2
Wheelerstreet 29 E3
Wheelock 79 E2
Wheelock Heath 79 E2
Wheelton 100 C5
Wheen 160 B2
Wheldale 103 D5
Wheldrake 103 F3
Whelford 41 D3
Whelley 91 G2
Whelpley Hill 43 E2
Whelpo 117 G3
Whelston 90 D5
Whenby 103 F1
Whepstead 59 G2
Wherstead 60 C3
Wherwell 27 E3
Wheston 93 F5
Whetley Cross 12 A2
Whetsted 31 F4
Whetstone Gt.Lon. 44 B3
Whetstone Leics. 68 A3
Whicham 106 C4
Whichford 55 F4
Whickham 120 B1
Whiddon 21 E5
Whiddon Down 7 G1
Whifflet 142 B3
Whigstreet 160 C5
Whilton 56 B1
Whim 143 G4
Whimble 20 D5
Whimple 10 D3
Whimpwell Green 87 E3
Whin Lane End 99 G3
Whinburgh 86 B5
Whinny Hill 110 C1
Whinnyfold 179 F4
Whippingham 15 E3
Whipsnade 43 F1
Whipton 10 C3
Whirlow 94 A4
Whisby 83 E1
Whissendine 68 D1
Whissonsett 86 A3
Whisterfield 92 C5
Whistley Green 42 C5
Whiston Mersey. 91 F3
Whiston Northants. 56 D1
Whiston S.Yorks. 94 B3
Whiston Staffs. 80 B3
Whiston Staffs. 66 A1
Whiston Cross 65 G2
Whiston Eaves 80 B3
Whitacre Fields 67 E3
Whitacre Heath 67 E3
Whitbeck 106 C4
Whitbourne 53 G2
Whitburn T. & W. 120 D1
Whitburn W.Loth. 142 D3
Whitby C. & W.Ches. 91 E5
Whitby N.Yorks. 112 B1
Whitbyheath 91 E5
Whitchurch B. & N.E.Som. 24 D1
Whitchurch Bucks. 56 D5
Whitchurch Cardiff 38 A4
Whitchurch Devon 7 E3
Whitchurch Hants. 27 F3
Whitchurch Here. 39 E1
Whitchurch Pembs. 48 A5
Whitchurch Shrop. 78 C3
Whitchurch Warks. 55 E3
Whitchurch Canonicorum 11 G3
Whitchurch Hill 42 B5
Whitchurch-on-Thames 42 B5
Whitcombe 12 D4
Whitcott Keysett 64 B4

White Ball 11 D1
White Colne 59 G5
White Coppice 92 A1
White Cross Cornw. 4 C4
White Cross Devon 10 D3
White Cross Here. 53 D3
White Cross Wilts. 25 E4
White End 54 A5
White Hill 25 F4
White Houses 95 E5
White Kirkley 119 G4
White Lackington 12 D3
White Ladies Aston 54 B2
White Lund 100 A1
White Mill 50 A5
White Moor 81 E3
White Notley 45 G1
White Ox Mead 25 E2
White Pit 97 D5
White Rocks 52 D5
White Roding 45 E1
White Waltham 42 C5
Whiteacen 176 B5
Whiteash Green 59 F4
Whitebirk 100 D5
Whitebog 179 E2
Whitebridge High. 187 E1
Whitebridge (An Drochaid Bhàn) High. 165 F3
Whitebrook 39 E2
Whiteburn 144 C5
Whitecairn 122 D5
Whitecairns 169 G3
Whitecastle 143 E5
Whitechapel 100 B3
Whitechurch 49 E4
Whitecote 102 B4
Whitecraig 144 A2
Whitecroft 39 F2
Whitecrook 122 C5
Whitecross Cornw. 2 C3
Whitecross Cornw. 5 D2
Whitecross Dorset 12 A3
Whitecross Falk. 143 D2
Whiteface 174 D1
Whitefield Aber. 169 E2
Whitefield Devon 22 A4
Whitefield Dorset 13 F3
Whitefield High. 165 G2
Whitefield High. 187 E3
Whitefield P. & K. 151 G1
Whiteford 169 E2
Whitegate 78 D1
Whitehall Devon 11 E1
Whitehall Hants. 28 C2
Whitehall Ork. 190 C2
Whitehall W.Suss. 29 G5
Whitehaven 116 C5
Whitehill Aber. 179 E2
Whitehill Hants. 28 C4
Whitehill Kent 32 B3
Whitehill Midloth. 144 A3
Whitehill N.Ayr. 141 D4
Whitehills 177 F3
Whitehouse Aber. 168 D3
Whitehouse Arg. & B. 139 G3
Whitehouse Common 66 D3
Whitekirk 144 C1
Whitelackington 11 G1
Whitelaw 145 F4
Whiteleen 187 F4
Whitelees 132 B2
Whiteley 15 E2
Whiteley Bank 15 E4
Whiteley Green 92 D5
Whiteley Village 29 F1
Whiteleys 122 B5
Whitemans Green 17 F1
Whitemire 175 F4
Whitemoor 5 D4
Whiteoak Green 41 F1
Whiteparish 26 D5
Whiterashes 169 F2
Whiterow 187 F4
Whiteshill 40 A3
Whiteside Northumb. 118 D1
Whiteside W.Loth. 143 D3
Whitesmith 18 A2
Whitestaunton 11 F1
Whitestone Aber. 168 D5

Whitestone Arg. & B. 130 C2
Whitestone Devon 10 B3
Whitestreet Green 60 A4
Whitestripe 179 E2
Whiteway 40 B1
Whitewell Aber. 179 E1
Whitewell Lancs. 100 C3
Whitewell Wrex. 78 B3
Whiteworks 7 F3
Whitewreath 176 B4
Whitfield Here. 52 D4
Whitfield Kent 33 F4
Whitfield Northants. 56 B4
Whitfield Northumb. 119 D2
Whitfield S.Glos. 39 F3
Whitford Devon 11 F3
Whitford (Chwitffordd) Flints. 90 C5
Whitgift 104 A5
Whitgreave 79 F5
Whithorn 115 E2
Whiting Bay 131 F3
Whitkirk 102 C4
Whitlam 169 F2
Whitland (Hendy-Gwyn) 35 F1
Whitland Abbey 35 F1
Whitleigh 8 A1
Whitletts 132 B3
Whitley N.Yorks. 103 E5
Whitley Read. 28 C1
Whitley W.Mid. 67 F5
Whitley Wilts. 25 F1
Whitley Bay 129 F4
Whitley Chapel 119 F2
Whitley Heath 79 F5
Whitley Lower 93 G1
Whitley Row 31 G3
Whitlock's End 66 D5
Whitminster 39 G2
Whitmore Dorset 13 G2
Whitmore Staffs. 79 F3
Whitnage 10 D1
Whitnash 55 F1
Whitnell 23 F3
Whitney-on-Wye 52 B3
Whitrigg Cumb. 117 F1
Whitrigg Cumb. 117 F3
Whitsbury 14 A1
Whitsome 145 F4
Whitson 38 C4
Whitstable 32 D2
Whitstone 6 C1
Whittingham 137 E5
Whittingslow 64 D4
Whittington Derbys. 94 A5
Whittington Glos. 54 C5
Whittington Lancs. 108 B5
Whittington Norf. 71 F3
Whittington Shrop. 78 A4
Whittington Staffs. 66 A4
Whittington Staffs. 67 D2
Whittington Worcs. 54 A2
Whittlebury 56 B3
Whittle-le-Woods 100 B5
Whittlesey 70 A3
Whittlesford 58 C3
Whittlestone Head 92 B1
Whitton Gt.Lon. 44 A5
Whitton N.Lincs. 104 B5
Whitton Northumb. 128 C1
Whitton Powys 52 B1
Whitton Shrop. 65 E5
Whitton Stock. 120 C5
Whitton Suff. 60 C3
Whittonditch 41 E5
Whittonstall 119 G2
Whitway 27 F2
Whitwell Derbys. 94 C5
Whitwell Herts. 44 F5
Whitwell I.o.W. 15 E5
Whitwell N.Yorks. 110 B3
Whitwell Rut. 69 E2
Whitwell Street 86 C1
Whitwell-on-the-Hill 103 G1
Whitwick 67 G1
Whitwood 102 D5
Whitworth 92 C1
Whixall 78 C4

Whixley 102 D2
Whorlton Dur. 110 A1
Whorlton N.Yorks. 111 D2
Whygate 127 F4
Whyle 53 E1
Whyteleafe 30 C3
Wibdon 39 E3
Wibsey 102 A4
Wibtoft 67 G4
Wichenford 53 G1
Wichling 32 B3
Wick Bourne. 14 A3
Wick Devon 11 E2
Wick (Inbhir Ùige) High. 187 F3
Wick S.Glos. 39 G5
Wick Som. 23 F3
Wick Som. 24 C4
Wick V. of Glam. 37 D5
Wick W.Suss. 16 C3
Wick Wilts. 26 C5
Wick Worcs. 54 B3
Wick Airport 187 F3
Wick Hill Kent 32 A4
Wick Hill W'ham 28 C1
Wick St. Lawrence 24 A1
Wicken Cambs. 71 D5
Wicken Northants. 56 C4
Wicken Bonhunt 58 C4
Wickenby 96 A4
Wicker Street Green 60 A3
Wickerslack 108 B1
Wickersley 94 B3
Wicketwood Hill 82 B3
Wickford 45 G3
Wickham Hants. 15 E1
Wickham W.Berks. 41 F5
Wickham Bishops 46 B1
Wickham Heath 27 F1
Wickham Market 61 E2
Wickham St. Paul 59 G4
Wickham Skeith 60 B1
Wickham Street Suff. 59 F2
Wickham Street Suff. 60 B1
Wickhambreaux 33 E3
Wickhambrook 59 F2
Wickhamford 54 C3
Wickhampton 87 F5
Wicklewood 86 B5
Wickmere 86 C2
Wickstreet 18 A3
Wickwar 39 G3
Widcombe 25 E1
Widdington 58 D4
Widdop 101 F4
Widdrington 129 E2
Widdrington Station 129 E2
Wide Open 129 E4
Widecombe in the Moor 10 A5
Widegates 5 G4
Widemouth Bay 20 C5
Widford Essex 45 F3
Widford Herts. 44 D1
Widford Oxon. 41 E1
Widgham Green 59 E2
Widmer End 43 D3
Widmerpool 82 B5
Widnes 91 G4
Widworthy 11 F3
Wigan 91 G2
Wiganthorpe 111 F5
Wigborough 12 A1
Wiggaton 11 E3
Wiggenhall St. Germans 71 D1
Wiggenhall St. Mary Magdalen 71 D1
Wiggenhall St. Mary the Virgin 71 D1
Wiggenhall St. Peter 71 E1
Wiggens Green 59 E3
Wigginton Herts. 43 E1
Wigginton Oxon. 55 F4
Wigginton Shrop. 78 A4
Wigginton Staffs. 67 E2
Wigginton York 103 F2
Wigglesworth 101 E2
Wiggonby 117 G1
Wiggonholt 16 C2
Wighill 103 D3
Wighton 86 A2
Wightwizzle 93 G3

Wigley 14 C1
Wigmore Here. 52 D1
Wigmore Med. 32 A2
Wigsley 95 F5
Wigsthorpe 69 F4
Wigston 68 B3
Wigston Parva 67 G4
Wigthorpe 94 C4
Wigtoft 84 A4
Wigton 117 F2
Wigtown 123 F5
Wike 102 C3
Wilbarston 68 D4
Wilberfoss 103 G2
Wilburton 70 C5
Wilby Norf. 72 C3
Wilby Northants. 57 D1
Wilby Suff. 72 D4
Wilcot 26 C1
Wilcott 64 C1
Wilcrick 38 C2
Wilday Green 94 A5
Wildboarclough 79 G1
Wilde Street 71 F5
Wilden Beds. 57 F2
Wilden Worcs. 66 A5
Wildern 27 E2
Wildhern 44 B2
Wildmoor 66 B5
Wildsworth 95 F3
Wilford 81 G4
Wilkesley 78 D3
Wilkhaven 175 F1
Wilkieston 143 F3
Wilksby 84 A1
Willand Devon 10 D1
Willand Som. 11 E1
Willaston C. & W.Ches. 91 E5
Willaston Ches.E. 79 D2
Willaston Shrop. 78 C4
Willen 57 D3
Willenhall W.Mid. 66 B3
Willenhall W.Mid. 67 F5
Willerby E.Riding 104 C5
Willerby N.Yorks. 112 D5
Willersey 54 C3
Willersley 52 C3
Willesborough 32 C4
Willesborough Lees 32 C4
Willesden 44 B4
Willesleigh 21 F2
Willesley 40 A4
Willett 23 E4
Willey Shrop. 65 F3
Willey Warks. 67 G4
Willey Green 29 E2
William's Green 60 A3
Williamscot 55 G2
Williamthorpe 81 F1
Willian 58 A4
Willimontswick 119 D1
Willingale 45 G1
Willingdon 18 A3
Willingham 70 C5
Willingham by Stow 95 F4
Willingham Green 59 E2
Willington Beds. 57 G2
Willington Derbys. 81 D5
Willington Dur. 120 A4
Willington Kent 31 G3
Willington T. & W. 120 C1
Willington Warks. 55 E4
Willington Corner 78 C1
Willisham 60 B2
Willitoft 103 G4
Williton 23 D3
Willoughbridge 79 E3
Willoughby Lincs. 97 E5
Willoughby Warks. 56 A1
Willoughby Waterleys 68 A3
Willoughby-on-the-Wolds 82 B5
Willoughton 95 G3
Willow Green 92 A5
Willows Green 45 G1
Willsbridge 39 F5
Willslock 80 B4
Willsworthy 7 F2
Willtown 24 A5
Wilmcote 55 D2
Wilmington B. & N.E.Som. 25 D1
Wilmington Devon 11 F2
Wilmington E.Suss. 18 A3
Wilmington Kent 45 E5

Wilmslow 92 C4
Wilnecote 67 E2
Wilney Green 72 B3
Wilpshire 100 C3
Wilsden 101 G4
Wilsford Lincs. 83 F3
Wilsford Wilts. 26 C4
Wilsford Wilts. 26 C2
Wilsham 22 A3
Wilshaw 93 F2
Wilsill 102 A1
Wilsley Green 31 G5
Wilsley Pound 31 G5
Wilson 81 F5
Wilstead 57 F3
Wilsthorpe E.Riding 105 D1
Wilsthorpe Lincs. 69 F3
Wilstone 43 E1
Wilton Cumb. 116 C5
Wilton Here. 53 E5
Wilton N.Yorks. 112 B4
Wilton R. & C. 111 E1
Wilton Sc.Bord. 135 F4
Wilton Wilts. 27 D1
Wilton Wilts. 26 B4
Wiltown 11 E1
Wimbish 59 D4
Wimbish Green 59 E4
Wimblebury 66 C1
Wimbledon 44 B5
Wimblington 70 C3
Wimborne Minster 13 G2
Wimborne St. Giles 13 G1
Wimbotsham 71 E2
Wimpole 58 B2
Wimpole Lodge 58 B3
Wimpstone 55 E3
Wincanton 25 E5
Winceby 84 B1
Wincham 92 A5
Winchburgh 143 E2
Winchcombe 54 C5
Winchelsea 19 E2
Winchelsea Beach 19 E2
Winchester 27 E4
Winchet Hill 31 G4
Winchfield 28 C2
Winchmore Hill Bucks. 43 E3
Winchmore Hill Gt.Lon. 44 C3
Wincle 79 G1
Wincobank 94 A3
Windermere 107 F3
Winderton 55 F3
Windhill 174 B5
Windle Hill 91 E5
Windlehurst 93 D4
Windlesham 29 E1
Windley 81 E3
Windmill 93 F5
Windmill Hill E.Suss. 18 B2
Windmill Hill Som. 11 G1
Windmill Hill Worcs. 54 B3
Windrush 41 D1
Windsor 43 E5
Windsor Green 59 G2
Windy Nook 120 B1
Windygates 152 B4
Windy-Yett 141 F4
Wineham 17 E1
Winestead 105 E5
Winewall 101 F4
Winfarthing 72 C3
Winford I.o.W. 15 E4
Winford N.Som. 24 C1
Winforton 52 B3
Winfrith Newburgh 13 E4
Wing Bucks. 57 D5
Wing Rut. 69 D2
Wingate 120 C4
Wingates Gt.Man. 92 A2
Wingates Northumb. 128 C2
Wingerworth 81 E1
Wingfield Beds. 57 F5
Wingfield Suff. 72 D4
Wingfield Wilts. 25 F2
Wingfield Green 72 D4
Wingham 33 E3
Wingham Well 33 E3
Wingmore 33 D4
Wingrave 43 D1
Winkburn 82 C2
Winkfield 43 E5
Winkfield Row 43 D5

Winkhill **80** B2
Winkleigh **21** G5
Winksley **110** B5
Winkton **14** A3
Winlaton **120** A1
Winlaton Mill **120** A1
Winless **187** F3
Winmarleigh **100** A3
Winnard's Perch **4** D3
Winnersh **42** C5
Winnington **92** A5
Winscombe **24** B2
Winsford *C. & W.Ches.* **79** D1
Winsford *Som.* **22** C4
Winsham *Devon* **21** E2
Winsham *Som.* **11** G2
Winshill **81** D5
Winsh-wen **36** C3
Winskill **118** B4
Winslade **28** B3
Winsley **25** F1
Winslow **56** C5
Winson **40** C2
Winsor **14** C1
Winster *Cumb.* **107** F3
Winster *Derbys.* **80** D1
Winston *Dur.* **110** A1
Winston *Suff.* **60** C1
Winston Green **60** C1
Winstone **40** B2
Winswell **21** E4
Winterborne Came **12** D4
Winterborne Clenston
   13 E2
Winterborne Herringston
   12 C4
Winterborne Houghton
   13 E2
Winterborne Kingston
   13 E3
Winterborne Monkton
   12 C4
Winterborne Stickland
   13 E2
Winterborne Whitechurch
   13 E2
Winterborne Zelston
   13 E3
Winterbourne *S.Glos.*
   39 F4
Winterbourne *W.Berks.*
   41 G5
Winterbourne Abbas
   12 C3
Winterbourne Bassett
   40 D5
Winterbourne Dauntsey
   26 C4
Winterbourne Earls **26** C4
Winterbourne Gunner
   26 C4
Winterbourne Monkton
   40 D5
Winterbourne Steepleton
   12 C4
Winterbourne Stoke
   26 B3
Winterbrook **42** B4
Winterburn **101** F2
Wintercleugh **134** A4
Winteringham **104** B5
Winterley **79** E2
Wintersett **94** A1
Wintershill **15** E1
Winterslow **26** D4
Winterton **95** G1
Winterton-on-Sea **87** F4
Winthorpe *Lincs.* **85** D1
Winthorpe *Notts.* **82** D2
Winton *Bourne.* **13** G3
Winton *Cumb.* **108** C1
Wintringham **112** B5
Winwick *Cambs.* **69** G4
Winwick *Northants.*
   68 B5
Winwick *Warr.* **92** A3
Wirksworth **81** D2
Wirksworth Moor **81** E2
Wirswall **78** C3
Wisbech **70** C2
Wisbech St. Mary **70** C2
Wisborough Green **29** F5
Wiseton **95** E4
Wishaw *N.Lan.* **142** B4
Wishaw *Warks.* **67** D3
Wisley **29** F3
Wispington **96** C5
Wissett **73** E4

Wissington **60** A4
Wistanstow **64** D4
Wistanswick **79** D5
Wistaston **79** D2
Wistow *Cambs.* **70** A4
Wistow *N.Yorks.* **103** E4
Wiswell **100** D4
Witcham **70** C5
Witchampton **13** F2
Witchburn **130** C3
Witchford **70** D5
Witcombe **24** B5
Witham **46** B1
Witham Friary **25** E3
Witham on the Hill **69** F1
Withcall **96** C1
Withcote **68** C2
Withdean **17** F3
Witherenden Hill **18** B1
Witherhurst **18** B1
Witheridge **10** B1
Witherley **67** F3
Withern **97** E4
Withernsea **105** F5
Withernwick **105** D3
Withersdale Street **73** D3
Withersfield **59** E3
Witherslack **107** F4
Witherslack Hall **107** F4
Withiel **5** D3
Withiel Florey **22** C4
Withielgoose **5** E3
Withington *Glos.* **40** C1
Withington *Gt.Man.*
   92 C3
Withington *Here.* **53** E3
Withington *Shrop.* **65** E1
Withington *Staffs.* **80** B5
Withington Green **92** C5
Withington Marsh **53** E3
Withleigh **10** C1
Withnell **100** C5
Withnell Fold **100** C5
Withybrook *Som.* **25** D3
Withybrook *Warks.*
   67 G4
Withycombe **22** D3
Withycombe Raleigh
   10 D4
Witham **35** D5
Withypool **22** B4
Witley **29** E4
Witnesham **60** C2
Witney **41** F2
Wittering **69** F2
Wittersham **19** D1
Witton *Angus* **161** D2
Witton *Norf.* **87** E5
Witton *Worcs.* **54** A1
Witton Bridge **87** E2
Witton Gilbert **120** B3
Witton Park **120** A4
Witton-le-Wear **120** A4
Wiveliscombe **23** D5
Wivelsfield **17** F1
Wivelsfield Green **17** F2
Wivenhoe **60** B5
Wiveton **86** B1
Wix **60** C5
Wixford **54** C2
Wixhill **78** C5
Wixoe **59** F3
Woburn **57** E4
Woburn Sands **57** E4
Wokefield Park **28** B1
Woking **29** F2
Wokingham **28** D1
Wolborough **10** B5
Wold Newton *E.Riding*
   112 D5
Wold Newton *N.E.Lincs.*
   96 C3
Woldingham **30** C3
Wolfelee **135** G3
Wolferlow **53** F1
Wolferton **85** E5
Wolfhampcote **56** A1
Wolfhill **151** G1
Wolfpits **52** B2
Wolf's Castle **48** C5
Wolfsdale **48** C5
Woll **135** F3
Wollaston *Northants.*
   57 E1
Wollaston *Shrop.* **64** C1
Wollaston *W.Mid.* **66** A4
Wollaton **81** G4

Wollerton **78** D5
Wollescote **66** B4
Wolsingham **119** G4
Wolston **67** G5
Wolsty **117** E1
Wolvercote **42** A2
Wolverhampton **66** B3
Wolverley *Shrop.* **78** B4
Wolverley *Worcs.* **66** A5
Wolvers Hill **24** A1
Wolverton *Hants.* **27** G2
Wolverton *M.K.* **56** D3
Wolverton *Warks.* **55** E1
Wolverton *Wilts.* **25** E4
Wolverton Common
   27 G2
Wolvesnewton **39** D3
Wolvey **67** G4
Wolvey Heath **67** G4
Wolviston **121** D5
Womaston **52** B1
Wombleton **111** F4
Wombourne **66** A3
Wombwell **94** A2
Womenswold **33** E3
Womersley **94** B1
Wonastow **39** D1
Wonersh **29** F3
Wonford **10** C3
Wonson **7** G2
Wonston **27** F4
Wooburn **43** E4
Wooburn Green **43** E4
Wood Bevington **54** C2
Wood Burcote **56** B3
Wood Dalling **86** B3
Wood Eaton **66** A1
Wood End *Beds.* **57** F3
Wood End *Beds.* **57** F1
Wood End *Bucks.* **56** C4
Wood End *Herts.* **58** B5
Wood End *W.Mid.* **66** B2
Wood End *Warks.* **54** D3
Wood End *Warks.* **66** D5
Wood End *Warks.* **67** E4
Wood Enderby **84** A1
Wood Green *Essex* **44** D2
Wood Green *Gt.Lon.*
   44 C3
Wood Green *Norf.* **72** D2
Wood Lane **78** B4
Wood Norton **86** B3
Wood Seats **94** A3
Wood Stanway **54** C4
Wood Street **87** E3
Wood Street Village **29** E2
Woodacott **21** D5
Woodale **109** F5
Woodall **94** B4
Woodbastwick **87** E4
Woodbeck **95** E5
Woodborough *Notts.*
   82 B3
Woodborough *Wilts.*
   26 C2
Woodbridge *Devon* **11** E3
Woodbridge *Dorset*
   12 D1
Woodbridge *Suff.* **61** D3
Woodbury *Devon* **10** D4
Woodbury *Som.* **24** C3
Woodbury Salterton
   10 D4
Woodchester **40** A2
Woodchurch *Kent* **32** B5
Woodchurch *Mersey.*
   91 D4
Woodcombe **22** C3
Woodcote *Oxon.* **42** B4
Woodcote *Tel. & W.*
   65 G1
Woodcote Green **66** B5
Woodcott **27** F2
Woodcroft **39** E3
Woodcutts **13** F1
Wooddditton **59** E2
Woodeaton **42** A1
Woodend *Aber.* **169** D3
Woodend *Cumb.* **106** C3
Woodend *High.* **166** B2
Woodend *High.* **155** G3
Woodend *Northants.*
   56 B3
Woodend *P. & K.* **158** C5
Woodend *W.Suss.* **16** A3
Woodend Green **59** D5
Woodfalls **26** C5
Woodfield *Oxon.* **56** A5
Woodfield *S.Ayr.* **132** B3

Woodfoot **108** B1
Woodford *Cornw.* **20** C4
Woodford *Devon* **9** E2
Woodford *Glos.* **39** F3
Woodford *Gt.Lon.* **44** D3
Woodford *Gt.Man.* **92** C4
Woodford *Northants.*
   69 E5
Woodford *Som.* **23** D4
Woodford Bridge **44** D3
Woodford Green **44** D3
Woodford Halse **56** A2
Woodgate *Devon* **11** E1
Woodgate *Norf.* **86** B4
Woodgate *W.Mid.* **66** B4
Woodgate *W.Suss.* **16** B3
Woodgate *Worcs.* **54** B1
Woodgreen **14** A1
Woodhall *Include* **141** E2
Woodhall *N.Yorks.*
   109 E3
Woodhall Hills **102** A4
Woodhall Spa **83** G1
Woodham *Bucks.* **42** B1
Woodham *Dur.* **120** B5
Woodham *Surr.* **29** F1
Woodham Ferrers **45** D3
Woodham Mortimer
   46 B2
Woodham Walter **46** B2
Woodhaven **152** C2
Woodhead *Aber.* **169** E1
Woodhead *Staffs.* **80** B3
Woodhey **91** E4
Woodhey Green **78** C2
Woodhill *Shrop.* **65** G4
Woodhill *Som.* **24** A5
Woodhorn **129** E3
Woodhouse *Cumb.*
   107 G4
Woodhouse *Leics.* **68** A1
Woodhouse *S.Yorks.*
   94 B4
Woodhouse *W.Yorks.*
   102 B4
Woodhouse *W.Yorks.*
   102 C5
Woodhouse *W.Yorks.*
   102 A5
Woodhouse Down **39** F4
Woodhouse Eaves **68** A1
Woodhouse Green **79** G1
Woodhouses *Gt.Man.*
   92 C2
Woodhouses *Staffs.*
   67 D1
Woodhouses *Staffs.*
   66 C2
Woodhuish **9** F2
Woodhurst **70** B5
Woodingdean **17** F3
Woodington **27** E5
Woodland *Devon* **9** D1
Woodland *Dur.* **119** G5
Woodland *Kent* **32** D4
Woodland Head **10** B3
Woodlands *Dorset* **13** G2
Woodlands *Hants.* **14** C1
Woodlands *N.Yorks.*
   102 C2
Woodlands *Shrop.* **65** G4
Woodlands *Som.* **23** E3
Woodlands Park **43** D5
Woodlands St. Mary
   41 F5
Woodlane **80** C5
Woodleigh **8** D3
Woodlesford **102** C5
Woodley *Gt.Man.* **92** D3
Woodley *W'ham* **42** C5
Woodmancote *Glos.*
   40 C2
Woodmancote *Glos.*
   54 B5
Woodmancote *Glos.*
   39 G3
Woodmancote *W.Suss.*
   17 E2
Woodmancote *W.Suss.*
   15 G2
Woodmancott **27** G3
Woodmansey **104** C4
Woodmansterne **30** B3
Woodmanton **10** D4
Woodmill **80** C5
Woodminton **26** B5
Woodmoor **64** B2
Woodnesborough **33** F3
Woodnewton **69** F3

Woodperry **42** A1
Woodplumpton **100** B4
Woodrising **86** A5
Woodrow **13** D1
Wood's Corner **18** B2
Woods Eaves **52** B3
Wood's Green **31** F5
Woodseaves *Shrop.*
   79 D4
Woodseaves *Staffs.*
   79 E5
Woodsend **41** E5
Woodsetts **94** C4
Woodsford **13** D3
Woodside *Aberdeen*
   169 G4
Woodside *Beds.* **43** F1
Woodside *Brack.F.* **43** E5
Woodside *Cumb.* **108** B3
Woodside *D. & G.* **125** D3
Woodside *Fife* **152** C4
Woodside *Fife* **152** C4
Woodside *Gt.Lon.* **30** C2
Woodside *Hants.* **14** C3
Woodside *Herts.* **44** B2
Woodside *N.Ayr.* **141** E4
Woodside *P. & K.* **151** G1
Woodside *Shrop.* **64** C4
Woodside *W.Mid.* **66** B4
Woodside *Oxon.* **41** G1
Woodside Green **32** B3
Woodstock *Oxon.* **41** G1
Woodstock *Pembs.*
   48 D5
Woodthorpe *Derbys.*
   94 B5
Woodthorpe *Leics.* **68** A1
Woodthorpe *Lincs.* **97** E4
Woodthorpe *S.Yorks.*
   94 A4
Woodton **73** D2
Woodtown **21** E3
Woodvale **91** E1
Woodville **67** F1
Woodwall Green **79** E4
Woodwalton **70** A4
Woodworth Green **78** C2
Woodyates **13** G1
Woofferton **53** E1
Wookey **24** C3
Wookey Hole **24** C3
Wool **13** E4
Woolacombe **21** E1
Woolage Green **33** E4
Woolage Village **33** E3
Woolaston **39** E2
Woolaston Slade **39** E2
Woolavington **24** A3
Woolbeding **29** D5
Woolcotts **22** C4
Wooldale **93** F2
Wooler **137** D4
Woolfardisworthy *Devon*
   10 B2
Woolfardisworthy *Devon*
   20 D3
Woolfold **92** B1
Woolfords Cottages
   143 E4
Woolgarston **13** F4
Woolgreaves **94** A1
Woolhampton **27** G1
Woolhope **53** F4
Woolland **13** D2
Woollard **24** D1
Woollaston **21** E4
Woollensbrook **44** C2
Woolley *B. & N.E.Som.*
   25 E1
Woolley *Cambs.* **69** G5
Woolley *Cornw.* **20** C4
Woolley *Derbys.* **81** E1
Woolley *W.Yorks.* **94** A1
Woolley Green *W. & M.*
   43 D5
Woolley Green *Wilts.*
   25 F1
Woolmer Green **44** B1
Woolmere Green **54** B1
Woolmersdon **23** F4
Woolpit **60** A1
Woolpit Green **60** A1
Woolscott **55** G1
Woolsgrove **10** A2
Woolstaston **65** D3
Woolsthorpe **82** D4
Woolsthorpe by
   Colsterworth **83** E5
Woolston *Devon* **8** D3
Woolston *S'ham.* **14** D1

Woolston *Shrop.* **78** A5
Woolston *Shrop.* **64** B1
Woolston *Warr.* **92** A4
Woolston Green **9** D1
Woolstone *Glos.* **54** B4
Woolstone *M.K.* **57** D2
Woolstone *Oxon.* **41** E4
Woolton **91** D4
Woolton Hill **27** F1
Woolverstone **60** C4
Woolverton **25** E2
Woonton **52** C2
Wooperton **137** E5
Woore **79** E3
Wootten Green **72** D4
Wootton *Beds.* **57** F3
Wootton *Hants.* **14** B3
Wootton *I.o.W.* **15** E3
Wootton *Kent* **33** E4
Wootton *N.Lincs.* **96** A1
Wootton *Northants.*
   56 C2
Wootton *Oxon.* **41** G1
Wootton *Oxon.* **41** G2
Wootton *Shrop.* **65** D5
Wootton *Shrop.* **78** A5
Wootton *Staffs.* **79** F5
Wootton *Staffs.* **80** C3
Wootton Bassett **40** C4
Wootton Bridge **15** E3
Wootton Common **15** E3
Wootton Courtenay
   22 C3
Wootton Fitzpaine **11** G3
Wootton Green **57** F3
Wootton Rivers **26** C1
Wootton St. Lawrence
   27 G2
Wootton Wawen **55** D1
Worcester **54** A2
Worcester Park **30** B2
Wordsley **66** A4
Wordwell **71** G5
Worfield **65** G3
Worgret **13** F4
Workhouse End **57** G2
Workington **116** D4
Worksop **94** C5
Worlaby *Lincs.* **96** C5
Worlaby *N.Lincs.* **96** A1
World's End *Bucks.*
   43 D2
Worlds End *Hants.* **15** F1
World's End *W.Berks.*
   41 G5
Worlds End *W.Mid.* **66** D4
Worle **24** A1
Worleston **79** D2
Worlingham **73** F3
Worlington **71** E5
Worlingworth **60** D1
Wormald Green **102** C1
Wormbridge **52** D2
Wormegay **71** E1
Wormelow Tump **53** D2
Wormhill **93** F3
Wormingford **60** A4
Worminghall **42** B2
Wormington **54** C4
Worminster **24** C3
Wormiston **153** E4
Wormit **152** B2
Wormleighton **55** G2
Wormley *Herts.* **44** C2
Wormley *Surr.* **29** G4
Wormley West End **44** C2
Wormshill **33** A3
Wormsley **52** D3
Worplesdon **29** E2
Worrall **94** A3
Worsbrough **94** A2
Worsley **92** B2
Worstead **87** E3
Worsted Lodge **58** D3
Worsthorne **101** E4
Worston **101** D3
Worswell **8** C3
Worth *Kent* **33** F3
Worth *W.Suss.* **30** B5
Worth Matravers **13** F5
Wortham **72** B4
Worthen **64** C2
Worthenbury **78** B3
Worthing *Norf.* **86** A4
Worthing *W.Suss.* **16** D3
Worthington **81** F5
Worting **28** B2
Wortley *Glos.* **39** G3

Wortley *S.Yorks.* **94** A3
Wortley *W.Yorks.* **102** B4
Worton *N.Yorks.* **109** E4
Worton *Wilts.* **26** A2
Wortwell **73** D3
Wothersome **102** D3
Wotherton **64** B2
Wotter **8** B1
Wotton **29** G3
Wotton Underwood **42** B1
Wotton-under-Edge **39** G3
Woughton on the Green **57** D4
Wouldham **31** G2
Wrabness **60** C4
Wrae **177** G4
Wrafton **21** E2
Wragby **96** B5
Wragholme **97** D3
Wramplingham **86** C5
Wrangaton **8** C2
Wrangham **168** D1
Wrangle **84** C2
Wrangle Lowgate **84** C2
Wrangway **11** E1
Wrantage **24** A5
Wrawby **96** A2
Wraxall *N.Som.* **39** D5
Wraxall *Som.* **24** D4
Wray **100** C1
Wray Castle **107** E2
Wrays **30** B4
Wraysbury **43** F5
Wrayton **108** B5
Wrea Green **99** G4
Wreay *Cumb.* **118** A5
Wreay *Cumb.* **118** A3
Wrecclesham **28** D3
Wrekenton **120** B2
Wrelton **111** G4
Wrenbury **78** C3
Wrench Green **112** C4
Wreningham **72** C2
Wrentham **73** F3
Wrenthorpe **102** C5
Wrentnall **64** D2
Wressle *E.Riding* **103** G4
Wressle *N.Lincs.* **95** G2
Wrestlingworth **58** A3

Wretham **72** A2
Wretton **71** E2
Wrexham (Wrecsam) **78** A3
Wrexham Industrial Estate **78** A3
Wribbenhall **65** G5
Wrightington Bar **91** G1
Wrightpark **150** B5
Wright's Green **45** E1
Wrinehill **79** E3
Wrington **24** B1
Writhlington **25** D2
Writtle **45** F2
Wrockwardine **65** F1
Wroot **95** E2
Wrose **102** A4
Wrotham **31** F3
Wrotham Heath **31** F3
Wrotham Hill Park **31** F2
Wrottesley **66** A2
Wroughton **40** D4
Wroxall *I.o.W.* **15** E5
Wroxall *Warks.* **67** E5
Wroxeter **65** E2
Wroxham **87** E4
Wroxton **55** G3
Wstrws **49** G3
Wyaston **80** C3
Wyberton **84** B3
Wyboston **57** G2
Wybunbury **79** D3
Wych Cross **30** D5
Wychbold **54** B1
Wychnor **67** D1
Wychnor Bridges **67** D1
Wyck **28** C4
Wyck Rissington **55** D5
Wycliffe **110** A1
Wycoller **101** F4
Wycomb **82** C5
Wycombe Marsh **43** D3
Wyddial **58** B4
Wye **32** C4
Wyesham **39** E1
Wyfordby **68** C1
Wyke *Devon* **10** B3
Wyke *Dorset* **25** E5
Wyke *Shrop.* **65** F2
Wyke *Surr.* **29** E2

Wyke *W.Yorks.* **102** A5
Wyke Champflower **25** D4
Wyke Regis **12** C5
Wykeham *N.Yorks.* **112** C4
Wykeham *N.Yorks.* **112** B5
Wyken *Shrop.* **65** G3
Wyken *W.Mid.* **67** F4
Wykey **78** A5
Wylam **120** A1
Wylde Green **66** D3
Wyllie **38** A3
Wylye **26** B4
Wymering **15** F2
Wymeswold **82** B5
Wymington **57** E1
Wymondham *Leics.* **69** D1
Wymondham *Norf.* **86** C5
Wyndham **37** F3
Wynford Eagle **12** B3
Wynnstay Park **78** A3
Wynyard **120** D5
Wyre Piddle **54** B3
Wyresdale Tower **100** C2
Wysall **82** B5
Wyson **53** E1
Wythall **66** C5
Wytham **41** G2
Wythburn **117** G5
Wythenshawe **92** C4
Wyton *Cambs.* **70** A5
Wyton *E.Riding* **105** D4
Wyverstone **60** B1
Wyverstone Street **60** B1
Wyville **83** D5
Wyvis Lodge **174** A2

Y

Y Bryn **76** B5
Y Fan **63** F4
Y Felinheli **75** E1
Y Ffôr **74** C4
Y Fron (Upper Llandwrog) **75** E2
Yaddlethorpe **95** F2
Yafford **14** D4

Yafforth **110** C3
Yalberton **9** E2
Yalding **31** F4
Yanley **24** C1
Yanwath **118** B5
Yanworth **40** C1
Yapham **103** G2
Yapton **16** B3
Yarburgh **96** D3
Yarcombe **11** F2
Yardley **66** D4
Yardley Gobion **56** C3
Yardley Hastings **57** D2
Yardro **52** B2
Yarford **23** F5
Yarkhill **53** F3
Yarlet **79** G5
Yarley **24** C3
Yarlington **25** D5
Yarm **110** D1
Yarmouth **14** C4
Yarnacott **21** G2
Yarnbrook **25** F2
Yarnfield **79** F4
Yarnscombe **21** F3
Yarnton **41** G1
Yarpole **53** D1
Yarrow *Sc.Bord.* **135** E3
Yarrow *Som.* **24** A3
Yarrow Feus **135** E3
Yarrowford **135** F3
Yarsop **52** D3
Yarwell **69** F3
Yate **39** G4
Yatehouse Green **79** E1
Yateley **28** D1
Yatesbury **40** C5
Yattendon **42** A5
Yatton *Here.* **52** D1
Yatton *N.Som.* **24** B1
Yatton Keynell **40** A5
Yaverland **15** F4
Yawl **11** G3
Yaxham **86** B4
Yaxley *Cambs.* **69** G3
Yaxley *Suff.* **72** C4
Yazor **52** D3
Yeabridge **12** A1
Yeading **44** A4
Yeadon **102** B3

Yealand Conyers **107** G5
Yealand Redmayne **107** G5
Yealand Storrs **107** G5
Yealmbridge **8** B2
Yealmpton **8** B2
Yearby **121** F5
Yearsley **111** E5
Yeaton **64** D1
Yeaveley **80** C3
Yeavering **136** D3
Yedingham **112** B5
Yelford **41** F2
Yell **191** F2
Yelland *Devon* **21** E2
Yelland *Devon* **7** F1
Yelling **58** A1
Yelvertoft **68** A5
Yelverton *Devon* **8** B1
Yelverton *Norf.* **87** D5
Yenston **25** E5
Yeo Mill **22** B5
Yeo Vale **21** E3
Yeoford **10** A3
Yeolmbridge **6** D2
Yeomadon **20** D5
Yeovil **12** B1
Yeovil Marsh **12** B1
Yeovilton **24** C5
Yerbeston **35** D2
Yetholm Mains **136** C4
Yetlington **137** E5
Yetminster **12** B1
Yettington **11** D4
Yetts o'Muckhart **151** F4
Yew Green **55** E1
Yielden **57** F1
Yieldshields **142** C4
Ynys **75** E4
Ynys Tachwedd **62** C3
Ynysboeth **37** G3
Ynysddu **38** A3
Ynyshir **37** G3
Ynyslas **62** C3
Ynysmaerdy **37** G4
Ynysmeudwy **36** D2
Ynystawe **36** C2
Ynyswen **37** F3
Ynysybwl **37** G3
Yockenthwaite **109** E5

Yockleton **64** C1
Yokefleet **104** A5
Yoker **141** G3
Yonder Bognie **177** F5
York **103** F2
Yorkletts **32** C2
Yorkley **39** F2
Yorton **78** C5
Yorton Heath **78** C5
Youldon **20** D5
Youldonmoor Cross **20** D5
Youlgreave **80** D1
Youlthorpe **103** G2
Youlton **103** D1
Young's End **45** G1
Yoxall **66** D1
Yoxford **61** E1
Ysbyty Cynfyn **63** D5
Ysbyty Ifan **76** B3
Ysbyty Ystwyth **62** D5
Ysceifiog **90** C5
Ysgubor-y-coed **62** C3
Ystalyfera **37** D2
Ystrad **37** F3
Ystrad Aeron **50** B2
Ystrad Meurig **50** D1
Ystrad Mynach **38** A3
Ystradfellte **37** F1
Ystradffin **51** D3
Ystradgynlais **37** D1
Ystradowen *Carmar.* **36** D1
Ystradowen *V. of Glam.* **37** G5
Ystumtuen **62** D5
Ythanwells **168** D1
Ythsie **169** F1

Z

Zeal Monachorum **10** A2
Zeals **25** E4
Zelah **4** C4
Zennor **2** B3
Zouch **81** G5